THE LATIN AMERICA REA[DER]
Series edited by Robin Kirk and Orin Sta[rn]

The Brazil Reader
SECOND EDITION

THE

BRAZIL

READER

HISTORY, CULTURE, POLITICS

SECOND EDITION, REVISED AND UPDATED

James N. Green, Victoria Langland,
and Lilia Moritz Schwarcz, editors

DUKE UNIVERSITY PRESS   *Durham and London*   2019

© 2019 Duke University Press
All rights reserved
Printed in the United States of America on acid-free paper ∞
Typeset in Monotype Dante by BW&A Books, Inc.

Library of Congress Cataloging-in-Publication Data
Names: Green, James Naylor, [date] editor. | Langland, Victoria, editor. |
Schwarcz, Lilia Moritz, editor.
Title: The Brazil reader : history, culture, politics.
Description: Second edition, revised and updated / edited by James N. Green,
Victoria Langland, and Lilia Moritz Schwarcz. | Durham : Duke University Press,
2018. | Series: The Latin America Readers | Includes bibliographical references
and index.
Identifiers: LCCN 2018023531 (print)
LCCN 2018026379 (ebook)
ISBN 9780822371793 (ebook)
ISBN 9780822370925 (hardcover : alk. paper)
ISBN 9780822371076 (pbk. : alk. paper)
Subjects: LCSH: Brazil—History. | Brazil—Civilization. | Brazil—
Politics and government.
Classification: LCC F2521 (ebook) | LCC F2521 .B768 2018 (print) |
DDC 981—dc23
LC record available at https://lccn.loc.gov/2018023531

Cover art: Luiz Braga, *Casa Miritis.* © Luiz Braga.

Valerie Millholland
In memoriam
Editor par excellence

Contents

Acknowledgments

The editors of this volume would like to thank Gisela Fosado for her patience as we slowly produced the second edition of *The Brazil Reader*, as well as the three reviewers who offered many valuable suggestions about how to improve its contents. Lorien Olive, Anna Tybinko, and Lydia Rose Rappoport-Hankins from Duke University Press helped us immeasurably in obtaining permissions for art and texts.

James N. Green offers special appreciation to Molly Quinn and Emma Wohl for having dedicated so much time, energy, and talent to translating numerous items for this volume. Other Brown students who assisted with this endeavor through their translation of texts include Caroline Landau, Benjamin Legg, Lanna Leite, Erica Manouselis, Isadora Mota, João Nascimento, and Jennifer Gonçalves Reis. Gregory Childs, Roquinaldo Ferreira, Johanna Richlin, and Natan Zeichner also generously assisted us in translating material. Marycarolyn G. France deserves particular gratitude for having spent endless hours carefully reading, editing, and correcting those translations.

Victoria Langland thanks the many colleagues—too numerous to mention here—who offered enormous assistance with individual entries, and thanks Nico, Cal, and Theo Howson for providing both unceasing support as she worked on this *Reader* and an equally limitless source of joyous distraction from it. She is particularly appreciative of Theresa Bachmann, Augusto de Moraes Guimarães, Page Martell, and Lonny Ivan Meyer for their work in translating some of the documents here.

Lilia Moritz Schwarcz extends her gratitude to Sonia Balady and Vladimir Sachetta, as well as her colleagues at Princeton University, Bruno Carvalho and Pedro Meira Monteiro.

In addition, we are grateful for the help of Vicente Arruda Camara Rodrigues at the Brazilian Arquivo Nacional; the Arquivo Público do Estado de São Paulo; Martina Spohr and her staff at CPDOC/Fundação Getúlio Vargas; the Edgard Leuenroth Archive at UNICAMP; the Instituto Moreira Salles; Neil Safier, the director of the John Carter Brown Library at Brown University; and Valeria Ganz and other staff at the Museu da República.

Introduction

When the governing body for world football, FIFA, confirmed in 2007 that Brazil would host the 2014 World Cup, many Brazilians across the country celebrated this latest affirmation of the nation's global importance. Two years later crowds again rejoiced when the International Olympics Committee chose the city of Rio de Janeiro as the site for the 2016 summer Olympic games.

Brazil's selection as host for these two enormous events seemed to confirm domestic and international confidence about the country's current status and future promise. Two decades of sustained economic growth had led to a vast movement of people into the middle class for the first time, while a series of government-sponsored poverty eradication initiatives had made real and material differences in the lives of the very poor. Brazil had long led others in developing and using renewable energy sources, such as hydroelectricity and biofuels, and in 2006 the government announced that it was now self-sufficient in oil production. That same year the discovery of enormous oil and natural gas reserves off the coast of Rio de Janeiro quickly drew predictions that Brazil would soon be one of the largest oil exporters in the world. Meanwhile, the nation's status as the world's third-largest democracy meant that since 1985 the country had enjoyed not just stable democratic transitions but also, due to compulsory voting laws, regular voter turnout of around 80 percent of eligible voters. Thus, the decisions of FIFA and the International Olympics Committee to hold their sporting events there were simply symbolic manifestations of what the international media had been enthusiastically proclaiming for some time: that for the country of the future, as many have called Brazil, its time had finally arrived.

While these decisions fueled an initial wave of optimism within Brazil that the country might finally be reaching its long-promised potential, they also provoked fierce critiques of the government's priorities when pressing domestic concerns still begged for redress. Serious infrastructural deficiencies complicated both personal and business lives, while political corruption at times seemed endemic. These tensions were brought into stark relief in 2013 and 2014, when the juxtaposition of government spending on items like stadium construction with the perseverance of long-standing flaws in public services, such as education, health care, and transportation, contributed to

Map of Brazil.

an explosion of street protests that made manifest this popular frustration. Meanwhile, the international media descended on Brazil, describing each delay in World Cup preparations as a disaster waiting to happen. As it turned out, these pessimistic predictions turned out to be wrong, but social discontent did not wane.

The 2014 elections that followed immediately after Brazil's stunning defeat in the World Cup semifinals brought new surprises. Brazilian Socialist Party presidential candidate Eduardo Campos died in an airplane crash in August, and Marina Silva, the former minister of environment and Campos's running mate, then stepped in to replace him, soaring in the polls for a brief time. In the first round of the presidential contest, Aécio Neves, the former governor of the state of Minas Gerais and the nominee of the centrist Brazilian Social Democracy Party, ended up coming in second place to incumbent President Dilma Rousseff of the Workers' Party. She then defeated him in the second round by a slim 3.2 percent margin. It was the closest presidential race since 1989.

Soon after Dilma Rousseff's inauguration, a series of scandals erupted that linked members of the Workers' Party and other parties to massive fraud in Petrobras, the state-owned oil monopoly. Ongoing corruption charges against her administration and Rousseff's narrow electoral victory fed a growing political polarization in the country between a center-left coalition led by the Workers' Party and a center-right coalition under the leadership of the Brazilian Social Democracy Party. Soon over a million people mobilized in marches calling for Rousseff's impeachment, while hundreds of thousands of others marched in counterdemonstrations of support. In late August 2016, the Senate impeached President Rousseff for violations of fiscal procedures related to the budget and government disbursements, although she was not accused of corruption. Michel Temer, the vice presidential candidate on her coalition slate and a leader of the Party of the Brazilian Democratic Movement, assumed the presidency for a two-year term, marking a sudden and dramatic shift to the center-right in national politics. As this edition of *The Brazil Reader* goes to press, it is hard to predict Brazil's political future.

Mixtures of optimism and critique have long characterized Brazilians' understanding of their country as a place with boundless potential yet seemingly intractable inequalities. By the same token, the recent spotlight on Brazil portraying it alternately as an emerging global power or a place ill equipped for such a position reminds us that it has been an object of international fascination and evaluation since the colonial period. This new edition of *The Brazil Reader* showcases these domestic and international dynamics of optimism and critique that have pervaded Brazil's past and continue to shape its present. The contents of the volume offer the reader multiple paths for exploring and understanding how the legacies of the past continue to both inspire and weigh on Brazil today.

Examining some of these paths is an enormous, if extremely gratifying, undertaking. Anyone interested in Brazil is familiar with the repeated comments on its immense size, enormous wealth, and environmental and cultural diversity. Indeed, it is a real intellectual challenge to present the complexities of how different societies and cultures have interacted over time and how economic, political, and social structures have developed, without reducing these histories to simplified clichés. This is especially the case given the sheer magnitude and significant regional diversities in Brazil. Nonetheless, in the pages that follow, the *Reader* presents documents, essays, poems, manifestos, speeches, images, and other materials (many published in English for the first time) that, taken together, try to capture some part of the great variety of lived experiences and political, social, economic, and cultural processes that have taken place in Brazil over five hundred years.

In order to best facilitate readers' explorations of these materials, the *Reader* is organized following a conventional historical periodization that will be familiar to those who have studied some Brazilian history. Divided into eleven parts, it begins with the contact between Portuguese explorers and indigenous peoples in 1500 and ends with essays on recent developments in the country. Of course, any division of a historical narrative into distinct time periods conveys only certain ways of looking at the past, and ostensible historical ruptures can lead to as much continuity as change, even if new forms of government or different political figures take power. Yet this periodization highlights the fact that important modifications in forms of government or types of regimes, such as the transition from monarchy to republic, and significant economic and social transformations, such as the discovery of gold in 1695 and the end of the Atlantic slave trade in 1850, helped to shape and constrain the lives of those who lived in these periods. This organizational structure seeks to respond to the needs of both students and a broader audience interested in an overview of Brazilian history, politics, and culture and an understanding of how the past is linked to the present.

Within this chronological approach, six interrelated and underlying themes appear throughout the volume: (1) the structure of the colonial, imperial, and republican economies in relationship to local production and international demands for goods produced in Brazil; (2) the complex social hierarchies that developed in a society based on extracting labor from the indigenous population, enslaved Africans, free people of color, and immigrants; (3) the legacy of slavery, the ideologies that have justified it, and their relationship to notions of race, equality, and democracy in Brazil; (4) the roles that women of all social classes have played in Brazilian public life and the importance of ideas about masculinity and femininity that undergird relationships of power; (5) the dynamic between political and social movements, popular rebellions, uprisings, revolts, and mobilizations, on the one hand, and social change, on the other; and (6) the multifaceted intellectual production that reveals much about the nature of Brazil, its people, and their cultures, from poetry and short stories to various forms of nonfiction. These themes and their varied facets emerge in the documents, essays, portraits, and images in all of the selections that follow.

All three editors of this volume teach and study the history and culture of Brazil. We work with students in the United States who often know very little about the country when they first enter the classroom, although they have generally picked up enough information to be deeply intrigued by Brazil and its history. One of the three editors also teaches history and anthropology at a leading Brazilian university where one of the pedagogical challenges is to encourage students to critically reassess long-standing assumptions about race, class, and social difference that are pervasive in Brazilian society. We have designed this *Reader* with both groups of students in mind, hoping to offer something to all of those curious and motivated to learn more about Brazil. We have therefore embedded in the selections and short introductory essays background knowledge and interesting materials that will enable all readers to develop, over time, a more variegated and multifaceted understanding of the country. Although Brazilian songwriter, singer, and composer Tom Jobim noted about anyone trying to decipher Brazil and its people, history, politics, and culture that "Brazil is not for beginners," we nonetheless think the attempt is worthwhile.

I

Conquest and Colonial Rule, 1500–1579

Long before the accidental arrival of Portuguese navigators in 1500, the land we now call Brazil had an extensive history. For thousands of years some two to five million people lived, worked, and traveled throughout this vast area, speaking over 170 different languages, creating a wide variety of cultures and political organizations, and interacting with their environment in diverse ways. Scholars today are acutely aware of the importance of these Amerindian peoples whose material and cultural impact extended beyond current national borders. If they did not leave behind the ruins of large cities, their cosmologies were nonetheless enormously complex. Today many scholars use the term "perspectivism," as elaborated by the anthropologist Eduardo Viveiros de Castro, to refer to indigenous philosophies that questioned the seeming boundaries between the human and animal worlds, and they continue to learn from these rich sets of ideas.

When we speak of the history of Brazil, however, we generally mean the history after 1500, when the area became marked by the encounters between its original inhabitants, the indigenous peoples, and the waves of new arrivals who came from Portugal, Africa, and elsewhere, and when Brazil's natural resources became directed toward a growing system of global trade that transformed the land and resulted in the development of a new society. These encounters date to April 1500, when a fleet of thirteen Portuguese ships bound for India via Vasco da Gama's newly discovered route around the southern tip of Africa instead found themselves pulled westward to Brazil. Headed by Pedro Álvares Cabral, the fleet laid anchor near present-day Porto Seguro, Bahia, and spent eight days exploring the coast in an effort to estimate the value this discovery might offer the Portuguese Crown. The Spanish had recently begun to establish outposts in the Caribbean and consequently laid broader claims to much of the Western Hemisphere. While Pope Alexander VI supported the Spanish claims in a papal bull of 1492, the Portuguese reached a separate agreement with Spain two years later. In this 1494 agreement, called the Treaty of Tordesillas and also brokered by the pope, everything east of an imaginary north-south line was ceded to Portugal. Written with the intention of staving off potential conflicts between the two crowns, the treaty was drawn up before both parties knew the dimensions of South America. When, in 1500, Cabral's fleet touched land, the Treaty of Tordesillas seemed to legitimize Portugal's claim to the area. Thus one ship quickly returned to Lisbon to report the news, and the rest continued on their journey. Remaining in Brazil were two Portuguese convicts deliberately left behind so that they might live among the indigenous populations, learn their languages, and thereby facilitate Portuguese interactions when the main party returned.

European explorers and mapmakers originally called their "discovery" the Land of the True Cross, the Land of the Holy Cross, Portuguese America, or even the Land of Parrots. Once it became clear that its most immediately lucrative resource was *pau-brasil* or brazilwood, a tree that could be used to produce a rich, red dye, the name Brasil (Brazil) soon stuck. Demand for brazilwood was so high that the Portuguese Crown decreed the trade a royal monopoly. This meant that traders needed special permission, usually granted in exchange for further exploring the coast and for building a *feitoria*, or fortified trading post. In this way the Portuguese Crown duplicated the trading system it had established in Africa. A few delegates within the *feitorias* traded for brazilwood and other items, including Indian slaves, but without the expense or administration of a permanent Portuguese colony. Indeed, Portugal initially viewed Brazil as only moderately important, focusing instead on its trade with the East. But French incursions into the brazilwood trade and their refusal to recognize Portuguese claims to the area led the Portuguese Crown first to send in naval expeditions to repel them and, when this failed, to seek a more established presence in the area.

To minimize royal expenditures on an area of indeterminate value, the Crown eventually devised a new system in which private individuals would essentially colonize Brazil at their own expense. Dividing Brazil into fifteen captaincies, or enormous parcels of land stretching from the coast westward, between 1533 and 1535 the Crown gave hereditary rights to these lands and the power to tax and police their inhabitants to twelve individuals. The *donatários*, as the recipients were called, were expected to encourage Portuguese settlement and economic development, thereby securing the Crown's possession of the colony and its revenues. They received the title of captain and the honor and prestige of their selection.

Nearly two decades later, several of the captaincies still had not been settled, and only two of them—those of Pernambuco and São Vicente—were economically successful. In both of these captaincies, the settlers benefited from the presence of go-betweens, linguistically and politically powerful interlocutors and cultural brokers such as Portuguese-born convicts like those noted earlier or shipwreck survivors who had integrated into particular indigenous communities, or the mixed-race descendants of Portuguese men

Come ce peuple couppe et porte le Bresil és nauires by André Thevet. Sixteenth-century woodcut of indigenous people collecting brazilwood for the Portuguese. From *La Cosmographic universelle d'André Thevet cosmographe du roy* (Paris: Chez Pierre L'Huillier, 1575). Courtesy of the John Carter Brown Library at Brown University.

and indigenous women known as *mamelucos*. The two captaincies also both produced sugar for export, using slave labor to do so. They first relied on enslaved Brazilian natives, inserting themselves into ongoing intraindigenous conflicts by forging alliances with groups like the Tupiniquim and enslaving their traditional enemies the Tupinambá. Over time, however, economic expansion led to growing Portuguese demand for slaves and a consequent increase in violence that impacted all nearby indigenous groups. The Portuguese thus soon began to introduce enslaved Africans, especially those with experience in the highly technical work of sugar processing. Meanwhile the vast majority of the captaincies remained unproductive for the Crown.

In 1549, Portugal once again shifted course, appointing a royal governor of Brazil for the first time and ordering the construction of a capital city in the former captaincy of Bahia (reclaimed by the Crown after the donatary captain's death), where there was already a small Portuguese settlement. So it was that Tomé de Sousa, governor-general of Brazil, arrived in March of that year. He came with an armada of six ships carrying over three hundred soldiers, some six hundred colonists (most of them convicts with skills in carpentry, blacksmithing, and stonemasonry, sent to Brazil as a form of penal exile), and six Jesuit priests, establishing the town of Nossa Senhora do Salvador da Bahia de Todos os Santos (today's Salvador da Bahia).

The six Jesuits, members of a new religious order that ministered to the poor, sick, and outcast, set to work studying indigenous languages and cultures in order to convert the indigenous populations, whom they considered lost souls with low moral standards, to Catholicism. Yet they soon found themselves at odds with Portuguese settlers, as they considered the settlers' moral lives worthy of reproach, especially their extensive concubinage with native women.

In the ensuing decades, waves of epidemic disease led to high death rates among native Brazilians, while growing settler demands resulted in increasingly violent interactions. The Jesuits tried to defend indigenous communities from the worst of these abuses, especially slavery, but the protective laws they helped establish were often disregarded. The Jesuits also ran into conflicts with Brazil's first bishop, Pedro Fernandes Sardinha, who arrived in 1551 and began to criticize their practice of incorporating Indian cultural practices into Catholic rituals. Ironically, perhaps, Sardinha became transformed into a martyr honored by the Jesuit order when his ship ran aground in 1556, and native peoples cannibalized him. By the arrival of Governor Mem de Sá in 1557, indigenous resistance was so strong that even many Jesuits supported the governor's decision to launch an extremely violent campaign against them. The Jesuit's missionary villages, or *aldeias*, originally founded to help protect native Brazilians from slavery expeditions, grew exponentially as the military campaigns destroyed indigenous settlements and soldiers forcibly relocated the natives to these enclaves. Such large concentrations of people in *aldeias* augmented the spread of epidemic disease, and a new wave of native deaths ensued.

Throughout the sixteenth century, foreign contests over Brazil continued, especially conflict with the French, who disputed the Portuguese and Spanish rights to territorial possession through the Treaty of Tordesillas. The French built strong alliances with indigenous groups along the coast, particularly the Tupinambá. Indeed, when Hans Staden, a German mercenary working for the Portuguese, was captured sometime in the early 1550s by Tupinambá warriors, he urgently tried to convince them he was not Portuguese in order to save himself. In 1555, the French decided to build their own formal colony in Guanabara Bay, near what is today Rio de Janeiro, which Governor Mem de Sá repeatedly attacked. Their leader in this venture, Nicolas Durand de Villegaignon, returned to France in 1559 in the face of intense internal conflict in the colony, and the Portuguese succeeded in expelling the French by 1567. Continued attacks on Portuguese farms by the Tupinambá led the

Portuguese to establish their own settlement in the area, founding the city of Rio de Janeiro.

By the late 1570s, most major foreign rivals to the Portuguese had been expelled from eastern Brazil, and indigenous resistance along its coast had been minimized. Sugar production began to expand significantly.

Letter to King Manuel I of Portugal

Pêro Vaz de Caminha

Pêro Vaz de Caminha, a Portuguese knight, accompanied explorer Pedro Álvares Ca-bral on his fateful voyage to India, when the fleet inadvertently stumbled upon the coast of Brazil. Born around 1450, Vaz de Caminha was at a rather advanced age to be undertaking such a voyage, but he had been awarded a position as secretary of a trading post to be built in Calcutta, and so needed to move there to take up office.

After the fleet spent eight days exploring the northeastern coast of Brazil, Cabral instructed Vaz de Caminha to write King Manuel I of Portugal informing him of their findings. The resulting letter, considered one of the most accurate accounts of how this area of Brazil looked at the time of first contact, describes vast forests of the brazil-wood trees that would later bring explorers to the coast to trade in their timber. The letter also includes detailed descriptions of the Tupi indigenous peoples they encoun-tered, whom Vaz de Caminha describes as innocent, simple, and free from shame or modesty, attributes he sees confirmed in their nakedness. The original letter, often referred to as the birth certificate of Brazil, is held in the National Archive of Torre do Tombo in Lisbon.

This same day, at the hour of vespers, we sighted land, that is to say, first a very high rounded mountain, then other lower ranges of hills to the south of it, and a plain covered with large trees. The admiral named the mountain Easter Mount, and the country the Land of the True Cross. . . .

We caught sight of men walking on the beaches. The small ships that ar-rived first said that they had seen some seven or eight of them. We let down the longboats and the skiffs. The captains of the other ships came straight to this flagship, where they had speech with the admiral. He sent Nicolau Coelho on shore to examine the river. As soon as the latter began to approach it, men came out on to the beach in groups of twos and threes, so that, when the longboat reached the river mouth, there were eighteen or twenty wait-ing. . . .

They are of a dark brown, rather reddish color. They have good, well-made faces and noses. They go naked, with no sort of covering. They attach no more importance to covering up their private parts or leaving them uncovered than they do to showing their faces. They are very ingenuous in that matter. They had both holes in their lower lips and a bone in them as broad as the knuckles of a hand and as thick as a cotton spindle and sharp at one end like a bodkin. They put these bones in from inside the lip, and the part that is placed between the lip and the teeth is made like a rook in chess. They fit them in in such a way that they do not hurt them nor hinder them talking or eating or drinking. . . .

The admiral had said when we had left the boat, that it would be best if we went straight to the cross which was leaning against a tree near the river ready to be set up on the next day, Friday; we all ought then to kneel and kiss it so that they could see the respect we had for it. We did so and signaled to the ten or twelve who were there to do the same, and they all at once went and kissed it.

They seem to be such innocent people that, if we could understand their speech and they ours, they would immediately become Christians, seeing that, by all appearances, they do not understand about any faith. Therefore if the exiles who are to remain here learn their speech and understand them, I do not doubt but that they will follow that blessed path which Your Majesty is desirous they should and become Christians and believe in our holy religion. May it please God to bring them knowledge of it, for truly these people are good and have a fine simplicity. Any stamp we wish may be easily printed on them, for the Lord has given them good bodies and good faces, like good men. I believe it was not without cause that He brought us here. Therefore Your Majesty, who so greatly wishes to spread the Holy Catholic faith, may look for their salvation. Pray God it may be accomplished with few difficulties.

They do not plough or breed cattle. There are no oxen here, nor goats, sheep, fowls, nor any other animal accustomed to live with man. They eat only *inhame* [yams], which are very plentiful here, and those seeds and fruits that the earth and the trees give of themselves. Nevertheless, they are of a finer, sturdier, and sleeker condition than we are for all the wheat and vegetables that we eat.

While they were there that day they danced and footed it continuously with our people to the sound of one of our tambourines, as if they were more our friends than we theirs. If we signed to them asking them if they wanted to come to our ships, they at once came forward, ready to come. So that, if we had invited them all, they all would have come. We did not, however, take more than four or five with us that night. The admiral took two: Simão de Miranda, whom he took as a page, and Aires Gomes, also as a page. One of those whom the admiral took was one of the guests who had been brought with him when we first arrived here; on this day he came dressed in his shirt and his brother with him. That night they were very handsomely treated,

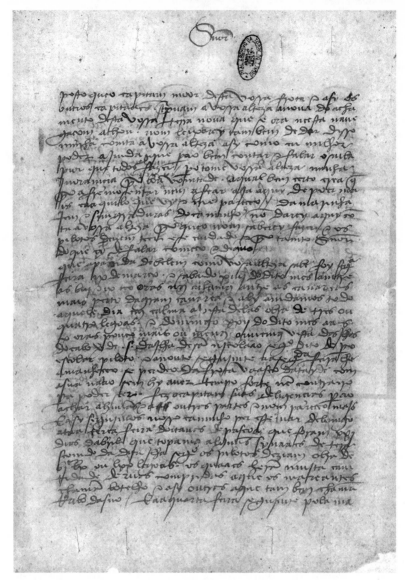

Letter from Pêro Vaz de Caminha to King Manuel I of Portugal. *Carta de Pêro Vaz de Caminha a El-Rei D. Manuel* (Bahia: Ed. Reis, 1900). Source: Biblioteca Nacional de Portugal.

not only in the way of food, but also to a bed with mattress and sheets, the better to tame them.

Today, Friday, 1st May, in the morning, we went on shore with our banner. We made our way up the river and disembarked on the southern bank at a place where it seemed best to us to set up the cross so that it might be seen to the best advantage. There the admiral marked the place for a pit to be made to plant the cross in. Whilst they were digging this, he and all of us went for the cross, down the river to where it was. We brought it from there as in a procession, with the friars and priest singing in front of us. There were many people about, some seventy or eighty. When they saw us coming, some of them went to help us to support the cross. We passed over the river along by the beach. We then went to set up the cross where it was to be, at some two bow-shots from the river. When we went to do this, a good hundred and fifty of those people and more came up. The cross was then planted, with Your Majesty's arms and motto on it, which had before been fastened to it, and they set up an altar by its side. Friar Henrique said Mass there, and the others who have been already mentioned did the singing and the officiating. About fifty or sixty of the people of the place were at the Mass, all on their knees as we were. When the Gospel came and we all stood with uplifted hands, they arose with us, lifted their hands, and stayed like that till it was ended. After which they again sat, as we did. When God's Body was elevated and we knelt, they all knelt and lifted their hands as we did and were so silent that I assure Your Majesty it much increased our devotion.

They stayed with us thus until the Communion was over. . . . Amongst those who stayed was a man of fifty or fifty-five years old—or rather he came up amongst those already there and also called others to come. He went in amongst them and spoke to them, pointing to the altar and afterwards at Heaven, as if he were speaking to a good purpose. We took it so.

When Mass was over, the priest removed his vestments, and mounted on a chair near the altar in his surplice. He preached to us on the Gospel and about the Apostles whose day it was. At the end of the sermon, he referred to the aim of your most holy and virtuous quest, which caused much devoutness.

The men who stayed all through the sermon looked at him as we did. The one I have spoken of called others to come. Some came and some went. At the end of the sermon, Nicolau Coelho brought a number of tin crucifixes that had remained over from his former journey. It was thought well that those people should each have one hung round their necks. Friar Henrique stood beside the cross for this purpose. There he hung a crucifix round each of their necks, first making him kiss it and raise his hands. Many came for this. All who came, some forty or fifty, had crucifixes hung round their necks.

At last, a good hour after midday, we went to the ships to eat. The admiral took with him the man who had pointed out the altar and Heaven to the others; he also took a brother of his. The admiral did him much honor and gave him a Moorish shirt and his brother a shirt like the others had had.

My opinion and every one's opinion is that these people lack nothing to become completely Christian except understanding us; for they accepted as we do all they saw us do, which makes us consider that they have no idolatry or worship. I believe that if Your Majesty could send someone who could stay awhile here with them, they would all be persuaded and converted as Your Majesty desires. Therefore, if anyone is coming out here, let him not omit to bring a clergyman to baptize them. For, by that time, they will have knowledge of our religion through the two exiles that are remaining with them, who also took communion today.

Only one woman came with those who were with us today. She was young and stayed throughout the Mass. We gave her a cloth to cover herself with and put it around her. But she did not pull it down to cover herself when she sat down. Thus, Sire, the innocence of Adam himself was not greater than these people's, as concerns the shame of the body. Your Majesty will judge if people who live in such innocence could be converted or not, if they were taught the things that belong to their salvation.

Our last action was to go and kiss the cross in their presence. We then took our leave and went to eat.

I think, Sire, that two cabin boys will also stay with the exiles we are leaving here, for they escaped to land in the skiff tonight and have not returned again. We think, I say, that they will stay, because, if God be willing, we are taking our departure here in the morning.

It appears to me, Sire, that the coast of this country must be a good twenty or twenty-five leagues in length from the most southerly point we saw to the most northerly point we can see from this port. In some parts there are great banks along by the shore, some of which are red and some white; inland it is all flat and very full of large woods. All the coastal country from one point to the other is very flat and very beautiful. As to the jungle, it seemed very large to us seen from the sea; for, look as we would, we could see nothing but land and woods, and the land seemed very extensive. Till now we have been unable to learn if there is gold or silver or any other kind of metal or iron there; we have seen none. However, the air of the country is very healthful, fresh, and as temperate as that of Entre Douro e Minho; we have found the two climates alike at this season. There is a plentitude of waters. The country is so well favored that, if it were rightly cultivated, it would yield everything, because of its waters.

For all that, the best fruit that could be gathered hence would be, it seems to me, the salvation of these people. That should be the chief seed for Your Majesty to scatter here. It would be enough reason, even if this were only a rest-house on the voyage to Calicut. How much more so will it be if there is a will to accomplish and perform in this land what Your Majesty so greatly desires, which is the spreading of our holy religion.

Thus, I have given Your Majesty an account of what I have seen in this land. If at some length, Your Majesty will pardon me, since my desire to tell you all made me relate it with such minuteness. And since, Sire, Your Majesty may be sure of my very faithful service in my present duties as in whatever may do you service, I beg of you as a signal favor that you send for Jorge de Ossório, my son-in-law, from the island of São Tomé—I should take this as a great kindness from you.

I kiss Your Majesty's hands.
From this Pôrto-Seguro, in Your Majesty's
island of Vera Cruz, today, Friday, 1st May 1500.

Pêro Vaz de Caminha

Captaincy Charter Granted to Duarte Coelho

King Dom João III

The Portuguese were noted sailors and explorers in the fifteenth and sixteenth centuries, and many of their early settlements, including Brazil, functioned largely as trading posts and sojourns during longer voyages. A small nation, Portugal relied on both the militarized character of its trading posts and agreements such as the Treaty of Tordesillas of 1494 to protect its colonial holdings. However, neither this treaty nor any other had much success in regulating the multiple and contested territorial claims in the New World, and the Portuguese Crown soon realized it would have to physically settle these lands if it wanted to protect them from European challengers. Because it did not have the resources to populate a new territory many times its size, especially one without the obvious and immediate sources of material wealth that drew the Spanish to present-day Mexico and Peru, the Portuguese Crown reconfigured a system they had first developed in Madeira.

As explained in the introduction to this part, in the 1530s royal administrators rather arbitrarily divided Brazil into fifteen donatary captaincies. Large land tracts, the captaincies began along the coastline and extended westward to an imaginary point, the supposed dividing line between Portuguese and Spanish territories in the New World as established by the Treaty of Tordesillas. The Crown then made certain citizens donatários, giving them the honor and the responsibility of colonizing one or more of these areas at their own expense, as well as the title of captain. These donatários were generally merchants, soldiers, sailors, and petty nobility who had served the king in some capacity; the high nobility had better prospects and did not feel the need to risk their lives and wealth in such dangerously unreliable and distant ventures.

In the following charter from 1534, King João III granted Duarte Coelho Pereira the captaincy of Pernambuco for his services to the Crown, including his help expelling the French from the Brazilian coast in 1532. The grant, drawn up by Manuel da Costa, who was likely a royal scribe, offers a view of the extensive rights the king granted to donatários. Pernambuco ended up being one of the two captaincies that flourished during this time, aided by go-betweens and relying on sugar produced by enslaved laborers. By the eighteenth century, all of the captaincies reverted to the Crown, as it sought a firmer grasp on the colony.

Dom João, etc.

To whom it may concern, I make it known that I now grant and award Duarte Coelho, nobleman of my lineage, to him and all his children, grand-children, heirs, and successors, by law and inheritance, forever, the captaincy and territory of sixty leagues of land along the coast of my colony of Bra-zil which begins at the river São Francisco, which is from the cape of São Agostinho toward the south, and ending at the river Santa Cruz. This is from the cape to a line according to a more explicit description in the grant that I have given him for the land. It is very necessary to have here a charter stating the taxes, rents, duties, and things that are to be paid in the land, in those of the territories that belong to me and the Crown, as well as those which be-long to the captain by the authority of the grant. I, because I enjoy rewarding him, thought it best to draw up and execute the charter for land, where he must now go to dwell, to populate it and exploit it. The sooner this is done the better, for the service of God and myself and for the good of the captain and inhabitants of the land.

Item: first of all, the captain of the land and his successors will give and di-vide the allotted land to any persons of any rank or status, so long as they are Christians, freely, without rent or tax at all, except for the tenth that they will be obliged to pay to the order of the mastership of our Lord Jesus Christ from everything that there is in the land. They will give these lands in the form and manner set forth in my ordinances. They cannot take allotted lands for themselves nor for their wives nor children. If they have any children who are not heirs of the captaincy, they can give them the land and likewise to their relatives as set forth in the grant. If any of the children who are not heirs of the captaincy or any other person who has any of this land should come to inherit the captaincy, he will be obliged to give the land up and to pass it on to another person within a year after inheriting the captaincy; and if he does not pass the land on within the prescribed time he will lose the land and be fined an additional sum equal to the price of the land. In such a case, I shall order my administrator or royal clerk who is in the captaincy on my behalf to take possession of the land for me and write it down in my courier's book and foreclose for the price of it. If he does not do this, he will lose his job and will pay me the equivalent value of the land.

Item: if there is any type of precious stones on the lands, coast, seas, rivers, and bays of the captaincy, such as pearls, seed pearls, gold, silver, coral, cop-per, tin, lead, or any other type of metal whatsoever, a fifth of it will be paid to me. The captain will have his tenth from this fifth as set forth in the grant and it will be paid to him at the same time that my officials collect my fifth.

Item: brazilwood from the captaincy and likewise any spice whatever or drug of any kind that might exist there will belong to me and will always be mine and my successors', without the captain or any other person being permitted to deal in the things. Neither can they sell them there in the land, or take them out for export to my kingdoms or holdings nor outside them under penalty of losing their property to the crown and being exiled to the island of São Tomé forever. Nevertheless, it is all right for the captain and also the inhabitants of the captaincy to use the wood as they find it necessary, except for burning, in which case the aforesaid penalties apply. . . .

Item: all the people of my kingdoms and estates as well as those outside of them who go to the captaincy may not deal with or buy from or sell anything to the heathen of the land. They will deal only with the captain and inhabitants of the land, buying, selling, and paying for all they have. He who does to the contrary will lose double the amount of his goods and things he is dealing in with the heathen. A third of such goods will go to my royal council, a third to the accuser, and the other third to the spiritual establishment that might be in the land. If there is no such establishment, the money shall go toward building a church for one. . . .

Item: the inhabitants and settlers and people of the captaincy will be obligated in time of war to serve in it with the captain if it be necessary. Thus I give notification to the present captain of the captaincy and those who will be captains in the future, and to my administrator and clerk and officials, judges and justices of the captaincy, and the other justices and officials of my kingdoms and estates, officials of justice as well as property; I command that all in general and each one in particular comply with, preserve, and make obeyed and preserved this my charter in the manner set forth by it without any doubt, restriction, or contradiction whatsoever, for this is my will. For the sake of consistency, I had this letter circulated, signed by me, and sealed with my seal, pending its recording in the books of my administration of the captaincy and also in my customs house in Lisbon. Likewise, it will be recorded in the books of the councils and villages and settlements of the captaincy so that all may know the contents of this charter and comply in every way.

> Manuel da Costa drew up [this document]
> in Évora the 23rd of September in the year of
> our Lord Jesus Christ 1534.

Translated by Emma Wohl

Letter from a Jesuit Friar

Manuel da Nóbrega

When the first governor-general of Brazil, Tomé de Sousa, disembarked in Bahia in 1549, one of the Jesuits who accompanied him was thirty-two-year-old Manuel da Nóbrega, brimming with optimism and enthusiasm for the missionaries' task of converting the numerous and diverse indigenous population to the Catholic faith. He quickly set about learning Tupi, one of the predominant native languages, and soon began to campaign fiercely for restrictions on Indian slavery, arguing that religious conversion depended upon it. His efforts contributed to the Crown's decision to allow enslavement only of those Indians captured by other tribes and thereby slated for human sacrifice, a practice the Portuguese called resgate *(rescue). But he faced repeated conflicts with settlers who abused the* resgate *provision to justify illegal enslavement, and whose relationships with Indian women Nóbrega criticized. By 1558, he became so discouraged by the challenges of conversion that he supported the use of military attacks against the Indians and their forcible relocation into aldeias, or villages, where they would be under Church supervision and supposed protection from abusive settlers.*

A decade after he arrived, Nóbrega wrote to Tomé de Sousa, now in Portugal, to update him on the situation in Brazil and request his counsel. In this letter Nóbrega's commitment to protecting the indigenous people from settler abuses remains, but his acceptance of the use of force to do so, and the fatigue of his ten years of effort, are also apparent. Nonetheless, in an ironic tone he directs most of his ire at Bishop Sardinha, who was killed by the native population and who had not shared Nóbrega's commitment to indigenous conversion, and at the Christian colonists themselves, whose sexual practices and abuse of the resgate *law continued to scandalize the Jesuit.*

May the peace and love of Christ our Lord always be in your continuous favor and assistance. Amen. . . .

First, I want to lament about this land and offer you an account of the particular things that I most have in my soul . . . because I see the evil path that this land takes, always deserving from our Lord great chastisement. Although punished for its sins, it deserves other, greater punishments, because it becomes ever more incorrigible and obstinate.

Since I have been in this land, to which I came with Your Excellency, two wishes have tormented me: one is to see the customs of Christians of these parts reformed so that there would be good seeds transplanted in these parts by the fragrance of good example; and another, to see a disposition in the heathens to be able to understand the word of God, so that they would become capable of grace and able to enter into the church of God. . . .

From these two wishes that I mentioned, others came to me, which were hopes for the means of fulfilling the first two. To these ends, I chose two that seemed best. One was to seek a bishop, such as Your Excellency did, as I envisioned reforming the Christians. Another was to see the heathens subjugated and thrown under the yoke of obedience to the Christians, so that they can understand all that we might want. The heathen is of a nature that, once subdued, the faith of Christ will be written very well in his understandings and desires, as was done in Peru and the Antilles, since the heathen [in Brazil] appear to be in a condition similar to theirs. We now are starting to see through the hindsight of experience, as I will relate below, that if they are left to liberty and free will, as they are brutal heathens, nothing will come of them. Through experience we have seen that this entire time we have spent a lot of work on them, but without reaping more fruit from it than a few innocent souls that we have sent to heaven.

Our Lord brought the Bishop Dom Pedro Fernandes [Sardinha], such a virtuous person, whom Your Excellency knows, and very zealous about reforming the customs of the Christians. However, as to the heathens and their salvation, he gave little of himself because he did not believe in it. They seemed to him incapable of [learning] the entire doctrine because of their brutishness and bestiality. Nor did he consider them sheep in his flock. He also did not feel that Christ our Lord would see fit to have them as such. However, Your Excellency helped me in this, to the praise of our Lord in his providence, by permitting [the bishop] to flee from the heathens and the land, having little desire to die in their hands and to be eaten by them. As for me, I always desired this and asked our Lord for it, and also asked that he send me, when he had the opportunity, someone greater than the bishop; but this was denied to me. What I judge from this, seeing that I was not the counselor of Your Excellency, is that whoever did this perhaps wanted to pay the bishop for his virtues and great kindness, and punish him simultaneously for his carelessness and the negligible zeal that he had for the salvation of the heathen. He [God] punished him [the bishop], giving him the death penalty, which He did not love [doing], and compensated him with the punishment, being as glorious as they now claim to Your Excellency that it was, given that he [the bishop] was in the power of the unfaithful with as many and as good circumstances as he did have.

The bishop, seeing that he was very zealous in the salvation of the Christians, did little because he was alone and brought with him some clerics as companions, who followed his example and badly used and dispensed the church's sacraments, giving them to everyone in perdition. . . . And when they came, they introduced into the land [the practice] that clerics and dignities would cohabit with their [Indian] slaves, and for this end they chose the best and most expensive they could find, with the resulting sin that they were reconciled to having whomever served them, and soon started to make children and propagate. . . .

They also started to dispense the sacraments, and untied the cords with which we saved souls, giving jubilee in place of condemnation and perdition to the souls, sanctifying dogs and throwing pearls to swine. . . . Thus, the land is . . . full of moral sins, full of adultery, fornication, incest, and abominations, so much so that I no longer care if Christ has anyone pure in this land, and there are no more than one or two who remain pure, at least without committing public sin. . . .

Another sin, also born from this infernal root, is that the Christians teach the heathens to kidnap their own people and sell them as slaves. I found this custom in Espirito Santo, under the rule of Vasco Fernandez, seeing more of it occurring there throughout the better part of his captaincy.

In São Vicente, those heathens, the Topinachins [Tupiniquim], do not do this, but the Christians of São Vicente . . . negotiated [to obtain] from the heathens . . . many females whom they sought as wives, giving their fathers some payment, but they [the women] will remain slaves forever. In Pernambuco, there also is much conduct of this sort, principally after the past wars that the Indians waged, although they are no longer capable [of waging wars].

The same was introduced into Bahia in the time of Dom Duarte, because in the time of Your Excellency, none of this was yet accepted. After the past war, from which the Indians emerged timid, and because of fear and subjugation by the Christians, as well as the greed for the ransom, the Indians sell the most forlorn who are among them. Those of Porto Seguro and Ilheus never will sell their own, but the Christians taught them that they might attack and sell those of the backlands who come to produce salt from the sea. Thus, those of the sea sell those of the backlands for as much as they can, because the depredation that the Christians have taught them seems fine.

Because this is the general conduct of everyone, it befitted me to stop listening to confessions because no one wants to do what is required of that [sacrament], and all of the other clergy absolve and support them.

From this same root evil is born [the situation] that Christians were little disposed to the salvation of the slaves whom they brought from the heathens, allowing them to live according to their law, with neither doctrine nor teaching, in a state of sin. And, if they die, they bury them in the dunghills, because they only want their service. So that Christians might have more of those who might serve them, they bring heathens into their houses and find pleasure with the female slaves, and thus the Christians are cohabiting with heathens.

I now have told Your Excellency most of my sorrow. . . . I beseech you through the charity of Christ our Lord to rescue this poor Brazil. . . . May he give you, through his mercy, his peace on earth and glory in heaven. Amen.

From Bahia, 5 July 1559
Servant of Your Excellency in Christ,
Manuel da Nóbrega

Translated by Robert M. Levine and John J. Crocitti

Impressions of a French Calvinist

Nicolas Barre

France tried to colonize Brazil twice in the sixteenth and seventeenth centuries. The first attempt, in 1555, became known as Antarctic France. Nicolas Durand de Villegaignon led an expeditionary force of soldiers and artisans that established Fort Coligny on an island in Guanabara Bay. However, the experiment was fraught with internal conflicts. In an effort to resolve some of these problems, in early 1556, Villegaignon wrote to a former classmate from law school in Orleans, John Calvin, a French theologian and an important figure in the Protestant Reformation, requesting that he send some of his followers. The next year fourteen French Protestants (Huguenots) arrived, but their presence merely exacerbated the tensions among the colonists. In reaction to the authoritarian way that Villegaignon administered the settlement, the Calvinists soon abandoned Fort Coligny, set up their own fortifications on coastal land, and allied themselves with the Tupinambá Indians.

Among the colonists were André Thevet, who would later become a royal cosmographer, and Jean de Léry, who, shocked by stories of ritualistic cannibalism among the Tupinambá, wrote what would become one of the most often quoted accounts of the so-called Brazilian savages (see his History of a Voyage to the Land of Brazil). *Villegaignon stayed in the colony until 1559, recording his impressions in letters he sent back to Europe. There was such interest in Villegaignon's experiment in Brazil that these and other letters were immediately published in France, where they circulated widely. Below are extracts of a letter dated 1556 that was written by Nicolas Barre, one of the Calvinist settlers, in which he comments on the idyllic nature of the land. Barre praises its mild climate and sweet water and registers his horror of and repulsion toward the indigenous people, observations that were quickly becoming familiar literary tropes.*

They go about completely nude with their bows and arrows, saying—in their tongue—that we are welcome, offering us their goods, making fire, and saying that we had come to defend them against the Portuguese and other of their mortal enemies. . . .

The place is naturally beautiful and easy to guard, seeing as its entrance is narrow and closed in by mountains.

French Franciscan priest and cosmographer André Thevet's depiction of monsters he allegedly saw in the French Antarctic. From *Les singularitez de la France Antarctique, autrement nommée Amerique* (Antwerp: Christophle Plantin, 1558). Courtesy of the John Carter Brown Library at Brown University.

The land is irrigated and has beautiful rivers of fresh water, the healthiest I ever drank. The air is temperate, tending more to heat than cold. . . . This is what I noted about the fertility of the land, its healthfulness, and the disposition of the air. . . .

This nation is the most barbarous and strange, in all honesty, that can be found under the sky, I believe. They live without knowledge of God, without worries, without law or whatever religion; they are no more than brute beasts driven only by their feelings. They are naked, not having any shame of their pubic parts, the men as much as the women. Their language is very rich in manner of speech, but limited in vocabulary, such that when they want to signify five they show five fingers. They make war with five or six nations, from which they take prisoners and give them in marriage to the most beautiful daughters they have. . . .

These savages are very cruel . . . who divide their prisoner in many pieces and eat him with great pleasure. . . . They greatly enjoy the weapons of the French and all that comes from our country, above all gold, silver, and other stones. . . .

Well, my brothers, that is what I can remember or describe in writing of that whole voyage, in that moment to Guanabara, in the country of Brazil in Antarctic France and below the Tropic of Capricorn on that first day of February of 1556.

Your perfect friend,
N.B. Thursday, July 23, 1556.

Translated by Emma Wohl

Indigenous Experiences of Colonization

Eduardo Viveiros de Castro

*Works such as those by French anthropologist Claude Lévi-Strauss (1908–2009) tes-
tify to the profound and complex mythologies of the indigenous peoples of Brazil. In
this text, ethnologist Eduardo Viveiros de Castro, professor of anthropology at the
National Museum in Rio de Janeiro, explains how observers of Brazil from the early
colonial period to the twentieth century have attached certain stereotypical images to
the indigenous population, stereotypes that still persist today.*

In a magnificent page of the *Sermon of the Holy Spirit* (1657), Antonio Vieira
writes:

> You who have walked through the world and have entered the homes
> of princes have seen in those rooms and on garden paths two very dif-
> ferent types of statues, those made of marble, and those made of myrtle
> [topiaries]. The marble statue is expensive to create, due to the mate-
> rial's rigidity and resistance; but once it's done, no one needs to touch
> it again: it always conserves and sustains the same shape. The myr-
> tle statue is easier to mold, for the ease with which one can bend the
> branches, but one must constantly adjust it and work on it so it keeps
> it shape. If the gardener stops attending to it, in four days a branch
> escapes and crosses the eyes, another escapes and disfigures the ears,
> and two escape from the five fingers to make seven, and what was once
> a man soon becomes a confusion of green myrtle. This is the differ-
> ence between some nations and others in doctrines of faith. There are
> some naturally tough, tenacious, and constant nations, those that only
> after great struggle accept faith and leave behind the errors of their
> ancestors. They resist with weapons, they doubt enlightenment, they
> repel it at will, they close themselves off, they fear, they argue, they of-
> fer retorts, they struggle until they surrender; but, once surrendered,
> once they have received the faith, they believe firmly and constantly,
> like statues of marble: it is not necessary to work on them further. But
> there are other nations—among them, Brazil—that receive everything

that is taught to them with great docility and ease, without arguments, without retorts, without doubts, without resistance; but these are the statues of myrtle that, once the gardener lifts his hand and shears, soon lose their new figure and return to their ancient and natural brutality, and the nation becomes the backwoods of before. The master of these statues must always keep watch on them: first, he must cut what grows around the eyes, so that they believe in that which they do not see; next, he must restrict what grows around the ears, so that they do not listen to the fables of their ancestors; then, he must trim that which grows around the feet so that they refrain from their barbaric acts and customary behaviors. It is only in this manner, always working against the nature of the body and the mood of the roots, that one can conserve in these uncultured plants the unnatural form and behavior of the branches.[1]

Fernando Pessoa, known as the emperor of the Portuguese language, has elaborated on this passage in his writings about Jesuit literature on the Amerindians. The topic was raised at the beginning of Jesuit activities in Brazil in 1549 and can be summed up in one sentence: the people of the country were exasperatingly difficult to convert. Not that they were made of refractory and intractable material; on the contrary, they were excited by new things, but at the same time incapable of being indelibly impressed by them. A people receptive to any figure but impossible to configure, the indigenous people were—to use a simile that is less European than topiary—like the jungle that surrounded them, always ready to close in on the spaces precariously taken over by European culture. They were like their land, deceptively fertile, where everything seemed like it could be planted, but where nothing sprouted that wasn't suffocated by weeds. This people without faith, without law, and without king would not provide a psychological and institutional ground in which the Gospel could lay its roots.

Among the pagans of the Old World, the missionary knew the obstacles that he had to overcome: idols and priests, liturgies and theologies—religions worthy of the name, despite rarely being as exclusionary as their own. In Brazil, on the other hand, the word of God was joyfully received by one ear and carelessly ignored by the other. The enemy here was not another dogma, but an indifference to dogma, a refusal to choose. Fickleness, indifference, forgetfulness: "the people of these lands are the most brutish, the most ungrateful, the most unstable, the most backward, the most difficult to teach of all that there are in the world," the disillusioned Vieira lists off. This is why Saint Thomas was appointed by Christ to preach in Brazil; just punishment for the apostle of doubt, he was to bring faith to those unable to believe—or able to believe in everything, which amounts to the same problem: "other peoples are incredulous until they believe; Brazilians, even after they believe, are incredulous."[2]

The savage is mobile. The theme of Amerindian fickleness is extensive, within and beyond missionary reflections and far beyond their primordial example of the coastal Tupinambá. Serafim Leite, a historian from the Society of Jesus in Brazil, grounds himself in the observations of the first missionaries to identify the "deficiency of will" and the "superficiality of feelings" as principal impediments to converting the Amerindians; but he also resorts to the opinion of laypeople, some unsuspicious of the Jesuits: Gabriel Soares de Souza, Alexandre Rodrigues Ferreira, Capistrano de Abreu, all unanimous in pointing out the amorphousness of the savage spirit.[3] This proverbial fickleness was not just limited to issues of faith. It became a defining feature of the Amerindian character, consolidating into a stereotype in the national imagination: the newly converted Indian who, at the first opportunity that God allows, gives his garden hoe and clothing to the Devil and happily returns to the jungle, imprisoned in an incurable atavism. This fickleness is a constant in the savage equation.

The image of the fickle savage is conspicuous in historiography since the eminent and reactionary [nineteenth-century historian] Varnhagen: "they were false and unfaithful, fickle and ungrateful."[4] The importation of African manual labor, it is widely known, was frequently justified by the inability of the indigenous people to tolerate work on the sugarcane plantations. The racialist anthropology of Gilberto Freyre emphasizes the contrast between the animal vigor of Africans and the vegetative laziness of the Amerindians.[5] More politically correct authors than these two also explore the Amerindian/African opposition in terms of the instability of the Brazilian people:

> [The ancient residents of this land] adapted poorly . . . to the precise and methodic work that sugarcane production requires. Their spontaneous nature was suited for less sedentary activities that could be carried out without forced regularity, vigilance, or the supervision of outsiders. Versatile to the extreme, for them certain notions of order, stability, and exactness were inaccessible, notions that form a sort of second nature in the European and seem like fundamental requirements for the existence of civil society.[6]

The theme of "three races" in the formation of Brazilian nationality tends to attribute to each race the predominance of one trait: to the Indian, perception; to the Africans, emotion; and to Europeans, reason, on a scale that, as in Freyre, evokes the three souls of Aristotelian doctrine. And while referring to Aristotle, patron of the sixteenth-century debate about the nature and condition of the American people, I ask myself, with due fear of the ridiculous, if he [Aristotle] does not have a part in the history of the vegetative image of the Amerindian, precisely because of this proverbial fickleness and indifference to faith. . . .

Translated by Molly Quinn

Notes

1. António Vieira, "Sermão do Espirito Santo," in *Sermões, 1657*, vol. 5 (São Paulo: Editora das Américas, 1957), 216.
2. Vieira, "Sermão do Espirito Santo," 216.
3. Serafim Leite, *História da Companhia de Jesus no Brasil*, vol. 11 (Lisbon/Rio de Janeiro: Livraria Portugália/Civilização Brasileira, 1938), 7–11.
4. Francisco Adolfo de Varnhagen, *História Geral do Brasil antes da sua separação e independência de Portugal* (1854; repr., São Paulo: Melhoramentos, 1959), 51.
5. Gilberto Freyre, *Casa-grande e senzala: Formação da família brasileira sob o regimen da economia patriarcal* (Rio de Janeiro: Maia e Schmidt, 1933), 316–18.
6. Sérgio Buarque de Holanda, *Raizes do Brasil* (Rio de Janeiro: José Olimpio, 1936), 43.

On Cannibals

Michel de Montaigne

Michel de Montaigne (1533–1592) exemplified European fascination with the Tupi-nambá practice of ritualistic cannibalism of enemy fighters, writing an essay about it even though he had never been to Brazil. Montaigne began thinking about canni-balism in Brazil when a handful of Indians were taken to Rouen, France, in 1550, where the French attempted to stage an authentic Indian ritual for the monarchs. Indeed, the very notion of cross-cultural differences sparked curiosity on both sides. While the Europeans wondered about the souls of the indigenous people of the Ameri-cas and brought them to Europe in an effort to scrutinize and civilize them, the na-tives of the New World drowned a number of Europeans in lakes in order to discover whether or not they had souls.

In Montaigne's case, however, he used what he heard about Brazil to reflect on and critique his own society. In his 1580 essay "On Cannibals," excerpted below, the French philosopher achieves an exercise in comparative sociology, arguing that Tu-pinambá warfare, as he understood it, was more valid and humane than many Eu-ropean practices. The violent and fratricidal religious wars that consumed Europe at the time no doubt influenced Montaigne's questions about Western civilization: at least the Tupinambá knew why they fought. Yet in the process of using stories of the Tupinambá to critique European violence, he romanticizes native Brazilian men as naturally noble, generous and brave, while also labeling them barbarous, in this sense prefiguring Jean-Jacques Rousseau's later idea of the noble savage. He also un-derstands Tupinambá warfare as an exclusively male phenomenon, as if indigenous women played no role whatsoever.

These people have continual war with the nations that live further from the mainland, beyond their mountains, to which they go naked, and with no other arms than their bows and wooden swords sharpened like the heads of our javelins. The resolve with which they fight is admirable, and they never end without great effusion of blood, for they are ignorant of flight and fear. Each one brings home the head of a slaughtered enemy as a trophy, and each one fixes the head over the door of his house. As for the prisoners, after guarding them for some time, they treat them well and provide for them all their needs until the day they decide to finish them off. The one to whom the prisoner belongs invites a great assembly of his friends. In the right moment, he ties a rope to one of the arms of the prisoner, holds the one end himself, and gives the other arm to his best friend to hold in the same manner, leaving the condemned a few steps' distance and unable to resist. After this, they both dispatch him with their swords in the presence of the whole assembly, then roast and eat him, and send some chops to their absent friends. They do not do this, however, for nourishment, as the ancient Scythians did, but as a sign of vengeance. The proof comes in observing the Portuguese, who were in league with their enemies, upon whom they inflicted another sort of death when taking them prisoner, which was to bury them up to the waist in the earth, shoot at the remaining part till it was stuck full of arrows, and then hang them. They thought that these people from the other world, being men who had sown the knowledge of many vices among their neighbors and were much greater masters than themselves in every sort of wickedness, did not adopt this sort of vengeance without some reason, and that it must be more painful than their own; so they began to give up their old method and to follow this one.

I am not sorry that we notice the barbarous horror of such acts, but I am heartily sorry that, judging their faults rightly, we should be so blind to our own. I think there is more barbarity in eating a man alive than in eating him dead; and in tearing by tortures and the rack a body still full of feeling, in roasting a man bit by bit, in having him bitten and mangled by dogs and swine (as we have not only read but seen within fresh memory, not among ancient enemies, but among neighbors and fellow citizens, and what is worse, on the pretext of piety and religion), than in roasting and eating him after he is dead. . . .

So we may well call these people barbarians, in respect to the rules of reason, but not in respect to ourselves, who surpass them in every kind of barbarity. Their warfare is wholly noble and generous, and as excusable and beautiful as this human disease can be; its only basis among them is their rivalry in valor.

They do not fight for the conquest of new lands, for those they already possess are so fruitful by nature as to supply them without labor or concern with all things necessary, in such abundance that they have no need to enlarge their borders. And they are, moreover, happy in that they only covet so much as their natural necessities require: all beyond that is superfluous to them. They treat each other as brothers when they are the same age, and those who are younger, children; and the old men are fathers to all. When they die, they leave their belongings to their natural heirs, who hold in common the full possession of goods, with no other designation than what nature bestows upon them to sustain them. If their neighbors come down from the mountains to attack them and are victorious, the only benefit of victory is glory and the advantage of having proved themselves superior in valor and virtue, for they would not know what to do with the spoils of victory. Presently, they return to their own country where they want for nothing and where they may enjoy their condition and to be content. And if they are conquered, their enemies in turn do the same. They demand of their prisoners no other ransom than acknowledgment that they are overcome.

But there is not one among them, of any age, who would not rather die than belie, by word or disposition, that courage that they wish to display above all. There is not a man among them who had not rather be killed and eaten than beg for mercy. They grant them full liberty, so that their lives may be so much the dearer to them, and frequently entertain them with menaces of their approaching death, of the torments they are to suffer, of the preparations for the sacrifice, of the mangling of their limbs, and of the feast that is to be made. All this is done to pry from them some word of complaint or weakness or to make them run away, by which they show that they have terrified their victims and shaken their constancy. Indeed, it is in this and only this that victory exists: "True victory is that which constrains one's enemies to confess themselves defeated."

On the Customs of the Indians of the Land

Pero de Magalhães Gândavo

The literature left by sixteenth-century travelers tends to oscillate between enchant-
ment and horror—enchantment at the sight of the impressive natural environment of
Portuguese America, and horror at the practices of the "new humanity" that inhab-
ited it. Cannibalism, polygamy, and nudity, for example, generated such intense sus-
picion of indigenous peoples that many Europeans debated whether or not they were
even human. It was only in 1534 that the papal bull of Paul III asserted that humanity
was one and indivisible.

Pero de Magalhães Gândavo was a sixteenth-century traveler to Brazil, likely a
scribe at the Torre do Tombo Portuguese National Archive, a servant and attendant
at the Chamber of King Sebastião I, and an administrator of the treasury in 1576. He
lived in Brazil in the 1560s and early 1570s, and wrote Tratado da Terra do Brasil
(Treaty of Brazil) sometime before 1573 and História da Província de Santa Cruz
(History of the province of Santa Cruz) in 1576. These two works became some of the
best-known Portuguese accounts of the indigenous inhabitants of the land that would
be called Brazil. They provided an almost canonical shape to Portuguese debates
about the nature of the indigenous peoples they encountered and the justification for
their own treatment of them.

It is impossible to count or to comprehend the multitude of barbaric pagans
that nature has planted throughout the land of Brazil, because nobody can
walk safely through the *sertão* nor pass through the land without encoun-
tering populations of Indians armed against all other peoples. As they are
so numerous, God allowed that they oppose one another, and that there be
fierce hatred and discord between them, because if this were not the case the
Portuguese would not be able to live in this land nor conquer such a powerfully large people.

There were many of these Indians along the coast near the Captaincies;
the area was full of them when the Portuguese began to populate the land.
But because these same Indians rose against them and betrayed them, the
governors and captains of the land destroyed them little by little and killed
many of them. Others fled to the *sertão*, and in this way the coast was de-

populated of pagans in all of the Captaincies. Next to the Captaincies other, peaceful Indians remained in the *aldeias* and were friends of the Portuguese.

The pagans along all the entire coast share one language: it lacks three letters—namely, you do not find in it an F, nor an L, nor an R, which is a frightening thing, for without these letters you cannot have Faith, nor Law, nor King [*Rei*], and in this manner they live without Justice and in complete disorder.

These Indians walk naked without any kind of covering, men as well as women; they do not cover any part of their body; and they display uncovered all that nature gave them. They all live in villages; there could be in each of them seven or eight houses, which are as long as rope factories, and each of them is full of people from one part or another, and each person has his own place and own hammock strung up where he sleeps. Thus they are all together, in order, and through the middle of the house is an open corridor they can use. There is not among them any King or Justice; each village only has one principal that is like a Captain, who is obeyed by choice and not through force. If this principal dies, then his son is put in this same role. He does not do anything besides go with them to war and tell them how to act in battle, but he does not punish their mistakes or order them to do anything against their will. This principal has three or four wives; the first is the most important, and he pays more attention to her than to the others. He has this as a matter of his position and honor. They do not worship anything at all nor believe that there will be glory in the next life for the good and punishment for the wicked; every person's existence ends in this life, and the soul dies with the body. This is how they live like animals without responsibility, regret, or restraint. . . .

These Indians are inhuman and cruel; they are not moved by piety. They live like brute animals without order or human concord. They are very dishonest and given to sensuality, and they give themselves over to vice as if they had no human reason, even though the males and females are always reserved in their congress, and in this they show that they have some shame. All of them eat human flesh and consider it the greatest delicacy: not the flesh of their friends with whom they have peace, but of their enemies. There is this quality to them: whatever they eat, no matter how small, they must share it with all who are present, this is the only intimacy to be found among them. They eat all the creatures of the land and will not reject anything, no matter how poisonous, except for spiders.

The male Indians have a custom of ripping out their beards, and they do not permit hair to grow anywhere on their body except for the top of their head, even removing all the hair on the sides of their heads. The females pay much attention to their hair and wear most of it long and combed, and the rest braided. The males customarily pierce their lips and place a rock in the hole as a form of gallantry. Others have their faces full of holes and look very ugly and deformed: they do this to them when they are children. Some Indians walk around with their whole bodies painted, doing this by scratching writing into their flesh; only those who have committed some act of bravery can do this. And both males and females have the custom of dyeing themselves with the juice of a fruit known as the *genipapo*, which is green when it is cut, but once it is put on the body and dries it becomes very black. Even with a great deal of washing, it does not come off for nine days. This they do for gallantry.

These Indian women are faithful to their husbands and are their great friends, because they do not tolerate adultery. Many of the men marry their nieces, daughters of their brothers or sisters. These are their true wives, and fathers cannot refuse requests for these marriages.

Some of the Indian women found in these parts swear and promise chastity. They do not marry and do not know any man at all, nor would they consent to even if threatened with death. These women stop doing any women's work and imitate the men and take on men's work as if they were not women. They cut their hair in the same way as the men, and they go to war with bows and arrows and hunt. They are always in the company of men, and each has a woman who serves and cooks for her as if they were married.

These Indians have a very calm existence; they do not worry about anything other than eating, drinking, and killing people, and for this reason they are extremely fat. With any sorrow, however, they become very skinny, as they become irritated easily and begin to eat dirt. In this way, many of them die like beasts. All of them follow the advice of the old women. Whatever the old women say, they do, and they consider their advice very correct. Due to this, many of those who live here will not buy any old women so they will not make their slaves run away. When these Indian women give birth, the first thing they do after the birth is wash themselves in a creek and they become as [sexually] willing as if they had not given birth. Their husbands lie in their place in the hammock, and the new mothers visit and take care of them as if the husbands were the ones who had just given birth.

When one of the Indians dies, it is the custom to bury him in a grave seated on his feet with the hammock in which he slept around his shoulders. For the first few days, food is left on top of the grave. These Indians practice many other bestial acts that I will not describe here because my intention was not to be lengthy but to touch on all of this briefly.

Translated by Molly Quinn

A Description of the Tupinambá

Anonymous

Unlike the Aztecs and Incas encountered by Spaniards, Brazil's diverse and heterogeneous first peoples produced few artifacts and no monuments or codices from which historians might piece together their pre-sixteenth-century way of life. Furthermore, by 1600, European diseases, warfare, trade, and culture had drastically altered life for those indigenous groups who dwelled along the coast. Sixteenth-century descriptions written by Europeans are therefore valuable yet problematic tools for retrieving, at least partially, the indigenous past.

After seventeen years of Brazilian travels, an anonymous author left the following account in 1587. Focusing on one Tupi tribe, the Tupinambá, this account belies the idyllic image that some Europeans of this era assigned to Brazilian Indians. The tribe's sexual practices and war rituals particularly fascinated its author. We should be cautious about assuming that all of the details described in this account are accurate or entirely inaccurate. While accounts such as this contain some reflections of what the observer witnessed firsthand, they also reflect their interpretations of what they saw, their preconceived ideas, and their creative imagination.

The Tupinambá live arranged in villages; in each one, everybody recognizes one person as their leader, or chief, so that in war he directs them; this is the only act in which they offer him any demonstration of obedience. They elect him by the proof he has given of having more power and valor than others; yet outside of instances of war, he does not receive better treatment, esteem, or respect than the rest, from whom he is not distinguished.

When this chief heathen settles his village, he always looks for some high, clear site, bathed by winds, that there might be good and nearby water, and that the land might be compatible for their crops. After the site is chosen and approved by the oldest men, the leader makes his home very long, covered with palms; and the rest, by the same method, also go about forming their houses, arranging them in squares that appear like plazas, in which they conduct their gatherings and dances. In each house there is an old Indian, who serves as head of the household and is related to the rest.

These houses last as long as the palms, which serve as a roof, keep from rotting, which is always past three or four years; as often as this happens, they move the site. In the houses, there is not any quality of a room other than the beams, which fall between the branches where each clan is sheltered. The old heathen chooses a place for his hut, where he settles with his woman, friends, children, and the old unmarried women who serve him. And soon, the rest go about settling. They do not move from these huts, except when a single male marries and wants to make a hut for himself because, in this instance, he does it with his woman.

On top of the beams of the houses, they insert some tightly joined poles, in which they store their utensils, vegetables, and everything else they have. When they eat, the whole hut gathers and, squatting over their legs (except the chief, who remains resting in the hammock), they eat what they have. In these same houses, they engage in their carnal couplings without safeguards or discretion for sex and age, with all the public display of brutes.

If the villages adjoin those of their rivals, they make fences of wattle and daub, strong and tightly joined, with their doors and openings from twenty to thirty palms [spans of a hand] distant from the houses; and of a manner that a rampart is formed, which is sufficient, which hinders entrance to the enemy, and defends the villagers and facilitates shooting arrows from inside, if the enemies intend to assault them, as very often occurs. . . .

The true woman of the Tupinambá is the first whom he knows [in the carnal sense]. In their marriages, the ceremonies are nothing more than the father giving the daughter to the son-in-law, and as long as they know each other carnally, they remain married. In addition to this, each one has whomever else he wants; and the best nobility or dignity among them is judged by the greatest number of women had. However, all the women recognize the superiority of the first one and serve her, and she is not offended to have them as companions in the art of cohabitating with her husband. She is the one who has her hammock joined to that of the husband; the others are more distant, and between each a fire is always burning at night.

In that which regards cohabitation, however, there is neither subordination nor discretion among the women; the husband gets up from his hammock when it strikes him and lies down in the hammock of the one whom he craves, and in view of the rest, satisfies his desires, without the others being upset for being passed over. Still, he can be with the first woman as much time as it strikes him and with the rest only the time necessary for the conclusion of his lustful act.

Despite this, secret jealousies gravely torment the women, especially the first woman; although they might not be able to complain about these relationships, by custom, this does not avoid nor impede stimuli for rivalry because of the knowledge of there being women more to the liking of the common husband, those whom he more often seeks for cohabitation.

[For] the Indian who is not chief of the village, the more children he has, the more honorable his reputation among the rest. They seek daughters from him (especially single men seeking their first woman) and serve [him for] two or three years, primarily so that the father might facilitate the daughters' relationship with them. The daughters are awarded to those who better serve the father, and for that the lovers willingly care about doing good for him, in order to win their intended loves. This service consists of going to cultivate the field for him, to kill game and fish, to bring him firewood from the forest, and to perform every salutation to him with fine diligence.

As soon as the father awards the daughter to the pretender, he lies down with her in the hammock of the said father, from which they arise married, and the daughter, then leaving the father's hut, parting from siblings and relatives, goes with the husband to his hut. If she still is not a woman, she is not offered to the husband until she arrives at that age, which is known easily.

[This is] because the female, until she is a perfect woman, walks about without wearing any article of distinction; and, as soon as she is [a perfect woman], she has the obligation to wear a string of cotton around the waist, and another around the wrists, by which is given the news that she is fit for marriage. However, if some man who is considered one of the most important of the village asks for a woman from some father whose daughter is still a girl, the father awards her to him, and the husband offers the infallible guarantee in which he specifies that he will not touch her too early. The father brings her immediately with him and sends her to grow in his hut; until the said time, the son-in-law does not offend [have sexual relations with] her.

If some Indian deflowers an Indian woman, although no one might know about it, she immediately breaks the cords that she has worn on her waist and wrists since she reached womanhood, so that all might know that she already was penetrated, and the Indian will not consider her a virgin, which she now is not. This is not a misdeed, whether the husband knows about it or any other man knows; nor by this fact is the father offended, nor does the daughter lose the husband, since there is never lacking anyone who might want her for a woman if the man who deflowered her rejects her. . . .

They are so barbarous that, not satisfied to deny quarter to whoever surrenders, they cut the parts natural to men and the female ducts [internal female reproductive organs] to carry back to their women, who dry them with smoke, and make those of the same nation whom they have captured eat these parts before they kill them.

Translated by Robert M. Levine and John J. Crocitti

History of a Voyage to the Land of Brazil

Jean de Léry

Jean de Léry (1538–1613) was a young shoemaker and theology student in Geneva when Nicolas Durand de Villegaignon sought Calvinist volunteers for his colony, Antarctic France. Joining a group of Protestant ministers and artisans who took up the call, Léry left for Brazil in 1558, where he witnessed the disintegration of the French colony and ended up living with the Tupinambá people. Léry eventually returned to Geneva and, years later, published this account of his travels. It met with immediate editorial success. Five editions were published soon after its release in 1578, and at least an additional ten, in French and Latin, appeared by 1611. His descriptions and reflections greatly influenced historical ideas about Brazil in the European imagination.

In his account, Léry describes the immense power that he believed emanated from the natural world in Brazil. Yet it was the native inhabitants who had an even greater impact on him. Besides recounting how the "Brazilian savages" prepared flour, made bread, produced wine, and roasted meat, Léry considered their ideas about war and vengeance the most remarkable aspects of indigenous life. And while he criticized the centrality of war to indigenous culture, Léry confided that he both understood the local logic at work and found parallels with the ways in which the French waged war. Indeed, when Léry was leaving Brazil for Geneva, he learned of the St. Bartholomew's Day Massacre (August 24, 1572), when Catholics slaughtered Protestants in France, and civil war ensued, and this series of events doubtlessly colored his understandings of his Brazilian experiences.

Of the Natural Qualities, Strength, Stature, Nudity, Disposition and Ornamentation of the Body of the Brazilian Savages, Both Men and Women, Who Live in America, and Whom I Frequented for about a Year

Thus far I have recounted both what we saw on the sea on our way to the land of Brazil, and what took place on the Island and Fort of Coligny, where Villegaignon was staying while we were there; I have also described the bay called *Guanabara*. Since I have gone so far into these matters, before re-embarking for France I also want to discuss what I have observed concerning the savages' way of life, as well as other singular things, unknown over here, that I have seen in their country.

*Du naturel, force, stature,
nudité, disposition &
ornemens du corps,
tant des hommes que
des femmes sauuages
Bresilliens, habitans en
l'Amerique,* illustration
by Jean de Léry. Jean
de Léry's vision of
indigenous people
reflects two representa-
tions of Brazil: Eden
and Hell. Here, the man
has a perfect, idyllic
body, whereas in the
subsequent image, the
artist depicts people
engaged in beastly
activities. From *Histoire
d'un voyage fait en la
terre du Bresil* (Geneva:
Antoine Chuppin, 1580).
Woodcut, 13.8 × 8.2 cm.
Courtesy of the John
Carter Brown Library at
Brown University.

In the first place then (so that I begin with the chief subject, and take things
in order), the savages of America who live in Brazil, called the Tupinambá,
whom I lived among and came to know for about a year, are not taller, fatter,
or smaller in stature than we Europeans are; their bodies are neither mon-
strous nor prodigious with respect to ours. In fact, they are stronger, more
robust and well filled-out, more nimble, less subject to disease; there are almost none among them who are lame, one-eyed, deformed, or disfigured.

Furthermore, although some of them reach the age of a hundred or a hundred and twenty years (for they know how to keep track of their ages and
count them by moons), few of the elderly among them have white or gray
hair. Now this clearly shows not only the benign air and temperature of their
country (in which, as I have said elsewhere, there are no frosts or great cold,

and the woods, plants, and fields are always greening), but also—for they all truly drink at the Fountain of Youth—they little care or worry about the things of this world. And indeed, as I will later show in more detail, since they do not in any way drink of those murky, pestilential springs, from which flow so many streams of mistrust, avarice, litigation, and squabbles, of envy and ambition, which eat away our bones, suck out our marrow, waste our bodies, and consume our spirits—in short, poison us and kill us off before our due time—nothing of all that torments them, much less dominates or obsesses them.

As for their natural color, considering the hot region where they live, they are not particularly dark, but merely of a tawny shade, like the Spanish or *Provençals*.

Now this next thing is no less strange than difficult to believe for those who have not seen it: the men, women, and children do not hide any parts of their bodies; what is more, without any sign of bashfulness or shame, they habitually live and go about their affairs as naked as they come out of their mother's womb. And yet, contrary to what some people think, and what others would have one believe, they are by no means covered with hair; in fact, they are not by nature any hairier than we are on any part of the body. They remove their hair, even the beard and eyelashes and eyebrows. It is plucked out, either with their fingernails, or, since the arrival of the Christians, with tweezers that the latter have given them—which makes their gaze seem walleyed, wandering, and wild. It has been written that the inhabitants of the island of Cumana in Peru do the same. As for our Tupinambá, they make an exception only of the hair on the head, which on all the males, from their youth onward, is shaved very close from the forehead to the crown, like the tonsure of a monk; behind, in the style of our forefathers or of those who let their hair grow, they have it trimmed on the neck.

To leave nothing out (if that is possible), I will also add this. There are certain grasses in that land with leaves about two fingers wide, which grow slightly curved both around and lengthwise, something like the sheath that covers the ear of all grain that we call "Saracen wheat." I have seen old men (but not all of them, and none of the young men or children) take two leaves of these grasses and arrange them together and bind them with cotton thread around their virile member; sometimes they wrapped it with handkerchiefs and other small pieces of cloth that we gave them. It would seem, on the face of it, that there remains in them some spark of natural shame, if indeed they did this on account of modesty, but, although I have not made closer inquiry, I am still of the opinion that it is rather to hide some infirmity that their old age may cause in that member.

To go on, they have the custom, which begins in the childhood of all the boys, of piercing the lower lip just above the chin; each of them usually wears in the hole a certain well-polished bone, as white as ivory, shaped like one of those little pegs that we play with over here, that we use as tops to spin on a table. The pointed end sticks out about an inch, or two fingers' width, and is held in place by a stop between the gums and the lip; they can remove it and put it back whenever they please. . . .

Our Brazilians often paint their bodies in motley hues; but it is especially their custom to blacken their thighs and legs so thoroughly with the juice of a certain fruit, which they call *genipap,* that seeing them from a little distance, you would think they had donned the hose of a priest; and this black dye is so indelibly fixed on their skin that even if they go into the water, or wash as much as they please, they cannot remove it for ten or twelve days. . . .

During that year or so when I lived in that country, I took such care in observing all of them, great and small, that even now it seems to me that I have them before my eyes, and I will forever have the idea and image of them in my mind. But their gestures and expressions are so completely different from ours, that it is difficult, I confess, to represent them well by writing or by pictures. To have the pleasure of it, then, you will have to go see and visit them in their own country. . . .

Before closing this chapter, however, I must respond both to those who have written and to those who think that the frequenting of these naked savages, and especially of the women, arouses wanton desire and lust. Here, briefly, is what I have to say on this point. While there is ample cause to judge that, beyond the immodesty of it, seeing these women naked would serve as a predictable enticement to concupiscence; yet, to report what was commonly perceived at the time, this crude nakedness in such a woman is much less alluring than one might expect. And I maintain that the elaborate attire, paint, wigs, curled hair, great ruffs, farthingales, robes upon robes, and all the infinity of trifles with which the women and girls over here disguise themselves and of which they never have enough, are beyond comparison the cause of more ills than the ordinary nakedness of the savage women— whose natural beauty is by no means inferior to that of the others. If decorum allowed me to say more, I make bold to say that I could resolve all the objections to the contrary, and I would give reasons so evident that no one could deny them. Without going into it further, I defer concerning the little that I have said about this to those who have made the voyage to the land of Brazil, and who, like me, have seen both their women and ours.

Portraits: Hans Staden

Victoria Langland

Over four hundred years after its publication in 1557, Hans Staden's book continues to both fascinate readers and inspire controversy. Originally written in High German, but almost immediately translated into Latin and Dutch, its full title is a sensationalistic mouthful in any language: *The True History and Description of a Country Populated by a Wild, Naked, and Savage Man-Munching People, Situated in the New World, America.* Its descriptive text and fifty-five accompanying woodcut illustrations tell the riveting story of the author's two trips to Brazil, including, most especially, his nine and a half months of captivity by Tupinambá Indians, his conviction that his captors planned to kill and eat him, and his numerous efforts to avoid this fate and eventually orchestrate his release. In some ways Staden, a German from the town of Hesse who never even planned to go to Brazil, was an unlikely protagonist for such a tale. Nonetheless his two residencies reflect the increasing interconnectedness of the Atlantic world, where sailors and ships' crews carried and commingled with people, goods, ideas, and diseases, while books like Staden's became important transmitters of understandings and misunderstandings about these connections.

Staden took his first trip in 1547, after his plans to join a fleet bound for India were frustrated when he arrived in Lisbon a few weeks after the ships' departure. Rather than wait months for their return, he signed on with a Portuguese trading vessel headed to Pernambuco, working as an arquebusier, or gunner. Charged with attacking any French traders found along the Brazilian coasts, Staden was also called upon to use these skills against indigenous people when a Portuguese sugar plantation found itself under siege.

In 1550, after Staden's return to Europe, he joined a Spanish expedition headed for the Rio de la Plata region but once again ended up in Brazil. This time his ship sank shortly after he and about 120 others had landed in an uncolonized area, leaving them marooned for over two years. Eventually, Staden made it north to the new settlement of São Vicente, where he accepted work as a gunner for a Portuguese fort.

Staden's military skills were especially valuable at São Vicente, as it was still a small settlement in an area of limited Portuguese control. Not only did

Ceremonies by which the Tuppin Ikins kill their enemies and eat them. This image by Theodor De Bry, the illustrator of Hans Staden's work, introduces the idea of cannibalism instead of anthropophagy, or ritual cannibalism, in which victors ate the brave warriors that they had vanquished. Yet here it appears that the members of the community are actually hungry and want to eat meat. The involvement of women and children in this ritual was uncommon, yet in this depiction for a European audience they are actively involved. From *Dritte Buch Americae, darinn Brasilia* (Frankfurt: Theodor De Bry, 1593), 85. Courtesy of the John Carter Brown Library at Brown University.

the French trade extensively in the region, but they also developed an alliance with the Tupinambá. The French and their indigenous allies actively opposed the Portuguese practice of enslaving the Tupinambá and encroaching on Tupinambá fishing and hunting grounds. The Portuguese in turn built alliances with the Tupiniquim, the Tupinambá's long-standing rivals. The result was a web of interconnected American and European territorial contests that helped redefine the area. These rivalries influenced Staden's life directly, as the fort he was sent to guard lay where Tupinambá and Tupiniquim influence intersected, just north of São Vicente. There he learned Tupi-Guarani, the language shared by both of these groups, and heard accounts of Tupiniquim and Tupinambá political rivalries and military practices. And it was there, when out hunting, that he was seized by Tupinambá warriors who recognized him as an enemy aggressor.

As Staden would have known, the Tupinambá practiced a ritualized cannibalism of their enemies. These symbolic and communal events allowed past deaths to be avenged and granted honors and special names to the warrior who killed the prisoner. Hence, Staden describes being terrified when the group suddenly surrounded him, tore off his clothes, bound his hands, and declared that they planned to eat him, some even biting their arms to dramatize their designs. In his telling, he initially staved off such a fate by convincing his captors that he was not Portuguese but a friend of their French allies. His story unraveled when a French trader who visited their village denied it, telling the Tupinambá to go ahead and eat the man. When at one point Staden managed to swim out to a French boat, he was literally pushed back into the water and forced to return to captivity. However, shortly after Staden was captured, a series of calamitous events befell the Tupinambá, including an outbreak of epidemic disease, brought to Brazil by Europeans, and an attack by the Tupiniquim. Staden was able to characterize these events as signs of the displeasure of his god with their plans, thereby sowing enough doubt among his captors that they kept putting off his execution. This allowed enough time for other French traders to appear, who helped him orchestrate his release, finally securing it through a combination of ransom and elaborate deception. Throughout, Staden credits his prayers to God for his salvation.

Upon his return to Hesse, Staden wrote an account of his experiences that soon became one of the most widely read travel accounts of this period. Written as a story of religious faith and redemption, the book's exotic and at times gruesome depictions of cannibalism undoubtedly contributed to its appeal. Portrayals of New World cannibalism were by no means unique, as French, Portuguese, and Italian observers both before and after Staden remarked on it, often in great detail. These stories often describe Native Americans as savages and thus helped justify indigenous slavery and the colonial project itself. Some scholars have questioned the truthfulness of Staden's account. Others have declared him a remarkable ethnographer, whose linguistic abilities and extended immersion in the Tupi world allowed him to understand, participate in, and describe Tupi cultural and political life with a level of detail not seen elsewhere. Meanwhile, contemporary Brazilian artists and authors have turned to his text to reclaim the Tupi as figures who literally consumed colonialism and in the process forged the nation of Brazil. While the accuracy of Staden's account is questionable, the long-standing importance of his book is undisputed.

II

Sugar and Slavery in the Atlantic World, 1580–1694

It is impossible to overestimate the importance of sugar and slavery to the transformation of Brazil. Steadily rising European demand for sugar for most of this period offered the possibility of enormous profits to those involved in its production. The efforts of numerous investors, planters, traders, and others to reap these rewards led to the razing of huge swaths of Brazilian Atlantic forest in the northeast, replaced by sugarcane plantations, as well as to the forced migration of hundreds of thousands of enslaved Africans who were set to work planting, harvesting, and processing sugar. Brazil became the leading producer of sugar in the world and the largest importer of enslaved Africans in the Americas. Sugar and slavery led to enormous profits for some and also resulted in the construction of a particular kind of society in Brazil. This society was marked by concentrated land ownership and the consequent concentration of economic and political power in the hands of a few. It was a society in which the reliance on race-based slave labor shaped nearly every aspect of colonial life.

Indeed, for those wanting to produce sugar, the Brazilian northeast was an area of unparalleled potential. The coastal region offered ideal conditions of abundant sun, adequate rain, and areas of incredibly rich soil, especially the soil the Portuguese came to eulogize as *massapé*, which was dark with organic matter that worked as a natural fertilizer for sugarcane. The system of streams and rivers in the area allowed plantation owners to use hydroelectric power to run the mills that pressed the cane into syrup, while the region's most dominant feature, its vast tropical forest, provided the wood necessary to heat the syrup as it was transformed into sugar. Finally, the same waterways allowed easy transportation to the coasts where slave laborers could be imported and sugar could be exported.

Thus, after the early success of those captaincies that produced sugar, the Portuguese Crown actively promoted the sugarcane industry, granting large tracts of land to those who promised to develop it, and offering inducements such as ten-year exemptions from the tithe, or the percentage of revenues due to the crown, to newly built *engenhos*, or sugar mills. Technically the word *engenho* referred only to the part of the plantation that converted cut sugarcane into sugar—a complex technical process that required both significant capital investment and a highly skilled workforce—but the name soon came to refer to the plantation as a whole, an enterprise that required an enormous workforce.

As seen in part I, plantation owners originally turned to indigenous populations to provide this labor, but they soon began importing enslaved Africans for the more technical positions. By the 1580s, as epidemic diseases ravaged the indigenous populations and the Jesuits helped induce the Crown to pass laws protecting them from slavery, planters in the sugarcane growing areas turned almost exclusively to African slave labor.

During the period covered by part II of this *Reader*, Brazil imported 4,000–5,000 enslaved Africans each year, the majority of whom were sent to sugar plantations. There the work demanded of them was grueling and ceaseless, as the cycle of sugarcane planting, weeding, and cutting takes place throughout most of the year, including seven to nine months of round-the-clock milling and processing during the critical harvest period. This cycle led to extremely high mortality rates for slaves.

The name *senhor de engenho*, or mill owner, soon emerged to describe the small but powerful group of plantation owners who saw both sugar revenue and control over land and laborers as the means and markers of social ascendance. Generally not members of the nobility themselves, they nonetheless formed a colonial aristocracy in Brazil. In between the great mass of enslaved workers and a small number of landed elites lay intermediate groups such as free people of color—those former slaves and their descendants who were either granted or who purchased their freedom—and the many smaller cane farmers who did not own their own mills but usually did own slaves. Together these people made Brazil the world's largest producer of sugar for over a hundred years, from 1580 until 1680, when competing sugar growers from the Caribbean challenged Brazil's position. For much of this period they rendered more profit to the Portuguese Crown than did all of its trade from India.

Colonists in other areas, such as in the northern province of Maranhão and the region surrounding São Vicente, continued to rely upon indigenous slavery throughout the seventeenth century. Notwithstanding continued Jesuit efforts against this, landowners, prospectors, and others relied on the idea of *resgate* (rescue) to justify indigenous enslavement, and groups of private slave hunters, explorers, and adventurers known as *bandeirantes* traveled further and further away from settled areas in search of Indians they could "rescue" and accordingly press into bondage.

As this suggests, Portuguese settlement remained limited, concentrated along the Atlantic coast. Effective colonial government was similarly constrained to the sugar-producing areas, especially Bahia and Pernambuco in the northeast, and, to a lesser degree, São Vicente in the south. This limited

Brasilise suyker werken. Engraving by Simon de Vries of a sugar mill complex (*engenho*), depicting sugar production. From *Curieuse aenmerckingen der bysonderste Oost en West-Indische verwonderens-waerdige dingen* (Utrecht, 1682). Courtesy of the John Carter Brown Library at Brown University.

presence provided the conditions necessary for escaped slaves (African or indigenous) to form alternative communities in the interior, known as *mucambos* or *quilombos*, where they established farms, hunted game, traded with small colonial towns, or launched raids on local estates. Yet Portuguese and, increasingly, Brazilian-born *bandeirantes* continued to expand the limits of the Portuguese presence. Official expeditions navigated the formidable Amazon River, while the unofficial *bandeirantes* pushed the western and southern frontiers in search of escaped slaves, new indigenous captives, and mineral deposits, such as gold or silver.

The resulting expansion of Brazil's territories was facilitated by the fact that for sixty years (between 1580 and 1640) Spain and Portugal shared a single monarch, as the lack of royal heir to the Portuguese crown led to the ascension of Philip I (simultaneously Philip II of Spain) to the Portuguese throne in what was known as the Iberian Union. While both kingdoms maintained separate legal systems and empires, they did experiment with new policies, such as briefly sanctioning direct commerce between Spanish America and Brazil. But the administrative complexity of this period of shared rule, along with Spain's focus on its silver-producing areas of Mexico and Peru and consequent absence from the frontier region, allowed the Portuguese to spread their presence and their de facto claims to new areas.

The period of a shared monarchy led to another significant consequence for Portugal's claims in South America: the intervention of the Dutch. The

United Provinces of the Netherlands had been at war with Spain since 1568, and they saw the unity of the two crowns as reason to direct assaults against Brazil as well. In 1621, they founded the Dutch West India Company to trade within the Caribbean, South America, and the Atlantic, using military and naval force to do so. In 1630 they took control of Pernambuco itself, one of the centers of Brazilian sugar production. They held the area until 1654, establishing their own colony, exporting sugar, and experimenting in religious tolerance, including allowing Jews to settle and establish religious communities and synagogues. They encouraged scientific investigation of the plants and animals of the region, promoted cultural and artistic expressions, and greatly expanded the city of Recife.

Throughout this period, the Catholic Church continued to play an important role in shaping colonial life. The Jesuits and other missionary orders continued in their efforts to convert the indigenous populations, a process made difficult by settler abuse. Yet the Jesuits also became wealthy owners of great tracts of land and enslaved Africans to work these plantations. Meanwhile the parish clergy, those sent to minister to the colonists, had added concerns about the moral lives of their charges. Thus the Catholic Church, and in particular the Portuguese Inquisition, began to broaden its scope of concerns to address the perceived religious transgressions of colonists.

Letter from a Portuguese Trader

Francisco Soares

As the Portuguese struggled to hold onto and profit from the new colony of Brazil, their Spanish neighbors to the west were capitalizing on the immense wealth of silver deposits located in the viceroyalty of Peru. The huge quantities of precious metals mined in this area and transported to Spain meant a boom in transatlantic trade as Spanish and Portuguese colonies thirsted for European goods. While Spain tried to keep close control over this commerce, smugglers worked to avoid taxes by bypassing the Spanish Crown's central presence in Lima and utilizing the more remote ports in the north (Panama and Cartagena) and the southeast (the River Plate). After 1580, however, Portuguese traders had a distinct advantage in this boom, helped by the union between Spain and Portugal in that year. While both kingdoms maintained separate legal systems and empires, they experimented with new policies, including briefly sanctioning direct commerce between Spanish America and Brazil from 1592 to 1596, and again from 1602 to 1618.

The following letter from a Portuguese trader in Rio de Janeiro to his brother in Lisbon was written in 1596 shortly before the end of this first legal period of commerce. His description of the large number of small boats that routinely traveled from Rio de Janeiro to the River Plate in order to trade in Peru, and the unbridled enthusiasm with which he discusses the profitability of this enterprise, suggest some of the reasons why such legalized commerce did not continue for long. His letter also exemplifies the breadth of the transatlantic trade in which he and other Portuguese traders participated, as they moved between Portugal, Brazil, Peru, and Africa (in his case, Angola), trading goods and slaves for silver.

One final note about his letter deserves mention here. We owe our access to it to the English, who, always interested in trade to and from the Americas, intercepted it, translated it into English, and eventually published it in a multivolume collection of information about overseas exploration. The Portuguese original is long lost.

Sir, we set sail from Lisbon the fourth of April 1596 and arrived here in this river of January [Rio de Janeiro] the twenty-seventh of June next ensuing. And the same day the *Visitadores* visited our ship with great joy, thinking that those commodities which we brought with us had been for the merchants of this country; but it proved to the contrary. . . . I hired a warehouse by myself, and landed my commodities. And now I am selling them as fast as I can; and sell them very well, and to great profit: for I have sold all our hats. I would I had brought forty or fifty dozen, by reason of the great utterance of them [public sale of goods] up into Peru and into the new kingdom of Granada, by the way of the river of Plate. For here is passage every three or four months with boats of thirty and forty [tons] a piece, which are laden with sugars, rice, taffetas, hats, and other kinds of commodities of this country, which are carried up the said river of Plate in the said boats, and thence are conveyed up into Peru. And these boats are but ten or twelve days going up the said river to Peru. And within four and five months after, the said boats come down this river again laden with *reales* of silver and bring down from those places no other commodities but treasure. It is a wonderful thing to behold the great gain and profit which is gotten in this river and in this country. I am ashamed to write it, fearing that I shall not be believed. For the employment of one hundred ducats in Spain, being brought hither, will yield between twelve hundred and fifteen hundred ducats profit. This trade has been used but within this year. For we can go up to the mines of Potosi, which are the best and the richest mines in all Peru. If the merchants of Spain and Portugal did know this trade, they would not send nor venture so much merchandise to Cartagena as they do. For up this river is a great deal the nearer way, and the easier to go to Peru. For the merchants of Peru, which dwell there, come down to this harbor and river of Janeiro, and bring with them between fifteen thousand and twenty thousand ducats in *reales* of silver and gold, and employ it here in this river in commodities: and when there are no commodities to be had for money in this place, then these merchants of Peru are constrained to go to Bahia and [Pernambuco], and there to employ their money. I would I had brought good store of silks and not these kind of commodities which I did bring. For here is more profit to be had, a great deal more than in the voyage of Angola. . . . If I had sold all my cloth for ready money for four hundred and fifty and five hundred *reyes*, the merchants would have bought it all from me: but I would sell no more, because I meant to exchange it in Angola for Blacks. Howbeit with ready money in hand in Angola a man shall buy better Blacks, and better cheap. . . . These letters I do send by the way of [Pernambuco], and have directed them to my cousin: for I do determine to settle myself here in this country. . . .

Your loving brother,
Frances Suares
[spelling changed by the British translators]

Exploration of the Amazon

Father Cristóbal de Acuña

In 1639, Cristóbal de Acuña (1597–c. 1676), a Jesuit priest from Spain then living in Quito, accompanied the Portuguese explorer Pedro Teixeira on an expedition into the Amazon rain forest. Teixeira and his crew had already traveled from Pará to Quito, the first journey from northern Brazil all the way up the Amazon River to what is today Ecuador, and it was on the return journey to Pará that Acuña joined them. He was asked to do so by Spanish officials in Peru, most likely including his brother, then a corregidor, *or an important judicial official in the Spanish Empire. Concerned about the westward flow of Portuguese settlements, and about Teixeira's motives, the Spanish instructed Acuña to document what he noted about the landscape, inhabitants, and ports he saw.*

At the conclusion of the trip, Acuña returned briefly to Europe to present his observations in a report to the Spanish government, arriving just as tensions between the Spanish and Portuguese boiled over as the Portuguese revolted against Spanish rule in 1640. Nonetheless, in 1641 Acuña's findings were published in Madrid under the title New Discovery of the Great River of the Amazon. *The text was read widely enough that it was translated into French in 1682 and into English in 1698. Yet recently some scholars have asserted that* New Discovery *was actually just one of two reports Acuña wrote, and that he also penned a second, more detailed account for the king that included maps with the locations of Portuguese garrisons along the river.*

In the excerpts of the 1641 report below, Acuña's observations are marked by his focus on how the environment and its inhabitants could most be profitable for the Spanish, yet they also reveal his real wonder at the richness and magnificence of the Amazon region.

The famous Amazon river, which traverses the richest, most fertile, and most densely populated regions of Peru, may be, from this day forth, proclaimed as the largest and most celebrated river in the whole world. For if the Ganges irrigates all India, and, with the great volume of its waters, eclipses the sea itself, which loses its very name and is called the Gangetic Gulf (or sometimes the Bay of Bengal); if the Euphrates, the famed river of Syria and Persia, is the joy and delight of those countries; if the Nile irrigates and fertilizes a great part of Africa, the Amazon river waters more extensive regions, fertilizes more plains, supports more people, and augments by its floods a mightier ocean. It only desires, in order to surpass them, that its source should be in Paradise, as is affirmed of those other rivers, by serious authors.

Histories say of the Ganges that thirty great rivers fall into it, and that the sands on its shores are full of gold, but the Amazon also has sands of gold and irrigates a region that contains infinite riches. . . .

The regions bordering on the Amazon require no supplies from foreign lands. The river is full of fish, the forests of game, the air of birds, the trees are covered with fruit, the plains with corn, the earth is rich in mines, and the natives have much skill and ability, as we shall see in the course of this narrative. . . .

The narrowest part in which the river collects its waters is little more than a quarter of a league wide. A place, doubtless, which has been provided by divine Providence, where the great sea of fresh water narrows, so that a fortress may be built to impede the passage of any hostile armament of any force what so ever, in case it should enter by the principal mouth of this mighty river.

The depth of the river is great, and there are parts where no bottom has yet been found. From the mouth to the Rio Negro, a distance of nearly six hundred leagues, there is never less than thirty or forty *brazas*[1] in the main channel. Above the Rio Negro it varies more, from twenty to twelve or eight *brazas*, but up to very near its source there is sufficient depth for any vessel. Though the current would impede the ascent, yet there is not wanting usually, every day, three or four hours of a strong breeze, which would assist in overcoming it. . . .

Timber and Material for Ships

The woods of this river are innumerable, so tall that they reach to the clouds, so thick that it causes astonishment. I measured a cedar with my hands, which was thirty *palmas*[2] in circumference. They are nearly all of such good wood that better could not be desired. There are cedars, cotton trees, iron wood trees, and many others now made known in those parts, and proved to be the best in the world for building vessels. In this river vessels may be built better and at less cost than in any other country, finished and launched, without the necessity of sending anything from Europe, except iron for the nails. Here, as I have said, is timber; here are cables made from the bark of a certain tree, which will hold a ship in the heaviest gale. Here is excellent pitch and tar. Here is oil, vegetable, as well as from fish. Here they can make excellent oakum [tarred fiber], which they call *embira*, for caulking the ships, and also there is nothing better for the stock of an arquebus [muzzle-loading firearm]. Here is cotton for the sails, and here finally is a great multitude of people, so that there is nothing wanting, for building as many vessels as may be placed on the stocks [of the shipyard]. . . .

The Multitude of Tribes, and of Different Nations

All this new world, if we may call it so, is inhabited by barbarians, in distinct provinces and nations, of which I am enabled to give an account, naming them and pointing out their residences, some from my own observations, and others from information of the Indians. They exceed one hundred and fifty, all with different languages. These nations are so near each other, that from the last villages of one they hear the people of the other at work. But this proximity does not lead to peace. On the contrary, they are engaged in constant war, in which they kill and take prisoner great numbers of souls every day. This is the drain provided for so great a multitude, without which the whole land would not be large enough to hold them.

But though, among themselves, they are so warlike, none of them showed courage to face Spaniards, as I observed throughout the voyage, in which the Indians never dared to use any defense against us, except that of flight. They navigate in vessels so light that, landing, they carry them on their shoulders, and, conveying them to one of the numerous lakes near the river, laugh at any enemy who, with heavier vessels, is unable to follow the same example. . . .

A Province Where They Find Gold

Twenty-eight leagues below the river Yurua, on the same (that is, the south) side, in a land full of deep ravines, commences the populous tribe of Curuziraris, who extend, always along the banks, for a distance of about eighty leagues, with settlements so close together that one scarcely passed before, within four hours, we came upon others. While sometimes, for the space of half a day at a time, we did not lose sight of their villages. Most of these we found to be uninhabited, as the Indians had received false news that we came destroying, killing, and making prisoners, and they had retired into the forests. These Indians are more ingenious than any others on the river. They do not display less order and civilization, both in the quantity of provisions they possess, and in the ornaments of their houses, than any other tribe on the river. They find very good clay in ravines near their dwellings for all kinds of hardware, and taking advantage of it, they have large potteries, where they make earthen jars, pots, ovens in which they make their flour, pans, earthenware cooking pots, and even well formed frying pans. All this diligence is caused by the traffic with the other tribes, who, forced by necessity, (as these things are not made in their country), come for large cargoes of them, giving, in exchange, other things which are wanted by the Curuziraris.

The Portuguese, in ascending the river, called the first village of these Indians they came to, *"the town of gold,"* having found and procured some there, which the Indians had in small plates, hanging from their ears and noses. This gold was tested in Quito, and found to be twenty-one carats. As the natives saw the desire of the soldiers, and how much they coveted the gold, they were diligent in procuring more of these little plates, and soon collected all they had. We found the truth of this in returning, for, though we saw many Indians, only one brought a very small earring of gold, which I obtained by barter. . . .

Opposite this village, a little higher up, on the north side, is the mouth of a river called Yurupazi, ascending which, and crossing a certain district by land, in three days another river is reached called Yupura, by which the Yquiari is entered, called also *"the river of gold."* Here, at the foot of a hill, the natives get a great quantity. This gold is all in grains and lumps of a good size so that by beating it, they make plates, which, as I said before, they hang to their ears and noses. The natives who communicate with those who extract the gold are called Managus, and those who live on the river and work at the mine are called Yumaguaris, which means, "extractors of metal," for *yuma* is a "metal," and *guaris* "those who extract." They give every kind of metal this name of *yuma*, and thus they called all the tools, hatchets, mattocks, and knives we had by this same word *yuma*.

Notes

1. A *braza* is 5.48 feet or 1.67 meters.
2. A *palma* is approximately 8 inches.

The Inquisition in Brazil

Various authors

The Portuguese Inquisition was created in 1536 in order to police religious beliefs and moral practices in the Portuguese Empire. It was especially concerned that conversos, or the descendants of Jews who had forcibly or willingly converted to Catholicism in the fourteenth and fifteenth centuries, were secretly continuing to practice Judaism. While the Church soon established inquisitional tribunals in Lisbon, Coimbra, and Évora in Portugal, and in Goa, India, it at first showed little concern with doing so in Brazil. Brazil's growing settlement and increasing economic importance, however, led to both the migration of numerous conversos and the arrival of the Inquisition. Meanwhile, the Inquisition began to extend its topical reach to matters such as sexual practices, witchcraft, and Protestant influence.

Rather than creating a permanent inquisitional tribunal in Brazil, the Church preferred sending visiting individual inquisitors. The first of these was Heitor Furtado de Mendonça, who visited Bahia, Pernambuco, Itamaracá, and Paraíba between 1592 and 1595. In each city, officials publicly read edicts of faith listing a series of crimes and demanded that people confess to anything they had done while also accusing others of any crimes. Those who confessed within thirty days of the edicts' reading were supposed to be granted extra leniency, while those who did not come forward risked excommunication.

Both this window of supposed leniency and the Inquisition's attention to sexual behavior are especially important for understanding the two confessions below: that of Father Frutuoso Álvares, offered just six days after the edict of faith, and that of Jerônimo Parada, who knew Álvares.

Confession of Frutuoso Álvares, Vicar of Matoim, in the Time of Grace, on July 29, 1591

On the twenty-ninth day of the month of July of the year one thousand five hundred and ninety, in the dwelling-place of the Lord, before the visitor Heito Furtado de Mendonça, appeared the father Frutuoso Álvares, vicar of Our Lady of Piety of Matoim, saying that he had to confess to the investigating body without being called.

For which he was judged by the Saintly Gospels, on which he placed his right hand, pledging to tell the truth.

And, making confession, he said that fifteen years from the founding of the captaincy of the Bay of All Saints, he committed the weakness of indecent touching with some forty people, more or less, embracing, kissing, namely, Cristóvão de Aguiar, a youth of eighteen years, as this was now two or three years ago, the son of Pero d'Aguiar, a resident of the parish, having touched his privates with his hands, gathering them together and there being pollution [an ecclesiastical term meaning ejaculation or orgasm] on the part of the youth two times.

And so he also, during more or less one month, touched the sexual member of Antônio, a seventeen-year-old boy, servant, or nephew of a merchant who lives in this city, named something like de Siqueira, and with this boy there was not pollution.

He also had congress to join the indecent members together, without there being pollution, with a Spanish youth named Medina, eighteen years of age, resident of the island of Maré, being the overseer of the master of that city, and another time with this same boy there were embraces and kisses and touches on the face, with this Spaniard some three or four years ago.

And with many other boys and youths who he does not know, not even their names or where they are from, he has vilely and indecently touched their privates, embraced and kissed them, drawn them to him, and sometimes slept in a bed with them, committing acts through the rear orifice with some of them, being himself the agent of penetration, and accepting that they would commit acts on him through his own orifice, being the recipient, launching himself with the stomach downward and placing the boys on top of him and also placing the boys with their stomachs down and placing himself, he confessed, on top of them, penetrating their orifices with his member and doing his part to commit, but never committing, the sin of sodomy by penetration.

And he particularly remembers that he committed such an act some ten times in the city where he is now vicar with a boy named Geronimo, who would then have been twelve or thirteen years old, and this would have been two or three years ago, who was the brother of the canon Manuel Viegas, who is now a student in this city.

And this also occurred just so with many other boys and youths whose names he does not even know, or where they are from, or what he chanced to do with them.

And he declared that in the visit made by the official the year before, someone denounced him, accusing him on these grounds, and that nothing was done to him because there was not enough proof.

And being asked, he responded that no one had seen him commit the said acts to which he confessed.

Die Inquisition in Portugall. Engraving by Jean David Zunner. As a result of the visits of representatives of the Inquisition in Brazil, colonists could be sent to Portugal to be tried. From *Description de L'Univers, Contenant les Differents Systemes de Monde, Les Cartes Generales & Particulieres de la Geographie Ancienne & Moderne* (Frankfurt, 1685).

And asked if he had said to these people with whom he sinned that to commit those weaknesses was not a sin, he responded no, but that some of them understood it to be a sin and some, being young, did not understand it, but he, he confessed, knows very well what large sins he has committed, and he repents them greatly and asks for pardon, and of their current relationship he said nothing.

And he was admonished to remove himself from interaction with these people and with any other who could cause harm to his soul, it being certain that doing otherwise he will be gravely punished, and he was commanded to return to this same investigating body of the visiting lord next month.

And in this judgment he declared that he is an Old Christian of all texts, born in Braga, son of João Álvares, a canner, and Maria Gonçalves, now deceased.

And in the said city of Braga, some twenty years ago, he committed and consumed the sin of sodomy one time with Francisco Dias, a student, son of Aires Dias, a locksmith, putting his foul member in his anal orifice, being with him from behind as a man should be with a woman in the natural way.

And thus he committed indecent touching with other people, for which he was denounced by the bishop in that city and denigrated to the galleys and, not having committed the same degradation, he went to Cape Verde where he was also accused of sinful touching with two youths and of presenting a false confession, for which he was sent to prison in Lisbon, where for the said faults he was sentenced and condemned to permanent exile in these parts of Brazil.

And being in this city he was also accused of the same sin with Diogo Martins, who now is married to the baker Pinheira, a resident of this city of Our Lady of the Savior, from whence he left absolved, not being at fault.

Likewise, he was accused in this city, by four or five statements from Antônio Álvares, Manuel Álvares, his brother, both of them skilled sugar workers, and others he does not know at all, of indecent touching, and in this case he was charged with a fine, which he paid, and with the suspension of his orders for some time that has now been carried out.

And not saying anything else, the visiting lord admonished him strongly, as he was a clergyman and pastor of souls, and so old—he said that he is more or less sixty-five years old—and has committed so many immoral acts offending Our Lord God, and only stopped a month ago, that he distance himself from them and return to this investigating body at the appointed time, and he said that he would do just so and signed here. I, Manuel Francisco, notary of the Holy Office, wrote it.—Heitor Furtado de Mendonça—Frutuoso Álvares.

Confession of Jerônimo Parada, Student, Old Christian, in Grace,
August 17, 1591

He said he was an Old Christian, born here in Bahia, the son of Domingos Lopes, a carpenter from Ribeira, and his wife Leonor Viegas, resident of this city, seventeen years old.

And confessing, he said that two or three years ago, on Easter Day, he went to confess in the house of Frutuoso Álvares, a cleric and old man with a white beard, because he had a friendship with the boy's father and his brother, and the said Frutuoso Álvares began to touch him, telling him that he was plump and other sweet words, and he put his hands in his pants and touched his member, playing with it with his hand, before taking off his pants and taking him to bed, and the said cleric also took off his, and they lay in bed together, and the clergyman joined their members together and with his hand coaxed their members together in order to have pollution, although in that instance there was not pollution from either of them.

And long after that time, when Frutuoso Álvares was vicar of Matoim, the confessor went to the house of his father, who lived half a league outside of Matoim, and arriving in Matoim at night, he went to stay in the house of the said Frutuoso Álvares and lay in his bed, where [Álvares] began to touch him and provoke him to do the same like the time before, and the confessor, in the same way, touched the cleric's member with his hand, and this second time there was nothing further than touching.

And many days after this, Frutuoso Álvares came to this city and stayed in the house of the confessor's grandmother, and the two of them being left alone, Frutuoso Álvares said they should do as on the other occasion, and the confessor responded that he did not want to, and so he gave him a coin, and not contenting him with one coin, gave him another, so they both took off their pants and lay on the bed, and after having done as on previous occasions, the said cleric lay on his stomach and told the confessor to get on top of him, and he did so and slept with the cleric, carnally, from behind, consummating the sin of sodomy, putting his dishonest member in from behind as a man does to a woman in the natural orifice, and this sin culminated in his having pollution, which he said happened only once, and for this he said that he begged forgiveness and confessed himself during this period of grace.

And asked if he knew that this was a sin, the confessor responded that he knew.

And asked again, he said he had heard that Frutuoso Álvares was fond of performing these depravities with boys and for this he was degraded by the Kingdom, and he said nothing of the ongoing relationship.

And he was admonished by the visiting lord to stay away from conversation with similar people that can cause harm to his soul, it being certain that, doing the contrary, he would be severely punished, and for saying that he was making amends and because he had stopped sinning long ago, he was ordered to confess to the guardian father of Santo Antônio, that is, of São Francisco, and that he bring written proof to this table.

And he declared that he did not want to confess to the said Frutuoso Álvares, and that he had already confessed these sins to the fathers of the Company, and they absolved him, and he completed the penances and showed himself repentant.

Translated by Emma Wohl

Excerpts from the Sermon on the Rosary

António Vieira

António Vieira was born in Portugal, but when still a small child his family moved to the northern province of Maranhão in Brazil, where he received his education. He became a Jesuit pastor, as well as a prolific writer, a well-traveled diplomat, and a missionary to indigenous populations in Brazil. In the 1650s he made numerous appeals to the Portuguese court against the continued practice of indigenous slavery, denouncing abuses against Indians, demanding restrictive laws, and advocating for increased Jesuit powers in order to protect them. Opposition to some of these laws, as well as jealousy over the Jesuits' increasing wealth and influence, eventually led to a campaign against Vieira, resulting in a twenty-year period of exile and imprisonment between 1661 and 1681.

In this early sermon, delivered to enslaved Africans and other workers on the Engenho Sergipe in 1633, before he was even ordained, Vieira condemns masters for their greed but also counsels slaves that they must serve God in order to maintain the freedom of their souls.

Vieira died in Brazil in 1697.

One of the remarkable things witnessed in the world today, and which we, because of our daily habits, do not see as strange, is the immense transmigration of Ethiopian peoples and nations who are constantly crossing over from Africa to this America. The fleet of Aeneas, said the Prince of Poets, brought Troy to Italy . . . ; and with greater reason can we say that the ships which one after the other are entering our ports are carrying Africa to Brazil. . . . A ship enters from Angola and on a single day unloads 500, 600 or perhaps 1,000 slaves. The Israelites crossed the Red Sea and passed from Africa to Asia, fleeing captivity; these slaves have crossed the Ocean at its widest point, passing from that same Africa to America to live and die as slaves. . . .

Now if we look at these miserable people after their arrival and at those who call themselves their masters, what was observed in Job's two conditions is what fate presents here, happiness and misery meeting on the same stage. The masters few, the slaves many; the masters decked out in courtly dress, the slaves ragged and naked; the masters feasting, the slaves dying of hunger; the masters swimming in gold and silver, the slaves weighted down

with irons; the masters treating them like brutes, the slaves adoring and fearing them as gods; the masters standing erect, waving their whips, like statues of pride and tyranny, the slaves prostrate with their hands tied behind them like the vilest images of servitude, spectacles of extraordinary misery. Oh God! What divine influence we owe to the Faith You gave us, for it alone captures our understanding so that, although in full view of such inequalities, we may nevertheless recognize Your justice and providence! Are not these people the children of Adam and Eve? Were not these souls redeemed by the blood of Christ? Are not these bodies born and do they not die as ours do? Do they not breathe the same air? Are they not covered by the same sky? Are they not warmed by the same sun? What star is it, so sad, so hostile, so cruel, that decides their fate?

There is not a slave in Brazil—and especially when I came upon the most miserable among them—who for me is not an object of profound meditation. When I compare the present with the future, time with eternity, that which I see with that which I believe, I cannot accept the idea that God, who created these people as much in His own image as He did the rest of us, would have predestined them for two hells, one in this life and another in the next. But when today I see them so devout and festive before the altars of Our Lady of the Rosary, all brothers together and the children of that same Lady, I am convinced beyond any doubt that the captivity of the first transmigration is ordained by her compassion so that they may be granted freedom in the second.

Our Gospel mentions two transmigrations, one in which the children of Israel were driven from their country "in the transmigration of Babylon" [Matt. 1:11] . . . ; and the other in which they were brought back to their country "after the transmigration of Babylon" [Matt. 1:12]. . . . The first transmigration, that of captivity, lasted for seven years; the second, that of freedom, had no end, because it lasted until Christ's coming.

Behold in the following, black brothers of the Rosary, . . . your present condition and the hope it gives you for the future: "and Josias begot Jechonias and his brethren" [Matt. 1:11]. You are the brothers of God's preparation and the children of God's fire. The children of God's fire of the present transmigration of slavery, because in this condition God's fire impressed the mark of slavery upon you and, granted that this is the mark of oppression, it has also, like fire, illuminated you, because it has brought you the light of the Faith, the knowledge of Christ's mysteries, which are these which you solemnly profess on the rosary. But in this same condition of the first transmigration, which is that of temporal slavery, God and His Most Holy Mother are preparing you for the second transmigration, that of eternal freedom.

It is this which I must preach to you today for your consolation. Reduced to a few words, this will be my topic: that your brotherhood of Our Lady of the Rosary promises all of you a Certificate of Freedom, with which you will not only enjoy eternal liberation in the second transmigration of the other life, but with which you will also free yourselves in this life from the most terrible captivity of the first transmigration.

Although banished Children of Eve, we all possess or all expect a universal transmigration, which is that from Babylon to Jerusalem, from this world's exile to our true home in heaven. You, however, came or were brought from your homelands to these places of exile; aside from the second and universal transmigration, you have another, that of Babylon, in which, more or less moderated, you remain in captivity. And so you may know how you should conduct yourselves in it, and so that you will not yourselves make it worse, I want first to explain to you what it consists of. I will try to say it so clearly that you will all understand me, so that they may more slowly teach you what for you and for them is very important to know.

Let it be known, all of you who are slaves, that not all of what you are is a slave. Every man is composed of a body and a soul, but that which is a slave and is known as one is not the whole person, but only half of him. . . . And which is the enslaved half that has a master whom it is forced to serve? There is no doubt that it is the more abject half,—the body. . . .

Therefore, black brothers, the slavery you suffer, however hard and grinding it may be, or seems to be to you, is not total slavery, or the enslavement of everything you are, but rather only half slavery. You are slaves in your exterior part, which is the body; however, in the other interior and noble half, the soul . . . you are not a slave, but free.

The Sugar Industry

Giovanni Antonio Andreoni

This careful description of people in the sugar industry comes from an Italian Jesuit who lived in Bahia for thirty-five years. Giovanni Antonio Andreoni first came to Brazil in 1681, under the urging of António Vieira, and he remained there until he died in 1716. Using the pen name André João Antonil, he wrote an encyclopedic volume about numerous aspects of Brazilian commercial and social life, from minute explanations of agricultural methods to practical advice for those who wished to come and make their fortunes in Brazil. His accounts of life on a sugar plantation, published in Lisbon in 1711, are some of the most detailed we have from this period. In the extracts that follow, he delineates the power of the senhor de engenho, *or sugar mill owner (translated here as sugar planter) and describes his view of the slaves who were the* senhor de engenho's *"hands and feet." Although published after the other documents in this part, his descriptions offer a rich portrayal of the world of sugar during the late seventeenth century, from the diversity of free and enslaved workers who produced the product to the violence and human degradation of slavery that undergirded it.*

To be a sugar planter is a title to which many people aspire. It brings with it the service, the obedience, and the respect of many others. If he is, as he ought to be, a man of wealth and command, a sugar planter in Brazil can be esteemed proportionally to the titled nobility in the Kingdom of Portugal. There are some sugar mills in Bahia that yield the owner four thousand loaves of sugar, and others a little less. This figure includes the cane from tenants that has to be pressed in the mill, and from which the mill is entitled to at least half, as well as that which is pressed with no obligation. In some other places in Brazil the mill receives even more than half.

Tenants depend on the planters. They rent fields on the lands belonging to the mill, as citizens do from nobles. When the planters are wealthier and have all the necessary provisions and are good-natured and truthful, then they are all the more sought after as landlords. This is true even for those who do not have their cane held captive, either by long-standing obligation or for the price that they receive for it.

Slaves serve the sugar planter in various capacities with hoes and sickles, which he keeps on the plantation and in the mill. Mulattoes and blacks also serve him, both male and female, occupied in household duties or in other jobs such as boatmen, canoe men, caulkers, carpenters, ox cart drivers, potters, cowboys, herdsmen, and fishermen. Each of these planters is also bound to have a sugar master, sugar masters in training, a refiner, a bookkeeper on the plantation and another in the city, overseers in the fields and allotments, and a head overseer of the plantation, as well as chaplains for the spiritual side, and each one of these employees receives wages. . . .

The slaves are the hands and the feet of the planter, for without them it is impossible in Brazil to create, maintain, and develop a plantation, or to have a productive mill. Whether the slaves turn out to be good or bad for the work depends on how the planter treats them. For this reason it is necessary to buy some slaves each year and to spread them out in the sugar fields, the allotments, the sawmills, and the boats. Since they are usually from different nations, and some are more ignorant than others, and their physiques differ greatly, this distribution must be made carefully and intelligently, and not haphazardly. Those who come to Brazil are Ardas, Minas, Congolese, from São Tomé, from Angola, and from Cape Verde. Some are brought from Mozambique in the homeward-bound East Indiamen. Those from Ardas and Minas are the strongest, while those from Cape Verde and São Tomé are the weakest. Those from Angola who have been brought up in Luanda are better fitted to become skilled craftsmen than those from the other regions I have mentioned. Some of the Congolese are also fairly good and industrious, not only for work in the cane fields, but in the workshops and in household management.

Some of them arrive in Brazil very uncouth and sullen, and so they remain for the rest of their lives. Others become fluent in Portuguese in a few years and are clever, both regarding their ability to learn the catechism as well as in seeking a livelihood. These can be entrusted with a boat, or to deliver a message, or do anything they might normally be told to do. The women use the sickle and the hoe like men, but only the male slaves can use axes in the woods. From among the Portuguese-speaking slaves are chosen the boiler, carpenters, skimmers, boatmen, and sailors, since these jobs need greater expertise. Those who are placed on an estate when they are very young should not be moved from it against their will, for otherwise they mope and die. Those who are born in Brazil, or who are brought up in white households, give a good account of themselves if they take a liking to their masters. If they are well treated, any one of them is worth four raw hands.

Still better for any function are the mulattoes; but many of them, abusing the favors of their masters, are proud, vicious, and pride themselves on being ruffians, ready to commit any outrage. They, both male and female, are usually luckier than anyone else in Brazil. For, thanks to that portion of white blood in their veins—which is perhaps derived from their own masters—they bewitch these to such an extent that some masters will put up with anything from them, and forgive them any excess. It would seem as if their owners not only dare not scold them, but also deny them nothing. It is not easy to decide whether masters or mistresses are more blameworthy in this matter. For among both of them alike can be found persons who let themselves be ruled by mulattoes who are none of the best, thus verifying the proverb that says that "Brazil is Hell for Blacks, Purgatory for Whites, and Paradise for Mulattoes," both male and female. Save only when on account of some suspicion, or jealousy, this love changes into hate and becomes armed with every sort of cruelty and rigor. It is a good thing to profit from their abilities when they are prepared to make good use of them, as some indeed do. But they should not be indulged so far that they, being given an inch, take a mile, and from being slaves they become masters. To emancipate unruly female mulattoes leads straight to perdition. The gold buying their freedom rarely comes from mines other than their own bodies by way of recurring sins. After they are freed, they continue to be the ruin of many.

Some planters do not like their slaves (of either sex) to live in lawful wedlock. Not only are they indifferent to their living together in an unmarried union, but they virtually encourage and initiate it. They say, "You, so and so, in due time will marry with so and so," and thenceforward they let them live together as if they were really man and wife. The planters excuse themselves by saying that they do not legally marry the slaves because, if they got tired of being married, they would kill themselves quickly with poison or through witchcraft. These means are not lacking among the slaves, who are noted practitioners of diabolical arts. Other masters, after slaves have been married for some time, separate them for years on end just as if they were single, which cannot be done in good conscience. Others are so negligent regarding the salvation of their slaves that they do not have them baptized for a long time while they work in the cane fields or the mill. Many of those who are baptized do not know who their creator is, what they ought to believe, and what law they ought to keep. Nor do they know how to pray to God, why Christians go to church, why they worship the consecrated Host, or what they ought to say to the priest when they kneel down and whisper in his ear. They also do not know whether they have a soul and whether it dies, and where it goes when it leaves the body. The most ignorant newcomers quickly learn who their master is and his name, how many holes of cassava they must dig each day, how many stands of cane they have to cut, how many loads of firewood they have to deliver, and other things belonging to their master's normal service. They likewise know how to ask his forgiveness when they have done wrong and persuade him not to punish them by promising to behave better. Yet, in spite of all this, there are planters who maintain that these people cannot learn how to make confession, or how to beg God for forgiveness, nor pray with their rosary beads, nor learn the Ten Commandments! This is merely for want of teaching, and because the planters do not consider the lengthy account they must one day render to God, for as Saint Paul says, Christians who neglect their slaves are behaving worse than unbelievers who do so. Nor do such planters compel them to hear Mass on Holy Days, but, on the contrary, they keep them so busy that they have no time for it. Nor do they ask the chaplain to catechize them, paying him a larger stipend for his work if need be.

It is obvious that the slaves should not be denied adequate feeding and clothing, and should not be overworked. For the owner rightfully ought to give whoever serves him sufficient food, medicines when sick, and the wherewithal to dress himself decently, as befits the servile state, and not let him appear nearly naked in the streets. The owner should also regulate the work in such a way that it is not more than his laborers can perform, if he wishes them to last. It is customary in Brazil to say that the three p's are necessary for the slave—namely, *pao* [stick], *pão* [bread], and *panno* [cloth]. Although they begin badly by placing the stick—punishment—first, yet would to God that the feeding and clothing were equally plentiful as the punishment often is. This castigation is often inflicted for a doubtful or fanciful reason, and with very cruel means (even when the crimes are undeniable), which would not be used on a brute beast. Some owners pay more attention to a horse than a half a dozen slaves. Their horse has attendants and someone to cut grass for him and is wiped down when in a sweat, and his saddle and bridle are decorated with gold. . . .

Slaves should not be completely forbidden from enjoying their traditional pastimes, which are their only solace in captivity. Otherwise, they will become miserable, melancholy, unhealthy, and disheartened. For this reason, the planter should not object to the slaves crowning their kings, singing, and dancing respectably on some days in the year. Nor should he object to their enjoying themselves innocently in the evenings after morning celebrations of their feast days of Our Lady of the Rosary, Saint Benedict, and of the patron saint of the plantation chapel. These celebrations should be at no cost to the slaves. The planter should liberally give to the judges of their festivities and bestow some reward for their continued toil. If the male and female judges of the feast have to spend their own money, this will be the cause of many offenses and insults to God. There are few of them who can lawfully save enough money for these festivities.

One thing that must be avoided on the plantation is the slaves getting drunk on fermented sugarcane wine, or on rum. It will be enough to allow them some sweet wine, which is harmless, and with which they can barter for flour, beans, sweet cassava, and potatoes.

It is a good thing if the planters take care sometimes to give surplus goods to the little black children, for this makes the slaves serve them willingly and propagate new male and female slaves. On the other hand, some female slaves deliberately try to abort their pregnancies on the plantations where they are ill-treated, so that the children inside them will not suffer as they have.

Translated by Timothy J. Coates and Charles R. Boxer

The Dutch Siege of Olinda and Recife

Ambrósio Richsoffer

As the United Provinces of the Netherlands (what would become the Dutch Republic) expanded its economic power in the early seventeenth century, it looked to Brazil as a potentially profitable place for colonization and trade. In 1621 it granted monopoly trading rights to the Dutch West India Company, but in the same year a truce with Spain, then part of the Iberian Union with Portugal, fell apart, leading the Dutch to seize a portion of Brazil and its lucrative sugar trade. In 1624, the Dutch sent a large expeditionary force to Bahia, where they captured Salvador and managed to hold onto the colony for a year before Spanish and Portuguese forces pushed them out. The Dutch then set their sights on the major sugar-producing captaincy of Pernambuco, including Olinda, the capital of Portuguese colonial settlement, which they seized in 1630 with ships from the Dutch West India Company. For over twenty years, until 1654, they controlled much of the northeastern coastline, from Pernambuco to Maranhão (see "Portraits" at the end of this part for a fuller account of the Dutch in Brazil).

The document below is a selection from a diary entry by Ambrósio Richsoffer, an eighteen-year-old soldier from Strasbourg, who participated in the siege.

. . . After every soldier had entrusted himself to God in his morning prayers, the forces were divided into three units. . . . We marched along beach and shore toward the city of Olinda, which we could make out perfectly, situated on top of the mountain. Nevertheless, we had two more hours of marching to reach Olinda from the place to the north where we had disembarked. During the journey there were various small skirmishes, the enemy showing himself on foot and on horse, but still not preventing us from approaching closer and closer until we arrived at the Rio Doce, a small river that we needed to cross.

In this part of the trip, we found the first and strongest resistance, as there were over eighteen hundred men on horse and on foot behind a low wall. A fight consequently broke out, leaving many on both sides on the ground, and no fewer injured. After a long battle, we managed to expel the enemy from its advantageous position. During the retreat, they were joined by fresh troops, but we advanced toward them with resolve and pursued them with constant skirmishing so that they left in flight. Some of them took to the

Diogo de Mendonça, the Portuguese governor of Salvador who surrendered to the Dutch in 1624, with the Jesuit priest Domingo Coinia. From *Steyger-Praetjen Tusschen Jan Batavier en Maetroos ober het apprehenderen van den Gouverneur ende Provinciael van gantsch Brazilien, met haer Geselschap* (Amsterdam: Claes Jansz Visscher, 1624). Courtesy of the John Carter Brown Library at Brown University.

forests and others took refuge near the city, in the flanks and behind a trench in a narrow passage. Again, we attacked with such force that there was great carnage on both sides.

In this same way, we attacked the Jesuit convent with great force, using fire and sword against all who dared resist us. After this, we flew our flags from the tower and windows. When our enemies, who were [held up] in the two stone forts and the trench located on the beach, saw this from the other side of the city, they realized that it was not just our rearguard that was resolutely overtaking them, because on the south side reinforcements that the admiral had sent were disembarking. They did not spend long resisting us. After firing a few pieces of artillery, they fled, abandoning everything.

The leading citizens had done the same days before, hiding their finest possessions in the forest, even though the Spanish governor prohibited this under penalty of death, so that in seeking to protect their possessions, they would more faithfully aid in the defense of the city. As they had disobeyed him, and feared the Dutch even more, they set fire to their storehouses in the town of [Recife], where the fires destroyed fifteen thousand boxes of sugar, along with a considerable amount of Brazilian tobacco and Spanish wine, causing enormous damage to the West India Company. Following this, the governor evacuated the plaza, leaving his officers in command of the forts.

In this way we conquered the city with the help of God, fortunately not losing more than sixty men, although many hundreds were injured. The enemy, however, certainly lost three or four times this figure. During the night, most of us stayed in the Jesuit convent, keeping up our guard. However, many that filled themselves with Spanish wine were left lying on streets and in houses like irrational brutes, raising the alarm for many false surprise attacks, such that we could catch little rest until daybreak. Despite being very fatigued from constant battle and intolerable heat, we soon replenished ourselves with delicious Spanish wine and refreshed ourselves with lemons, oranges, and sugar.

On the seventeenth of February, all units were given lodging in the city, a few of us fitting into comfortable quarters where we found a barrel of Spanish wine and all sorts of food. We took two blacks into our service, who collected many good and beautiful fruits (mainly coconuts), taking them from the tallest trees and bringing them to our quarters, to which we again treated ourselves, feeling more refreshed.

During the days of the eighteenth and nineteenth, the admiral continued to bombard the forts of Recife. He ordered two ships to the entrance of the port to discover if it was possible to enter the port in boats or other vessels. Next, he ordered six ships, which must have been continuously bombarding the great fort of São João, followed by twelve boats, to travel with their sails lowered until they could, at the right time and occasion, enter the port and anchor there.

To this end, 223 soldiers and 350 sailors were deployed. The enemy, however, realizing our intention, wrecked a number of ships entering the port carrying sugar and tobacco, and, when the sugar dissolved, [the boxes] floated until they dried. We were thus forced to withdraw, having suffered losses. . . .

Translated by Molly Quinn

An Eyewitness Account of
the First Battle of Guararapes

Francisco Barreto de Meneses

During the administration of Count de Nassau-Siegen (1637–43) in the regions of the northeast controlled by the Dutch West India Company (see "Portraits" at the end of this part), many sugar plantation owners found ways to adapt to the Dutch presence and even prospered. However, after Nassau was removed from his post in 1643, the new company administrator aroused considerable opposition by demanding that planters quickly repay long-standing debts they had incurred. By 1648, an irregular army led by the large landowners André Vidal de Negreiros and João Fernandes Vieira; by Henrique Dias, the son of freed slaves who organized a regiment of people of color; and by Felipe Camarão, of indigenous origins, who headed an Indian militia force, rose up against the Dutch occupation. Together they faced a superior number of European mercenary troops, largely from the German countries. In 1648, commanded by Francisco Barreto de Meneses, these combined forces defeated the Dutch in the First Battle of Guararapes, a hill in Pernambuco where the battle took place. A year later they repeated the victory at the same site at the Second Battle of Guararapes, and by 1654 the Dutch were forced to leave Brazil. Many of the departing Dutch planters and traders who had been prosperous in Brazil moved their operations to the Caribbean and eventually developed a sugar industry that competed successfully with Brazilian production.

The following rather self-congratulatory account of the First Battle of Guararapes in 1648, written by Barreto de Meneses to the king of Portugal, is also a rich source for considering his understanding of black and indigenous soldiers and their contributions to this historical battle.

On March 17 the enemy's fleet arrived and disembarked in Recife. They prepared their infantry, and on April 18 they marched into the countryside with an army of 5,500 soldiers, 500 sailors, and 300 Tapuya Indians. Their battalions carried sixty flags and one large standard with the coats of arms of the United Provinces and the Estates General, five pieces of bronze artillery, many supplies, munitions, and much money. . . . They marched along the south shore and on the same day, April 18, they beheaded forty of the one hundred men who had been stationed along the shore to defend it. I heard news of how they quartered themselves at that place. Only two days had passed since I received an order from the Count-General in Bahia to govern these captaincies, a command I did not refuse to accept in order to serve Your Majesty. Despite the miserable state of the land, the great power of the enemy, and the limited forces which I had to oppose them, I immediately called a council of the principal leaders: André Vidal de Negreiros, João Fernandes Vieira, and the infantry captains. After informing them of the state of affairs, the council resolved to go out to meet the enemy, even though our strength did not exceed more than 2,200 men, among whom was the unit of Blacks led by Governor Henrique Dias and the Indians of militia captain [Felipe] Camarão, which left our base guarded with only three hundred men. With that limited force, I marched to the hills of Guararapes. After passing them, I stopped in the foothills to set up the infantry in the best manner and shape that the terrain permitted. I spent the night at that place. The following day, which was Sunday, April 19, the enemy broke camp and came marching toward us. The mounted scouts began the battle. As soon as we discovered the enemy invading Guararapes, I ordered our troops into battle. I had stationed Commander André Vidal de Negreiros in the vanguard and behind him Commander João Fernandes Vieira, while the militia Captain Camarão guarded the flanks on one side and Governor Henrique Dias on the other. After the first shots were fired on both sides, we drew our swords and broke through the enemy lines. Because two of the enemy's reserve battalions, which had not engaged in battle, detoured around the main battle front and attacked the flank guarded by Henrique Dias, I dispatched five hundred men, whom I had kept in reserve, to come to his aid. They aided him in his stand against the attackers. But our captains, who in two volleys of shots halted the enemy, did not recognize the continuing danger and turned toward another part of the battle where they thought they could inflict greater injury on the enemy. As a result of this mistake, we did not completely destroy our adversaries, who fell upon Henrique Dias. Since he was unable to hold back their full force, he retreated toward our main body. There were few of us, and we already were exhausted. So we, too, were forced to fall back. I immediately swung into action everywhere in order to prevent the enemy from recovering its artillery, munitions, and money, which we already had captured, but I was not able to do so because with the defeat we had inflicted on our enemy our troops became more disorganized than the very opponents we had defeated. However, in a few minutes, I took a stand at a creek located on the battlefield where, encouraging some and striking others, I forced our infantry to halt and I began to regroup them, ordering Commander João Fernandes Vieira to do the same. I put André Vidal de Negreiros in the vanguard. With few soldiers but with great energy, he again attacked the troop detachments the enemy sent against him. Skirmishing with them, he began to defeat them by killing some of their captains and many of their soldiers. The battle began anew all across the field and lasted for four hours, during which we performed wondrous acts of bravery in which the commanders and the other officers distinguished themselves. The enemy retreated to occupy some high ground within our sight, and behind the hills they gathered their wounded who had fallen in that vicinity. Then I considered how tired our own soldiers were. They had not eaten in twenty-four hours, and many of them were busy rescuing the wounded and recovering the dead. I ordered them to collect the flags we had won, which numbered thirty-three, including the large standard bearing the arms of the United Provinces to which I already have referred. I sent that standard, along with nineteen flags, to the Count-General in Bahia. Our Black and Indian soldiers destroyed the other thirteen flags because they saw no other value in them except as bright material to tear up for ribbons and other ornaments. . . .

I gave orders to Governor Henrique Dias to march to the town of Olinda with his unit of Blacks, some companies of mulattoes, and one of white soldiers. Their orders were to enter and seize the town from many sides, which they did so valiantly that they put to flight the six hundred Dutchmen who were there, who fled to Recife, a distance of one league. In this skirmish we killed 150 or more who were left in the fields. Some officers, and doubtless others, must have died in the waters where they jumped to escape. We captured a Frenchman, and we recovered the five iron cannons that we had left there. I ordered them transported to this base in case we abandon the town again, because it is indefensible and requires too many troops to garrison it, when we could use them to better advantage elsewhere or we could use them also to attack the enemy when it tries to engage us in battle. We did not have more than six wounded, among whom was a captain; none of them was in danger of dying. From these happy victories with which God favors Your Majesty's arms, at a time when the well-known superiority of the enemy presaged total destruction without any hope of success, I can take heart that there will be further great victories in which our Lord will free this Christian State threatened by the Dutch tyrant.

Translated by James N. Green

Two Documents in the War against Palmares

Various authors

The most common way that enslaved men and women openly resisted slavery in colonial Brazil was through flight. Fugitive slaves frequently joined runaway slave communities called mucambos *(also spelled* mocambos*) or, later,* quilombos. *These settlements could harbor groups of just a few dozen or grow to contain hundreds and even thousands of residents. Colonial officials, who saw them as a threat to both slavery and colonial order, struggled to suppress and eliminate them. But both fugitive slaves and* quilombos *remained a constant feature of colonial life.*

The largest, most well-known, and one of the longest-lasting of these communities was Palmares, located within the captaincy of Pernambuco (in an area of present-day Alagoas), with a population that reached over ten thousand people. Really a series of interconnected quilombos *that shared a political and legal system, Palmares might be best understood as an alternative state within Brazil, albeit unrecognized by either the Portuguese or Dutch colonial governments. While both colonial governments launched numerous military campaigns against it, Palmares was nonetheless a political reality for nearly a century, from about 1605 to 1694.*

The two documents below reflect Luso-Brazilian officials' views of Palmares. In the first, an unknown author connected to the Pernambucan government tries to explain its resilience, offering a fascinating description of Palmares itself, at least as understood by outside observers. In the second document, the governor of Pernambuco contracts Domingos Jorge Velho, a slave trader from São Paulo, to help attack the quilombo. *When Palmares was finally destroyed in 1694, five hundred residents were captured for resale as slaves, while the final two hundred survivors reportedly committed suicide rather than surrender. The rest of the community had perished earlier or possibly fled elsewhere.*

Since 1992, archaeologists have been excavating the former site of Palmares and uncovering new information about the lives and culture of its residents. Palmares and its leaders have become symbols of resistance to slavery and of black pride.

The Imalê Ifé Afro Group dances in the celebration on the Day of Black Consciousness at the monument in Rio de Janeiro to Zumbi dos Palmares, the last leader of the *quilombo*. Photograph by Fernando Frazão. Courtesy of Agência Brasil.

Reports on the Wars against Palmares by Pernambuco Governor Pedro de Almeida, 1675–1678

The captaincies of Pernambuco have been returned to the dominion of Your Highness and are now free from the foreign enemies who came to conquer them. Our weapons are powerful enough to beat that enemy who oppressed us for so many years, but were never effective in destroying the opposite enemy who infested us internally and who inflicted losses just as great. Neglect did not cause this failure, because every governor who lived in Recife carefully engaged in this campaign. However, the difficulties of the terrain, the ruggedness of the roads, and the impossibility of transportation made the campaign unrealistic for those lacking prowess. The best commanders in the ranks and the most battle-tested soldiers were occupied in these levies, and the labors that they endured were not trivial, but they reaped very little fruit.

To prove the uniqueness of these campaigns, I will briefly recapitulate the information that I discovered through experience. Extending through the upper reaches of the Rio São Francisco is a cord of untamed forest that bounds the *sertão* [backlands] of Cabo de Santo Agostinho, running almost north to south, paralleling the coast. The *palmares agrestes* [wild palms of the region] are the principal trees and gave the region its name. The trees are so richly endowed that people use them to make wine, oil, salt, and clothing. Their leaves are used as roofing, the branches for supports, and the fruit for sustenance. And the texture that covers the stalks in the trunk makes string for all types of bonds and rope. These *palmares* do not run so uniformly that other forests with diverse trees do not separate them, and within a distance of sixty leagues are found distinct *palmares*. To the northwest, sixteen leagues from Porto Calvo, is the *mucambo* of Zambi; five leagues north of that is Arotireui; a little east of that are the two *mucambos* of the Tabocas; fourteen leagues northwest of these is Dambrabanga; eight leagues to the north is the walled city called Subupira; six more leagues to the north, the royal walled city called Macaco; five leagues to the west is the *mucambo* of Osenga; nine leagues northwest from our settlement of Serinhaem, the city of Amaro; and twenty-five leagues northwest from Alagoas is the Palmar of Andalaquituxe. These are the largest and most defendable, but there are others of less importance and with fewer people. These *mucambos* are various distances from our settlements, according to the direction, because they are spread out over forty or fifty leagues.

The area is naturally rugged, mountainous, and wild, supporting all varieties of known and unknown trees with such thickness and entangled branches that, in many places, it is impenetrable by light. A diversity of thorns and creeping, harmful plants and intertwined trunks impedes passage. Spread out among the hills are very few fertile plains for cultivation. To the west of the *sertão* of Palmares stretch extensive, infertile fields useful only as pastures.

In this uncultivated and natural refuge are gathered some Blacks to whom, either because of their crimes or the stubbornness of their masters, Palmares seems less punishing than what they fear [as slaves]. With so much imagination, they felt more secure where they could be more at risk. The open pastures of cattle ranches facilitated their escape. By taking prisoners and persuading others with hopes of liberty, they started to spread out and multiply.

People think that once Black slaves arrived in these captaincies, Palmares started to have inhabitants. When Holland occupied Recife, the number of inhabitants increased, since a disturbance for the masters was a release for the slaves. Over time, Palmares grew, and the nearness of settlers made them deft with arms. Today, they use all types of arms. They make bows and arrows, but steal and purchase firearms. Our assaults have made them wary and experienced. They do not all live in the same place, so that one defeat will not wipe them out. Distinct functions exist in Palmares as much for sustenance as for security. There are great workers who plant all the land's vegetables, and prudently store fruits for the winter and at times of war. Their main sustenance is coarse corn, from which they make various appetizing foods. Hunting provides much food because those forests are abundant.

They wage all forms of war, with all the superior commanders and inferiors, as much for victory in battle as for assistance to the king. They all obey the one who is called Ganga Zumba or, in other words, Great Lord. As the king or lord, he enjoys everything produced in Palmares in addition to imported goods. He has a palace and a royal cloak, and is attended to by guards and officers who are accustomed to royal houses. In all respects, he receives a king's treatment and the ceremonies proper for a lord. People immediately kneel in his presence, applaud him, and affirm his excellence. They speak to him as His Majesty and obey him out of admiration. He lives in the royal city called Macaco, a common name for death, which they associated with an animal [the monkey]. This city is the metropolis among the rest of the cities and settlements. It is fortified entirely by a wall of wattle and daub, with openings aimed so that the combatants might harm your safety. The area outside the wall is entirely planted with iron spikes, and such clever traps that even the most vigilant will be imperiled. This city occupies a wide area and is composed of more than fifteen hundred houses. Among the residents are ministers of justice for the necessary execution of laws. They imitate everything found in a republic.

Although these savages have completely forgotten bondage, they have not entirely lost recognition of the church. In this city, crowds have recourse to a chapel and entrust their worries to religious images. At the chapel's entrance is a very perfect image of the child Jesus, and others of Our Lady of Conception and Saint Bras. They choose one of the smartest to revere as the priest who baptizes and marries them. However, baptism does not follow the form determined by the church, and marriages are not the special events that the law of nature still demands. Lust is the rule for selection of mates, and each has the women he desires. Some Christian prayers are learned and documents of faith compatible with their abilities are observed. The king who lives in this city was accompanied by three women, a mulatta and two *crioulas* [Brazilian-born black women]. By the first, he had many children, but from the others none. Their style of dress is the same as observed among us: more or less clothed according to the possibilities.

This is the principal city of Palmares and the king who dominates it. The rest of the cities are the responsibility of sovereigns and superior commanders, who govern and live in them. . . .

This is the enemy who lasted for so many years within these captaincies, who defended the area, who perseveres. Our injuries from this enemy are innumerable because they endanger the Crown and destroy the settlers. . . .

Vassals are destroyed because the enemy wreaks havoc on life, honor, and possessions. Regarding the latter, they demolish property and steal slaves. As for honor, women and daughters are irreverently treated. As for life, vassals are always exposed to sudden assaults. Furthermore, the roads are not free and journeys not safe, so that one only travels with troops who can repel the enemy.

*Conditions Arranged with the Governor of the Paulistas [i.e., the Leader
of the* Bandeirantes*], Domingos Jorge Velho, on August 14, 1693, for the
Conquest and Destruction of the Blacks of Palmares*

Articles and conditions that the Governor [of Pernambuco] João da Cunha
Souto Maior concedes to Colonel Domingos Jorge Velho to conquer, destroy,
and suppress totally the rebellious Blacks of Palmares with his people and
officers who accompany him, and the governor is obliged in these articles to
execute the inferred [conditions]. . . .

1. The governor gives to the said colonel two hundred kilograms each of
    powder and lead for the first expedition.
2. The governor will order given to him six hundred *alqueires* (measures)
    of flour . . . placed in the villa of Alagoas, and the said colonel is then
    obliged to transport it with his Indians.
3. The governor gives more than one thousand *cruzados* (units of cur-
    rency) from the public treasury, contributing firearms and other sup-
    plies for the campaign.
4. The governor relinquishes to the colonel the prisoners' jewels and the
    quintos (tax revenues), which they took from Your Majesty, so that the
    said Colonel Domingos Jorge Velho can divide everything between
    himself and his officers as he sees fit.
5. After suppressing the said Blacks, they cannot use their services in
    these captaincies, and he, Domingos Jorge, will be obliged to have all
    the prisoners put in the plaza in Recife, from there to sell them to Rio
    de Janeiro or Buenos Aires . . . and only the Black children of Palmares
    from seven to twelve years of age can stay in these captaincies, some
    who will be sold according to their value for the account of the said
    colonel and his people.
6. The governor will give to the said conquerors land grants in the same
    Palmares region, so they can populate and cultivate the land as their
    own, living as subjects and with the same lands under the dominion of
    Your Majesty, whom God watches over.
7. Said Domingos Jorge is obliged to prevent any Blacks from fleeing his
    masters to the said lands and settlements; instead, he will quickly re-
    turn them to their masters.

Translated by Robert M. Levine and John J. Crocitti

Bandeirantes

Anonymous

Throughout most of the seventeenth century, the captaincy of São Vicente and its major township São Paulo remained much poorer and smaller than their counterparts in the northeast, and far fewer Portuguese women migrated there. Meanwhile the indigenous populations and Jesuit missionaries that lived in the surrounding area had an enormous impact on colonial life. Male Paulistas (residents of São Paulo) had numerous children with indigenous women (the offspring were called mamelucos). They owned indigenous slaves, notwithstanding growing legislation against the practice, and adopted a variety of indigenous practices and customs.

By the mid-1600s, however, the indigenous population there began to decline, and the price of indigenous slaves increased, while rumors emerged that the backland area contained precious metals, such as gold, silver, and emeralds. Both developments led to the rise of bandeirantes, militarized groups of Portuguese, mameluco, and indigenous men who traveled through the hinterlands. Theoretically in search of minerals and escaped slaves for recapture and sale, they also enslaved many free indigenous peoples, sometimes raiding Jesuit missions in order to do so. In the process, they opened up much of the Brazilian interior for future colonization and expanded Portuguese claims to the area.

The bandeirantes have often been lionized for their supposed masculine vigor, their extensive backwoods travels in difficult conditions, and for the impact of their slave-raiding trips in expanding Portuguese control of lands also claimed by the Spanish. A romanticized image of the bandeirantes is not a modern construct, but as we can read in the following document, was already well established in the seventeenth century. This anonymous writer from the 1690s praises them to the king and recommends them for special honors.

. . . [To populate other areas,] Your Majesty could make use of the men of São Paulo, granting them honors and favors. For these men, [the chance to earn] honors and interests makes all kinds of danger easy. These men are capable of penetrating all the *sertões* [backlands], where they ceaselessly traipse without any more sustenance than scrubland quarry, animals, cobras, lizards, wild fruits, and various roots. It does not bother them to walk through the *sertões* for years and years, for the life they have lived has made this a force of habit.

Forêt Vierge Les Bords du Parahiba. Illustration by Jean-Baptiste Debret. *Bandeirantes* from São Paulo, oftentimes presented as brave backwoodsmen, were mostly involved in tracking down runaway slaves or capturing indigenous people and placing them in bondage. From *Viagem Pitoresca e Histórica ao Brasil* (Paris: Firmin Didot Frères, 1834), plate 1. Courtesy of the John Carter Brown Library at Brown University.

And assuming that these Paulistas were taken as insolent, as has happened in some cases, no one could deny that they conquered all of the *sertão* that we have populated in Brazil. In the time of Governor Affonso Furtado de Mendonça, they wrested it from the brave savages who had destroyed and devastated the towns of Cayrú, Boipeba, Camamú, Jaguaripe, Maragogipe, and Peruasseu, something previous governors had been unable to do no matter how diligent they were. Nor could anyone deny that they were the ones who conquered Palmares of Pernambuco. And one would be deluded to think that without the Paulistas and their heathen we would ever have conquered the brave primitives who rose up in Ceará, in Rio Grande, and in the *sertão* of Parahiba and Pernambuco. The brave savages of the mountains, of the cliffs, of the scrublands, and of the scrub brush can only be conquered with tame heathens, and not with any other power, hence Your Majesty should make use of the Paulistas to conquer your lands.

Translated by Victoria Langland

Portraits: Count Johan Maurits von Nassau-Seigen

James N. Green

Johan Maurits von Nassau-Seigen (1604–1679) was a nobleman who governed the Dutch colony in northeastern Brazil on behalf of the Dutch West India Company from 1637 to 1644. While administering these territories, Maurits saw himself as a military man, a humanist thinker, and a firm but benevolent ruler who imposed order while bringing European culture to the Brazilian wilderness. Historians have referred to him as a "humanist prince," someone who supported some degree of religious tolerance, free trade, and consultative rule, even if he also prized and supported military conquest and could flex his administrative powers in authoritarian ways. Yet even today, scholars continue to benefit from the artistic and scientific works produced under his patronage.

Founded in 1621 to pursue commercial transactions in the Atlantic, the Dutch West India Company had a powerful board of directors and relied on relatively limited support from the bicameral legislature, known as the States-General of the Republic of the United Netherlands. The corporation modeled itself after the successful Dutch East India Company, which controlled most trade between Europe and Southeast Asia. Obtaining sugar from Brazil was the primary aim of the Dutch West India Company, and it relied on Johan Maurits to help it pursue this. Yet he had additional ambitions as well.

The count's first piece of business upon arriving in Brazil was to drive the Portuguese out of the northeast. Accordingly, he made alliances with the Tapuya, the indigenous peoples most antagonistic to the Portuguese and their Tupi allies, and waged a campaign to expel the Portuguese from Pernambuco. However, he did not pursue them southward into Bahia, seeing the São Francisco River as a suitable boundary between the new Dutch colony and Portuguese possessions.

Maurits then began to transform Recife, the capital of the province, from a pioneer settlement into a model colonial city and a symbol of his authority. He established representative councils for local governance and offered

Count Johan Maurits von Nassau-Seigen (1604–1679) in a portrait by Jan de Baen, probably painted around 1668–70. As in most of his portraits, Maurits had himself painted as a military man. Photograph by Margareta Svensson. Courtesy of Mauritshuis, The Hague.

Portuguese residents of the city the same protections under colonial laws granted to the Dutch. He improved the transportation system, and he built a palace for himself called Vrijburg on undeveloped lands around the existing town of Recife, converting swamps into magnificent gardens that functioned both as rationally ordered ornaments and as practical sources of food.

Almost immediately upon arriving, he had declared Brazil one of the most beautiful places in the world, and he spent considerable energy and resources encouraging his European entourage to discover, understand, and document its natural wonders. He also invited forty-six scholars from the Netherlands, all of them experts in an art, a craft, or science, to come to Brazil to do the same. Among those who joined him in Recife were Albert Eckhout, a painter of portraits and still lifes, who depicted the flora, fauna, and peoples of the northeast, including numerous paintings of cannibalism; Frans Janszzon Post, the first European to paint American landscapes; and Abraham Willaerts, a Dutch baroque painter who depicted marine and harbor scenes. Some of the pictures they left are the only images we have from this colonial town. Moreover, Maurits himself amassed an enormous collection of ethnographic objects or curiosities, often gifts from friends or allies, such as jewelry, ornamental decorations, housewares, and weapons, which visitors said he deeply appreciated and enjoyed showing to others. And he commissioned various works, such as ethnographic and zoological illustrations, that point to the extent of his interest in the colony.

As a colonial administrator, Maurits was pragmatic. Despite his Calvinist upbringing, he was tolerant of the Catholics and Jews in Pernambuco, allowing them freedom not just of conscience but of worship. Sephardic Jews, whose ancestors had fled religious persecution in the Iberian Peninsula and settled in the Low Countries, sought opportunities in the Dutch colony, using their knowledge of Portuguese as an advantage to trade and entering the sugar industry. Maurits's religious tolerance and his role as a benefactor also helped to reduce the animosity between the Protestant Dutch and the Catholic Portuguese living in northeastern Brazil, and his investment in the colony helped diminish Portuguese bitterness toward the Dutch presence.

His popularity among the various factions of the colony was likely the most significant reason Johan Maurits remained in power as long as he did. Increasingly, however, the directors of the Dutch West India Company, interested in profits from sugar production, grew frustrated as Maurits focused on expensive patronage of the arts and sciences and building projects. Yet it was not until the 1640s, after the successful conclusion of a truce with Portugal, that the company took serious action to remove him from control of the colony. In May 1644, more than two years after the directors had sent him a letter calling him back to Europe, Johan Maurits departed from Paraíba for the Netherlands.

Whatever the motivations behind Maurits's efforts to bring European artists and scientists to Brazil, he had an undeniable influence on European understandings of the region. From his collection of ethnographic objects and commissioned art, he made gifts to the electors of the United Provinces of the Netherlands, the king of Denmark, the king of France, and a number of other European leaders, guaranteeing the inclusion of these works in the great museums of Europe. And for over 150 years, until the nineteenth century, the written sources amassed in Brazil under his direction stood as the most authoritative body of information available on the country.

In the last century, Brazilian intellectuals have been ambivalent and divided in their analysis of the Dutch occupation of the Brazilian northeast. Most have considered the Dutch colonization an unjustifiable incursion on Portuguese rights to possess the region. Some scholars insist that the Portuguese monarchy's strategy of not investing in the colony left it vulnerable to the Dutch incursion. Gilberto Freyre, a tremendously influential social scientist from the early twentieth century, has argued that Maurits's artistic and scientific interests, as well as his relatively tolerant rule over the Portuguese in the region, helped reconcile the local Brazilian population to the Dutch colonial experiment, much as the Jesuits played a mediating role between indigenous and Portuguese populations in the sixteenth century. However, early twentieth-century diplomat and historian Manuel de Oliveira Lima considers the failure of the Dutch conquest a result of the weaknesses of Protestant mercantilism when compared with the strengths of Portuguese-Brazilian Catholicism. He has viewed Johan Maurits's religious tolerance, his building projects, and his artistic and scientific achievements as mere attempts to get a firmer hold on the colony, and has judged Maurits's motivations as more of a desire for control than genuine interest in the welfare of the people.

In his recommendations to his successor, Johan Maurits emphasized tolerance of religious differences and courtesy to the Portuguese, who, he claimed, valued manners and hospitality over material comforts. While some Portuguese residents of northeastern Brazil did begin plotting revolts against Dutch control during Maurits's administration, it was not until the years after his removal from power that the Portuguese in Brazil began to seriously chafe at their subjugation. A series of revolts in Maranhão, Pernambuco, and Bahia shook the Dutch West India Company's confidence that its treaties with Portugal would hold. Ultimately, faced with the precarious position of his throne, King João IV of Portugal cracked down on the Dutch, resolving to drive them out of Brazil. In 1654 the combined forces of local landowners, militias, and irregular fighters finally ended the Dutch experience in Brazil.

Gold and the New Colonial Order, 1695–1807

In order for the Portuguese government to complete the destruction of the Palmares *quilombo* in 1694, the Crown relied in part on *bandeirantes*, the back-woodsmen from São Paulo. Their experience in surviving in the wilderness as bounty hunters pursuing runaway slaves, or as traders capturing and enslaving indigenous people, suited them well for that disreputable task. Throughout the seventeenth century, *bandeirantes* also trekked over rugged terrain hundreds of leagues from the coast in pursuit of gold, silver, and precious stones. Finally, a year after the annihilation of Palmares, they found gold in an area of the hinterlands located north of São Paulo and northwest of Rio de Janeiro. This area eventually became known as Minas Gerais, or General Mines, an apt description for the mountainous region that over the next half century provided hundreds of tons of revenue in gold to the Portuguese Crown.

From São Paulo or Rio de Janeiro, adventurers crossed through the dense vegetation covering the hilly backlands, winding their way through low valleys and over rocky passes to reach the gold district. Young men from Portugal, many from the poor region of Minho in the north, crossed the Atlantic, landed in Salvador or another northern port, traveled down the São Francisco River, and then proceeded overland to seek their fortunes. They brought slaves with them to do the heavy labor: blocking and rerouting streams and rivers in order to find gold in the riverbeds, digging pits and mines to engage in underground prospecting, and transporting supplies and equipment to the remote region.

The discovery of gold in the faraway backlands transformed colonial Brazil in many ways. First, it pulled people into regions of the country that had previously seen very few Europeans, Africans, or their descendants. Some historians estimate that as many as 600,000 Portuguese and as many, if not more, slaves came to the region to extract gold. This movement of free and enslaved people inland further weakened sugar production along the coast, as the price of slaves rose in response to increased demands in the mining district. While many slaves labored in mining enterprises, others were engaged in supplying the area with food, animals, tools, and equipment that, over time, created a complex regional economy with links to the coastal area.

The population explosion also displaced those indigenous people who had survived the influx into the region, pushing them further away from the mining centers. And as the early alluvial mining diminished, miners and adventurers moved on to other parts of the region, seeking new sources of wealth and expanding Portuguese influence in heretofore inaccessible areas. At the same time, gold, and later diamonds, offered a significant boost to the Portuguese economy and increased prosperity for the colony.

In the first two decades of the gold rush, incessant conflicts broke out among the different groups trying their luck in the mining district. The most notable tension was between the Paulista prospectors, who claimed the rights to control the region due to their role in the first discoveries of rich gold deposits, and newly arrived fortune hunters from Portugal. Because the Portuguese generally reached the gold mining region only after first landing in Salvador, Bahia, where they equipped themselves for the arduous trip in high leather boots and elaborate gear, the Paulistas mocked their exaggerated footwear by pejoratively calling the newcomers *Emboabas,* a Tupi term for birds with feathers that covered their legs and feet. Violent confrontations over control of the region, known as the Emboabas War, broke out in 1708–9 and pitted Portuguese prospectors and their Bahian supporters against Paulista *bandeirantes*. The fighting ended in a stalemate, although an independent captaincy called São Paulo e Minas de Ouro was established in 1709. Minas Gerais became a separate entity in 1720.

Gold promised considerable revenue for the Portuguese government if it could successfully tax the miners and prevent smuggling of the precious metal out of the region. Edicts from Lisbon attempted to restrict access to the mining area, especially the entrance of friars and priests, who the government was convinced were deeply involved in illicit trade. The Crown also employed different taxation methods, ranging from a head tax on all residents in the region, free and enslaved alike, to decrees that gold had to be smelted in official government foundries in order to pay the 20 percent tax called the royal *quinto*. When prospectors discovered diamonds in the 1720s, the Portuguese ordered restricted access to the region where they had been found and granted licenses to diamond miners with exclusive rights to dig for the precious stones under royal supervision.

As a result of the gold trade, Rio de Janeiro became a much more important urban center. Merchants and mule drivers transported slaves and supplies from the port to the mining district and returned with gold, oftentimes smuggled past checkpoints along the roads and trails that connected Minas Gerais to the coast. In order to more successfully control the movement and taxation of gold and to shore up royal garrisons that had become vital in re-

Negroes Washing for Diamonds, Gold, & c. Illustration by John Mawe. In addition to gold mining, Minas Gerais became the most important source of diamonds in the eighteenth century. From *Travels in the interior of Brazil* (London, 1823).

sponding to border disputes with the Spanish Empire in the south, in 1763 the Portuguese decided to move the seat of the viceroyalty from Salvador to Rio de Janeiro. The new capital of the colony was a growing city with a population of forty thousand, equaling the number of inhabitants of Salvador. Yet by the time the capital was moved, gold extraction had begun to significantly decline, forcing the Portuguese government to reform its colonial operations in order to more efficiently obtain revenues and increase profitability.

Sebastião José de Carvalho e Melo (1699–1782), minster to King José I, who received the title of marques of Pombal in 1770, was the official who took on this ambitious task. From 1750 to 1777, Carvalho e Melo carried out a series of measures, known as the Pombaline Reforms, designed to strengthen Portugal's economy and increase its control over its colonies. Having served as Portuguese ambassador to Great Britain, Carvalho e Melo was well aware of Britain's position as an emergent industrial power. He also understood the problems inherent in the Methuen Treaty of 1703, by which Britain supplied Portugal with industrialized woolen goods and manufactured products in

As profetas de Aleijadinho. Photograph by Horácio Coppola, 1945. Statues of biblical prophets sculpted by Antônio Francisco Lisboa (1738–1814), also known as Aleijadinho. Coppola's sensitive series of photographic images of the baroque artwork by Brazil's most important colonial sculptor contributed to the consecration of Aleijadinho as an iconic figure in the post–World War II period when national tourism to Minas Gerais increased significantly. Instituto Moreira Salles Collection.

exchange for Portuguese wines. While it seemed to benefit both economies, in reality it weakened Portugal's possibilities for industrialization, while also reinforcing a long-term political alliance between the two nations against their historic rivals, Spain and France.

Carvalho e Melo tried to overcome this disadvantage through increased efficiency in imperial operations. He established state-supported monopoly trading companies in the Amazon and northeastern Brazil, enacted new regulations to increase tax collection, and initiated a series of measures designed to eliminate the Inquisition and reduce the power of the Jesuits, who had enjoyed relative autonomy in Portugal and its possessions. The trading companies that he created in Brazil sought to encourage the extraction of medicinal drugs and other products from the Amazon region and stimulate cotton and rice production in the northeastern captaincy of Maranhão. Carvalho e Melo also issued an edict eliminating slavery in Portugal and Portuguese India, presumably to more efficiently direct enslaved Africans to Brazil, and another prohibiting indigenous slavery in Brazil. A complementary provision encouraged the marriage of Portuguese men to indigenous women, especially in the Amazon and the southern borderlands, as a means of integrating indigenous people into the empire and encouraging Portuguese settlements in frontier areas that were in dispute with Spain.

Carvalho e Melo's anti-Jesuit campaigns resulted in their expulsion from Portugal and its empire in 1759. The religious order's vast properties were taken over by other sectors of the church or sold to provide revenue for the Crown. The measure, however, diminished educational opportunities in Brazil, as the Jesuits had provided much of the schooling in the colony. At the same time, it freed indigenous people in the north who had been under Jesuit control. Carvalho e Melo also eliminated legal restrictions on New Christians, whose ancestors had been Jews, and weakened the power of the Inquisition.

The marquis of Pombal lost power and influence at the court when José I died and his daughter Queen Maria I assumed the throne in 1777. Still, most of his policies continued under her reign, including the ongoing pressure to extract taxes from the richest regions of Brazil, which provoked regional discontent and conspiracies against the Crown.

By the late 1780s, Minas Gerais had become a cultural center that produced art, music, and literature. The wealth of the gold-mining region financed opulently decorated baroque churches, as well as European-style paintings and fine sculptures. The most prominent artist of the period in the region was Antônio Francisco Lisboa (1738–1814), also known as Aleijadinho, or the Little Cripple, because he suffered from a debilitating disease that disfigured his hands and arms. The son of a Portuguese carpenter and an African slave, this late baroque architect and sculptor created gracious soapstone carvings of Old Testament prophets in the town of Congonhas do Campo, as well as imaginative wooden sculptures of religious figures for the interiors of churches that included black saints and cherubic angels. As an architect, he designed and luxuriously decorated beautiful churches.

In the same wealthy city of Vila Rica (today called Ouro Preto) where Aleijadinho produced his masterpieces, a conspiracy formed in the late 1780s against the Crown and its policies toward the region. The plot, later called the Mineira Conspiracy, involved members of the local elite, including intellectuals, writers, and members of the Arcadian literary group. Quashed before it could be carried out, the plot marked the first time that Brazilians organized for emancipation from Portugal and a possible Republican regime. The planners were harshly punished—exiled or imprisoned for life—while the person of the lowest social rank involved in the conspiracy, Joaquim José da Silva Xavier, popularly known as Tiradentes, was executed.

A decade later, in 1798, free people of color, slaves, and artisans organized another rebellion in Salvador, Bahia, known as the Tailors' Revolt, this time against slavery and racial discrimination. Because it involved members from other social groups and not just elites, it was considered more dangerous, and the rebellion was violently repressed. Although in both cases the causes of unrest revolved around local or regional concerns, these incidents suggest a more widespread uneasiness in Brazil's most prosperous regions among different sectors of the population. Both members of the elite and those from other social groups were beginning to seriously consider independence from Portugal.

The Brazilian Gold Rush

Antonio Giovanni Andreoni

Antonio Giovanni Andreoni, the Italian Jesuit mentioned earlier in this volume who wrote rich descriptions of sugar plantation life under the pen name André João Antonil, also included in his book a chapter on the newly discovered gold mines. Indeed, it may have been this chapter that caused the king of Portugal to ban the book immediately after its publication, and to confiscate all existing copies, for the chapter describes the huge quantities of gold being found and mined, and the mechanisms by which a large number of people were avoiding paying royal taxes. Only seven original copies of the book remain, although since the nineteenth century it has been reedited and republished numerous times because of its historical importance.

While Antonil's earlier chapters on sugar plantation life were based on his personal experiences and observations in Bahia, the chapter on gold mining came from information gleaned from others. In the passages below, he recounts the story of how gold was first discovered, a tale that leaves anonymous the mixed-race person who supposedly first found gold, but carefully names each subsequent official discoverer and the rivers named after him. He also describes the transformation this discovery wrought on the area of Minas Gerais.

It has been just a few years since the general mines of Caraguá were discovered. Artur de Sá was governing Rio de Janeiro at the time. They say that the first person to discover gold was a mulatto who had been at the mines in Paranaguá and Curitiba. This fellow went into the interior with Paulistas to look for Indians. After they arrived at Tripuí Mountain, he went down the mountain to draw water from the creek with a wooden bucket at a stream they today call Ouro Preto. Putting the bucket into the river to get some water, he scraped it at the side of the river and noted that inside were some small steel-colored flakes. He did not know what he had discovered, nor did his companions when he showed them these flakes. They did not appreciate what they had so easily found. They only remembered that at this place there was a metal that was poorly formed and, for that reason, was unknown. Once they arrived in Taubaté, they did not forget to inquire about what kind of metal it was. Without any additional examination, they sold some of it to Miguel de Sousa. . . . This was without knowing what they were selling, nor did the buyer know what he purchased. They sent a sample to the governor in Rio de Janeiro, Artur de Sá. He made some tests and discovered it was very fine gold.

At a distance of half a *legoa* from the creek to Ouro Preto, another mine was found called the mine at the Antonio Diaz Creek. From there, proceeding another half-legoa, there is the mine of the Father João de Faria Creek. Next to it, a little more than a legoa distant, is the mine of the Bueno Creek and the mine of Bento Rodrigues. From there, three days' moderate journey, travelling each day until dinner time, there is the mine of Our Lady of Carmo Stream. It was discovered by João Lopes de Lima, not counting the other mine on the creek of Ibuprianga. All of these were named for their discoverers and all were Paulistas. . . .

The unquenchable thirst for gold motivated so many to leave their lands and follow the very rough roads of Minas that it is difficult to count the number of people who are currently there. Taken together—those who have been there these past few years, for a long time, and those who have recently moved there—they say that more than thirty thousand souls are working there. Some are prospecting, others supervising the mining, others negotiating, selling, and buying not just the necessities but also gifts, more than in the ports.

Each year masses of Portuguese and foreigners arrive and head for the mines. From the cities and towns, bays and backlands of Brazil come whites, *pardos*, blacks, and many Indians serving the Paulistas. This mixture is composed of all sorts of people: men and women, young boys and old men, rich and poor, nobles and peasants, as well as secular and clerical figures. Religious figures come from diverse institutions, many of which do not have a monastery or house in Brazil.

As far as governing the daily lives of these people, until presently there has not been any constraint or government that is effective. They obey only some laws—that is, those pertaining to rights and shares of the mining areas, disregarding everything else. There are no agents or justices that enforce or who can address punishments for crimes, which are not few, and are mainly homicides and thefts. In regard to their spiritual welfare, until now the ecclesiastical prelates have disputed the proper jurisdiction.

The king had Justice José Vaz Pinto as his superintendent of these mines. After two or three years, he settled in Rio de Janeiro. I assume he is well informed as to what is happening there because of his vast experience. I also assume that he has pinpointed the disarray, its remedies, and the possibilities of their enforcement.

Also assisting in the region of the mines is a royal attorney and a customs officer, who are paid stipends. Until now, there have been places where the royal fifth [*quinto*] is collected in Taubaté, in the town of São Paulo, in Parati and in Rio de Janeiro. In each of these Customs Houses there is a supervisor, a secretary, and a foundry man. The latter casts the gold into bars and stamps them with the royal sign, showing that the tax of a royal fifth has been paid from this gold.

If there were royal mints in Bahia and in Rio de Janeiro (since these are the two locations where all the gold arrives), His Majesty would collect greater profit than he currently does. This profit would be increased even more if the mints were well supplied with the necessary equipment, and if funds were available for immediate purchase of the gold from the miners.

We now understand that His Majesty has sent a governor and ministers of justice to better administer the mining regions and a regiment of soldiers to impose order.

The Minas Uprising of 1720

Anonymous

The discovery of rich gold deposits in the mid-1690s in what today is the state of Minas Gerais allowed many to make personal fortunes. Officially the Crown was to receive a tax on one-fifth of all gold produced, the quinto, *but in reality many evaded it as the official presence in the region was weak. In an effort to enforce tax collection, the Crown mandated that all exported gold be smelted at royal facilities and restricted the use of gold dust as specie. The following report to the Crown describes the miners' indignation with these new rules and the response of Pedro Miguel de Almeida Portugal e Vasconcelos (1688–1756). The governor of the captaincy of São Paulo and Minas Gerais from 1717 to 1721, who held the title of third count of Assumar, Almeida is referred to in the document as the Conde-Governador (Count-Governor). He later served as the viceroy of Portuguese India. Within the report one can notice several interesting subplots, such as the miners' resentment toward merchants, the church's standing in the community, and the specter of a slave rebellion. Perhaps the reader will notice others.*

On São Pedro eve, during the night, a mob of armed people descended from the hill of Ouro Preto, and another mob arose in the area of Padre Faria. Together they attacked the house of Doctor Martinho Vieyra, the *ouvidor* [a justice or magistrate]; and only by leaving the house did he escape the riot's rage and death. Some of these rioters, entering, destroyed everything that he had in the house, throwing from the windows the royal ordinances, the books of the Royal Treasury, and all the rest of the papers belonging to his ministry, while reading the sentences and rulings with mockery, and taunting the *ouvidor*, whose staff one of the rioters held. The latter shouted to the people that if they wanted him to do justice for them, then he was present. Accompanying this action were some voices and words of dishonor against the said magistrate.

The first assault completed, they started to chant: *Viva o povo, viva o povo* [Long live the people, long live the people]. And thus, they added partisans joining them in that riot, some willingly, others by force. . . . On the following day of São Pedro, they sent a bulletin with some demands to the Count of Assumar, who with prudence responded to them that some things that they asked for were being resolved by Your Majesty in the letters that he [Count of Assumar] would receive from the fleet, doing this so that they might calm down. . . .

On the following nights, until July 16, that entire village appeared to be an inferno with disorders, riots, and disturbances caused by some disguised people who descended from the hill of Ouro Preto, coming down accompanied by blacks and mulattoes; breaking into houses; injuring, beating, and killing those who resisted them. Residents of the villa of Ouro Preto emptied the goods of their stores and hid them in the woods because of the fear of robbery, and the insults that the rioters committed with such stubbornness made them seem to be unleashed demons with the power to scatter the village and all its population. . . .

The Count-Governor ordered the arrest of those whom he prudently judged the cause, motive, and occasion for this uprising, and not even with these imprisonments was the rebellion calmed, but instead, it was provoked further and inflamed with greater rage, and now with evident suspicion of greater ruin to Minas. On July 14, the rioters that descended from the hill were so horrific, and acted with such vehemence that they went to the home of the schoolmaster, the vicar of the jurisdiction of Ouro Preto, and made him get out of bed, so that he would open the door of the church for them, supposing that the rest of the people were in it, and they went into the church and indecently overturned even the altars. On this night there were the greatest disorders, breaking the doors and windows of residents, and killing one man from the same hill, whom they supposed had given information to the Count-Governor.

On July 15, they acquainted the Count-Governor with the insolence already proclaimed in those uprisings, and of the ultimate goal and ruin coming from this rebellion; and rudely, they ordered him to say that he would take measures for leaving, because certainly they were expelling him from Minas. The residents of Ouro Preto, who now were appearing discouraged by that which they bore, insisted with supplications that the Count-Governor help them, and free them from the oppression that they suffered. The residents of Padre Faria, as most opposed to those of the hill (and so much so that they always opposed the expansion of that settlement or encampment on the hill), suffered these insolences with more impatience and were seen in such desperation on the first night of the riot that they wanted to climb the hill and declare war, killing each other with hostility, and destroying all the houses on the hill, going from place to place wielding weapons simultaneously with the uproar. Many fatalities would have followed with the confrontation of the two parties if the Reverend Doctor Luiz Ribeiro had not dissuaded them from that action, telling them that they should seek the remedy for this oppression from the Count-Governor.

The Count-Governor—laden with reason, patience, prudence, and justice

—finally decided to leave Ribeirão on July 16, a most happy day, since it was the day of Our Lady of Carmo, patron saint of Ribeirão, and he marched to Villa Rica accompanied by dragoons and residents of this village, and with their slaves also armed, to confront the rebellion, which with so much prudence and patience he sought to quell. And entering Villa Rica, knowing for certain that on the hill the assassins, rioters, and rebels were still currently lodged, and that throughout the neighboring woods they had been placing armed people, either for an invasion or for defense of their rebellion (which they certainly would execute if the intention were not obstructed or cut off from them), the Count-Governor seized the initiative to order the homes of the principal originators and agents of the uprising to be burned.

And thus he sent the captain of the dragoons, João de Almeida de Vasconcelos, to climb the hill, designating to him Sergeant-Major Manoel Gomes da Silva, Captain Antonio da Costa Gouvêa, and Second Lieutenant Balthasar de Sampaio, all residents of the hill, so that they would show him the houses of those who publicly and openly were rebels and agents of this uprising, and accomplices in this crime, and put fire to them. When the captain of the dragoons arrived at the hill with the men whom the Count-Governor named to him, he asserted that by no manner would they entrust their consciences with any hatred or private passion, and would only signal to him the homes of those known actors, agents, and accomplices in the crime, which they thus did. And soon, the said captain of the dragoons, arriving at the house of the camp master, Pascoal da Silva Guimarães, ordered a captain of the orderlies, whom he brought with him, to pull out the images and ornaments from the small chapel in the said house, and ordered him to hand over everything that pertained to divine worship to the venerable vicar of the cathedral, Antônio Dias, according to the order of the Count-General. When they started the fire, three neighbors came running to complain, imagining that fire was being set to all the houses, to which Captain Antonio da Costa Gouvêa replied quickly and assured them that the fire was only for the houses of the known originators [of the uprising], and that they might have calmed down, as some had done, and because of that they had saved their homes.

But since on the said hill, two thousand, or close to three thousand, blacks mined, on seeing that spectacle of fire they were changed; and exiting the holes in the ground, from which they excavated gold, imagining that fire would be set generally to all the houses without distinction, the blacks entered those that they found deserted, and robbed and burned them. And Captain João de Almeida could not respond quickly to that because not only did the fire and the rough terrain hinder him, but also it was necessary, according to the order of the Count-General, to be with his soldiers in formation while the home of Pascoal da Silva was being destroyed, because of the risk of armed people who were said to be in the neighboring woods and thereby to avoid the danger of some unexpected assault. And moving on to execute the same order at Ouro Podre (another place situated on the same hill), this captain put guards in a narrow passageway so that the blacks would not mix with the soldiers; and that caused the order here to be executed only in the houses of the guilty, and with neither confusion nor ruin for those who were not guilty.

Translated by Robert M. Levine and John J. Crocitti

Expulsion of the Jesuits from Brazil

King Dom José I

After two hundred years of missionary service in Brazil, the Society of Jesus, known as the Jesuits, came into open conflict with the Crown. In addition to monopolizing indigenous labor, they had built profitable endeavors in sugar, cotton, and cattle based on African slave labor, while avoiding taxes and royal control over their operations. The order's autonomy from local government authority and profitable activities with the Spanish Empire from the Amazon to the borderlands in the south provoked widespread opposition from other colonists, who resented the Jesuits' favorable economic standing and control over indigenous labor. Under the leadership of Sebastião José de Carvalho e Melo, the Portuguese state moved to limit the Jesuits' economic and temporal influence in the colony in the 1750s. Among other measures, the Crown ended indigenous peoples' state of legal dependency on ecclesiastical authority, which removed them from Jesuit control, and it encouraged indigenous integration into Portuguese society through the legalization of interethnic marriages. When the Jesuits resisted these measures, the Crown suppressed the temporal power of the Jesuits throughout Brazil in 1758 and formally expelled them the next year from the empire. This led to other measures against the Society of Jesus in Europe. Finally, in 1773, Pope Clement XIV prohibited the Jesuits from operating anywhere in the Catholic world, which included prohibiting any remaining members of the order who were still working in schools and hospitals from continuing their activities.

In the following royal ordinance, Portuguese King Dom José I complies with the papal decree by suppressing all former Jesuit educational institutions and hospitals that had continued to operate in Brazil after 1759.

*Dom José, by the Grace of God, King of Portugal and the Algarves,
on this side of the ocean, and beyond the sea, in Africa, Lord of Guinea,
and of the Conquest, Navigation, and Enterprise of Ethiopia, Arabia,
Persia and of India, to the Vassals of all the States of My Kingdoms,
and Lordships.*

Our most holy Father Clement XIV, now President of the Universal Church of God: having observed, examined, and agreed to . . . not only all the facts concerning the founding, progress, and ultimate state of the Company of Jesus; directed to the Universal Church, and to the monarchies, sovereigns, and people of the four parts of the discovered world; but also in recognition of all the revolutions, tumults, and scandals that the aforementioned Company has caused; all the remedies, which no less than twenty-four of the Pope's predecessors had sought to implement against those great evils . . . had no other effect than that the most frequent day-to-day complaints and clamors against the Company were not expressed, and seeking to abort at the same time, in different kingdoms, and states of the world, seditions, riots, discords, and very dangerous scandals, that, destroying and almost breaking the bonds of Christian charity, inflamed the minds of the faithful with feelings of division, hatred, and enmity; when these referred-to insults, and their consequent dangers, became extremely urgent, such that the same monarchs, who had once distinguished the Company in piety and with hereditary liberalism, became necessarily constrained; . . . all of the Societies from their kingdoms, provinces, and dominions, because this extreme solution was the only one that permitted them to prevent equally extreme dangers, such as the provocation, offense, and injury to the Christian people of their respective kingdoms and dominions within the bosom of the Church of the Holy Mother, and within the same fatherlands. . . .

After the Holy Father had conclusively demonstrated that the aforementioned Company not only failed to produce, for the benefit of the Church and for faithful Christians, the copious fruits which were the object of its institution, and the many privileges with which it was honored; but that, much to the contrary, it was impractical that the conservation of the said Society would be compatible with the restitution, conservation, and permanent peace of the Universal Church, civil society, and the Christian Union. . . .

[Thus,] the Pope ordered his papal bull, on the twentieth day of July of this fifth year of his papacy. By his mature counsel, sure knowledge, and plenitude of apostolic power, he extinguished and wholly suppressed the same Company named of Jesus: Abolishing, and derogating all and every one of their offices, ministries, administrations, houses, schools, colleges, hospitals, residences, and whatever other places that pertained to them, in whatever kingdom, state, or province in which they exist; likewise all their statutes, constitutions, decrees, mores, and habits; all of their privileges, and general pardons, . . . declaring entirely revoked, and perpetually extinct the authority of the general function of all the provincials, visitors, and all other superiors of the said Society, regarding things spiritual as well as temporal. . . .

And I mandate to Doctor João Pacheco Pereira of my counsel, and palace judge, who serves the Chancellor Mor [Keeper of the Royal Seal] of these kingdoms, to publish this in the chancellery, and deliver copies under my seal to all of the tribunals, the district and town heads of these kingdoms, and to all of their captaincies, and to send the original document to the Torre do Tombo Royal Archive.

Decreed in the palace of Our Lady of Assistance, on the ninth day of the month of September in the year of Our Lord Jesus Christ one thousand seven hundred seventy and three. The King under Protection.

September 9, 1773

Translated by Johanna Richlin

Portugal, Brazil, and *The Wealth of Nations*

Adam Smith

In these selections from Adam Smith's magnum opus, An Inquiry into the Wealth of Nations, *the Scottish economist and philosopher discusses the importance of gold in facilitating foreign trade. An advocate of free trade among nations, Smith argues that a direct exchange of consumable goods is generally the most advantageous. But, he argues, Portuguese gold and silver greatly facilitate Britain's ability to trade around the world.*

Book IV: Of Systems of Political Economy

CHAPTER 6: OF TREATIES OF COMMERCE

Portugal receives annually from the Brazils a greater quantity of gold than can be employed in its domestic commerce, whether in the shape of coin or of plate. The surplus is too valuable to be allowed to lie idle and locked up in coffers. As it can find no advantageous market at home, it must, notwithstanding any prohibition, be sent abroad, and exchanged for something for which there is a more advantageous market at home. A large share of it comes annually to England, in return either for English goods, or for those of other European nations that receive their returns through England. . . .

Our merchants were, some years ago, out of humor with the crown of Portugal. Some privileges, which had been granted them, not by treaty, but by the free grace of that crown, at the solicitation, indeed, it is probable, and in return for much greater favors, defense and protection, from the crown of Great Britain, had been either infringed or revoked. The people, therefore, usually most interested in celebrating the Portugal trade, were then rather disposed to represent it as less advantageous than it had commonly been imagined. The far greater part, almost the whole, they pretended, of this annual importation of gold, was not on account of Great Britain, but of other European nations. . . .

Let us suppose, however, that the whole was on account of Great Britain. . . . This trade would not, upon that account, be more advantageous than any other in which, for the same value sent out, we received an equal value of consumable goods in return.

It is but a very small part of this importation, which, it can be supposed, is employed as an annual addition either to the plate or to the coin of the kingdom. The rest must all be sent abroad and exchanged for consumable goods of some kind or other. But if those consumable goods were purchased directly with the produce of English industry, it would be more for the advantage of England, than first to purchase with the produce the gold of Portugal, and afterward to purchase with that gold those consumable goods. A direct foreign trade of consumption is always more advantageous than a round-about one. . . .

Though Britain were entirely excluded from the Portugal trade, it could find very little difficulty in procuring all the annual supplies of gold which it wants, either for the purposes of plate, or of coin, or of foreign trade. Gold, like every other commodity, is always somewhere or another to be got for its value by those who have that value to give for it. The annual surplus of gold in Portugal, besides, would still be sent abroad, and though not carried away by Great Britain, would be carried away by some other nation, which would be glad to sell it again for its price, in the same manner as Great Britain does at present. In buying gold of Portugal, indeed, we buy it at the first hand. Whereas, in buying it of any other nation, except Spain, we should buy it at the second, and might pay somewhat dearer. This difference, however, would surely be too insignificant to deserve the public's attention.

Almost all our gold, it is said, comes from Portugal. With other nations, the balance of trade is either against us, or not much in our favor. But we should remember, that the more gold we import from one country, the less we must necessarily import from all others. The effectual demand for gold, like that for every other commodity, is in every country limited to a certain quantity. If nine-tenths of this quantity is imported from one country, there remains a tenth only to be imported from all others. The more gold besides that is annually imported from some particular countries, over and above what is requisite for plate and for coin, the more must necessarily be exported to some others; and the more that most insignificant object of modern policy, the balance of trade, appears to be in our favor with some particular countries, the more it must necessarily appear to be against us with many others.
. . .

The great annual importation of gold and silver is neither for the purpose of plate nor of coin, but of foreign trade. A roundabout foreign trade of consumption can be carried on more advantageously by means of these metals than of almost any other goods. As they are the universal instruments of commerce, they are more readily received in return for all commodities than any other goods; and, on account of their small bulk and great value, it costs less to transport them backward and forward from one place to another than almost any other sort of merchandize, and they lose less of their value by be-ing so transported. Of all the commodities, therefore, which are bought in one foreign country, for no other purpose but to be sold or exchanged again for some other goods in another, there are none so convenient as gold and silver. . . .

Poems from Baroque Minas

Various authors

Tomás Antonio Gonzaga (1744–1810) and Cláudio Manuel da Costa (1729–1789) are the most famous poets of Brazil's late eighteenth-century period. Residents of the mining district known for its baroque churches, whose luxurious interiors reflected the region's wealth, both left important poetic works and were involved in the Minas Conspiracy of 1789 against the Portuguese monarchy. Banished to the Portuguese colony of Mozambique, Gonzaga wrote the poem "Marília de Dirceu" as a romantic ode to Maria Dorotéia Joaquina de Seixas, to whom he had been engaged before his arrest. The complete poem includes three parts, published in 1792, 1799, and 1812. The first lyric of the first book appears below.

Cláudio Manuel da Costa introduced neoclassical poetry to Brazil, established a literary society, the Overseas Colony in Ouro Preto, and was involved in theater. Arrested for his involvement in the Minas Conspiracy, on the morning of July 4, 1789, he was found dead with a cord around his neck, less than forty-eight hours after his questioning had incriminated many of his friends. Below are four of his sonnets.

Marília de Dirceu

TOMÁS ANTONIO GONZAGA

Part I

LYRIC I

Oh Marília, I am not a simple cowherd,
Who lives his life caring for others'
    cattle;
Poorly mannered and using coarse
    expressions,
Burnt and weather'd from hot suns
    and bitter cold.
I have my homestead upon which I
    labor;
That yields wine, vegetables, fruit
    and olive oil;

Parte I

LIRA I

Eu, Marília, não sou algum
    vaqueiro,
Que viva de guardar alheio gado;
De tosco trato, d'expressões
    grosseiro,
Dos frios gelos, e dos sóis
    queimado.
Tenho próprio casal, e nele
    assisto;
Dá-me vinho, legume, fruta,
    azeite;

From the small white sheep I receive sweet milk,	Das brancas ovelhinhas tiro o leite,
And furthermore the fine wool in which I dress.	E mais as finas lãs, de que me visto.
Thanks to you, fair Marília,	Graças, Marília bela,
Thanks to my shining star!	Graças à minha Estrela!
I've seen my reflection in a clear fountain,	Eu vi o meu semblante numa fonte,
And it has not yet been ravaged by the years:	Dos anos inda não está cortado:
The shepherds who inhabit this mountain,	Os pastores, que habitam este monte,
With such deft art do I play my concertina,	Com tal destreza toco a sanfoninha,
That I am the envy even of Alcestis:	Que inveja até me tem o próprio Alceste:
To its tones I attain a heavenly voice;	Ao som dela concerto a voz celeste;
Nor do I even sing fair verse that is not my own,	Nem canto letra, que não seja minha,
Thanks to you, fair Marília,	Graças, Marília bela,
Thanks to my shining star!	Graças à minha Estrela!
Though I may possess so many gifts of fortune,	Mas tendo tantos dotes da ventura,
I shall only value them dear shepherdess,	Só apreço lhes dou, gentil Pastora,
After your sweet affection has secured me,	Depois que teu afeto me segura,
When you want to be the mistress of what's mine.	Que queres do que tenho ser senhora.
Oh Marília, it is good, so good, to be the master	É bom, minha Marília, é bom ser dono
Of such a flock that covers hill and meadow;	De um rebanho, que cubra monte, e prado;
However, gentle shepherdess, your pleasure	Porém, gentil Pastora, o teu agrado
Is worth more than that flock, or than a throne.	Vale mais q'um rebanho, e mais q'um trono.
Thanks to you, fair Marília,	Graças, Marília bela,
Thanks to my shining star!	Graças à minha Estrela!
Your eyes illuminate the world with divine light,	Os teus olhos espalham luz divina,
One which the sun's rays vainly dare to challenge:	A quem a luz do Sol em vão se atreve:

Red poppies and roses delicate and fine,
Cover your cheeks, which are the color
of snow.
The hairs on your head equal threads
of gold;
And your body exudes rich balsams,
Ah gentle shepherdess, Heaven has
not made,
Such a treasure for the great glory
of Love.
Thanks to you, fair Marília,
Thanks to my shining star!

Take far away from me the seeds I
have sown,
The river risen o'er its banks in the
fields:
Oh decimate my herd, vile murderous
plague,
Without leaving a single shimmering
head.

For these earthly goods, Marília, I
have no need:
Nor shall the passion that this world
drags take my sight;
To live happily, Marília, all I need
Is for you to move your eyes and
smile upon me.
Thanks to you, fair Marília,
Thanks to my shining star!

You shall amuse yourself in the lush
forest,
Supported, dear Marília, on my arm;
There I shall rest through the hot
afternoon,
Sleeping lightly in the shelter of
your dress:
While the shepherds play at wrestling,
And two by two they run across the
meadows.
I shall touch your hair the color of
daisies,

Papoula, ou rosa delicada, e fina,
Te cobre as faces, que são cor de
neve.
Os teus cabelos são uns fios
d'ouro;
Teu lindo corpo bálsamos vapora.
Ah! Não, não fez o Céu, gentil
Pastora,
Para glória de Amor igual
tesouro.
Graças, Marília bela,
Graças à minha Estrela!

Leve-me a sementeira muito
embora
O rio sobre os campos
levantado:
Acabe, acabe a peste
matadora,
Sem deixar uma rês, o nédio
gado.

Já destes bens, Marília, não
preciso:
Nem me cega a paixão, que o
mundo arrasta;
Para viver feliz, Marília, basta
Que os olhos movas, e me dês
um riso.
Graças, Marília bela,
Graças à minha Estrela!

Irás a divertir-te na
floresta,
Sustentada, Marília, no meu braço;
Ali descansarei a quente
sesta,
Dormindo um leve sono em teu
regaço:
Enquanto a luta jogam os Pastores,
E emparelhados correm nas
campinas,
Toucarei teus cabelos de
boninas,

And on tree trunks I shall engrave
   praise for you.
Thanks to you, fair Marília,
Thanks to my shining star!

After death's cold hand has wounded
   both of us,
Whether on this hillside or another
   mountain,
Our bodies shall have, oh they shall
   have the luck
To be consumed together by the
   same soil.
And on the grave encircled by
   cypresses,
The shepherds shall be able to read
   these words:
"Who wants to be happy in their
   romances,
Follow the examples that these two
   gave us."
Thanks to you, fair Marília,
Thanks to my shining star!

Nos troncos gravarei os teus
   louvores.
Graças, Marília bela,
Graças à minha Estrela!

Depois de nos ferir a mão da
   morte,
Ou seja neste monte, ou noutra
   serra,
Nossos corpos terão, terão a
   sorte
De consumir os dois a mesma
   terra.
Na campa, rodeada de
   ciprestes,
Lerão estas palavras os
   Pastores:
"Quem quiser ser feliz nos seus
   amores,
Siga os exemplos, que nos deram
   estes."
Graças, Marília bela,
Graças à minha Estrela!

Sonnets

CLÁUDIO MANUEL DA COSTA

I.
So that I may sing the tender
   concerns of love,
Among you, oh mountains, I take
   my instrument,
Oh, hear then my funereal
   lamentation;
If you are so inspired by your
   compassion:
You have already seen that the
   wounded echoes
Of Orpheus the Thracian stopped
   the wind itself;
The sweetly accented playing of
   Amphion's lyre
Shook and overturned great stones
   and boulders.

I.
Para cantar de amor tenros
   cuidados,
Tomo entre vós, ó montes, o
   instrumento;
Ouvi pois o meu fúnebre
   lamento;
Se é, que de compaixão sois
   animados:
Já vós vistes, que aos ecos
   magoados
Do trácio Orfeu parava o mesmo
   vento;
Da lira de Anfião ao doce
   acento
Se viram os rochedos abalados.

I know that Destiny, of other talents,
Could crown Apollo with a wreath
    of green branches,
Inspired their lyres with divine
    poetic grace:

The poetic song, then, that spills
    forth in my voice,
Because at least one exceptional
    verse resounds,
Also makes itself worthy of fame
    among you.

II.
Oh my native river, read in posterity,
Your good name celebrated in my
    verses;
So that one day you see that name
    awakened
From the vile slumber of cold oblivion:

You do not see upon your banks the
    cool shade,
Sweet resting place beneath a leafy
    hornbeam;
You do not see the nymph sing or
    herd her cattle
In the bright afternoon of a sultry
    summer.

Your cloudy waters bathing the
    pale sandy banks
With small pieces of the richest of
    all treasures,
The vast field that you create by
    your ambition.

Through your tributaries the
    golden blond planet
Enriches the cresting high flow
    inside your veins,
Such that in flames it fertilizes
    and flows with gold.

Bem sei, que de outros gênios o Destino,
Para cingir de Apolo a verde r
    ama,
Lhes influiu na lira estro
    divino:

O canto, pois, que a minha
    voz derrama,
Porque ao menos o entoa
    um peregrino,
Se faz digno entre vós também
    de fama.

II.
Leia a posteridade, ó pátrio Rio,
Em meus versos teu nome
    celebrado;
Por que vejas uma hora
    despertado
O sono vil do esquecimento frio:

Não vês nas tuas margens o
    sombrio,
Fresco assento de um álamo
    copado;
Não vês ninfa cantar, pastar o
    gado
Na tarde clara do calmoso
    estio.

Turvo banhando as pálidas
    areias
Nas porções do riquíssimo
    tesouro
O vasto campo da ambição
    recreias.

Que de seus raios o planeta
    louro
Enriquecendo o influxo em
    tuas veias,
Quanto em chamas fecunda,
    brota em ouro.

III.

Oh cowherds who bring your cattle
    to this mountain,
Take caution there as you stroll
    upon those hillsides;
Because you can contaminate all
    of that land,
Just by looking upon my hurt and
    wounded face:

I amble (can't you see me) so heavily;
And the traitorous herd girl who is
    at war with me,
Is the same one who contains in her
    countenance
The cause of such an exhausted
    martyrdom.

If you want an introduction to her,
    come with me,
You shall see the stunning beauty
    that I adore;
Best not to, I have not yet become
    your enemy:
Leave her, don't look upon her,
    I implore you;
If you desire to follow what I have
    followed,
You shall lament and weep, oh
    cowherds, like I weep.

IV.

I am a cowherd; I don't deny it, my
    goods
Are those you see over there, I live
    happily
By guiding among the fresh flowering
    grasses
The sweetest company of my herd
    of cattle;

And there's where they hear me,
    the love-struck trunks of trees,

III.

Pastores, que levais ao monte o
    gado,
Vêde lá como andais por essa
    serra;
Que para dar contágio a toda a
    terra,
Basta ver se o meu rosto
    magoado:

Eu ando (vós me vêdes) tão pesado;
E a pastora infiel, que me faz
    guerra,
É a mesma, que em seu semblante
    encerra
A causa de um martírio tão
    cansado.

Se a quereis conhecer, vinde
    comigo,
Vereis a formosura, que eu
    adoro;
Mas não; tanto não sou vosso
    inimigo:
Deixai, não a vejais; eu vo-lo
    imploro;
Que se seguir quiserdes, o que
    eu sigo,
Chorareis, ó pastores, o que eu
    choro.

IV.

Sou pastor; não te nego; os meus
    montados
São esses, que aí vês; vivo
    contente
Ao trazer entre a relva
    florescente
A doce companhia dos meus
    gados;

Ali me ouvem os troncos
    namorados,

Into which the ancients have been transformed;	Em que se transformou a antiga gente;
Each and ev'ry one of them feels their own ruin;	Qualquer deles o seu estrago sente;
In the way that I too feel all of my worries.	Como eu sinto também os meus cuidados.
You, oh trunks of great trees, (I say to them) at one time	Vós, ó troncos, (lhes digo) que algum dia
Considered yourselves to be so firm and secure	Firmes vos contemplastes, e seguros
Within the arms of a beautiful companion;	Nos braços de uma bela companhia;
Console yourselves in me, oh solid, sturdy trunks;	Consolai-vos comigo, ó troncos duros;
Because I, at one time, also once witnessed joy;	Que eu alegre algum tempo assim me via;
And today I do weep at the falsehoods of Love.	E hoje os tratos de Amor choro perjuros.

Translated by Benjamin Legg

Tiradentes's Sentence

Queen Maria I of Portugal

The reforms promoted by the Portuguese government at the initiative of the marquis of Pombal were not widely welcomed in the gold mining area of Minas Gerais, where royal efforts to extract more revenue led to greater colonial oversight and taxes. It is not surprising, then, that the first real rebellion of elites who articulated a goal of independence took place there. In what became known as the Inconfidência Mineira, in 1789 a small group of prominent citizens from the town of Vila Rica (now Ouro Preto) plotted to proclaim Minas Gerais an independent country. Much of the information about their intentions has come from testimonies taken down after interrogations, and therefore the original program of the conspirators is not entirely clear. They seem to have demanded an end to restrictions on diamond mining, the cancellation of all debts to the Portuguese Crown, the establishment of a university, and the foundation of a vaguely defined democratic republic. They insisted, however, on the maintenance of the African slave trade. After an informer alerted the governor to their plans, the plotters were arrested, interrogated, and tried, and eleven of them were condemned to death. Yet soon after the trial Queen Maria commuted the death sentences of ten of them, who were instead banished to Africa. The eleventh, Joaquim José da Silva Xavier, a member of the militia, a cattle driver, and a dentist, who during his trial was given the pejorative nickname Tiradentes or Tooth Puller, took responsibility for the conspiracy. The person of lowest social rank among the conspirators, his punishment by execution, detailed below in his legal sentence, was meant to serve as warning for others. Instead it served as the basis for his later canonization as a national hero and symbol of independence.

Therefore, the criminal Joaquim José da Silva Xavier, known as Tiradentes, formerly second lieutenant of the troops in Minas Gerais, is condemned to be paraded with hangman's noose and public proclamation through the public streets to the place of hanging, where he will be executed, and after death his head will be cut off and taken to Vila Rica where, in the most public place, it will be fastened to a tall pole until consumed by time; his body will be divided into four quarters and fastened to poles along the road to Minas at Varghina and Sevolas, where the criminal carried on his infamous practices, and the rest at places of greatest population, until consumed by time. The criminal is declared infamous and his sons and grandsons infamous and his goods [will be] confiscated and the house in which he lived in Vila Rica will be leveled and the ground salted so that nothing more can be built there; and if they [goods found at his house] do not belong to him, they will be appraised and the owner paid for the confiscated goods, and on that same spot will be placed a sign to preserve forever the infamy of this abominable criminal.

Translated by Emma Wohl

The Tailors' Revolt

Luís Gonzaga das Virgens e Veiga

On August 12, 1798, Bahian authorities apprehended a group of men distributing leaflets at a church in the capital of Salvador and posting handwritten signs on the wall
that suggested some kind of conspiracy, movement, or possible revolt. Their arrests
led to hundreds of denunciations and the trials of forty-nine people, largely from the
lower classes. Most of their material was confiscated and burned, but twelve of these
pamphlets ended up in archives. Taken together, they articulated a series of demands:
better pay for laborers and soldiers, freedom from the despotism of the Crown, an end
to racial discrimination, the abolition of slavery, free trade with other countries, and
the execution of priests who stood in the way of liberty.

Luís Gonzaga das Virgens e Veiga was charged with authorship of the papers.
Veiga and three other free men of color, all of them either soldiers or tailors (and in
two cases both soldiers and tailors), were found guilty and executed, hence the name
Tailors' Revolt, also known as the Bahian Conspiracy. The remaining conspirators
were exiled or received other forms of punishment. The seized material emphasized
popular support for their demands and announced the possibility of also enlisting foreign support, mostly French, for their movement. Although the exact meaning of the
call for French aid is not entirely clear, scholars attribute it to the conspirators' knowledge of both the French Revolution and the slave revolt that had recently erupted in
the French colony of Saint-Domingue (now Haiti). The first of the two documents
that follow refers to demands regarding race, slavery, and the clergy. The second is a
petition to Queen Maria, penned by Luís Gonzaga, concerning racial discrimination
in the military.

Notice to the Clergy and to the Bahian People

The Powerful and Magnificent Republican Bahian People of this Republican City of Bahia, considering the many and repeated thieveries done in the
name of fair taxes that are levied by order of the Queen of [Portugal], concerning the uselessness of the slavery of the sacred People who are worthy
of freedom; with respect to liberty and equality, we urge and wish that in
the future, in the City and its outskirts, there will be a revolution so that the
terrible, ruinous yoke of Europe may be eliminated forever; according to the

promises made by 392 Most Dignified Representatives of the Nation in individual consultation with 280 persons who embrace total National Liberty, debated in the general body of 676 Men. . . . Therefore we make it known and notify the press that measures have been taken by means of aid from Foreigners, and in establishing free trade in sugar, tobacco, and brazilwood, and all other products, it being certain that all Foreigners, especially the French nation, will come here as long as we maintain free trade. Likewise the People demand that any priest, regular or secular, be punished, who hearing confession or in the pulpit, indoctrinates the ignorant fanatics and hypocrites, saying that Popular liberty is useless; in addition, any man who is guilty of the same crime will be punished, with punishment fitting his guilt. The People wish that all members of the regular army and the militia, white, brown, and black men, work together for Popular liberty; the People demand that each soldier receive in pay two pence each day, in addition to his relevant benefits. Officers will have an increase in pay and will be promoted, according to regulations. Each person should inquire and identify those who are the tyrants [who are opposed] to liberty and the freedom of the People. Each representative will follow the actions of the Church to note which Priests oppose liberty. The People will be free from the despotism of the tyrant king, and each one of them will be subject to the Laws of our Code and its reforms. All men and women who plot against [fair liberty] for all men will be cursed in our National society, and the graver blame will be that of the Church officials. So may it be understood.

A Petition to Queen Maria of Portugal

Luís Gonzaga das Virgens e Veiga, soldier of the first Regiment and fourth company of Grenadiers of this garrison, with the deepest respect, appeals to Your Excellency with the following plea.

That the brown men [*pardos*] being recruited for the Military Guild of the paid troops, all the tasks of the warlike work of infallible loyalty falling on them, so that they give their lives for the good of the Royal Crown of the State, of the nation, and all that is inherent to those who join the military profession voluntarily or through coercion, as those brown men are equal to other, white individuals within military and civil society, with no greater difference than that of color, a distinct feature by which nature distinguished them . . . but these men of color being nevertheless equivalent to white men, in their physical substance as well as their spiritual essence or microcosmic consistency, but being included in and considered indissolubly a part of the sovereign union, they are however reduced, by unacceptable abuse and supreme ignorance, to the least reasonable distinction in the regular and irregular troops, and considered as objects of slavery, contempt . . . and disposable, as undeserving of minimal promotion and access to ranks; but considering these said brown men are obligated to military service for many long years from adolescence until they lose their strength, their health, and even their lives, without rest or reward, to the point of making past labors seem appealing. These persons are encouraged to endure future suffering, but they are not even rewarded by simple flattery and a promised hope of access, of praise, of promotion to the privileged status of white men, but rather they are relegated to the fourth regiment, erected by Royal Order for those mentioned above, because reason and humanity and justice demand this; and because the supplicant is an individual of the class of these men, he has the sorrow, the inconsolable sorrow, of [not] rising through the ranks due to not having white skin, there being no other relevant motives than different [false] standards and the rule by noble men.

Translated by Gregory Childs, Emma Wohl, and Roquinaldo Ferreira

Letter from a Sugar Mill Owner

João Rodrigues de Brito

In the early nineteenth century, Portugal's economic trade began to stagnate as the French and English economies boomed. Mercantilist policies prohibiting Brazil from trading with nations other than Portugal and from producing items that competed with Portuguese products and exports came increasingly under fire. Portugal's reliance on revenue from Brazilian sugarcane led to a series of studies of Brazilian agriculture and economy. In this context, the governor of Bahia, Dom João de Saldanha da Gama Melo e Torres, asked four prominent members of the community to respond to several questions regarding Bahia's economic situation. The extracts below are from one of the letters he received in response. They showcase both planters' frustrations with the economic interventions of the colonial government and their close familiarity with global economic thinkers of their day, such as Adam Smith.

Illustrious President, Representatives, and Senators:

Honored by your letter of the twentieth of this month, through which your Excellencies condescend to consult me on the forces that depress agriculture and trade in this country, and over other items of public interest, . . . I am obliged to respond. . . .

[Question:] Do you recognize some oppressive force working against agriculture in this city? What is this force and how can it be avoided?

I have observed various forces, that, in my view, retard agricultural progress in this country, and many of these are easy to remedy. . . . I will speak only of principles. Since, according to the best economists, all that a government can do in favor of agriculture is limited to [providing] freedom, infrastructure, and instruction, I will organize [my answers] following this division.

On forces arising from the lack of freedom: For farmers to achieve the full freedom that farming requires, they must be able to: first, cultivate whatever goods they best see fit; second, construct any buildings or factories they deem appropriate for harvesting their products; third, sell their products anywhere, through any means, and with the assistance of anyone they want, without any burdensome charges or formalities; fourth, choose any buyer who pays them the best price; and fifth and finally, sell to them whenever they find it most convenient. Unfortunately, in none of these respects are farmers of this captaincy currently successful. . . .

[On the first force,] frequent laws . . . oblige farmers from the Recôncavo [the area around the Bay of All Saints] to plant five hundred beds of manioc for each slave in their service, and oblige slave traders to grow enough manioc for their ships' needs. The goal of these laws was not simply to support the slave trade, but also to ensure the survival of that class of citizens who purchase the most flour [and other milled grains] by preventing rises in the price of these basic goods and thus any corresponding periods of hunger.

We don't doubt the purity of the laws' intentions; however, they don't suffice to achieve the public good, . . . and in fact they . . . threaten sugar and grain production, without profit to the slave trade. They threaten sugar production because they make farmers plant the insignificant manioc, which grows in any type of soil, in the rare and precious plots of *"massapé"* soil, to which nature gives sugarcane the privilege of producing very good sugar and other crops of great value. This causes the farmers to lose a part of the earnings of their land that, if occupied with valuable plants for which the soil is appropriate, would give them considerably higher returns. This would also position them to produce all the grains needed and even allow for excess product. . . . These laws equally threaten flour production because, by forcing sugar farmers, tobacco farmers, and other citizens to produce for themselves more grain than their households can consume, actual grain farmers cannot easily sell their produce. And as it is sales that stimulate production, sales diminish proportionally with irreparable damage to grain farmers, who cannot reallocate their lands to another purpose, as the lands are unable to produce sugar, cotton, coffee, etc.

All of this is without profit to the slave traders, who by the division of labor principles developed by [Adam] Smith, cannot make better use of their industry and capital than by employing these entirely to the vocation that they already practice. The proof is that slave traders prefer to buy flour and other grains at the current market price rather than distracting themselves by cultivating them. By the same principles, other seemingly annoying laws harm agricultural production . . . forbid[ding] citizens from practicing certain kinds of industry, such as raising cattle within ten leagues of the coast. The farmer suffers as much in being obliged to cultivate a type of crop that renders him less as he does in failing to cultivate another that could render him more. In general, every time the public administration intervenes in prescribing labor for its citizens, [telling them] what they should do with their land, laborers, and capital, it upsets the equilibrium and natural distribution of those wealth-producing agents, as no one can better direct their use than the owners themselves, who are the most interested parties. . . .

Our farmers do not enjoy any more freedom regarding the second force because they are prohibited from establishing factories, distilleries, fishing enterprises, or sugar mills without a license, and these licenses require certain costly formalities. Everything that hampers the establishment of these factories aggravates a type of natural monopoly enjoyed by the current owners of the few existing ones, principally the sugar mills, as their expense makes them rare. This consequently worsens the already harsh conditions for those farmers who do not have such [mills]; over many years they see their sugarcane lost due to their inability to find a place to have it pressed. . . .

How different are our laws versus those of China! For many thousands of years in that civilized empire, not only has everyone been freely able to establish sugar mills anywhere, but they can even travel from place to place with portable mills, offering their services to anyone who has cane to press. For us to establish mills in our own homes we must kiss the Governor and flatter the Judge and the County Scribe, while these expect exorbitant payments before they'll even undertake the necessary first inspections. Poor farmers! . . .

Those who should grasp the sword and the quill to protect your liberty are those who will take it from you, or sell it to you! It is true that some owners of established sugar mills do not look favorably on the construction of new ones, arguing that they make the prices of firewood and lumber rise, but these are complaints that stem from their own self-interest. . . . If the price of firewood rises, it is a necessary effect of agricultural progress, for by enlarging the area of planted land, the woods become more distant, and one must pay a higher transportation cost. This kind of price increase, like that of meat, is a symptom of civilization's progress, and it grows in the same proportion and for the reasons that Smith explained in his *An Inquiry into the Nature and Causes of the Wealth of Nations*, book 1, chapter 11.

[Regarding the third force,] those crops that farmers do have the freedom to plant and tend cannot be sold freely by them in any city, village or other place that planters choose, nor by their slaves or any other agent. Instead these products suffer constraints, formalities, and taxes. . . . Regulations on meat, flour, and vegetables came about due to fear of hunger at home. . . . But even the fact that tobacco's production greatly exceeds local consumption has not given it more freedom, and its owners are prohibited from sending it to Europe, the place where it carries the highest price, if they do not get approval first. In this case it is not because there is any shortage of tobacco, but instead due to the goal of accrediting this national commodity, which seemingly has no other way of competing in Europe with some kinds of foreign tobacco. I, however, cannot help but consider this kind of prohibition as noxious as others like it. . . .

This prohibition is founded on the same principles as the old system of corporations and storehouses, instituted to sustain manufacturing credit, a system that is today completely refuted by the new economists, like Smith in the work previously cited, book 1, chapter 10, and, most recently, by Mr. Simonde [Jean Charles Léonard Simonde de Sismondi] in his *Commercial Wealth* [1803], book 3, chapter 5, and in [Jean-Baptiste] Say's *A Treatise on Political Economy* [1803], books 1 and 2, chapters 37 and 38. These and a thousand others have made us see that customers' boldness, [producers'] emulation, and rivals' competition, along with the spread of reason in the country, are the real forces obliging a producer to perfect a product's quality, and not prohibitions against selling it without a seal of approval.

[In the fourth case,] the prohibiting system adopted by us has not been limited to preventing planters from selling their products where they carry the highest price, . . . but has gone on to prohibit certain kinds of buyers, whose business should make prices rise to their benefit. These are the traveling salesmen, resellers, and middlemen, etc. And this is the fourth way in which the lack of liberty impedes the progress of labor. . . .

[In the fifth case,] planters and their agents [are] hindered in their timing and do not have freedom to sell the fruits of their labors. Per the provision of October 27, 1785, and other later orders, tobacco cannot leave the ports of the Recôncavo before the twentieth of January, meaning that before this their growers cannot benefit as they ought to. This prohibition gives tremendous advantage to those who come from the ports that are closest to the city, and over those who are further away, as they can be the first approved and the first shipped to Europe. There they will take advantage of being part of the first sales, a very advantageous position because the Lisbon market will be without tobacco owing to this same prohibition. I do not know what advantage this can bring us.

Translated by Augusto de Moraes Guimarães

Portraits: Chica da Silva de Oliveira

Victoria Langland

As is the case with many of those born into slavery, there is little documentation about the birth and early life of Chica da Silva de Oliveira. No baptismal or birth certificates for her remain, although she was almost certainly baptized, so historians have had to approximate her date of birth to sometime between 1731 and 1735. When she does emerge in the written record in her early years, she is generally referred to as Francisca *parda*, or the brown-skinned Francisca, a reflection of the fact that the enslaved in Brazil did not officially receive surnames. Considered interchangeable human property, rather than individual people connected to families with meaningful histories and genealogies, they were described by simply a first name, followed by an indication of their skin color, if born in Brazil, or their general place of origin, if born in Africa. Yet by the time she died in 1796, Francisca *parda* had become widely known as Chica da Silva de Oliveira, mother of fourteen successful children, godmother to many more, owner of slaves and extensive property, member of the most prestigious religious and social associations of her community, and accorded in death all of the religious honors usually reserved for the local white elite, including burial in the nave of the church of the Brotherhood of Saint Francis of Assisi. Indeed, not only does more abundant documentation of her later years exist, but much of it bears her own handwriting, as she by then had learned to sign her own name and quite possibly to read.[1]

Moreover, in the years following her death, historians, novelists, film directors, and television producers have popularized her image, making Chica da Silva one of the most well-known figures of eighteenth-century Brazil, generally presented as a rare example of upward mobility within Brazilian slave society. In much of this treatment, her relationship with the father of thirteen of her children, a wealthy, white diamond contractor, looms large. Perhaps nowhere was this more evident than in the 1976 film by Carlos Diegues, *Xica da Silva*, in which the title character is portrayed as a scheming sexual seductress with an insatiable thirst for power and wealth. Yet the real Chica, or at least what can be gleaned about her from surviving documents, lived a much more interesting life than such clichéd visions of a sexualized female slave would suggest, and her biography reveals a great deal about the limited choices faced by enslaved women in eighteenth-century Brazil.

Of Chica's early life, we know that she was born in a small village in Minas Gerais sometime between 1731 and 1735, when the rush for gold and diamonds was in full swing and the population swelled dramatically. Her mother was Maria da Costa, an enslaved woman who had been brought to Brazil from the Mina coast while still a child and whose owner at the time was Domingos da Costa, a former slave himself. Chica's father was a white man named Antônio Caetano de Sá, about whom we know little. At some point in her childhood Chica was sold to a Portuguese physician and slave owner named Manuel Pires Sardinha, for whom she worked as a domestic slave in his home in the town of Tejuco. In 1751, she bore him a son named Simão. While Sardinha did not legally acknowledge his paternity, he manumitted Simão at his baptism and would later make him an heir in his will, as he did with two other sons he bore with enslaved women. Unmarried, Sardinha had no legitimate children who might have contested this arrangement. While the teenaged and enslaved Chica undoubtedly had little choice in the decision to bear a child with the sixty-year-old Sardinha, she may have taken some comfort in knowing her son was legally free, almost from birth. Nor was she alone in this experience, as Minas Gerais was characterized by a heavy imbalance in the sex ratio among both free and enslaved populations, such that many white men not only sought out sexual relationships with enslaved women, but also often manumitted their resulting offspring.

Simão's birth also led to Chica's sale to a new owner and to a new chapter in her life. A year before Simão was born, the Inquisition investigated Sardinha for supposedly having an illicit relationship with a female slave, presumably Chica, but insufficient evidence had been found. After Simão and a child from another of Sardinha's slaves were born, however, ecclesiastical authorities convicted Sardinha (along with Chica and the other woman) of concubinage, and Sardinha signed a document promising to break off all "illicit communication" with them. Soon thereafter he sold Chica, presumably to fulfill this commitment.

Chica's purchaser was João Fernandes de Oliveira, the twenty-six-year-old son of a wealthy white family from Minas Gerais who had recently completed his legal studies at Coimbra University in Portugal and seemed poised to begin a legal career in Lisbon. Instead, he came to Brazil on behalf of his father, one of the diamond contractors named by the Portuguese Crown. Since the discovery of diamonds in Minas Gerais in the 1720s, the Crown had struggled to control production so as not to glut the market and see their prices drop, eventually settling on the establishment of limited-term concession contracts to a select few contractors. The father of João Fernandes de Oliveira had been one of the first contractors, had renewed the position several times, and had

The Church of Saint Francis of Assisi in Ouro Preto, with its stark exterior and richly gilded interior, is representative of the architecture of religious buildings throughout Minas Gerais during the height of gold and diamond production. Photograph © Harry-Strharsky.Pixels.com.

amassed a considerable fortune from it. But he had returned to Lisbon and wished to stay there, so when he received a new diamond contract, he sent his son to represent him in Tejuco, the center of diamond production.

It is unclear how, exactly, the sale of Chica from Manuel Pires Sardinha to João Fernandes de Oliviera transpired, nor what that transition meant for her. But we do know that within a few months of the sale João Fernandes manumitted Chica, who officially took on the last name da Silva as a marker of her freedom, and that the date of her manumission papers was Christmas Day (December 25), 1753. While the granting of manumission was not uncommon, especially for adult women, when it occurred it usually took place after years of service, and generally only after an owner's death. Manumission so soon after purchase was extremely rare. Did João Fernandes free Chica (but not other slaves he owned) as a gesture of Christian faith for Christmas? Did he do so as an act of love for Chica? Did he do so in order to secure her affection or cooperation? We do not know. But we know that she continued to live with him after gaining her freedom, and that after the birth of their first child, Francisca de Paula, in 1755, Chica added his name to hers, becoming Francisca da Silva de Oliviera. As a freedwoman, she could acquire property, including slaves, and it appears that the first slave she purchased was a wet nurse for Francisca. Women of the elite typically used wet nurses rather than breastfeeding themselves, in part because the contraceptive effects of breastfeeding were thought to limit their ability to produce numerous heirs. Indeed, Chica went on to have twelve more children with João Fernando, a fact that meant she was pregnant, on average, every thirteen months, a detail that is left out of portrayals of her as the licentious Xica.

Chica and João Fernandes never married, as the requirement that spouses be of equal social standing precluded that. Lacking the status of a wife, Chica had no legal access to João Fernandes's estate and no claim to an inheritance, which was strictly regulated by Portuguese law. And while both she and João Fernandes were often asked to serve as godparents to others' children, a sign of their social importance in local society, they rarely attended baptisms or any other religious ceremony together, as the church, as we have seen, condemned concubinage. But they and their children became active members of the main religious brotherhoods in Tejuco, including those theoretically organized for whites, blacks, or those of mixed race. And the two of them worked to ensure the best possible future they could for their children, first educating them with tutors, then sending the girls to a prestigious convent for further study and sending the boys to Portugal with their father to be introduced into powerful social circles. In the final years of his life, João Fernandes established an entail that was designed to keep the bulk of his assets together to be passed on to his oldest child, as well as to set standards of behavior that the heirs needed to follow, thereby attempting to ensure their place in respected social circles. Chica was, by definition, left out of his will, but by the time of his death in 1779 she owned enough property in her own name that she lived very comfortably for the rest of her life.

Chica's story epitomizes the demographic transformation then taking place in Minas Gerais that led to a growing population of free people of color. By 1805, two-thirds of the free population was nonwhite. Most of this growth came from the high rate of manumission for the children of enslaved women and white men. Another important source came from the manumission of enslaved women, often as acknowledgment of long-standing relationships with their owners, be these sexual, nurturing, or otherwise. And a small part of it came from the possibilities for gold and diamond wealth that allowed some slaves to purchase their own freedom. Yet obtaining freedom did not always result in true autonomy, especially for women. Without the ability to earn a living through a trade or craft, or without a network of family and friends able to offer material support, manumission did not necessarily lead to stability, let alone upward mobility for one's children. Chica's decision to remain with João Fernandes after gaining her freedom ought to be understood within this context, while the stability and endurance of their relationship ought to remind us that informal unions that did not conform to ecclesiastical or social norms might have nonetheless reflected lasting affective bonds.

Note

1. This portrait is drawn from Júnia Ferreira Furtado, *Chica da Silva: A Brazilian Slave of the Eighteenth Century* (Cambridge: Cambridge University Press, 2009).

IV

The Portuguese Royal Family
in Rio de Janeiro, 1808–1821

Political crises can have unexpected consequences. Such was the case with Napoleon Bonaparte's efforts to block Great Britain from trading with countries under French control or influence during the Napoleonic Wars (1803–15). When Portugal refused to abrogate its treaty agreements with its longtime British ally in order to comply with France's demands, Napoleon sent his armies to the Iberian Peninsula to enforce the blockade. The Napoleonic invasion of Portugal provoked the panicked flight of the royal family to the New World. Suddenly, the capital of the Portuguese Empire was located in Brazil.

The idea of moving the seat of the Portuguese Empire across the Atlantic Ocean was not an entirely new one. In 1738, the Portuguese diplomat and statesman Dom Luis da Cunha proposed the transfer, arguing that Rio de Janeiro would be a better place from which to rule the maritime and commercial empire. A similar proposal was made in 1803 by the Portuguese nobleman and politician Dom Rodrigo de Sousa Coutinho to establish a "great and powerful empire" in South America, since Portugal was "neither the best nor the most essential part of the monarchy."[1] The actual decision to make the move, however, was driven by the immediacy of events and the fear that the Portuguese monarchy might be overthrown by Napoleon's invading armies.

On January 22, 1808, Prince Regent Dom João, his wife, Princess Dona Carlota, and their eight children, along with his mentally ill mother, Queen Maria I, and nearly the entire Portuguese court landed in Salvador. The royal entourage barely understood the city that it encountered. The streets of Salvador were narrow, dirty, and poorly paved. The local elite paraded around "covered in jewels, crosses, medals, rosaries, and scapulars, wearing the same dress as the slaves who transported them in velvet-covered sedan chairs."[2] The slaves, who lived on the outskirts of town, wore clothing that was not only colorful, but also revealing, drawing the attention of the new arrivals, who were not accustomed to such unseemly public displays of the body. Yet what caused the most bewilderment among members of the royal family and its entourage was witnessing black slaves perform every type of labor—they were barbers, nannies, porters, artisans, street vendors, day laborers, prostitutes, and nurses. The casual acceptance of human captivity and the ways in which slaves were treated were also shocking. It was not uncommon to see them being whipped in the streets, bearing disproportionately heavy loads on their shoulders, or carrying sedan chairs with chambray curtains so that white ladies could be protected from the gazes of passersby. Noise and commotion dominated the public space and crowded streets. The smells, people, colors, and customs all declared this a strange new locale. Instead of the soft colors of blossoming almond trees that swept Lisbon at that time of the year, the Portuguese saw a lush landscape of exuberant hues illuminated by the tropical sun, creating a unique play between shadow and light.

On January 28, just a few days after the court's arrival in Salvador, and without the presence of ministers or counselors, Dom João signed the first royal decree to be issued from this part of the Portuguese Empire: a letter "opening Brazilian ports to friendly nations." From this point on, the import "of all and any provision, material, or good transported in foreign ships from nations that maintained peace and harmony with the Royal Crown" was permitted, along with products carried in Portuguese vessels.[3] Brazil thus gained freedom of trade, and the Portuguese fulfilled the first of many agreements with Great Britain in exchange for the protection of its most important ally. Brazil also acquired more freedom in "coming and going." Not only were residents of Brazil able to leave the colony with greater ease, but non-Portuguese, who had previously been prohibited from entering Portuguese America, began to come to Brazil at an ever-accelerating pace. After the Treaty of Trade and Navigation, which created a tariff structure favoring British exports to Brazil, the British came to dominate the Brazilian market.

With the Portuguese Crown now in Brazil, Prince Regent Dom João ordered the creation of the Medical and Surgical School of Salvador in 1808, since the colony lacked doctors and faced notable public health problems. Heretofore, no opportunities had existed for educating the sons of the landed elites and urban upper classes on Brazilian soil.

On February 26, the royal family and its entourage continued the journey to their final destination: Rio de Janeiro. In the new imperial capital, Dom João proclaimed that royal orders in the Portuguese Empire would emanate from Brazil. The responsibilities for foreign affairs fell to Dom Rodrigo de Sousa Coutinho. Foreign embassies and their representatives soon began to energize local diplomatic life. There was, however, some cause for irritation. Among the Portuguese bureaucracy, the number of officials grew, inflating and stalling the administrative machinery.

The unprecedented transformation of a colony into the capital of the empire had other consequences. The imperial government in Rio de Janeiro

Embarque da Família Real Portuguesa. Painting by Giuseppe Gianni, c. nineteenth century. In this depiction of the arrival of the Portuguese royal court in Rio de Janeiro, everything looks dark, including the sky and the expression of the king and his subjects.

had to publish the decisions, legislation, and diplomatic papers produced by its royal offices, but printing presses had been prohibited in the colony prior to 1808. On May 13, 1808, the Royal Press was created in Rio de Janeiro. Along with an obligation to publish official documentation, the decree founding the press also provided for the printing of other works, in particular those that helped to promote the monarchy's official image. Changes in the name of the press reveal important political developments. In 1815, the year in which the colony was elevated to the United Kingdom of Portugal, Brazil, and Algarves, it became the Regal Printing Office. In 1818, when Maria I died and Dom João was proclaimed king, the institution's name was changed to the Royal Printing Office. The press's board of directors had among its many duties the examination of all printed material to prevent the issuing of papers and books with content that opposed the government, religion, or morality.

The presence of a king also required the presence of nobility, which would provide continuity and support to the monarchy. The Crown established the Chamber of Noble Registry and the Corporation of Arms in order to organize the creation of new titles and appropriate Brazilian heraldry. Before his return to Portugal in 1821, Dom João granted no less than 254 titles, including eleven dukes, thirty-eight marquises, sixty-four counts, ninety-one viscounts, and thirty-one barons. He was even more generous in dispensing the

Un employé du govern[men]t. sortant de chez lui avec sa famille. This 1839 painting by Jean-Baptiste Debret of an elite family, their slaves, and their servants leaving church offers a naturalized portrayal of the system of slavery and its racial and gender hierarchies. Courtesy of the John Carter Brown Library at Brown University.

titles of commander, knight, and Grand Croix to those who found favor with the Crown.

Brazil also lacked an effective structure for military defense and training that could guarantee the integrity of the empire. Therefore, minister Dom Rodrigo established a naval academy and a military academy, and also installed a gunpowder factory. Additionally, the government established the military archives for the drafting and safekeeping of charts and maps of Brazil and overseas holdings.

After tending to the new capital's protection, the Crown could now focus on its beautification. Dom João established a botanical garden in Rio de Janeiro, developing it as an area for the transfer of plants to Brazil and the display of exotic species found in the colony. A royal museum was created nearby to stimulate studies of botany and zoology in the area, initiated with a donation from the prince regent himself of artwork, prints, mineral samples, indigenous artifacts, taxidermy animals, and natural specimens. To further Europeanize the capital, the Crown also established the São João Royal Theater in 1813, and the Royal Library, which opened its doors to the public in 1814.

Gradually the city gained a new flavor, taking on airs of an imperial capital. However, the monarchy was dangerously spendthrift. Even the eighty million *cruzados* in gold and diamonds it brought to Brazil would have been insufficient to sustain the imperial government. The Bank of Brazil, created by Dom João in 1808, barely covered royal expenses such as pensions, wages, and the functioning of courts and military before declaring bankruptcy. The Crown increased taxes, which provoked general dissatisfaction, while conspicuous consumption and waste in the royal palace soon became a subject of mockery.

On balance, the political and administrative changes imposed on the colony created a modernizing trajectory for Brazil. The unexpected development of the American territory and the inversion of its position with the imperial capital did not go unnoticed. "Almost Europe, almost empire"; these were the terms of the era describing Brazil. While it was not the sole imperial capital with dominion over Portugal, neither was it a colony in the traditional sense. Instead Brazil was, first, the administrative center of the Portuguese Empire and, after 1815, a kingdom theoretically coequal to Portugal.

Notes

1. Abílio Diniz Silva, "Introduction," in *Instruções políticas* (Lisbon: Comissão Nacional para as Comemorações dos Descobrimentos Portuguesas, 2001), 165.
2. Oliveira Lima, *Dom João VI no Rio* (1906; repr., Rio de Janeiro: Top Books, 1996), 109.
3. Therezinha de Castro, *História Documental do Brasil* (Rio de Janeiro: Biblioteca do Exército, 1995), 108–9.

The Royal Family's Journey to Brazil

Thomas O'Neill

This concise report offers an eyewitness account of the departure of the royal family from Portugal in 1808. In his testimony, the Irishman Thomas O'Neill claims he was a lieutenant in the squadron that brought Prince Dom João and part of his court to the distant Brazilian colony in America. He constructs his text with two expressly declared objectives: to elevate the heroic character of British action and to condemn the evil atrocities of the French.

Although the lieutenant asserted that he was on board one of the ships of the English squadron that accompanied the royal family to the New World, in fact, he arrived in Brazil after the royal family, disembarking directly in Rio de Janeiro. His diary is thus a mixture of firsthand accounts and other reports, but this fact does not detract from his description of the hasty departure from Portugal.

By the 27th, the royal family had all embarked. His Royal Highness the Prince Regent and his sons were on board the *Prince Royal*; her Majesty, the Princess of Brazil, and the Infantas, were in the *Ilfonza*; the Dowager Princess on board the *Count Henrick*; and the ladies of distinction were accommodated as circumstances would admit in the respective ships. Is there a heart that will not sympathize with the misfortunes of these illustrious personages, when their forlorn situation is for a moment considered? For, in addition to the destitute state in which they were now placed, it should be observed, that numbers of their followers had to encounter the perils of a long and tedious voyage through (to them at least) unknown seas, without even a single bed on which to repose their weary heads.

28th—The wind continued to blow from the same quarter, so that it was impossible for his Royal Highness's ships to quit the Tagus River; and the French troops were now within fifty miles of Lisbon. At eight o'clock on the same day, General Junot arrived in that city, and was not more disappointed than he was surprised to learn that the Royal Family had been informed of his approach with the French troops. His mortification was beyond description on finding that the Prince had embarked, the seizing of his person being the principal object of his mission, if the wind had not providentially allowed him to quit the Tagus.

Letter from a Son in Brazil
to His Father in Portugal

Luíz Joaquim dos Santos Marrocos

Luíz Joaquim dos Santos Marrocos (1781–1838) was a librarian at the Royal Portuguese Library in Lisbon. In 1811, he accompanied the transfer of the Royal Library's collection of nearly sixty thousand volumes from Portugal to Brazil and then continued as its librarian in Rio de Janeiro. The cargo was precious, as the library possessed rare and antique books, drawings, maps, and important Portuguese documents. It was during the trip that Santos Marrocos began a protracted exchange of letters with his father, a correspondence that is today considered one of the period's richest historical sources. The collection includes nearly two hundred letters. The first letter, reprinted here, was written by Marrocos while aboard a Portuguese ship on April 12, 1811. He wrote the last one on April 26, 1821, one month before King João returned to Portugal. The letters are filled with the complaints of someone who seemed to especially suffer from the arduous nature of these transatlantic journeys—trips that took a physical toll on one's body and health as well as an emotional toll due to forced separations from family members. Nonetheless, Marrocos stayed in Brazil until his death in 1838 at age fifty-seven. During this period, he married a woman born in Brazil to Portuguese parents and served for several years as the senior secretary of affairs for the kingdom.

April 12, 1811

My Father and Dear Sire,

I have arrived safely, having braved the seas with the blessings of Heaven, through thousands of afflictions, troubles, and labors that I never thought I would suffer. Having left Lisbon's inlet in windy conditions, we barely made it to the high seas when a crosswind hit us, driving us toward the coast of Africa. With the coast in view we passed the Azores and the Canary Islands, having to make many backward turns, often suspending all navigation because of doldrums and headwinds that exposed us to immense dangers. Now we are hoping tomorrow to view the Island of Santiago, one of the islands of Cape Verde. In order not to miss out on such a fine occasion, I intend to step onto land despite the island's bad air so that I can post this letter, as I do not trust it with anyone else. It is unnecessary to explain to Your Grace the anguish I have experienced these past twenty-seven days of the journey, thinking of all of the family, without exception. I am sure that Your Grace believes me, especially with Mother's illness and Your Grace's sudden bouts of dizziness, but I pray God will ensure that my suffering is not exacerbated by poor health. I have had great discomfort in my throat, mouth, and eyes, such that I am using remedies. I did not experience any nausea while leaving the inlet of Lisbon, but this caused me to feel great compassion upon seeing the general vomiting of everyone on the ship. Among the five hundred people on board, few escaped seasickness. At night I cannot sleep for more than one hour, because the rest of the night I spend thinking about the current and future experiences in my life. On the eighth day of the trip the rationed water was already spoiled and contaminated, so they had to throw the animals overboard so that there would be water for people to drink. They also had to throw to sea many barrels of rotten meat. In all, everything here is in chaos for the lack of any type of planning. All of the ship's ropes are rotten, except for the rigging. All of the sails are defective, such that they tear at the slightest breeze, and the crew is incompetent. If this state continues we will get lost, if by mischance we are stricken by a long storm. There is not enough medicine for the sick. There are not more than half a dozen herbs, and illnesses are rampant. There are no hens, nor is there any fresh meat for the sick. Finally, to summarize, if I had known the state of the *Princesa Carlota* frigate, I would have been absolutely repulsed by the thought of involving myself with her and the library. By merely involving myself in the library, I have done a great service for His Royal Highness [Prince Regent Dom João]. Despite all of this, I trust in Divine Mercy to free us from the dangers to which we are exposed. To your Providence, I have submitted myself with the greatest patience. I trust Your Grace will have the generosity of sending my regards to our friends, and I hope that you include me in your prayers, praising me with your blessing, and to my Mother and Aunt, to whom I cannot explain the turmoil in my head, which at times loses all sense, as I wonder how and when I will see them again.

I hope that Your Grace writes to me soon after receiving this, sending your letter to Rio de Janeiro.

The loving and affectionate Son of Your Mercy

P.S. I deeply miss Mana [Bernarda Maria da Conceição] and Inês, and having still so much to say but such little time, I am obliged to put aside my pen, leaving this pleasure for Rio, if God allows me to arrive there.

On Good Friday at 10 PM, having already received two requests from the patrol to turn out the light.

Translated by Molly Quinn

Treaty between Portugal and Great Britain

Various authors

In recognition of Great Britain's help in bringing the Portuguese Crown to Brazil, the prince regent signed several agreements with King George III in 1810 that were beneficial to Great Britain. In the treaty excerpted below, they reduced the tariffs on British goods sold in Brazil to 15 percent, much lower than the 24 percent added to goods from most other countries and even lower than the 16 percent added to Portuguese goods. Trade with Great Britain consequently boomed in the following years. The treaty also granted British citizens in the Portuguese Empire the right to be subject only to British laws and courts, a privilege that underscored the immense bargaining power of Great Britain at that moment. Another provision allowed British citizens to worship in non-Catholic churches, albeit with restrictions, which set the precedent for religious tolerance in Brazil. A subsequent agreement promised that Brazil would take steps to end its participation in the international traffic in slaves, something that it continually delayed in doing.

In the Name of the Most Holy and Undivided Trinity.

His Majesty the King of the United Kingdom of Great Britain and Ireland, and His Royal Highness the Prince Regent of Portugal, being equally animated with the desire not only of consolidating and strengthening the ancient friendship and good understanding which so happily subsist, and have during so many ages subsisted, between the two Crowns, but also of improving and extending the beneficial effects thereof to the mutual advantage of their respective subjects, have thought that the most efficacious means for obtaining these objects would be to adopt a liberal system of Commerce, founded upon the basis of reciprocity and mutual convenience, which by discontinuing certain prohibitions and prohibitory Duties might procure the most solid advantages on both sides, to the National Productions and Industry, and give due protection at the same time to the Public Revenue, and to the interests of fair and legal trade. . . .

 I. There shall be a sincere and perpetual friendship between His Britannic Majesty and His Royal Highness the Prince Regent of Portugal, and between their heirs and successors; and there shall be a constant and universal peace and harmony between themselves, their heirs and successors, Kingdoms, Dominions, Provinces, Countries, Subjects, and Vassals, of whatsoever quality or condition they be, without exception of person, or place; and the stipulations of this present Article shall, under the favor of Almighty God, be permanent and perpetual.

II. There shall be reciprocal liberty of Commerce and Navigation between and amongst the respective subjects of the two high Contracting Parties, in all and several of the Territories and Dominions of either. They may trade, travel, sojourn, or establish themselves, in all and several the Ports, Cities, Towns, Countries, Provinces, or places whatsoever belonging to each and either of the two high Contracting Parties, except and save in those from which all foreigners whatsoever are generally and positively excluded, the names of which places may be hereafter specified in a separate Article of this Treaty. Provided, however, that it be thoroughly understood that any place belonging to either of the two high Contracting Parties, which may hereafter be opened to the Commerce of the subjects of any other country, shall thereby be considered as equally opened, and upon correspondent terms, to the subjects of the other high Contracting Party, in the same manner as if it had been expressly stipulated by the present Treaty. And His Britannic Majesty, and His Royal Highness the Prince Regent of Portugal, do hereby bind and engage themselves not to grant any favor, privilege, or immunity in matters of Commerce and Navigation to the subjects of any other State, which shall not be also at the same time respectively extended to the subjects of the high Contracting Parties, gratuitously, if the concession in favor of that other State should have been gratuitous, and on giving *quam proxime*, the same compensation or equivalent, in case the concession should have been conditional.

III. The subjects of the two Sovereigns respectively shall not pay in the Ports, Harbors, Roads, Cities, Towns, or Places whatsoever, belonging to either of them, any greater duties, taxes, or imposts (under whatsoever names they may be designated or included) than those that are paid by the subjects of the most favored nation, and the subjects of each of the high Contracting Parties shall enjoy within the Dominions of the other, the same rights, privileges, liberties, favors, immunities, or exemptions, in matters of Commerce and Navigation that are granted or may hereafter be granted to the subjects of the most favored nation.

IV. His Britannic Majesty, and His Royal Highness the Prince Regent of Portugal, do stipulate and agree that there shall be a perfect reciprocity on the subject of the duties and imposts to be paid by the ships and vessels of the high Contracting Parties, within the several ports, harbors, roads, and anchoring places belonging to each of them; to wit, that the ships and vessels of the subjects of His Britannic Majesty shall not

Les refraichissemens de l'après diner sur la Place du Palais. Illustration by Jean-Baptiste
Debret. The commercial treaties with Great Britain opened the port of Rio de Janeiro
to international trade. From *Voyage pittoresque et historique au Brésil* (Paris: Firmin Didot
Frères, 1835). Courtesy of the John Carter Brown Library at Brown University.

pay any higher duties or imposts (under whatsoever name they be designated or implied) within the Dominions of His Royal Highness the
Prince Regent of Portugal, than the ships and vessels belonging to the
subjects of His Royal Highness the Prince Regent of Portugal shall be
bound to pay within the Dominions of His Britannic Majesty, and vice
versa. And this agreement and stipulation shall particularly and expressly extend to the payment of the duties known by the name of port
charges, tonnage, and anchorage Duties, which shall not in any case,
or under any pretext, be greater for British ships and vessels within the
Dominions of His Royal Highness the Prince Regent of Portugal, than
for Portuguese ships and vessels within the Dominions of His Britannic Majesty, and vice versa. . . .

VII. The two high Contracting Parties have resolved, with respect to the
privileges to be enjoyed by the subjects of each of them within the
Territories or Dominions of the other, that the most perfect reciprocity shall be observed on both sides. And the subjects of each of the
high Contracting Parties shall have a free and unquestionable right to
travel and to reside within the Territories or Dominions of the other,
to occupy houses and warehouses, and to dispose of personal property of every sort and denomination, by sale, donation, exchange, or

testament, or in any other manner whatsoever, without the smallest impediment or hindrance thereto. They shall not be compelled to pay any taxes or imposts under any pretext whatsoever, greater than those that are paid or may be paid by the native subjects of the Sovereign in whose Dominions they may be resident. They shall be exempted from all compulsory military service whatsoever, whether by sea or land. Their dwelling-houses, warehouses, and all the parts and appurtenances thereof, whether for the purposes of commerce or of residence, shall be respected. They shall not be liable to any vexatious visits and searches, nor shall any arbitrary examination or inspection of their books, papers, or accounts be made under color of the supreme authority of the State. . . .

XII. His Royal Highness the Prince Regent of Portugal declares and engages, in His own name and in that of His Heirs and Successors, that the subjects of His Britannic Majesty residing within His Territories and Dominions, shall not be disturbed, troubled, persecuted, or annoyed on account of their religion; but that they shall have perfect liberty of conscience therein, and leave to attend and celebrate Divine Service to the honor of Almighty God, either within their own private houses, or in their own particular churches and chapels, which His Royal Highness does now and for ever graciously grant to them the permission of building and maintaining within His Dominions: provided however, that the said churches and chapels shall be built in such a manner as externally to resemble private dwelling houses; and also, that the use of bells be not permitted therein, for the purpose of publicly announcing the time of Divine Service: and it is further stipulated, that neither the subjects of Great Britain, nor any other foreigners of a different communion from the religion established in the Dominions of Portugal, shall be persecuted or disquieted for conscience-sake, either in their persons or property, so long as they conduct themselves with order, decency, and morality, and in a manner conformable to the usages of the country, and to its constitution in Church and State; but if it should be proved that they preach or declaim publicly against the Catholic religion, or that they endeavor to make proselytes or converts, the parties so offending may, upon manifestation of their delinquency, be sent out of the country in which the offence shall have been committed; and those who behave in public with disrespect or impropriety towards the forms and ceremonies of the established Catholic religion, shall be amenable to the civil police, and may be punished by fine, or by confinement within their own dwelling houses. And if the offence be so flagrant and so enormous as to disturb the public tranquility, or endanger the safety of the institutions of Church and State (as established by law), the parties so offending may, on due proof of the fact, be sent out of the Dominions of Portugal. Liberty shall also be granted to bury the subjects of His Britannic Majesty who may die in the Territories of His Royal Highness the Prince Regent of Portugal, in convenient places to be appointed for that purpose; nor shall the funerals or sepulchers of the dead be disturbed in any way, nor upon any account. In the same manner the subjects of Portugal shall enjoy within all the Dominions of His Britannic Majesty a perfect and unrestrained liberty of conscience in all matters of religion, agreeably to the system of toleration established therein. They may freely perform the exercises of their religion publicly or privately within their own dwelling houses, or in the chapels and places of worship appointed for that purpose, without the smallest hindrance, annoyance, or difficulty whatsoever, either now or hereafter. . . .

XV. All goods, merchandizes, and articles whatsoever of the produce, manufacture, industry, or invention of the Dominions and subjects of His Britannic Majesty shall be admitted into all and singular the Ports and Dominions of His Royal Highness the Prince Regent of Portugal, as well in Europe as in America, Africa and Asia, whether consigned to British or Portuguese subjects, on paying generally and solely duties to the amount of fifteen per cent, according to the value which shall be set upon them by a tariff or table of valuations, called in the Portuguese language *pauta*, the principal basis of which shall be the sworn invoice cost of the aforesaid goods, merchandizes, and articles, taking also into consideration (as far as may be just or practicable) the current prices thereof in the country into which they are imported. . . .

XXXIV. The several stipulations and conditions of the present Treaty shall begin to have effect from the date of His Britannic Majesty's ratification thereof; and the mutual exchange of ratifications shall take place in the City of London, within the space of four months, or sooner if possible, to be computed from the day of the signature of the present Treaty.

In witness whereof, we, the undersigned Plenipotentiaries of His Britannic Majesty and of His Royal Highness the Prince Regent of Portugal, in virtue of our respective full powers, have signed the present Treaty with our hands, and have caused the seals of our arms to be set thereto.

Done in the City of Rio de Janeiro, on the 10th day of February, in the year of our Lord, 1810.

Signed Strangford, Conde de Linhares

Rio de Janeiro's First Medical School

Count of Aguiar

The move of the Portuguese court to Rio de Janeiro in 1808 led to many new develop-
ments in the city and the colony: the first printing press in Portuguese America, a new
home for the Royal Library, new theaters, and new opportunities for higher educa-
tion. For the first time, the sons of the elite in Brazil could now study at law schools
in São Paulo and Recife and medical schools in Salvador and Rio de Janeiro. Brazil's
first school of anatomy, medicine, and surgery, designed along the model of medical
schools in Portugal, was built in Salvador, and its second was established in Rio de
Janeiro. In 1826, the royal government authorized the school in Rio de Janeiro to issue
diplomas and certificates to doctors who received their training in Brazil.

At the medical school in Rio de Janeiro, the course of study was extremely difficult,
and many students struggled to meet its rigorous standards. It was not exclusively for
the elite, however, since medicine was seen as a less illustrious profession than law.
A registry book from 1815 shows that the school enrolled several students of African
origin, including a slave of the prince regent, alongside students of predominantly
Portuguese descent. In its early days, barbers, bleeders, and pharmacists, as well as
those studying to be surgeons, attended the school. The institution did not have a
female graduate until 1888.

DECREE:

With the notice of the eighteenth of March ordering its enactment, I propose
to establish in this State of Brazil the Course of Surgery, which is part of the
Medical Course, at the Hospital of the Sacred House of Mercy of this Court.
I, for the benefit of all, approve the Plan of Surgery Studies . . . Palace of Rio
de Janeiro on the first of April of one thousand eight hundred and thirteen.

With the Signature of Prince Regent

PLAN OF SURGERY STUDIES

I.

The students who matriculate to the first year of the Surgery course
should know how to read and write correctly.

II.

It would be desirable for them to understand the French and English languages; we expect French by the time of the first exam in the second year of matriculation, and English the third year.

III.

The first matriculation can be done from the fourth until the twelfth of March, and the second from the first through sixth of December.

IV.

The entire Course will last five years.

V.

During the first year, students will learn General Anatomy until the end of September, and from this time until the sixth of December, Chemistry, Pharmaceutics, and the knowledge of nonapplied Medical Material and Surgery will be taught, and will be repeated in the following years.

VI.

All students from the first year will attend a course on healing, which will be from seven until eight thirty in the morning; from then until ten or later will be the time for Anatomy classes, and in the afternoon when necessary.

VII.

In the second year that study will be repeated, with explanations about the internal organs and other parts necessary to human life, that is, Physiology, from ten until three quarters past eleven in the morning, and in the afternoon if it is convenient.

VIII.

The students who know Latin or Geometry, a sign that their spirit is accustomed to Studies, can matriculate to the second year; no other student may do so because it cannot be presumed that he will have the necessary knowledge of the material for the second-year exam, which like any other exams of this Course, will always be public.

IX.

From the second year until the last there will be a weekly review, and every month an oral exam in the Portuguese language.

X.

Beginning in the third year, from four until six in the evening a medical professor will give lessons in Hygiene, Etiology, Pathology, and Therapy.

XI.

After the end of the fourth year, days off will not be spent in Infirmaries, only in classes, if there is not an important operation to attend.

XII.

In the fourth year, Surgery instructions and operations will be from seven to eight thirty in the morning, and at four in the afternoon there will be lessons and practice in the art of Obstetrics.

XIII.

In the fifth year, students will practice medicine from nine until eleven in the morning; from five in the afternoon there will again be reviewing of fourth-year lessons and Obstetrics.

XIV.

The year after the exam, students can obtain an Approved Surgery certificate.

XV.

Those who have been fully approved in all years, and want again to attend the fourth or fifth year and complete the exams with distinction, will be awarded a Bachelor in Surgery.

XVI.

Graduated surgeons will enjoy the following prerogatives: 1. They will be preferred by all parties to those who do not have this distinction; 2. They will be able to, by virtue of their Certificate, treat all illnesses when no doctor is present; 3. They will from then on be members of the Surgical College, and candidates for the chairs of these schools and of those that are established in the cities of [Salvador da] Bahia and Maranhão, and in Portugal; 4. All of those who become enriched by the principles and practices, upon completing the exams that doctors will determine, will graduate with the degree of Doctorate in Medicine.

XVII.

The exams are those of preparatory schools, final exams, and oral exams in Latin.

Palace of Rio de Janeiro on the first of April of
one thousand eight hundred and thirteen.
Count of Aguiar

Translated by Molly Quinn

The Influence of the Haitian Revolution in Brazil

Paulo José Vianna

The rebellion of slaves and freed people of color in the French colony of Saint-Domingue (present-day Haiti) from 1791 to 1804 shook slave owners in the entire Atlantic world, as it offered a successful example of how the enslaved could rise up and obtain their freedom. The revolt in Haiti loomed so large in the imagination of the elite in Brazil that they invented the word haitismo *to talk about any slave rebellion. The events in the Caribbean led the governor of the Amazonian province of Grão-Pará, for example, to strengthen security measures along the border with French Guiana. Slave flight from Brazil to this adjoining French colony had been a problem since the late eighteenth century, but after slavery was abolished in French Guiana in 1794, the number of Brazilian slaves seeking freedom there increased. After the Haitian Revolution, they also feared that news of the event might spread to Brazil and inspire similar slave rebellions. In 1809, the Portuguese preemptively attacked and occupied Cayenne, the capital of French Guiana, to forestall a possible invasion by Napoleonic forces in northern Brazil, and immediately became concerned about the fact that the French had armed many of their former slaves to fight against the Portuguese. The Portuguese did not leave until 1817.*

The following document offers glimpses into the fascinating story of Father Joaquim de Souza Ribeiro, who was imprisoned by the Portuguese in Cayenne in 1814 for allegedly inciting slaves to revolt, and then sent to Rio de Janeiro for further interrogation. The priest, who was from Bahia, claimed that he was the bishop of Saint-Domingue and had been invited to the island by the revolutionary military leader André Rigaud to spread the Christian faith. He also reported that he had witnessed the coronation of Jean-Jacques Dessalines as Emperor Jacques I of Haiti in 1804.

Regardless of the veracity of his account, the Portuguese clearly worried that news about revolts and abolition in the Caribbean might incite slaves in Brazil to rebellion. The report below, produced by an official in Rio de Janeiro, tries to make sense of Father Ribeiro's story.

Because of the Order that Your Excellency sent me dated April 4, I was put in charge of examining the papers that came from Cayenne with Father Joa-

Boutique de la Rue du Val-Longo. Illustration by Jean-Baptiste Debret. Elites considered slavery essential to the economy, and the slave trade was a very profitable business. In this image, the French artist Jean-Baptiste Debret portrays the frailty of the slaves and the seeming indifference of the corpulent trader, but he does not depict the slave owner in an unfavorable light. Courtesy of the John Carter Brown Library at Brown University.

quim de Souza Ribeiro, who calls himself the Bishop of São Domingos, and who is secluded in the Monastery of São Bento in this city.

After reading all the aforementioned papers, I only judged it necessary to make him confirm the responses that he had given to the Administrator [*intendente*] of Cayenne and hear about the conversation that the same Administrator notes that he had had with some slaves lamenting their luck and the injustice of their captivity, as if preparing them to revolt, pointing to examples of blacks and mulattoes he had seen become Sovereign [free] in São Domingos, which the Father [Joaquim de Souza Ribeiro] considered dangerous and impudent both in that Colony as well as all over Brazil. If this single fact were certain, and confirmed, it alone would be enough to be established as a cause of rioting and of Revolution; but as it could not be proven in any way, that Administrator passed over this business, otherwise so essential, in such a superficial way that he didn't provide me with facts or a basis to question or convince him of the absolute trap he had gotten himself into. This news shocked him, and he took it as a calumny and trickery meant to make his luck even worse.

Dispensing, therefore, with this accusation, which I do not judge to be worthy of the effort of verifying circumstantially in Cayenne, so that it could serve as the only basis for prosecution, I find in examining his papers suffi-cient proof for him to be considered an imposter at many stages of his life. I also find in the diary, which he offered up at the time of his interrogation and is written in his own hand, proof that he has lost his mind, proudly deem-ing himself such an authoritative virtuoso, who in his trips to Cayenne and from there to Pernambuco suffered stabs, blows, and poisons without being harmed, which could only occur by miracle. It is evident that he already con-siders himself a Saint, and this is the most conclusive proof of the miserable state of his mind.

It is my recommendation, and the most favorable one he could get, that he be sent to the Government of Portugal, to spend his [last] days in one of the asylums of Rilhafolles, where he can rest without the freedom to wander the streets, seeing as he has confessed to having established [contact with the] Bishopric in Rome against royal authorization, and even, against the recom-mendations of the Ministry [in Portugal], [made contact with] the Minister in residence there. [For this offense,] he was subject to punishment according to the Order Book 2, volume 13. We can readily take this action, sending him on one of the ships that are about to sail, and giving him all of his papers, in which he trusts so much, and which in no way show him to have the Episcopal position he believes himself to possess. I am sending all papers in accordance with the instructions given to me in the Order, which is all that remains in my possession.

Rio de Janeiro, May 1, 1815.

For the Marquis of Aguiar

Paulo José Vianna

Translated by Emma Wohl and Isadora Mota

Petition for Pedro I to Remain in Brazil

Anonymous

On August 20, 1820, a military revolt in the northern city of Porto, Portugal, unleashed a process that threatened the monarchy. Receiving widespread popular support, the leaders of the Porto revolt demanded that the king return to Portugal and that commerce with Brazil be placed under the exclusive control of the Portuguese. They also convoked a National Assembly (Cortes) to draw up a constitution. Fearing that he might lose his crown, João VI left for Lisbon in April 1821. Before departing Rio de Janeiro, the king declared that Pedro de Alcântra, his twenty-three-year-old son and heir apparent to the Portuguese throne, be the prince regent of the kingdom of Brazil. He also counseled Pedro that he should seize the throne should any "adventurer" attempt to do so in his stead.

Meanwhile, the majority of National Assembly delegates wanted to strip Brazil of its designation as a united kingdom with Portugal and were suspicious of Pedro's intentions. To that end, they issued Decrees 124 and 125 that demanded that the prince regent immediately return to Portugal. The Cortes also wanted to avert the danger posed by radical liberals in Brazil who formed the Partido Brasileiro (Brazilian Party) and had organized an eight-thousand-signature petition pressuring Pedro to remain in the country. Their concerns proved valid, as Pedro sided with the Brazilians' request in direct conflict with the Portuguese authorities, declaring, "If it is for the good of all and the general happiness of the nation, I am ready! Tell the people that I will stay." The date of the pronouncement, January 9, 1822, is now commemorated as the Dia do Fico (I Will Stay Day). This decision initiated the process of Brazil's independence, which culminated on September 7, 1822. Below is the Partido Brasileiro–sponsored petition asking the prince regent to remain in Brazil.

The people of Rio de Janeiro . . . are convinced that in the current circumstances we bear the responsibility for future generations if we do not express our sentiments regarding the frightful prospect facing us with the removal of His Royal Highness, and appeal to you, Your Lordship, as our legitimate representative, believing that our arguments deserve your full attention, to suspend the execution of the Decree of the National Assembly [demanding] the return of His Royal Highness to the ancient seat of the Portuguese Monarchy. . . .

In the current crisis, the return of His Royal Highness should be considered an entirely tragic fate for the national interests in both hemispheres. No, it is not the glory of possessing a prince of the reigning dynasty that obliges the People to cry out for him to reside in Brazil in light of this decree that calls him across the Atlantic. We would lose this glory with nostalgic tears, which unforeseen and mysteriously combined events brought us, opening among us an epoch that is not only represented by providence in our ceremonies, but also has allowed for the emancipation of Brazil at the time in which, possessed by an indisputable idea, it begins to rise up to reject the colonial system. But the loss of this eminent office is equally a loss of security and prosperity for this rich and vast continent; we even go so far as to respectfully say that this loss will have a very immediate influence on the destiny of the Monarchy in general. . . .

If it retains its current status, Brazil will never lose sight of the ideas regarding the illustrious and ancient Metropolis; never will it break this chain of friendship and honor, which should connect the two continents across the vast seas that separate them. . . . This same distance will never be able to loosen the ties of our alliance, nor will it impede Brazil from going ahead with great joy, full of riches, as before, adding wealth to the Nation.

The people of Rio de Janeiro, knowing that these are the sentiments of their fellow Brazilians, protest to the Nations out of a desire to ensure the necessary union that is indispensable to consolidating the bases of national prosperity: nevertheless, the most august agent of these sentiments is the Royal Prince in Brazil himself, because in him resides the grand idea that will enable the execution of these plans, as the first defender of the Constitutional system. . . .

There is a very considerable difference between midday in Europe and midday in America; human nature here experiences a noticeable change, a new Sky, and for this a new influence on individual character; it is possible that people in physical opposition can meet under the same system of government: industry, agriculture, arts in general demand in Brazil a particular legislation, and the bases of this new Code should be outlined for local areas, where later they will be executed. If Brazil, restrained in its infancy and with very little recognition in its youth, advanced rapidly across these same barriers that hinder its march, how will it not advance after having been visited and perfectly known by the Heir Prince to the Monarchy, who in his journey will see the justice that he has done by removing the colonial rings and giving Brazil the Crown? The People of Rio de Janeiro have in view the fulfillment of this truly philanthropic project, and knowing that His Royal Highness announces the most energetic enthusiasm in realizing this great advantage for the Nation in general, cannot agree to his return. . . .

Thus it is time to wait for all of the provinces of Brazil to meet around these ideas. As soon as the positive news is spread that His Royal Highness has not returned, the people charge His Lordship to see the absolute necessity of suspending Decrees 124 and 125 of the National Assembly, because it cannot be presumed to be the public intention of the Sovereign Congress [to close, for the Congress] does not accede to such just motives, and does not perceive the relationship of this measure to the general good of the Nation.

Rio de Janeiro, 29th of December, 1821.

Translated by Molly Quinn

Speech Given at the Cortes
(National Assembly) of Lisbon

Diogo Antônio Feijó

As Dom Pedro considered whether or not he should heed the Cortes's demand that he return to Portugal, propertied men in various provinces of Brazil were electing delegates to attend the National Assembly in Lisbon, entrusted with writing a new Portuguese constitution. Among the members of the São Paulo delegation was Diogo Antônio Feijó (1794–1843), a slave-owning Catholic priest and teacher. A defender of the constitutional monarchy, he was a liberal who advocated political decentralization. Yet he also bristled at the efforts of Portuguese delegates to reassert a hierarchical relationship between Portugal and Brazil. In the excerpts of his April 1822 speech at the National Assembly that follows, he powerfully argued that Brazil had the right to separate from Portugal.

By the time Feijó returned to Brazil, independence had been declared. In the new Brazilian Empire, he served in Congress as a national representative from the province of São Paulo in 1826 and in 1830, as a senator in 1833, as the minister of justice from 1831 to 1832, and as regent of the empire from 1835 to 1837.

No association is just when its foundation is not the free agreement of those who are associated; no society is true when it does not strive to act in the best interests of the individuals who compose it. One man cannot, should not, impose law on another man; a people does not have the right to force another group to submit to its social institutions. Despotism has trampled over these truths, but the essence of them can never be entirely stifled in the hearts of men. It is, however, of the nature of political institutions to endure as long as all are content. This principle of eternal justice holds back the ambitious, while free peoples have not hesitated to include it in their constitutions, as they are not afraid of it. This is what justifies the [Porto] revolution of August 24, [1820] and is what shall bring glory to all who employ it in posterity.

But how dangerous are these times! Men are united by desires and emotions instead of social ties that no longer exist. How easy it is to err in one's resolve and, becoming weak through division, succumb as prey to the ambitious (be they one or many)! Portugal, animated by its past wisdom, protests separating from other Portuguese people and considers itself a nation with them, and by this manifesto forms an article that will be the foundation for a future constitution. Portugal, however, never wanted this act to cause its destiny to waver or depend on external will. Only its inhabitants, united in heart and strong in resolve, establish representation, forge the basis of the Constitution, and swear on it without delay so that nothing can stand in the way of their august march in the organization of the new social pact.

Brazil heard the echo of liberty, jealous of Portugal's future destiny in spite of the obstacles that lay ahead and the sacrifices it would have to make, and broke the old and forcefully imposed association. Each province, on its own behalf and on its own time, without communication or help, will in-state a government over the remains of the ruins of the old one and elect representatives to send to the National Congress so that they may organize a Constitution, which in the future may govern and require the obedience of those who sanctioned it.

Brazil, like Portugal, fears division and its terrible effects; Brazil thus en-dorses the Constitution created by the Portuguese Cortes because it refuses to take part in the Parliament to which the King is committed and swears to this Constitution that the Cortes has made because it does not want to subject it to royal sanctions. Brazil protests obedience because it ought to disobey the authority of the King so that it may establish a foothold, which will rightfully be the basis of the agreement. . . .

Each province has a government that is as legitimate as the one that Por-tugal installed on September 15 [1820]. The province created it, and only it can change the government until the Constitution, organized by provincial representatives in accordance with those of Portugal, determines and marks the destiny of the province. Benefactors in Portugal controlled the political events in Brazil during this risky crisis. The people went along with every-thing because they were assured that it was all being done for their benefit. However, the time for peace has come; they united, they elected us, they sent us—not to receive the fundamental law of their future government, but to make it. This may all be a mistake, but it is a widespread mistake in Brazil that can only be destroyed by force. . . .

My Sovereign Congress, Brazil already knows that the Constitution is the establishment of order and the way by which a people is governed. It is a free expression of a contractual agreement, the fundamental basis of a society of free men.

We were sent to forge an agreement. Only two clauses were imposed on us, and the rest has been left to our discretion. It is therefore necessary that you honor our requests or that you reject our association. We are still not rep-resentatives of the nation, which ceased to exist the moment it broke with the old social compact. We are not representatives of Brazil, of which we were an immediate part in another time, because today each province independently governs itself. We each represent the province that has elected and sent us. We thus need to obtain a plurality of votes, not of all of the representatives collectively but of each province, which can require him [each representative] to serve in accordance with his mandate. If we reach an agreement, if the Constitution makes us equal, then from this day on we become one State, one Nation, and each representative will belong with equal rights to the province that has elected him.

However, let's suppose for one moment that the nation exists, and that we all are uncommitted delegates representing it. In such a system, can the will of one half oblige the other half? The nation has decided, and who else could decide this? Doesn't the nature of agreement, the rights of man, demand unanimous consensus of the parties that enter the agreement? The agreed-upon foundation has deemed that there must be a two-thirds consensus to amend any constitutional article. Constitutions of civilized peoples, which serve as our examples, despite having two chambers and a more extensive veto, require a two-thirds vote in order to validate some decisions. Additionally, to organize an entire Constitution, half of the nation's vote would suffice in these countries that serve as our examples. . . .

My Sovereign Congress, the Constitution regulates the creation of administrative laws; but who will regulate fundamental laws? All of us, or at least the most noteworthy majority that represents and unequivocally expresses the general will of the nation, but never just a few of us. We shall not imitate the power-hungry despots who do not listen to man's rightful claims. Brazil presents each day an even more unfortunate prospect; her fight is only to salvage her rights, which she sees as violated. We must take advantage of this moment, which may have already passed. We do not want the entire world to brand us as ignorant of the evils of humanity; we do not want posterity to accuse us of abandoning a brother, who will undoubtedly help to affirm our power, our independence, and our glory.

I therefore propose, as the only way to stop the progress of disgrace that threatens Brazil, as the most secure measure to consolidate the great Portuguese family, and as a way to give the world the irrefutable testimony of our prudence, our objectivity, and our justice, the following:

1. May it be declared that the Congress of Portugal, until the Constitution is formalized, acknowledge the independence of each of Brazil's provinces.
2. May the Constitution be enforced only in provinces in which a plurality of deputies has approved it.
3. May the Cortes provide assistance to any province that feels it is being threatened by factions and that has requested such assistance in order to guarantee perfect freedom of choice.

4. May it be declared to the government to suspend all provisions and decisions affecting Brazil, except when it is legitimately requested by a specific province.
5. That the governments of Brazil, wherever detachments from Portugal may be found, recuse themselves as soon as it is convenient.

Translated by Lanna Leite and Molly Quinn

Portraits: Empress Maria Leopoldina of Brazil

Lilia Moritz Schwarcz

Contrary to popular belief, the life of a princess is not an easy one. At least, that is what more than eight hundred letters written by the Princess Maria Leopoldina (1797–1826), dispersed in archives in Austria and Brazil, seem to show. Through the letters, it is possible to experience the drama of this young woman. A daughter of Emperor Francis of the powerful Hapsburg dynasty of Austria, she was educated according to the most traditional rules of European monarchies. But because of her marriage to Pedro I, she ended up living in Brazil during its separation from Portugal.[1]

The letters serve as a type of diary, with Leopoldina frequently writing to her sister, Maria Luísa (who married and then later separated from Napoleon), as well as to her father. Through their correspondence, we get a sense of the glamour of the European court, where princesses mixed with figures like Haydn and Beethoven, and of the responsibilities and obligations of her position. We also come to understand Princess Leopoldina's fear of revolution, her interest in mineralogy, her desire to fall in love with her husband, Dom Pedro, and her eventual discontent in Brazil.

Dona Carolina Josefa Leopoldina Francisca Fernanda of Habsburg-Lorraine was born in Vienna in 1797 and grew up there in Schönbrunn Palace, where she seems to have received a conservative and meticulous education. Maria Leopoldina, as she was known in Brazil, belonged to the powerful House of Hapsburg, one of the oldest dynasties of Europe, which reigned over Austria from 1282 until 1918. Her father was the Emperor Francis II (1768–1835), the last emperor of the Holy Roman Empire. After his defeat by Napoleon and the dissolution of the Holy Roman Empire in 1806, his title became Francis I, emperor of Austria.

When Leopoldina was around eighteen years old, marriage negotiations on her behalf began with the arrival of a representative of Prince Pedro, heir to the throne of the United Kingdom of Portugal, Brazil, and Algarve. The son of King Dom João VI and Queen Carlota Joaquina de Bourbon from the House of Braganza, Pedro lived in what must have seemed a very distant and exotic place, Brazil.

In many ways, the story has a fairy-tale beginning. The Marquis of Mari-

Empress Maria
Leopoldina of Brazil
(1797–1826). Painting by
Joseph Kreutzinger, 1815.

alva, the Portuguese envoy sent to negotiate the marriage, arrived in Vienna
with a beautiful jewel and a picture of the proposed fiancé in a small box, as
well as a negotiation document. According to the terms of the proposed contract, the royal family was to return to Portugal once the Napoleonic Wars
were over. Although Klemens von Metternich, the powerful foreign minister
of the Austrian Empire, feared for the fate of the princess, he was soon persuaded to approve the marriage by her father and Leopoldina herself, who
both saw the fiancé as a very suitable partner for a princess of such a noble
house. The marriage was planned as a strategic mission, as marriage among
royalty. Its purpose was to form a link between states, rather than to create
a sentimental bond between individuals. Thus without so much as having
met one another, the two were officially married in a wedding by proxy on
May 13, 1817, in St. Augustine's Church in Vienna; the Archduke Carlos Luís
represented the groom.

As soon as the marriage was arranged, the future princess of Brazil began
to study Portuguese as well as the history, geography, and economy of her
new empire. On June 3, the princess and her party set out for Rio de Janeiro.
Particularly interested in mineralogy and botany, Leopoldina packed botanical specimens she hoped to acclimatize to Brazil, and invited scientists to

join her in Brazil to study the flora and fauna of the land. Her entourage also carried samples of Austrian commercial products, decorative objects, and scientific instruments to be used in various expeditions in Brazil.

Meanwhile, in Brazil, preparations were being made for the princess's arrival. News of the marriage was lavishly celebrated with holy masses, the ringing of bells, and artillery salvos, as the royal union was seen to benefit both the internal and foreign relations of the new nation. The Portuguese monarchy had triumphed in finding a princess of such distinguished lineage willing to live in a far-off tropical colony.

Despite differences in their upbringings and education and rumors of Dom Pedro's dissatisfaction with Leopoldina's appearance, the couple soon adapted to one another. They moved into a home on the grounds of the royal palace at the Quinta da Boa Vista, and she joined her husband in hunting and horsemanship, activities they both enjoyed.

However, the situation rapidly deteriorated. The princess found the colony narrow minded and missed the company of the nobility. Furthermore, her husband was often absent, and his numerous extramarital affairs soon became public, especially his long-term relationship with Domitila de Castro Canto e Melo, whom Pedro ennobled with the title Marchioness of Santos. To make things worse, the Liberal Revolution of Porto in Portugal in 1820 meant the return of the king to Lisbon. Dom João was the member of the royal family she had grown closest to, and the princess lamented her father-in-law's departure, but did not wish to go with him and leave her husband alone in Brazil.

The deadlock that led to the proclamation of independence in 1822 is described in part V, but the role of Leopoldina is worth highlighting here. She quickly took up the Brazilian cause and firmly encouraged Dom Pedro to declare independence from Portugal. In the buildup to independence, Leopoldina and José Bonifácio de Andrada e Silva, who is described in the portrait in part V, became the strongest voices influencing the prince. When, in August 1822, Dom Pedro had to travel to São Paulo to try to pacify the rebellious province, Leopoldina temporarily assumed full powers, acting as head of the State Council and interim princess regent of Brazil. It was she—along with José Bonifácio—who received the news that Portugal was preparing action against Brazil, demanding Dom Pedro's immediate return. In response, she affirmed, "The apple is ripe, pick it now or it will rot." In letters that she wrote to Bonifácio, she positioned herself in favor of independence, even before her husband, and insisted that her sister help convince their father to support emancipation of her "dear country."

The letters from the National Assembly demanding Pedro's return, along with a letter containing Leopoldina's advice to her husband favoring independence from Portugal, reached Dom Pedro on September 7, 1822. From that point on, the story is well known: Pedro proclaimed the independence of Brazil, without a large audience and in the middle of a trip with only a few officials as witnesses (see part V, From Independence to the Abolition of the Slave Trade).

Notwithstanding Leopoldina's initial enchantment with the regency and her critical support for Brazilian independence, in her letters she often complained of isolation, of the lack of books, and even of the unfulfilled promise to return to Portugal after she became disillusioned with Brazil. Most of all, she expressed profound discontent with her husband, who she said liked to enjoy himself, but did not allow others the same right. Nevertheless, she still tried to fulfill her socially inscribed role as princess and later empress, providing the monarchy with six children. After 1819 when her first daughter, Maria da Glória, was born, she had nearly one child per year until her death at age twenty-nine in 1826. However, her sadness with the marriage was palpable in her letters: Leopoldina wrote that "she wasn't loved" and that she "swallowed everything in secret."

Similar strains of disappointment inflected her comments about Brazil over time, which she came to describe as that "horrible America," "a country where everything is driven by villainy"—and where "to find virtuous women, one needed a microscope." The last letter, dated December 8, 1826, and addressed to her sister, Maria Luísa, shows her total despair. Dom Pedro had become a "seductive monster," who publicly humiliated her, and the empress no longer hid her situation. "He just gave the final proof of his total neglect in my respect, mistreating me in the presence of she who is the cause of my disgrace," she wrote, referring to the Marchioness of Santos, who by that point had come to occupy all of the young monarch's time.

Leopoldina died before her youngest child (the future emperor, Dom Pedro II) reached his first birthday. Her life, reflected in her letters, allows consideration of the history of Brazil from an unusual perspective, that of an Austrian noblewoman who came to find her Prince Charming hidden in an exotic kingdom, but who ended up a central player in the land's political plots and intrigues, and who ultimately became disenchanted with her prince. They reveal a tormented character who knew how to mock her own situation. "Poor princesses," said Leopoldina, "they are what is given out in a game, the result of which determines their luck or misfortune." Unfortunately for her, her story did not have a fairy-tale ending.

Note

1. Dona Leopoldina, *Cartas de uma Imperatriz* (São Paulo: Compnhia das Letras, 2000).

V

From Independence to the Abolition
of the Slave Trade, 1822–1850

While the process of Brazilian independence shares much with the movement toward colonial emancipation that took place throughout the rest of Latin America in the early 1820s, it also had distinct features. As in the rest of the Americas at this time, the spread of liberal ideas led many to believe that the colonial situation was not a natural fact, but something that could be changed through human action. At the same time, these ideas were often reinterpreted and translated in Latin America in conservative ways. In Brazil, the principal reasons for this revolved around the deeply embedded nature of slavery. Large landowners, who relied on enslaved labor, had little interest in changing the nation's status quo or general social structure. Even the relatively small middle classes relied on slave labor for domestic service and additional income. Thus, the rural elite, the group that assumed leadership of the independence process, did so in order to keep intact the great pillars of the nation: slave labor, large landholdings, and an export-oriented monoculture economy.

The Italian writer Giuseppi Lampedusa used an expression in his book *The Leopard* (1958) that is particularly apt in relation to Brazilian independence: "Something needs to change so that everything can remain exactly as it is." That is, the powerful in Brazil wanted a shift in the external political situation that would not in any way affect the nation's internal political and social order.

And that is essentially what happened. While across Spanish America former colonies were becoming republics, Brazil would adopt neither a republican nor a presidential form of government. On the contrary, the elites, especially those from Rio de Janeiro, preferred a monarchy, judging a royal figure to be a strong symbol that could prevent the disintegration of the country after independence. Brazilian politicians had before them the examples of what had happened in Spanish America, when the four viceroyalties shattered into many small and medium-sized countries. By and large they wanted to avoid a similar fate for Brazil.

Dom Pedro I, emperor of Brazil (1798–1834). Painting by unidentified artist after John Simpson (1782–1847).

Thus following Dom Pedro's declaration of Brazilian independence from Portugal on September 7, 1822, he remained in Brazil as a monarch. But rather than becoming king, he chose instead the title emperor of Brazil, a designation that seemed an appropriately august term for a monarch of such an immense territory. It also held local relevance, for in choosing the title Pedro heeded the advice of José Bonifácio de Andrada e Silva, one of his closest advisors, who affirmed that the people already knew the term "emperor" because of the popular Feast of the Divine, which each year elected an emperor. At the same time, it reflected Pedro's secret admiration for Napoleon Bonaparte, who had also been acclaimed emperor. Thus, through a much more complex process than can be fully explained here, Brazil became an independent constitutional monarchy surrounded by republics on all sides.

This is not to say that the Portuguese gave up their most valuable colony without a fight. Portuguese garrisons stationed in Brazil combated would-be separatists, but they were short of men, arms, and supplies and failed to win any decisive battles. When a reorganized Brazilian navy finally forced the withdrawal of Portuguese vessels from coastal waters in 1823, this ended the conflict. Unlike the hundreds of thousands who died during the wars of independence in Spanish America, only around six thousand are estimated to have perished during the conflict. Thus, in contrast to the independence wars of many of its neighbors, Brazil's struggle for independence was a relatively peaceful affair.

Soon after Pedro I's lavish coronation ceremony on December 1, 1822, he convened a constitutional convention to write a new national charter. The body quickly found itself divided between those delegates who wanted a liberal document that would limit the powers of the emperor and those who supported granting the monarch greater authority. Frustrated by the proposed limitations on his rule, Pedro dissolved the convention and appointed a new commission to draft the document. The final version, the Constitution of 1824, established the usual three branches of government—executive, legislative, and judicial—but added a fourth power, known as the moderating power (*poder moderador*), granting additional authority to the emperor in order to moderate conflicts between the legislative and judicial branches. Through this moderating power, the emperor could convene or dismiss the legislature at will, appoint lifetime senators from a list of three nominees, choose members of a Council of State, select and remove judges without restrictions, and approve ecclesiastics of the Roman Catholic Church. While the charter adopted some liberal elements, such as the inherent right of citizens (a status denied to slaves) to liberty, individual security, and property, elections for the legislature were indirect, and the moderating power deposited considerable control of the government in the hands of the monarch.

The United States was the first country to recognize Brazil in 1824, followed by a few African countries involved in the slave trade. Although Great Britain supported Brazilian independence and was anxious to continue having access to its markets, the British had to play a cautious diplomatic game. On the one hand, London wanted to maintain the close relations it had developed with Brazil since 1808, when British ships escorted the royal family across the Atlantic, and Great Britain received a most favored nation trading agreement in return. On the other hand, the British did not want to alienate Portugal, a longtime European ally. So Britain acted as a friendly intermediary and negotiated Portugal's recognition of Brazilian independence in 1825. In return for Portuguese acknowledgment of its independence, Brazil agreed to compensate it with £2 million for lost property that had remained in Brazil when João VI returned to Lisbon in 1821. British bankers then generously loaned Brazil the exact amount needed to compensate Portugal, giving the emergent nation its first hefty foreign debt.

In recognition of this support from Great Britain, Pedro I agreed in 1827 to British requests to end Brazil's slave trade with Africa. But the Brazilian government only half-heartedly implemented this commitment in 1830 and then, for all intents and purposes, ignored it for the next two decades. During the same period, when the slave trade was officially illegal, the expansion of coffee production in the southeast increased the demand for forced labor, and Brazilian officials routinely looked the other way when ships bearing slaves landed near the country's major ports, and when boats clandestinely whisked the captives to shore. Until the slave trade was definitively ended in 1850, again due to British pressure, more Africans were illegally transported to Brazil on an annual basis than in the years prior to the ban.

Pedro I stayed in power for only nine years and could point to few successes in his time as emperor. He failed to win a war with the Confederation of La Plata (present-day Argentina) over disputed southern territories in what is today Uruguay. The conflict lasted from 1825 to 1828 with no clear victor and placed additional strains on the new country's finances. Moreover, Pedro engaged in incessant fights with Congress over his powers. Frustrated with these repeated conflicts, in 1831 he suddenly renounced the throne and returned to Portugal, where he worked to ensure that his daughter Maria da Glória would inherit the Portuguese Crown. He left his five-year-old son Pedro in Brazil as his heir.

Because the Constitution stipulated that regents rule on behalf of a young emperor until he became an adult, the period from 1831 until 1840 is known as the Regency. It was characterized by tensions between a centralized government in Rio de Janeiro and regional power in the provinces. In 1834, liberal forces in Congress succeeded in passing an amendment to the 1824 Constitution that decentralized some state power and put it in the hands of regional politicians. With greater local authority, various groups around the country began to raise the possibility of establishing a federal system of government or even a republic. And in various outlying areas of the empire, violent outbreaks and regional revolts, such as Cabanagem in Pará (1835), Balaiada in Maranhão (1838), Sabinada in Bahia (1837–38), and the Farroupilha [Ragamuffins] War in Rio Grande do Sul (1835–45) epitomized a rising demand for more regional self-rule. Although none of these uprisings was explicitly directed against the monarchy, as the strength of the central government grew, so did demands for regional autonomy, which implicitly challenged imperial rule. As the statesman Joaquim Nabuco later said, "In Brazil, the Regency was a republic, a provisional republic."[1]

Alarmed by this wave of regional revolts, a group of liberal and conservative politicians set aside their differences to urge fourteen-year-old Pedro to take the throne as a way of reinvesting power in the central government. He did so at the age of fifteen in 1840, and thus began his long forty-nine-year reign as Emperor Pedro II of Brazil (see Portraits: Emperor Dom Pedro II in part VI). In his first decade as ruler, one of the major issues Pedro II faced was the mounting pressure from Great Britain to end Brazil's illicit international slave trade. Although an expanding agricultural export sector of the economy profited considerably from the use of imported slave labor, Brazil finally conceded to British pressure and ended trafficking in African slaves in 1850. The international slave trade ended, but the abolition of the institution of slavery took another thirty-eight years to achieve.

Note

1. Maria Ligia Prado, *A formação das nações latino-americanas*, 2nd ed. (Campinas: Atual/ Editora da Unicamp, 1986), 61.

On the Declaration of Brazilian Independence

Padre Belchoir Pinheiro de Oliveira

The demand of the Portuguese Cortes (National Assembly) that Prince Regent Pedro follow his father back to Portugal—and that Brazil revert to its former, subordinate status—prompted some Brazilians, led by Pedro's tutor and adviser José Bonifácio de Andrada e Silva, to encourage Pedro to imitate Brazil's Spanish American neighbors and seek independence. Pedro himself preferred to stay in Brazil and reacted with growing displeasure to the pressure from Lisbon for him to return. In January 1822, he announced that he would indeed remain by declaring "Fico," which means "I will stay" (see in part IV, "Petition for Pedro I to Remain in Brazil"). On September 7 of that year, while riding on horseback along the banks of the Ipiranga River in São Paulo, Pedro received letters from his father, his wife, his chief adviser, and the British consul general, Sir Henry Chamberlain, offering him counsel on whether or not to continue to stay in Brazil. After reading them, he made the final break and declared independence. A priest, Father Belchoir Pinheiro de Oliveira, who was present at the event, wrote the following description of this moment.

Pedro's declaration of independence, however, did not mean he envisioned a democratic Brazil, governed by the majority; he quickly became an authoritarian monarch and later forced José Bonifácio de Andrada into exile. Becoming increasingly unpopular with his Brazilian subjects, he abdicated in 1831 and returned to Portugal, leaving his five-year-old son Pedro behind.

The prince ordered that I read aloud the letters transported . . . from the Cortes, a letter from Dom João, another from the princess [Leopoldina], another from José Bonifácio, and still another from [Sir Henry] Chamberlain, the secret agent of the prince. The Cortes demanded the immediate return of the prince, and the imprisonment and trial of José Bonifácio; the princess recommended prudence and asked that the prince heed his minister. José Bonifácio told the prince that he must choose one of two roads to follow: leave immediately for Portugal and hand himself over to the Cortes, as was the situation of Dom João VI, or remain and proclaim the independence of Brazil. . . .

Dom Pedro, trembling with anger, seized the letters from my hands and crumpled them. He threw them on the ground and stomped on them. . . .

Dom Pedro walked silently toward our horses at the side of the road. Suddenly, he halted in the middle and said, "The Cortes is persecuting me and calling me an adolescent and a Brazilian. Well now, let them see their adolescent in action. From today on, our relations with them are finished. I want nothing more from the Portuguese government, and I proclaim Brazil forevermore separated from Portugal."

Translated by Robert M. Levine and John J. Crocitti

Acclamation of Pedro as Emperor of Brazil

José Martins Rocha

The following account from the Correio Braziliense *newspaper describes the ceremony in which Pedro I was publicly acclaimed as emperor of Brazil on October 12, 1822. Considered Brazil's first newspaper, the* Correio Braziliense *circulated from 1808 to 1822. It was not printed in Brazil, however, but London, where it not only escaped Portuguese censorship but where its editor, the journalist Hipólito da Costa, fled after suffering Portuguese imprisonment. Da Costa was born in 1774 in the colony of Sacramento, a Portuguese settlement that today is part of Uruguay. He moved with his family to Rio Grande do Sul when Sacramento reverted to the Spanish Crown in 1777. When da Costa became old enough for university study, he, like other elite Brazilian men, went to Portugal to study at the University of Coimbra. In 1798 the Portuguese government sent him on an official mission to Mexico and the United States to study those countries' economies and learn about industrial innovations in the United States, and in 1802 he was sent to London to acquire books for the Royal Library and machinery for the Royal Press. Upon his return to Portugal, however, he was accused by the Inquisition of spreading Freemasonry and imprisoned. He fled to London in 1805, where he met the Duke of Sussex, son of the king of England and also a Mason, who protected him from extradition. As a cosmopolitan center, London hosted many future leaders of the Latin American independence movement who passed through, including Simón Bolívar, Francisco de Miranda, and José de San Martín, figures da Costa met.*

The journal circulated monthly in the form of a book of around one hundred pages and attracted a relatively limited audience—close to five hundred subscribers. Through the Correio Braziliense, *da Costa criticized the corruption and inertia of the Portuguese government. He believed the Portuguese Empire needed to enact reforms, but shied away from criticizing the figure of the sovereign himself or advocating for other forms of government, instead proposing that the monarch himself undertake these reforms. Da Costa also defended freedom of the press, based on the liberal English model, which, he argued, allowed for the spread of scientific advances and new cultural and artistic ideas. He also advocated for an end to the Inquisition and to slavery. Those who read the* Correio Braziliense *could follow national and international events, learn the theories of the Enlightenment, and become familiar with new economic concepts.*

Cérémonie de Sacre de D. Pedro 1er. Empereur du Brésil, à Rio de Janeiro, le 1er. Decembre 1822.
Illustration by Jean-Baptiste Debret. Coronation of Pedro I as emperor of Brazil. From
Voyage pittoresque et historique au Brésil (Paris: Firmin Didot Frères, 1839). Courtesy of
the John Carter Brown Library at Brown University.

In the account that follows, the ceremony in which Dom Pedro was declared em-
peror of Brazil by acclamation is described in some detail. In addition to his royal
lineage, Dom Pedro drew on declarations by loyal members of local town councils
throughout the province of Rio de Janeiro and Minas Gerais to establish his legiti-
macy as the new ruler of Brazil.

On the festive day of October 12, 1822, the first year of the Independence of
Brazil in this city and capital of Rio de Janeiro, at the palace at the Field of
Santa Ana, the High Court Judge; members of the Town Council; and the
Attorney of the Senate, who, along with the undersigned, is a scribe; gentle-
men and masters of the city; the attorneys of the councils of the towns of the
province; and the people who have signed below have all gathered to acclaim
Dom Pedro the Constitutional Emperor of Brazil, while keeping the title of
Perpetual Defender. . . .

And, finding the majority of the people of this city present, covering the
Field of Santa Anna with their incalculable numbers, whereto the Honor
Corps also went, and the second line of the Garrison of this same city, at
ten in the morning the same Lord [Pedro] came out with his august wife
[Maria Leopoldina], and the Princess Dona Maria da Glória, being received
in said palace by a thousand cries of the people and the troops, by the Senate,
gentlemen and masters of this city, and officials of the noted town councils,
with the ex-senator Antônio Alves de Araújo bearing the standard with the

new crest of the Empire of Brazil. A message of the people of this province was presented to the same Lord by the President of the Senate, who dedicated his speech to him, showing that the universal will of the people of this province and of all others, who had made themselves known through the declarations of many legislatures, was to support the Independence of Brazil, which the same Lord, in agreement with the general will, had already declared, and to acclaim the same Lord on this auspicious day the Constitutional Emperor of Brazil and its Perpetual Defender, preserving for him and his noble successors the title of Perpetual Defender of Brazil. His Constitutional Imperial Majesty deigned to give the following response: "I accept the title of Constitutional Emperor, and Perpetual Defender of Brazil, because, having heard my Council of State and other officials, and having examined the declarations of the Legislatures of different provinces, I am entirely convinced there is such consensus among these others, that only due to lack of time have they not yet arrived." With this response announced to the people and the troops from the balcony of the said palace, where this whole act was celebrated, the same Lord was acclaimed legally and solemnly by the Council of State, noblemen and lords, the people and the troops of the city, and by the officials of the councils of all villages of this province, the President of the Senate raising the following cries, which were repeated with unfeigned enthusiasm by all the people: "Long live our holy Religion! Long live the Lord Dom Pedro, first Constitutional Emperor of Brazil and its Perpetual Defender! Long live the Constitutional Emperor of Brazil and Brazil's Imperial Bragança Dynasty! Long live the Independence of Brazil! Long live the Constitutional and Legislative Assembly of Brazil! Long live the Constitutional People of Brazil!" At the end of this solemn and majestic act, his Imperial and Constitutional Majesty went down under a canopy to the Imperial Chapel where a solemn Te Deum was given in thanks. And this act, which was ordered so that all should remain, was undertaken by His Imperial and Constitutional Majesty and the Council of State with the noblemen and lords and the Officials of the village councils. . . .

Translated by Emma Wohl

On Slavery

José Bonifácio de Andrada e Silva

José Bonifácio de Andrada e Silva, an adviser to Dom João VI, and later the close confidante of Dom Pedro I, is often remembered in Brazilian history as the Patriarch of Independence because of his role as a leader in steering Brazil's separation from Portugal (see also "Portraits" at the end of part V). During the ensuing empire, Bonifácio, as he was known, served as the minister of foreign affairs from January 1822 to July 1823, when he broke with the emperor and joined the opposition. In November 1823, when Pedro dissolved the constitutional convention tasked with writing a new constitution, Bonifácio was banished from Brazil and took refuge in France. After later reconciling with Dom Pedro, he returned to Brazil and, when Dom Pedro abdicated, he accepted the outgoing emperor's request to become tutor to his young son, the future Pedro II. This position did not last, as Bonifácio was dismissed from this post in 1833, this time by the Regency government, worried about rumors of a return by Dom Pedro I and about Bonifácio's influence.

As this brief slice of his biography suggests, Bonifácio did not shy away from controversial positions. Among these was his criticism of slavery. In 1823, many years before official abolition (which would not come until 1888), he wrote the following proposal to both end the slave trade and gradually emancipate the enslaved. Yet his proposal found little support at the time as the economy was inextricably tangled with chattel labor, especially the agricultural export sector, and slave owners constituted a powerful political force. Nonetheless it reveals an early current of criticism about the toll of slavery and demonstrates the ways in which proposals for abolition could be built on racist beliefs.

A happy epoch of political regeneration in the Brazilian nation has arrived, obligating all honorable and educated citizens to work toward so great a task. I flatter myself to think that I can bring some ideas to the General Constitutional and Legislative Assembly, which I have developed through study and experience.

As a free citizen and assemblyman of the nation, two objectives beyond the design and intent of the Constitution appear to me to be essential for the prosperity of this empire. The first is a new regulation to promote the general civilization of the indigenous people of Brazil who, with the passing of

Rideau d'Avant Scène Exécuté au Théatre de la Cour, Pour la Réprésentation d'Apparat, à l'occasion du Couronnement de l'Empereur D. Pedro 1er. Illustration by Jean-Baptiste Debret. Allegorical portrayal of the empire suggesting the popularity of Pedro I's rule. Courtesy of the John Carter Brown Library at Brown University.

time, will make the use of slaves ineffectual. I have already submitted a draft of the regulation to this Assembly. Secondly, a new law on the slave trade and treatment of those miserable captives. That topic is the subject of this presentation, in which I seek to show the need to abolish the slave trade, improve the lot of current captives, and to promote their gradual emancipation.

When true Christians and philanthropists raised their voices for the first time in England against the commerce in African slaves, there were many self-interested and worried people who shouted that abolition was impossible or unwise because the British colonies could not conclude such a trade without total destruction. . . . But I hope that the fairness and the generosity of the English people will achieve emancipation, as they already have obtained the abolition of so disgraceful a trade. And why is it only the Brazilians who continue to be deaf to the cries of reason, of the Christian religion, and, I will go further, of honor and national pride? For we are the only nation of European blood that still openly and publicly trades in African slaves.

I am also a Christian and philanthropist, and God emboldens me to dare to raise my weak voice in the midst of this venerable Assembly in favor of the cause of justice and sane politics for a noble and holy cause, which can move generous and humane hearts. Legislators, do not fear the roars of sordid interests: Follow the path of progress and do not fear justice and political reform. But, nevertheless, we must take care to be cautious and prudent.

If the old despotism was numb to everything, it was because it was in their interests that we exist as a mixed and heterogeneous people, without nationality, without brotherhood, allowing them to enslave us more. Thank heaven and our geographical position, we are already a free and independent people. But how can there be a lasting liberal Constitution in a country that continues to be populated by an immense multitude of brute slaves and enemies? So let us start this already great work of the expiation of our old crimes and sins. Yes, this cannot be handled solely with dispassionate behavior. We must [also] be penitent. We must demonstrate to God himself and to mankind that we repent everything in this area that we have done for centuries against justice and religion, that we scream aloud that we will not do unto others that which we would not do unto ourselves. Thus it is necessary to end at once the thefts, fires, and wars that we foment among the savages of Africa. Thousands and thousands of blacks, who die smothered in the holds of our ships, more overcrowded than bales of hay on a farm wagon, must no longer come to our ports. We need to stop at once all these countless deaths and martyrdoms, and the beatings of these poor creatures in our land. For it is time, and past time, that we stop this barbaric and gory trade; it is time for us to gradually eliminate the last vestiges of slavery among us, so that we can build a homogenous nation in the course of a few generations, for, failing this, we will never be truly free, respectable, or happy. It is essential to terminate so much physical and civil disparity. Let us take care to wisely harmonize the many discordant and contrary elements, and to amalgamate the many diverse metals so that we end as a homogenous and compact whole that does not crumble at the slightest touch of any new political disturbance.

Translated by Molly Quinn

From the Journal of Maria Graham

Lady Maria Dundas Graham Callcott

Travelers from Europe and the United States increasingly made their way to Brazil and the rest of Latin America in the nineteenth century, propelled by their nations' expanding economic interests in the region and facilitated by the diminishing travel restrictions that followed independence. As they did, many of them wrote about their experiences for audiences back home, fueling a market for travel literature: firsthand descriptions of the places they visited that were supposed to be both informative and entertaining.

Maria Graham was an especially prolific travel writer. Born in England in 1785, she wrote her first two books about India after traveling there with her father in 1808. While in India she met her first husband, Thomas Graham, an officer in the British Royal Navy, whose position brought them to Italy and led to her third book. When he became commander of a British ship sent to patrol the Brazilian coast, their trip to Brazil and Chile provided the material for her subsequent two books (published in 1823 and 1824). Thomas Graham died in Chile six months after their arrival, but Maria Graham stayed on in Chile for a year and then returned to Brazil for an additional seven months, where she met the emperor. After going home to England, she returned once more to Brazil to become royal tutor to Maria da Glória, the eldest daughter of Dom Pedro and Maria Leopoldina (see part IV, "Portraits: Empress Maria Leopoldina of Brazil"). With time, Maria Graham became the empress's confidante, closely following Maria Leopoldina's disappointment in love and the infidelities of her husband. Maria Graham returned to England in 1826, where she married the painter Augustus Callcott and wrote several history books before dying of tuberculosis in 1842.

These selections from her published journal entries describe her time in Recife, in a Rio de Janeiro sugar mill, and at the Brazilian court.

[Pernambuco, Monday, September 24, 1821.] We had hardly gone fifty paces into Recife, when we were absolutely sickened by the first sight of a slave-market. It was the first time either the boys or I had been in a slave-country; and, however strong and poignant the feelings may be at home, when imagination pictures slavery, they are nothing compared to the staggering sight of a slave-market. It was thinly stocked, owing to the circumstances of the town, which cause most of the owners of new slaves to keep them closely shut up in the depots. Yet about fifty young creatures, boys and girls, with all the appearance of disease and famine consequent upon scanty food and long confinement in unwholesome places, were sitting and lying about among the filthiest animals in the streets. The sight sent us home to the ship with the heartache and resolution, "not loud but deep," that nothing in our power should be considered too little or too great that can tend to abolish or to alleviate slavery. . . .

[Rio de Janeiro, August 21, 1823.] This morning looked at least as threatening [with rain] as yesterday, but we determined to go as far as the Engenho dos Affonsos, for whose owner, Senhor João Marcus Vieira, we had letters [of introduction] from a friend in town. Accordingly we took leave of our kind hostess [a cottage dweller who gave them shelter from the storm], who had made coffee early for us, and proceeded along a league of very pretty road to the Affonsos. Where that estate joins Campinha there is a large tiled shed where we found a party of travellers, apparently from the mines, drying their clothes and baggage after the last night's storm. A priest, and two or three men apparently above the common, appeared to be the masters of the party; the baggage was piled up on one side of the shed, and the arms were stuck into the cordage which bound it. There was a great fire in the middle, where a negro was boiling coffee, and several persons round drying clothes. Generally speaking, the men we met on their way from the mines are a fine, handsome race, lightly and actively made. Their dress is very picturesque. It consists of an oval cloak, lined and bordered with some bright color such as rose or apple green, worn as the Spanish Americans wear the poncho. The sides are often turned up over the shoulders, and display a bright colored jacket below. The breeches are loose, and reach to the knee, and loose boots of brown leather are frequently seen on the better sort, though it is very common to see the spurs upon the naked heel, and no boot or shoe of any kind. The higher classes have generally handsome pistols or great knives, the others content themselves with a good cudgel.

A short league from the last house of Campinha brought us to Affonsos, where we presented our letter, and were most kindly welcomed. The estate belongs in fact to the grandmother of Senhor João Marcus, who is a native of St. Catherine's, and a widow. His mother, and sister, and brother, and two dumb cousins also reside here, but he is only an occasional visitor, being married, and living near his wife's family. The dumb ladies, no longer young, are very interesting; they are extremely intelligent, understanding most things said in Portuguese by the motion of the lips, so that their cousin spoke in French, when he wished to say any thing of them; they make themselves understood by signs, many of which, I may say most, would be perfectly intelligible to the pupils of Sicard or Braidwood. They are part of a family of eight children, four of whom are dumb, the dumb and the speakers being born alternately. One of them made breakfast for us, which consisted of coffee, and various kinds of bread and butter.

After breakfast, as the day continued cold and showery, we were easily prevailed upon by our host to remain all day at Affonsos. I was indeed glad of the opportunity of spending a whole day with a country family. The first place we visited after breakfast was the sugar-mill, which is worked by mules. The machinery is rather coarse, but seems to answer its purpose.

The estate employs 200 oxen and 180 slaves as labourers, besides those for the service of the family. The produce is somewhere about 3000 arobas of sugar, and 70 pipes of spirits. The lands extend from Tapera, the place where we met the travellers, and where 200 years ago there was an aldea of reclaimed Indians, about a league to Piraquara. There are about forty white tenants who keep vendas and other useful shops on the borders of the estate near the roads, and exercise the more necessary handicrafts. But a small portion of the estate is in actual cultivation, the rest being covered with its native woods; but these are valuable as fuel for the sugar-furnaces, and timber for machinery, and occasionally for sale. The owners of estates prefer hiring either free blacks, or negroes let out by their masters, to send into the woods, on account of the numerous accidents that happen in felling the trees, particularly in steep situations. The death of an estate negro is the loss of his value, of a hired negro, only that of a small fine; and of a free black, it is often the saving even of his wages, if he has no son to claim them. . . .

By the time we had examined the sugar-work, and seen the garden, it was two o'clock, and we were summoned to dinner. Every thing was excellent in its kinds, with only a little more garlic than is used in English cookery. On the side-table there was a large dish of dry farinha, which the elder part of the family called for and used instead of bread. I preferred the dish of farinha moistened with broth, not unlike brose, which was presented along with the bouillie and sliced sausage after the soup. The mutton was from the estate, small and very sweet. Every thing was served up on English blue and white ware. The table-cloths and napkins were of cotton diaper, and there was a good deal of plate used, but not displayed. After dinner some of the family retired to the siesta; others occupied themselves in embroidery, which is very beautiful, and the rest in the business of the house, and governing the female in-door slaves, who have been mostly born on the estate, and brought up in their mistress's house. I saw children of all ages and colors running about, who seemed to be as tenderly treated as if they had been of the family. Slavery under these circumstances is much alleviated, and more like that of the patriarchal times, where the purchased servant became to all intents one of the family. The great evil is, that though perhaps masters may not treat their slaves ill, they have the power of doing so; and the slave is subject to the worst of contingent evils, namely, the caprice of a half-educated, or it may be an ill-educated master. Were all slaves as well off as the house slaves of Affonsos, where the family is constantly resident, and nothing is trusted to others, the state of the individuals might be compared with advantage to that of free servants. But the best is impossible, and the worst but too probable; since the unchecked power of a fallible being may exercise itself without censure on its slaves.

One of the dumb ladies made tea, and afterwards we passed a couple of hours at a round game of cards, where the sisters felt themselves quite on an equality with the speakers, and enjoyed themselves accordingly. . . .

The cards made way for the supper, a meal almost as ceremonious, and quite as constant, as the dinner. After it, toasted cheese was introduced, with griddle cakes of farinha freshly toasted, and spread with a very little Irish butter; they are the same as the Casava bread of the West Indies, but prepared here more like Scotch oat-cakes.

On retiring to my room at night, a handsome young slave entered, with a large brass pan of tepid water, and a fringed towel over her arm, and offered to wash my feet. She seemed disappointed when I told her I never suffered any body to do that for me, or to assist me in undressing at any time. In the morning she returned, and removing the foot bath, brought fresh towels, and a large embossed silver basin and ewer, with plenty of tepid water; which she left without saying a word, and told her mistress I was a very quiet person, and, she supposed, liked nobody but my own people, so she would not disturb me.

[Rio de Janeiro, October 12, 1823.] This is the Emperor's birthday, and the first anniversary of the coronation. I was curious to see the court of Brazil; so I rose early and dressed myself, and went to the royal chapel, where the Emperor and Empress, and the Imperial Princess were to be with the court before the drawing room. I accordingly applied to the chaplain for a station, who showed me into what is called the *diplomatic* tribune, but it is in fact for respectable foreigners; there I met all manner of consuls. However, the curiosity which led me to the chapel would not allow me to go home when the said consuls did; so I went into the drawing-room, which, perhaps, after all, I should not have done, being quite alone, had not the gracious manner in which their Imperial Majesties saluted me, both in the chapel and afterwards in the corridor leading to the royal apartments, induced me to proceed. I reached the inner room where the ladies were, just as the Emperor had, with a most pleasing compliment, announced to Lady Cochrane and that she was Marchioness of Maranham; for he had made her husband Marques, and had conferred on him the highest degree of the Order of the Cruzeiro. I am sometimes absent; and now, when I ought to have been most attentive, I felt myself in the situation Sancho Panza so humorously describes, of sending my wits wool-gathering, and coming home shorn myself: for I was so intent on the honor conferred on my friend and countryman; so charmed, that for once his services had been appreciated,—that when I found the Emperor in the middle of the room, and that his hand was extended towards me, and that all others had paid their compliments and passed to their places, I forgot I had my glove on, took his Imperial hand with that glove, and I suppose kissed it much in earnest, for I saw some of the ladies smile before I remembered anything about it. Had this happened with regard to any other prince, I believe that I should have run away, but nobody is more good-natured than Don Pedro: I saw there was no harm done, and so determining to be on my guard when the Empress came in, and then to take an opportunity of telling her of my fault, I stayed quietly, and began talking to two or three young ladies who were at court for the first time and had just received their appointment as ladies of honor to the Empress.

Her Majesty, who had retired with the young Princess, now came in, and the ladies all paid their compliments while the Emperor was busy in the presence-chamber receiving the compliments of the Assembly and other public bodies. There was little form and no stiffness. Her Imperial Majesty conversed easily with everybody, only telling us all to speak Portuguese, which of course we did. She talked a good deal to me about English authors, and especially of the Scotch novels, and very kindly helped me in my Portuguese; which, though I now understand, I have few opportunities of speaking to cultivated persons. If I had been pleased with her before, I was charmed with her now. When the Emperor had received the public bodies, he came and led the Empress into the great receiving room, and there, both of them standing on the upper step of the throne, they had their hands kissed by naval, military, and civil officers, and private men; thousands, I should think, thus passed. It was curious, but it pleased me, to see some black officers take the small white hand of the Empress in their clumsy black hands, and apply their pouting African lips to so delicate a skin, but they looked up to *Nosso Imperador*, and to her, with a reverence that seemed to me a promise of faith *from* them, a bond of kindness *to* them. The Emperor was dressed in a very rich military uniform, the Empress in a white dress embroidered with gold, a corresponding cap with feathers tipped with green. Her diamonds were superb, her head-tire and ear-rings having in them opals such as I had supposed the world did not contain, and the diamonds surrounding the picture of the Emperor she wears were the largest I have seen.

Portugal Recognizes the Brazilian Empire

Charles Stuart, Luiz José de Carvalho e Mello,

and Barão de Santo Amaro

Eager to maintain good diplomatic and trading relations with both Portugal and the newly independent Brazil, Great Britain maneuvered carefully between them. It delayed recognizing Brazil until successfully negotiating for Portugal to do the same, sending its diplomat Sir Charles Stuart to undertake the delicate operation. Just a few months later, Brazil and Portugal signed the treaty below. As a mutual agreement to divide the two empires, and, by extension, to define the new roles of Dom João VI and Dom Pedro I, it at times reads more like a familial reconciliation between a father and his son than an administrative act of statecraft.

In an "Additional Convention" to the treaty, not shown here, Brazil agreed to pay Portugal two million pounds sterling to end all outstanding Portuguese monetary claims against it.

Treaty of Friendship and Alliance between King D. João VI and D. Pedro I, Emperor of Brazil, made through the mediation of His British Majesty, signed in Rio de Janeiro on August 26, 1825; ratified by Portugal on November 15 of the same year and by Brazil on August 30 of the same year.

His Most Loyal Majesty, having steadfastly in his royal spirit a vivid desire to re-establish peace, friendship and good harmony between brother communities, and to bring together and unite in perpetual alliance the most sacred ties; in order to achieve such important goals, to promote general prosperity and to assure the political existence of and future destiny of Portugal, as well as of Brazil, and wanting once and for all to remove those obstacles that might impede such an alliance, agreement and happiness between one State and the other, by his official document of May 13 of this year recognized Brazil in the category of independent Empire, separated from the Kingdom of Portugal and the Algarve, and [recognized] his own son, loved and respected above all others, D. Pedro, as Emperor, ceding and transferring by free will the sovereignty of said Empire to this same son, and to his legitimate successors, and only taking and reserving for himself the same title.

And these august gentlemen, accepting the mediation of His British Majesty for the settlement of all questions related to the separation of the two States, have named as plenipotentiaries, namely, His Most Faithful Highness, to the Most Illustrious and Most Excellent Gentleman Sir Charles Stuart, Private Counselor to his British Majesty, Knight Grand Cross of the Order of the Bath. His Imperial Majesty, to the Most Illustrious and Most Excellent Luiz José de Carvalho e Mello, of his Counsel of State, Dignitary of the Imperial Order of the Cross, Commander of the Orders of Christ and of Conception, and Minister and Secretary of State of Foreign Affairs; to the Most Illustrious and Most Excellent Baron of Santo Amaro, Great Figure of the Empire, of the Counsel of State, Gentleman of the Imperial Congress, Dignitary of the Imperial Order of the Cross and Commander of the Orders of Christ and of the Tower and Sword; and the Most Illustrious and Most Excellent Francisco Villela Barbosa, of the Counsel of State, Grand Cross of the Imperial Order of the Cross, Knight of the Order of Christ, Coronel of the Imperial Corps of Engineers, Minister and Secretary of State for Naval Affairs, and Inspector-General of the Navy. And having seen and exchanged their full powers, they agreed, in conformity with the principles expressed in this preamble, to create the present treaty.

ART. I—His Most Loyal Majesty recognizes Brazil in the category of independent Empire and separated from the Kingdom of Portugal and the Algarve; and his own son, loved and respected above all others, D. Pedro, as Emperor, ceding and transferring by free will the sovereignty of said Empire to this same son, and to his legitimate successors. His Most Loyal Majesty only takes and reserves for his person the same title.

ART. II—His Imperial Majesty, in recognition of respect and love to his august father Sir D. João VI, agrees that his Most Loyal Majesty takes for his person the title of Emperor.

ART. III—His Imperial Majesty promises not to accept any proposition by any Portuguese Colonies to join the Empire of Brazil.

ART. IV—From now on there will be peace and alliance and the most perfect friendship between the Kingdoms of Portugal and Algarve and of Brazil with the forgiveness of past quarrels between their respective peoples.

ART. V—The subjects of both the Portuguese Nation and the Brazilian Nation will be considered and treated in the respective States like those of the most favored and friendly nations, and their rights and properties will be religiously guarded and protected; it is understood that the current owners of immovable goods [real estate] will continue in peaceful possession of those same goods.

ART. VI—All sequestered or confiscated immovable or moveable goods and shares belonging to subjects of both the Sovereigns of Portugal and of Brazil will be soon reinstated, as well as their lost income, after the costs of administering them are deducted, and the property owners will be reciprocally indemnified in the manner set up in ART. VIII.

ART. VII—All confiscated shipments and cargos belonging to subjects from both Sovereigns will be similarly restored and their proprietors indemnified.

ART. VIII—A commission named by both Governments, made up of Portuguese and Brazilians in equal number, will be established as the respective Governments deem most convenient, and will be charged with examining the subject of Articles VI and VII; understanding that the claims must be made within one year of the Commission's formation, and that, in the case of a tie vote, the question will be decided by the Representative of the Mediator Sovereign. Both Governments will indicate the resources to be used to pay the first of these liquidated claims.

ART. IX—All public Government to Government claims will be reciprocally received and decided, or decided through the restitution of reclaimed objects or through an indemnity of its just value. For the settlement of these claims both High Contracting Parties agree to have a direct and special Convention.

ART. X—Trade relations will soon be re-established between both the Portuguese and Brazilian Nations, reciprocally and provisionally paying on all merchandise 15 percent for rights of consumption; transfer and re-export charges will remain as they were practiced before the separation.

ART. XI—A reciprocal exchange of ratifications of the present Treaty will be made in the city of Lisbon within the space of five months or as soon as it is possible, counting the date of signature of the present Treaty. In testimony of this, we, the undersigned, Plenipotentiaries of His Most Loyal Majesty and of His Imperial Majesty, by virtue of our respective full powers, sign the present Treaty in our own hand, and we order it sealed with our coats of arms. Done in the city of Rio de Janeiro, on the 29th day of the month of August of 1825.

Charles Stuart
Luiz José de Carvalho e Mello
Barão de Santo Amaro

The Malê Revolt

João José Reis

In the early morning hours of January 25, 1835, a group of African-born slaves took over the streets of Salvador, capital of the province of Bahia, in what was the most effective urban slave rebellion in the history of the Americas. Led by African Muslims, called Malês in nineteenth-century Brazil, the uprising took place after months of careful organizing. The planning was facilitated by Malês' strong African identity, their Arabic literacy, and their prestigious position within Afro-Bahian society, as well as by the relative physical mobility of urban slave life and symbolic power of Islam as a source of non-European solidarity.

While the rebels managed to take control of the streets for a short period of time, they were eventually defeated. Suspects were tried and punished with death, whippings, prison terms, and deportation. The insurrection caused a prolonged panic among the local population, which led to legal and informal persecution of freed Africans, hundreds of whom decided to return to Africa. The most prominent specialist on the Malê Revolt is João José Reis, a historian from the Federal University of Bahia. The text below, authored by Reis, shows how enslaved and freed Africans were not mere victims of the system but also protagonists in fighting for their emancipation.

On January 25, 1835, an African slave revolt occurred in Salvador. This movement is known today as the Malê Revolt, as the Yoruba Muslims who led the revolt were known as Malês, from "Ìmàle," a term that signifies Muslim in the Yoruba language. Although numerous individuals belonging to more densely Muslim ethnic groups—such as the Hausa, Nupe, and Borno—were initially indicted, just a few actually took part in the revolt. And although its leaders and perhaps most of its rank-and-file were Muslims enslaved in wars of Islamic expansion and other political conflicts in Africa, the movement also had a pronounced ethnic, namely Yoruba, dimension. The revolt was the last of a cycle of more than twenty African revolts or plots that had begun with a carefully planned conspiracy that was nonetheless crushed in the cradle in 1807.

In 1835, close to six hundred men participated in the uprising. Although this number seems small, as a proportion of Salvador's population it would be the equivalent of close to thirty thousand people today. The rebels had planned the uprising to occur in the early hours of the morning of the twenty-fifth, but news about the plot reached the authorities in advance. A patrol that was sent out to check several suspect addresses arrived at a house where a group of conspirators was meeting, and while they were trying to force open the door, nearly sixty African warriors came out shouting and fighting with swords and knives. A small battle ensued in front of this house, following which the rebels headed to the City Hall, located a few yards away.

The rebels attacked the City Hall because its basement prison held one of the most respected Malê leaders, the aged Pacífico Licutan, also known by his Muslim name, Bilal, and his Yoruba name, Licutan. This slave had been imprisoned not for rebellion, but for being property: his master's possessions had been confiscated in order to be auctioned off and thereby repay his creditors. But the attack on the prison did not succeed. Both the prison guards and the provincial government's palace guards, located in the same plaza, fired upon the group.

This first group of rebels then marched through the city streets, fighting and shouting in an attempt to awaken the city's slaves to join them. They headed to Vitória, a district where there lived numerous Muslim slaves belonging to foreign traders, particularly Englishmen. After gathering in the areas surrounding a nearby field, they crossed in front of an army barracks, São Pedro Fort, under its soldiers' heavy fire, and returned to the city's center, where they attacked two police stations, one adjacent to the Monastery of São Bento, and another next to the Lapa convent. The Muslims also fought in the Square of Jesus and in other parts of the city that bore Christian names. Next, they went down through Pelourinho (the heart of today's historic quarters) and reached the lower city—for Salvador was and still is divided into upper and lower districts, the latter located on hilltops, the former at sea level. From there, they attempted to reach the sugar plantation area where they had planned to meet with local slaves, many of whom had been forewarned about the imminent rebellion. However, the African rebels were stopped at the cavalry barracks in Água de Meninos, a beach formerly used (i.e., before the official but loosely enforced prohibition of the slave trade in 1831) for the disembarkation and accommodation of slaves in nearby warehouses. Here, the final battle of the uprising took place, resulting in a true massacre of the Malês and their non-Muslim allies, although many managed to escape into the bush; some tried to flee by swimming and succeeded, while others drowned.

The revolt left the city in turmoil for several hours, having caused the deaths of more than seventy rebels and some ten of their opponents or passersby. The alarm that another uprising could occur, however, was ingrained for many years in Salvador's free residents. This fear spread to other provinces of the Empire of Brazil. In almost all of them, and particularly in the capital of Rio de Janeiro, newspapers published stories about the events in

Bahia, thus helping the spread of panic, while local authorities tried to subjugate the African population, as well as Brazilian-born blacks and mulattoes, submitting them to cautious vigilance and often abusive repression.

At the time of the revolt, Salvador had approximately 65,500 residents, of whom 42 percent were slaves. The nonslave population was also primarily composed of Africans and their descendants, called *crioulos* when referring to blacks born in Brazil, as well as black and white mestizos, known as *pardos* [brown], mulattoes, and *cabras*. Together, black and mixed-blood free and freed people, along with slaves, represented 78 percent of the population. Among the slaves, the vast majority (63 percent) was born in Africa. In the Recôncavo, the sugar plantation region, this figure was even higher.

These slaves were brought from various ports along the African coast. A good number of them came from Luanda, Benguela, and Cabinda, but at the time of the revolt in the 1830s, the vast majority came from ports in the Gulf of Benin (Ouidah, Porto-Novo, Badagry, and especially Lagos), a coastal area known in Brazil as Costa da Mina, the Mina Coast. In Bahia the majority of these slaves were known by ethnic names different from those that they had used in Africa: those who spoke Yoruba were known as Nagôs; the Gbe-speakers were known as Jejes; and the Nupes were known as Tapas. The Hausas kept their original ethnic identification term. Some of the Costa da Mina groups were among those most directly linked to the revolt, mainly the Nagô/Yoruba.

In 1835, the largest group of African-born slaves in Bahia, constituting around 30 percent of them, was Yoruba-speaking Nagôs. While many among them practiced Islam, the majority of Nagôs worshiped the traditional Yoruba gods, the Orishas. Numerous devotees of the latter also joined the uprising led by their ethnic brothers and sisters, the Malês. Therefore, the Muslim revolt had an important ethnic dimension as well.

Translated by Molly Quinn

How to Write the History of Brazil

Carl Friedrich Philipp von Martius

In the nineteenth century, the elite of imperial Brazil sought to define and assert a national identity for newly independent Brazil. But they faced the challenge of acknowledging Brazil's reliance on African-based slavery and the presence of numerous indigenous populations with European ideas of racial and cultural superiority that they shared. In 1838, a group of prominent civilians formed the Brazilian Historical and Geographic Institute, modeled on the Institut Historique in Paris, to produce and disseminate studies of Brazilian national and natural history. The Emperor Dom Pedro II became a member the following year, and within five years the Brazilian government was providing the majority of the institute's budget.

In 1840, the institute offered a prize for the best essay on how to write the history of Brazil. Ironically, the winner was not a Brazilian but a foreigner: Carl Friedrick Phillipp von Martius (1794–1868), a German naturalist, doctor, botanist, and researcher. Martius came to Brazil in 1817 as part of the scientific mission that accompanied Princess Leopoldina when she moved to Brazil as the new bride of Prince Pedro. Together with Johann Baptiste von Spix, he spent over three years traveling vast stretches of Brazilian territory, collecting botanical, zoological, and mineral samples for the Museum of Vienna, samples he later used in his extensive writings about Brazilian flora.

In his winning essay (published in 1844 and awarded the prize in 1847), Martius portrays the uniqueness of Brazil through the metaphor of a single river forming out of mixed racial waters—one white, one black, and one red. But in his telling, the rivers are of different lengths: the white river very long, the red one short, and the black one even shorter. In many ways, Martius's essay foreshadows later interpretations of Brazil as a country defined by a peculiar racial harmony, an idea that would become a pervasive notion by the 1930s.

Whoever takes on the task of writing the History of Brazil, a country with so much promise, must never lose sight of those elements that converge there and that are part of the development of man.

These are, however, very diverse natural elements that have been brought together for man's formation of three races, namely, the copper-colored or American, the white or Caucasian, and finally the black or Ethiopian. Out of the encounter, the mixture, out of the mutual relations and the changes in these three races, today's population was formed, which is why its history has a very particular hallmark.

One could say that each of the human races, according to its intrinsic nature, according to the circumstances under which it lives and develops, participates in its own distinctive historic movement. Therefore, seeing a people be born and develop out of the meeting and coming together of such different human races, we can suggest that its history ought to develop according to a particular law of diagonal forces.

Each of the physical and moral particularities that distinguish the diverse races offers in this respect a special engine; and each of these races will have a greater influence on the common development [of man] the greater is its population in terms of size, energy, and dignity. From this it necessarily follows that the Portuguese, who, as discoverer, conqueror, and master, powerfully influenced this development. The Portuguese created the moral and physical conditions and guarantees for an independent kingdom, and the Portuguese appear as the most powerful and essential engine. But it would also certainly be a great error in regard to all the principles of pragmatic historiography if one were to neglect the force of the indigenous peoples and the imported blacks, forces that equally contributed to the physical, moral, and civil development of the whole population.

Both the indigenous peoples and the blacks reacted to the predominant race.

I know very well that there will be *whites* who consider any contribution by these inferior races a mark of contempt for their ancestry, but I am also certain that they will not be those whose voices are raised for a *Philosophical Historiography of Brazil*. On the contrary, the deepest and most enlightened spirits will find that investigating the role that the Indian and Ethiopian races had and still have in the historical development of the Brazilian people provides a new stimulus for the humane and profound historian.

The history of groups, as well as the history of individuals, shows us that the genius of history (of the world), that moves the human species along paths, whose wisdom we should always recognize, not infrequently allows races to cross in order to achieve the most sublime results in the world order. Who can deny that the English nation owes its energy, its solidity, and its perseverance to that mix of Celtic, Danish, Roman, Anglo-Saxon, and Norman peoples!

Similarly and perhaps more importantly, the genius of history proposes mixing up not just people of the same race, but even races that are completely diverse in their individualities, in their particular moral and physical nature, in order to form out of them a new and marvelously organized nation.

Never can we doubt that the will of providence predestined this mix for Brazil. The powerful river of Portuguese blood ought to absorb the small tributaries of the Indian and Ethiopian races. It is in the lower classes that this mixture takes place, yet in Brazil, as it is in all countries, the upper classes are built on elements of the lower ones, and it is through them that they vitalize and fortify themselves. So while nowadays this mix of races occurs in the lowest class of the Brazilian population, centuries from now it will have a powerful influence over the elevated classes and will communicate to them that historical activity for which the Empire of Brazil is known.

I believe that a philosophical author, influenced by the doctrines of true humanity and an enlightened Christianity, would think nothing of this opinion that could offend Brazilians' susceptibility. Appreciating man according to his true value, as the most sublime work of the Creator, and ignoring his color or his past development, is today a *conditio sine qua non* [prerequisite] for the true historian. The invigorating spirit of the true historian is that transcendent philosophy that evaluates man in whatever situation in which he is destined to labor and serve as an instrument to the world's infinitely wise order. And I am even inclined to suppose that individual relations, through which the Brazilian permits the black to influence the development of Brazilian nationality, determine the destiny of the country. This is preferable to the situation in other states within the New World, where those two inferior races are excluded from the general movement [toward national development], either because they are unworthy due to their birth or because their numbers, compared with those of whites, are small and insignificant.

Thus for the reflective historian it should be critical to show how, in the successive development of Brazil, conditions become established for the improvement of three human races, which in this country live side by side, in a manner unheard-of in ancient history, and which should serve one another mutually as a means and as an end.

This reciprocity offers to the history of the development of Brazil's general population a portrait of an organic life. To appreciate it appropriately will also be the work of truly humane legislation. Using what has so far been done for the moral and civil education of Indians and blacks, and from the results of the respective institutions, historians can judge the future and—turning history into a Sybil to prophesize the future—can suggest useful projects, etc. The more passion and vitality with which they defend in their writing the interests of those races who were abandoned in so many ways, the more meritorious will be their work, earning the mark of that noble philanthropy that our century justly demands of the historian. The historian who shows himself to mistrust the perfectibility of part of the human race allows readers to doubt that he knows how to rise above biased or hateful views.

Translated by Emma Wohl

Scenes from the Slave Trade

Various authors

Over the course of three hundred years, more than twelve million African men, women, and children were captured, branded, placed in heavy iron manacles, and transported on gruesome voyages across the Atlantic to be enslaved in the Americas. Of these, at least five million reached Brazil alive, while 500,000 to one million more died aboard ships making the journey. Just between 1807, when the British suspended their involvement in the transatlantic slave trade, and 1850, when Brazil finally began to enforce its own 1831 law against importing slaves, more than 2.4 million enslaved Africans arrived in Brazil.

In the 1840s, the British began seizing slave ships and freeing their captives, conferring upon them the status of free Africans. Some of them were then transported to Freetown, Sierra Leone, while some of those found in Brazilian waters remained in Brazil. Although technically not enslaved, free Africans were legally bound to work for the Brazilian state for fourteen years or to be rented out by the state to other employers. Only once this period of apprenticeship was finished and free men or women had shown that they had learned a trade and "good customs" could they make use of their freedom. In reality, the administration of free African status was so precarious that many were indeed fully enslaved. Moreover, when captains of slave ships saw hostile naval vessels approaching, they often threw their human cargo into the sea to avoid fines and the confiscation of their ships.

Below is an assortment of documents testifying to the immense human toll of the slave trade. The first two selections are passages from the logbooks of British naval ships written in February 1841. The third selection was written by João Dunshee de Abrantes, a Brazilian abolitionist, writer, journalist, jurist, musician, and later politician, who lived in the northern port city of São Luís do Maranhão.

Logbook from the Warship Fawn

ANONYMOUS

The living, the dying, and the dead, huddled together in one mass. Some unfortunates in the most disgusting state of smallpox, distressingly ill with ophthalmia [inflammation of the eye], a few perfectly blind, others, living skeletons, with difficulty crawled from below, unable to bear the weight of

Négres à fond de calle. Illustration by Johann Moritz Rugendas. Although officially outlawed in 1831, the Atlantic slave trade to Brazil only ended in 1850. From *Moeurs et usage des négres. Quatrième Division Pr.1., 1835.*

their miserable bodies. Mothers with young infants hanging at their breasts, unable to give them a drop of nourishment. How they had brought them thus far appeared astonishing. All were perfectly naked. Their limbs were excoriated from lying on the hard planks for so long a period. On going below, the stench was insupportable. How beings could breathe such an atmosphere and live appeared incredible. Several were under the soughing, which was called the deck, dying—one dead.

Logbook from the British Hospital Ship Crescent

THOMAS NELSON

Huddled together on deck, and clogging up the gangways on either side, cowered, or rather squatted, 362 blacks, with disease, want, and misery stamped on them with such painful intensity as utterly beggars all powers of description. In one corner . . . a group of wretched beings lay stretched, many in the last stages of exhaustion, and all covered with the pustules of small-pox. Several of these, I noticed, had crawled to the spot where the water had been served out, in the hope of procuring a mouthful of the precious liquid; but, unable to return to their proper places, lay prostrate around the empty tub. Here and there, amid the throng, were isolated cases of the same loath-some disease in its confluent or worst form, and cases of extreme emacia-tion and exhaustion, some in a state of perfect stupor, others looking around piteously, and pointing with their fingers to their parched mouths. . . . On every side, squalid and sunken visages were rendered still more hideous by the swollen eyelids and the putrid discharge of a virulent ophthalmia, with which the majority appeared to be afflicted; added to this were figures shriveled to absolute skin and bone, and doubled up in a posture that originally want of space had compelled them to adopt, and that debility and stiffness of the joints compelled them to retain.

Captives

JOÃO DUNSHEE DE ABRANTES

Removed from the ship into barges, they came in neck chains, or *libambos*, leashed to one another to stop them from running away or throwing themselves into the water. Often, they had already been divided into lots before leaving the ship. And they were delivered in batches to the merchants or the bush captains, representatives of the planters of the interior of the province. Since, in certain seasons, the ships remained two or three days in view of the harbor entrance without being able to enter, the buyers went out to meet them in boats to complete the transactions. The traffickers did everything they could to land those horrible cargoes at once. And after a certain number of years in the business, their service was perfected, and usually only sick slaves or those of a weak constitution set foot on the soil of São Luís. These were sold at any price, while the other unfortunates, descended from good races, were haggled over and high offers were made.

Cruelty to Slaves

Thomas Ewbank

Thomas Ewbank followed in the travel writing tradition of Maria Graham and others who found an eager audience for their observations about Brazil. Born in England in 1792, Ewbank migrated to the United States in 1819, where he opened a manufacturing business. He had sufficient financial success to travel to Brazil of his own accord in 1845 and 1846 to visit his brother, then resident in Rio de Janeiro. Several years after his return, he began writing and publishing an account of his trip, first with two articles in Harper's *magazine, and then, in 1856, with his book* Life in Brazil, or A Journal of a Visit to the Land of the Cocoa and the Palm.

Ewbank focused his gaze on various aspects of Brazilian society that he found noteworthy, from Catholic rituals to the workings of the monarchy, and from signs of technological progress to examples of quotidian life such as local foods and customs. But perhaps what most caught his readers' attention were his vivid descriptions of the ways in which slave owners and overseers literally tortured the enslaved, such as those in the passage below. Through accounts such as his, outsiders came to see Brazil as a slave nation that tolerated and defended the most inhumane institution.

It is said slaves in masks are not so often encountered in the streets as formerly, because of a growing public feeling against them. I met but three or four, and in each case, the sufferer was a female. The mask is the reputed ordinary punishment and preventative of drunkenness. As the barrel is often chained to the slave who bears it, to prevent him from selling it for rum, so the mask is to hinder him or her from conveying the liquor to the mouth, below which the metal is continued, and opposite to which there is no opening.

Observing one day masks hanging out for sale at a tin and sheet iron store, I stopped to examine them, and subsequently borrowed one, from which the attached sketch is taken. Except for a projecting piece for the nose, the metal is simply bent cylinderwise. Minute holes are punched to admit air to the nostrils, and similar ones in front of the eyes. A jointed strap (sometimes two) of metal on each side goes round below the ears and meets one that passes over the crown of the head. A staple unites and a padlock secures them.

At most of the smiths' shops, collars are displayed, as horseshoes are with our blacksmiths; at one shop in Rua das Violas, there was quite a variety, with leg shackles, chains, etc. Most of the collars were of five-eighths-inch-round iron, some with one prong, others with two, and some with nothing except a short upright tubular lock.

Here, too, were the heaviest and cruelest instruments of torture—shackles for binding the ankles and wrists close together, and consequently doubling the bodies of the victims into the most painful and unnatural positions. Had I not seen them, I could hardly have thought such things were [possible]. While making a memorandum of their form and dimensions, the proprietor or his adjutant, a black man in his shirt sleeves, came from the rear, and handling them, spoke by way of recommending them, supposing I was a customer. They were made of bar iron, *three inches wide and three-eighths of an inch thick!* Each consisted of three pieces, bent, jointed, and fastened, as shown in the margin [of his journal]. The large openings were for the legs, the smaller for the wrists. A screw bolt drew the straight parts close together. . . . The distance from joint to joint was two feet.

Such are the tortures that slaves privately endure in the cellars, garrets, and outhouses of their masters. T_____, a native merchant, says another common punishment is to enclose the legs in wooden shackles or stocks. Some owners fasten their slaves' hands in similar devices, and others retain relics of the old thumbscrews to lock those members together. In the northern provinces, he says, the slaves are much worse used than in Rio; that it is no uncommon thing to tie their hands and feet together, hoist them off the ground, and then "beat them as near to death as possible." A heavy log fastened by a chain to the neck or leg of a slave who has absconded, or who is supposed to be inclined to run away, is a usual punishment and precaution. He is compelled to labor with it, laying it on the ground when at work, and bearing it under his arm or on his shoulder when he moves.

I observed one day a slave wearing a collar, the largest and roughest of hundreds I have seen. . . . Of inch-round iron, with a hinge in the middle, made by bending the metal of its full size into loops, the open ends flattened and connected by a half-inch rivet. The upright bar terminated in a *death's head*, which reached above that of the wearer, and to it another piece, in the form of the letter S, was welded. The joint galled him, for he kept gathering portions of his canvas shirt under it. Rest or sleep would seem impossible.

A Bahian planter, the brother of an ex-councilor, dined with us one day and spoke with much freedom on slavery. Like most men, he thinks the land can never be cultivated in the northern provinces by whites. The city slaves of Bahia, he said, are principally Minas (from El Mina on the West African coast). Shrewd and intelligent, they preserve their own language, and by that means, organize clubs and nurture schemes of revolution that their brethren of Pernambuco have repeatedly attempted to carry out. Some write Arabic fluently and are vastly superior to most of their masters. In the interior, he remarked, the slaves are badly fed, worse clothed, and worked so hard that the

Feitors corrigeant des negres. Illustration by Jean-Baptiste Debret. This image provoked a scandal in the Brazilian Historical and Geographical Institute because it portrayed a harsh image of the institution and implied that this treatment was sanctioned by the state. Courtesy of the John Carter Brown Library at Brown University.

average duration of their lives [after enslavement] does not exceed six years. In some districts it reaches eight, while the number that see ten years after leaving Africa is small indeed. Deceptions are perpetrated on foreign agents of the slavery commissions. These [agents] visit the *engenhos* once or twice a year. The planters, informed when they set out, have their slaves decently garbed and *well oiled*, to make them look supple and in good condition. On a late visit, the examiners were so highly gratified that one left and wrote home a flattering account of the treatment of the helots. The other continued his inquiries, came to a *fazenda* where he was not looked for, and there beheld what he did not expect—a black slave about to be *boiled to death* for some act of insubordination. His owner had invited, according to custom in such cases, neighboring proprietors to witness the tragedy.

From the little I have seen, I should suppose the country slaves are the worst off. Every morning, while nature was enshrouded in the blackness of darkness, I heard them driving wagons through the thick mist, and as late as ten at night they were shouting at the oxen as the jolting and groaning wheels rolled by. (This was, however, in the busiest season.) I often wondered how they found their way over the horrid roads, how their naked feet and limbs escaped unharmed, and how they then worked in the fields, unless the pupils [of their eyes] had the expansile and contractile powers of night animals.

On large estates, a few days' rest are given them every three or four weeks during the sugar season, but on smaller ones, where owners commonly have difficulty in keeping out of debt, they fare badly and are worked to death. Staggering into their huts, or dropping where their labors end, hardly do their aching bones allow the angel of sleep to drive away the memory of their sorrows, than two demons, lurking in the bell and lash, awaken them to fresh tortures. To say these poor creatures are better off than when ranging their native lands is an assertion [so false] that language lacks the power justly to describe. It may be true, if the life of an omnibus hack is better than that of a wild horse of Texas. I would rather, a thousand times [over], be a sheep, pig, or ox, [and] have freedom, food, and rest for a season, and then be knocked on the head, than be a serf on some plantations. I say *some*, because there are in Brazil, as in other lands, humane planters.

Suicides continually occur, and owners wonder [why this is so]. The high-souled Minas, both men and women, are given to self-destruction. Rather than endure life on the terms it is offered, many of them end it. Then they that bought them grind their teeth and curse them, hurl imprecations after their flying spirits, and execrate the saints that let them go. If individuals are ever justified in using the power that heaven has placed in their hands to terminate at once their earthly existence, it must be these. Those who blame them for putting the only barrier between them and oppression could not endure half their woes. And how characteristic of human frailties! Here are slave dealers who weep over the legendary sufferings as [if they are] saints and laugh at [far] worse tortures they themselves inflict; who shudder at the names of old persecutors and dream not of the armies of martyrs they make yearly; who cry over Protestants as sinners doomed to perdition and smile in anticipation of their own reception in the realms above. . . .

The Praieira Revolution Manifesto to the World

Antônio Borges da Fonseca

Of the numerous revolts that broke out during the imperial period—including the Cabanagem in Pará, the Farroupilha in Rio Grande do Sul, and the Sabinada in Bahia—the Praieira in Pernambuco was the last. It took place nine years after young Pedro II assumed the throne, as conservative politicians in Rio who blamed the instability of the Regency years on liberal reforms worked to reassert the primacy of the central government. Named after the rebellious liberals whose party newspaper was published on the Rua da Praia, or Beach Street, in the city of Recife, the Praieira Revolution was a liberal, federalist revolt that lasted from 1848 to 1850.

Conflicts between liberal and conservative political elites in Pernambuco marked the 1840s, but the spark for revolt came in 1848, when conservative senators rejected the nomination of the liberal candidate Antônio Pinto Chichorro da Gama to a seat in the National Senate. Election to this important position, a lifelong appointment, was a two-step process, in which a very narrow pool of possible voters chose three candidates for the position, and the emperor then appointed one of the three. But in this case, when the emperor chose Chichorro da Gama from the names on the list, conservatives in the Senate blocked his appointment, declaring the election in Pernambuco invalid due to irregularities. They thereby maintained conservative dominance of the Senate. For political liberals in Pernambuco, the act was unbearable. They soon began to arm themselves and to seek popular support, in part by criticizing conservatives' connections to Portuguese residents of Brazil, appealing to and stoking nationalistic resentment against the Portuguese. Thus while the uprising began within the political elite, it soon spread to different sectors of the population and tapped into anti-Portuguese sentiments, especially against Portuguese merchants and retailers. It also led to growing expressions of dissatisfaction from those who were unhappy with the lack of political autonomy granted to the provinces, the moderating power of the monarchy, and the centralization of decision making in Rio de Janeiro. As the revolution grew, the praieiros managed to take the city of Olinda but were defeated in early 1850. Many of the leaders were imprisoned and sentenced, but granted amnesty the following year.

Below are the principal items listed in a document produced by some of the most radical praieiros, including its author, Antônio Borges da Fonseca. This "Manifesto ao Mundo" (Manifesto to the world), inspired by the 1848 French Revolution, was issued on January 1, 1849.

—Free and universal suffrage for the Brazilian people;
—Complete and absolute freedom to communicate one's thoughts in the press;
—Guaranteed work for Brazilian citizens;
—Retail trade limited to Brazilian citizens;
—Complete and effective independence of the governing powers;
—An end to the [monarch's] moderating power and of the right to bestow [titles];
—A new federal organizational structure;
—Complete reform of judiciary power so as to guarantee the individual rights of citizens;
—An end to the current system of military recruitment;
—Expulsion of the Portuguese.

Translated by Molly Quinn

Portraits: José Bonifácio de Andrada e Silva

Lilia Moritz Schwarcz

At first glance, it might seem surprising that José Bonifácio de Andrada e Silva (1763–1838) would become the Patriarch of Independence, as he is now widely known in Brazil. Although born in Santos, São Paulo, as a member of the wealthy and politically active Andrada family, he spent the bulk of his adulthood—from age twenty to fifty-six—in Europe. Like other elite men of his generation, he originally went to Portugal to attend the University of Coimbra. There he studied law and the natural sciences, eventually distinguishing himself as a mineralogist. But rather than returning to Brazil upon graduation, he remained in Europe, traveling extensively, conducting scientific research, and publishing his results in French and English journals. Eventually he became a professor of mineralogy at the University of Coimbra and was named a member and, later, secretary of the prestigious Lisbon Academy of Sciences. During his years in Portugal, Bonifácio joined a group of scholars led by Rodrigo de Sousa Coutinho, the count of Linhares, that sought to modernize the Portuguese state and solve the economic and political crises facing the country. These intellectuals considered themselves heirs of the political enlightenment of the marquis of Pombal. While the group included a number of Brazilians, they did not advocate separation or independence. In fact, the essays that Bonifácio wrote during this period highlight his view that Brazil was an integral part of the Portuguese Empire.

Once Bonifácio returned to Brazil in 1819, he became deeply involved in Brazilian political life and soon showed himself to be a strongly opinionated and influential figure. He joined a group of scholars linked to the Royal Palace in Rio de Janeiro often referred to as a hard-core group surrounding the emperor. Conservative and pragmatic, they were given to compromise, while supporting traditional institutions and the preservation of order. Yet Bonifácio at times broke with them, such as in his argument for the abolition of the slave trade (see "On Slavery" in this part).

Following the 1820 Porto Revolution, an uprising of liberals in Portugal who demanded a constitutional monarchy, Bonifácio was named vice president of the provisional junta of São Paulo. When São Paulo sent delegates to Lisbon in 1822 to draft and approve a new constitution, he was influential in

José Bonifácio de Andrada e Silva (1763–1838) by Sébastien Auguste Sisson. From *Livro Galeria dos Brasileiros Ilustres*, vol. 1, Coleção Brasil 500 anos (Brasília: Senado Federal, 1999).

designing instructions for them to follow, while his brother was one of those selected. The delegates intended to discuss the abolition of slavery and the religious education of indigenous peoples (two themes for which Bonifácio was well known). They also planned to propose that the seat of the monarchy alternate between Brazil and Portugal, that Brazil continue as a co-kingdom with Portugal, and that both kingdoms have an equal number of representatives in the constitution-drafting process. As these proposals suggest, at first, the liberal colonial elite, including Bonifácio, welcomed the Porto Revolution, and saw it not only as a movement aimed at limiting the absolutist power of King João VI, but also as an initiative that might guarantee the autonomy that Brazil had won when the royal family moved to Rio de Janeiro. In this context, the idea of independence was not seriously considered.

As the revolution unfolded in Portugal, however, it soon became clear that the Crown sought to reestablish the old order in which the empire was one kingdom with two divisions—European and American—rather than two kingdoms under one monarch. While the Porto Revolution had a liberal program for Portugal, its advocates sought the tacit recolonization of Brazil. Thus, the instructions of the São Paulo delegates proved useless. Even before the Brazilian representatives arrived, the National Assembly met and endorsed measures to subordinate all local governments to Lisbon, and to revoke commercial treaties with Great Britain that had benefited Brazilian producers.

It was in this context that Bonifácio spearheaded a push by sectors of the national elite to suspend the recolonizing aims of the court in Lisbon and soon thereafter to promote independence. In January 1822, Prince Regent Pedro invited him to become a minister, and Bonifácio became convinced that a unified co-kingdom was unsustainable. In this regard, the path to independence and Bonifácio's own position on the matter were not premeditated and conscious, but processes that were improvised as events unfolded.

Following independence, Bonifácio endeavored to transform Brazil into a European country in the Americas. He was part of the first group of Brazilian intellectuals to produce literature about their homeland, which stopped being considered Portuguese-Brazilian and became instead national. As the literary scholar Antonio Candido has argued, for this generation of educated men such writing was understood as a kind of mission, one in which their work could create a "civilizing" model—celebrating the uniqueness of Brazil's tropical kingdom, yet also trumpeting the characteristics it shared with Europe.[1]

Bonifácio also continued to advocate for a variety of reforms designed to create what he called a more homogenous nation and to combat what he considered to be colonial vices and laziness that marked the country. Thus he pressed for the end of slavery, the creation of some social support mechanisms for the disadvantaged, and efforts to integrate indigenous people into the dominant society. In his opinion, miscegenation was the only way to create a Brazilian race capable of bringing not just homogeneity but also a common culture to Brazil's citizens. In his texts, he repeatedly directed criticism at the "terrible consequences of the persistence of slavery in the national territory," not only for the enslaved but, above all, for the white elite.[2] Slavery, according to Bonifácio, led to violence and ignorance, and impeded citizenship and modernity: "Without individual liberty, there can neither be civilization nor great wealth; there can be no morality or justice, and without these virtues there can be no pride, strength, or force within a nation."[3]

In his "Notes on *Sesmarias* [colonial land grants]," he also defended a kind of agrarian reform as a way of achieving modernity. In this essay, he laid out a plan that called for the sale of unproductive lands to the government for settlement by indigenous peoples, mulattoes, freed blacks, and European immigrants.[4] He also used his position as a scientist to argue against deforestation and to suggest its implications for Brazil.

Yet politically Bonifácio's career was as short as it was spectacular. In March 1823, he took a seat as a representative from São Paulo in the Constituent Assembly charged with writing a constitution for Brazil. But his attempts to give the constitution a liberal content proved fruitless after Pedro I dissolved the assembly. What's more, Pedro had him arrested and deported to

France. Indeed, Bonifácio wrote a substantial number of his political texts in Bordeaux and Paris.

With Pedro's permission, Bonifácio returned to Brazil in 1829. Two years later he briefly returned to Brazilian politics when he became a representative in the national Parliament and, later that same year, assumed the responsibility of tutoring young Pedro II following the abdication of his father, Pedro I. He remained in these positions only briefly, however; liberals forced him out of his seat in the Parliament and then deposed him from his tutoring duties in 1832. Charged with treason for allegedly trying to restore Pedro I to the throne, he was acquitted in 1835, but the trial ended his career in politics.

Bonifácio's political life was marked by the ambiguities of a thinker who was both conservative and innovative. On a continent where nearly all the neighboring countries had republican governments, Bonifácio fought for a constitutional monarchy, the only kind of regime, in his opinion, that would bring civilization to Brazilians. He also believed that only the monarchy and the symbolic figure of the emperor could guarantee the constitution and allow Brazil to avoid the fragmentation that plagued the rest of South America. Whereas in other parts of the Americas federalist and republican ideas prevailed, Bonifácio fought for unity, centralization, and monarchy.

While Bonifácio was innovative in some of his social plans, he vehemently held that control over these processes should remain in the hands of the "government of the wise," an educated elite and, above all, a constitutional monarchy organized around the Parliament. Only a strong, modern state would have the capacity to manage conflicts, prepare for the gradual emancipation of slaves, and mediate relations between masters and slaves.

The elite citizen that Bonifácio idealized and imagined in his texts, however, did not exist, and his frustration with his fellow citizens soon became evident: "Brazilians are ignorant but vain; before independence, not only did they not respect Portugal, but today they actually consider themselves better than the Portuguese. . . . Brazilians laze around as priests or swindlers, because those are the lifestyles that do not require work."[5] This critique captures the dominant view of many elites and intellectuals during the early years of the empire, who imagined a beneficent constitutional monarchy yet benefited from the existing structure of concentrated landholdings, acknowledged the state's and the elite's need for slavery, and disdained the masses. They proposed some changes but were often opposed by other members of the elite and limited by the conservative nature of the monarchy, which ultimately held power over emancipation and other reforms.

The implementation of Bonifácio's ideals was also limited by his own personality. He hoped to act as a guide for the elite citizen, but he constantly quarreled with the elites (as well as the royal family). In many ways Bonifácio was always an outsider. His political career was brief, and his writings only made a significant impact years later, when the fight over slavery and abolition in Brazil became unavoidable.

Notes

1. Antonio Candido, *Formação da literatura brasileira*, vol. 1 (São Paulo: Martins, 1957), 26–29.
2. José Bonifácio, "Representação à assembléia geral constituinte e legislativa do Império do Brasil sobre a escravatura," in Miriam Dolhnikoff, *José Bonifácio de Andrada e Silva* (São Paulo: Companhia das Letras, 1998), 63.
3. Bonifácio, "Representação à assembléia geral constituinte," 82.
4. Bonifácio, "Representação à assembléia geral constituinte," 152–54.
5. José Bonifácio de Andrada e Silva, "Apontamentos autobiográficos de José Bonifácio sobre corografia, história, etnografia, etc. do Brasil" (Coleção José Bonifácio, Museu Paulista, São Paulo), I.1 I-2-1 272.

VI

Coffee, the Empire, and Abolition, 1851–1888

Coffee was so important in Brazil in the late nineteenth century that it became known as black gold. From the 1850s to the 1880s, the Paraíba Valley in the province of Rio de Janeiro produced more coffee than any other place in the world, and was only supplanted by its own neighbor, western São Paulo, in the 1880s. The economic windfall that accompanied the coffee boom was fundamental to the economic and political stability of the reign of Pedro II from 1840 to 1889 and to the preservation of legal slavery until 1888. The monarchy increased its investments in the country's infrastructure, while the economic possibilities brought by coffee encouraged the introduction of new technologies. New roads, railroads, and telegraph lines, as well as the use of steamships in both coastal and transatlantic travel, improved transportation and communications (at least in those regions with a dynamic agro-export economy), and laid the groundwork for Brazil's uneven development. The imperial government oversaw a massive urban renewal project for the imperial capital of Rio de Janeiro with better public lighting and a new sewage and water system, while entrepreneurs such as Irineu Evangelista de Souza, the later viscount of Mauá, became prominent backers of infrastructural development.

Culturally, Pedro II promoted policies that encouraged patriotic sentiments toward the nation and offered important financial and symbolic support to young cultural institutions like the Academy of Fine Arts (est. 1826), the Brazilian Historical and Geographic Institute (est. 1838), and the public high school Colégio Pedro II (est. 1837), among many other projects. During this period, artists and writers developed a romantic movement later termed Indianism, in which the imaginary figure of the native Brazilian—above all of the idealized Tupi Indian—became a prominent theme in literature, painting, poetry, and music, even while the fate of contemporary indigenous populations was often ignored. In the symbolic world of the arts, noble, pure, and courageous Indians committed valiant acts of heroism but died in the process, sacrificing themselves so that the nascent Brazilian nation could live on.

The political stability that the monarchy generally enjoyed was shaken,

D. Pedro II antes da maioridade by Félix Taunay, 1837. Young Dom Pedro II (1825–1891) soon after assuming the throne as emperor of Brazil.

Desfile militar em 1° de março de 1870, depois da vitória sobre a Guerra do Paraguai by Angelo Agostini. Celebration of the victory of the Paraguayan War in 1870.

De volta do paraguai by Angelo Agostini, 1870. Soldiers who fought valiantly in the war returned to the daily reality of slavery.

however, by the Paraguayan War (1864–70), also known as the War of the Triple Alliance, when Argentina, Brazil, and Uruguay joined forces against Paraguay in a contest over the strategic control of the Plata River. Despite this seeming imbalance, the conflict turned out to be long and brutally destructive, leading to an enormous loss of life. An estimated 60 percent of the Paraguayan population died as a result of combat, diseases, and food shortages. Among its allies, the Brazilian troops suffered the greatest number of casualties, with an estimated fifty thousand deaths. If the onset of the war represented the height of support for the empire, and people initially responded enthusiastically to patriotic appeals for military volunteers, as the conflict dragged on they began to openly criticize its handling. Indeed, the war exposed Brazil's military weakness and its reliance on unprofessional militias organized by local and regional political elites and landowners. To fill the need for soldiers, slaves were promised their freedom if they would fight, and their participation contributed to growing popular sentiment in favor of abolition. The war's end marked the beginning of the empire's decline. In the 1870s, a variety of diverse groups that opposed the empire began to form: the Republican Party, the abolitionist movement, and sectors of the military that had become somewhat more autonomous after the end of the Paraguayan War.

This lithograph by Victor Frond titled *The countryside kitchen* (*A cozinha na Roça*) and originally published in a French photo album, *Brazil Pittoresco* (Picturesque Brazil), portrayed a harsh but pacific life for Brazilian slaves.

Coffee replicated and reinforced some of the economic and social characteristics that had long marked Brazil, such as the importance of large agricultural estates worked by slave labor. Thus, it solidified a conservative elite that was committed to the maintenance of this system, and an internal slave trade led to a large movement of slaves from northern Brazil to the south. The landholding class was instrumental in preserving the international slave trade until 1850 and the legality of slave labor until 1888. Of course, enslaved Africans and their descendants did not merely act as spectators of this process. Through everyday forms of resistance, flight, or individual or collective rebellions, mutinies, and/or assaults on the various overseers of this system, they expressed their opposition to the institution. The enslaved and their families also crafted elaborate strategies to gain freedom through manumission. These efforts only grew in the final years of slavery. For example, *quilombos* (runaway slave communities), which had been a vehicle for fleeing slavery since the sixteenth century, expanded in number in these years, while abolition societies, many times led by free people of color, proliferated. By the late 1880s, abolitionists could count as one of their supporters Princess Isabel, heir to Dom Pedro II, who was said to deliberately pin camellias to her dress when in public, as the flower was a known symbol of the abolition movement.

Notwithstanding the persistence of slavery within Brazil, the desire to seek new forms of labor led to early efforts to bring foreign workers and immigrants to Brazil. Even after independence, Portuguese emigrants had continued to settle in Brazil, and in the early years of the empire modest efforts to encourage other European immigrants had led to the establishment of a few German-speaking communities in southern Brazil. But the number of immigrants was quite small. After the international slave trade ended in 1850, efforts began anew. The imperial government signed labor contracts for temporary Chinese workers in the 1850s, inspired in part by the role of Chinese laborers in expanding the economies of Cuba and Peru, but both these and similar private initiatives led to vigorous racist polemics about the future of Brazilian civilization and, eventually, a ban in 1890 on the entry of any Asian or African person without prior congressional approval. European immigrants continued to be seen as desirable, and some planters and government officials sought ways of encouraging their arrival. Nonetheless, the flow of European immigrants continued to be small in this period, in large part because potential immigrants did not want to compete with slave labor.

Internationally, the political and cultural leaders of the Brazilian empire sought to present Brazil as a civilized nation imbued with Western culture. They also took pains to distinguish it from other Latin American republics that struggled with political instability in the wake of independence, pointing to the fact that Brazil's unparalleled political stability was guaranteed by a monarch related to the noble families of Europe. Yet a stubborn barrier for Brazilian elites who wanted to achieve equal footing with the European countries they so admired was the continuation of slavery. The institution was so deeply rooted in the fabric of Brazilian society that newspaper announcements of the rental, pawning, sale, and insurance of slaves abounded, and owners were not ashamed to publish advertisements looking for runaway slaves that relied on descriptions of scars they carried from wounds obtained in the course of forced labor or inflicted on them as punishment for displeasing their masters. Closely intertwined in almost every aspect of Brazilian political, social, and economic life, the slave trade and slavery created fortunes, reinforced racial hierarchies, and shored up the political power of those who benefited from the system of forced labor. Moreover, slaveholding was common even among more modest segments of Brazilian society, not just among the elites. Thus it was difficult to maintain the image of Brazil as a cultured and civilized nation ruled over by an enlightened monarchy when slavery remained the mainstay of the economy.

As the abolition movement picked up steam and it became clear that there was formidable opposition to slavery, elites delayed the inevitable by supporting a policy of gradual emancipation, in which a series of laws gradually limited, but did not abolish, slavery. For example, after nearly two decades of campaigns to free the newborn children of slave women, Brazilian legislators passed the Law of the Free Womb in 1871, guaranteeing freedom to those born after the law's passage (thenceforth called *ingênuos*, or freeborns), but with restricting stipulations until they turned twenty-one (see "Law of the Free Womb" later in this part). The Sexagenarian Law was passed in 1885 and freed all slaves over the age of sixty, but this meant emancipation only for those who were too weak to work anyway. While proponents of this kind of legislation proclaimed that these measures signified the end of the system, in fact, they worked to sustain it for as long as possible.

Linked as they were, the monarchy and slavery had a mutual fate. On May 13, 1888, parliament passed a brief law ending the institution of forced captivity in Brazil, and Princess Isabel, acting as princess regent while Dom Pedro II was in Europe, signed it (see "Abolition Decree" later in this part). Notwithstanding slave owners' demands that abolition include remuneration for the loss of their property, the law made no such provision. Nor did it provide financial or other support for freed slaves.

Just eighteen months later, on November 15, 1889, the monarchy collapsed. The republican regime began with new models of citizenship, of social inclusion and exclusion, while a sector of the population that had fought for a new political and social situation now employed concepts of freedom and liberty as they tried to take advantage of these changing circumstances. However, as in other postemancipation societies, new forms of racial hierarchy quickly developed. Promises of equality and freedom were challenged by racial theories, many imported from Europe, that defended such hierarchies through biology and natural law. While the new regime arrived with novel ideas about democracy and republicanism, it continued to maintain policies of social exclusion for large portions of the population.

Memoirs of a Settler in Brazil

Thomas Davatz

As coffee planters began exploring new sources of labor and looked to possible Euro-pean immigration, some devised a system of sharecropping that proved very beneficial to them. In exchange for transportation to Brazil and the right to farm a certain area or tend a certain number of coffee trees, European immigrants signed contracts prom-ising to divide their harvests with their employer and to pay back all debts, starting with the cost of their passage from their home country. They also had to pay for basic tools and seeds needed to get started. Their debts quickly extended to goods acquired at the plantation store (usually at inflated prices) and a host of other services, such as schooling and health care.

Among the thousands of immigrants who were seduced by the possibilities of a new life in Brazil was Thomas Davatz (1815–1888), a relatively well-educated schoolmaster from the village of Fanas in the canton of Graubünden, Switzerland. He and his wife and children became colonos, or sharecroppers, on the Ibicaba coffee plantation owned by Senator Nicolau Pereira de Campos Vergueiro. But Davatz quickly became disillusioned with the poor working conditions and the crushing debt that impeded them in improving or leaving their situation. Davatz ended up leading a settler revolt against Vergueiro in 1856. While no injuries were reported, the repercussions were im-mense. A Brazilian inspector and the Swiss consul both went to Ibicaba to investigate conditions there. Consular authorities paid to return Davatz to his native country, where he wrote an account of his experiences as a cautionary tale for other potential immigrants. His book, The Treatment of the Settlers in the Province of São Paulo and their Uprising Against the Oppressors: A Cry for Mercy and Help from the Authorities and the Philanthropists of those Countries and States where the Colonos Reside, *suggests the continued importance of the slave system in both real and symbolic ways. For example, it describes the colonos as "the property of the Vergueiro Company . . . simple merchandise, or slaves." Davatz's book was translated into Portuguese and published in Brazil for the first time in 1951 under the title* Memories of a Settler, *by the renowned historian Sérgio Buarque de Holanda.*

It is a notorious fact that some years ago the immigrant question became a vital problem for the poor populations of many European countries. Nu-merous people included in this category share the opinion that in current circumstances—when everything seems to conspire to aggrandize the powerful and belittle the existence of the humble—it is already impossible for them to remain in their old fatherland; they do not lack reasons that entice them [to leave]. Many dared to take a decisive step, seeking better days in distant lands overseas. The result is that a widespread opinion, justifiable to some extent, ultimately evaporated like a dream.

Beautiful descriptions; enticing accounts of countries that the imagination beheld; portraits painted in a partial and inexact way, in which reality is sometimes deliberately falsified; fascinating and seductive letters or reports from friends and relatives—the efficacy of all these aspects of propaganda and, above all, a relentless activity of the emigration agents, more committed to fill their own pockets than to alleviate the condition of the poor . . . —all this contributes to immigration reaching a truly sickening degree and has turned into a legitimate fever that has already contaminated many people. Just as with a physical fever that dissipates with tranquil reflection and clear reason, a similar thing seems to occur with fevers of immigration. People are contaminated by dreams of an ideal country while they are asleep and when they are awake, during work and during rest. They cling to leaflets and brochures that deal with their favorite theme, relying on them completely (as a rule, however, they stoke their aspirations). At the same time, however, they mostly disregard the warnings and advice of wise men and, as soon as an opportunity offers itself, they often decide to carry out their plans until the day when—how many times!—nothing but confessing the sad mistake remains. "I was cheated!" or: "This time I am lost!" "I have to endure the trick and put my heart into it!" "I bitterly regret the day on which I decided to embark, but now I must bear everything in silence. So-and-so frequently warned me, but it is too late to confess my error to him!" I do not make up these statements; I limit myself to only reproducing that which, unfortunately, I have heard many times with my own ears.

I myself was a victim of the emigration fever. For a long time I contemplated going to the United States of North America, but without doing so. Eventually certain circumstances allowed me to settle in the Brazilian province of São Paulo. In the company of numerous other emigrants I embarked for this land in the spring of 1855, but it did not take me long to arrive at the same conclusion reached by many others who expressed their pain in the laments I've described.

"This time I am lost!" The saddest day is when we discover this, when we perceive that a new slavery subjugates us and that this slavery is more difficult to escape than the traditional one, which for a long time yoked the black Africans. . . . Thanks to the Lord we are finally free, my family and me. But there are many people from Switzerland, many German states, Holland, etc., who still find themselves there. In leaving these people, a painful farewell in many aspects, I promised them firmly that I would . . . paint an accurate portrait of the situation and the condition of those settlers.

Serving both this pledge and my major objective, which is to weigh in with all my strength so that the poor settlers lost over there (who are so dear to me today after we have suffered together and because of loyal assistance that they gave me for my efforts), can save themselves from the deplorable conditions that they are in. Another objective of greater importance is to warn against the folly of emigration and calm the fever of immigration, even when it is directed to other centers (North America, Australia, etc.), so as to spare many people from bitter disappointments. . . .

In order to successfully achieve similar objectives, I intend to describe the treatment of emigrants in the colonies in the province of São Paulo, Brazil, showing how they were dealt with soon after their arrival in Santos, and then how they were given housing, food, work, etc. In sum, I have tried to offer a portrait of the lives of the settlers. Then I will try to show how to remedy the situation. It is not possible, however, to obtain a clear vision of the treatment of settlers without a notion of the aspects, conditions, customs, and practices of this land which was the setting of my narratives, because they are considerably different from what we know in Switzerland and in Germany. . . .

Translated by Erika Manouselis

O Guarani

José de Alencar

*No one better represents the mid-nineteenth-century Brazilian literary movement
known as Indianism than José Martiniano de Alencar (1829–1877). Born in the northeastern city of Fortaleza, Ceará, he earned a law degree but worked as a journalist for
the* Correio Mercantil *and the* Diário do Rio de Janeiro. *Alencar was also a politician, speaker, critic, writer, debater, novelist, and playwright. His works include
books that focused on urban, regional, and historical topics. However, today he is
most known for his three novels with indigenous themes:* Iracema *(1865),* Ubirajara
(1874), and O Guarani *(1857).*

O Guarani *takes place in the early 1600s and portrays a struggle between good
and bad whites, and more importantly between good and bad Indians. In the novel,
the Portuguese nobleman Dom Antônio de Mariz lives in a fortress-like castle with his
wife Dona Lauriana, his son Diogo, his beautiful (and blonde) daughter Cecília, and
a character he refers to as his niece Isabel, who is in fact his daughter with an Indian
woman. In the passage below, the author describes Cecília's three suitors: Loredano,
a strong, handsome, and passionate Italian, who had abandoned his vocation as a
priest and lusts after Cecília; Álvaro, a young man whose fondness for Cecília is not
reciprocated; and Peri, an indigenous Guarani leader who has a platonic and idealized love for Cecília. The story is one of impossible love, where Peri embodies the trope
of Rousseau's noble savage: good, free, and incorruptible. However, there is a happy
ending to Alencar's romantic tale, as Cecília and Peri promise their love for each other
and sail off together into the horizon on a raft made from a palm tree.*

Together with Iracema, O Guarani *is among a collection of uniquely Brazilian
novels that reflect a romantic fascination with an idealized image of the country's
indigenous past that also distracted from the actual violence being committed against
indigenous peoples in the nineteenth century.*

O Guarani *was made into an opera by the Brazilian-born composer Carlos Gomes
and debuted before Emperor Pedro II at the Scala Theater in Milan on March 18, 1870.
It was performed throughout Europe and had its Brazilian debut in Rio de Janeiro on
December 2, the emperor's birthday. The opera was popular with the Brazilian monarchy, as it suggested an image of benign colonization giving rise to a noble empire.*

The window curtains closed; Cecília had gone to bed.

Near the innocent girl, asleep in the freedom of her pure and virgin soul, were watching three deep passions, were palpitating three very unlike hearts.

In Loredano, the adventurer of low extraction, this passion was an ardent desire, a thirst for enjoyment, a fever that burned his blood: moreover, the brutal instinct of his vigorous nature was heightened by the moral impossibility that his condition created; by the barrier that rose between him, a poor colonist, and the daughter of Dom Antônio de Mariz, a rich nobleman of rank and fame. To break down this barrier and equalize their positions, some extraordinary occurrence would be necessary; some event that should change completely the laws of society, at that time more rigid than today: there was demanded one of those situations in the presence of which individuals, whatever their rank, noble or pariah, are leveled, and descend or ascend to the condition of men. The adventurer knew this; perhaps his Italian penetration had already sounded the depth of that idea. At all events he hoped, and hoping watched his treasure with a zeal and constancy equal to every trial. The twenty days he had passed in Rio de Janeiro had been a real torment.

In Álvaro, a courteous and refined cavalier, the passion was a pure and noble affection, full of the pleasing timidity that perfumes the first flowers of the heart, and of the knightly enthusiasm that lent so much poetry to the loves of that time of faith and loyalty. To feel himself near Cecília, to see her and exchange a word, stammered with difficulty, both blushing without knowing why, and avoiding each other while desiring to meet, this was the whole history of that innocent affection which surrendered itself carelessly to the future, balancing on the wings of hope. Tonight Álvaro was about to take a step, which in his habitual timidity, he compared almost to a formal request of marriage; he had resolved to make the maiden accept in spite of herself the gift she had refused, by laying it on her window; he hoped that when she found it on the following day Cecília would pardon his boldness and keep his present.

In Peri the passion was a worship, a kind of fanatical idolatry, into which entered no thought of self; he loved Cecília, not to feel a pleasure or experience a satisfaction, but to dedicate himself wholly to her, to fulfill her slightest desire, to anticipate her very thoughts. Unlike the others, he was not there either from a restless jealousy or a ridiculous hope; he braved death solely to see whether Cecília was contented, happy, and joyous; whether she did not desire something that he could read on her countenance, and go in search of that same night, that very instant.

Thus love was so completely transformed into those organizations that it assumed three very different forms; one was a madness, the other a passion, the last a religion. Loredano desired; Álvaro loved; Peri adored. The adventurer would give his life to enjoy; the cavalier would brave death to deserve a look; the savage would kill himself, if need be, merely to make Cecília smile.

. . .

Some moments had passed since the window curtain was closed; only a dim and fading light reflected on the dark green foliage of the *oleo* tree that outlined the window. The Italian, who had his eyes fixed upon this reflection as upon a mirror where he saw all the images of his mad passion, suddenly started. In its light a moving shadow was depicted; a man was approaching the window.

Pale, with glowing eyes and clenched teeth, hanging over the precipice, he followed the slightest movements of the shadow. He saw an arm stretched toward the window, and the hand leave on the sill some object so small that its form was not discerned. By the wide sleeve of the doublet, or rather by instinct, the Italian divined that this arm belonged to Álvaro, and comprehended what the hand had laid in the window.

And he was not mistaken. Álvaro, steadying himself by one of the posts of the garden-fence, placed one foot on the inclined plane, pressed his body against the wall, and leaning forward succeeded in accomplishing his purpose. Then he returned, divided between fear at what he had done and hope that Cecília would pardon him.

No sooner did Loredano see the shadow disappear and hear the echoes of the young man's footsteps, than he smiled, and his eyes shone in the darkness like those of a wildcat. He drew his dagger and buried it in the wall, as far around the corner as his arm would reach. Then supporting himself by this frail prop, he was able to climb the inclined plane and approach the window; the least indecision or the slightest movement was enough to cause his foot to fail him, or if the poniard should move in the cement, to precipitate him headlong upon the rocks.

In the meantime, Peri, seated quietly on the branch of the *oleo* tree, and hidden by the foliage, witnessed without a movement the whole scene. As soon as Cecília closed her window curtains, the Indian had seen the two men standing on either hand and apparently waiting. He waited also, curious to know what was to occur; but resolved, if it were necessary, to hurl himself at one bound upon the one that should offer the least violence, and to fall with him from the top of the esplanade. He had recognized Álvaro and Loredano; for a long time he had known the cavalier's love for Cecília, but of the Italian he had never had the least suspicion.

What could these two men want? What came they to do there at that silent hour of the night? Álvaro's action explained part of the enigma; Loredano's was about to make plain the rest. For the Italian, who had approached the window, succeeded with an effort in pushing the object that Álvaro had left there off, over the precipice. This done, he returned in the same way, and retired enjoying the pleasure of that simple revenge, the result of which he foresaw.

Peri did not move. With his natural sagacity he had comprehended the love of the one and the jealousy of the other, and reached a conclusion that for him, with his savage understanding and fanatical adoration, was very simple. If Cecília thought this ought to be so, the rest mattered little to him; but if what he had seen caused her a shade of sadness and dimmed for a moment the luster of her blue eyes, then it was different. Quieted by this idea he sought his cabin, and slept dreaming that the moon sent him a ray of her white and satiny light to tell him that she was protecting her daughter on earth.

And in reality the moon was rising above the trees, and illuminating the front of the house. Then anyone approaching one of the windows at the end of the garden would have seen in the obscurity of the room a motionless figure. It was Isabel, watching pensively, wiping away from time to time a tear that trickled down her cheek.

She was thinking of her unhappy love, of the solitude of her soul, so bereft of pleasing recollections and bright hopes. All that evening had been a martyrdom to her; she had seen Álvaro talking with Cecília, and had divined almost his very words. Within a few moments she had seen the shadow of the young man crossing the esplanade, and knew that it was not on her account that he passed.

From time to time her lips moved, and some imperceptible words escaped, "If I could make up my mind!"

She took from her bosom a golden phial, under whose crystal lid was seen a lock of hair coiled in the narrow metal container. What was there in this phial so powerful as to justify that exclamation, and the brilliant look that lit up Isabel's black eyes? Could it be a secret, one of those terrible secrets that suddenly change the face of things, and make the past rise up to crush the present? Could it be some inestimable and fabulous treasure, whose seduction human nature has not power to resist? Could it be some weapon against which there is no possible defense except in a miracle of Providence? It was the fine dust of the *curare*, the terrible poison of the savages.

Translated by James W. Hawes

The U.S. Civil War and Slave Rebellions in Brazil

Francisco Primo de Souza Aguiar

At a time when bonded labor was coming under attack throughout the Atlantic world, the U.S. Civil War became an important reference point for both free and enslaved peoples within Brazil. Slaves learned about and discussed the conflict abroad, using their own channels of communication, including literate slaves with access to newspapers. News of the U.S. Civil War was especially accessible on the northern coast of Brazil, where both Union and Confederate warships routinely docked in search of fuel and provisions. In this letter, the president (governor) of the maritime province of Maranhão reports on the repression of a rebellion that took place in sugar and cotton plantations in the county of Anajatuba in 1861. Led by a slave called Agostinho, several Anajatuba slaves proclaimed themselves free in anticipation of armed support from American troops, whom they presumed to be abolitionists.

In a letter dated the second day of the current month, which was sent by the police chief, he informs me of having ordered the arrest of several slaves and the punishment, by order of his master, of the slave of Cristóvão Vieira called Agostinho, who confirmed having declared to his peers that they were all free because he had heard so from several blacks in this Capital, and that they only waited for the warship to disembark its troops.

Such an idea originates from the entrance into this port of two warships, one of the United States of America and another from the states that seek to become a separate confederation.

According to this police authority's opinion, they have no organized plan and only hope for their freedom. Despite that, judging it to be an issue of concern, I ordered the deployment of more provincial troops there.

It is my duty to let Your Excellency know all this, while assuring Your Excellency that I will do whatever I can to neutralize any plan that the matter concerning the United States of America might create here among the slaves.

Translated by Isadora Mota

The Slave Ship

Antônio Frederico de Castro Alves

Just twenty-four years old when he died of tuberculosis in Salvador on July 6, 1871, Antônio Frederico de Castro Alves had already made a name for himself as a poet and an abolitionist. Known as the Poet of the Slaves for his works that condemned slavery, Castro Alves was born in Curralinho, Bahia, on March 14, 1847, to a prominent family. He attended various law schools during this period of fierce debates about abolition but ultimately eschewed the legal treatise in favor of other forms of writing to promote abolition and the republican cause. Alves instead became a writer of poetry and plays that took on social topics. He formed part of a romantic literary movement called Condorism, in which the writers imagined viewing their topics from above, like the sharp-eyed Andean condor, and used this perspective to educate others. His dynamic public speaking style furthered the popularity of his writings.

"The Slave Ship" is one of Castro Alves's most famous poems; it was often recited at public events organized by abolitionists in which slaves were granted their freedom. In the poem, an epic account of the African slave trade, he treats his subject with enormous emotional intensity. His condor-like gaze moves from the beauty of the ocean to the humanity of the ships' crews, until, finally, it gazes below deck at the horrors of the ships' holds.

The Slave Ship

I.
We're on the high sea . . . Mad in space
The moonlight plays—a golden butterfly;
And the waves run behind it . . . and tire
Like the unsettled babble of infants.

We're on the high sea . . . From the firmament
The stars jump like a golden froth . . .

I.
'Stamos em pleno mar . . . Doudo no espaço
Brinca o luar—dourada borboleta;
E as vagas após ele correm . . . cansam
Como turba de infantes inquieta.

'Stamos em pleno mar . . . Do firmamento
Os astros saltam como espumas de ouro . . .

The sea, in return, sparks its ardent
glow,—
Constellations of liquid treasure.

We're on the high sea . . . Two infini-
ties, over there,
Join together in a mad embrace,
Blue, golden, placid, sublime . . .
Which of the two is the sky? Which
the ocean? . . .

We're on the high sea . . . Unfurling
the sails
To the warm gasp of the sea's breezes,
The sailing brig runs on the surface
of the sea,
Like the swallows that skim the
waves . . .

Where does it come from? Where
does it go?
Who knows the path of errant
ships
When the space is so vast?
In this Sahara the stallions raise dust,
Gallop, fly, but don't leave a trace.

Happy is the one who, at this
moment,
Can feel the majesty of this scene!
Below—the sea. Above—the heavens
. . .
And in both sea and sky—immensity!

Oh what sweet harmony the breeze
brings to me!
What soft music sounds in the
distance!
My God! How sublime is the ardent
song
On the endless waves, floating
aimlessly!

Men of the sea! Oh humble sailors,
Tanned by the sun of the four worlds!

O mar em troca acende as
ardentias,—
Constelações do líquido tesouro.

'Stamos em pleno mar . . . Dois
infinitos
Ali se estreitam num abraço insano,
Azuis, dourados, plácidos, sublimes . . .
Qual dos dous é o céu? qual o oceano?
. . .

'Stamos em pleno mar . . . Abrindo as
velas
Ao quente arfar das virações marinhas,
Veleiro brigue corre à flor dos
mares,
Como roçam na vaga as
andorinhas . . .

Donde vem? onde vai? Das naus
errantes
Quem sabe o rumo se é tão grande o
espaço?
Neste saara os corcéis o pó levantam,
Galopam, voam, mas não deixam
traço.

Bem feliz quem ali pode nest'
hora
Sentir deste painel a majestade!
Embaixo—o mar em cima—o firma-
mento . . .
E no mar e no céu—a imensidade!

Oh! que doce harmonia traz-me a
brisa!
Que música suave ao longe
soa!
Meu Deus! Como é sublime um canto
ardente
Pelas vagas sem fim boiando
à toa!

Homens do mar! Ó rudes marinheiros,
Tostados pelo sol dos quatro mundos!

Children that the tempest has rocked
In the cradle of these deep seas!

Wait! Wait! Leave me to drink
This savage, free poetry.
Orchestra—it is the sea, that roars by
   the prow,
And the wind that whistles among
   the lines . . .

Why do you flee so, nimble boat?
Why do you flee from the frightened
   poet?
Oh how I wish to accompany your
   wake
Which in the sea looks—like a mad
   comet!

Albatross! Albatross! Eagle of the
   ocean,
You who sleep among the gauze of
   the clouds,
Ruffle your feathers, Leviathan of
   space,
Albatross! Albatross! Give me your
   wings.

II.
What does the navigator care for the
   cradle,
Where are you son, where is your
   home?
He loves the cadence of the verse
That the old sea teaches him!
Sing! That death is divine!
Shift the brig windward
Like a speedy dolphin.
Trapped on the mizzen mast
The melancholy flag waves
At the swells that it leaves behind.

From the Spaniard, the languid
   crooning,
That reminds one of brown-haired
   girls,

Crianças que a procela acalentara
No berço destes pélagos profundos!

Esperai! Esperai! Deixai que eu beba
Esta selvagem, livre poesia.
Orquestra—é o mar, que ruge pela
   proa,
E o vento, que nas cordas
   assobia . . .

Por que foges assim, barco ligeiro?
Por que foges do pávido
   poeta?
Oh! quem me dera acompanhar-te a
   esteira
Que semelha no mar—doudo
   cometa!

Albatroz! Albatroz! Águia do
   oceano,
Tu que dormes das nuvens entre as
   gazas,
Sacode as penas, Leviathan do
   espaço,
Albatroz! Albatroz! dá-me estas
   asas.

II.
Que importa do nauta o
   berço,
Donde é filho, qual seu
   lar?
Ama a cadência do verso
Que lhe ensina o velho mar!
Cantai! que a morte é divina!
Resvala o brigue à bolina
Como golfinho veloz.
Presa ao mastro da mezena
Saudosa bandeira acena
As vagas que deixa após.

Do Espanhol as
   cantilenas
Requebradas de langor,
Lembram as moças morenas,

The flowering maids of Andalusia!
The indolent son of Italy
Sings of slumbering Venice,
—Land of love and betrayal,
Or of the sheltered gulf
Recalls Tasso's verse,
Together with the volcano's lava!

The Englishman—cold sailor,
Who at birth found himself at sea,
(Since England is a ship,
That God anchored in the Channel),
Intones, upright, the homeland's
    glory,
Proudly remembering tales of Nelson
    and Aboukir . . .
The Frenchman—preordained—
Sings the laurels of the past, and those
    yet to come!

The Hellenic sailors, raised by Ionic
    waves,
Handsome swarthy pirates
From the seas Ulysses sailed,
Men that Phidias sculpted,
Go on singing in the clear night
Verses that Homer moaned . . .
Navigators of all shores,
You know how to find at sea
The melodies of the sky! . . .

III.
Descend from the immensity, oh
    eagle of the sea!
Descend more . . . and even more . . .
    no human can see as you do
When you plunge to the flying
    brig!
But what do I see there . . .
What scene of bitterness!
It's a funereal dirge! . . .
Such gloomy figures! . . .
Such a vile, dishonorable scene. . . .
My God! My God! The horror!

As andaluzas em flor!
Da Itália o filho indolente
Canta Veneza dormente,
—Terra de amor e traição,
Ou do golfo no regaço
Relembra os versos de Tasso,
Junto às lavas do vulcão!

O Inglês—marinheiro frio,
Que ao nascer no mar se achou,
(Porque a Inglaterra é um navio,
Que Deus na Mancha ancorou),
Rijo entoa pátrias
    glórias,
Lembrando, orgulhoso, histórias
De Nelson e de Aboukir . . .
O Francês—predestinado—
Canta os louros do passado E os lou-
    reiros do porvir!

Os marinheiros Helenos, Que a vaga
    jônia criou,
Belos piratas morenos
Do mar que Ulisses cortou,
Homens que Fídias talhara,
Vão cantando em noite clara
Versos que Homero gemeu . . .
Nautas de todas as plagas,
Vós sabeis achar nas vagas
As melodias do céu! . . .

III.
Desce do espaço imenso, ó águia do
    oceano!
Desce mais . . . inda mais . . . não
    pode olhar humano
Como o teu mergulhar no brigue
    voador!
Mas que vejo eu aí . . .
Que quadro d'amarguras!
É canto funeral! . . .
Que tétricas figuras! . . .
Que cena infame e vil. . . .
Meu Deus! Meu Deus! Que horror!

IV.

It was a Dantesque dream . . . the
    deck below
Its blood-bathed shimmer reddened
    by the lights.
The clanking shackles . . . cracking of
    the whip . . .
Legions of men, black as
    night,
Dancing the horror . . .

Black women hang by the
    breast
Scrawny children from whose black
    mouths
Flows the blood of their mothers:
Other maidens, so nude and
    frightened,
Dragged in a whirlwind of specters,
Vainly racked by anxiety and pain!

The harsh, ironic orchestra
    laughs . . .
And the serpent, in a fantastic ring,
Makes mad spirals . . .
If the old man wheezes, if he slips to
    the floor,
Shouts sound out . . . the whip lashes.
And they fly more and more. . . .

Chained by the links of one single
    chain,
The starving mass staggers,
And weeps and dances right there!
One is delirious with rage, another
    goes mad,
Another, numbed by this martyrdom,
Sings, moans and laughs!

And yet the captain commands the
    maneuvers,
And after staring at the unfolding sky,
So pure above the sea,
Says smokily, among the dense fogs:

IV.

Era um sonho dantesco . . . o
    tombadilho
Que das luzernas avermelha o brilho.
Em sangue a se banhar.
Tinir de ferros . . . estalar de açoite
    . . .
Legiões de homens negros como a
    noite,
Horrendos a dançar . . .

Negras mulheres, suspendendo às
    tetas
Magras crianças, cujas bocas
    pretas
Rega o sangue das mães:
Outras moças, mas nuas e
    espantadas,
No turbilhão de espectros arrastadas,
Em ânsia e mágoa vãs!

E ri-se a orquestra irônica, estridente
    . . .
E da ronda fantástica a serpente
Faz doudas espirais . . .
Se o velho arqueja, se no chão
    resvala,
Ouvem-se gritos . . . o chicote estala.
E voam mais e mais. . . .

Presa nos elos de uma só
    cadeia,
A multidão faminta cambaleia,
E chora e dança ali!
Um de raiva delira, outro
    enlouquece,
Outro, que martírios embrutece,
Cantando, geme e ri!

No entanto o capitão manda a
    manobra,
E após fitando o céu que se desdobra,
Tão puro sobre o mar,
Diz do fumo entre os densos
    nevoeiros:

"Crack the whips hard, sailors!
Make them dance even more! . . ."

And the harsh, ironic orchestra
    laughs . . .
And the serpent, in a fantastic ring,
Makes mad spirals . . .
The shadows fly in such a Dantesque
    dream! . . .
Shouts, cries, curses and prayers
    echo!
And Satan cackles below! . . .

V.
Lord God of the wretched!
Oh tell me, Lord God!
If it is madness . . . if it is truth
Such horror beneath your skies?!
Oh sea, why not erase
With the sponge of your waves
This blot upon your cloak? . . .
Comets! Nights! Storms!
Roll in from the vastness!
Sweep these seas clean, oh typhoon!

Who are the wretches, who find in
    you
Nothing more than the calm laugh of
    the rabble
Which ignites the torturer's
    fury?
Who are they?
If the stars are snuffed out,
If the waves slip hurriedly by,
Like a fleeing accomplice,
In the chaos of the night . . .
Tell it yourself, severe Muse,
Freest Muse, most audacious! . . .

They are the sons of the desert,
Where the land weds the light.
Where the tribe of nude men
Live on open land . . .
They are daring warriors

"Vibrai rijo o chicote, marinheiros!
Fazei-os mais dançar! . . ."

E ri-se a orquestra irônica, estridente
    . . .
E da ronda fantástica a serpente
Faz doudas espirais . . .
Qual um sonho dantesco as sombras
    voam! . . .
Gritos, ais, maldições, preces
    ressoam!
E ri-se Satanás! . . .

V.
Senhor Deus dos desgraçados!
Dizei-me vós, Senhor Deus!
Se é loucura . . . se é verdade
Tanto horror perante os céus?!
Ó mar, por que não apagas
Co'a esponja de tuas vagas
De teu manto este borrão? . . .
Astros! noites! tempestades!
Rolai das imensidades!
Varrei os mares, tufão!

Quem são estes desgraçados
Que não encontram em vós
Mais que o rir calmo da
    turba
Que excita a fúria do
    algoz?
Quem são?
Se a estrela se cala,
Se a vaga à pressa resvala
Como um cúmplice fugaz,
Perante a noite confusa . . .
Dize-o tu, severa Musa,
Musa libérrima, audaz! . . .

São os filhos do deserto,
Onde a terra esposa a luz.
Onde vive em campo aberto
A tribo dos homens nus . . .
São os guerreiros ousados

Who with mottled tigers	Que com os tigres mosqueados
Do solitary combat.	Combatem na solidão.
Yesterday simple, strong, and brave.	Ontem simples, fortes, bravos.
Today miserable slaves,	Hoje míseros escravos,
Without light, or air, or reason . . .	Sem luz, sem ar, sem razão . . .
They are the disgraced women,	São mulheres desgraçadas,
Like Hagar was too.	Como Agar o foi também.
How parched, how broken,	Que sedentas, alquebradas,
From far . . . so far they come . . .	De longe . . . bem longe vêm . . .
Bringing in their weak steps,	Trazendo com tíbios passos,
Children and shackles in their arms,	Filhos e algemas nos braços,
In their soul—tears and bitterness . . .	N'alma—lágrimas e fel . . .
Like Hagar suffering so,	Como Agar sofrendo tanto,
That Ishmael cannot be nursed	Que nem o leite de pranto
Even on the tears of mourning.	Têm que dar para Ismael.
There in the infinite sands,	Lá nas areias infindas,
Of the palm groves of their land,	Das palmeiras no país,
Lovely children were born,	Nasceram crianças lindas,
Gentle maidens lived.	Viveram moças gentis.
. . . One day the caravan passes,	. . . Passa um dia a caravana,
When the virgin in her hut	Quando a virgem na cabana
Suspicion in the night of her veils . . .	Cisma da noite nos véus . . .
. . . Farewell oh shack on the hillside,	. . . Adeus, ó choça do monte,
. . . Farewell palm groves of the foun-	. . . Adeus, palmeiras da
tain! . . .	fonte! . . .
. . . Farewell, my loves . . . farewell!	. . . Adeus, amores . . . adeus!
. . .	. . .
After this, the extensive sand seas . . .	Depois, o areal extenso . . .
After this, the ocean of dust.	Depois, o oceano de pó.
After this on the immense horizons	Depois no horizonte imenso
Deserts . . . and only deserts . . .	Desertos . . . desertos só . . .
And the hunger, the fatigue, the thirst	E a fome, o cansaço, a sede
. . .	. . .
Oh! how many unfortunates yield,	Ai! quanto infeliz que cede,
And fall to never rise again! . . .	E cai p'ra não mais s'erguer! . . .
A space opens in the chain,	Vaga um lugar na cadeia,
But the jackal on the sands	Mas o chacal sobre a areia
Finds a corpse to devour.	Acha um corpo que roer.
Yesterday in Sierra Leone,	Ontem a Serra Leoa,
War and lion hunts,	A guerra, a caça ao leão,
Idly slept slumber	O sono dormido à toa

Beneath tents of bounty!
Today . . . the deep, black cargo hold,
Infested, cramped, filthy,
Hunting plague instead of jaguars . . .
And slumber always broken
By the rattle of the fallen,
And the smack of a corpse on the sea
        . . .

Yesterday total freedom,
The power of will . . .
Today . . . the accumulation of evil,
Not even free to die . . .
The same chain binds them
Gloomy, iron serpent
In the threads of slavery.
And mocking death in this way,
The gloomy cohort dances
To the sound of the whip . . . Scorn!
        . . .

Lord God of the wretched!
Tell me, oh Lord,
If I am delirious . . . or if it is true,
Such horror beneath your skies?! . . .
Oh sea, why not erase
With the sponge of your waves
This blot from your cloak?
Comets! Nights! Storms!
Roll in from the vastness!
Sweep these seas clean, oh typhoon!
        . . .

VI.
There is a people who puts out the
    flag
To cover up such dishonor and cow-
    ardice! . . .
And allows it to be transformed into
    this feast
Into the impure cloak of the cold Bac-
    chante! . . .
My God! My God! But what flag is
    this,

Sob as tendas d'amplidão!
Hoje . . . o porão negro, fundo,
Infecto, apertado, imundo,
Tendo a peste por jaguar . . .
E o sono sempre cortado
Pelo arranco de um finado,
E o baque de um corpo ao mar
        . . .

Ontem plena liberdade,
A vontade por poder . . .
Hoje . . . cúm'lo de maldade,
Nem são livres p'ra morrer . . .
Prende-os a mesma corrente
Férrea, lúgubre serpente
Nas roscas da escravidão.
E assim zombando da morte,
Dança a lúgubre coorte
Ao som do açoute . . . Irrisão!
        . . .

Senhor Deus dos desgraçados!
Dizei-me vós, Senhor Deus,
Se eu deliro . . . ou se é verdade
Tanto horror perante os céus?! . . .
Ó mar, por que não apagas
Co'a esponja de tuas vagas
Do teu manto este borrão?
Astros! noites! tempestades!
Rolai das imensidades!
Varrei os mares, tufão!
        . . .

Existe um povo que a bandeira
    empresta
P'ra cobrir tanta infâmia e cobardia!
        . . .
E deixa-a transformar-se nessa
    festa
Em manto impuro de bacante
    fria! . . .
Meu Deus! meu Deus! mas que ban-
    deira é esta,

That gloats impudently from the
    topsail?
Silence.
Muse . . . weep and weep so much
That the ensign is cleansed by your
    mourning! . . .

Green and gold pendant of my land,
That the breeze of Brazil kisses and
    sways,
Standard that the sun's light encases
And the divine promises of hope
    . . .
You, who for freedom after the war,
Was raised by heroes on their lances
Before they had torn you in battle,
So that you will serve as a shroud for
    a people! . . .

Merciless fate that squelches the
    mind!
Extinguish at once this filthy brig
The trail that Columbus blazed
    through the waves,
Like an iris in the deep sea!
But it is too dishonorable! . . .
From the ethereal shore
Rise up, you heroes of the New
    World!
Andrada! Tear this banner from the
    skies!
Columbus! Close the door to your
    seas!

Translated by Benjamin Legg

Que impudente na gávea
    tripudia?
Silêncio.
Musa . . . chora, e chora tanto
Que o pavilhão se lave no teu pranto!
    . . .

Auriverde pendão de minha terra,
Que a brisa do Brasil beija e
    balança,
Estandarte que a luz do sol encerra
E as promessas divinas da esperança
    . . .
Tu que, da liberdade após a guerra,
Foste hasteado dos heróis na lança
Antes te houvessem roto na batalha,
Que servires a um povo de mortalha!
    . . .

Fatalidade atroz que a mente
    esmaga!
Extingue nesta hora o brigue imundo
O trilho que Colombo abriu nas
    vagas,
Como um íris no pélago profundo!
Mas é infâmia demais! . . .
Da etérea plaga
Levantai-vos, heróis do Novo
    Mundo!
Andrada! arranca esse pendão dos
    ares!
Colombo! fecha a porta dos teus
    mares!

Victims and Executioners

Joaquim Manuel de Macedo

Joaquim Manuel de Macedo (1820–1882) was a writer, novelist, playwright, journalist, and teacher. Born in Rio de Janeiro, he earned a degree in medicine in 1844, but in the same year his first novel became such an immediate success that he abandoned medicine for writing. That book, A Moreninha *(often translated as* The Brunette *but which also means* The Brown-Skinned Woman*) is considered the first typically Brazilian novel, written about contemporary bourgeois youth in the city of Rio de Janeiro, and still widely read today. Following its publication, Macedo became a professor of history and geography at the elite Pedro II High School, the most important secondary school in Brazil at the time, as well as a founding member of the prestigious Brazilian Historic and Geographic Institute. Along with Gonçalves Dias and Manuel Araújo Porto-Alegre, he also founded* Guanabara *magazine in 1849, which emphasized topics considered particularly Brazilian, especially focusing on nature and indigenous people. Macedo was close to the royal family, serving as tutor to the princesses and becoming active in the Liberal Party.*

His book Victims and Executioners *was one of his last novels, published in 1869, nineteen years before the abolition of slavery. The work attacked slavery and portrayed the institution as the root of society's problems, but at the same time it demonized slaves. According to the book's introductory note, Macedo was not interested in "educational or moralizing stories." Rather, he preferred to show "the portrait of evil that the master, even unintentionally, does to the slave" and "the portrait of evil that the slave intentionally, or at times unintentionally, does to the master." In other words,* Victims and Executioners *argued that abolition was necessary not for humanitarian reasons, but because the enslaved caused the physical and moral corruption of white families. In the book's three stories, dissolute figures, all black, abound: a witch doctor, a deceitful boy, a female slave assassin, seductresses who sleep with their masters, a lascivious maid, drunkards, wily mulattoes, and so forth. With this cast of characters, Macedo's book denounces the evils of slavery (considered a social cancer), while portraying slaves as immoral and vice ridden.*

In the interior, and in particular, far from the village, the parish, and the towns, there is always a store close to the farm: it is the parasite that always sticks to the tree; worse, it is the hypocritical enemy that pays homage to his victim.

The store that I speak of is a very special tavern that could not exist, maintain itself, thrive in other local or rural work conditions, nor be confused with the regular tavern that is found everywhere, nor with the tavern found in small or large trading houses in which rich and poor workers are provided with their household needs when it is not possible for them to wait for remittances from their partners or clients.

This parasite of farms and neighborhood agricultural establishments is easily known for its characteristic features and ways of being, such that it is permissible to say the following: one looks like all the others, and there is no case in which one, as different as it may seem, manages to lose the family character.

It is a small mud hut with a tile roof, at times keeping its front porch open on three sides. The porch also has a tiled roof, supported by pillars that are strong yet at the same time crude and crooked. The walls are rarely whitewashed, the floor has neither floorboards nor tile; when the porch is open, a door and a window are opened inside. It is inside that you find the store: between the door and the window a wooden bench leans against the wall; against a rough counter and in the pantry or the space behind it there is a grotesque frame of planks containing bottles, jars, cans of powdered tobacco, a few rolls of tobacco, and a bad piece of dried meat in a corner. This is the store.

Many do not even reach the opulence of what was described above; all of them thus appear humble, with the bottom of their pantries nearly empty. Through the short door, the filthy hallway leads out to two or more dark rooms, where the storekeeper, who incidentally has no farm of his own, collects profits from agricultural crops.

The store is not crowded on weekdays; but never, or rarely ever, is it empty. Even on those days when work is a holy duty, vagabonds, men of leisure, and ruffians play on the counter with a pack of worn, oily black cards from morning until late afternoon, but miraculously, a tireless guitar player is absent. Arriving only at night, he begins the competition and heats up business.

Exploiter of the protective darkness of vice and crime, the low, ignoble, conscienceless storekeeper scandalously charges double the price for bottles of liquor and rolls of tobacco, and a tragically high price for coffee, sugar, and grain that slaves steal from their masters. An accomplice in the robberies of slaves is a criminal in his own right, robbing these amounts at these types of prices.

The store does not sleep: in the dead of the night come the *quilombolas* [residents of *quilombos*, colonies of runaway slaves and their descendants] and fugitive slaves taking refuge in the forests, bringing the tribute of their depredations from neighboring or distant fields to the storekeeper, who selects from them a second harvest which he does not distribute; for the *quilombolas*, he always keeps this on reserve—food supplies that they could not do without, and often gunpowder and pellets to resist attacks against their *quilombos*.

And the storekeeper is as a rule the vigilant protector of the *quilombola*. He is a disguised spy who has an interest in opposing both the police and the owners in the tracking of fugitive slaves.

Despicable and noxious during the day, the store is squalid, grisly, criminal, and atrocious at night: the slaves who meet there get drunk, fight, and are incapable of work the following morning. The brawls and the blows mix with the most indecent conversation about the characters and lives of their masters, whose reputations are ravaged to the sound of wicked chuckling. Inspired by hate, by horror, by the inherent suffering of slavery, they enter into terrible slander that at times offends the honor of the wives and daughters of their masters; they stir up the rage that they all feel toward the overseers, telling grim tales of excessive punishments and cruel vengeance, an idea which takes hold of their discussion. In their stupid and unlimited gullibility, these wretches listen agape to the wonders of witchcraft, and they agree upon nighttime witchcraft gatherings; some finally learn from the wiser slaves the evil plants and poisonous roots that produce insanity or bring death, and all of this is even more wrapped in drunkenness, with the disorder and the frame of abjection and of shamelessness already natural in the words, the actions, and the pleasures of the slave.

On Sundays and on holy days, the store boasts one hundred times more of its nefarious glories, taking advantage of the sunlight and the darkness, day and night, and exactly because of this the fields count fewer laborers, and the infirmary more slaves the following morning.

Ordinarily, or at least often, it is in these meetings and in this hub of moral disease that slaves premeditate and plan the crimes that bring bloodshed and stir up trouble on the farms. In the case of an insurrection, the store will always have had something to do with the event.

Still, the store is tolerated: the government cannot ignore it, the local police know, the farmers and laborers know and feel that this ignoble dump is the source of vice and crime and the murky and hideous fountainhead of profound corruption, constant threats to property, the death of reputation, and in certain cases the foundry for murder weapons; because it is and always will be the meeting place of slaves to conspire or begin conspiring; and even so the store survives and there is no force capable of destroying it.

Why? . . .

It is because if they prohibited the store that I speak of, if they closed its door, if they destroyed its roof, it would be reborn with another name; and however and wherever it is, it will live on, though hidden and abused.

The logic is implacable.

It is not possible to have slaves without all of the scandalous consequences of slavery: it is to desire the ulcer without the pus, the cancer without the decay; to do so is insanity or a child's fancy.

Dangerous and repugnant certainly, and yet still not one of the most formidable consequences of slavery, the store of which I am speaking is inevitable, because it is born from life, from the conditions, and from the overwhelming demands of the situation of the slaves.

The store is the mirror that gives a live portrait of the face and the spirit of slavery.

If it weren't for this, if it were not called the store, it would have a thousand other names in the jargon of the slave; it would be a house in the desert or a place in the undergrowth. It would be found in a forest cave or a beast's den, but the slave and the *quilombola* would always go there to sell stolen goods, to become intoxicated, to insult the honor of their master and their master's family whom they hate, to engulf themselves in vice, to hear poisoned advice, to become inflamed with hatred, to accustom themselves to the idea of crimes of revenge; because the slave, as well as he is treated, is, as a general rule, by virtue of being a slave, always, naturally, and logically the first and most spiteful enemy of his master.

The slave needs to express his incessantly boiling rage and forget for moments or hours the miseries and bottomless torments of slavery. It is in the store that he expresses himself and forgets; there, hate is licentiously expressed and liquor drowns memory in vapors and haze.

Nevertheless, the store is horrible: it is the sanctuary of a savage assembly of the slaves, a place where lascivious evil, disgusting defamation, and crime without remorse take the stage; there, the venerable matron, the honest wife, and the angelic maiden are all judged and measured by the gauge of morality of the slaves; scandal is applauded and sanctioned as a proven truth and is described with squalid forms of savagery and the eloquence of alcohol-sublimated anger. In the store, furies ascend against overseers and masters. There, they rob the farm and make fierce vows for the death of those whom they detest, those who are undeniably oppressors.

And there is no other way to abolish the store, this fatal store that robs, demoralizes, corrupts, slanders, and sometimes kills, than to abolish slavery.

There is only this one way, because the store intimately adheres and is indispensably joined to the life of the slave; without it, slave suicides would reach terrifying proportions.

Where there are plantations, there will by force be the perverse, threatening, infamous store as I have described and as every single laborer knows.

There is no king without a throne, there is no family without a home, nor birds without a nest, nor beast without a den; the throne, the home, the nest, the den of the slave is, more than the *senzala* [slave quarters], the store.

The store, which to you seems merely repugnant, corrupt, thieving, and

disgraceful, is, more than that, formidable and cruel; but, in all of these attributes, it is a dignified, legitimate child of slavery, which created it, raised
it, sustained it, imposed it, and which will maintain it ingrained as long as
slavery exists.

It is an absolutely dependent ill, inseparable from the other ill; it is not the
cause, it is the effect; it is not the tree, it is the fruit of the tree.

If you wish to abolish the hell that is the store, you must first abolish the
demon that is slavery.

Translated by Molly Quinn

The Republican Manifesto

Members of the Republican Party

At the end of the Paraguayan War, a growing number of Brazilian intellectuals and politicians took a more aggressive stance against the empire. One faction, linked to the Paulista liberal elite, formed the federal Republican Party in 1870. They drafted the manifesto excerpted below as their founding document, where they laid out their criticism of the empire and its centralizing power, and called for various reform measures. They were particularly staunch advocates of federalism, which they painted as both a natural part of Brazil's heritage and a common characteristic of American states.

In Brazil, even before the idea of democracy, nature led to the establishment of federalism. The topography of our territory, the diverse zones that divide it, the various climates and different modes of production, the mountains and the waters, indicated the necessity of modeling an administration and a local government that followed and respected the divisions created by nature and imposed by the immense size of our territory.

It was this necessity that demonstrated, since the beginning, the efficacy of the grand principle that cements the unifying forces that the central regime has tried to undo and destroy.

As a colony, no fear could lead the Portuguese Crown to divert the power it delegated to its favorite and beloved vassals. Rather, this was the way to maintain the strict unification demanded by the absolute rule of the metropolis [Portugal]. . . .

The Independence officially proclaimed in 1822 saw and respected the forms of colonial division.

The democratic idea represented by the first Brazilian Constitution tried, it is true, to give the principle of federation all of the development that it required and that the country needed to move forward and progress. But the dissolution of the National Assembly suffocated democratic aspirations, devalued the idea of federalism, and robbed it of acceptance, and the Constitution of 1824 helped maintain the status quo of territorial division, amplifying the sphere of centralization through the dependency it imposed on the provinces and through administrators who wielded intrusive and dominating power. . . .

The autonomy of the provinces is, for us, more than a by-product of the solidarity of provincial rights and relations; it is a cardinal and solemn principle that we inscribed in our flag.

The regime of the federation, based then on the reciprocal independence of the provinces, which elevates them to the category of proper States, uniquely linked by the bond of the same nationality and of the solidarity of grand interests of representation and international defense, is the one that we have adopted in our program, as it is the only one capable of maintaining the communion of the Brazilian family.

Lacking a formula to demonstrate before the national conscience the effects of another regime, we would summarize it in the following manner: Centralization equals dismemberment. Decentralization equals union. . . .

In conclusion:

Exposed to the general principles that serve as the basis of a modern democracy, the only [institution] that consults and respects the rights and opinions of the people, we have made our thoughts known.

As our aim has to be satisfied by the preliminary condition established in the Constitution; the convocation of a Constitutional Assembly with ample faculties to implement a new regime is of cardinal importance. The reforms that we aspire to are complex and encompass our entire social mechanism.

To deny them absolutely, as if it [implementing reform] were a wicked deed, would provoke resistance. To delay them indefinitely is a disgusting and dangerous maneuver.

Strengthened, then, by our rights and by our conscience, we present ourselves before our fellow Brazilians, resolutely raising the flag of the federal Republican Party.

We are from America and want to be Americans.

Our [current] form of government is, in its essence and in practice, opposed to autonomy and hostile toward the rights and interests of the American States.

The permanence of this form would be, in addition to the origin of internal oppression, the font of perpetual hostility and wars with the people that surround us.

We appear to be a democratic monarchy that inspires no sympathy and provokes no adherence in Europe, but in America we have become a monarchical democracy, where the instinct and strength of the people cannot predominate against the will and omnipotence of the ruler.

Because of such conditions, Brazil considers itself an isolated country, not only in America, but also in the world.

Our efforts are directed to suppress the current state of things, putting us in fraternal contact with all peoples, and in democratic solidarity with the continent of which we are a part.

Translated by João Nascimento

Law of the Free Womb

José Maria da Silva Paranhos and Princess Isabel

Notwithstanding the growing abolition movement, the imperial government took no major legislative steps to end slavery within Brazil until 1871, when parliament passed the Law of the Free Womb. Also known as the Rio Branco Law because it was proposed during the Cabinet of Prime Minister José Maria da Silva Paranhos, the viscount of Rio Branco (1819–1880), it generated fierce debate and was only narrowly approved, with a 65–45 vote. Those who voted in favor were overwhelmingly representatives from the northeast, while those from the center-south, where coffee producers relied on slave labor, generally opposed it. Acting as princess regent while Dom Pedro II was abroad, Princess Isabel signed the bill into law on September 28, 1871.

The major provision of the law declared all children free who were born to slave mothers after its passage. As the mothers remained slaves, the law left strict legal connections between the new ingenûos (innocents), or children who were born free, and their mothers' masters. The masters had legal authority over such children until they turned eight, at which point they could either turn them over to the state in exchange for an indemnity designed to compensate them for the eight years of support they supposedly offered, or they could keep them on as unpaid laborers until age twenty-one, using their services to pay back those first eight years. Among the other provisions in the law, slave owners were no longer allowed to separate married slaves and their young children through sale; the state freed abandoned slaves or those the Crown owned; and the government established a national slave registry.

The law served as a response to pressure from the national and international abolitionist movements, which had picked up steam following the end of the war with Paraguay in 1870. It signaled that slavery in Brazil would have to end, as slaves could no longer be imported from Africa nor born henceforth in Brazil, and implicitly delegitimized the institution by casting it as something that needed, eventually, to be eliminated. Yet it also provided reassurance to slaveholders that their legal rights to own other human beings would, for the time being, be upheld.

The Imperial Princess Regent, in name of His Majesty the Emperor Dom Pedro II, informs all citizens of the empire that the General Assembly has decreed and sanctioned the following law:

Art. 1.—The children of female slaves born in the empire after the date of this law will be considered free.

§ 1.—Said minor children will be placed in the power and under the authority of their mothers' owners, who will have the obligation to raise them and be responsible for them until they reach eight full years of age. Once the child of the slave reaches this age, the mother's owner will have the option of either receiving an indemnity of 600$000 [600,000 réis] from the state, or of using the services of the minor until twenty-one full years of age. In the first case, the government will receive and provide for the minor, conforming to this law. . . .

§ 6.—The provision of services to the children of slave mothers will be stopped prior to the period indicated in § 1., if by criminal sentence a judge recognizes that the masters mistreat them or inflict excessive punishments. . . .

Art. 2.—The government may submit the children of slave mothers to authorized associations if these children are born after the date of this law and are abandoned or relinquished by their mothers' masters, or if they are taken from the masters in accordance with Art. 1., § 6.

§ 1.—Said associations will have the right to use the free services of the minors until twenty-one full years of age and will have the power to rent out these services, but must also:

1. Raise and tend to these same minors;
2. Create for each of them a savings fund, consistent with the quota that is reserved for them for this purpose in the respective statutes;
3. Find them an appropriate placement after the period of service comes to an end.

§ 2.—The provision of this article shall apply to orphanages and to people that judges place in charge of the education of said minors, in the absence of associations or establishments created for such purpose. . . .

§ 4.—The government retains the right to order said minors to return to public establishments, transferring to the state the obligations that § 1. imposes on the authorized associations.

Art. 3.—In each imperial province, a number of slaves corresponding to the quota annually available from the emancipation fund will be liberated. . . .

Art. 4.—The slave is permitted to form a savings fund that may come from donations, legacies, and inheritances, and to which, by consent of the master, he may contribute with his own work and savings. The government will implement regulations on the spending and security of the savings fund.

§ 1.—Upon the slave's death, half of his savings fund will belong to the surviving spouse, if there is one, and the other half will be transmitted to his heirs under civil law. In the absence of heirs, the savings will be awarded to the emancipation fund, which is discussed in Art. 3. . . .

§ 4.—A slave who belongs to joint owners and who is freed by one of them has the right to his freedom, compensating the other masters the share of value that belonged to them. This indemnity can be paid with services provided for a period no greater than seven years. . . .

§ 7.—In any case of sale or transfer of slaves, it is prohibited, under penalty of nullifying the transaction, to separate spouses or to separate minor children under twelve years from the father or the mother.

§ 8.—If the division of property among heirs or partners is not successfully negotiated among family members, and if none of the family members wish to keep the slave under his or her ownership either through restitution based on quota or on the part of interested stakeholders, then the family's wealth will be sold and its proceeds distributed. . . .

Art. 6.—The following are declared free:

§ 1.—The slaves belonging to the nation, who will be given the occupation that the government sees fit.

§ 2.—The slaves used by the Crown for enjoyment or profit.

§ 3.—The slaves of unclear inheritance.

§ 4.—The slaves abandoned by their masters. If the masters abandon them for being disabled, they will still be obliged to feed them, except in the case of famine, with food being established by the Judge of Orphans.

§ 5.—In general, the slaves freed by this law will be subject to inspection by the government for five years. They are required to contract out their services, with the penalty of being required to work in public establishments if they are living as vagrants. The work requirement will be ceded as long as the freed slave is seeking work.
. . .

Art. 8.—The government will arrange for the special registration of all existing slaves in the Empire, with declaration of their name, sex, marital status, ability to work, and the affiliation of each one, if it is known.

§ 1.—The period in which the registry will be initiated and completed will be announced as far in advance as possible via repeated announcements that will include this provision in the paragraph below:

§ 2.—The slaves that, for fault or omission of interested stakeholders, are not registered one year after the closing of registration, will thus be considered free. . . .

§ 4.—The children of slave women who are freed by this law will also be registered, but in a different book. Masters who fail to register their slaves will incur a fine of 100$000 to 200$000 [100,000 to 200,000 réis], repeated for as many individual slaves [as] are omitted, for negligence and fraud under penalty of Art. 179 of the criminal code.

§ 5.—Parish priests will be required to have special books for the registry of births and deaths of the children of slave women born after the date of this law. Each omission will subject the parish priest to a fine of 100$000.

Art. 9.—The government, in its regulation and enforcement, may impose fines of up to 100$000 [100,000 réis] and prison sentences of up to one month.

Art. 10.—All provisions contrary to this law are revoked. This law orders all authorities to whom the knowledge and execution of the referred law applies to comply, enforce, and protect all measures contained in the law. The Secretary of State Agricultural Business, Commerce, and Public Works will print, publicize, and oversee this law.

*Presented at the Palace of Rio de Janeiro on
the twenty-eighth day of September, 1871, the
fiftieth year of Independence of the Empire.*

Imperial Princess Regent—
Teodoro Machado Freire Pereira da Silva

Translated by Molly Quinn

Early Brazilian Feminism

Francisca Senhorinha da Motta Diniz

In the later part of the nineteenth century, a small number of educated women be-came advocates of what was then called women's emancipation. Although the vast majority of the population remained illiterate (the 1872 census found illiteracy rates of 80 percent for men and 88.5 percent for women), a growing number of women received an education, especially in urban centers. Many of them became schoolteachers, an occupation that was increasingly becoming acceptable for women, as teaching chil-dren came to be seen as consistent with socially ascribed ideas about women as nur-turers. Women schoolteachers also formed the vanguard of efforts to secure increased educational and other opportunities for women.

Among these pioneering feminists was Francisca Senhorinha da Motta Diniz, a schoolteacher from the small town of Campanha, Minas Gerais. Like other early feminists, she saw newspapers as an important venue for women to learn about their rights, to consider their collective challenges, and to circulate ideas about women's roles elsewhere. In 1873 she began to publish the periodical O Sexo Feminino *(The feminine sex), a paper directed at women readers. Within its pages she argued, among other things, that women should have access to education not simply so that they could raise their children properly. Rather, they should also be able to understand financial matters that affected themselves and their families. In this she proposed that women should be equal partners with their husbands and directly challenged mar-ried women's legal subordination to their spouses, especially the provision whereby a married woman could not administer property, even her own dowry, without her husband's consent.*

What Do We Want?

It is quite natural that more than one of those backward souls who form part of our present-day society have asked this question. It is very probable that those who are unconcerned or pessimistic or willfully blind have asked the same question. We will try hard to give them answers.

It is definitely a verifiable fact that men have overlooked the need to en-lighten women's minds: instead, they remain content to adorn their bodies and flatter their vanity.

It cannot be denied that women (with few exceptions) live in complete ignorance of their rights, unaware even of those due them under our nation's laws—particularly that their public consent is necessary for the conveyance of *real estate*. How many married women are ignorant of the fact that a husband cannot dispose of any piece of the couple's property in any way without the wife's informed consent? How many married women are deceived in such matters by husbands who force them to sign those legal documents on which they *automatically scrawl* their names? How many married women write out in their own hand the words dooming all the savings their parents suffered to accumulate but which their wastrel husbands pledged to repay *debts* that were not even contracted for the couple's benefit?

The state of crass and apathetic ignorance in which women languish, always deceived by their husbands, allows them often to fool themselves into thinking that they are *rich* when someday, in fact, they will awake to the *sad reality* of not owning anything, of being *poor, in abject poverty*, because their husbands have squandered their *inheritance*, wasted it, handed it over to *creditors* who *legally* claim their money. Only then will such women see the abyss in front of their eyes! It is not surprising that in such cases, after all this has happened, these husbands culminate their previous knaveries by abandoning their wives and children.

Many husbands perceive that their wives lack sufficient training to take over affairs in their absence and carry on as they would do. Other husbands *praise* such ignorance and give thanks for their luck in having wives who understand nothing about those affairs in which men say women *should not meddle!*

How many parents labor unceasingly under the harshest conditions to amass a dowry for their daughter and then deliver her, body and soul, to a *son-in-law* who will soon squander this dowry? After all, he secured the dowry through a marriage which he viewed not as an *end* in itself but just as a means of obtaining a fortune *without working*. While the true purpose of marriage has always been the legitimization of the *union of man and woman*, so that they will live together as one and love each other as Christ loved his church, in this corrupt, immoral, and irreligious society, *marriage is a means of making one's fortune*. Marriage is the goal of the rascal who does not want to work and who acts like some strange kind of acrobat turning *somersaults* to snare a dowry, no matter if the woman attached to it is pretty or ugly, young or old—anyone will do. With the social goal of marriage thus perverted, love of family, children, and homeland easily disappears.

Girls must be prepared for *reversals of fortune*. They must receive *education* and *instruction*, so that whether married, single, or widowed, they will know their rights and will be able to judge the *intentions* and hearts of men requesting their hand in marriage.

To summarize the thesis of this article: We want our emancipation and the regeneration of our customs; we want to regain our lost rights; we want *true* education, which has not been granted us, so that we can educate our children; we want complete instruction so we can know our rights and use them appropriately; we want to become familiar with our family affairs so that we can administer them if ever obliged to. In short, we want to *understand* what we do, the *why* and *wherefore* of matters; we want to be our husbands' companions, not their slaves; we want to know how things are done outside the home. What we do not want is to continue to be *deceived*.

Translated by June E. Hahner

Letters to the French Mineralogist Claude-Henri Gorceix

Emperor Dom Pedro II

Dom Pedro II left behind a vast collection of correspondence. In particular, he enjoyed communicating with scientists and scholars. He sent the following three letters to Claude-Henri Gorceix, a French mineralogist who founded and served as the first director of the School of Mines in Ouro Preto, Minas Gerais. The emperor had invited Gorceix to Brazil to found the school, and he paid considerable attention to its development. As the first letter shows, although Pedro II was traveling in Europe when the school was inaugurated in 1876, he made a point of writing to Gorceix about its progress. In the following letters, one can see that over the years the emperor continued to write to Gorceix about scientific matters, while he worked to recruit other European scientists, such as French chemist and microbiologist Louis Pasteur, to come to Brazil.

August 17, 1876

Dear Sir,

It was only yesterday that I received the letter you sent on May 19. Since my departure from Rio, I have imposed on myself a rule of non-interference in Brazil's public matters; however, I shall give you my opinion in regard to what you wrote, but only as a man who likes to occupy his mind with scientific matters as much as time allows, considering the position that I hold and the many responsibilities it entails.

A preparatory school such as Your Lord has proposed can only provide service to my homeland, and in particular, to the province of Minas; but as Your Lord said, this measure should only be implemented when the circumstances require it, which I hope do not last long. It is necessary to allow these exceptions until a true educational system may be established. You should soon try all possible means to initiate the operation of a more regular system.

You are aware of the credit that I give to M. Gobert. I understand the exceptional position in which he finds himself in relation to the Ecole

Polytechnique; the course of study that he promised would be useful in the development of certain fields of knowledge in Brazil, and I ask you to think of this as you rightfully solicit his involvement in your school.

The time I have taken during this trip to be of service to my country does not permit me to go on any longer; moreover, I fear that I am breaking my aforementioned rule of abstention.

I vow to secure the success of your school and am assured by your obvious zeal. I ask that you trust my support, and know that my intention is always firm.

With my encouragement and affection.

Yours truly,

Dom Pedro of Alcântara.

January 7, 1885

Dear Sir,

Your November 18 and December 4 letters were of great interest to me.

I am awaiting Pasteur's response to the letter I wrote after his departure, and I shall do everything in my power so that he comes. I am always afraid of personally meddling in economic issues and I hope that Pasteur will understand this about the Brazilian delegation.

I have already told my grandson, Pedro, to respond to the December 4 letter that you sent. I ask you to thank the Mineralogy Society for the likely nomination of Pedro as an effective member. Currently, he is solely focused on his studies at Génie; but, along with this, he could also continue the course of study in the natural sciences. The publications of the Mineralogy Society should thus serve him quite well. I hope that you have recovered entirely from your ill health and that I may have the pleasure of seeing you soon. Keep me updated on what is being done with respect to Brazil's minerals. The study of monazites shall be of great importance to science.

The name M. Radaud is very familiar to me from reading *Revue des Deux Mondes* and the book on Pasteur's findings.

Send my regards to all those who remember me, and always believe in the sincerity of my sentiments.

Yours truly,

Dom Pedro of Alcântara.

January 31, 1885

Dear Sir,

Your extremely interesting letter can only receive a brief response. It arrived on a Saturday, and, as you know, that day is usually very busy for me.

I hope you convince the Pasteur family to come here. I touched upon the delicate matter of finances in my previous letter to you. I know that Pasteur will speak of this frankly and will allow plenty of time to ask the Chambers, which open on the first of March, for the necessary authorization. I would be very surprised if the Legislative Body does not handle this matter with diligence.

I attribute equally great importance to the trip taken by Father David. I spoke this morning with the Ministers about sending that information, as well as [the information] about what you mentioned regarding the Biology Department Chair, which is entirely acknowledged here.

I hope that you continue to write me during your absence, which I am sure will not be too prolonged.

Farewell! Many greetings to all who have shown me good will. I assure them of my love for the progress of science, to which I unfortunately can only contribute indirectly.

I await the Centennial of Chevreul in order to properly express to the Dean of the Students of France all of my high esteem.

I must bring this letter to an end.

Yours truly,

Dom Pedro of Alcântara

Translated by Lanna Leite and Molly Quinn

Selections from *Abolitionism*

Joaquim Nabuco

*Joaquim Aurélio Barreto Nabuco de Araújo was among Brazil's most important abo-
litionists. Born in Recife on August 19, 1849, to a powerful and wealthy sugar planter
family, he died in Washington, DC, on January 17, 1910, while serving as Brazil's first
ambassador to the United States. During his lifetime he was one of Brazil's great
thinkers, working as a politician, jurist, diplomat, journalist, and historian. He became especially well known for his abolitionist views, arguing against slavery as an
elected representative between 1878 and 1881, and founding the Brazilian Antislavery
Society in 1880. When he and other well-known abolitionist politicians were defeated
in the parliamentary elections of 1881, and the abolitionist movement seemed to be
waning, Nabuco went into a self-imposed exile in London. There he wrote his powerful and extended argument against slavery in Brazil, titled O abolicionismo (Abolitionism). The selection below offers a sense of his long-term vision of Brazil's future
after slavery, and the work that needed to be done to remedy the effects of the institution on the nation's economy and society.*

. . . In 1850 it was hoped that slavery could be suppressed with the ending
of the traffic; in 1871 it was to be done by freeing the infant still to be born,
though only in fact when he reached the age of twenty-one. Today what is
desired is to abolish it by freeing the slaves *en masse* and by rescuing the *ingênuos* [freeborn children of slaves] from the servitude of the Law [of the Free
Womb] of September 28 [1871]. Only this last movement, which is called abolitionism, will resolve the real problem of the slaves by the gift of freedom
itself. Public opinion of 1845 regarded the purchase of Africans, treacherously
shipped from the shores of their continent and smuggled illegally into Brazil,
as legitimate and honest. The opinion of 1875 condemned the transactions of
the slave traders but judged it legitimate and honest to register the victims
of that same traffic after thirty years of illegal captivity. Abolitionism is the
point of view which, in turn, must replace this last outlook, for all dealings
in [the enslavement of] human beings are crimes that differ only in their level
of cruelty.

Abolitionism, however, is not only this. As a movement it is not satisfied to
be the advocate ex officio of that part of the black race still enslaved. It does

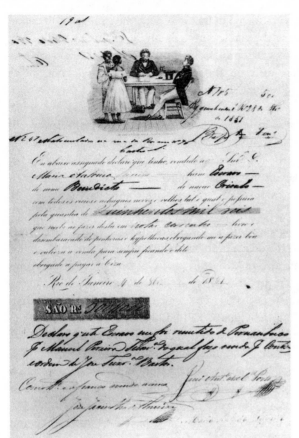

A document granting manumission on the eve of abolition. Courtesy of the Brazilian National Archive (Arquivo Nacional).

not limit its mission to achieving the redemption of the slaves and the *ingênuos* in the shortest time possible. This work of ours—of reparation, of shame, of repentance, however it may be termed, of the emancipation of the existing slaves and their children—is only the immediate task of abolitionism. Apart from this, there is even greater work to be done, that of the future: that of blotting out all the effects of a system which for three centuries has been a school of demoralization and inertia, of servility and irresponsibility for the master caste, which made of Brazil the Paraguay of slavery.

Even if total emancipation were decreed tomorrow, the liquidation of that system would give way to an unending series of questions which could only be resolved in accordance with the vital interests of the country, by the same spirit of justice and humanity that gives life to abolitionism. After the last slaves have been wrested from the sinister power which represents for the black race the curse of color, it will still be necessary to eliminate, through vigorous and forthright education, the gradual stratification of three hundred years of slavery, of despotism, superstition, and ignorance. The natural process by which slavery fossilized in its own shape the exuberant lifeblood of our people lasted during the whole period of our development; and as long as the nation does not know that it is essential to adapt to freedom every part of its being which slavery usurped, the effects of servitude will continue to exist, even when there are no more slaves.

Thus abolitionism is a new concept in our political history, and, as a result of it, as will be seen, divisions in the present political parties will very probably develop. Until very recently it could be anticipated that slavery would end in Brazil as it did in the Roman Empire, that it would be allowed to disappear without convulsions or violence. The whole policy of our statesmen was, until now, inspired by the desire to see slavery dissolve imperceptibly in our country.

Abolitionism is a protest against that dismal outlook, against the expedient of waiting for death to solve a problem, which requires not only justice and moral rectitude but also political vision [for a solution]. Furthermore, our system is much too corrupt to withstand the prolonged effects of slavery without damage. Each year of that system, which degrades the entire nation to the advantage of a few individuals, will be harmful. Perhaps today, the appearance of a new generation, educated in different principles, will create a new response and cause society to enter again into the [currently] retarded process of spontaneous development. In the future only a major operation will save us, at the cost of our national identity: the transfusion into our system of the pure and vigorous blood of a free race.

Our character, our temperament, our whole physical, intellectual, and moral organization are profoundly afflicted by influences which during three hundred years were infused into Brazilian society. The task of annulling those influences is certainly beyond the ability of one generation, but as long as this work has not been completed abolitionism will have a reason to exist.

Thus, like the word "abolitionism," the word "slavery" is used in this book in its broadest sense. It does not mean merely the relationship of the slave to the master. It means much more. It signifies the sum of the power, influence, capital, and patronage of all the masters; the feudalism established in the interior, the dependence in which commerce, religion, the poor, industry, Parliament, the Crown, the entire State find themselves before the amassed power of the aristocratic minority, in whose slave huts hundreds of thousands of human beings live brutalized and morally mutilated by the system to which they are subjected. Finally, it signifies the spirit, the living principle, which animates the entire institution, particularly at the moment in which it begins to fear a loss of the timeless power with which it is endowed, a spirit in which the whole history of slave countries has been the source of backwardness and ruin.

. . . In other countries the propaganda of emancipation was religious, preached from the pulpit, fervently supported by the various churches and religious communities. Among us the abolitionist movement unfortunately owes nothing to the state church. On the contrary, the ownership of men and women by the convents and by the entire secular clergy completely demoralized the religious feelings of masters and slaves. The slaves saw nothing in the priest but a man who could who buy them, while the masters saw in him the last person who would think to accuse them. Our clergy's desertion of the role which the Gospel assigned to it was as shameful as it could possibly have been. No one observed it taking the side of slaves; no one saw it using religion to ease the burdens of their captivity, or to propose moral truths to the masters. No priest ever tried to stop a slave auction; none ever denounced the religious regiment of the slave quarters. The Catholic Church, despite its immense power in a country still greatly fanaticized by it, *never* raised its voice in Brazil in favor of emancipation.

If what gives strength to abolitionism is not mainly religious feeling, deformed by the clergy itself and so not the lever of progress which it should be, the abolitionist cause is also not generally inspired by a spirit of charity and philanthropy. In England the struggle against slavery was a religious and humanitarian movement, determined by feelings unrelated to politics, except to the extent that one can refer to the social morality of the Gospel as political. By contrast, abolitionism in Brazil is above all a *political* movement, with which, undoubtedly, the interests of the slaves and compassion for their fate powerfully concur, but which is born of a different purpose: the hope of reconstructing Brazil on the basis of free labor and of uniting the races in freedom.

A Critique of José de Alencar's *O Guarani*

Joaquim Maria Machado de Assis

One of Brazil's great novelists of the late nineteenth century, Joaquim Maria Machado de Assis (1839–1908) had an unusual background. The son of an Afro-Brazilian house painter and a Portuguese immigrant washerwoman, Machado received little formal education. Nevertheless he taught himself English and French, and became a well-read journalist who wrote regularly for Rio de Janeiro's newspapers and a prolific author of short stories, novels, poetry, and plays. In his journalistic career, Machado became known for producing crônicas, short literary pieces that appeared in newspapers, in which he offered critical and insightful commentary on daily life, politics, and culture.

In this delightful crônica, under the pretense of commenting on the thirtieth anniversary of the publication of O Guarani *(The Guarani) by José de Alencar (see* O Guarani *in this part), Machado recalls the literary generation of Indianist romantics who came before him. If the early works of Machado owe much to romanticism, his later, more mature works are more influenced by a realism that depicted late nineteenth-century Brazilian society critically. When Machado penned this crônica, the empire was no longer experiencing its moment of glory. Rather, a crisis was approaching. The tone is nostalgic, recalling a time when the city was "less animated" and when "neither progress, nor life" was the same. Yet the text still reflects a celebratory spirit. It is a fine example of the way Machado de Assis experimented with the crônica, a genre that is still identified with Brazil to this day.*

One day, responding to Alencar in an open letter, I told him, in reference to a matter of his, that he kept a conspiracy of posterity rather than a conspiracy of silence. It was easy to foresee: *O Guarani* and *Iracema* were published, and many other books granted our author the first place in Brazilian literature. He died just ten years ago; and behold what is reborn in commemorative editions, but the first of those works, as fresh and as new as when it first saw the light of day, thirty years ago in the columns of the *Diario do Rio*. The conspiracy begins.

O Guarani was his grand debut. The first drafts appeared in the *Correio Mercantil* in 1853, where he replaced Francisco Otaviano as a columnist. The space was small, and the contents meager; but Alencar's imagination overcame or stretched things, and he sprinkled the ordinary events of the week with his gold dust. Life in the province then was different, more circumscribed, less noisy. The world did not yet speak to us over the telegraph, nor did Europe send us its papers, by the armful, two or three times a week. Farms in 1853 were not, as they are today, linked to the Ouvidor Street [in Rio de Janeiro] by a number of tramways, but rather were truly on the outskirts of the city, connected to downtown by slow transports and private or public coaches.

Naturally, our main street was much less crowded. There were few theaters, where spectators go calmly to view dramas and comedies that soon lose their luster. The city was less animated and had a different character. Today's city is the natural product of the progress of time and of population, but it is clear that neither progress nor life is free. Ease and rapidity of movement produce scattered attention and shortness of breath, and innumerable new curiosities cause many things to lose their cordial and lasting interest. Alencar's imagination, however, profited from his work, and it was soon apparent that the debutant would be a future master . . . and would be repaid for his effort.

Sure enough, three years later *O Guarani* appeared. . . . The critics caught the attention of the city, which analyzed *O Guarani* for many days, and there were many attempted imitations, debates, conversations about it. . . . Here comes the book that was the foundation of our author's reputation as a romanticist. It is the vibrant work of youth. This writing goes to the heart of the publication, the material adjusting itself to the space on a page, a situation that is adverse to art, but excellent for garnering public attention. To conquer these conditions, which were obstacles, and to make them favorable to his writing, was Alencar's great victory, as it had been for the author of *The Three Musketeers*.

I am not here to criticize *O Guarani*. Preserved there, in well-worn pages, is my judgment of him. Whatever strange influences he had to obey, this book is essentially national. Brazilian nature, with the exuberances that Burke assumes to be the profession of our civilization, is here seen through various aspects; and its interior life at the beginning of the seventeenth century ought to be as our author describes it, save for the literary color and the touches of imagination that, even when he abuses them, are a delight. Here is the expert note, so characteristic of the author, alongside the manly touch, as if he intended to compare and contrast the savage and the civilized life. From the beginning we are in pure and unabashed Romanticism. . . . The imagination gives a feeling of realism to the most opulent embellishments. What does it matter if they are sometimes overused? What of the healing they can bring to the psyche of the native Brazilian? This strikes us as a model of dedication, just as Cecília is one of candor and coquettishness; altogether, a work in which the best of the Brazilian spirit throbs. . . .

I could not reread this book without remembering and comparing the first phase of the author's life with the second. His life in 1856 compared with that in 1876 serves to illuminate two souls of the same person. The first date is that of the initial period of production when the soul devotes itself, and the imagination does nothing but flourish, without gaining from its fruits or benefiting those who collect them. In the second, he was disenchanted. Discounting his personal life, his final years were those of a misanthrope. It emanated through his writing and his appearance. I am still reminded of those mornings when I would go looking for him on the solitary lanes of the Public Road, where he would be walking and meditating, and I would walk with him and listen to his melancholy words, without a sign of hope or of nostalgia. He felt the worst that the pride of a great genius can feel: public acclaim followed by public indifference. Beginning like Voltaire and ending like Rousseau. . . .

These and other signs of the times had soured his soul. The echo of the noisy block contrasted with the present silence; he did not find loyalty in admiration. He entered into politics and rose, only to fall just as quickly, bringing forth the first drops of bitterness. When a minister of state, questioned by him, retorted with words that conveyed, more or less, this sense—that partisan life demands ranking of positions and submission to bosses—he used language that was precise and clear to the whole *Câmara* [legislative body] but unintelligible to Alencar, whose sensibilities would not accommodate the inferior disciplines of partisans. . . .

Posterity will give this book the position to which it aspires. Not all works arrive intact to be read by the public; there are cases in which a summary is all the author leaves to the world. . . . The author of *Iracema* and *O Guarani* can confidently hope for more. There is an unconscious allegory here. When the Paraíba River floods everything, Peri, to save Cecília, seizes a palm tree with all his might. No one can forget that magnificent page. The palm tree falls. Cecília is deposited safely on it. Peri murmurs so that the girl can hear, "You will live," and they both plunge ahead between water and sky, until the two merge in the horizon. Cecília is the soul of the great author; the tree is the nation that bears [his work] in the grand tumult of the times. You will live!

Translation by Emma Wohl

Abolition Decree

Princess Isabel and Rodrigo Augusto da Silva

It took nearly four decades after the end of the slave trade in 1850 to abolish slavery entirely. As noted earlier, in the intervening years the imperial government of Dom Pedro II had passed a number of conservative edicts whose supposed goal was the gradual end of slavery, such as the Law of the Free Womb of 1871. The Sexagenarian Law, which went into effect September 28, 1885, freed all slaves over sixty-five years of age and granted those aged sixty to sixty-five eventual freedom after three more years of servitude. It did little to undermine the institution of slavery, however, as slaves at that age, for the most part, were too old to work. These conciliatory measures may have slowed the process of abolition, but they did not reverse support for it. By the mid-1880s voluntary and even some instances of provincially decreed manumission became increasingly common.

In May 1888, the minister of agriculture, Rodrigo Augusto da Silva, with the support of Princess Isabel, sent a proposal for full abolition to parliament. After a quick debate, the two houses passed the measure and on May 13, 1888, Princess Isabel, again acting as regent while Dom Pedro II was in Europe, signed it into law. Though slave owners had hoped the government would provide them financial compensation for their lost property, the decree offered no such measure, a fact that alienated many wealthy landowners from the monarchy. The law is now known as the Golden Law, and May 13 is often commemorated.

The Imperial Princess Regent, in the name of His Majesty the Emperor Dom Pedro II, makes known to all subjects of the Empire that the general assembly has decreed, and she has approved, the following law:

Article 1. From the date of this law, slavery is declared abolished in Brazil.

Article 2. All contrary provisions are revoked.

She therefore orders all the authorities to whom belong the knowledge and execution of the said law to execute it, and cause it to be fully and exactly executed and observed.

The secretary of state for the Departments of Agriculture, Commerce, and Public Works, and *ad interim* for Foreign Affairs, Rodrigo Augusto da

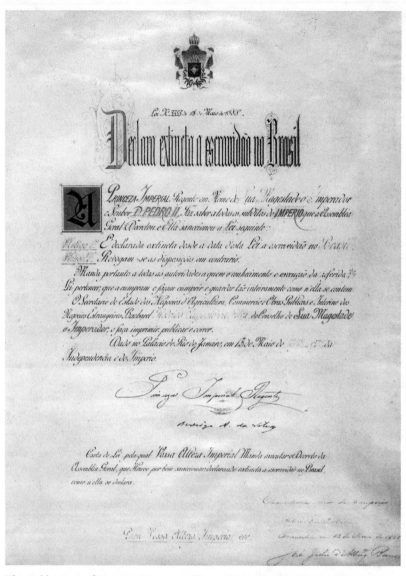

The Golden Law of May 13, 1888, granted immediate emancipation to all slaves without compensation to their former owners. Courtesy of the Brazilian National Archive (Arquivo Nacional).

Silva, of the council of His Majesty, the emperor, will cause it to be printed, published, and circulated.

Given in the Palace of Rio de Janeiro, May 13, 1888, the sixty-seventh year of Independence and of the Empire.

Translated by Robert M. Levine and John J. Crocitti

Portraits: Emperor Dom Pedro II

Lilia Moritz Schwarcz

On December 2, 1825, the city of Rio de Janeiro awoke to the roar of salvos from forts and ships. The crown prince was born, the first genuinely Brazilian prince and the promise and embodiment of national aspirations. Pedro de Alcântara João Carlos Leopoldo Salvador Bibiano Francisco Xavier de Paula Leocádio Miguel Gabriel Rafael Gonzaga was a long name for such a small child. Nevertheless, the length of the name served to reveal the size of the hopes for the little prince.

Dom Pedro II grew up to be the antithesis of his father, the Emperor Dom Pedro I (Pedro IV of Portugal), who proclaimed the independence of Brazil on September 22, 1822. While his father was seen as a volatile, strong-willed man, the son was the opposite: serene and calm, even as a child. But the childhood of the future emperor was far from tranquil. Just a few days after his first birthday, his mother, Dona Maria Leopoldina of the House of Habsburg, archduchess of Austria and daughter of the Austrian emperor Francis I, died of illness (see "Portraits: Empress Maria Leopoldina of Brazil" in part IV).

Little is known about this period in the life of Brazil's second emperor. All that remain are accounts of the monotony of everyday life and critical descriptions of his tutors. These accounts highlight the daily tedium and strict rules that, with clockwork precision, kept the prince tied to a schedule of work and study far from his subjects, revealing the tiresome routine of a child being shaped into a monarch.

His childhood, such as it was, was short, as in 1831 his father abdicated the throne and the five-year-old prince became the new emperor of Brazil. Pedro I had been facing criticism over what some in Brazil saw as his abuses of political authority, while the 1826 death of his own father, João VI, had led to a crisis of succession in Portugal. Thus, in 1831 the monarch departed for Portugal with the firm intention of claiming the throne for his firstborn child with Maria Leopoldina, their daughter, Dona Maria da Glória. The new Emperor Pedro II remained in Brazil, where he was placed under the care of a tutor, José Bonifácio de Andrada e Silva. To make matters worse, on September 24, 1834, Pedro I died in Portugal, making Pedro II an orphan.

Between 1831 and 1840, a series of regents ruled Brazil on behalf of the boy emperor. Although he was just fourteen years old in 1840, a series of rebellions against the regency in many areas of the country that year suggested the need for a more centralized power. It is difficult to imagine that a monarch of his age was ready to assume control of the nation, yet numerous documents describe Dom Pedro II as resolute and confident about the idea of ascending the throne. He was seen as poised, cautious with words, and sometimes distant. Not by coincidence, his consecration and coronation in 1841 was an elaborate spectacle, including ceremonies, processions, and the Portuguese custom of *beija-mão* (hand kissing).

The period from 1841, when he became emperor, to 1864, when the war with Paraguay began, represents an important phase in the consolidation of the Brazilian monarchy. Revolts against the regency in Bahia, Pará, and Maranhão had been quelled; only the Farroupilhas (Ragamuffins) War in the south continued to inconvenience the central government. It was also in this period that the country achieved improved financial stability due to the entrance of coffee into international markets, the end of the transatlantic slave trade, and the concurrent introduction of large amounts of capital into the economy. Pedro II kept away from state affairs and educated himself in the sciences and humanities. When it came time for the emperor to marry, he followed the custom of European courts, with a bride selected for him. On June 23, 1843, he married Tereza Maria Cristina, princess of the two Sicilies.

As the monarch matured, his popularity grew, and his reign became associated with economic and political stability. A generation of scholars, novelists, and painters redrew images of the country, using more imagination than reality in their representations. Pedro II was a great patron of the arts and sciences. He financed, often with his own personal funds, painters, writers, historians, and scientists. He wanted to create an image of Brazil that was at once tropical and possessed of universal values, an enlightened empire that lay in contrast with the warring and fractious Spanish American republics nearby.

However, as the nineteenth century advanced, domestic and international disputes disrupted the seeming tranquility of the empire. In 1870, the Republican Party was founded, and a fierce domestic debate over abolition helped lead, in 1871, to the passage of the Law of the Free Womb, which freed the children of slave mothers. Also in this period, the disastrous Paraguayan War (1865–70) came to an end. This conflict between tiny Paraguay and an alliance between Argentina, Brazil, and Uruguay had lasted much longer than anticipated, caused more deaths than expected, resulted in a sizeable financial debt, and caused considerable wear on Dom Pedro II. If the onset of the war represented the height of support for the empire, its end five years later marked the beginning of the empire's decline. Responsibility for a large loss of human life fell on the emperor, and a new institution, the military, began to grow beyond the monarchy's control.

Princess Isabel (1846–1921), the heir to the throne, and her father, Dom Pedro II, during the years of the Paraguayan War. Photograph by Joaquim Insley Pacheco.

After the war, Dom Pedro II, disillusioned with domestic politics, began to travel extensively outside of the country. The first of these trips began in 1871 with a lengthy itinerary that included Europe and North Africa. After a ten-month absence, the emperor returned to Brazil and soon began planning another trip abroad, this time to the United States, Canada, Europe, and the Middle East. The monarch visited schools and cultural institutions and met with famous scientists and intellectuals, notably the republican writer Victor Hugo. These were the activities most dear to the sovereign, who publicly expressed his alienation from everyday Brazilian politics and who preferred to contemplate questions of world culture and science.

Pedro II was becoming a foreigner in his own land. While he supported abolition and took some steps to promote it, he observed the growth of the Republican Party from the sidelines and did not actively engage in responding to the severe drought of 1877 that ravaged the northeast. Cartoons and political caricatures from the time show a tired monarch, sleeping during assemblies of the Brazilian Geographical and Historical Institute and napping among deputies and during exams at the Dom Pedro II High School.

It was in this context that the emperor left for his third trip abroad on

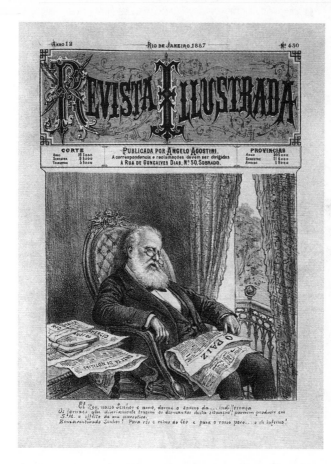

This cartoon by Angelo Agostini, a prominent abolitionist, criticizes the fact that the emperor is too old to rule. The caption reads, "The King, our Lord and Master, sleeps and dreams indifference." From *Revista Illustrada*, no. 450, 1887.

June 30, 1887. While the stated reason for his first journey was the death of a daughter, and the second was prompted by the illness of the empress, on the third journey, it was the emperor who required medical care. Exhausted, the sovereign retired to the hot springs of Baden-Baden spa and appeared even more lethargic in pictures. In 1888, Brazil abolished slavery, a decision he celebrated, as he and his heir, Princess Isabel, had been personally opposed to slavery. Nonetheless, the measure struck a severe blow to the imperial regime, which, by that time, depended largely on the support of slave owners in the Paraíba Valley. In this context the end of the empire was discussed almost openly. Yet some, including Deodoro da Fonseca, the military officer who would later head the new republican regime established in 1889, said they preferred to await the death of the old monarch rather than instigate a republican coup d'état.

Other military officers, however, chose not to wait. On November 9, 1889, Pedro hosted a luxurious ball to honor a delegation from Chile, and critics pounced on this seeming display of a wasteful monarchy. Soon thereafter,

Dom Pedro, o primeiro dos heróis, by Henrique Fleiuss. Dom Pedro II, emperor of Brazil, near the end of his reign. From *Semana Ilustrada*, 1865.

the Clube Militar (Officers' club) mobilized and proclaimed a republic on November 15, 1889. Dom Pedro II and his family were forced to leave Brazil for Portugal, accompanied by a number of friends and supporters who voluntarily joined the imperial family in exile. Fearful of public reaction, the Republicans thought it best to say little about the royal family's departure. Instead, they issued a decree only after Dom Pedro had left, banning Dom Pedro and all of his family from Brazil, prohibiting them from owning property there, and giving them six months to sell off what they had. Yet the decree also made a gesture of amicability, offering him a sum of money to help them resettle.

In his final years, Dom Pedro II lived in Europe and was supported financially by his friends, refusing to accept the aforementioned funds the new Republican regime had offered. Tereza Cristina died soon after they arrived in Portugal, on December 28, 1889, constituting another deep blow to Dom Pedro, who wrote in his diary, "I can hardly believe it. I always wanted to die before her. An emptiness has opened in my life that I do not know how to fill."[1] Following her death he moved to France, eventually settling in Paris. In 1891 the ex-sovereign began to suffer from a persistent cough, caused by pneumonia in his left lung, and on December 5, 1891, he died. The elaborate funeral proceedings for Pedro II in Paris befitted his previous status and also suggested an implicit critique of his exile. He was dressed in his imperial uniform and decorated with the insignia of two chivalric orders created by his father in the 1820s and abolished by the Republican government just a few months before his death. Across his lap lay two Brazilian flags, and next to his body was a sealed container of Brazilian soil, which he had brought himself with instructions that he be buried with it. The funeral rituals in Paris lasted three days, during which a large delegation of European royalty attended. Following this, his body was sent by train to Portugal to lie alongside that of his Tereza Cristina in the Pantheon of the House of Braganza.

At the time of his death, government officials in Brazil were disheartened by the honorifics accorded to him in France and tried to cast the events as the holdover of European monarchical values, irrelevant to Brazil's current trajectory of republican progress. Within three decades, however, Dom Pedro had been reimagined as a national hero, a magnanimous figure who loved Brazil and worked tirelessly to serve it. In 1922, as part of the celebrations of the centenary of Brazil's independence in 1822, the remains of Dom Pedro and Tereza Cristina were returned to Brazil. With great ceremony, they were interred in a specially built mausoleum in Petrópolis, the resort town that Pedro II had founded in the hills near Rio de Janeiro. Their arrival suggests how much more secure the republican system had become by the 1920s and the extent to which Brazilians could begin to reconcile their republican present with their imperial past.

Note

1. Lilia Moritz Schwarcz, *The Emperor's Beard: Dom Pedro II and the Tropical Monarchy of Brazil* (New York: Hill and Wang, 2004), 344.

VII

Republican Brazil and the Onset
of Modernization, 1889–1929

Three days after the military led the overthrow of the monarchy and pro-claimed Brazil a republic, the *Diário Popular* (People's daily) newspaper pub-lished an article describing the events in Rio de Janeiro on that November 15, 1889. Penned by the republican advocate Aristides Lobo, it enthusiastically applauded the intervention: "For now the color of the government is purely military and should be so. The event was theirs, theirs alone because the col-laboration of civilians was almost nil. The people cried, bestialized, stunned, surprised, without knowing what it meant. Many seriously believed they were watching a parade."[1]

Indeed, the event garnered no popular rebellions, neither in support nor opposition, and not even any widespread civilian participation. Instead it was the result of a handful of republicans, many of whom were adherents of posi-tivist philosophy, who had managed to draw military allies into their plans to bring down the empire. Over time, as politicians consolidated the republican regime, the new state would retain this elitist, exclusionary character, even as outbursts of discontent from the lower and middle classes challenged the republic's oligarchic nature until it too was overthrown in 1930.

Positivism was hugely influential in the military and among urban middle-class intellectuals in the early days of the republic, a fact that both re-flected and had an impact on the restrictive nature of republican politics. The movement drew from the ideas of French philosopher Auguste Comte, who offered an account of the social evolution of humanity in which enlightened technicians and scientists should play a crucial role in establishing a modern, industrialized society. Slavery had been abolished just sixteen months before the declaration of the republic, and the country remained overwhelmingly rural and economically dependent on agricultural exports. At abolition, the state offered no assistance to freed slaves, who were forced to scrape by in the countryside or in the cities. While Europe and the United States indus-trialized, Brazil remained a largely agrarian nation. Positivism offered a plan to improve that situation, and many looked to the state to play a key role in

A poster announcing the declaration of the republic. Credit: Museu da República, Ministério de Cultura, 35/2013.

the country's transformation. Symbolic of this sentiment was the positivist motto emblazoned on the new republican flag announcing that "Order and Progress" would define the nation.

Under the Constitution of 1891, church and state became legally separate, and the government assumed the role of registering births, marriages, and deaths. According to the Constitution, the new federal republic would be characterized by decentralized power, and it transformed the provinces into states and granted them more autonomy and fiscal control over certain affairs.

During the empire, suffrage had been limited to certain male property owners; in 1874, only about 10 percent of the population was legally eligible to vote. Under the republic, lawmakers further restricted the franchise, adding a literacy requirement and other measures. By 1910, out of a total population of 22 million, only 627,000 people, all men, had the right to vote. Throughout the 1920s the percentage of eligible voters hovered at between 2.3 percent and 3.4 percent of the total population.

In the early years of the republic, from 1889 until 1894, the army assumed

Alegoria à proclamação da república e à partida da família imperial, anonymous. Military officers and politicians offer a new national flag to the female symbol of the republic.

a preeminent role in the new government. Marshal Deodoro da Fonseca, the symbolic leader of the republican movement, became the head of the provisional government in 1889 and then the republic's first president in February 1891, and army marshal Floriano Peixoto was made his vice president, both elected by Congress. Yet by the end of 1891, facing severe congressional opposition to his efforts to strengthen executive power, and an economic crisis stemming from rampant stock market speculation, da Fonseca suddenly resigned. When Peixoto assumed the presidency in his place, he soon faced both a naval revolt in Rio de Janeiro and a military rebellion in several southern states. These conflicts ended only after the presidential elections of 1894, when São Paulo coffee elites successfully promoted the election of one of their own, Prudente de Morais, the first directly elected civilian president of Brazil.

Prudente de Morais's administration (1894–98) crafted a new political system that favored the state's economic interests and gave tremendous impetus to the modernization of the city of São Paulo. Indeed, the election of successive Brazilian presidents who hailed from São Paulo consolidated the state's influence on national politics and the importance placed on the coffee industry. De Morais also oversaw the military's annihilation of the rural community of Canudos in the interior of Bahia, an act that was reminiscent of the destruction of Palmares two hundred years earlier. Framed as a battle

580 Emigrants Coming to the "Lan

Millions of people from Europe, the Middle East, and Japan immigrated to the Americas in the late nineteenth and early twentieth centuries. Photograph by William H. Rau. Courtesy of the U.S. Library of Congress.

between civilization, as defended by the federal government, and barbarity, as manifested by the religious and popular folk beliefs of Canudos's mainly mixed-race and African-descendant backland residents, the decision to invade and destroy Canudos symbolized a larger debate among elites about the country's future. Would the majority, predominantly nonwhite, population impede modernization and progress? As Brazilian intellectuals and other elites engaged with racist ideas that circulated among European and U.S. thinkers, they pondered the future of their nation.

One proposed solution to this seeming problem was to encourage European immigration, revamping efforts that had been relatively unsuccessful under the empire. Following abolition, immigrants, mostly from southern and eastern Europe and the Ottoman Empire, flooded into the country, and after 1907 immigrants from Japan joined them.

Although most newcomers initially went to work on the coffee plantations of São Paulo, many soon settled in urban areas where they provided cheap labor for the slowly developing light industrial sectors. Some of the Spanish, Italian, and Jewish immigrants from eastern Europe and Russia embraced anarchist and socialist ideas, contributing to the emergence of mutual aid societies, workers' organizations, and trade unions that fought to improve labor and living conditions.

In the capital city of Rio de Janeiro, the federal government carried out an extensive urban renewal plan that involved tearing down low-income housing and creating broad avenues lined with modern buildings that imitated the latest architectural styles of Europe. It also authorized public health campaigns designed to combat the unsanitary and insalubrious conditions in much of the city. Yet the federal government's heavy-handed approach to these efforts, especially the authorization of mandatory, house-to-house smallpox vaccinations, provoked an urban riot in 1906. Known as the Vaccine Revolt, the incident exposed the limits of the government's reach as popular classes fiercely resisted what they saw as intrusive and authoritarian invasions of their homes and bodies.

Popular revolts were not the only threat to the stability of the republic. Feuding among different factions and sectors of the economic and social elite risked political volatility at a time when the nation was experiencing dramatic social and demographic changes. In response, politicians and powerful families from the three wealthiest and most populous states—São Paulo, Minas Gerais, and Rio de Janeiro—developed a tacit power-sharing agreement. This pact, known as the politics of *café com leite* (coffee with milk) in reference to the importance of coffee production to all three states and of the cheese and milk produced in Minas Gerais, sought to rotate the office of the presidency among representatives from the three states. The candidate, usually the former governor of one of the states, bargained for political support among local power brokers in other parts of the country by promising federal resources and local autonomy. This arrangement managed to secure a stable and elite-dominated political system until the Great Depression, when coffee prices plummeted and new political forces pushed for access to the central government.

The early twentieth century also gave rise to new forms of social and cultural discontent. A growing number of intellectuals questioned the scientific racism propagated by Brazilian scholars, which often merely echoed European ideas about the existence of superior and inferior races. One expression of this questioning can be seen in the modernist movement that surfaced in São Paulo in 1922, a city whose population skyrocketed from 64,000 in 1890 to 239,820 in 1900, and then more than doubled to 579,033 in 1920. The mod-

The cover of the first edition of *Klaxon*, a literary magazine of the modernist movement.

ernist movement criticized the staid conventions of Brazilian high society and its slavish imitation of European styles and tastes. These artists instead privileged Brazilian themes, praised popular culture, and featured people of color in artistic and literary works. Many modernists, such as the writers Mário de Andrade and Oswald de Andrade (who were unrelated) and the artist Tarsilia do Amaral (who designed the official invitations to an exhibition called *Modern Art Week* in São Paulo in 1922), embraced this popular culture in their work.

At the same time, sectors of the lower and middle classes demonstrated their critiques of the exclusionary and conservative policies of the national government through their participation in the General Strike of 1917 and the formation of the Brazilian Communist Party (PCB) in 1922. Discontent had permeated the armed forces as well. In 1910, several thousand navy sailors carefully organized and carried out a mutiny to protest the use of corporal punishment by the officers, nearly all of whom were white, against the enlisted sailors, who were mostly black or of mixed race. Later called the Revolta da Chibata (Revolt of the whip), the event exposed racism within the navy and the abuse of enlisted troops, including their poor working conditions and pay. In 1922, noncommissioned officers revolted at the Copacabana Fort in Rio de Janeiro, critical of what they saw as persistent fraud and abuse ignored by high-ranking officers. Meanwhile millenarian revolts such as the Contestado, which shook up the south of Brazil between 1912 and 1916, exemplified popular protests against the incursion of railroads and capital into rural regions. The great stock market crash of October 1929 and the subsequent collapse of the Brazilian economy set the stage for even more economic hardship and consequent political reshuffling.

The new political leader that emerged in 1930 was Getúlio Vargas, a politician from the southernmost state of Rio Grande do Sul who came to office via a military coup. In order to mark a sharp break between his presidency and the government that he had overthrown, his administration began to refer to the period from 1889 to 1930 as the Old Republic (República Velha), implying that his predecessors defended conservative and antiquated values. Nowadays, most historians name this period the First Republic, and consider it a time when the country experimented with new ideas about political authority, race, and nation.

Note

1. Aristides Lobo, "Cartas ao Rio," *Diário Popular*, November 15, 1989.

Hymn of the Proclamation of the Republic

José Joaquim de Campos da Costa de Medeiros

e Albuquerque and Leopoldo Miguez

As soon as the republic was established, its founding leaders created symbols to represent the new regime and to signal its break from the past. Thus, in January 1890, the provisional government of Marshal Deodoro da Fonseca sponsored a song contest to choose a new national anthem, with the entries to be performed at the Lyric Theatre of Rio de Janeiro. The award went to a piece composed by Leopoldo Miguez (1850–1902), with lyrics by José Joaquim de Campos da Costa de Medeiros e Albuquerque (1867–1934). Miguez had originally studied music in Europe but returned to Brazil in 1878; by 1889 he had become the director of the National Institute of Music. Medeiros e Albuquerque had also studied in Europe, at the School of the Academy of Lisbon, but in Brazil he became a protégé of the well-known folklorist Silvio Romero and a great enthusiast of republican ideals, serving in several public and administrative posts in the new government.

Despite choosing their song as the winner of the competition, the government ultimately decided not to make it the national anthem. Rather, they continued to use "Hymn of the Empire" for that role and stipulated that Miguez and Medeiros e Albuquerque's creation would be called "Hymn of the Proclamation of the Republic."

The lyrics promote patriotic ideals of liberty, a challenge given the fact that legal slavery had only been abolished a year and a half earlier.

May this be a cloak of light unfurled,	Seja um pálio de luz desdobrado,
Across the broad expanse of these skies.	Sob a larga amplidão destes céus.
This rebel song that the past	Este canto rebel, que o passado
Comes to redeem from the vilest disgraces!	Vem remir dos mais torpes labéus!
May this be a hymn of glory that speaks	Seja um hino de glória que fale
Of the hopes of a new future!	De esperanças de um novo porvir!
With visions of triumphs may it cradle	Com visões de triunfos embale

Those who come forward to defend it!

Liberty! Liberty!
Spread your wings above us,
Through struggles in the storm
Let us hear your voice.

We cannot believe that formerly
There were slaves in so noble a country . . .
Today the rosy flash of dawn
Finds brothers, not hostile tyrants.
We are all equal! In the future,
United, we will know to lift
Our august banner that, pure,
Shines triumphant from the altar of the fatherland!

Liberty! Liberty!
Spread your wings above us,
Through struggles in the storm
Let us hear your voice.

If it must be that from brave breasts
Our flags are bloodied,
The living blood of the hero Tiradentes
Baptized this bold flag!
Messenger of peace, it is peace we desire,
From love comes our strength and power,
But in war, in the greatest ordeals
You will see us fight and win!

Liberty! Liberty!
Spread your wings above us,
Through struggles in the storm
Let us hear your voice.

From Ipiranga the shout must be
A magnificent cry of faith!
Brazil has already emerged free,

Quem por ele lutando surgir!

Liberdade! Liberdade!
Abre as asas sobre nós,
Das lutas na tempestade
Dá que ouçamos tua voz.

Nós nem cremos que escravos outrora
Tenha havido em tão nobre País . . .
Hoje o rubro lampejo da aurora
Acha irmãos, não tiranos hostis.
Somos todos iguais! Ao futuro
Saberemos, unidos, levar
Nosso augusto estandarte que, puro,
Brilha, ovante, da Pátria no altar!

Liberdade! Liberdade!
Abre as asas sobre nós,
Das lutas na tempestade
Dá que ouçamos tua voz.

Se é mister que de peitos valentes
Haja sangue em nosso pendão,
Sangue vivo do herói Tiradentes
Batizou neste audaz pavilhão!
Mensageiro de paz, paz queremos,
É de amor nossa força e poder,
Mas da guerra, nos transes supremos
Heis de ver-nos lutar e vencer!

Liberdade! Liberdade!
Abre as asas sobre nós,
Das lutas na tempestade
Dá que ouçamos tua voz.

Do Ipiranga é preciso que o brado
Seja um grito soberbo de fé!
O Brasil já surgiu libertado,

From the purple vestments of
   royalty.
Oh, Brazilians, advance!
May we reap green laurels!
May our Country be triumphant,
A free land of free brothers!

Liberty! Liberty!
Spread your wings above us!
Through struggles in the storm
Let us hear your voice!

Sobre as púrpuras régias
   de pé.
Eia, pois, brasileiros avante!
Verdes louros colhamos louçãos!
Seja o nosso País triunfante,
Livre terra de livres irmãos!

Liberdade! Liberdade!
Abre as asas sobre nós!
Das lutas na tempestade
Dá que ouçamos tua voz!

Translated by Erika Manouselis and Victoria Langland

The Human Races

Raimundo Nina Rodrigues

Race was one of the themes most frequently addressed by intellectuals under the new republic, as they imagined what kind of future Brazil would have. An important participant in these debates was Raimundo Nina Rodrigues (1862–1906), a professor of the Bahia School of Medicine. Influenced by models of racial determinism and positivist criminology, and notwithstanding his own mixed-race background, Rodrigues believed that blacks, the indigenous, and their descendants were innately inferior to whites. He further drew on models of criminal anthropology proposed by Cesare Lombroso in Italy to argue that people of color were especially prone to crime. In 1894, just a few years after the abolition of slavery, he published As raças humanas e a responsabilidade penal no Brasil *(The human races and penal responsibility in Brazil), in which he favored the creation of two penal codes—one for whites and one for those of other races. Given the purportedly different attributes of whites and nonwhites, he argued, they should be subject to different liabilities.*

In the passage below extracted from the introduction to that work, Rodrigues presents his theory about the inherent inferiority of non-European races, advancing racist notions couched in scientific language. He also points to the impossibility of successfully educating the native populations. While many of his ideas remained outside of the mainstream, and his proposal to develop two penal codes was not taken up by jurists, his publications were widely read by other intellectuals and reflect an important strain of racist thought at the turn of the twentieth century.

The spiritualist understanding that a soul of the same nature exists in all peoples consequently supposes an intelligence of the same capacity in all races, which only varies in their level of culture. However, considering the idea that a representative of the inferior races is capable of achieving the elevated degree to which the superior races have arrived is a concept that must be irredeemably refuted in the face of modern scientific understanding.

The root causes of the inequality that diverse races and species face around the world are not so simple or contingent. On the contrary, they reproduce, more or less reliably, the stages or phases through which, over time and under the force of relentless, powerful causes, certain anthropological groups achieve perfection as a result of their ability to triumph through adaptation, occupying the vanguard in social evolution.

The slow and gradual perfection of psychic activity, intelligence, and morality allows evolutionary perfection in the animal kingdom. In their underlying anatomical makeup, simple organic functions occur that evolve toward gradual perfection, through the growing complexity of the nervous systems of organisms.

But in the animal kingdom, this growing complexity in the microscopic biochemical composition of the brain only occurs very slowly with the help of adaptation and heredity through many generations. In the same way successive degrees of mental development have occurred in different peoples. Mental evolution not only assumes a very different cultural capacity in the different phases of development of a race, which is capable of becoming progressively more perfect, but it also affirms the impossibility of preventing the intervention of time in adaptations and imposing on one people a civilization that is incompatible with the degree of its intellectual development. . . .

Today, what have become of the brilliant, complex, and powerful barbarian civilizations that, at the time of the discovery of America, occupied Mexico and Peru?

They dissolved. They disappeared completely in their social interactions with European civilization, which was much more polished and advanced. Where are the prosperous, civilized colonies of the Brazilian savages, whom our sincere and dedicatedly selfless missionaries uplifted, having conquered them with saintly ingenuity and made them followers of the Lord?

The truth is that the American savage still roams today in the deserted depths of our virgin forests, always resistant and always on the run from European civilization, which harasses and hems in [the native] from all sides, preparing at the same time for its total extinction. The truth is that only through miscegenation have natives been able to integrate into our population, incapable as they are of receiving and adopting as their own the European civilization imported with the colonizers.

No one can believe now that the tremendous failure of this great campaign of civilizing and converting the savages, sustained by men of elevated intellect, whose faith and religious conviction motivated them and made them heroes, was caused by errors and defects of orientation and leadership.

The misconceptions of spiritualist psychology prepared, in fact, with their false promises, the failure of such drowned hopes.

The cause was positive and material—the need for time and the organic incapacity of the aboriginals to achieve the social adaptation that was demanded of them.

"If the moral nature of a people," a man profoundly convinced of their capacity to be educated wrote, "were a piece of paper, where we inscribed whatever came to mind, it would be as easy to change customs as it is to write. Fortunately or unfortunately, it is not like that. Their rude customs are more persistent than those of a civilized people; they become intimately involved with feelings, needs, and even religious beliefs and superstitions. The most rudimentary understanding of nature makes one see that it is impossible to change such things without the passage of some generations and without some means other than the education of one special child, cultivated in an attempt to reduce him to an interpreter who serves as a link between the Indian and the Christian."[1]

The study of inferior races has furnished science with well-observed examples of this organic cerebral incapacity.

Translated by Emma Wohl

Note

1. José Vieira Couto de Margalhães, *O Selvagem* [The savage] (Rio de Janeiro: Typographia da Reforma, 1876), 191.

Os Sertões or Rebellion in the Backlands

Euclides da Cunha

Many intellectuals in turn-of-the-twentieth-century Brazil held deeply racist conceptions about people of non-European background. Such is the case with Euclides Rodrigues da Cunha (1866–1909), a writer, reporter, historian, geographer, and engineer, who is best known for his 1902 book, Os Sertões, translated into English as Rebellion in the Backlands. *The book recounts his experiences as a correspondent for the* O Estado de São Paulo *newspaper in 1897, when he accompanied federal troops sent to the interior of Bahia to suppress a messianic community of some thirty thousand impoverished rural residents. The community of Canudos, led by a charismatic Catholic folk preacher named Antônio Conselheiro, threatened state and federal authorities because it challenged the legitimacy of the secular republic and garnered widespread appeal among the destitute populations of the interior. Three previous military expeditions had been sent to disband the community, stoking sensationalistic news reports of fanatical backlanders.*

Da Cunha's account of events surrounding the Canudos campaign became a best seller. The book is divided into three parts. In the first two sections, "The Land" and "The Man," da Cunha adopts a geographically and racially deterministic posture, portraying the harsh environment of the backlands as shaping the fierce character and degenerate physical attributes of its inhabitants. But in the last part, titled "The Rebellion," da Cunha lauds the residents for their resistance and criticizes the barbaric violence of federal troops who annihilated the community. By the book's end, da Cunha makes it clear that he no longer knows how to distinguish who was more degenerate or more backward.

Canudos Did Not Surrender

Let us bring this book to a close.

Canudos did not surrender. The only case of its kind in history, it held out to the last man. Conquered inch by inch, in the literal meaning of the words, it fell on October 5 [1897], toward dusk—when its last defenders fell, dying, every man of them. There were only four of them left: an old man, two other full-grown men, and a child, facing a furiously raging army of five thousand soldiers.

Political cartoon showing Antônio Conselheiro (1830–1897), the leader of Canudos, under assault by republican troops. From *Revista Ilustrada*, no. 728, 1897.

We shall spare ourselves the task of describing the last moments. We *could* not describe them. This tale we are telling remained a deeply stirring and a tragic one to the very end, but we must close it falteringly and with no display of brilliancy. We are like one who has ascended a very high mountain. On the summit, new and wide perspectives unfold before him, but along with them comes dizziness.

Shall we defy the incredulity of future generations by telling in detail how women hurled themselves on their burning homes, their young ones in their arms?

And, words being what they are, what comment should we make on the fact that, from the morning of the third on, nothing more was to be seen of the able-bodied prisoners who had been rounded up the day before, among them that same "Pious Anthony" who had surrendered to us so trustingly— and to whom we owe so much valuable information concerning this obscure phase of our history?

The settlement fell on the fifth. On the sixth they completed the work of destroying and dismantling the houses—5,200 of them by careful count.

The Counselor's Corpse

Previously, at dawn that day, a commission assigned to the task had discovered the corpse of Antônio Conselheiro. It was lying in one of the huts next to the arbor. After a shallow layer of earth had been removed, the body appeared wrapped in a sorry shroud—a filthy sheet—over which pious hands had strewn a few withered flowers. There, resting upon a reed mat, were the last remains of the "notorious and barbarous agitator." They were in a fetid condition. Clothed in his old blue canvas tunic, his face swollen and hideous, the deep-sunken eyes filled with dirt, the Counselor would not have been recognizable to those who in the course of his life had known him most intimately.

They carefully disinterred the body, precious relic that it was—the sole prize, the only spoils of war this conflict had to offer!—taking the greatest of precautions to see that it did not fall apart, in which case they would have had nothing but a disgusting mass of rotting tissues on their hands. They photographed it afterward and drew up an affidavit in due form, certifying its identity; for the entire nation must be thoroughly convinced that at last this terrible foe had been done away with.

Then they put it back in its grave. Later, however, the thought occurred to them that they should have preserved the head, that head on which so many maledictions had been heaped; and, since it was a waste of time to exhume the body once more, a knife cleverly wielded at the right point did the trick, the corpse was decapitated, and that horrible face, sticky with scars and pus, once more appeared before the victors' gaze.

After that they took it to the seaboard, where it was greeted by delirious multitudes with carnival joy. Let science here have the last word. Standing out in bold relief from all the significant circumvolutions were the essential outlines of crime and madness. . . .

The Owner's Pastry Shop

Joaquim Maria Machado de Assis

Literary scholars and critics, both in Brazil and internationally, acclaim Joaquim Maria Machado de Assis (1839–1908) as one of Brazil's greatest authors. Born into a modest mixed-race family, he did not receive a strong formal education as a child, but as an adolescent and young man worked as a typographer's assistant at a government printing office. He would become a poet, columnist, playwright, journalist, short story writer, novelist, and literary critic (see his critique of José de Alencar's 1887 novel O Guarani *in part VI), as well as one of the founders of the Brazilian Academy of Letters in 1896. Today one of the most prestigious literary prizes awarded by the Brazilian Academy of Letters is named the Machado de Assis Prize.*

Living in Rio de Janeiro, Machado de Assis witnessed important changes in the capital as the country changed from an empire to a republic, and he often wrote ironic, shrewd, and veiled political commentary about them, as in this excerpt from his novel Esau and Jacob. *The book tells the story of twin brothers, Pedro and Paulo, who began fighting when inside their mother's womb and never stopped: one became a doctor, the other a lawyer; one a republican, the other a monarchist. The brothers only agreed on one thing: they both fell in love with the same woman.*

The excerpt below is a subplot of the novel that takes place immediately after republican forces take control of the government and are about to send the emperor and his family into exile. Custódio, the owner of a pastry shop, has just ordered a brand-new sign for his business, the Imperial Pastry Shop. Worried that his sign might cause political problems, he seeks advice from a neighbor and prominent politician, Conselheiro Aires, who offers a pragmatic solution. Throughout Machado's novel, the author implies that there are few real differences between the old and the new regime, at least as far as politics are concerned. The ellipses in the text are in the original.

LXIII. A New Sign

When he had reported the above, Custódio disclosed all the money he had lost on the name [on the shop's sign] and the other expenses, the trouble that the preservation of the shop's name would cause him, the impossibility of finding another name, an abyss of woe in short. He did not know where to turn; he did not have any ideas or any peace of mind. If he could, he would

Joaquim Maria Machado de Assis (1839–1908) by Joachim José Insley Pacheco, 1864.

liquidate the pastry shop. And, after all, what did he have to do with politics? He was a simple maker and seller of sweets, esteemed, with a host of customers, respected, and especially a respecter of public order. . . .

"But what's the trouble?" asked Aires.

"The Republic has been proclaimed."

"There's already a government?"

"I think there is. But tell me, Your Excellency, have you ever heard anyone accuse me of attacking the government? Nobody ever has. And yet . . . A cruel stroke of Fate! Come to my rescue, most honored sir! Help me to get out of this difficulty. The sign is finished, the name all painted, *Confeitaria do Império* [Imperial Pastry Shop], the paint is bright and nice. The painter insists on my paying for the work before he does any more. If the sign were not finished I would change the name, no matter how painful it would be for me, but must I lose the money I've spent? Do you believe, Your Excellency, that if the *Império* remains, they will come and break my windows?"

"Well, I don't know."

"Really, there is no reason why they should. It's the name of the shop, has been for thirty years, no one knows it by any other name. . . ."

"But you could call it *Confeitaria da República*. . . ."

"This occurred to me, on my way home, but it also occurred to me that if in a month or two from now there is a counter-revolution, I'll be in the same spot I'm in today, and once again lose money."

"You are right. . . . Sit down."

"I'm all right."

"Sit down and have a cigar."

Custódio refused the cigar; he did not smoke. He accepted the chair. They were in Aires' study, where there were curiosities that would have attracted his attention, if it had not been for his distraught state of mind. He went on imploring his neighbor to rescue him. His Excellency, with the great intelligence that God had given him, could save him. Aires proposed a middle term, a name that would fit both contingencies, *Confeitaria do Governo* [Government Pastry Shop].

"It will serve as well for one political system as another."

"I don't say that it won't, and, if it weren't for the money I've lost. . . . There is, however, one thing against it. Your Excellency knows that there is no government that doesn't have an opposition. When members of the opposition come down the street they may pick a fight with me, get the idea that I am defying them, and break up my signboard, while all I want is the respect of everybody."

Aires understood very well that fear went hand in hand with avarice. To be sure, his neighbor did not want rows at his shop door, nor gratuitous ill will, nor the hatred of no matter whom, but he was no less terrorized by the expenditures he would have to make from time to time if he did not find a name that was definitive, popular, and impartial. In losing what he had, he had already lost celebrity, besides losing the cost of the painting and having to pay more money to boot. No one would buy a condemned, criminal signboard from him. It was bad enough to have his name and the name of his shop in the Laemmert *Almanac* where some busybody might read it and come with others to punish him for what had been printed way back at the beginning of the year. . . .

"Oh no, sir," interrupted Aires, "there is no need for you to withdraw the whole edition of an almanac from circulation."

And after several moments: "Look, I'll give you an idea that may prove useful, and if you do not think it good I have another ready, and it will be the last. But I believe that either of them will serve. Leave the signboard painted as it is, and, to the right, on the lower edge below the name, paint in these words to explain the name, Founded in 1860. Wasn't it in 1860 that you opened the shop?"

"It was," answered Custódio.

"Well then. . . ."

Custódio reflected. One could read neither *yes* nor *no* in him. Astonished, mouth half open, he kept looking not at the diplomat, nor at the floor, nor at the walls or furniture, but at the air. As Aires insisted, he came to and admitted that it was a good idea. As a matter of fact, it would keep the name and take from it its seditiousness, which had increased with the fresh paint. Still, the other idea might be as good or better, and he wanted to compare the two of them.

"The other idea does not have the advantage of showing the date of the founding of the house, but only that of defining the name, which will remain the same, but in a manner unconnected with the monarchy. Let the word *império* stand and add below it, in the center, these two words that need not be large, *das leis*—of law. Look, like this," concluded Aires, seating himself at the secretary and writing what he had said on a strip of paper.

Custódio read it, reread it, and thought the idea practical: yes, it was not bad. He saw only one defect in it: Since the letters below were smaller, they might not be seen so quickly and easily as those above, and it was these that caught a person's eye as he walked along the street. And so, some politician, or even a personal enemy, might not understand right away, and. . . . The first idea, when he came to think of it, had the same drawback, and besides this additional one: it might appear that the pastry-man, in marking the date of the establishment, was making a trademark of being old. Who knows if it was not worse than nothing?

"Everything is worse than nothing."

"Let's try to think of something else."

Aires thought of another name, the name of the street, *Confeitaria do Catete*, without noticing that since there was another pastry shop on the same street, it meant assigning the local designation exclusively to Custódio's. When his neighbor made his weighty observation Aires found it just and rejoiced to see the fellow's delicacy of feeling, but he soon discovered that what made Custódio speak out was the idea that the name would be common to the two shops. Many people would not bother to look for the sign but would buy at the first shop they came to, so that he alone would have the expense of painting the sign, and on top of it he would lose customers. On perceiving this, Aires was no less struck with admiration at the sagacity of the fellow, who, in the midst of so many tribulations, was able to calculate the bad results of an ambiguous word. Then, he told him, the best thing was to pay the expense he had incurred and not put up anything, unless he preferred his own name: *Confeitoria do Custódio*. Many people, surely, did not know the shop by any other name. A name, the owner's own name, did not have any political significance or historical aspect, hatred or love; it had nothing to attract the attention of the two rival political systems and consequently put his St. Clare turnovers in jeopardy, not to mention the lives of the proprietor and his employees. Why didn't he adopt this proposal? He would spend something on the changing of one word for another, *Custódio* in place of *Império*, but revolutions always entail expense.

"Yes, I'll think about it, most honored sir. Perhaps it will be best to wait a day or two, to see where the fad will end," said Custódio gratefully.

He bowed, backed away, and left. Aires went to the window to see him cross the street. He imagined that he would carry away from an ex-minister's house a special glow that would momentarily make him forget the crisis of the signboard. Expenses are not everything in life, and the glory of one's connections can soothe the roughnesses of this world. It did not happen this time. Custódio crossed the street without stopping or looking back and disappeared into the pastry shop with all his despair.

Revolt of the Whip, *A Revolta da Chibata*

João Cândido Felisberto and Bulcão Vianna

Following the end of the Paraguayan War in 1870, the Brazilian navy declined signifi-
cantly as the imperial government invested little in new ships, weapons, and equip-
ment. The officers were almost all white, and most of the sailors were black or of
mixed racial background. Many had been forcibly pressed into service; others were
slaves who had fled their masters. Conditions were dismal, wages low, and corporal
punishment pervasive.

After the establishment of the republic in 1889, the navy immediately banned cor-
poral punishment, but a year later it reinstituted whipping, permitting twenty-five
lashes for serious infractions. The punishment, which harkened back to the days of
slavery, outraged sailors. Led by João Cândido Felisberto and others, sailors began
meeting in secret groups to plan a rebellion that was scheduled for November 1910,
shortly after Hermes da Fonseca was to be inaugurated as president. However, the
punishment of a sailor with 250 lashes, deliberately delivered in front of his peers,
precipitated the revolt, which began a few days earlier than planned. Thousands of
sailors seized battleships in Rio's harbor and demanded better pay, improved work-
ing conditions, and a definitive end to flogging. The mutiny initially ended peace-
fully with an amnesty for the rebels and the acceptance of their demands, including
a decree abolishing whipping. But the government soon reneged on the amnesty guar-
antees, leading to a second revolt. This was violently repressed as the government
arrested hundreds of sailors, summarily executed numerous others, and expelled two
thousand men from the navy.

In the first document below, João Cândido Felisberto, whom the press called the
Black Admiral, describes the prison conditions he faced from the end of 1910 until
April 1911, when he was moved to an insane asylum. He and other defendants were
finally acquitted of charges in December 1912, as shown in the second document writ-
ten by Dr. Bulcão Vianna on behalf of the War Council.

Incarceration

The prison was small; water leaked in from all sides. And the doors were
covered in graffiti. We felt the stifling heat. The air was sweltering. It was as
if we were being cooked inside a cauldron. Some, worn down from thirst,

João Candido (*right*) reading the amnesty decree in the *Diário Official*, the government publication that recorded official occurrences. Photograph by Augusto Malta, Rio de Janeiro, 1910. Instituto Moreira Salles Collection.

drank their own urine. We took care of our needs in a barrel that was so full that it overflowed, inundating a corner of the prison. With the pretext of disinfecting the cell, they tossed in water and a considerable amount of lime.

The floor was sloped, causing the liquid at the bottom of the dungeon to evaporate, leaving just the lime. At first we were still so as not to disturb the lime dust. We thought we could endure the six days of solitary with bread and water. But the heat, beginning at ten in the morning, was suffocating. We screamed. We tried to break down the grate. The effort was draining. Clouds of lime rose off the ground and entered our lungs, choking us. The darkness was profound. The only light was a kerosene lamp. The moans gradually diminished, until a silence fell inside that hell, where the Federal Government, which we had blindly trusted, threw eighteen Brazilians along with their political rights guaranteed by the Constitution and by a law passed by the National Congress. When they opened the door, the dead bodies were already rotting. The doctor from the Naval Battalion, Dr. Guilherme Ferreira, was a very dear man, who refused to provide death certificates stating natural deaths. They removed the bodies and washed the cell with clean water. The two of us, the only survivors, were placed back into that miserable prison. There I stayed, until being sent to an insane asylum.

One day, the guard opened the door and said that I would be leaving. They put me inside a car, and I observed the car's route. At first, I passed along the

Avenida Beira-Mar, and came to Botafogo. At Praia Vermelha, the vehicle entered the grounds of an old mansion. It was the Hospital for the Insane. I was thrown inside as a lunatic for after the removal of the cadavers from my prison cell, I began to hear the wails of my dead friends, envisioning these miserable people screaming desperately and rolling on the damp clay floor, covered in clouds of dust. The infernal image would never leave my mind.
. . .

Result of the Proceedings against the Sailors

Considering, in sum, that there is no evidence in the record that the defendants have practiced any act that constitutes suspicion of participating in said revolt in view of the legal provision in Art. 93 of the Military Code, and that the mistakes they made are simple disciplinary infractions beyond the scope of the War Council, citing Regiment Art. 219, we unanimously vote that the accusation has not been proved and move to absolve. We thus absolve the defendants João Cândido, Ernesto Roberto dos Santos, Deusdedit Teles de Andrade, Francisco Dias Martins, Raul de Faria Neto, Alfredo Maia, João Agostinho, Vitorino Nicácio de Oliveira, Antônio de Paula, and Gregório do Nascimento, with their sentences suspended by virtue of this appeal, as provided by law by the Supreme Military Tribunal.

Translated by Molly Quinn

Three Types of Bureaucrats

Afonso Henriques de Lima Barreto

Not all brilliant writers receive critical recognition in their lifetime. Such was the fate of Afonso Henriques de Lima Barreto, who was born in Rio de Janeiro on May 13, 1881, seven years to the day before the abolition of slavery, and who died in the same city in November 1922. He worked as a journalist for a number of important newspapers of the era, and also as an essayist, critic, and novelist, defining himself as a black writer in a country in which the elite of nearly all backgrounds made a point of character- izing themselves as white. Barreto's father was a freeborn mulatto who worked as a printer and typographer; his mother was a schoolteacher who had been born a slave. She was his first teacher but died of tuberculosis when he was around seven years old. Barreto was able to continue his education at several prestigious schools, thanks to the financial assistance of a wealthy godfather, but when his father began suffering from mental illness, Barreto had to suspend his formal education in order to help take care of him and to provide for his sisters. He found work instead as a clerk in the Ministry of War, a position that he detested, as we shall see below. While there, he began to write and to publish in various newspapers and magazines, and eventually wrote several novels.

Barreto was a critical voice in the First Republic, opposing government policies that limited political participation and the racial theories in vogue at the time. He de- fined his literature as realistic and engaged, as opposed to the formalism that marked the Brazilian Academy of Letters, and his writings often took on the topics of racism, classism, and women's roles. He died in 1922 from heart failure after years of strug- gling with alcoholism and depression.

In the parody excerpted below, Barreto describes life as an employee at the Office of Religious Rites, an imagined bureaucratic division of the Brazilian government. The story reflects Barreto's criticisms of the growing bureaucracy of the First Republic and the nepotism and laziness that he saw as characterizing public employment.

These memoirs of mine, which I have tried to begin for days, are difficult to write, for they suggest that my office has a small staff and that little of note happens here. What dire straits I find myself in trying to add breadth to my memories as a long-term employee. Nonetheless, not yielding to obstacles, but rather skirting them, I will go on, without worrying about dates or discomforting myself with the order in which things happened. Relating what strikes me as important as I write, I embark on my task.

On the very first day I worked in the office I felt strongly that we were all born to be public employees. It was the reflection I made, judging myself the same as all men while (after investiture and the swearing-in ceremony) I sat perfectly at ease at the table they chose for me. Nothing surprised me, nor did I feel the least bit of shame. I was twenty-one, going on twenty-two, and I sat as if what I was doing I had done for a long time. So swift was my adjustment that I judged myself born to help the state in its mission to regulate the progress and activity of the nation even with my limited grammar and my terrible handwriting.

With familiarity and conviction, I handled the books—huge mountains of thick paper and leather covers, which were destined to last as long as the pyramids of Egypt. I paid much less heed to the registers of decrees and ordinances, and they seemed to eye me respectfully and plead for the caress of my hands and the sweet violence of my writing.

They put me to work copying official documents as well, and my script was so poor and so sloppy that it caused me to waste much paper. Yet this did not cause a major disturbance in the course of government matters.

But, as I said, we were all born to be public employees. The calm of the office, without discord or violent encounters; the smooth slide over a five-hour workday; the mediocrity of position and fortune, guaranteeing without fail a run-of-the-mill life—all this fits well with our outlooks and our temperaments. Days working for the state contain nothing unexpected; it does not demand any extra effort whatsoever to live until the next day. Everything runs calmly and smoothly, without collisions or shocks, the same papers and notices written, the same decrees and ordinances issued in the same way throughout the year, except for religious holidays and sick days, one of the best inventions of our Republic. As for the rest, everything is peaceful and quiet. The body remains in a comfortable state; the spirit calms itself and is neither elated nor distressed; habits are fixed and formulas already known.

I even thought about marriage, not only to have squabbles with the wife, but also to become even more of a simpleton, to worry about influence in order to rise in the ranks. I did not do it, and now, seeing as I do not speak to a human being but to the discreet page, I can confess why. To be married with my social rank would be to abuse myself with a wife who lacked education, intellect, and culture; to marry up would be to make myself a lackey of the bosses, to let them give me tasks, tips, and rewards that would satisfy the demands of the wife. I did not want either one. There was an occasion on which I tried to solve the difficulty by marrying, or something like it, below my station. It is that story of the maid. . . . In that case it was my personal dignity and my chivalry that prevented me from doing so. I could not, nor should I, hide from anyone in any fashion the woman I was sleeping with and who was the mother of my children. I would quote Saint Augustine, but I will stop myself to continue my story. . . .

When in the morning, new or old to the job, we sit at the official table, there is no kind of novelty, and, it is shameful to relate, we write slowly: "I have the honor," etc., etc.; or, in a republican way, "I declare to you, for convenient ends," etc., etc. If there is a change, it is small and the beginning is already well known: "I have in view" . . . or "In the form provided." . . .

At times the official paper ends up like a strange mosaic of formulas and clichés; and the most difficult are those in which Doctor Xisto Rodrigues shone like an unequaled master.

Doctor Xisto is now known among the masters, but he is not of the sort typical of the Office of Religious Rites. Xisto is old-fashioned. He began honestly, doing a decent job on the tests and without patrons. Despite his poor education and his intellectual limitations, he deserves respect for the honesty he puts into everything he does in life, including as a bureaucrat. He leaves at the correct time and starts at the correct time; he does not flatter, nor does he receive bonuses.

Two others, however, are more modern. One is a "puzzle master," the man the director consults, who gives confidential information so that the president and the minister know whom among the secretaries to promote. No one knows how this one entered the office; but he immediately gained the confidence of all, befriended everyone and, in short, rose three steps in the hierarchy and arranged four (monthly extra) bonuses. He is not a bad person, no one can be annoyed with him: he is a creation of a profession of those who only pester the others, in such a way that these others know nothing for sure when it comes to promotions. There are very interesting cases, but I will omit the prowess of his bureaucratic subtlety, which, stemming from his primitive love of puzzles, logographs, and picturesque enigmas, sparks in his soul a warmth of feeling toward mysteries and a need to impart to others predictions concerning his future.

I leave him, you could say, in order to speak of the "Office Assistant." This is the strangest figure in modern civil service. He is always a doctor in something; he can be a hydraulic engineer just as easily as an electrician. He can have come from any part of Brazil, from Bahia or Santa Catarina. He studied whatever in Rio, but he did not come to study, he came to arrange secure employment that carried him smoothly to the depths of the earth, from whence he might emerge as a plant, or an animal, or, possibly as some kind of mineral. He is useless, a vagabond, mean and pedantic, or even pretentious.

Installed in Rio, with the fantasies of a student, he dreamed about arranging a marriage, not to find a woman but to gain an influential father-in-law who would employ him in something that is solid. For someone like him, life is merely a path to the grave. He does not want much: a place in whatever office will do. There are those who aim higher and advance the same way, but they are quintessentially of the same species.

In the Office of Religious Rites, the typical and celebrated "Office Assistant" found the father-in-law of his dreams in an old seminary professor, someone with connections to priests, friars, sextons, sisters of mercy, doctors of canon law, vestrymen, purveyors, and other ecclesiastical personnel.

The ideal father-in-law, the old professor, taught in the seminary a branch of physics that fit well with the ends of the [Church] establishment, but which would have horrified the most mediocre student in any lay institution.

He had a daughter to marry, and the "Office Assistant" soon saw in marriage to her the easiest way to ensure a full belly and a cane with a golden pommel.

There was an exam in the Office of Religious Rites, and the "father-in-law," without any scruples, had himself named examiner of the contest to choose the position and place "the groom" in it.

What could he do? The boy needed the help.

The boy was put in first place, nominated, and the old father-in-law (now it was fact) arranged for him the position of "Office Assistant" to the minister. Never again would he leave the position. Once, when he went, as a matter of course, to say goodbye to the new minister, he started to lift the curtain to leave; but, at this, the minister smacked his forehead and shouted:

—"Are you Doctor Blotting Paper?"

The little man turned and responded with a tremor in his voice and hope in his eyes.

—"I am, Excellency."

—"Stay, sir. Your 'father-in-law' has told me you have many needs."

He is like that, in the office, among the powerful; but when he speaks to his equals, it is as a progeny of Napoleon that Josephine didn't know about.

Anyone whom he sees as a competitor, he duplicitously discredits: he is a drunk, gambles, neglects his wife, does not know how to write the word "commission," etc. He acquires literary titles, publishing *A List of the Patron Saints of the Main Cities of Brazil*; and when his wife speaks of him, she doesn't forget to say, "Like Rui Barbosa, or like Machado de Assis, my husband only drinks water."

A domestic and bureaucratic genius, Blotting Paper will not even manage, despite his opportunistic slander, to enter Hell. Life is not only a march to the grave; it's more than that, and not even Beelzebub will accept someone like him. He would be demoralizing to Satan's empire, but bureaucracy longs for such empty souls. Bureaucracy is the social creation that tries most assiduously to numb the spirit, the intelligence, and the natural physical impulses of the individual. It is an expression of inverse selection that characterizes our whole bourgeois society, allowing in its special field, with the annulment of the greatest minds, to explain, by character and creation, the unexpected success in that place of a Blotting Paper.

Just like its exact copy.

Translated by Emma Wohl

On the Mestizo in Brazil

João Batista Lacerda

Between July 26 and 29, 1911, a diverse group of intellectuals, state officials, and reformers from around the world convened in London for the First Universal Races Congress, a transatlantic effort to promote interracial and international understanding. To represent Brazil, President Marshal Hermes da Fonseca chose João Batista Lacerda and financed his trip. Lacerda was a physician and the director of the National Museum in Rio de Janeiro, a center for natural history and anthropology.

At the time, many foreign and Brazilian intellectuals alike advanced theories of innate biological differences between the races and of white superiority. Lacerda himself, for example, had studied the Botocudo indigenous groups and argued in the annals of the National Museum that they were inferior remnants of the "infancy of humanity." Yet, if many Brazilian intellectuals generally accepted ideas of racial differences and hierarchies, some were beginning to challenge another common idea of the time, the belief that racial mixing inevitably led to racial degeneration. This idea had particular importance for Brazilian officials who wanted the nation to be recognized as modern, civilized, and white.

Lacerda was one of a small group of intellectuals who both accepted the premise of white superiority and rejected the idea of mixed-race degeneration. He believed instead in a redemptive form of miscegenation that would eventually lead to both physical and cultural whiteness. He insisted that Brazil's black and indigenous populations were already in a progressive decline, and argued that mixed-race Brazilians naturally chose whiter partners, making the whitening of the population a "scientifically observed fact." Moreover, he argued, this process could be sped up with increased European immigration. According to Lacerda, in three generations, or the course of a century, everyone in Brazil would be white.

What follows are excerpts from the speech he delivered at the 1911 Congress. They reflect some beliefs commonly held by elite white Brazilians, such as the romantic visions of Brazilian slavery he describes. They also express Lacerda's ideas about whitening that were then quite new. Some in Brazil chafed at his estimation that it would take a full century to achieve whiteness. Internationally some were unconvinced that this could happen at all. Yet Lacerda's theory of whitening proved influential during its day among anthropologists and others.

This question of the mestizo, considered from an anthropological and social position, is of extraordinary importance in Brazil, above all because in the mixed population of that country the proportion of mestizos is very high, and the descendants of the crossing between black and white have an equally considerable social and political representation.

In order to establish some indications as to the fate of the mestizo in Brazil sometime in the future, we see ourselves, initially, obliged to retain as a point of departure an anthropological question that many consider unresolved, and which consists of knowing if whites and blacks should be considered as two races or two species. The polygenists consider them two species of the genus *Homo*, basing that theory in the different physical characteristics that separate the black from the white and that, according to them, are deeper than those which exist between many species of the animal kingdom. . . . Science does not yet possess an infallible criterion by which to distinguish races from species, and the only method that allows us to establish this difference for certain is the fertility or infertility of the descendants of the cross between two supposed species. . . .

Accepting this criterion, which seems to me more physiological and natural than any other, I do not have any difficulty in admitting that whites and blacks are two races and not two species, given that mestizos, descendants of the crossing of white and black, have been fertile for many generations. If, however, the white and the black in isolation conserve for an undefined period the individual characteristics of their race—what constitutes fixity—it is not the same for the product of their crossing, the mestizos. These do not form a true race, owing to their lack of fixity of many physical characteristics, which vary with each new crossing, tending now to whiteness, now to blackness.

This innate tendency of the mestizo, depriving them of the qualities of a fixed race, has a considerable value in the transformations suffered over the years by racially mixed populations, in which mixing does not obey precise social rules; in which mestizos have full liberty to unite with whites, begetting products that become each time more white than black.

This is precisely the present condition of the mixed populations of Brazil. The black, almost entirely savage, bought from African overseers and transported to the coast of Brazil by Portuguese traffickers until the middle of the last century, arrived here in the most complete state of stultification to which it is possible for a human race to fall. The adventurers who explored the fertile lands of Brazil in this century treated them worse than domestic animals, inflicting on them the cruelest and most humiliating tribulations. During the ocean crossing, at the slightest sign of rebellion, they suffocated them in the ship's hold, closing the hatch and dumping sacks of lime into this confined atmosphere. Some died of hunger, others of thirst, still others were asphyxiated by their own odor which, in great quantities, tainted the surrounding air. . . . This nefariously forced immigration of slaves has weighed on the destiny of Brazil up until the present, implicating it in disastrous moral results that will not disappear except slowly, over time. . . .

Naturally, the union between whites and blacks quickly became commonplace. In a few years the outskirts of rural estates were populated by mestizos. They shared the treatment of their ancestors, being also under the yoke of ordinary gentlemen. Because they were more active and intelligent than blacks, they soon entered the master's mansions and worked as domestic servants. Many earned the esteem of their masters and that social circle. Some made a show of real intelligence and devotion to their patrons, who, in recognizing their service, liberated these exceptional individuals and obtained for them the basics of an education as artisans. In this way, many turned into able mechanics, carpenters, woodworkers, and even tailors. The ascension of mestizos up the social ladder, which began during slavery, continued slowly until today, following the laws of intellectual selection.

One ought to also credit the general sentiments of the majority of Brazilian slaveholders; they evinced a truly Christian spirit in sweetening as much as possible the fate of the children of slaves born on their lands. How many times did we see slave masters who had no problem with including their small mulatto slaves at the family table? They provided them food and clothes and cared for them with sweetness and generosity when they were ill. The mulattas often appeared dressed in fashionable clothes, bedecked in jewels, accompanying the daughters of their masters on outings, to the church or public festivals, taking on the role of chaperones. Nor was it rare to see the master's son accompanied by a mestizo of the same age at hunts, on horseback rides, at the country balls attended by people of all classes. In general, the slave owners chose black or mulatta women to breastfeed their children. These lucky creatures, once their duty was done, were freed; they almost always continued living freely under the same roof and enjoying a variety of privileges. They used the old blacks only for very light tasks, and the rest of the time they entertained the children of their owners, telling them picturesque stories to delight their childish imaginations.

We cite these facts on purpose, because we judge them very important to explain how the vices of blacks were injected into the white race and among mestizos. Vices of language, vices of blood, false conceptions about life and death, coarse superstitions, fetishism, incomprehension of every elevated sentiment of honor and human dignity, base sensuality: such is the sad inheritance we received from the black race. It poisoned the well of modern generations; it irritated the social body, demeaning the character of mestizos and lowering the level of whites. The encounter of the Portuguese and the black in the territories of the New World took on a very different character from that which the Anglo-Saxons learned to maintain in the presence of the same race. While the Portuguese did not fear mixing with the black to engender offspring, the Anglo-Saxons, more zealous about the purity of their line, maintained a distance from the blacks, using them only as a tool of labor. It is a curious and notable fact that neither the work of time nor other factors could ever change this initial attitude of the North Americans, who to this day keep the black race separate from the white population. To the disgrace of Brazil, it is precisely the inverse that took hold here; the white mixed with the black with so little discrimination that a mixed race formed, which is today dispersed throughout a large part of the country. . . .

In Brazil today, mestizos have become poets of great inspiration, painters, sculptors, distinguished musicians, magistrates, jurists, eloquent orators, notable authors, doctors and engineers without compare, thanks to their technical aptitude and professional capacity. As politicians, they are skillful, ingratiating, knowing admirably how to take advantage of favorable events to gain positions; in general they are energetic and courageous in the fight, where they employ all available weapons in equal measure. With all this in mind, it is easy to see that, contrary to the opinions of many different authors, the mixing of the black race with the white does not result, in general, in products of an inferior intellect. And, if these same products cannot rival in other qualities the stronger Aryan races, if they do not have a fully formed instinct for civilization like the latter, there is no doubt that these mestizos should not be placed on the level of truly inferior races: that they are physically and intellectually much superior to the blacks who constituted one ethnic element of their formation.

The collaboration of mestizos in the progress and advancement of Brazil is notorious and far from being of little worth. It was they who had the greatest role in the campaign, carried out over many years in Brazil, in favor of abolishing slavery. I could cite here the celebrated names of more than one of those of mixed race involved in the emancipation movement. . . .

Preconceptions of race and color, which were never as firmly rooted in Brazil as we could always see among the populations of North America, have lost even more force since the Proclamation of the Republic. This regime's open door to all aptitudes will allow many talented mulattoes to enter even the highest political organizations of the nation. In the National Congress, in the courts, in higher education, in diplomacy, in the highest administrative corps, mulattoes occupy a very prominent position today. They are a great influence on the country's government. . . . Continuous sexual selection always helps to suppress atavism and purges the descendants of mestizos of all traits characteristic of blacks. Thanks to this procedure of ethnic reduction, it is logical to suppose that, in the space of a new century, mestizos will disappear from Brazil, which will coincide with the parallel extinction of the black race among us. After abolition, the black returned to his own kind and began to disappear from the grand civilized centers, without managing to improve his social position, fleeing from movement and progress, to which he could not adapt. . . . The mixed population of Brazil should therefore have, within a century, a very different nature from what it has now. The flow of European immigration, which each day increases greatly the white element in this population, will finally, after a certain time, suffocate the elements within which some traits of the black race might persist.

Thus Brazil will turn itself into one of the principal civilized centers of the world.

Translated by Emma Wohl

Demands of the São Paulo General Strike of 1917

Proletarian Defense Committee

After the abolition of slavery in 1888, immigrants from Italy, Spain, Portugal, and later Japan flooded into southern and central Brazil with hopes of greatly improving life for themselves and their families, either in the countryside laboring in the coffee fields or as workers in urban areas. Owners of coffee plantations introduced a form of sharecropping in which immigrant families planted and cared for coffee bushes, dividing the production with the landowners. Some immigrants prospered; many did not, finding themselves in isolated and unproductive lands and owing debts to the landowners.

Many immigrants who settled in urban areas in the south-central and southern parts of Brazil joined native-born workers to participate in the emergent industrial sector of the economy. There they helped build unions that were heavily influenced by anarchist and socialist ideologies, organizing strikes in Rio de Janeiro and São Paulo.

After the outbreak of World War I, the international demand for foodstuffs increased and Brazilian manufacturing expanded. Even though factory workers labored longer hours, their real earnings dropped as inflation soared. In July 1917, a Spanish worker was killed during a demonstration in front of a São Paulo factory. His death sparked a massive protest and general strike with the participation of an estimated seventy thousand men and women, both foreign and Brazilian born. Newspaper reporters and other middle-class São Paulo residents, who also suffered from the effects of inflation, viewed the strikers favorably. After the strike had endured for about a month, employers agreed to meet many of the workers' wage demands and to look into the other questions they had raised. But employers and the state government not only failed to follow through on some of their commitments but also worked to deport those labor activists who were foreign born.

The workers' demands below, published in O Estado de São Paulo, offer a sense of the kinds of rights workers sought in this period, as well as the impact of the current economic situation on their daily lives.

The representatives of the workers league [associated with] the businesses currently on strike and of the sociopolitical associations that make up the

Proletarian Defense Committee, having met on the evening of June 11, and having consulted with the entities of which they are a part, [wish] to explain the aspirations not only of the working masses on strike but also of the population as a whole, which is distressed due to its urgent needs, [and] considering the failure of the state to deal with this matter other than by violent repression, hereby make public the immediate goals of these demonstrations, formulated in a way that considers working conditions, which are presented here in detail:

1   That all persons detained due to the strike be freed;
2   That the absolute right of association be respected for all workers;
3   That no worker be fired for having participated in the strike movement;
4   That the exploitation of minors be abolished for those working under age fourteen in factories, workshops, etc.;
5   That workers under the age of eighteen not engage in night work;
6   That night work for women be abolished;
7   That a 35 percent increase in salaries lower than 53$000 [53,000 réis] and a 25 percent increase for salaries higher than that [be implemented];
8   That the payment of salaries be made punctually, every fifteen days, or, at the latest, five days after the due date;
9   That permanent employment be guaranteed to all workers;
10 That a half-day workday on Saturdays [be stipulated];
11 That a 50 percent increase for all overtime work [be enacted];

In addition, the Proletarian Defense Committee, focusing particularly on the working class and considering that wage increases, as it almost always happens, can be undercut by an increase—and not a small one—in the cost of basic necessities and considering that current economic conditions, for many reasons, are felt by the whole population, suggests some other measures of a general character that are summarized in the following proposals:

1   That immediate measures be taken to lower the prices of basic necessities, as has been done elsewhere, so that the reduced prices will not go up due to hoarding;
2   That, if necessary, all products essential to public nutrition be regulated, to avoid speculation;
3   That real and immediate measures be implemented [by the government] in order to impede the adulteration and misrepresentation of food products, a task that has been carried out, up to this point, by industries, importers, and manufacturers;
4   That the rent of houses up to 100$000 [100,000 réis] be reduced by 30 percent, and that tenants not be evicted nor dispossessed for failure of payment of residencies whose owners may be opposed to this reduction.

The proposed actions are, above all, reasonable and humane measures. To judge them subversive and deny them would require that the current movement be put down by force of arms, an act that we believe would be a dangerous provocation and demonstrate a lack of good faith.

The Proletarian Defense Committee believes that they have found the way toward an honest and achievable resolution [of the strike]. This resolution will certainly have the support of all of those who are not deaf to the protests of the hungry.

Translated by Jennifer Gonçalves Reis

Brazil and World War I

Anonymous

On April 5, 1917, a German submarine torpedoed the Brazilian merchant ship Paraná *off the coast of France, killing three people, injuring many more, and sinking a cargo of 93,000 sacks of coffee beans. Although Brazil had been neutral in the European war, the Germans nonetheless sank the ship without warning, purportedly because it was inside their blockade zone. As revealed in this report from the newspaper* O Estado de São Paulo *on April 12, 1917, the incident inspired Brazilians throughout the state of São Paulo to come out in patriotic marches demanding an end to diplomatic relations, while similar demonstrations took place in other parts of the country. Six months later, after an attack on yet another commercial vessel, Brazil declared war on Germany. At that point, Brazilians looted the businesses of German immigrants, and soon thereafter the Brazilian government expropriated many German establishments.*

Brazil's actual participation in World War I was minimal, consisting of a small fighting unit that joined the French army, a medical detachment of fewer than one hundred doctors, and a troubled naval mission that arrived in Europe a few days before the Allied victory. Nonetheless, Brazil provided significant help through the export of foodstuffs and raw materials to the Allied powers. Although its contribution to the fighting was small, Brazil's entrance into the war increased its international status. (Argentina, a major rival, remained neutral throughout the war.) Brazil participated in the talks at Versailles and was a founding member of the League of Nations. The government campaigned for a seat on the Permanent Council, but its initiative failed, resulting in Brazil's withdrawal from the league in 1926.

During the war, Germany's increased control over the Atlantic Ocean led to a dramatic drop in foreign imports to Brazil. Some historians have argued that this decrease in imported goods stimulated national production and industrialization; others insist that domestic production could not have sufficiently substituted for imports. After the war, however, the surplus of foreign exchange helped finance an influx of capital goods into Brazil.

Porto Feliz. Since news of the torpedoing of the *Paraná*, the newspapers here have waited in anticipation. Yesterday at 8 in the evening, people gathered at the main church to protest German actions toward Brazil and to demand severing relations. Colonel Silvino de Moraes Fernandes and Professor Octavinao Martins spoke, and then after a short march, Mr. Armando Seglia spoke on behalf of the Italian colony, and Mr. Guilherme Pelegrino was widely applauded.

With the national flag and those of the allied powers leading the march, demonstrators paraded through the city frenetically shouting "Long Live Brazil" and "Long Live the Allies," while the municipal band played the Brazilian, French, and Italian national anthems.

The crowd only dispersed at 10 p.m.

PATRIOTIC DEMONSTRATIONS IN TAUBATÉ

A crowd estimated to be around five thousand marched through the streets of our city last night shouting "Long Live Brazil" and protesting the torpedoing of the *Paraná* steamship.

All of the local public officials were present, as well as the press, and the Italian consul. There was complete order throughout the rally. Enthusiasm was widespread.

DISPLEASURE OF THE PEOPLE OF ITAPETININGA

Today at 7 p.m. a great crowd protested the attack on our flag by the torpedoing of the *Paraná*.

During the demonstration, Alcides Torres and Sixto Briccolla spoke.

The people, following behind the flag and accompanied by a band, marched through the city.

There is general enthusiasm among the people of Itapetininga. The city is perfectly calm, and up to this point no disagreeable incidents have occurred.

Translated by Emma Wohl

The Cannibalist Manifesto
(Manifesto Antropófago)

Oswald de Andrade

At once ironic and critical, outrageous and insightful, humorous and theoretically astute, the Cannibalist Manifesto *is the most celebrated text of the Brazilian modernist movement and its founding document. This artistic and literary movement first emerged in São Paulo, Brazil, in the early 1920s, where a group of intellectuals embraced European cultural trends like cubism and futurism but also sought to transform them into something authentically Brazilian. Inspired by an image painted by his wife, Tarsila de Amaral (see "Portraits" in this part), Oswald de Andrade (1890–1954) wrote the* Cannibalist Manifesto *(also translated as the Anthropophagic Manifesto) around 1928 and first read it aloud to others in the movement at one of their gatherings. Soon thereafter Raul Bopp, a poet and diplomat, and Antônio de Alcântara Machado, a journalist, politician, and writer, joined with Andrade to create a new magazine, the* Revista de Antropofagia *(Magazine of anthropophagy], that could serve as a creative outlet for the group. They published the manifesto in its first issue, in May 1928, with a painting by Tarsila de Amaral on the front cover.*

In the manifesto, Andrade draws on metaphors, aphorisms, and sixteenth-century travelers' accounts about the supposed cannibal activity of native Brazilians who "devoured" their enemies in order to obtain their strength and valor. Yet he does so in order to argue that one had to "swallow" European cultural legacies and "digest" them in order to create an entirely new and original Brazilian culture—a synthesis of the colonized and the colonizer, the barbarous and the modern.

Cannibalism alone unites us. Socially. Economically. Philosophically.

The world's single law. Disguised expression of all individualism, of all collectivisms. Of all religions. Of all peace treaties.

Tupi or not tupi, that is the question.[1]

Down with every catechism. And down with Gracchi's mother.[2]

I am only concerned with what is not mine. Law of Man. Law of the cannibal.

We're tired of all the suspicious Catholic husbands who've been given starring roles. Freud put an end to the mystery of Woman and to other horrors of printed psychology.

What clashed with the truth was clothing, that raincoat placed between the inner and outer worlds. The reaction against the dressed man. American movies will inform us.

Children of the sun, mother of the living. Discovered and loved ferociously with all the hypocrisy of *saudade*,[3] by the immigrants, by slaves and by *touristes*. In the land of the Great Snake.[4]

It was because we never had grammars, nor collections of old plants. And we never knew what urban, suburban, frontier and continental were. Lazy in the *mapamundi* of Brazil.[5]

A participatory consciousness, a religious rhythmics.[6]

Down with all the importers of canned consciousness. The palpable existence of life. And the pre-logical mentality for Mr. Lévy-Bruhl to study.[7]

We want the Carib Revolution. Greater than the French Revolution. The unification of all productive revolts for the progress of humanity. Without us, Europe wouldn't even have its meager declaration of the rights of man.[8]

The Golden Age heralded by America. The Golden Age. And all the *girls*.

Heritage. Contact with the Carib side of Brazil. *Où Villegaignon print terre.*[9] Montaigne. Natural Man. Rousseau. From the French Revolution to Romanticism, to the Bolshevik Revolution, to the Surrealist Revolution and Keyserling's technicized barbarian.[10] We push onward.

We were never catechized. We live by a somnambulistic law. We made Christ to be born in Bahia. Or in Belém do Pará.[11]

But we never permitted the birth of logic among us.

Down with Father Vieira.[12] Author of our first loan, to make a commission. The illiterate king had told him: put that on paper, but without a lot of lip. The loan was made. Brazilian sugar was signed away. Vieira left the money in Portugal and brought us the lip.

The spirit refuses to conceive a spirit without a body. Anthropomorphism. Need for the cannibalistic vaccine. To maintain our equilibrium, against meridian religions.[13] And against outside inquisitions.

We can attend only to the oracular world.

We already had justice, the codification of vengeance. Science, the codification of Magic. Cannibalism. The permanent transformation of the Tabu into a totem.[14]

Down with the reversible world, and against objectified ideas. Cadaverized. The stop of thought that is dynamic. The individual as victim of the system. Source of classical injustices. Of romantic injustices. And the forgetting of inner conquests.

Routes. Routes. Routes. Routes. Routes. Routes. Routes.[15]

The Carib instinct.

Death and life of all hypotheses. From the equation "Self, part of the Cosmos" to the axiom "Cosmos, part of the Self." Subsistence. Experience. Cannibalism.

Down with the vegetable elites. In communication with the soil.

We were never catechized. What we really made was Carnaval. The Indian dressed as senator of the Empire. Making believe he's Pitt.[16] Or performing in Alencar's operas,[17] full of worthy Portuguese sentiments.

We already had Communism. We already had Surrealist language. The Golden Age.

Catiti
Imara Notiá
Notiá Imara
Ipejú.[18]

Magic and life. We had the description and allocation of tangible goods, moral goods, and royal goods.[19] And we knew how to transpose mystery and death with the help of a few grammatical forms.

I asked a man what the Law was. He answered that it was the guarantee of the exercise of possibility. That man was named Galli Mathias.[20] I ate him.

Only where there is mystery is there no determinism. But what does that have to do with us?

Down with the histories of Man that begin at Cape Finisterre. The undated world. Unrubrified. Without Napoleon. Without Caesar.

The determination of progress by catalogues and television sets. Only machinery. And blood transfusers.

Down with the antagonistic sublimations. Brought here in caravels.

Down with the truth of missionary peoples, defined by the sagacity of a cannibal, the Viscount of Cairu[21]—it's a lie told again and again.

But those who came here weren't crusaders. They were fugitives from a civilization we are eating, because we are strong and vindictive like the Jabuti.[22]

If God is the consciousness of the Uncreated Universe, Guaraci is the mother of the living.[23] Jaci is the mother of plants.[24]

We never had speculation. But we had divination. We had Politics, which is the science of distribution. And a social system in harmony with the planet.

The migrations. The flight from tedious states. Against urban scleroses. Against the Conservatories and speculative tedium.

From William James and Voronoff.[25] The transfiguration of the Taboo into a totem. Cannibalism.

The paterfamilias and the creation of the Morality of the Stork: Real ignorance of things + lack of imagination + sense of authority in the face of curious offspring.

One must depart from a profound atheism in order to arrive at the idea of God. But the Carib didn't need to. Because he had Guaraci.

The created object reacts like the Fallen Angels. What do we have to do with that? Next, Moses daydreams. What do we have to do with that?

Before the Portuguese discovered Brazil, Brazil had discovered happiness.

Down with the torch-bearing Indian. The Indian son of Mary, the stepson of Catherine of Medici and the godson of Dom Antonio de Mariz.[26]
    Joy is the proof of nines.

In the matriarchy of Pindorama.[27]

Down with Memory as a source of custom. The renewal of personal experience.

We are concretists. Ideas take charge, react, and burn people in public squares. Let's get rid of ideas and other paralyses. By means of routes. Believe in signs; believe in sextants and in stars.

Down with Goethe, the Gracchi's mother, and the court of Dom João VI.[28]

Joy is the proof by nines.

The struggle between what we might call the Uncreated and the Creation— Illustrated by the permanent contradiction between Man and his Taboo. Everyday love and the capitalist way of life. Cannibalism. Absorption of the sacred enemy. To transform him into a totem. The human adventure. The earthly goal. Even so, only the pure elites managed to realize carnal cannibalism, which carries within itself the highest meaning of life and avoids all the ills identified by Freud—catechist ills. What results is not a sublimation of the sexual instinct. It is the thermometrical scale of the cannibal instinct.
    Carnal at first, this instinct becomes elective, and creates friendship. When it is affective, it creates love. When it is speculative, it creates science. It takes detours and moves around. At times it is degraded. Low cannibalism, agglomerated with the sins of catechism—envy, usury, calumny, murder. We are acting against this plague of a supposedly cultured and Christianized peoples. Cannibals.

Down with Anchieta singing of the eleven thousand virgins of Heaven,[29] in the land of Iracema[30]—the patriarch João Ramalho, founder of São Paulo.[31]

Our independence has not yet been proclaimed. An expression typical of Dom João VI: "My son, put this crown on your head, before some adventurer puts it on his!"[32] We expelled the dynasty. We must still expel the Bragantine spirit,[33] the decrees and the snuff-box of Maria da Fonte.[34]

Down with the dressed and oppressive social reality registered by Freud—reality without complexes, without madness, without prostitutions and without penitentiaries, in the matriarchy of Pindorama.

OSWALD DE ANDRADE
In Piratininga, in the 374th Year of
the Swallowing of Bishop Sardinha[35]

Notes

Translation of Oswald de Andrade's "Manifesto Antropófago," *Revista de Antropofagia* 1:1 (São Paulo, May 1928) by Leslie Bray. [The following notes are from Bray's translation.] I want to thank Margaret Abel-Quintero, Wilton Azevedo, Aloísio Gomes Barbosa, José Niraldo de Farias, Dalila Machado, Sonia Ramos, and Lisa Fedorka-Carhuaslla at *Latin American Literary Review*, who read and commented on earlier versions of this translation.

1. In English in original. *Tupi* is the popular, generic name for the Native Americans of Brazil and also for their language, *nheengatu*.

2. A student of Greek and Latin literature, Cornelia is said to have been virtuous, austere, and extremely devoted to her sons. In the *Manifesto* she is the bad mother who (in contrast to the mother-goddesses Jaci and Guaraci) brings her children up as subjects of a "civilized" culture.

3. *Saudade* or yearning, homesickness, nostalgia, is a sentiment traditionally associated with the Portuguese national character.

4. In his annotated French translation of the *Manifesto*, Benedito Nunes points out that the sun is a maternal deity here. As Nunes points out as well, The "Great Snake" (*Cobra Grande*) is a water spirit in Amazonian mythology, and is the theme of Raul Bopp's poem *Cobra Norato* (1928). See Oswald de Andrade, "Le manifeste anthropophage," trans. Nunes, *Surréalisme périphérique*, ed. Luis de Moura Sobral (Montréal: Université de Montréal, 1984) 180–192, esp. 181, n. 3.

5. Nunes writes, "Oswald establishes an analogy between the absence of grammatical discipline and the absence of a split between Nature and Culture [in Brazil]. [As they were] so close to nature, [Brazilians] did not need to gather herbs (collections of old plants) as Rousseau and Goethe did." ("Le manifeste anthropophage" 182, n. 4). "Old plants" (velhos vegetais) also seems to allude to the entrenched, inactive, vegetative attitude of the Brazilian literary and cultural establishment Oswald wants to displace.

6. References to the work of Lévy-Bruhl on the structure of "primitive" thought. See below, n. 7.

7. Lucien Lévy-Bruhl, French philosopher and ethnologist (1857–1939). Among his publications are *Les fonctions mentales dans les societies inférieures* (1910), *La mentalité primitive* (1927), and *La mythologie primitive* (1935). The "primitive" mentality, according to Lévy-Bruhl, is not a deformation of the "civilized" one, but rather a completely different structure of thought. The primitive mind is mystical, collective and pre-logical.

8. Neil Larsen writes, "The *Manifesto* itself plays ironically on the 'theory' that the Enlightenment discourse of natural right, leading from Locke through Rousseau and ultimately to the *Declaration of the Rights of Man* and the Bourgeois Revolution as such, has its origins in Montaigne's 'noble savage,' based on the first reports from Brazil of 'cannibalism' among members of the Tupinamba tribal aggregate." *Modernism and Hegemony* (Minneapolis: University of Minnesota Press, 1990) 80.

9. In Montaigne's essay "Des cannibales," "où Villegaignon print terre" is Antarctic France

(the French colonial settlement in sixteenth-century Brazil). Montaigne argues in this essay that ritual cannibalism is far less barbaric than many "civilized" customs.

10. Count Herman Keyserling, German philosopher, world traveller and European Orientalist (1880–1946). His works propose the (Spenglerian) ideas that the Western world must be compenetrated with Eastern philosophy and that Latin America will rise as a world power while Europe declines. Nunes informs us that Keyserling, whose "visit to São Paulo in 1929 was welcomed by the *Revista de antropofagia*, set forth the idea of *technical barbarism* in his book *Die neuentstehende Welt*" ("Anthropophagisme et surréalisme," *Surréalisme périphérique*, ed. Luis de Moura Sobral, Montréal: Université de Montréal, (1984), 159–79, esp. 173, n. 15). Oswald inverts Keyserling's idea that a soulless "technical barbarism" is the sign of the modern world. In Oswald's utopia, primitive man enjoys the fruits of modernization.

11. The Brazilian city of Belém, or Bethlehem (state of Pará). Christ is thus not *brought* to the New World in Oswald's text, but born in His own Bethlehem.

12. António Vieira (1608–1697), Portuguese Jesuit instrumental in the colonization of Brazil. He came to be known as "the Judas of Brazil." In the war between Portugal and Holland over Pernambuco, Vieira negotiated a peace treaty by which Pernambuco was given to Holland so that Portugal would not have to pay Holland to end the war (with money made in Brazil). A noted orator and writer, Vieira is associated with formal, elegant rhetoric—a language directly opposed to the poetic idiom Oswald is forging for Brazil. Nunes writes that Vieira "is for Oswald the strongest of all emblems of Brazilian intellectual culture. . . . Oswald refers to Vieira's 1649 proposition to organize a company to exploit the sugar produced in the state of Maranhão" ("Le manifeste anthropophage" 183, n. 11).

13. According to Nunes, "meridian" religions are religions of salvation. "Antropofagia ao Alcance de Todos," in Oswald de Andrade, *Do Pau Brasil à Antropofagia e às Utopias* (1972); Rio de Janeiro: Civilização Brasileira, (1978) xxxi. *Meridian* as a dividing line seems, in the context of the *Manifesto*, to connote the divisions body/soul, native/foreign, and so on, which Oswald is attempting to dismantle.

14. In *Totem and Taboo* (1913, tr. 1918), Freud argues that the shift from "totemistic" to "taboo" systems of morality and religion consolidated paternal authority as the cornerstone of culture. Subjects of the taboo system are "civilized" because they have internalized the paternal rule. Oswald's advocacy of totemistic cannibalism, then, constitutes a rejection of patriarchy and the culture of the (Portuguese) "fathers." See also Nunes' more detailed explanation in "Anthropophagisme et surréalisme," 169–70.

15. The original *roteiros* (from *rotear*, to navigate) can also signify ships' logbooks or pilots' directions. Oswald can thus be construed here as referring to a rediscovery of America.

16. William Pitt, (1759–1806), British statesman influential in the formation of colonial policy for India.

17. José de Alencar, Brazilian writer and conservative politician, (1829–1877). His Indianist novel *O Guarani* (1857) was turned into an opera, with music by Carlos Gomes (1836–1896), which opened in the Teatro Scala, Milan, 2 December 1870. Nunes points out that "Peri, the hero of *O Guarani*, [has] civilized manners, imitating the great Portuguese lords" ("Le manifeste anthropophage" 186, n. 18).

18. In a footnote, Oswald provides a Portuguese translation of this Tupi text, running "New moon, oh new moon, blow memories of me into [the man I want]." The note gives the source of this text as *O Selvagem*, a work by José Vieira Couto de Magalhães, the politician and folklorist (1836–1898). Nunes quotes Couto de Magalhães' complete translation of the Tupi text: "Lua Nova, ó lua Nova! assoprai em . . . lembranças de mim; eisme aqui, estou

em vossa presença; fazei com que eu tão somente ocupe seu coração." [New moon, oh new moon! Blow memories of me into . . . ; I stand here before you; let me and no other fill his heart. "Le manifeste anthropophage" 186, n. 19].

19. The original here reads "dos bens físicos, dos bens morais, dos bens dignários." Oswald is playing with legal terms for various kinds of property, so as to ridicule "civilized" European institutions and show that they are superfluous to Brazilian culture. *Bens físicos* are probably the land and natural resources of Brazil, and *bens morais* the native culture. *Bens dignários*, property granted by the king, suggests both the aspects of Brazilian culture held in common with Portugal and also property "granted" by the Portuguese king that was in fact originally Brazilian.

20. "Galli Mathias" is a pun on *galimatias*, or nonsense.

21. José de Silva Lisboa, Viscount of Cairu (1756–1835), Brazilian politician. After Dom João VI established his court in Rio de Janeiro (1808) in the wake of Napoleon's invasion of Portugal, the Viscount of Cairu convinced him to open Brazilian ports to "all nations friendly to Portugal."

22. Tortoise of northern Brazil; in the popular culture of the Indians, he is a trickster figure. The jabuti is astute, active, comical, and combative.

23. Tupi sun goddess, mother of all men.

24. Tupi moon goddess, creator of plants.

25. William James, American philosopher (1842–1910), is the author of *Principles of Psychology* (1890), *The Varieties of Religious Experience* (1902), and *A Pluralistic Universe* (1909). Serge Voronoff, Russian-born, is the author of *Etude sur la vieillesse et la rajeunissement par la greffe* (1926) and *La conquête de la vie* (1928), a method of rejuvenation by the grafting of genital glands. James's demystifying interpretation of religion can be contrasted to the *catachesis* Oswald rejects, and Voronoff's interest in grafting, as well as the return to youth and defiance of death, has affinities with Oswald's project. Nunes writes that "one could consider [Voronoff] to represent a biological pragmatism, towards which the Anthropophagy Manifesto leans" ("Le manifeste anthropophage" 188–89, n. 26).

26. Nunes writes that this is a "[s]uperimposition of three images: that of the sculpted Indians of the chandeliers of certain Baroque churches, that of the Indian Paraguassu, who went to France in the 16th century, accompanied by her husband, the Portuguese Diogo Alvares Correia, and [that of] D[om] Antonio de Mariz, the noble rural lord, father of Ceci, with whom Peri falls in love, in *O Guarani*. Paraguassu was baptized as Saint-Malo. A false version [of the story], spread through schoolbooks, made Catherine of Medici the godmother of this native" ("Le manifeste anthropophage" 189–90, n. 28).

27. Pindorama is the name of Brazil in the Tupi language. It may mean "country or region of palm trees."

28. Dom João VI, King of Portugal (reigned 1816–26). As Prince Regent, he fled the Napoleonic invasion of Portugal (1807) and installed the Portuguese court in Rio de Janeiro (1808–21). He made Brazil a kingdom (1815), equal in status to Portugal, and was Brazil's last colonial monarch before independence (1822).

29. Father Anchieta (1534–1597), Jesuit missionary among Indians; known as "The Apostle of Brazil" and generally considered to be the first Brazilian writer. He helped found São Paulo in 1554, after founding a Jesuit school at Piratininga (São Vicente). Anchieta is the author of a long Latin poem to the Virgin Mary, which he composed and committed to memory while a captive of the Indians, and a dramatic poem in Portuguese about the arrival of a relic of the Eleven Thousand Virgins (legendary companions of St. Ursula, martyred at Cologne in the early 4th century, after whom the Virgin Islands are named) in Brazil. Anchieta

thus embodies the catechesis, importation of culture, and inscription of Brazil as colony that Oswald rejects.

30. Indian heroine in Alencar's novel of the same name (1865).

31. João Ramalho was one of the first Portuguese colonizers of Brazil. Shipwrecked off the coast near São Paulo in 1512, he made friends with the Tamoia Indians, married the daughter of a chief, had many children by her and other Tamoias, and created a small empire. He founded what is now Santo André and also the village of Piratininga. He was opposed to the Jesuits' founding of São Paulo, and organized the Indians' resistance against the missionaries.

32. Dom João VI's son, Dom Pedro I, became Emperor of Brazil when Independence was declared in 1822. According to tradition Dom João, already sensing that Brazil would separate itself from Portugal, had given Dom Pedro the directions Oswald quotes here before returning to Lisbon in 1821.

33. The Portuguese kings of the period were of the Bragança dynasty.

34. The legendary figure Maria da Fonte became the symbol of a popular rebellion in the Minho (1846) against higher taxation to finance the improvement of roads and reforms in public health. The uprising strengthened conservative forces in Portugal, associated with absolution and colonialism. In the context of the *MA*, Maria da Fonte is an emblem of allegiance to Portuguese tradition and a patriarchal woman, parallel to the Gracchi's mother and opposed to Jaci and Guaraci.

35. Sardinha was Bishop of Bahia from 1552 to 1556, when he was killed and apparently eaten by the Caltis Indians, into whose hands he fell when the ship that was taking him back to Lisbon sank in the São Francisco River. Sardinha had favored punishing Portuguese settlers who, enraged at the Jesuits' opposition to the enslavement of Indians, attacked the school at Piratininga in 1554.

Macunaíma

Mário de Andrade

Poet, novelist, musician, historian, art critic, folklorist, and photographer Mário Raul de Moraes Andrade (1893–1945), a native of São Paulo, was a founder and leader of Brazilian modernism and one of the most eminent personalities of his generation. Andrade (no relation to Oswald de Andrade) was responsible for bringing an innovative cultural agenda to Brazil. His most famous novel, Macunaíma, *the source of the excerpt below, was an instant classic, inspired a film by the same name in 1969, and continues to be read and interpreted to this day. It is based on de Andrade's interests in Brazilian folklore, languages, cultures, and musical forms, and draws heavily on indigenous legends culled from anthropological studies. Indeed, he never referred to the piece as a novel, calling it instead a rhapsody or an anthology of Brazilian folklore, one that used a mixture of Portuguese and indigenous languages.*

The novel presents the misadventures of the antihero Macunaíma, an indigenous figure who travels from the Amazon to São Paulo in search of a lost amulet, and who goes through a series of fantastic physical transformations. Labeled by the author a "hero without character," Macunaíma represents a transformative Brazilian national culture, unrooted to any singular source.

The passage translated below is often understood as a rereading of the myth of Brazil's three founding races: indigenous, black, and white. As the story goes, through the use of magical water, Macunaíma, born with dark black skin, becomes white, and his brother Jiguê turns the color of bronze, while another brother, Maanape, remains black, although the palms of his hands and soles of his feet turn red. The scene reads like a parody of the idea of racial whitening and a critique of Catholic evangelizing.

In one instant, the sun covered the three brothers with a wave of sweat, and Macunaíma remembered to take a bath. However, bathing was impossible in the river because of the ravenous piranhas. . . . Macunaíma then noticed a sheltered area in the middle of the river with a cavity filled with water. . . . They turned the bow [of their boat] in its direction. The hero, after shouting because of the cold water, descended into the cavity and washed himself. But the water was enchanted, because the big foot of Sumé had left that hole from the time when he preached the Gospel of Jesus to the Brazilian Indians. When the hero left the bath, he was white, blonde, and blue-eyed, for the water had washed off his blackness. . . . Barely understanding the miracle, Jiguê threw himself into Sumé's footprint. However, the water was already very dirty from the hero's blackness, and as much as Jigué vigorously rubbed water all over himself, he only managed a bronze color. . . . Maanape then went to wash himself, but Jiguê had splashed all of the enchanted water out of the hole. There was only a bit at the bottom, and Maanape managed to dampen only the palms of his feet and hands. He thus stayed as black as a son of the Tapanhuma. Only the palms of his hands and feet were red because of being washed in the holy water. . . . The sight was beautiful; the three brothers— one blonde, one red, and the other black, standing naked in the sun. . . .

Translated by Emma Wohl

Revolutionary Manifestos from the Tenentes Revolts

Various authors

Between 1922 and 1927, junior army officers led a series of uprisings that became known as the Tenentes (Lieutenants') Revolts. The immediate cause of these uprisings was the election of President Artur da Silva Bernardes instead of the military-supported candidate, Nilo Peçanha. But there were deeper dissatisfactions that animated the rebels. Many junior officers and poor conscripted servicemen believed that the high-ranking officers were ineffective at preventing electoral fraud or at curbing abuse within the military. Overall the Tenentes Revolts reflected the growing frustrations of midlevel sectors of society with the continued political exclusion they faced and with the federal government's failure to modernize the country.

In 1924 during one of these revolts, rebels occupied the city of São Paulo and held it for three weeks as federal troops sought to dislodge them. After the rebels eventually retreated, one group of officers and army recruits, led by Captain Luís Carlos Prestes, fled to the hinterlands of Brazil. Known as the Prestes Column, the group marched for three years through the backlands, evading capture and hoping to stir a popular uprising. Their endurance demonstrated both the ineffectiveness and the unpopularity of the government due to oligarchic abuse of political powers.

It was not only army officers and conscripted soldiers who supported the Tenentes Revolts. In the two documents that follow, both from São Paulo in 1924, one can get a sense of their political message and its appeal. In the first, the rebels who held São Paulo published a manifesto in all the local newspapers to justify their actions. In the second, a group of workers offered their response.

A Communiqué of the Leaders of the Movement

The leaders of the revolutionary movement are anxious to meet the representatives of the press of this capital because they urgently want to make public the main reasons for their movement and to define its objectives, not having done so previously due to the restrictions of the press law and the circumstances resulting from the state of siege.

First, it is necessary to note that this revolution is not an isolated movement that has only managed to have a limited effect on the Republic. It is a patriotic movement of the utmost social and political significance and, consequently, its operations have a national character—such that, carefully prepared for many months, it sought to take action simultaneously in São Paulo, Paraná, Santa Catarina, Rio Grande do Sul, Minas Gerais, and Matto Grosso.

Although unforeseen circumstances prevented [the revolt] from taking place simultaneously [throughout the country] as planned, this certainly did not dampen the determined convictions and the efficient action of the other parts of the revolutionary movement. With this historic act, which sought to affect the whole nation, there was a total shift in the situation of the federal and state governments of the Republic, where a revolutionary program needs to be carried out.

As to the government of the Republic, it should be noted that in the long run the National Army cannot and will never accept Dr. Arthur Bernardes or his government. Even disregarding well-known facts, [there remains the reality that] he directed his gravest offenses against the army. However, the revolution does not target Dr. Arthur Bernardes personally; this would diminish the noble character that inspired it and which it presents to the Brazilian people. The leaders and advisors [of the Revolution] have as one of their objectives the replacement of the current government of the Republic, which is not capable of tending to the best interests of the nation for well-known reasons that need not be mentioned, and it has been shown to be the continuation of [previous] governments riddled with vices that have governed Brazil. These governments full of nepotism, of self-promotion, of technical incompetency in the highest ranks of the administration, of concessions upon concessions, of deals upon deals, continue to destroy their own internal and external vitality.

The army does not have ambitions and does not want posts in the government. It fights selflessly and fundamentally because of patriotic Brazilian altruism, and, in that sense, the leaders of the revolutionary movement wish to set the example that will lend authority to their critique of the republicans who, until now, occupied the highest positions in the administration of the country and who, with rare exceptions, did not know how to serve its general interests. The army wants a nation like the one at the end of the Empire with the same principles of moral integrity, patriotic awareness, administrative honesty, and deep political insight. . . .

When the Republic was proclaimed, the national army pledged loyalty to the Constitution and, as a consequence, implicitly assumed a promise to the people on its honor as citizens and soldiers to defend it [the Constitution]. Those circumstances alone were enough to justify the current gesture by the military, which, moreover, cannot stay removed from the life of the nation, its internal order and international prestige. . . .

We wish to declare that the people of São Paulo will find that the revolutionaries will exert all efforts in guaranteeing their security, as well as apply-ing principles of justice. In this sense, we affirm, with total confidence, that we are not responsible for or in collusion with any looting, destruction, or burning, and we will do everything possible to save as many lives as possible and prevent material damage to the city. . . .

This revolutionary movement is a gesture of indignation and patriotism. The current government of the Republic does not have the support of the na-tion nor of those whose ultimate responsibility is to defend its honor. It is not the government of the Brazilian people, and it does not have the support of the army, because the army is composed of those who signed the manifesto of the Military Club and others who are represented by it. If our ideas reveal the sentiments of the people, we hope that they will show their support for our work. We are willing to go forward and, if we are vanquished, with our defeat, the ideals of the nation will also be defeated.

We are informing the public that the leaders of all the cities in this state, including the capital, will remain in their positions.

Motion of the Workers of the Committee of Revolutionary Forces

Militants of the working classes of São Paulo, who have met to analyze the Manifesto that the Leaders of the Revolutionary Movement published in the newspapers of this capital, have resolved, after long consideration, to send by means of a commission the following motion:

São Paulo, July 15, 1924.

Members of the Revolutionary Committee.

The undersigned, militants of the working class of São Paulo, having stud-ied the Manifesto of this Revolutionary Committee now in charge of the State government, . . . and taking the necessary above-mentioned consider-ation of the Manifesto, at least the portion concerning the proletariat, the signatories judge, as they should, that they will try to respond to the invita-tion made by this Committee, which shows itself willing to fulfill the task of regenerating the political, social, and economic practices of the Brazilian Republic—"republicanizing it"—and to reclaim for the people the rights of liberty and life that until now had been no more than a utopian promise ex-isting only on the pages of the Brazilian Constitution; and, for these reasons:

considering that the proletariat has economic needs, as there are those who are constantly suffering the pangs of hunger;

considering that to avoid the continual exploitation of the working people it is necessary to balance their economic situation with the living conditions that they currently face;

considering that the proletariat must organize itself to defend its rights to life and liberty, rights that, until now, have been almost entirely curtailed by the slave-holding lords in collusion with police and governmental authorities;

considering that for the satisfaction of these rights the proletariat must defend itself;

considering that in the realm of education the proletariat feels a lack of instruction, not only due to the existing impediments preventing unions from opening schools able to shape the worker as a man with a free conscience, independent of the prejudices that dull and degenerate his mental function from all sides in the vicious circle of bourgeois Capitalist education, but also for the duty to recognize their role and value in the present society;

considering that one of the means to facilitate workers' instruction and education is to reduce the hours of work;

the following suggestions are presented:

1st. The establishment of a minimum wage for all working classes of the state, based on the index of basic necessities, including clothing and housing;

2nd. The establishment, as well, of an index of maximum prices for basic items, clothing, and housing, in accordance with the index referred to above;

3rd. The right to association for all working classes;

4th. The freedom of the workers' press and the right to express opinions in public demonstrations, as well as the revocation of the portion of the law that deports people because of social-political concerns;

5th. The right to found schools of instruction and education, equipped with methods that seem most practical and draw together the aspirations of liberty and justice;

6th. Finally, the general application of the eight-hour work day.

In conclusion, we remind the Members of the Revolutionary Committee, who find themselves in the state government, that all of the suggestions in the present proposal reflect not just the feelings of the *paulista* proletariat at the present time, but also the guarantees and rights that the Brazilian Constitution provides and, even more, it synthesizes a translated expression of the Manifesto made public by this committee, in joining with which we resolve to fulfill the conditions of the lines transcribed below:

"The people have been reduced to a situation of total impotence, their will choked by the constraints of those in political and administrative power."

"We are committed to declaring that the population of São Paulo will encounter on the part of the revolutionaries all efforts for their security and safety, as well as for the application of all principles of justice."

"The press, whatever its creed, will have total guarantee of free thought, revolutionaries being disposed to study and respond to all declarations that carry the mark of sincerity and patriotism. We are also, here, willing to receive any and all citizens who need our support for needs and hopes."

And, with the transcription of the sections above, without further ado, we sign below:

> Pedro A. Mota, graphic artist; José Righetti, weaver; José Ribeiro, stone cutter; Arsênio Palácios, commercial employee; Francisco De Simoni, shoemaker; Paulo Menkitz, weaver; Pasqual Martinez, launderer; Belmiro da Silva Jacintho, glass-blower; Nino Martins, graphic artist; Antonio Domingues, shoemaker; Fernando Ganga, shoemaker; Fernando Donaire, metalworker; Antônio Cordon Filho, carpenter; João Castellani, weaver; Mário Silva, cabinet-maker; José Sarmento, hatter; João Badué, shoemaker; Rodolpho Felippe, Francisco Pawlik, polishers; João Matheus, painter; Alberto Magagni, Marino Spagnolo, tailors; Antônio Lucas, painter; José Gomes, stone-cutter; Affonso Festa, shoemaker.

Translated by Emma Wohl

An Essay on Brazilian Sadness

Paulo Prado

The scion of an influential São Paulo family with lucrative ties to the coffee business, Paulo da Silva Prado (1869–1943) was a politician, coffee grower, and investor who became a patron of the modernists, supporting a group of artists and intellectuals known as the Pro-Modern Art Society. He also became a writer in his own right. Between 1926 and 1928, he wrote and published Retrato do Brasil: Ensaio sobre a tristeza brasileira *(Portrait of Brazil: An essay on Brazilian sadness), a work that discusses the so-called Brazilian national character. The book is divided into four chapters and is marked with Catholic undertones. In the first, titled "Lust," he uses Inquisition documents to describe a colonial past of sexual excess. In the second, "Covetousness," he paints Brazilian history as the craven search for easy wealth, focusing on figures such as the* bandeirantes. *It is in his third and fourth chapters that the sadness of the essay's title comes to the fore, as he defines Brazilians as a sad people, having inherited a collective melancholia from the colonial period.*

One of Prado's main points in the essay is to explain the influence of Portuguese cultural heritage, rooted in the European Renaissance, which coincided with the colonization of Brazil in the sixteenth century. Unlike more optimistic texts of the period, Retrato do Brasil *was noteworthy for its pessimistic assessment of Brazilian history and culture.*

In a radiant land there lives a sad people. This melancholia was bequeathed to the land by the discoverers who revealed Brazil to the world and peopled it. The splendid dynamism of this rough-hewn people obeys two great impulses that dominate the psychology of the discovery and never generated happiness: ambition for gold and freedom to pursue unbridled sensuality that, like a cult, the [European] Renaissance caused to rise from the dead.

From this Renaissance came a new man with a new way of thinking and feeling. His history will be the history of the conquest of the human spirit's conscious freedom. Thus the return to paganism—if it had a disastrous effect on the artistic evolution of humanity, which saw the creative imagination of the Middle Ages staunched—the return to ancient ideals had the best result in the enlargement, so to speak, of human ambition for might, knowledge, and pleasure.

Thus agitated, the peoples of that age felt themselves suffocated and stifled in strict European life. It was necessary to alter—in Nietzschean terminology —the negative effects of Christianity that daily sapped strength and audacity. War on the weak, war on the poor, war on the sick. It was necessary to open the doors of the Western prison. To substitute obedience with the will of the individual. To dissipate the constant and terrifying worries of Death and Hell—fear of God and fear of the Devil—that so tortured Christian souls. . . .

Among us [Brazilians], a vicious cycle resulted in a set of mutually reinforcing influences: sad verses made sad men; melancholy of the people created melancholy in the poets. Our first romantic generation was already sad, because it was religious and moralizing, observed José Veríssimo; in the second, the tendency was emphasized by the skepticism and disapproval of the schoolmasters. The continuously recurring idea of impending death followed them and, as for a desirable woman, they composed amorous verses to it.

Almost all our poets of that time died young and had foreknowledge of that finality.

Death and love. The two refrains of Brazilian poetry. The desire to die came out of the disorganization of the will and the disillusioned melancholy of those who dreamed of the romantic in everyday life. And physically weak from the expenditure of nervous energy, in an instinctive reaction of vitality, they managed to survive through a hallucinatory eroticism, almost feminine in nature. Thus they embodied the weakness of the race, the vice of our mestizo origins. They lived sad in a radiant land.

Translated by Emma Wohl

Portraits: Tarsila do Amaral

Victoria Langland

Tarsila do Amaral, best known as simply Tarsila, was a Brazilian painter whose work was foundational to the development and direction of the modern art movement. Born in 1886 to a wealthy, coffee-growing family from the interior of São Paulo, Tarsila grew up on their farm, São Bernardo. She enjoyed painting as an adolescent, but only began to study art formally in 1916 when she was nearly thirty years old. Then married and with a small daughter, but estranged from her husband, Tarsila enjoyed a degree of freedom not available to many women, due to her family wealth and social position. She lived in the city of São Paulo, where she studied painting, sculpture, and design with some of the best teachers available. In 1920 she and Dulce, her daughter, moved to Paris, where Tarsila took further lessons from renowned artists. There she began steps to formally end her marriage and came to experience the inspiration and dislocation of life abroad. Two years later she was one of only three Brazilians, and the only woman, to have a painting accepted in the Salon de la Societé des Artistes Français in Paris. Her work, then titled *Figura*, was a portrait of a woman painted in the French impressionist style. She later renamed the piece *Passaporte*.

Notwithstanding this early recognition for her impressionist work, Tarsila soon began to turn away from pure impressionism and instead began developing new, distinctive artistic styles that she believed could better capture Brazilian culture. Immersing herself in the artistic avant-garde of both France and Brazil, she traveled frequently between the two countries and sought to meld her European training with her Brazilian experiences and her own aesthetic sensibilities. Writing from Paris in 1923 in a letter to her family, she explained her quest thus: "I feel myself ever more Brazilian: I want to be the painter of my country. How grateful I am for having spent my whole childhood on the farm. My memories of those times are becoming precious for me. I want, in art, to be the *caipirinha* [little country girl] from São Bernardo, playing with straw dolls, like in the most recent picture I am working on."[1]

In this pursuit, Tarsila became an influential participant in the burgeoning modern art movement in Brazil. A member of the so-called Grupo dos Cinco

Tarsila do Amaral
(1886–1973).

(Group of five), a group of artists and writers that also included Anita Mal-
fatti, Oswald de Andrade, Mário de Andrade (no relation), and Menotti del
Picchia, she experimented with new techniques, forms, and subject matter
in a self-conscious drive for authentic nationalistic expression. Where indigenous and Afro-Brazilian cultural products had been traditionally dismissed as
craft rather than art, Tarsila and other modernist artists traveled the country
studying local artistic productions and visiting historic sites. The paintings
she produced showcased subjects previously ignored by formal artists in a
mélange of styles that incorporated both European and Brazilian influences.
For example, her 1923 work *A Negra* presented the figure of an Afro-Brazilian
woman. Painted in a cubist style that distorted her features, and with one
enormous breast as its visual center, the painting at once suggests the tropes
of an earth mother, a Madonna figure, and the enslaved black wet nurses of
eighteenth- and nineteenth-century Brazil, while at the same time evincing
modern sensibilities in its form and in the geometrical shapes that make up
its background. The Swiss poet Blaise Cendrars, a friend of Tarsila, used the
image on the cover of his 1924 book of poetry about Brazil, *Feuilles de Route*.

While Tarsila never demonstrated an interest in the burgeoning women's rights movement, some Brazilian feminists from the 1920s later said her successes proved an inspiration and an important example of women's abilities.

The late 1920s arguably marked Tarsila's most creative period, when she, Oswald de Andrade, whom she married in 1926, and others developed what became known as the anthropophagic movement. Appropriating the trope of the Brazilian cannibal, they argued, oftentimes with biting humor, that Brazilian artists must consume outside influences and digest them fully in order to thereby create something authentically their own. She painted one of her most well-known works in this period, an image of an enormous seated figure resting its tiny head on its hand, surrounded by only a cactus and a lemon-slice sun, and gave it to Oswald de Andrade as a birthday gift in January 1928. He and a fellow modernist artist, the poet Raul Bopp, dubbed the piece *Abaporu*, a Tupi-Guarani word that means "the man who eats people," and the piece's combination of surrealist elements with nativist aesthetics helped inspire the anthropophagic movement. It thus appropriately illustrated the cover of the *Revista de Antropofagia*, where Andrade's "Cannibalist Manifesto" was first published (see above in this part).

The 1930s brought difficult changes to Tarsila's life as a female artist. Her family lost São Bernardo due to the Great Depression, much as other wealthy families saw a good deal of their fortunes disappear. Members of their social class also experienced a considerable decline in previously enjoyed social and political privileges as a result of the so-called Revolution of 1930. In the same year, her marriage to Andrade ended, exacerbating her financial vulnerability. At age forty-four she took on her first paid job, working as the conservation director at a São Paulo museum, but this too was cut short by national political changes wrought by the Vargas presidency, and she was dismissed. She produced only one painting the entire year. The following year, 1931, she sold some of her paintings and traveled to the Soviet Union to organize an exhibit in Moscow, only to face a one-month imprisonment upon her return when President Vargas jailed numerous intellectuals suspected of being communist sympathizers. But she also came away from the trip with a renewed interest in her work, deploying social realist styles to portray human suffering and the plight of the proletariat around the world. She eventually returned to painting Brazilian people and landscapes from her home in São Paulo. She continued to show her work in numerous exhibitions in Brazil and abroad before her death in 1973. Since then her paintings have continued to be exhibited around the world.

Note

1. Letter from Tarsila to her family, April 19, 1923, cited in Aracy A. Amaral, *Tarsila: Sua obra e seu tempo* (São Paulo: Editora USP, 2003), 101.

First Mass in Brazil by Victor Meirelles, 1860. Nineteenth-century romantic vision of the first Mass in Brazil.

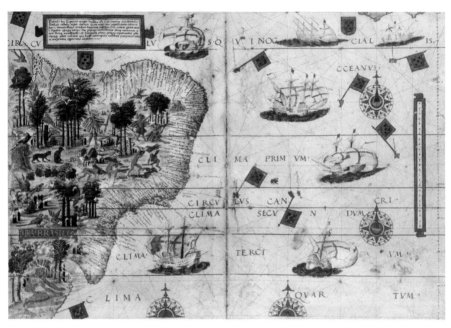

Terra Brasilis by Pedro Reinel and Lopo Homem. Early map of Brazil. From *Miller Atlas*, 1519.

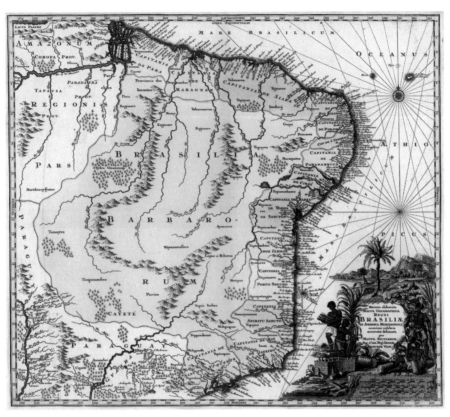

Recens elaborata Mappa Geographica Regni Brasiliae in America Meridionali by Matthias Seutter.
Map of Brazil indicating the captaincies created by the Portuguese Crown in 1534. Courtesy of
the John Carter Brown Library at Brown University.

The sugar mill complex. From Henry Koster, *Travels in Brazil* (London, 1816). Courtesy of the John Carter Brown Library at Brown University.

Dança dos Tapuias. Dutch artist Albert Eckhout's seventeenth-century rendering of the Tapuia people.

Baroque altar from church in Ouro Preto, Minas Gerais. Photograph © Harry-Strharsky.Pixels.com.

As shown in this image, the elite relied heavily on enslaved people from Africa or of African descent for transportation. Courtesy of the John Carter Brown Library at Brown University.

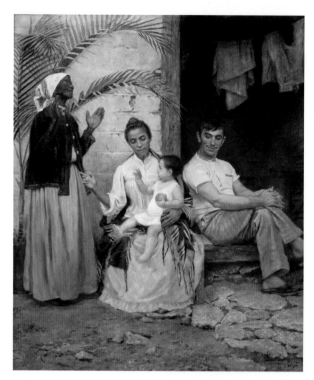

A redenção de Cã (The redemption of Cain) by Modesto Brocos, 1895, portrays the notion that miscegenation would whiten the Brazilian population. Source: Museu Nacional de Belas Artes.

Boutique de Cordonnier by Jean-Batiste Debret. A cobbler punishing an enslaved artisan with a wet nurse or the mother of an infant discreetly viewing the scene. The French artist captured everyday scenes in Rio de Janeiro that depicted both the mistreatment of Afro-Brazilians and racial miscegenation. Courtesy of the John Carter Brown Library at Brown University.

The Brazilian victory in the 1970 World Cup strengthened popular support for the dictatorship.

Military operations in the Rocinha favela of Rio de Janeiro after a battle of different drug traffickers for control of the community. Photograph by Fernando Frazão. Courtesy of Agência Brasil.

Women participating in the Third March of Black Women at the Center of the World along the Copacabana Beach in Rio de Janeiro, 2017. Photograph by Tânia Rêgo. Courtesy of Agência Brasil.

Indigenous representatives attending the 2015 First National Policy Conference for Indigenous People, which was held in Brasília. Courtesy of Agência Brasil.

VIII

Getúlio Vargas, the Estado Novo, and World War II, 1930–1945

After an intense presidential campaign in 1930 marked by multiple charges of corruption, the losing candidate from the opposition Liberal Alliance Party, Getúlio Vargas, a wealthy rancher, lawyer, and congressman from the southern state of Rio Grande do Sul, nonetheless assumed the presidency with the support of the armed forces. In doing so, Vargas and his allies began a process of intense political transformation in Brazil.

Vargas governed the country for a decade and a half, during the Great Depression and World War II, and then returned to power for four more years in the early 1950s. He was first the head of a provisional government (1930–34), next a constitutional president elected by the Constituent Assembly (1934–37), and then the dictator of an authoritarian New State (1937–45). As we will see in part IX, Vargas later returned to the presidency yet again (1951–54), this time popularly elected. He had a tremendous influence on Brazil throughout his political career and even after his death in 1954.

Vargas's rise to power in 1930 coincided with the devastation wrought by the Great Depression. The sale of coffee and other agricultural products on the international market plummeted, and the crisis in the countryside pushed more peasants and rural workers into urban areas. With low foreign reserves, Brazil was unable to import foreign goods, which reinforced the arguments of those who believed that Brazil needed to industrialize in order to modernize. As in many other countries whose economies collapsed in the 1930s, Brazil under Vargas witnessed the significant expansion of the powers of the federal government, often over the fierce opposition of entrenched economic and political interests in different states. In the context of increased labor organization, Vargas mobilized and channeled the popular demand for unionization and political participation of the laboring classes in supporting a new nationalist project for the country.

One of the ways that the Vargas administration strengthened the power of the federal government was by creating Brazil's first Ministry of Labor, Industry and Commerce immediately upon taking office, signaling a state

President Getúlio Vargas in a military uniform soon after taking power in 1930.
Used by permission from CPDOC/Fundação Getúlio Vargas.

commitment to regulating the economy. He also deposed political opponents, including state governors, and replaced them with *interventores*, federally appointed officeholders.

Vargas's campaigns to promote nationalism, from economic policies to cultural programs, became a hallmark of his presidency. In this, his efforts complemented and fostered intellectual and artistic attempts to celebrate some aspects of Brazil's multiracial heritage. Under Vargas, for example, the federal government began to officially sponsor carnival celebrations in Rio de Janeiro, transforming what had been a regional and largely Afro-Brazilian festival into a symbol of national culture and pride. This was also the case with capoeira, a martial art practiced by slaves and other Afro-Brazilians that had been outlawed in the nineteenth century. In the 1930s, capoeira became a national sport. Similarly, *feijoada*, a meal that had been associated with slaves, was hailed as a national dish. Even its main ingredients became transformed into symbols of the nation: white rice, brown or black beans, red peppers, and yellow oranges were metaphorically linked to Brazil's four races. In the 1930s, Our Lady of Aparecida, known as the black Madonna and venerated by Afro-Brazilians, became the patron saint of the country.

Vargas sought to cultivate popular support for these endeavors and his administration. During his first years in office he traveled over ninety thousand miles to visit almost every area in the country. His government also publicly committed itself to electoral reforms, the drafting of a new constitution, and an end to the restrictive political system of the former period that he disparagingly referred to as the Old Republic. Vargas's promises to implement constitutional reforms strengthened the long-standing demands of the feminist movement for women's suffrage. Women finally won the right to vote in 1932. The next year Vargas convened a Constituent Assembly to draft a new constitution that expanded other political rights. Provisions that guaranteed the secret ballot responded to middle-class concerns about vote buying and demands for greater electoral fairness. Lowering the voting age from twenty-one to eighteen expanded the electorate. The new Constitution of 1934 empowered the Constituent Assembly to choose the president for a four-year term in office. Not surprisingly, Vargas was elected to the post. Although his supporters referred to the military coup d'état that brought him to power as the Revolution of 1930, Vargas never intended to bring about a popular revolution, and the majority of the populace for whom schooling was unavailable (especially the rural population) remained disenfranchised due to the continuation of the literacy requirement for voters.

Another hallmark of Vargas's leadership in this period was his adherence to corporatism, or the belief that society should be organized into major interest groups, such as workers, students, capitalists, and so forth. According to this perspective, the state's task was to minimize conflict between groups (such as that between labor and capital) and to pursue policies that would benefit the greater social body (hence the name corporatism, from the Latin *corpus*). By encouraging the formation of officially sanctioned interest groups such as labor unions or student organizations, but repressing independent organizations, corporatism offered ways of simultaneously currying support and stifling opposition.

Vargas had powerful detractors, especially people from the state of São Paulo, who bitterly resisted the loss of their influence over national decisions and the intervention of the federal government in the coffee trade. In the city of São Paulo, an uprising against Vargas in 1932 led to a three-month insurrection before federal forces eventually quieted the rebellion. Meanwhile the growing conflicts between fascism and communism that marked Europe at this time had parallels in Brazil. Groups from both the left-leaning Aliança Libertadora Nacional (National Liberating Alliance) and the fascist Ação Integralista Brasileira (Brazilian Integralist Action) alternately opposed and courted Vargas and battled fiercely with one another. It is a testament to Vargas's political skills that both fascists and communists considered him an ally at certain moments, yet once he determined that they posed a threat to him, he effectively suppressed them. In 1937, Vargas canceled the upcoming elections that would have chosen his successor and instead decreed the dawn of an Estado Novo or New State, a dictatorial period of authoritarian state control that only ended when the military deposed him 1945.

Vargas's diplomatic skills also served him well during the years preceding and then during World War II, as both the Allied and Axis powers vied for the support of the Brazilian government. Brazil had significant commerce with Germany and Italy, and large sectors of the German and Italian immigrant communities in Brazil were sympathetic to their countries of origin. Thus, despite mounting pressure from the United States on Latin American nations to side with the Allies, Brazil maintained its neutrality. Even after German submarines began sinking Brazilian merchant ships, Brazil only broke off relations with the Axis powers in January 1942 and entered the war in August of that year. During World War II, Brazil became a close ally of the United States. Washington sought access to rubber, strategic minerals, and other Brazilian resources that were essential for the war effort. Vargas allowed the United States to set up bases in the northeast to be used as staging grounds for the air force and for naval supplies sent across the southern Atlantic, and sent 25,000 troops to Italy to fight alongside U.S. soldiers. Trade with the United States increased significantly, and the Roosevelt administration agreed to provide technology and capital to help establish the first steel mill in Brazil.

During the war years, opposition to Vargas began to mount among much of the Brazilian political elite, who chafed at their political exclusion and saw the fight for democracy abroad as propitious for political and economic liberalization at home. Sectors of the armed forces that trained and fought with the Allies on the Italian Front also aligned themselves with those politicians calling for Vargas's ouster. In October 1945 the military removed him from office and scheduled new presidential elections for the end of the year. Nevertheless, Vargas remained extremely popular and was elected senator in two states, which was permitted under Brazilian law. He chose to represent his home state of Rio Grande do Sul. From there he rebuilt his power base to return to the presidency in 1951.

From the Platform of the Liberal Alliance

Liberal Alliance

When, in 1929, incumbent President Washington Luis backed Júlio Prestes, another Paulista, as his successor for the upcoming elections, the act signified a break in the old café com leite political arrangement between São Paulo, Minas Gerais, and Rio de Janeiro. In response, a group from Minas Gerais, Rio Grande do Sul, and Paraíba, along with various nationalists, intellectuals, and important members of the tenentes movement, formed a coalition called the Liberal Alliance and nominated Getúlio Vargas and João Pessoa as their candidates for president and vice president. In September 1929 they released their electoral platform, calling for such reforms as the adoption of the secret ballot, greater judicial independence, amnesty for those who had participated in the Tenentes Revolts, and increased federal efforts for economic development, diversification, and modernization. As the extract from their platform below details, they also made social problems a major part of their campaign, promising to enact sweeping social legislation for the first time in Brazil, such as a minimum wage and worker protection laws. In this, the Liberal Alliance differed greatly from previous political campaigns in Brazil. Yet its program was very similar to that of political movements in other parts of Latin America in which national leaders increasingly saw the need to support the labor force on behalf of national economic development.

One cannot negate the existence of a social question in Brazil as one of the problems that will have to be dealt with seriously by public authorities. The little that we have in terms of social legislation either is not applied or [is applied] only sporadically in tiny measures, in spite of the promises that have been made by us as signers of the Versailles Treaty and of our responsibilities as members of the International Labor Organization, whose conventions and regulations we fail to observe. . . . The activities of women and children in factories and commercial establishments in every civilized nation are subject to special conditions that we, up to now, unfortunately do not heed. We need to coordinate activities between the states and the federal government to study and adopt measures to create a national Labor Code. Both the urban and rural proletariat require measures, applied to both, to address their respective needs. These should include instruction, education, hygiene, diet, housing, protection of women, children, invalids, and old people, credit, salary relief, and even recreation, including sports and artistic culture. It is time to think of creating agricultural schools and industrial learning centers, of making factories and mills safe, bringing sanitation to the countryside, constructing workers' villas, granting vacations, [establishing] a minimum salary, consumer cooperatives, and so forth.

Translated by Robert M. Levine and John J. Crocitti

Prestes's Declaration about the Liberal Alliance

Luís Carlos Prestes

In forging a new political coalition, the Liberal Alliance sought support from dissident groups throughout the country. Among them were the rebellious junior officers of the Tenentes (Lieutenants') Revolts. As seen earlier, one tenente leader, Luís Carlos Prestes, had become a larger-than-life figure, admired for his defiant challenges to traditional political authority, especially after he and his supporters occupied São Paulo for several weeks in 1924 and then, for over three years, successfully evaded the federal troops pursuing them. During this period they crossed into Bolivia and Argentina, where Prestes came into contact with members of the Communist Third International. He joined the Communist Party in 1929, traveled to Moscow, and soon adopted radically different perspectives on revolutionary possibilities in Brazil. In May 1930, prior to the coup d'état that brought Vargas to power, he issued a statement from Argentina in which he was strongly critical of the Liberal Alliance, notwithstanding their overtures to him. The May Manifesto, excerpted below, reflects the new anti-imperialist and anti-oligarchic political viewpoint that he had recently adopted.

These words are directed to the suffering proletariat of our cities, to the oppressed of the plantations and ranches, to the miserable masses of our backlands and especially to the sincere revolutionaries, to those who are willing to struggle and to sacrifice on behalf of the profound transformation that needs to take place.

Stripped of any rhetorical whims, [these words] were written with the principal objective of clarifying and stating in detail my opinion regarding the Brazilian revolutionary movement, and to show the necessity of a complete change in the political direction that we have been following, so that we might be able to reach a coveted victory.

The last political campaign [the 1930 presidential election] has just ended. It was another electoral farce, methodically and carefully prepared by petty politicians; it was carried out with the innocence of many and with a great number of dreamers still not convinced of the uselessness of such efforts.

Once again, the real popular interests were sacrificed and the people easily deceived by an apparently democratic campaign, which, deep down, was nothing more than the fight between two opposing interests of the oligarchy,

GENERAL LUIZ CARLOS PRESTES

BRA SIL

5 DE JULHO DE 1929

O BRASIL
"ESPERA QUE CADA UM CUMPRA
COM O SEU DEVER"

Propaganda promoting the Prestes Column, which presents its leader as a general. The caption reads, "Brazil 'hopes each person fulfills his [or her] duty.'"

supported and stimulated by the two greatest imperial powers that enslave us, and to whom petty Brazilian politicians deliver the entire Nation, bound hand and foot.

Even while making such statements, I cannot fail to recognize that there are a great number of sincere revolutionaries among the ranks of the Liberal Alliance, on whom, I believe, I can still count to join the genuine and determined struggle that I now propose against all of the oppressors. . . .

Despite all their revolutionary demagoguery and despite those who said that the liberals would stand up for the repeal of the latest oppressive laws, during the last electoral campaign no one within the Liberal Alliance protested against the brutal political persecution that the proletarian associations of the entire Country suffered; and in Rio Grande do Sul itself, during the height of the elections, the most violent persecution took place against workers fighting for their own rights. . . .

The Brazilian revolution cannot be carried out with the ineffectual program of the Liberal Alliance. A simple change in individuals, the secret ballot, promises of free elections, administrative honesty, respect for the Constitution, a stable currency, and other panaceas cannot solve [our problems], nor can they be of any interest to the great majority of our population, without whose support any revolution is nothing more than a fight between different sectors of the dominant oligarchies.

We are not fooled. A minority governs us who are the owners of the farms and plantations and the means of production and who are supported by foreign imperialists who exploit us and divide us. They will only be defeated by the true general insurrection and a conscious revolt of the vast masses of our people, from the backlands to the cities.

Translated by Robert M. Levine and John J. Crocitti

The Masters and the Slaves

Gilberto Freyre

While the implications of some of his ideas have long been debated, even today Gilberto de Mello Freyre (1900–1987) is considered one of the great interpreters of Brazilian culture. In a trilogy of books about Brazilian history and society that he wrote beginning in 1933, he critiqued then-current views of racial miscegenation as a source of social degeneration and instead celebrated the mixture of European, American, and African races and cultures that, in his view, explains the uniqueness of Brazil.

Freyre was raised in the northeastern state of Pernambuco, one of the centers of Brazil's sugar-producing and slaveholding colonial past. After finishing his early education in the city of Recife, he traveled to the United States, where he studied at Baylor College in Waco, Texas, and completed a master's degree at Columbia University, studying with the anthropologist Franz Boas, who greatly influenced his thinking. The Masters and the Slaves (1933) was his first and most famous work. Together with the other two books in the trilogy, The Mansions and the Shanties (1936) and Order and Progress (1957), it was an extended essay about the formation of Brazil and Brazilian identity. After an initial chapter on the process of colonization, excerpts of which appear below, the subsequent chapters each focus on one of the races that Freyre argued created Brazil, with one about the role of the indigenous, another on the Portuguese colonizer, and two long chapters explaining "the black slave in Brazilian sexual and family life." As this chapter title suggests, the topic of sexuality as a form of power and negotiation pervades the book, as Freyre's arguments center on the importance of patriarchal family structures.

His thinking provoked a monumental intellectual shift for Brazil. During the empire, writers largely ignored black and mixed-race populations, and in the First Republic most intellectuals adopted racial theories that understood racial mixtures as a cause of national inferiority. By contrast, Freyre declared that miscegenation had led to a panoply of racial gradations and to such a thorough mixing of cultural elements that the resulting Brazilian culture was a unique new hybrid. The Masters and the Slaves was an instant best-seller, and his vision of race—what later came to be known as the idea of racial democracy—proved immensely compelling to many for decades.

Gilberto Freyre (1900–1987) challenged scientific racism and reshaped national notions of race in Brazil. Courtesy of Acervo Iconographia.

I. General Characteristics of the Portuguese Colonization of Brazil:
Formation of an Agrarian, Slave-Holding, and Hybrid Society

When, in 1532, the economic and civil organization of Brazilian society was effected, the Portuguese already for an entire century had been in contact with the tropics and had demonstrated, in India and in Africa, their aptitude for living in those regions. The definitive proof of this aptitude is to be found in the change of direction that Portuguese colonization underwent in São Vicente and in Pernambuco, from an easy-going mercantile way of life to an agricultural existence. Colonial society in Brazil was organized upon a more solid basis and under more stable conditions than it had been in India or on the African plantations. The foundation was agriculture, and the conditions were a patriarchal stability of family life; the regularization of labor by means of slavery; and the union of the Portuguese male with the Indian woman, who was thus incorporated into the economic and social culture of the invader.

In tropical America the society that was formed was agrarian in structure, slave-holding in its technique of economic exploitation, and hybrid in composition, with an admixture of the Indian and later of the black. This was a society that in its evolution was protected less by a consciousness of race, which was practically non-existent in the cosmopolitan and plastic-minded Portuguese, than it was by a religious exclusiveness given expression in a system of social and political prophylaxis; less by official action than by the arm and sword of the individual. All this, however, was subordinated to a spirit of political, economic, and juridical realism that here, as in Portugal, from the first century on, was the decisive element in the forming of the nation. What we had in our country was great landowning and autonomous families, lords of the plantation, with an altar and a chaplain in the house and Indians armed with bow and arrow or blacks armed with muskets at their command; and from their seats in the municipal council chamber these masters of the earth and of the slaves that tilled it always spoke up boldly to the representatives of the crown, while through the liberal-toned voices of their sons who were priests or doctors of the law they cried out against every species of abuse on the part of the Metropolis and of Mother Church itself. In this they were quite different from the rich *criollos* [those of European descent born and raised in the colonies] and learned bachelors of Spanish America, who for so long were inert in the dominant shadow of the cathedrals and the palaces of the viceroys, or who, when gathered in *cabildos* [town councils], did little more than serve as a laughingstock for the all-powerful lords of the realm.

The singular predisposition of the Portuguese to the hybrid, slave-exploiting colonization of the tropics is to be explained in large part by the ethnic or, better, the cultural past of a people existing indeterminately between Europe and Africa and belonging uncompromisingly to neither one nor the other of the two continents; with the African influence seething beneath the European and giving a sharp relish to sexual life, to alimentation, and to religion; with Moorish or black blood running throughout a great light-skinned mulatto population, when it is not the predominant strain, in regions that to this day are inhabited by a dark-skinned people; and with the hot and oleous air of Africa mitigating the Germanic harshness of institutions and cultural forms, corrupting the doctrinal and moral rigidity of the medieval Church, drawing the bones from Christianity, feudalism, Gothic architecture, canonic discipline, Visigoth law, and Latin tongue, and the very character of the people. It was Europe reigning without governing: it was Africa that governed. . . .

In its ethnic and cultural indeterminateness between Europe and Africa, Portugal appears to have been always the same as other portions of the peninsula. A species of bi-continentalism that, in a population so vague and ill-defined, corresponds to bisexuality in the individual. It would be difficult to imagine a people in more fluctuation than the Portuguese, the feeble balance of antagonisms being reflected in everything that pertains to them, conferring upon them an easy and relaxed flexibility that is at times disturbed by grievous hesitations, along with a special wealth of aptitudes that are frequently discrepant and hard to reconcile for the purpose of a useful expression or practical initiative. . . .

Within this antecedent factor of a general nature—the bi-continentalism or, better, the dualism of culture and race—there are other, subordinate factors that call for our special attention. One of these is the presence among the elements that united to form the Portuguese nation of individuals of Semitic origin, or stock, individuals endowed with a mobility, a plasticity, and adaptability social as well as physical that are to be made out easily in the Portuguese navigator and cosmopolitan of the fifteenth century. Hereditarily predisposed to a life in the tropics by a long tropical habitat, it was the Semitic element, mobile and adaptable as no other, that was to confer upon the Portuguese colonizer of Brazil some of the chief physical and psychic conditions for success and for resistance—including that economic realism which from an early date tended to correct the excesses of the military and religious spirit in the formation of Brazilian society. . . .

As to their miscibility, no colonizing people in modern times has exceeded or so much as equaled the Portuguese in this regard. From their first contact with women of color, they mingled with them and procreated mestizo sons; and the result was that a few thousand daring males succeeded in establishing themselves firmly in possession of a vast territory and were able to compete with great and numerous peoples in the extension of their colonial domain and in the efficiency of their colonizing activity. Miscibility rather than mobility was the process by which the Portuguese made up for their deficiency in human mass or volume in the large-scale colonization of extensive areas. For this they had been prepared by the intimate terms of social and sexual intercourse on which they had lived with the colored races that had invaded their peninsula or were close neighbors to it, one of which, of the Mohammedan faith, was technically more highly skilled and possessed an intellectual and artistic culture superior to that of the blond Christians. . . .

In opposition to the legend of the "enchanted Moorish woman," although it never attained the same prestige, there evolved that of the "Moorish hag," representing, it may be, an outlet for the blonde woman's sexual jealousy toward her colored sister. . . . With reference to Brazil, as an old saying has it, "White woman for marriage, mulatto woman for f—, black woman for work," a saying in which, alongside the social convention of the superiority of the white woman and the inferiority of the black, is to be discerned a sexual preference for the mulatto. Moreover, in our national lyricism there is no tendency more clearly revealed than one toward a glorification of the mulatto woman, the *cabocla* or Indian woman, the brown-skin or brunette type, celebrated for the beauty of her eyes, the whiteness of her teeth, for her wiles and languishment and witching ways, far more than are the "pale virgins" and the "blonde damsels." . . .

All of these elements, beginning with a Christianity that was lyrically social, a cult of the family rather than a religion of the church or cathedral . . . All these elements and advantages, to repeat, were to favor a colonization that in Portuguese America, as in the "proprietary colonies" of the English in North America, was to rest upon the institution of the slaveholding family, the Big House, the patriarchal family, the only difference being that in our country the family was to be enlarged by a far greater number of bastards and dependents, gathered round the patriarchs, who were more given to women and possibly a little more loose in their sexual code than the North Americans were.

The true formative process of our society, as has been said, is to be viewed from 1532 on, with the rural or semi-rural family as the unit, whether it was a matter of married couples who had come from the homeland or of families that had been set up here through the union of colonists with Indian women, with orphan girls, or even with women whom matchmaking fathers had sent over at random from Portugal. . . .

The advantages of miscegenation in Brazil ran parallel to the tremendous disadvantage of syphilis. These two factors began operating at the same time: one to form the Brazilian, the ideal type of modern man for the tropics, a European with black or Indian blood to revive his energy; the other to deform him. . . .

Of all the social influences, perhaps syphilis has been, next to bad nutrition, the most deforming in its effects, the one that has to the greatest extent drained the economic energy of the Brazilian mestizo. It would appear to have come from the first unions of Europeans, wandering aimlessly along our shores, with those Indian women who offered themselves to the white man's sexual embrace. That initial ethnic "tare" of which Azevedo Amaral speaks was first of all a syphilitic tare.

It is customary to say that civilization and syphilis go hand in hand, but Brazil would appear to have been syphilized before it was civilized. The first Europeans to come here were swallowed up in the aboriginal mass without leaving upon the latter any traces of their origin other than those of syphilis and racial hybridism. They did not bring civilization, but there is evidence to show that they did bring the venereal plague to the population that absorbed them.

Speech by the First Woman Elected to Congress in Brazil

Carlota Pereira de Queirós

Carlota Pereira de Queirós (1892–1982) was a pediatrician and suffragist from São Paulo who was the only woman elected to the Constituent Assembly of 1933, the body charged with drafting a new constitution. She was also the first woman elected to the national Congress, joining the Chamber of Deputies as a representative of São Paulo, also in 1933. Coming from an elite and politically influential family in São Paulo, she represents an important sector of women suffragists—those well-educated and well-connected women who supplied much of the leadership for the suffrage movement but who also stressed mild political reform rather than radical social restructuring. She also reflects the gendered expectations of an era that saw women as the proper custodians for only certain kinds of public service. Her legislative work within the two congressional bodies revolved around issues of health and education, and the legislation she drafted focused on social welfare policies. As the extracts from her March 13, 1934, speech to the Constituent Assembly below reveal, she believed women held responsibilities to the nation just as men did, but that the form these obligations took was categorically different.

Her comments came at a time when women were just acquiring the right to vote. In the 1920s, bills to grant national political rights to women languished in both houses of Congress for years. But after President Vargas assumed the presidency in 1930 and publicly proclaimed his commitment to electoral reform, women suffragists saw a new opportunity and intensified their work. In 1931, the new government released a provisional electoral code granting suffrage to a very small group of women: those who were literate, and, if married, had their husbands' permission, or, if single or widowed, could prove financial independence. Several feminist and suffragist organizations denounced the code as insufficient and lobbied for its expansion. In 1932, a new electoral code enfranchised women equally to men (literacy remained a requirement for both sexes), making Brazil the fourth country in the Western Hemisphere to grant women the right to vote, a right later guaranteed in the 1934 Constitution. In 1933, during the first congressional elections following women's suffrage, Queirós ran for and was elected to the Chamber of Deputies, the only woman to join that body.

She won a succeeding reelection and remained in her position until 1937, when Vargas dissolved the Congress as part of the authoritarian changes of the Estado Novo.

Mr. President, Representatives, I thank your Excellencies for the kindness with which you have welcomed me in this moment.

Despite the silence I have maintained since this house began its activities, I have the honor, simply by my presence here, of creating a new chapter for the history of Brazil—that of female collaboration in the nation's politics. . . .

If the feminine voice, interpreting the classic texts of national politics, does not reach the depth and gravity of the voices that have echoed in this enclave, it will at least produce new vibrations, its sharpness reaching notes previously unheard by the usual listeners of these sessions. And it will thus be a complement to the musical scale, a simple expansion of the choruses, because we do not want to assume the role of mere soloists. In addition to being a female representative, the only one in this Assembly, I am, like everyone here, a Brazilian, involved in the destiny of the country and forever identified with its problems.

Today men and women must work together, simultaneously, using all of our resources to increase Brazil's potential. Such is the spirit that should be our conviction when we enter politics. A friendly environment always welcomes us. That is the impression the fellowship in this house gives me. Not once did I feel I was in the presence of adversaries.

Because we, as women, must always keep in mind that it was by the decision of men that we were granted the right to vote. And, if they treat us that way today, it is because the Brazilian woman has demonstrated how much she is worth and what she is able to do for her people. . . .

Here, we are all representatives of the Brazilian Nation. Based on this thought, I presented some amendments to the proposed Constitution submitted to this Assembly, which I respectfully request, Mr. President and my noble colleagues, to defend in front of this tribunal. The first of these amendments refers to Article 78 of the proposal, which is about obligatory military service. . . . I made light modifications to this section. . . . International conventions already exclude women from this obligation and for this reason I thought it unnecessary to mention this exclusion. . . .

But there is a new amendment by the São Paulo delegation, which I know has been considered by the subcommission, that requires all Brazilians to pledge allegiance to the flag in the form prescribed by law.

Now, Mr. President, I do not believe that women should also be excluded from this fundamental obligation to the Nation.

As our amendment states, pledging allegiance to the flag, besides being a necessity in a country like ours which accumulates so many successive waves of immigration, thus helping avoid dual nationalities, is also an important aspect in forging the national spirit. [Audience reaction: Very good!] What reason is there to distance women from this highly educative ceremony? If the right to vote is today conceded to them, if they are granted vast new responsibilities by this act of voting, that they receive by contract with the country, why not signal their civic maturity with this obligation, so noble and so wide-reaching? . . .

It would be woman's first contact with her responsibilities as a citizen. . . .

The day on which this ought to take place is to be established by law; it could be made to coincide with the completion of one's secondary school education, today so common even for girls.

That ceremony, performed throughout the country with great pomp and on a specially determined day, would be a great aid to the formation of the national spirit. It would resound like the voice of the Nation, echoing simultaneously in all corners and imparting to girls the image of its greatness. [Audience reaction: Very good!]

The completion of this rite would be highly educational for our girls, little accustomed still to civic responsibilities, and who need to become more interested in national problems in order to acquire the civic consciousness for the vote they will one day have. [Audience reaction: Hear, hear!] It would be the first effort to take advantage of female collaboration in the service of national defense. (Audience reaction: Very good!)

A first effort, I say, because I see no reason not to later consider, in just this way, literacy services and social assistance work, making them equivalent to military service, the example of which was already proposed vis-à-vis spiritual service for priests.

The sanitation and education campaigns, which our country needs so much, inarguably represent acts of national defense.

The first paragraph of Article 78 says that no Brazilians will be able to exercise rights or public functions without proving that they did not recuse themselves from their legally stated obligations regarding the defense of the nation.

Now, Mr. President, I would propose that the pledge to the flag, for one and the other sex, constitutes this initial obligation.

The granting of a document, which would come to replace the military reservists' passbook, would constitute a safe-conduct pass for Brazil's citizens. And, as in other countries, it could come with an attached copy of the Constitution, in order to inculcate youth in the traditions of the nation and the law.

Afterward, it could serve as a draft for men to fill the ranks of the armed forces.

And nothing stops us from thinking that this draft could one day be extended to women, too, in ways befitting their sex, of course. Once the programs for assistance to minors are created, as we proposed in a separate amendment, this whole female army could be utilized. And besides main-

Carlota Pereira de Queirós (1892–1982) during the 1934 Constitutional Assembly.
Source: Sec. Municipal de Cultura de São Paulo.

taining it for reasons of eventual national defense, like the military draft, it would offer constant benefits to the nation because it would give women a new understanding of their rights and would be hugely advantageous for the future of the race.

[The Swedish writer and suffragist] Ellen Key, considering women's issues in her notable book *The Century of the Child* [1900], affirmed that we could only be confident in the improvement of the race if the law that granted women the right to vote also imposed the draft on them, as on men, so that they too spent a residency, for the same amount of time that men spend in barracks, in which they would study nursing and public health. I recall that they were interned in boarding houses akin to schools of domestic arts. "For what purpose?" you might ask me. For the same purpose that barracks have. For the eventual defense of the Nation. In cases of mobilization, these would be the *leaders* [in English in original], organizing auxiliary services. And if their collaboration is never needed for this exact goal of national defense, the state will not have made useless expenditures. These notions of hygiene and first aid, learned generally by all young women, would be a great accomplishment of indisputable utility. Perhaps much more useful than young men's knowledge of how to use weapons.

This training for girls, whether it takes place in boarding houses or in organized welfare or literacy services, would indisputably have an educational effect. Coming from diverse areas, they would immediately come together to live collectively in civilized centers, which could only serve to clarify their spirit and prepare them better for their future duties as mothers of the family.

In order to avoid social disorder and keeping in mind the cautious education of our girls, we could, for example, impose a female draft only for those aged twenty-four or older and only for unmarried women—clearly always with the restrictions determined by law, as is the case with obligatory military service: precarious health, breadwinners of the family, etc. . . .

Pardon me, Mr. President and my colleagues, for these digressions. . . . They are the anxieties of one who desires a strong and united Brazil, granting the opportunity to all its children—men and women—to cooperate in its exaltation. . . .

It seems to me that we are not dreaming, nor do we mean to demand of women services that oblige them to act against nature. As a doctor, I know well that women cannot transgress the limits imposed on them by nature.

What we need is to create a new female mentality. And, for this, we must instill in them the notion of civic responsibility and teach them to uphold their duties.

Translated by Emma Wohl

Manifesto of the National Liberating Alliance

Luís Carlos Prestes

Like many other areas in the world, Brazil in the early 1930s experienced both the ascendancy of fascist and communist thought and ensuing political polarization. The Integralists, a fascist-inspired movement, grew in strength and numbers, as did the Brazilian Communist Party (PCB), their appeal augmented by the economic hardships of the Great Depression. In 1935, a group of PCB members joined forces with other left-leaning intellectuals and union leaders to form the Aliança Libertadora Nacional (ALN, National Liberating Alliance), a group designed to unite antifascist and anti-imperialist forces in a broad front. Among other demands, the ALN advocated for the nationalization of key industries, agrarian reform, and the cancellation of foreign debts.

Luís Carlos Prestes, the aforementioned leader of an important branch of the tenentes movement in the 1920s, and a member of the PCB since 1930, was in the Soviet Union when the ALN was founded. Despite his absence, he was declared the honorary president of the ALN, a position he actively took on following his clandestine return to Brazil in April 1935. But in July 1935 he issued a statement, extracts of which appear below, that called for the overthrow of the Vargas government and its substitution with "a people's revolutionary government." In response, Vargas used the newly approved National Security Law to outlaw the ALN, pushing left-wing activities underground throughout the 1930s and early 1940s.

Conditions for Joining the ALN

All people, groups, movements, organizations, and even political parties should join the National Liberating Alliance, whatever their programs may be, under only one condition: that they fight against fascism in Brazil, against imperialism and feudalism, and for democratic rights. To all people and groups, who wish, for whatever reason, to restrict the only national revolutionary front, we should oppose the iron will of their attempts. All persons, groups, associations, and political parties that participate in the Alliance should stop those efforts with all their might by relentlessly denouncing those at fault as traitors to Brazil and to its people.

Unification of the Proletariat

The forces of the National Liberating Alliance are now great, but they can and should be even greater, made up of millions because all those who work in the country and all those who suffer from imperialist and feudal domination are included in its program and are in the front lines of the proletariat and the great rural masses. The unification of the proletariat, a now unstoppable movement that will overcome all efforts to prevent it from happening, is one of the greatest forces of revolution. Recent strikes progressively expand the capacity of Brazil's heroic proletariat to fight as the leading class of the revolution, and they increase the confidence that they inspire in all Brazilian revolutionaries. The struggles of the peasants, while still spontaneous and disoriented, are the true index of the hatred and the energy accumulated over centuries of suffering and misery among the millions who seek better days. They, [along with] soldiers and sailors throughout Brazil, will stand with the revolution and therefore with the Alliance. . . .

Privileges of Race, Color, and Nationality

With the Alliance will stand the petty merchants and industrialists, who, stuck between the impositions and monopolies of imperialists on one side and the increasing misery of the popular masses on the other, earn less each day and become impoverished, humble, poorly paid intermediaries in the exploitation of the people by imperialism and indirect taxes. All those Brazilians of color, heirs to the glorious tradition of Palmares, will stand with the Alliance, because only broad democracy, from a truly popular government, will be able to permanently end all the privileges of race, color, or nationality, and give to blacks in Brazil the enormous perspective of freedom and equality, free of reactionary prejudices, for which they have fought boldly for more than three centuries.

Anti-imperialist Program

There are no excuses that justify, in the eyes of the people, the fight against the only Liberating Front. For this reason the ranks of the National Liberating Alliance are open to all those who want to fight for its anti-imperialist, antifeudalist, and antifascist agenda, which only the popular revolutionary government can carry out:

I. No recognition or payment of the foreign debt.
II. Denunciation of treaties with imperialists that hurt trade.
III. Nationalization of the most important public services and those imperialist businesses that do not submit to the laws of the people's revolutionary government.

IV. A maximum workday of eight hours, social security, retirement benefits, salary increases, equal pay for equal work, a guaranteed minimum wage, satisfaction of all other demands of the proletariat.

V. The fight against slave labor and feudal working conditions.

VI. Distribution of land and use of water resources for poor peasants and factory workers to be taken without compensation from imperialists, from the most reactionary estate holders, and from those elements within the Church who fight against Brazil's freedom and the emancipation of the people.

VII. The broadest freedom for the people, the complete elimination of all differences or privileges of race, color, or nationality, the most complete religious freedom, and the separation of Church and State.

VIII. Opposition to any and all imperialist warfare and strict unity with the National Liberating Alliances of other Latin American nations and with all oppressed classes and peoples. . . .

Implantation of a Popular Government

We march quickly toward the implementation of a people's revolutionary government in all of Brazil, a government of the people against imperialism and feudalism, which will demonstrate in practice what democracy and liberty are to the great working masses of the nation. The people's government, carrying out the program of the Alliance, will unify Brazil and save the lives of millions of workers threatened by hunger, plagued by illness, and brutally exploited by imperialism and large landholders. The distribution of the lands of great estates will increase the activity of internal commerce and open the path to a faster industrialization of the country, independent of imperialist control. The people's government will open the prospect of a new life for Brazil's youth that guarantees them work, health, and education. The power of the masses, which will support such a government, will be the greatest guarantee of the nation's defense against imperialism and counterrevolution. The military of the people, the national revolutionary army, will be able to defend the nation's integrity against imperialist invasion, eliminating, at the same time, all counterrevolutionary forces. . . .

An Appeal

Working population of the whole nation! On guard, in defense of your interests! Come occupy your post with the liberators of Brazil!

Soldiers of Brazil! Attention! The tyrants want to turn you against your brothers. Join the fight for the liberty of Brazil!

Soldiers of Rio Grande do Sul, heroic heirs to the greatest revolutionary traditions of the Gaúcho land! Prepare yourselves! Organize yourselves! Because only thus will you reverse the tyranny [of the past] that has brought on ongoing shame lasting until the present!

Honest democrats of all Brazil! Heroic people of Minas Gerais, traditional land of the great struggles for democracy! Only with the National Liberating Alliance will you be able to continue the fights begun by your forebears! Northerners and northeasterners! Formidable reserve of the great energies of the nation! Organize yourselves for the defense of a Brazil that belongs to you!

Peasants throughout Brazil, defenders of the backlands of the Northeast! The people's revolutionary government guarantees you the ownership of the lands and water reservoirs that you take! Prepare yourself to defend them!

Brazilians! All you who are united in the idea, in the suffering and humiliation of all of Brazil! Organize your hatred toward the dominators, transforming yourselves into the unstoppable and invincible force of the Brazilian Revolution! You who have nothing to lose and the immense richness of Brazil to gain! Seize Brazil by armed rebellion from the forces of imperialism and their lackeys! All hands to the fight for the national liberation of Brazil! Down with fascism! Down with the hateful government of Vargas! Up with a popular national revolutionary government!

All power to the National Liberating Alliance!

Luís Carlos Prestes, July 5, 1935.

Translated by Emma Wohl

The Cordial Man

Sérgio Buarque de Holanda

Of the many intellectuals who sought to understand and explain Brazilian culture in the 1930s, Sérgio Buarque de Holanda (1902–1982) was one of the most important. He was born and raised in São Paulo, but in 1921 his family moved to Rio de Janeiro, where he enrolled at the University of Rio de Janeiro, studying law and enthusiastically participating in the city's bohemian life and the country's modernist intellectual movement. After graduation, he worked as a journalist for several newspapers, one of which sent him to Berlin in 1929. Once there, he accepted a job with a bilingual German-Brazilian business magazine, where he often found it difficult to explain Brazil to his German readers. As he later recounted in an interview, when he returned to Brazil at the end of 1930, he had hundreds of pages of notes from these attempts that became part of his first book, Raízes do Brasil (Roots of Brazil), published in 1936. In this text, his only general essay on Brazil, Holanda builds on the ideal types modeled by the German sociologist Max Weber to understand Brazilian society through pairings of nondichotomous opposites, such as a tile worker and a planter, or work and adventure. His most well-known chapter, from which we draw the following excerpt, is called "The Cordial Man." Using the Latin notion of cor (heart), Holanda argues that the biggest obstacle to modernizing is the way in which Brazilians support themselves through personal relationships and a distrust of official spheres. His argument brings to mind the common Brazilian proverb, "For my friends, everything; for my enemies, the law."

The same year that he published this book, he began working as a history professor at the University of the Federal District in Rio de Janeiro and married Maria Amélia de Carvalho Cesário Alvim, who became his intellectual advisor and the mother of their seven children, among them the well-known singer and writer Chico Buarque de Holanda.

Even during the Empire, it had already become evident among us that overly narrow and often oppressive family ties can limit individuals' later lives. Undoubtedly, there were ways to overcome the disadvantages that often resulted from certain patterns of conduct imposed early on by the domestic circle. It would not be much of an exaggeration to say that, if the institutions of higher education, particularly law schools, operating since 1827 in São Paulo and Olinda, largely contributed to the formation of capable, public men, then we owe this to the fact that many adolescents, wrenched from their provincial and rural origins, were able to "live for themselves," progressively freeing themselves from their old ties to home and learning as much this way as from the teachings the schools provided.

Students' social personalities, molded in very particular traditions that, as everyone knows, tend to be decisive and crucial during the first four or five years of a child's life, were forced to adjust in the face of new situations and new social relationships. These new circumstances often necessitated revising, sometimes radically, the interests, activities, values, feelings, attitudes, and beliefs acquired when living with one's family.

Transplanted far from their parents while very young, these "landed sons," as [the historian] Capistrano de Abreu called them, managed to develop a sense of responsibility they were previously denied. Of course, these new experiences were not always enough to extinguish the domestic ties, the mentality created by contact with a patriarchal lifestyle, one so opposed to the demands of a society of free men of increasingly egalitarian inclination. For this very reason, Joaquim Nabuco can say that "in our politics and in our society . . . , it is the orphans, the abandoned, who overcome the struggle, rise and govern."[1]

The criticism of the recent tendency of some States to establish vast programs of social security and welfare has been seen to be based solely on the fact that such structures leave too little margin for individual action and that they condemn all kinds of competition. This argument belongs to an era in which, for the first time in history, competition between citizens, with all of its consequences, has been raised as a positive social value. . . .

In Brazil, only rarely have we had an administrative system founded on objective interests and a corps of public officials purely dedicated to these same interests. Rather, throughout our history one can see the constant predominance of private interests whose natural environment consists of closed circles that are inaccessible to impersonal organization. Among these circles, that of the family was doubtless the circle that most powerfully and boldly expressed itself in our society. One of the most decisive effects of the incontestable and absorbent supremacy of the family nucleus—the sphere par excellence for the so-called primary contacts of ties of blood and heart—is that the relationships created in domestic life always provided the obligatory model for any of our social connections. This occurs even where democratic institutions, founded on neutral and abstract principles, attempt to establish society with antiprivate norms.

A happy expression states that the Brazilian contribution to civilization will be cordiality—we will give to the world the "cordial man." Familiarity, hospitality, generosity, virtues lauded by foreigners who visit us, represent, in effect, defined features of the Brazilian character, at least insofar as the ancestral influence of patterns of human relationships, patterns informed by a rural and patriarchal setting, remains active and flourishing. It would be a mistake to suppose that these virtues signify "good manners" or civility. Primarily, they are legitimate expressions coming from an incredibly rich and overflowing emotional background. In civility, there is something coercive—it can reveal itself in orders and judgments. Among the Japanese, where, as we know, the most ordinary aspects of social relationships involve politeness, it can at times be confused with religious reverence. Some observers have noted the significant fact that external forms of venerating the divine in Shinto ceremonies are not essentially different from social ways of showing respect.

By adopting similar exterior forms of cordiality, which do not need to be legitimate in order to manifest themselves, a decisive triumph of the spirit over life is revealed. Armed with this mask, the individual is able to maintain his supremacy over society. In effect, politeness implies the continued and sovereign presence of the individual. . . .

There is nothing more significant to this aversion to social ritual, which at times demands a strongly homogenous and overall well-balanced personality, than the difficulty that Brazilians generally find in exhibiting prolonged reverence for a superior. Our temperament allows forms of reverence to a substantial degree, but only when they do not stifle the possibility of a more familiar relationship. The normal display of respect in other peoples has here its counterpart, as a general rule, in the desire to establish intimacy. And this is even more notable given the often pronounced affection of the Portuguese, so close to us in many aspects, for titles and signs of reverence.

In the linguistic domain, to cite an example, this way of being seems to be reflected in our exaggerated penchant for using diminutives. The ending *inho* (little), affixed to words, allows us to become more familiar with people or objects and, at the same time, to accentuate them. It is a way of making them more accessible to our feelings and of bringing them closer to our hearts. We know how common it is among the Portuguese to mock certain abuses of our affection for diminutives, abuses as ridiculous to them as the Portuguese sentimentality, tearful and bitter, is to us. A close study of our syntactic forms would surely offer precious revelations in this respect.

To this same order of manifestations certainly belongs the tendency to omit family names in social interactions. As a rule, it is the given name, the baptismal name, that prevails. This tendency, which among the Portuguese results from a tradition with ancient roots—as it is known that family names only began to predominate in Christian and medieval Europe beginning in the twelfth century—became oddly accentuated among us. It would perhaps be plausible to relate this fact to the suggestion that the use of just the first name is important in psychologically abolishing the barriers created by the existence of different, independent families. It corresponds to the natural attitude of human groups that accept a substantial degree of sympathetic order, or "concord," and reject relationships based on abstract reasoning, or those that do not have as a foundation, to use the terminology of [German philosopher Ferdinand] Tonnies, communities of blood, place, or spirit.

The rejection of any form of interaction not dictated by an emotionally based ethics represents an aspect of Brazilian life that few foreigners are able to understand easily. It is this characteristic among us, this way of being, that does not disappear even in types of activities that normally feed on competition. A businessman from Philadelphia once revealed to André Siegfried his astonishment upon realizing that, in Brazil as in Argentina, to gain a client he would first need to win his friendship.

Our old Catholicism, so characteristic of us, which permits us to treat our saints with an almost disrespectful intimacy that should seem strange to truly religious souls, comes from these same motives. The popularity among us of Saint Teresa de Lisieux—[who we call] Santa Teresinha—results from the intimate way in which we venerate her, a friendly and almost fraternal veneration, which doesn't fit well with ceremonies and minimizes distances. This is what also happens with our Baby Jesus, a child's playmate that makes one think less of the Jesus in the canonical gospels than of the Jesus in certain apocrypha. . . . Those who attend the feasts of Senhor Bom Jesus de Pirapora in São Paulo know the story of the Christ who came down from the altar to dance samba with the people.

This type of religious worship, which has antecedents in the Iberian Peninsula, also appears in medieval Europe and in the decadence of the palatial religion that subsumed the individual, in which the common will manifested itself in the construction of grandiose Gothic monuments. Following this period—affirms a historian—a more human and simple religious sentiment arose. Every home wants its own chapel, where residents kneel before the patron saint and protector. Christ, Our Lady, and the saints do not appear as privileged beings, exempt from any human feelings. Everyone, nobles and plebeians, wants intimacy with the sacred creatures, and even God himself is a familiar friend, domestic and close—the opposite of the "palatial" God, to whom the knight, on his knees, paid homage, as if to a feudal lord.

A similar attitude can be seen in our characteristic transferal of this horror of distance, a horror that seems to constitute the most specific trait of the Brazilian spirit, at least so far, to the religious domain. It is noted that even here we behave in a way that is perfectly contrary to the above-noted attitude of the Japanese, among whom ritualism invades the terrain of social conduct and gives it more rigor. In Brazil it is precisely the rigor of ritual that is relaxed and humanized.

Translated by Molly Quinn

Note

1. Joaquim Nabuco, *Um estadista do Império* (São Paulo: Civilização Brasileira, 1936), 5.

Vargas and the Estado Novo

Getúlio Vargas

On November 10, 1937, surrounded by members of his cabinet and military advisors, Getúlio Vargas canceled the upcoming presidential elections, suspended Congress, and announced that he would be promulgating a new constitution, one that would transform the Brazilian government into an Estado Novo (New State). The pretext for this act was the alleged existence of a communist plot, a fabricated threat that allowed Vargas to take this measure. But in fact Vargas and his allies had been planning for such a move for a long time, as they saw an authoritarian state as the best way of strengthening the federal government over the opposition of the states.

Notwithstanding the increased powers he accorded himself, Vargas still sought popular support for his actions. In this New Year's Day radio address of January 1, 1938, he appealed directly to the people to explain his decision to implement the Estado Novo, and to cast himself as their advocate and protector.

At the dawn of the new year, when in hearts and souls the call of hope and happiness is more lively and crackling and we feel more strongly and overwhelmingly the aspiration for victory, achievement, and progress, I come to communicate with you and speak directly to everyone, without distinction of class, profession, or hierarchy, so that united and in brotherhood, we might lift quite high the idea of an irrevocable vote for the greatness and happiness of Brazil.

I have received from the Brazilian people, in grave and decisive moments, unequivocal proof of a perfect communion of ideas and sentiments. And for that very reason, more than ever, I judge myself obligated to transmit to the people my word of faith, so much more opportune and necessary if we consider the responsibilities arising out of the recently instituted regime, in which patriotism is measured by sacrifice and the rights of individuals have to be subordinate to the obligations of the nation.

It was imperative, for the good of the majority, to change procedures and agree to a labor policy consonant with our realities and the demands for the country's development.

The Constitution of November 10 is not a document of simple, legal regulation of the state, made to order, according to fashions in vogue. It is adapted concretely to the current problems of Brazilian life, considered in origins of formation, defining, at the same time, the direction toward its progress and enrichment.

The actions and practices of these fifty days of government reflect and confirm the decisive will to act within the principles adopted.

We are suspending payment of the foreign debt, because of the imposition of circumstances alien to our desires. . . .

We are modifying the onerous policy followed in relation to coffee, and in the same manner the monetary regimen, which was in force for our trade. . . .

Alongside these resolutions of an economic and financial character, there figured others of not lesser significance in the political-administrative sphere. I want to allude to the acts of abolition of political parties, organization of the national court, and regulation of civil service pensions.

The first action was taken with a view toward the elimination of interference from factious interests and groups in the solution of problems of governance. The state, according to the new order, is the nation, and because of that, ought to dispense with political intermediaries in order to maintain contact with the people and consult their aspirations and needs. The second action created national courts, causing the dissolution of organizational contradictions and anomalies in which we had as many courts as existing federated units. The codification of national law, already initiated, will come to complete these measures, which have made great progress in strengthening national cohesion. Just as a single flag is supreme, protecting all Brazilians, the law also ought to ensure, in a uniform way, the rights of citizenship for the entire national territory. In the case of the last action, it is fitting to refer to the law that prohibits accumulation of public offices. For more than a century, this provision challenged legislators who had good intentions. The solution that we have come upon is, without doubt, severe. It will bring sacrifices for some people, but it represents a benefit for the populace as a whole and demonstrates, in an undeniable manner, a righteous plan to abolish all situations of privilege. Permitting more equitable access to public office, it implicitly benefits more people and offers an opportunity to ensure equivalent remuneration for services rendered.

We will persist in the willingness to eliminate barriers that separate zones and isolate regions, so that the national economic body might be able to evolve homogenously, and the expansion of the internal market might be undertaken without restraints of any type. . . .

In the regime of the revoked Constitution, it was not possible to take these initiatives, nor assume the responsibilities of such heavy duties. . . .

Until recently, our equipment for teaching was limited to the minimum necessities for individual competences. . . . There was an abundance of PhDs and a lack of qualified technicians; the man competent in his trade was rare;

Workers in Rio de Janeiro marching in support of Getúlio Vargas, 1942. Courtesy of the Agência Nacional, Arquivo Nacional.

artistic technique declined with the dominance of the machine, causing us to be unable to make full use of industrial workers.

The national government resolved to undertake, in this respect, a decisive task. In addition to modernizing the existing establishments, and increasing their capacity and efficiency, it initiated the construction of large professional schools, which should eventually constitute a vast network of popular teaching, radiating throughout the country. It also will support the initiatives of local governments, by means of auxiliary materials and technical guidance. . . .

The sentiment of human solidarity is one of the most noble and highest manifestations of the Christian spirit. When the state takes the initiative of projects of economic assistance and supports the struggle of the worker, it is to attend to an imperative of social justice, providing an example to be observed by all, without need of compulsion. . . .

The multiplicity of sectors in which the state acts does not exclude, but rather affirms, a fundamental rule: that of security for the work and achievements of general interest. The public order and tranquility will be maintained without vacillation. The government continues vigilant in the repression of extremism and is going to segregate, in fortified military prisons and agricultural colonies, all those agitating elements, recognized by their seditious activities or condemned by political crimes. We will not permit that the struggle and patriotic dedication of good Brazilians might come to endure turmoil and alarms originated by personalistic ambitions, or the ideological craziness of false prophets and vulgar demagogues. . . .

Brazilians! In this hour of good cheer and promise, I bring you my cordial greetings.

Like you, I believe in the high destiny of the fatherland and, like you, I work to achieve it. In the New State there will be no place for the skeptics and the hesitant, those who doubt themselves and others. There are those who, at times, interrupt your honestly earned repose with the alarm of their fears and the rumor of slanderous negativism. But, with trustful heart and uplifted enthusiasm, you should continue to devote yourselves to daily labor and to the cares of the home, where you have guarded hope of happiness and find the comforting shelter of dear ones.

To all those who live under the bright protection of the Southern Cross, I give, in this dawn of the new year, best wishes for good fortune and prosperity. And from all of you—Brazilians!—I ask and hope, at this moment, for a solemn promise to serve the fatherland well and to do everything possible for its enrichment.

Translated by Robert M. Levine and John J. Crocitti

Rubber and the Allies' War Effort

Various authors

The U.S. government spent considerable energy trying to convince Brazil to enter World War II on the side of the Allies. Early in the international conflict, Great Britain feared that Germany might use West Africa as a launching ground for invading South America and creating a front to the south of the United States. Later, when the Allies controlled North Africa, the U.S. military considered Brazil's strategic importance as a transshipment point for supplying the Middle Eastern and Italian fronts through Africa. Brazil also possessed rubber, crystals, and rare minerals that were of strategic value for the arms industry.

Brazil had dominated the international rubber trade until the 1910s, when rubber plantations in Southeast Asia surpassed production from the Amazon. With those supplies cut off with the Japanese occupation of much of Southeast Asia, the United States once again turned to Brazil to supply this raw material essential for the war effort. The following excerpts from articles in Agriculture in the Americas, *a publication of the U.S. Department of Agriculture's Office of Foreign Agricultural Relations, were written on the eve of the United States' entrance into the war. They express the concern that without Brazilian rubber, the war effort would not be successful. The U.S. government and the Vargas regime ended up collaborating in an effort to increase rubber production during the war years with mixed results.*

Can the Americas Live Alone?

JOSEPH L. APODACA

Robinson Crusoe was lucky!

When Robinson Crusoe chanced upon Juan Fernandez Island, he faced a deficit problem of major proportions. Marooned and alone in that wilderness, the problem of wrestling a subsistence from nature challenged his ingenuity to the limit. But Robinson Crusoe was lucky. He had his creator, Daniel Defoe, in command of the situation.

Suppose we in the Western Hemisphere were cut off from the rest of the world and left to our hemisphere resources. This is not so far-fetched an assumption as it sounds. With the American nations determined to preserve peace and independence in the midst of war, action to provide a strong de-

At a meeting between Presidents Getúlio Vargas and Franklin D. Roosevelt in Natal, Brazil, in 1942, the two negotiated cooperation agreements for the war effort against the Axis powers. Credit: Fundação Getúlio Vargas, CPDOC.

fense for this half of the world already has been taken. Plans call not only for adequate land, sea, and air power, but for economic measures, designed to weld the hemisphere into a unit capable of withstanding any form of penetration.

In this connection we face, like Robinson Crusoe, a serious deficit problem for a number of essential raw materials. But we are also caught in the throes of a surplus situation with respect to certain other agricultural commodities, which nations of the Western Hemisphere produce in common. These difficulties threaten hemispheric solidarity. They may weaken the links of hemispheric defense unless we can do something about them.

The possibilities of our being cut off from sources of essential commodities or to division from within by conflicting economic interests, is only part of the reason for desiring a greater coalescence of the hemisphere economies. Greater solidarity on the part of peace-loving democracies of the New World is important to defense right now. It would be just as important should the American republics ever have to deal with a United Europe dominated by one ruler with one trade policy.

There must be adequate export outlet to maintain production at a level of abundance. For these the American nations doubtless will rely upon each other to a growing extent. But only if the way is paved for a sound and lasting inter-American trade. Let us consider the possibilities of achieving this trade by examining the hemisphere's deficits and surpluses and the effect these have on trade developments.

RUBBER.—We are literally a nation on wheels and rubber is essential to keep those wheels moving. Although three-fourths of the natural rubber we use goes into tires, thousands of other products require it too.

Despite the tremendous demand in the United States for natural rubber, there is no production in this country and approximately 98 percent of our imports come from the Far East. Average annual imports, 1937–39, were 503,644 long tons. Less than 2 percent came from tropical America—the original source of rubber.

Speaking of Rubber . . .

EDGAR R. BURKLAND

It's news to many of us that the bounce in our rubber heels comes from a tree in the Dutch East Indies. Or that the rubber in our raincoats travelled 10,000 miles to keep us dry.

So familiar are we with rubber heels, rubber tires, rubber raincoats, and a thousand other rubber products that we seldom consider rubber itself. The adequacy and availability of the United States rubber supply, or what would happen should that supply suddenly be cut off, has never worried most of us.

To the tire manufacturer of Akron and Los Angeles, to the boot-and-shoe maker of New England, to the manufacturers of a host of other rubber products, this matter of an adequate rubber supply is vital at all times. In normal peace-time a continuous supply is necessary. In war-time it is imperative.

Unlike many other necessities, which we produce in abundance, rubber happens to be one which we do not. A product indispensible [*sic*] to our national economy, the vast bulk of it is now produced in the British and Netherlands East Indies, Ceylon, French Indo-China, and Thailand. These areas are located as much as 10,000 miles from our shores and the continuation of their prewar economic and political status, in the light of current history, should not be taken for granted.

True, we have made rapid strides during recent months in developing and perfecting synthetic products to meet any serious emergency that might arise, but production costs still are at least twice those of the natural product. From a struggling industry a century ago, giving employment to perhaps a hundred persons, an industry with an output [that is] possibly $20,000 annually, the rubber business has grown steadily. Employing more than 120,000 workers in 1939, the industry produced a wide variety of products valuated at $900,000,000.

It is centered in the State of Ohio, which accounts for about 40 percent of the entire output of rubber products. Other states important in United States rubber manufacturing are California, Massachusetts, Pennsylvania, and New Jersey.

By 1910, the rubber industry here had begun to assume a vital economic role. The fast-developing motorcar industry was established and the crude rubber production with scientific methods was becoming firmly entrenched in the East Indian plantations. Up to 1910 our rubber had come mainly from the wild trees of South America and Africa. From 1910 on, the well-developed and well-managed plantations of the Far East were to play an increasingly important part in crude rubber production. In a few years, wild rubber was practically out of the picture.

Automobile tires form the largest single outlet for crude rubber imported into the United States.

Recent statistics reveal that out of 45 million motor vehicles registered in the world, 68 percent are registered in the United States. More than 70 percent of all the passenger cars in the world are owned in the United States. About 54 percent of the world's trucks travel United States highways. During the four decades of this century we have manufactured some 79 million motor vehicles of one kind or another. When we say we are a nation on wheels, we are not kidding.

The number of tires required for the motor industry is tremendous. Due, however, to the fact that improved lasting qualities have been built into tires during recent years, giving them three to four times the mileage available before, a significant trend has been noted in the proportion of tires consumed in this branch of the industry. In 1929, of the total consumption of rubber in the United States, 86.6 percent was used in the manufacture of tires and inner tubes. By 1937 this figure has dropped to 72.9 percent in spite of vastly increased automobile production.

New outlets for rubber are being discovered every year. One of the most important is the use of rubber in the making of tires for farm implements. Other articles in which rubber has been found to be suitable include seat cushions, arm rests, and mattresses, and in aircraft construction where minimum weight is important. . . .

WHAT ABOUT TROPICAL AMERICA?

How much rubber can be obtained from the wild rubber trees in tropical America? The largest amount of rubber ever produced in the Western Hemisphere was 62,891 tons in 1910. Of this amount the Amazon Valley accounted for nearly 38,000 tons and Mexican guayule 9,500 tons. In 1939 crude-rubber shipments originating in these areas totaled some 17,000 tons, of which nearly 14,000 tons were shipped from the Amazon region and 2,200 tons from Mexico.

The sparseness of these wild trees is the reason why rubber production declined in the American tropics while scientific methods of cultivation succeeded on the Far Eastern plantations. Without regard for cost of production, it is possible that thousands of tons of wild rubber could be gathered and exported yearly from the Amazon area.

We have examined some of the possible solutions to be considered in the event of serious curtailment of our present rubber supplies.

Let us look into the possibilities of scientific rubber production in the native home of the rubber tree—the Amazon Valley—and other suitable tropical areas in the Western Hemisphere. There are millions of acres suitable for rubber production from the standpoint of soil, climate, rainfall, transportation, and accessibility. Labor, while not found in such abundance as in the Asiatic regions, could be recruited in fairly large numbers.

Considerable attention has been given to the South American leaf disease, and scientists believe that disease-resisting strains now being developed eventually will eliminate this malady. For many years, scientists of the United States Department of Agriculture have worked with others in the development of high-yielding strains of rubber trees. Success has been achieved to the extent that there now are rubber trees available, which will yield up to five times that of an average seedling of eastern plantations.

Among all the products being studied in the program to increase Latin-American agricultural production, none offers greater opportunities than rubber. The establishment of a successful plantation industry in the Western Hemisphere, along with the encouragement of other complementary crops, will go a long way toward improving the economic, financial, and social levels in many of these countries.

By taking advantage of the many resources in Latin America we will be supplying the nations to the south of us with the purchasing power needed to create a solid foundation for lasting trade relations. It is an economic postulate that trade is not a one-way proposition. In order to export we must import, and we cannot sell to those who do not have the dollar exchange with which to buy from us.

Portraits: Patrícia Galvão (Pagú)

James N. Green

São Paulo in 1930 was a teeming metropolis. The population had doubled from half a million inhabitants in 1920 to 1.3 million in 1940. Coffee cultivation in the state's hinterlands had created a wealthy elite that lived comfortably alongside a new industrialist class in large mansions along the wide, tree-lined Paulista Avenue, while migrants from the countryside and immigrants from Europe and Japan lived in cramped quarters or tenement houses and labored in factories in the industrial outskirts of the city. Skyscrapers arose alongside the three-storied nineteenth-century downtown buildings, heralding the city's modernity, while a conservative and traditional Catholic culture still dominated local high society. Even though the city was sprawling outward from the historic center, social and cultural life still clung close to the central area where Jesuits had founded the College of São Paulo de Piratininga in 1554.

As a teenager, Patrícia Galvão walked through downtown São Paulo every day on her way to and from the normal school where she was training to become a teacher. It was not an unusual career path for a young woman from a modest middle-class family, since the city's booming population had created a demand for more female educators. Normal schools offered the equivalent of a high school degree and trained students to become primary school teachers.

But Galvão already chafed at many social conventions, and it seemed unlikely that she would ever end up drilling students in their ABCs or teaching them how to do rudimentary arithmetic. As she passed through the bustling downtown streets every morning, she already sought to defy the strict social norms that guided proper behavior for young women. Audaciously, she would adjust the white blouse of her conservatively tailored school uniform to suggest a certain sensual daring. She'd apply yellowish makeup to her face to accent her dark lipstick. And she would flaunt her untamed and curly shoulder-length hair as she passed the male law school students at São Francisco Square, who openly commented on her unusual look. Though she may not have been aware of the term New Woman, she was in many ways performing this new role, in which new women ignored standards of properly gendered behavior by smoking cigarettes, using coarse slang, and showing more public confidence with their bodies and dress than would have been considered suitable for a well-brought-up young lady.

At some point Galvão was noticed by Raul Bopp, a poet and friend of Oswald de Andrade, a leader of the modernist movement that had shocked the city's high society in 1922 with a week of cultural activities at the stately Municipal Theater. By 1928, Andrade and his wife, the painter Tarsila do Amaral (see Portraits in part VII), had become the cultural leaders of modernism, which was moving toward more radical critiques of contemporary culture and society. Bopp found the young Galvão both charming and a talented writer and artist. He suggested she adopt the pen name Pagú, mistakenly thinking that her full name was Patricia Goulart and the nickname an appropriate composite. The name stuck.

Bopp also introduced Pagú to Andrade and Amaral, who quickly brought her into their circle of artists, poets, and avant-garde writers that was publishing the *Revista de Antropofagia* (see part VII, "The Cannibalist Manifesto"). Soon, Pagú was collaborating with drawings to illustrate contributions to the magazine, and within a year she had launched her own public literary career with a poetry reading at the Municipal Theater. Around this time she began an affair with Oswald de Andrade that would lead to a pregnancy, Andrade's divorce from Tarsila do Amaral, a marriage proposal, and a baby boy.

Although Andrade, Amaral, and their group had played the role of avant-garde critics of staid and proper São Paulo elite society, they still circulated comfortably among the rich and famous throughout the 1920s. Andrade's marriage to Galvão, however, shocked conventional circles, and Olívia Guedes Penteado, the wealthy patroness who had encouraged the young modernists, shunned the newlyweds.

The New York stock market crash of October 1929 and the subsequent collapse in coffee prices also changed the couple's life course. Like many in São Paulo's middle classes, they joined street demonstrations in favor of the Liberal Alliance's seizure of power in 1930 under the leadership of Getúlio Vargas. At the end of that year, Pagú traveled to Buenos Aires for a poetry festival, where she met Luís Carlos Prestes, who had recently joined the Communist Party. She returned to Brazil enthusiastic about Prestes's revolutionary ideas and convinced her husband to join the Communist Party along with her. In March 1931, the two founded the newspaper tabloid *Homem do Povo* (Man of the people), which was not officially linked to the still-illegal Communist Party but promoted "the revolutionary left." Pagú wrote a column titled "The Women of the People" in which she lambasted "elite feminists," hurling her newly found radicalism at the women of the social classes that had applauded her poetry.

There was a logical element to Andrade's and Pagú's shift from enfants terribles of the *paulistana* bourgeoisie to dedicated communist militants.

The modernists' rejection of traditional European art and literature and their search for authentic Brazilian cultural forms had led them to examine, embrace, and reproduce the art forms and representations of ordinary Brazilians. The role of the artist was to be on the side of *o povo*, the people. The economic crisis of the 1930s, the growing polarization of the left and the right, and revolutionary upheavals around the world led many Brazilian intellectuals to align with socialist or communist ideologies. Pagú enthusiastically joined the new radical movement that was sweeping the country. In 1931, she was arrested in the port city of Santos during a rally of striking construction workers. It was the first of many occasions when she would spend time in prison. She also had her first run-in with official Communist Party policy. Party officials criticized her harshly for having gotten herself arrested and forced her to sign a self-criticism declaring that she was an "individualist, sensationalist, and inexperienced agitator."

By 1932, Andrade and Galvão had broken up, and Pagú moved to Rio de Janeiro to live in a working-class neighborhood. The decision to mingle with the proletariat was part of Communist Party policy, which encouraged intellectual members to have daily contacts with the lower classes. The next year she published her first novel, *Industrial Park*; her former husband financed the edition. Although this work of fiction portrays the struggles and deprivations of the working class, especially women workers, it is a rather one-dimensional representation of the exploited and oppressed that was common in left-wing literature of the period. Even so, it did not receive official approval, and the Communist Party insisted that she publish it under the pseudonym Mara Lobo, so that it would not be too closely associated with publications by known party members.

In 1934, Pagú decided to travel to the Soviet Union to experience the revolution firsthand, and once again Andrade helped her by financing the trip. She made stops in the United States (where she interviewed Sigmund Freud), in Japan, and in China, then continued across the Trans-Siberian Railway to Moscow. She was profoundly disappointed with what she saw there: the ongoing poverty of the masses and privileged lives of party members shook her belief in communist ideals. Nevertheless, after she left the Soviet Union and traveled to Paris, she joined the French Communist Party and was arrested several times for being involved in street demonstrations. Before the year was out, she was deported to Brazil for being a foreign subversive.

Pagú arrived in Brazil at the end of 1935 in time to be caught in another police roundup after a failed uprising by the Communist Party led to widespread repression. She spent the next five years in prison, where she broke definitively with the party. Upon her release, she remarried, joined a Trotskyist organization, and helped edit the newspaper *Socialist Vanguard*. In 1950, she ran unsuccessfully for a seat in the state legislature on the Brazilian Socialist Party ticket and then turned toward theater and the arts. During the 1950s,

Patrícia Galvão (1910–1962) under arrest in 1935 for her involvement with the communist movement. Courtesy of Acervo Iconografia.

she became actively involved in cultural production in the city of Santos. She died of cancer in 1962.

In the late 1970s, when a second wave of feminism emerged in Brazil among left-wing women activists, many of whom had been involved in underground antidictatorship activities, Pagú was rediscovered and became an iconic image for many radical feminists. Patrícia Galvão, the young middle-class rebel artist and poet turned revolutionary, who maintained a free-spirited personal life while involved in politics, was an attractive historical symbol for a new generation of feminists. Unlike Berta Lutz, the more traditional pioneering campaigner for women's rights in the early twentieth century, or Carlota Pereira de Queirós, the first woman elected to Congress, Galvão challenged the state and its politicians rather than seeking them out to negotiate the incorporation of the women's rights agenda into government policies. Galvão's time in prison gave her an additional mystique, as a woman willing to endure great sacrifices for the cause. Even her iconoclastic attitude toward the Brazilian Communist Party made her popular among a new generation of activists who saw the pro-Soviet organization as moderate, reformist, and old-fashioned.

Her colorful life lends itself to fascinating reevaluations that suggest she was somehow unique in her radical feminism and commitment to political and cultural causes. Yet she represents a tradition of strong, dedicated, and determined women who have been actively engaged in social change over the course of Brazilian history.

IX

Democratic Governance and Developmentalism, 1946–1964

While almost two decades of democracy followed the authoritarian Estado Novo, Getúlio Vargas's influence on national politics nonetheless persisted. His endorsement of General Eurico Dutra in the 1945 elections helped the former minister of war win the presidency, although Vargas played little role in Dutra's administration. Instead, he spent time working as a senator for Rio Grande do Sul and building the Partido Trabalhista Brasileira (PTB, Brazilian Labor Party), a party that relied on support from organized labor and urban workers—groups that had benefited from social legislation enacted during the Estado Novo. In the subsequent presidential elections in late 1950, Vargas again returned to the presidency, this time via direct popular vote, defeating candidates from the centrist Partido Social Democrático (PSD, Social Democratic Party) and the conservative União Democrático Nacional (UDN, National Democratic Union) by a solid margin.

During this presidency, Vargas maintained his focus on economic nationalism and added a distinctly populist tone. Perhaps the best example of this is his support for the creation of a national oil company, Petrobras, approved by Congress in 1953. Yet he struggled throughout his presidency with fierce opposition from the UDN. In 1954 he faced a severe political crisis, and the military again threatened to depose him. Rather than allow himself to be forcibly removed from office, however, he enacted his final deed of grand political symbolism by taking his own life. He left behind a dramatic suicide letter that helped cement his legacy as a now-martyred president who loved his nation and the people for whom he claimed to have lived and died. Thus, even following his death, Vargas remained an important figure in national politics, and figures associated with his earlier presidencies (as allies or opponents) continued to struggle over his legacy and the future of Brazil.

Given these circumstances, the election to succeed him was especially tense and Vargas's legacy inescapable. It was in part the support of the Brazilian Labor Party that paved the way for the victory of Juscelino Kubitschek, the presidential candidate of the Social Democratic Party. Brazilian election

Getúlio Vargas during the 1950 presidential campaign. Courtesy of Acervo *Última Hora*, Arquivo Público do Estado de São Paulo.

President Juscelino Kubitschek visiting the Verlag automobile factory in 1956. Courtesy of Acervo *Última Hora*, Arquivo Público do Estado de São Paulo.

The modernist architecture of the Brazilian Congress. Credit: Fundação Getúlio Vargas, CPDOC.

law allowed for coalition tickets, and Kubitschek chose as his running mate the leader of the Brazilian Labor Party, João Goulart, a former minister of labor under Vargas. Kubitschek's campaign slogan, Fifty Years of Progress in Five, promised rapid economic and industrial development, echoing Vargas's earlier efforts.

But soon after the election, stalwart opponents in the National Democratic Union began pressuring the interim government to bar them from taking office. These conservative politicians saw Kubitschek, and especially Goulart, as left-wing demagogues who had won popular support by manipulating the ignorant masses. It was only following a preventative coup, in which Army Marshall Henrique Lott deposed the acting president, that Kubitschek and Goulart were able to assume office in January 1956.

Notwithstanding this inauspicious beginning, the Kubitschek presidency soon boasted multiple signs of prosperity and economic growth, from the successful development of an automobile industry in São Paulo that began churning out Ford, Volkswagen, and General Motors vehicles, to the construction and inauguration of the new modernist capital of Brasília in 1960. Meanwhile, Brazil's victory in the 1958 soccer World Cup, coupled with the international popularity of bossa nova, a new syncopated cool jazz sound, as well as the worldwide success of the film *Black Orpheus*, set in Rio de Janeiro's slums during Carnival, showcased the country as a dynamic, emerging nation. Television began to replace radio as popular entertainment, and young middle-class students and intellectuals crowded into downtown theaters to catch the latest Italian or French movie or a Brazilian Cinema Novo (New Cinema) production that captured the social reality of the country.

Despite these much-trumpeted successes and the ensuing feelings of optimism, little progress was made in reversing the extreme inequalities that marked the country. The continued out-migration from the countryside to the urban centers, a stream that had been flowing since the 1930s, led to rapid growth and increased social divisions and tensions in Brazilian cities. The economic expansion under Kubitschek had been financed through deficit spending, and when growth stalled, the country was hit with high inflation and rising government debt. This led to increases in the cost of living and decreases in public spending. Bitter disputes broke out over the extent to which foreign investment hobbled domestic economic sovereignty. Indeed, the very promise of progress led to a deep disillusionment for some about the power of Brazil's recent economic development to lead to meaningful social change.

Thus by the late 1950s and early 1960s, revolutionary cultural and political activity mounted across Brazil, as large numbers of peasants, urban and rural workers, low-ranking members of the military, intellectuals, artists, and members of the Catholic Church proposed radical solutions to Brazil's long-standing economic, social, and political inequalities. Academics and artists debated theories of dependency, cultural imperialism, colonialism, and neocolonialism. Figures such as Francisco Julião, a lawyer who organized peasant leagues in the countryside, demanded agrarian reform, while Paulo Freire, an educator, conceived of literacy training as a means to gain political consciousness.

The following presidential election in the late 1960s reflected the unfolding political and social polarization. Popular frustration with the status quo, a broad search for new solutions, and electors' unwillingness to give up on the promises of Vargas resulted in an unusual split ticket. Jânio Quadros, the center-right candidate, who had been endorsed by the National Democratic Union, was elected president. Quadros was a self-proclaimed political outsider. As the governor of São Paulo and a presidential candidate, he promised to sweep out corruption and bad government. Goulart, a figure from the left with a long political history and the leader of the Brazilian Labor Party, was elected vice president.

Quadros abruptly resigned the presidency only seven months into his term in a failed bid to leverage more power from Congress. Goulart, who happened to be in China on an economic mission at the time, was only allowed to return to Brazil ten days later, after intense negotiations between

Retirantes by Henri Ballot. During the 1950s, hundreds of thousands of peasants and rural workers migrated from the northeast to southeastern Brazil to seek jobs and opportunities for their families. Henri Ballot/Instituto Moreira Salles Collection.

political and military officials who opposed his ascendency to the office. These debates demonstrated the weakness of the country's political institutions and the tenor of distrust and division. In the resulting compromise, Congress approved a constitutional amendment that limited the president's powers by temporarily creating a parliamentary system of government. Only then was Goulart allowed to assume the presidency.

To many observers who sought deep changes, even Goulart's government was too cautious and incrementalist, and they called for revolutionary change. In the context of the Cold War and the recent advent of the Cuban Revolution in Latin America, many conservatives within Brazil and abroad became alarmed.

Soon after assuming the presidency, Goulart traveled to the United States in an attempt to gain financial support for his government. He met with President John F. Kennedy in the White House but did not allay the concerns

President João Goulart (*standing*) in a New York City ticker-tape parade during his 1962 trip to the United States. Photograph by World Telegram staff photographer Dick DeMarisco. Courtesy of the U.S. Library of Congress.

of U.S. officials, who considered Goulart's policies to be too left-wing. Over the course of Goulart's presidency, political divisions and mistrust intensified until eventually a coalition of both civilians and high-ranking members of the military resolved to overthrow him, a decision secretly supported by the U.S. government. After weeks of increasing tensions and rumors of military intervention, military troops set out on the night of March 31 and early morning of April 1, 1964, to unseat Goulart, who eventually went into exile in Uruguay. Newspapers supportive of the intervention originally celebrated the fact that the overthrow took place on April 1. But as April 1 coincided with an annual holiday known as the Day of Lies, military officials later came to refer to the event as the Revolution of March 31, an ironic parallel to Vargas supporters' celebration of the Revolution of 1930. What followed was twenty-one years of authoritarian rule.

Telenovelas in Constructing the Country of the Future

Esther Hamburger

The first television network in South America, TV Tupi, broadcast its inaugural program on September 20, 1950, in São Paulo. The communications media group Diários Associados, whose founder, Francisco de Assis Chateaubriand, was a politician, patron of the arts, and one of the country's most influential businessmen in the 1940s and 1950s, owned TV Tupi. Immensely popular in its day, the network offered a wide variety of programming, including news, dramas, sports, and later comedy, cartoons, and children's shows. The first logo of TV Tupi, seen in the accompanying image, portrayed a friendly, childlike Indian wearing television antennas on his head. It was an image that fit in with the network's nationalist project by showcasing the inclusion of Brazil's (idealized and infantilized) indigenous peoples in the forging of the technologically modern nation.

The following essay by Esther Hamburger, an anthropologist and scholar of Brazilian film and media, offers an overview of the history of the Brazilian telenovela, a unique genre that remains incredibly popular in Brazil.

The television industry was consolidated in Brazil thanks to a peculiar version of electronic entertainment known in Latin America as the telenovela, which unexpectedly became a national medium that crossed class, race, gender, and generational divides. The telenovela disrupted the traditional direction of transnational media flows, as it has been exported to other areas of both the Global South as well as the centers of the Cold War. The Brazilian telenovela mixes well-established melodramatic structures with references to ongoing events in well-known places. Its heterodox stylistic references include the Hollywood film industry, news broadcasting, and international cinema. Beyond the classification as hybrid melodrama, the telenovela might be thought of as the continuous dramatization of ongoing processes of social change. Researchers have noted the unplanned and unexpected ways in which this television genre, which has roots in the American soap opera and in the nineteenth-century French *feuilleton* (newspaper serials) and which was considered female, commercial, and lowbrow, has become a privileged

Logo of the Tupi TV channel.

daily prime-time space to problematize everyday social and political issues. As such, the telenovela might be thought of as prefiguring current world television serials.

In September 1950, Brazilian media tycoon Assis Chateaubriand inaugurated the first Brazilian television station. Like his radio chain, the pioneer TV station was named Tupi, after one of the main Brazilian indigenous groups and languages. In the absence of any specifically national legislation, Brazilian television adopted the U.S. commercial model. In 1967, the government of the state of São Paulo inaugurated TV Cultura, the country's first public TV station. Other public television stations followed, but the first national public network was only established in the early 2000s.

Improvisation marked the first twenty years of television transmission in Brazil. Until 1951 when the Invicta Company started to make TV sets, receivers were smuggled into the country through the black market. Stations were local; there was no cable; only a few cities had access to television signals; and few households were equipped with television sets. In 1970, when national broadcasting began, only 9 million out of 90 million Brazilians had access to television. Today almost the entire population of 190 million people has access to television.

During the military regime (1964–85) television spread throughout the national territory and across all social classes, becoming a profitable medium. With an instrumental vision of television as a vehicle for diffusing official culture, the authoritarian regime considered television strategic for what officials defined as "national security." Television was part of the country's economic growth between 1969 and 1974, a period known as the "Economic Miracle" and marked by a combination of urbanization, consumerism, inflation, and social inequality. Successive military governments helped to finance television networks by using them as a site of advertising for official campaigns, by promoting state-owned companies, and by investing in high-tech infrastructure, such as a microwave system and satellite communications. The authoritarian government also censored television in an attempt to control its content. Censorship prevented the discussion of certain taboo issues such as racial discrimination and abortion. Nonetheless, the virtual space of the telenovela addressed other questions related to gender and the family that had not previously been discussed on television, such as marriage, divorce, female orgasms, and sexual pleasure.

During the 1970s and 1980s, thanks to government technological, economic, and political input, Brazilian commercial television became a privileged "window" onto a specific "modern" world, one that echoed the film industry's focus on up-to-date fashion design, electronic devices, means of communication, and new forms of transportation. Indeed, contemporary telenovelas' tales of love and hate worked as privileged sites that showcased changing urban and human landscapes. Closely linked to consumerism, the telenovela also became a place for advertising within the narrative.

Blending formal conventions employed in television newscasts, such as direct camera work, contemporary stories shot on location, and Hollywood editing, telenovelas displayed continuously updated repertoires of fashion, furniture, domestic electronic devices, and modern means of transportation and communication, such as cars, airplanes, telephones, and computers. Audiences grew significantly as signals reached larger portions of national territory and greater segments of the population. As many critics have pointed out, in a highly unequal society, television broadcasts a world of consumerism that had once only been available to a few in a small number of locations. Although most viewers had little access to the world of consumption, they learned about its existence and use—as if buying certain goods signaled social inclusion. Television soaps and ads have worked as privileged venues for educating viewers to be consumers even before they had full democratic and civil rights.

Telenovelas have become so popular in Brazil that sometimes it seems that the genre has always been there, dominating prime-time programming on all networks. Indeed, the television version of the radionovela appeared on Brazilian television since its beginnings. Nonetheless it was only in 1963, when the recently inaugurated and short-lived Excelsior network introduced the videotape, that telenovelas started to be broadcast daily in prime-time slots. Unlike European and North American television, which, even after the advent of the videotape, used mostly 16 mm and 35 mm film to shoot newscasts, documentaries, and fiction, in Brazil film had not been common on television. It was only with videotape that television ceased to be limited to live local programming. Tapes started to circulate by bus and/or by plane. Delays depended on distance.

In the 1960s, networks began to compete by means of the telenovela.

2–5499 Busy, based on an Argentinian script, was the title of the first daily telenovela that Excelsior aired. As the title makes explicit, the story revolved around the telephone, which was an icon of nineteenth-century modernity but would not be accessible to most Brazilians until the last years of the twentieth century. Even though most viewers did not have telephones in their homes, successive telenovelas allowed them to follow the production of new types and colors of telephones, a recurrent device in telenovela narratives.

Unlike U.S. soap operas, telenovelas have clear endings. Each program lasts from six to eight months, sometimes more. When a telenovela starts, only a few installments are shot. Part of the rules of the genre is that the stories are written and filmed while the story is on the air, and there is where the *feuilleton* appeal resides. This write-shoot-edit-air dynamic incorporates the serial newspaper story's feedback appeal and retains some of the attraction of a live performance.

Tupi reacted to Excelsior's breakthrough program with *The Right to Be Born*, a well-known Latin American radio and television hit based on the Cuban original by Felix Cagnet. This melodramatic tale of patriarchy, race, and social discrimination attracted the first telenovela audience in Rio de Janeiro and São Paulo for live performances of the final installment. In 1968, Tupi produced and aired *Beto Rockfeller*, an original story by theater writer Braulio Pedroso, which defined some of the features that would structure the genre that became known as the Brazilian telenovela in the decades to come. This original and irreverent tale incorporated some of the global sentiment in favor of liberating social movements in Europe and in the Americas. The narrative was shot in São Paulo both in Tupi's studios and nearby locations. The telenovela depicted shifting urban landscapes, new avenues, and new construction, as well as new consumer items such as motorbikes, and situated the efforts of the antihero social climber in the present among young men and women ready to seek their personal dreams that reached beyond their given social status.

The Globo network was inaugurated in 1965, one year after the military coup d'état, and, like Tupi, it was an extension of a large and preexisting media group. Globo benefited from government support in establishing a vertical structure of production and distribution that the other networks would imitate. The Rio de Janeiro–based network hired Cuban exile Glória Magadan to direct the first drama department embedded in a network. Globo structured its prime-time programming around the concept of a "sandwich," meaning that they alternated between a telenovela, a newscast, and another telenovela. Magadan's style, however, insisted on stories with no reference to viewers' everyday lives. Her stories and the stories she produced spoke of remote times and places. Characters had unfamiliar names. This "classic" telenovela style attempted to be "universal" by not touching on polemical and/or site-specific issues. In 1969, Daniel Filho replaced Magadan, and highlighted the "modern" conventions introduced with *Beto Rockfeller*. Although Globo produced historical literary adaptations for its 6 p.m. slot, the most popular 7 and 8 p.m. (now 9 p.m.) programming specialized in contemporary tales that included on-location shooting. Even though the stories did not abandon a basic melodramatic structure, their contemporary settings and topics stimulated feedback excitement. References to a wide range of daily life issues—from furniture and clothing to literature and politics—intensified relations of contiguity between television and problems of daily life. Inspired by the structure of cinema, the telenovela industry included systematic routine production procedures and practices of audience feedback and control.

Different networks have produced hundreds of programs throughout the history of Brazilian television. Nonetheless, some remain as references, as spaces where art and the cultural industry interact and reverberate in modes that define new paths of imagination. During the second half of the twentieth century, in connection with telenovelas, television alluded in provocative ways to liberal ideas about the bourgeois family and sexuality. In the world of telenovelas, more liberal gender relations, technology, and consumerism contributed to the notion that Brazil was becoming the "Country of the Future," as Stefan Zweig, the Austrian writer, once predicted while living in exile in Brazil during World War II.

Translated by Emma Wohl

The Oil Is Ours

Getúlio Vargas

Prior to the 1930s, many experts believed that Brazil had no significant oil deposits, but efforts to promote national security and sovereignty under the Estado Novo led to new exploration. In 1938, the Vargas administration created a National Petroleum Council to promote the development of an oil industry. By 1941, it had drilled the first commercial well, located in Cadeias, Bahia, but Brazil continued to import the vast majority of the oil that the nation consumed.

Among the provisions of the Constitution of 1946 was an article that allowed foreign capital to be involved in mineral exploration, including oil. This item provoked a major debate between nationalists, who argued that the state should have total control over the extraction and processing of oil, and those who favored partnerships with international interests. When President Dutra proposed legislation that would have regulated international investment in the industry, nationalists mounted a campaign against it, forming the National Center for the Study and Defense of Oil. Its national campaign slogan was The Oil Is Ours, even inspiring a musical comedy film by the same name. The campaign was successful. On October 3, 1953, Getúlio Vargas signed Law No. 2,004, which established Petrobras, a state-owned enterprise with a legal monopoly over oil exploration and production. Sections of the law and Vargas's public statement on the day it was passed follow.

Law No. 2,004, of October 3, 1953 establishes National Petroleum Policy and defines the duties of the National Petroleum Council, establishing a stock corporation, Petroleo Brasileiro Corporation, among other provisions.

THE PRESIDENT OF THE REPUBLIC:
Let it be known that the National Congress decrees and I sanction the following Law:

CHAPTER I: *Preliminary Provisions*

Article 1. Establishes the Union's monopoly of:

> I—the prospecting and mining of petroleum and other hydrocarbon fluids and rare gases that exist in the country;

II—the refining of domestic or foreign petroleum;

III—the ocean transportation of crude petroleum of domestic origin or petroleum products produced in the country, as well as the transport of crude oil and its derivatives as well as rare gases from any source through pipelines.

Article 2. The Union shall exercise control over the monopoly established in the previous article:

I—through the National Petroleum Council, as the guiding and supervisory body;

II—through the joint stock company Petroleo Brasileiro SA and its subsidiaries, as established in this law, as the enforcement agencies.

CHAPTER II: *The National Petroleum Council*

Article 3. The National Petroleum Council, an autonomous body reporting directly to the President, is to supervise measures concerning the domestic oil supply.

§ 1. National oil supply includes production, import, export, refining, transportation, distribution, and trading of crude oil, pit, or shale, as well as its derivatives.

§ 2. The use of other fluid hydrocarbons and rare gases is within the supervisorial responsibilities of the National Petroleum Council.

Article 4. The National Petroleum Council will continue to be governed in its organization and functioning by the laws in force, along with the changes resulting from this law.

Single paragraph. The President shall issue the new Rules of Procedure of the National Petroleum Council to conform to the provisions of this article.

CHAPTER III: *The Petróleo Brasileiro Corporation (PETROBRAS) and Its Subsidiaries*

SECTION I: THE CONSTITUTION OF PETROBRAS

Article 5. The Union is authorized to establish, in accordance with this law, a corporation, to be called Petróleo Brasileiro, Inc., using the acronym Petrobras or an abbreviation.

Article 6. Petróleo Brasileiro, Inc., will carry out mining, refining, trade, and transport of oil from wells or shale, its derivatives, and any related or similar activities.

Single paragraph. The prospecting and mining carried out by the Company will follow the plan approved by the National Petroleum Council, without formalities, requirements, area limitations, and other actions deemed necessary under Decree-Law No. 3,236 of 7 May 1941, authorizing the Council on behalf of the Union.

Article 7. The President shall designate by decree the representative of the Union in the founding meeting of the Corporation.

§ 1. The articles of incorporation shall be preceded by:

I—A study and approval of the proposed organization of the basic services of the Corporation, both internally and externally;

II—All specifications of goods and rights that the Union holds regarding the use of capital;

III—The preparation of its bylaws that will be published for general public knowledge.

§ 2. The articles of association shall include:

I—Authorization of the assessment of registered assets and rights that will constitute the Union's capital.

II—Approval of the bylaws.

III—Approval of a transfer plan regarding the services authorized by the National Petroleum Council for the Company and its funds.

§ 3. The Company shall be established in public session of the National Petroleum Council, whose minutes shall contain the approved bylaws, as well as the history and a summary of the articles of incorporation, especially the value of the assets and rights converted into equity.

§ 4. The incorporation of the Company will be approved by decree of the Executive Branch, and its minutes shall be filed by certified copies with the Commercial Registry.

Article 8. The Articles of Incorporation shall comply with incorporation laws. Changes in the bylaws involving modification of this law will depend on legislative authorization and in other cases is subject to the approval of the President by decree.

★ ★ ★

Brazilians . . .

The Congress has just passed into law the government's plan for the use of our oil. Petrobras will ensure not only the development of the national oil industry, but it will also contribute decisively to eliminating currency flight. Established exclusively with Brazilian capital, technology, and labor, Petrobras is the result of a strong nationalist policy in the economic field, already established by other bold projects whose feasibility I have always trusted. When the Volta Redonda [National Steel Plant] was built, many disbelieved that possibility, but today the steel industry stands as irrefutable proof of national creative capacity. When the foundations of the Paulo Afonso Power Plant were laid, there were also those who expected the failure of a great public project that will soon be the mainstay of the entire northeastern economy. Achievements such as these confirm the power of the people to achieve goals, and they give us the assurance, against the advice of the naysayers, that we will make good use of Brazilian oil. It is therefore with satisfaction and pride that today I signed the law, passed by the Legislature, which represents another milestone in our economic independence.

Translated by Emma Wohl

An Unrelenting Critic of Vargas

Carlos Lacerda

One of Getúlio Vargas's fiercest critics was Carlos Lacerda, a founding member of the left-wing National Liberating Alliance in 1935, who a decade later had become an elected congressperson with the right-wing National Democratic Union party. In 1949, Lacerda founded the influential political newspaper Tribuna da Imprensa, which he used to attack Vargas throughout his 1951–54 presidency, calling for his impeachment on charges of illicit dealings with Argentina's Juan Perón.

Perhaps the most damning of Lacerda's editorials was the following, published on August 5, 1954. Shortly after midnight that day, unidentified attackers had attempted to assassinate Lacerda, out with his teenage son, but accidentally killed his bodyguard instead, air force major Rubens Vaz. It quickly came to light that members of Vargas's inner circle had been behind the attack. Wounded in the leg, Lacerda accused the president of the attack in an editorial published on his newspaper's front page.

It was later revealed that the chief of the president's security detail had indeed coordinated the assassination, although apparently unbeknownst to Vargas. A political crisis ensued, and the military threatened to remove the president from office. Vargas committed suicide just twenty days after this editorial first appeared.

The Blood of an Innocent

Rubens Florentino Vaz, hero of the Air Force Postal Service, father of four children, fell tonight by my side. With him, my own son also ran the risk of all Brazilians subjected to a regime of corruption and terror.

Those who don't give in to corruption fall to acts of violence.

We have said this: Is there anyone in this country who does not know that the corruption of the Vargas government breeds the violence perpetuated by his gang?

Day after day, night after night, the circle of violence closes in on those who don't give in to the coercion of money.

Today, what more can I say? The vision of Rubem [sic] Vaz [lying] on the street, shot twice at point-blank range, the interminable trip I took with him

Carlos Lacerda (1914–1977) speaking at the São Paulo Law School soon after the attempt on his life in 1954. Courtesy of Acervo Iconografia.

to the hospital, watching him die in my arms, makes it impossible for me right now to coldly analyze tonight's heinous ambush.

But, before God, I accuse only one man as responsible for this crime. He is the protector of thieves, whose impunity gives them the audacity to commit acts like the one that took place tonight.

That man is named Getúlio Vargas.

He is intellectually responsible for this crime. It was for his protection; it was the cowardice of those who cover up the crimes of his followers that armed the bandits with audacity.

In this way corruption generates violence, and impunity stimulates the criminal.

I think of the children [of Rubens Vaz] and of my son. Rubens Vaz died in war. He died, that dear friend, in the most terrible, the most insidious of wars: the struggle of an unarmed people against the bandits who make up the Getúlio Vargas government.

Translated by Victoria Langland

Vargas's Suicide Letter

Getúlio Vargas

A mounting campaign fueled by right-wing journalist Carlos Lacerda and supported by conservative political forces in the National Democratic Union led some sectors of the armed forces to support the overthrow of Getúlio Vargas. Unwilling to be forcibly removed from office, the veteran politician chose instead to commit suicide. In the bedroom of the presidential palace on the morning of August 24, 1954, still in his pajamas, he placed a revolver to his chest and fired one fatal shot. Hearing the gunfire, his family and staff quickly rushed into the room, where his son-in-law found a handwritten letter addressed to the Brazilian people on his dresser. The letter enumerates the ways that Vargas had transformed the country and lashes out against those political forces that opposed his nationalist policies and resented his support among Brazil's lower classes. Just hours after his death, Vargas's staff released typed copies of the letter to the press, and it was repeatedly read over the radio and widely published, contributing to the massive outpourings of grief by Brazil's poor and working classes, especially at his subsequent funeral in Rio de Janeiro. The letter is now referred to as Vargas's testament letter, and scholars have noted important differences in the handwritten version stored in the archive of Vargas's papers and the typewritten one released to the press. It was likely edited by the journalist José Soares Maciel Filho, Vargas's closest aide and speechwriter, who told interviewers he was the one who transcribed the document. The text below comes from the widely circulated, typed version of the letter.

Once more the forces and interests against the people are newly coordinated and raised against me. They do not accuse me, they insult me; they do not fight me, they slander me and refuse to give me the right of defense. They seek to drown my voice and halt my actions so that I no longer continue to defend, as I always have defended, the people, and principally the humble. I follow the destiny that is imposed on me. After decades of domination and plunder by international economic and financial groups, I made myself chief of an unconquerable revolution. I began the work of liberation, and I instituted a regime of social liberty. . . . I was forced to resign. I returned to govern in the arms of the people.

A subterranean campaign of international groups joined with national interests, revolting against the regime of workers' guarantees. The excess

Mourners at Getúlio Vargas's funeral. Credit: Fundação Getúlio Vargas, CPDOC.

profits law was held up in Congress. Hatreds were unleashed against the justice of a revision of minimum wages. I wished to create national liberty by developing our riches through Petrobras [the state-owned oil company], which had scarcely begun to operate when the wave of agitation clouded its beginnings. Eletrobrás [the state-owned power company] was obstructed to the point of despair. They do not want workers to be free. They do not want the people to be independent.

I took office during an inflationary spiral that was destroying the rewards of work. Profits by foreign companies reached as much as 500 percent annually. In declarations of goods that we import, frauds of more than 100 million dollars per year were proven. I saw the coffee crisis increase the value of our principal product. We tried to maintain that price, but the reaction was such violent pressure on our economy that we were forced to surrender. I have fought month after month, day after day, hour after hour, resisting constant, incessant pressures, unceasingly bearing it all in silence, forgetting everything and giving myself in order to defend the people that now are abandoned. I cannot give you more than my blood. If the birds of prey wish the blood of anyone, they wish to continue to suck the blood of the Brazilian people. I offer my life in the holocaust. I choose this means to be with you always. When they humiliate you, you will feel my soul suffering at your side. When hunger knocks at your door, you will feel within you the energy to fight for yourselves and for your children. When you are scorned, my mem-

Procession accompanying Vargas's coffin to the Santos Dumont airport in Rio de Janeiro to be transported to Rio Grande do Sul. Credit: Fundação Getúlio Vargas, CPDOC.

ory will give you the strength to react. My sacrifice will keep you united, and my name will be your battle standard. Each drop of my blood will be an immortal call to your conscience and will uphold the sacred will to resist.

To hatred, I reply with forgiveness. And to those who think that they have defeated me, I reply with my victory. I was a slave of the people and today I am freeing myself for eternal life. But this people, whose slave I was, will no longer be slave to anyone. My sacrifice will remain forever in your souls, and my blood will be the price of your ransom. I fought against the looting of Brazil. I fought against the looting of the people. I have fought bare breasted. The hatred, infamy, and calumny did not defeat my spirit. I have given you my life. I gave you my life. Now I offer you my death. Nothing remains. Serenely, I take my first step on the road to eternity, and I leave life to enter history.

Translated by Robert M. Levine

The Life of a Factory Worker

Joana de Masi Zero

Getúlio Vargas has been called the father of the poor and the mother of the rich for his seemingly contradictory policies that addressed many of the basic needs of the lower classes yet also favored industrial capitalists and large landholding interests. The Consolidated Labor Laws, adopted in 1943 during the Estado Novo, are a good example of the paradoxical relationship between Vargas and the Brazilian populace. The legislation established a minimum wage, required that employers register their workers so that they could receive social security and other benefits, and set up a system of labor courts that employees could use when they believed their rights had been violated. At the same time, it gave the state significant power to control unions and thereby restricted workers' ability to organize for better wages and working conditions.

Women workers constituted an important segment of the growing industrial sector, and the new laws stipulated that they should receive the same benefits as men, including equal pay for equal work. In practice, however, women were often assigned to the least-skilled and lowest-paying jobs. Moreover, the new labor laws included special provisions for women, who, legislators believed, needed extra protection from long hours, night work, or physically demanding labor, and thus were prohibited from working in areas such as mines or construction sites and from engaging in "dangerous or unhealthy activities." Moreover, the laws entirely excluded domestic workers, the vast majority of them women, declaring their labor "noneconomic."

Yet the legacy of Vargas is complex. He developed a strong link with ordinary working men and women in the 1930s and '40s that deepened during his presidency in the early 1950s. The following recollections by Joana de Masi Zero, a factory worker during the Vargas period, who spoke with an interviewer in 1996 about her life, capture one woman's response to the changes faced by working-class families over the century, including the social reforms introduced by Vargas and the erosion of worker benefits since then.

My name is Joana de Masi Zero. I was born in São Paulo on October 23, 1916, in the district of Mooca. In those days, Mooca wasn't like it is today. There were few houses; you could walk around. There wasn't much movement, although the streetcar passed by Ipanema Street. . . . You catch it and were downtown in ten minutes.

We lived on Guarapuava Street. The houses there were simple, like all of the ones on old streets, close together. Ours was a duplex, with large rooms with high ceilings. The privy was outside. Later on, we built one inside, but the old outhouse remained in use, too. Our yard was ample, with many plants, including guavas, oranges, and even a pear tree. We kept chickens in the back of the yard. We also had Angora cats, who jumped over the wall and ran around everywhere, but they didn't get close to the chickens. . . .

My sister Carmela and I stayed by the front door; when neighbors passed by we would chat with them. My mother didn't let us go out alone because we were girls, and it could be dangerous. When Carmela and I and our friends did go out, we all would hold hands; sometimes we walked while singing. I only went through primary school. It was a good school; I started when I was eight. In those days, you started then and went until you were twelve.

I studied in a private school, Sete de Setembro, and then went on to another. My sister Carmela and I finished, but our older sister had to stop and go to work. In school, boys and girls had separate classes. No one mixed in those days, even during recess. The boys stayed on one side and the girls on the other. The school yard was divided so that no one could have contact with anyone from the other group. They entered on the left side and we on the right. The boys' teacher was very energetic. Boys are more rebellious; sometimes the teachers punished the boys right in the corridor. We wore uniforms. On regular days, we had blouses with the school emblem embroidered on them. On special days, we wore uniforms of white linen, pleated skirts, and white blouses. We wore white pants for physical education. . . . Everyone was neat and well groomed.

We studied many things: Portuguese grammar, arithmetic, history, geography, science, sewing, singing, gymnastics, everything. We studied four hours each day, from eight to noon. . . .

My family worked hard. My father was a textile supervisor. In those days, they earned a good living . . . two hundred *mil-réis* a month in 1920. This was good money. Salaries weren't meager, like today. You could buy what you needed at home. My mother even saved a bit. We built our house and paid it off fairly quickly, but then my father had an accident and died. He was handling a machine when it injured him. He hung on for a month. On his death certificate it said he died of pneumonia, because he couldn't breathe. My mother wanted to give him medicine against infection, but he refused, saying, "I'm not going to take anything!" He said his blood was good, that he didn't need anything.

I was five when my father died. My grandfather came to live with us, but he died too. Only the women remained, my mother, my grandmother, and we three sisters.

The house was my mother's, but the rest? For food and clothing we had to work. First, my mother went to work in a chicken coop; later, she started to sew men's clothing at home. My oldest sister started working when she was still a girl. She was the first, when she was twelve. Then I went to work, and finally Carmela. At first, she stayed at home, doing chores: she would prepare lunch and keep house. My older sister worked in textile factories, going from one to another. It was she who taught Carmela how to do textile work. My first job was sewing carpets by hand. I was twelve. I worked for a year and a half. It was in a private house, and they hired girls to work. Then I went to a factory, the Santa Madalena, on Bresser Street. When I went to work there, my mother had to get me a work permit, because I was still a minor, fourteen years of age. Actually, I was younger; I started in July, but my birthday was in October. Only then did I work legally. Only my sisters and I left school. Our other friends continued because their parents could afford it. . . . When I was fifteen, I moved to a more difficult machine in the factory. You earned more . . . forty-five *mil-réis* a month if you produced up to your daily quota. . . .

I went from factory to factory . . . finding different jobs. . . . I worked in one factory for twenty-five years. Getúlio was president. Many people said that he was a dictator, but he did many things for us workers. His labor laws were good. There were no strikes, at least never at places where I was working. Sometimes, to avoid strikes, the bosses dismissed us early, saying to us, "You go home. We're going to stop the machines so we won't have any fights at the door." They meant with the militants. All the laws we have today were thanks to [Vargas]. . . . The first minimum wage was forty *mil-réis* a month. Then they started to withhold payments for pensions—three *mil-réis* a month. Everyone paid, whether they wanted to or not. It was taken out of your pay envelope. Later, this system changed for the worse; retirement paid almost nothing. Every time the politicians changed the laws, they took more from us. Getúlio's time was good; later, I don't know. We earned good wages, and prices didn't go up. You went out to buy milk, for example, and the price was always the same. We didn't live in luxury; we made our own clothes—we knew how to sew—we were well dressed, we had money to go to the movies every week, sometimes twice. We ate well, we lived well. They say he was a dictator, but for us he was good.

But when the factory moved to Mooca, with new machinery, production didn't go well. We earned little at the beginning. . . . Our salaries were affected. But then the law required that the employers give raises of 35 percent. My employer said that he couldn't, that he couldn't even pay 5 percent more. . . . He didn't even want to negotiate. We went to the union, and the union officials took our case. Unions worked well then—at least ours did. It had a lawyer who worked for it, Dr. Paranhos. We could talk to him about any problem we had. The complaint took more or less a year to be decided, and in the end we won. So the boss left Mooca and moved the factory to Vila

Maria, because he wanted to cheat us. He hired others and paid them less. On the whole, though, our bosses were decent, human. They came to visit; my mother invited them into the living room. They always asked about how my mother was.

When Getúlio died, it was like a death in the family. People were sad. No one talked; everyone was quiet. It was a really sorrowful day, especially for the workers. Things were closed for, I think, three days.

I retired when I turned sixty-five. The first month I earned the same as I had made when I was working, and after that, for a while as well. Then they began to take a little here and there, and the government took more and more, and now I earn almost nothing.

Translated by Robert M. Levine and John J. Crocitti

Operation Pan America

Juscelino Kubitschek

In the late 1950s, President Kubitschek (1955–60) proposed Operation Pan America, which would have been a massive development program designed to help bridge the growing economic gap between North and South America. Kubitschek drew his inspiration from the Marshall Plan of Europe, which was sold as a selfless act of U.S. American-funded reconstruction for the European continent following World War II. He also thought it fit into Cold War politics and the anticommunist campaigns of the United States in Latin America. Just a few years earlier, sixteen states had joined the United States in signing a mutual defense accord called the Inter-American Treaty of Reciprocal Assistance, better known as the Treaty of Rio de Janeiro, which was considered a collective agreement against foreign, that is, communist intervention in the region. Kubitschek believed poverty and hunger increased the appeal of communist ideology and thus were responsible for growing political instability across Latin America. Yet the development plan aroused little interest in the United States, mainly because the administration of Dwight Eisenhower (1953–61) saw trade and private investment as the best path for Latin American development. It was only after the 1959 Cuban Revolution that Washington politicians came to rethink their policy for Latin America. In 1961, the administration of President John F. Kennedy (1961–63) announced the Alliance for Progress, a proposal very similar to Operation Pan America, combining large-scale investments in government aid for economic development with funding for military, police, and counterinsurgency training.

I. Definition and Objectives

The Brazilian Government considers that a clearer definition of the objectives of Operation Pan America is necessary in order that this movement, which has been initiated at the right time and under the best auspices, may not be impaired or lose its impact.

A. *General definition:* Operation Pan America is not an undertaking limited by time, with objectives to be attained in a short period; rather, it is a reorientation of hemispheric policy, intended to place Latin America, by a process of full appraisement, in a position to participate more effectively in the defense of the West with a growing sense of vitality and a greater development of its capacities. Thus, Operation Pan America is more than a mere program; it is an entire policy.

B. *Strategic political concept:* Operation Pan America must be understood as a corollary of the general strategy of the West, and among its fundamental purposes the following are particularly outstanding: preservation of the democratic system, based on political and religious freedom and on respect for private ownership and free enterprise, and the defense of all areas that concern the security of the free world. Because of its intrinsic, political, economic, social and strategic importance, and because "a threat to the peace in any part of the world is now a threat to the peace of the entire world," it is opportune to re-examine, with a view to strengthening it, the contribution to the resources of the free world that may be made by the nations that are signatories of the Treaty of Rio de Janeiro.

C. *Economic concept:* The more rapid development of Latin America's economic strength will result in a growing sense of vitality and will enable it to increase its contribution to the defense of the West.

II. Characteristics

A. *Joint multilateral action:* Operation Pan America is conceived as involving the joint action of the twenty-one republics of the Western Hemisphere, the preservation of its strictly multilateral nature being indispensable. Bilateral matters will continue to be handled through the channels normally followed in such cases, without becoming part of the aforesaid Operation.

B. *Struggle for democracy:* Within the framework of Operation Pan America, the struggle for democracy becomes identified with the struggle against stagnation and underdevelopment. The underdevelopment that prevails in this hemisphere morally and materially involves the cause that we are defending. Underdeveloped areas are open to the penetration of anti-democratic ideology. From many standpoints and in all of its implications, the battle of the West is the battle for development. Materialist ideologies feed upon the poverty and misery that give rise to them in the first place; to combat these factors is the only sure way to combat those ideologies. Where there is poverty, our cause will always be in danger. It is illusory to expect positive action on behalf of a cause embracing such complex factors from peoples whose isolation in the rigors of extreme poverty prevents them from thinking or feeling anything beyond the narrow limits of their urgent needs for survival.

C. *Latin America's participation in world policy:* According to the Brazilian concept, Operation Pan America is a reflection of the need for more active and more vigorous participation and cooperation by the Latin American countries in international policy, and it reveals these countries' full awareness of their moral, political, and demographic importance. Latin America's contribution may become highly significant in the struggle for a balance of power.

III. Western Postwar Policy

A. Inter-American political reorientation: The Brazilian Government believes that the time has come for a revision of inter-American policy, with a view to strengthening hemispheric unity in the face of the increasing common danger. A stronger, more courageous, creative, and dynamic initiative is urgently needed in the Western hemisphere at this time.

It is imperative that the West become ever more conscious of its mission in the modern world. The principal objective of this mission is to defend and to perfect man's spiritual and moral achievements. Spiritual and moral forces should be the ones to guide and regulate a world expanded and profoundly transformed by technology. This is what is important to the West; this is its own cause.

B. Economic reorientation of Pan Americanism: The reasons for underdevelopment are many and complex. One could not in good faith fix responsibility for Latin America's chronically anemic condition and the consequent organic weakening of Pan Americanism. Although it is understood that efforts toward economic development devolve primarily upon each country individually, it is now understood better than ever before that there must be cooperation on an international basis.

IV. The Operation's Course of Action

A. Advance preparation: The Brazilian Government wishes to clarify the fact that it was never its intention or plan to hold a conference of American Chiefs of State without the most careful advance preparation. Furthermore, the Brazilian Government is not committed to any rigid plans for carrying out the operation in question, and it believes that only after a series of contacts and consultations among the countries of our community will it be possible to make a definitive determination of the best methods for achieving the common objective.

B. Preliminary inquiries: The Brazilian Government would now be willing to assume responsibility for making diplomatic inquiries with a view to the preparation of a basic agenda and toward ascertaining whether the [Latin] American governments would agree with the idea of reaching informal understanding and carrying out preliminary negotiations in Washington through the embassies accredited to the Government of the United States.

C. Initiation of the Operation: The preparatory work could be done at the diplomatic or technical level, and it is anticipated that the participation by members of the delegations accredited to the Organization of American States would be desirable. These informal understandings would become more clearly defined and be better coordinated if a *Committee of Twenty-one* were created. Brazil does not wish to propose any date, but nonetheless it does state that it would be ready to begin its work in the said committee during the latter part of September.

D. High-level meeting: Once the bases for an agreement have been established and significant results obtained that might be looked upon as substantial progress, then the competent organs of the Organization of American States could study the idea of a high-level meeting among the republics of the hemisphere to approve and to sign that group of resolutions and proclamations that could become the plan of action for achieving Pan American unity; among these would be included, with special emphasis, the preparation of a dynamic and progressive program for the struggle against underdevelopment, and this would be the crowning feature of Operation Pan America.

V. Basic Objectives of the Operation

The following points might be the basic objectives of the Operation:

1. Reaffirmation of the principles of hemispheric solidarity;
2. Recognition of underdevelopment as a problem of common interest;
3. Adaptation of inter-American organs and agencies, if necessary, to the requirements of more dynamic action to carry on the struggle against underdevelopment;
4. Technical assistance for increased productivity;
5. Measures to stabilize the market for basic commodities;
6. Adaptation to present needs and expansion of the resources of international financial institutions;
7. Reaffirmation of private initiative in the struggle against underdevelopment; and
8. Revision by each country, where necessary, of its fiscal and economic policy, for the purpose of assuring means to promote economic development.

Excerpts from *Child of the Dark*

Carolina Maria de Jesus

During the 1940s and '50s, millions of poor people from the countryside moved to Brazilian cities. They sought to escape grinding poverty and drought in the countryside and searched for steady employment and a better way of life. Unable to afford basic housing, many built or rented shacks in the poor, increasingly crowded, informal neighborhoods called favelas, where they survived on minimum wage in low-level service jobs, participated in the informal economy, or scavenged through garbage to find recyclable materials or leftover food.

Carolina Maria de Jesus, an Afro-Brazilian woman from Minas Gerais, settled in one such favela in São Paulo while in her early twenties. There she singlehandedly struggled to support her three children, often by scavenging. Although she had only a minimal formal education, she penned a diary over the course of several years describing her efforts to sustain her family and documenting daily life in her favela. In 1960, a journalist discovered her writings and arranged to have them published, catapulting Jesus to national and later international fame. Proceeds from this best-selling work allowed her to move to a lower-middle-class neighborhood of São Paulo, but she found the new surroundings and the media glare unwelcoming, and moved to the rural outskirts of the city where she eventually died impoverished.

In the early 1960s, the bleak and harsh everyday life depicted in her diary symbolized the ongoing existence of poverty and underdevelopment in Brazil. Jesus's will to survive, however, also represented the determined drive of the dispossessed to overcome these dire obstacles to achieving human dignity.

In the excerpt from her diary below, we have changed the term "Negro," used in the original translation of her diary into English, to "black."

1958

JUNE 3 When I was at the streetcar stop [my daughter] Vera started to cry. She wanted a cookie. I only had ten cruzeiros, two for the streetcar and eight to buy hamburger. Dona Geralda gave me four cruzeiros for me to buy the cookies. She ate and sang. I thought: my problem is always food! I took the streetcar and Vera started to cry because she didn't want to stand up, and there wasn't any place to sit down.

Writer Clarice Lispector with Carolina Maria de Jesus after she had become a literary sensation in the early 1960s. Instituto Moreira Salles Collection.

When I have little money I try not to think of children who are going to ask for bread. Bread and coffee. I sent my thoughts toward the sky. I thought: can it be that people live up there? Are they better than us? Can it be that they have an advantage over us? Can it be that nations up there are as different as nations on earth? Or is there just one nation? I wonder if the favela exists there? And if up there a favela does exist, can it be that when I die I'm going to live in a favela?

JUNE 16 [My son] José Carlos is feeling better. I gave him a garlic enema and some mint tea. I scoff at women's medicine but I had to give it to him because actually you've got to arrange things the best you can. Due to the cost of living we have to return to the primitive, wash in tubs, cook with wood.

I wrote plays and showed them to directors of circuses. They told me:

"It's a shame you're black."

They were forgetting that I adore my black skin and my kinky hair. Black people's hair is more educated than the white man's hair. Because with Black hair, where you put it, it stays. It's obedient. The hair of the white, just give one quick movement, and it's out of place. It won't obey. If reincarnation exists I want to come back black.

One day a white told me:

"If the blacks had arrived on earth after the whites, then the whites would have complained and rightly so. But neither the white nor the black knows its origin."

The white man says he is superior. But what superiority does he show? If the Black person drinks *pinga* [sugar-cane rum], the white drinks. The sickness that hits the black hits the white. If the white feels hunger, so does the Black person. Nature hasn't picked any favorites.

JULY 7 I went to Dona Juana and she gave me some bread. I passed by the factory to see if there were any tomatoes. There was a lot of kindling wood. I was just about to pick up some pieces when I heard a black man tell me that I wasn't to mess with that wood or he would hit me. I told him to go ahead and hit because I wasn't afraid. He was putting this wood into a truck. He looked at me scornfully and said:

"Nut!"

"And it's just because I am crazy that you'd better not mess with me. I've got all the vices. I rob and I fight and I drink. I spend 15 days at home and 15 days in jail."

He made a move toward me and I told him:

"I am from the favela of Candidé. I know how to cut with a razor and I'm learning to handle a fish knife. A *nortista* [person from Northern Brazil] is giving me lessons. If you want to hit me go ahead."

I started to search my pockets.

"Where's my razor? Today you're going to walk around with only one ear. When I drink a few *pingas* I go half crazy. It's that way in the favela, anybody who shows up there we can beat them, steal their money and everything they have in their pockets."

The black kept quiet. I went away. When someone insults us, all we have to do is tell what the favela is. They leave us in peace. We of the favela are feared. I dared the black because I knew he would go away. I don't like to fight.

When I was returning I met Nelson from Vila Guilherme. He said something I didn't like. I pretended I didn't understand what he said.

"But you with all your intelligence, you don't understand why I'm following you around?"

When I got back to the favela my children were not there. I called. None of them appeared. I went to Senhor Eduardo and bought half a liter of oil and 16 cruzeiros of sausage. I found the 46 cruzeiros that [my son] João received when he sold the scrap iron. 46 with my 20 gave me 66. On my return I kept watching the favela men. Most of them don't work on Monday. I went to Manuel and met João who was just coming back. He said he found some cans and got four cruzeiros. I asked him about Vera. He told me he left her at home. And she was with José Carlos.

Excerpts from Child of the Dark   393

Then I heard Vera's voice. She said:

"José Carlos. Here's Mama!"

They came running toward me. She said that she and José Carlos had gone out begging. He had one of my sacks on his back. I walked ahead of them so they wouldn't see my smile but told him he should be studying his lessons. I had to go into the city.

While I was dressing I heard the voice of Durvalino arguing with a strange drunk. Women started to appear. They never miss these things. They can stand hours and hours just watching. They don't think of anything even if they left a pot on the stove. A fight for them is just as important as the bull-fights in Madrid are for the Spanish. I saw Durvalino strike the drunk and try to strangle him. The drunk had no strength to fight back. Armin and some others took Durvalino's hands off the drunk's neck and carried him to the other side of the river. And Durvalino stayed, bragging about what he had done.

I went to register to vote. When I got to Semanario Street, I needed a photo for registration papers. I had a picture taken in Foto Lara. It cost me 60 cruzeiros. While I waited for the photographs, I talked to the people there. They were all pleasant. I got my pictures and went to stand in the line. I talked with a woman whose husband works in the mayor's office. She wanted to know whom I was going to vote for. I told her I was going to vote for Dr. Ademar.[1] I left the Board Room and took the streetcar. When I got off at the last stop I went to the butcher to buy hamburger. I bought a half kilo of rice. I asked the woman selling newspapers if she was going to vote. I was thinking of my children, who must be hungry. Vera started asking for something to eat. I heated it and gave it to her. João ate and so did José Carlos. They told me about Dona Aparecida's brother-in-law who went to the First Aid Station. He had been run over and was in a cast.

When I go into the city, I have the impression that I'm in paradise. I think it just wonderful to see all the women and children so well dressed. So different from the favela. The different-colored houses with their vases of flowers. These views enchant the eyes of the visitors to São Paulo who never know that the most famous city in South America is ill with ulcers—the favelas.

1959

APRIL 29 Today I am out of sorts. What saddens me is the suicide of Senhor Tomás. The poor man. He killed himself because he was tired of suffering from the cost of living.

When I find something in the garbage that I can eat, I eat it. I don't have the courage to kill myself. And I refuse to die of hunger!

I stopped writing the diary because I got discouraged. And I didn't have time.

MAY 1 I got out of bed at 4 a.m. I washed the dishes and went to get water. There was no line. I don't have a radio so I can't listen to the parade. Today is Labor Day.

MAY 2 Yesterday I bought sugar and bananas. My children ate a banana with sugar because I don't have any lard to cook food. I thought of Senhor Tomás who committed suicide. But if all the poor in Brazil decided to kill themselves because they were hungry nobody would be left alive.

MAY 3 Today is Sunday. I'm going to spend the day at home. I have nothing to eat. I'm nervous, upset and sad. There is a Portuguese here who wants to live with me. But I don't need a man. And I have begged him not to come around here bothering me.

Today the Father came to say Mass in the favela. He gave the favela the name of "The Rosary District." Many people came to the Mass. In his sermon the priest asked the people not to rob.

Senhor Manuel arrived and we started to talk. I told him about the girl of a year and a half who can't see anyone move his mouth without asking:

"What are you eating?"

She is the latest child of Tiger Benny. I can see that she is going to be intelligent.

MAY 4 I got out of bed at 6, because when Senhor Manuel sleeps here he doesn't let me get up early.

I was not born ambitious. I remembered this line from the Bible: "Do not hoard up Treasures, because your heart will be set on them."

I've always heard it said that the rich man doesn't have any peace of mind. But the poor doesn't have it either, because he has to fight to get the money to eat with.

MAY 28 Life is just like a book. Only after you've read it do you know how it ends. It is when we are at the end of life that we know how our life ran. Mine, until now, has been black. As black as my skin. Black as the garbage dump where I live.

Note

1. Dr. Ademar de Barros was the conservative populist mayor of the city of São Paulo and later governor of the state.

Education as a Practice of Freedom

Paulo Freire

Brazilian educator Paulo Freire (1921–1997) has influenced generations of teachers, organizers, and activists around the globe. Born in the state of Pernambuco, he both witnessed and experienced firsthand the ways in which educational inequalities reflected and reinforced other kinds of inequalities, and he eventually made adult education and literacy training the centerpiece of his life's work. Arguing that a successful educator did not simply transmit knowledge to his or her students, he advocated dialogue between students and teachers on collectively chosen topics, a process that led to conscientização, a term perhaps best translated as the development of critical consciousness.

In the early 1960s, Freire worked as a professor in the Cultural Extension program of the University of Recife, where he put his ideas into practice. He taught reading and writing to adults with few literacy skills, and he led what he called culture circles as part of a broader adult education program. He was so successful in these efforts that the Goulart government worked to extend his efforts nationwide until the military coup of 1964 put an end to these plans. Freire was imprisoned for over two months on charges of subversion, and upon his release he went into exile in Chile. There he continued to develop his educational ideas, working in a number of countries and earning an international reputation. In Chile, he wrote one of his most famous works, Pedagogy of the Oppressed *(1970), as well as the following account of his work in Recife in the early 1960s, in which he describes the centrality of education to democracy. Although he speaks of humanity in decidedly masculine terms, for many today his pedagogical approach is still considered revolutionary. This essay, written while in Chilean exile, explains the work he carried out in Brazil in the early 1960s.*

... The first literacy attempt took place in Recife, with a group of five illiterates, of which two dropped out the second or third day. The participants, who had migrated from rural areas, revealed a certain fatalism and apathy in regard to their problems. They were totally illiterate. At the twentieth meeting, we gave progress tests. To achieve greater flexibility, we used an epidiascope. We projected a slide on which two kitchen containers appeared. "Sugar" was written on one, "poison" on the other. And underneath, the caption: "Which of the two would you use in your orangeade?" We asked the group to try to read the question and to give the answer orally. They answered, laughing, after several seconds, "Sugar." We followed the same procedure with other tests, such as recognizing bus lines and public buildings. During the twenty-first hour of study, one of the participants wrote, confidently, "I am amazed at myself."

From the beginning, we rejected the hypothesis of a purely mechanistic literacy program and considered the problem of teaching adults how to read in relation to the awakening of their consciousness. We wished to design a project in which we would attempt to move from naïveté to a critical attitude at the same time we taught reading. We wanted a literacy program which would be an introduction to the democratization of culture, a program with men as Subjects [active participants] rather than as patient recipients, a program which itself would be an act of creation, capable of releasing other creative acts, one in which students would develop the impatience and vivacity which characterize search and invention.

We began with the conviction that the role of man was not only to be in the world, but to engage in relations with the world—that through acts of creation and re-creation, man makes cultural reality and thereby adds to the natural world, which he did not make. We were certain that man's relation to reality, expressed as a Subject to an object, results in knowledge, which man could express through language.

This language, as is already clear, is employed by men whether or not they are literate. It is sufficient to be a person to perceive the data of reality, to be capable of knowing, even if this knowledge is mere opinion. There is no such thing as absolute ignorance or absolute wisdom. But men do not perceive those data in a pure form. As they apprehend a phenomenon or a problem, they also apprehend its causal links. The more accurately men grasp true causality, the more critical their understanding of reality will be. Their understanding will be magical to the degree that they fail to grasp causality. Further, critical consciousness always submits that causality to analysis; what is true today may not be so tomorrow. Naïve consciousness sees causality as a static, established fact, and thus is deceived in its perception.

. . . It so happens that to every understanding, sooner or later an action corresponds. Once man perceives a challenge, understands it, and recognizes the possibilities of response, he acts. The nature of that action corresponds to the nature of his understanding. Critical understanding leads to critical action; magical understanding to magic response.

. . . We felt that even before teaching the illiterate to read, we could help him to overcome his magical or naïve understanding and to develop an increasingly critical understanding. Toward this end, the first dimension of our new program content would be the anthropological concept of culture—that is, the distinction between the world of nature and the world of culture; the active role of men *in* and *with* their reality; the role of mediation which nature plays in relationships and communication among men; culture as the addition made by men to a world they did not make; culture as the result of men's labor, of their efforts to create and re-create; the transcendental meaning of human relationships; the humanist dimension of culture; culture as a systematic acquisition of human experience (but as creative assimilation, not as information-storing); the democratization of culture; the learning of reading and writing as a key to the world of written communication. In short, the role of man as Subject in the world and with the world.

From that point of departure, the illiterate would begin to effect a change in his former attitudes, by discovering himself to be a maker of the world of culture, by discovering that he, as well as the literate person, has a creative and re-creative impulse. He would discover that culture is just as much a clay doll made by artists who are his peers as it is the work of a great sculptor, a great painter, a great mystic, or a great philosopher; that culture is the poetry of lettered poets and also the poetry of his own popular songs—that culture is all human creation.

. . . Many participants during these debates affirm happily and self-confidently that they are not being shown "anything new, just remembering." "I make shoes," said one, "and now I see that I am worth as much as the Ph.D. who writes books."

"Tomorrow," said a street-sweeper in Brasília, "I'm going to go to work with my head high." He had discovered the value of his person. "I know now that I am cultured," an elderly peasant said emphatically. And when he was asked how it was that now he knew himself to be cultured, he answered with the same emphasis, "Because I work, and working, I transform the world."

. . . To acquire literacy is more than to psychologically and mechanically dominate reading and writing techniques. It is to dominate these techniques in terms of consciousness; to understand what one reads and to write what one understands; it is to *communicate* graphically. Acquiring literacy does not involve memorizing sentences, words, or syllables—lifeless objects unconnected to an existential universe—but rather an attitude of creation and re-creation, a self-transformation producing a stance of intervention in one's context.

Thus the educator's role is fundamentally to enter into dialogue with the illiterate about concrete situations and simply to offer him the instruments with which he can teach himself to read and write. This teaching cannot be done from the top down, but only from the inside out, by the illiterate himself, with the collaboration of the educator. That is why we searched for a method which would be the instrument of the learner as well as of the educator, and which, in the lucid observation of a young Brazilian sociologist, "would identify learning *content* with the learning *process*."

Letter of Manumission for the Brazilian Peasant

Francisco Julião

Francisco Julião (1915–1999) was a native of Pernambuco, where he grew up on his grandfather's rural estate. There he saw firsthand the effects of a land tenure system in which a small minority held enormous plots of land called latifúndios, *while the large majority worked as sharecroppers, tenants, or day laborers. A legacy of the colonial period, the* latifúndio *system contributed to long-standing inequalities not just of land, but of political and social power as well.*

Julião dedicated his life to redressing these problems, earning a law degree at the Law School in Recife in 1939 and serving as a leading advocate for agrarian reform. In the mid-1950s he became a central figure in the newly founded Peasant Leagues (Ligas Camponesas), representing sharecroppers and smallholders in land tenancy courts. A self-described Catholic Marxist who was also inspired by the Cuban Revolution, Julião eventually came to argue, famously, for the implementation of agrarian reform "by law or by force."

The passages that follow are extracts from a document in which Julião uses accessible language colored with regional references to point out the injustices faced by peasants, encouraging them to unite to redress these problems.

From here in Recife, Pernambuco, the cradle of the Peasant Leagues, I send you this letter, Brazilian peasant, in the hope that it will reach your home.

Together with your brothers, you make up almost all of Brazil. It is you who satiates our hunger. And yet you die from hunger. It is you who dresses us. And yet you wear rags. You are the soldiers who defend the nation. And yet the nation forgets you. You are the overseer for the landowners. And yet the overseers oppress you. You give alms to the church. And the church demands from you submission in the name of Christ. Yet Christ was a rebel. And for this he sacrificed himself on the cross. And, like Christ, the good Francis of Assisi from Italy also stayed by your side. And of those who are still alive, Mao Tse-tung from China and Fidel Castro from Cuba were victorious because they were with you and because you were with them. You were and you are. You are and you shall remain so.

This letter, Brazilian peasant, has to reach you. Even if you are lost in the Amazon jungle. Or beneath the *babassu* [palm trees] of Maranhão. Or under the *carnauba* [palm trees] of Ceará. Or in the sugarcane plantations of the Northeast. Or in the shade of the cacao trees of Bahia. Or in the rice fields of the São Francisco river. And in the yerba mate region. And in the pampas. Or where there are only scrub brush and thorns. With your brother dressed in leather. And another with a broadax and firebrand in his hands, fighting the forest to win the land. Or with a "yellow tag" [an 1873 Winchester rifle] fighting against the land grabbers in order to defend the land. In the state of Rio de Janeiro. In Paraná. In Goiás. In Maranhão. Along the open roads across the heart of Brazil. Wherever you groan night and day, at the handle of the hoe, ax, sickle, machete, and plow.

This letter, Brazilian peasant, that I write to you from Recife, from the headquarters of the Peasant Leagues, points out the paths you must follow in search of your freedom.

I can tell you that the journey is arduous and full of traps, but your victory is as certain as the sunrise that comes each morning. The *latifúndio* is cruel. It relies on the police and its own henchmen. It elects your worst enemies. To get your vote, it uses two recipes: violence and cunning. It scares you with violence. It deceives you with cunning. The violence comes from the overseers; it comes from the police. It is the threat to expel you from the land. It is the threat to tear your house down, to take away your harvest, to kill you with hunger. It is the threat of calling you a communist and saying that God will punish you for that. As if there could be a greater punishment than the one in which you live, chained to the *latifúndio*, in the name of a freedom that is not your freedom. In the name of a God that is not your God.

The cunning [of the *latifúndio*] comes from acting like a protector. It comes from entering your house meekly like a lamb. With its claws hidden. With its poison concealed. The cunning comes from offering you a bottle of medicine, and the jeep with which to take your wife to the hospital. It comes from lending you a bit of money, or orders for a little credit at the corner store. It comes from catching you off guard at election time, saying, "Friend, get your ballot ready. If my candidate wins, everything is going to change." And then when the candidate wins, things don't change. And if they do change, it is for the worse. The *latifúndio* is bloated from gluttony. You are bloated from hunger. The years go by. Centuries pass. Listen to what I say: the one who needs to change is you, peasant. But you will only change if you kill fear. And there is only one way to kill fear: in unity. With only one finger you cannot hold a hoe, an ax, a sickle, or a plow. Nor can you with your hand open, because the fingers are separated. You have to close your hand so that all of your fingers are united. The League is a closed hand because it is the union of all your brothers. Alone you are just a drop of water. United with your brothers, you are a waterfall. Unity makes strength. It is a bundle of sticks. It is a swelling river. It is the people marching; it is the overseers running away. It is the police dismantled. It is justice being born. It is freedom arriving, carrying the League in its arms and the Syndicate in its hands. . . .

Many are the paths that will take you to freedom. Freedom means land. It means bread. It means a home. It means medicine. It means school. It means peace. I will point out these paths to you. But I have to tell you, and I repeat: there is no point in going on this journey if you go alone. Invite your landless brother or your brother with little land. And ask him to invite another. At first there will be two people. Then ten. Then a hundred. Then a thousand. And in the end it will be everybody, marching united together. Just as united you go to the farmers' markets, to parties, to Mass, to ceremonies, to funerals, to elections. I say and I repeat: unity is the mother of freedom.

Translation by Theresa Bachmann

Brazil's New Foreign Policy

Jânio Quadros

Jânio Quadros, a center-right political gadfly, won the 1960 presidential race on a program that included combating corruption in the federal government. He also articulated a nonaligned foreign policy that positioned Brazil between the two major blocs in the Cold War and alongside the countries of Africa, Asia, and Latin America that sought a disengaged third path. Quadros presented his ideas in the prestigious U.S. journal Foreign Affairs *shortly before he suddenly resigned from office in August 1961 in a dispute over presidential powers. Many of the main principles outlined in this article continue to be fundamental tenets of Brazil's foreign policy today.*

The interest shown in Brazil in international affairs is in itself proof of the presence of a new force on the world stage. Obviously, my country did not appear by magic, nor is it giving itself momentarily to a more or less felicitous exhibition of publicity seeking. When I refer to a new force, I am not alluding to a military one but to the fact that a nation heretofore almost unknown is prepared to bring to bear on the play of world pressures the economic and human potential it represents, and the knowledge reaped from experience that we have a right to believe is of positive value.

We are a nation of continental proportions occupying almost half of South America, relatively close to Africa and having European, indigenous, and African roots. Within the next decade our nation will amount to close to 100,000,000 inhabitants, and the rapid industrialization of some regions of the country heralds our development into an economic power. . . .

In time, the foreign policy of Brazil will reflect the craving for developmental progress. Obviously, underlying the decisions that we are compelled to take in order to meet the problems of material growth inherent in the desire of the Brazilian people for economic, social, political and human freedom lies the interweaving of the country's material needs. Keeping our aims ever in mind, we must choose those of our country's sources of inspiration that can best be mobilized to assist the national effort. . . .

Common ideals of life and organization draw us close to the major nations of the Western bloc, and on many issues Brazil can, in a leading position, associate itself with this bloc. This affinity is underlined by our participa-

Presidents Jânio Quadros (*waving*) and Juscelino Kubitschek (*to his right*) at Quadros's inauguration with a supporter waving a broom, the symbol of his campaign against corruption. Courtesy of Acervo *Última Hora*, Arquivo Público do Estado de São Paulo.

tion in the Inter-American regional system, which entails specific political commitment.

However, at the present juncture, we cannot accept a set national position exclusively on the basis of the above premises. It is undeniable that we have other points in common with Latin America in particular, and with the recently emancipated peoples of Asia and Africa, which cannot be ignored, since they lie at the root of the readjustment of our policy, and on them converge many of the main lines of the development of Brazilian civilization. If it is true that we cannot relegate our devotion to democracy to a secondary place, it is no less true that we cannot repudiate ties and contacts offering great possibilities for national realization.

The closeness of Brazil's relations with neighboring countries of the continent and with the Afro-Asian nations, though based on different reasons, tends to the selfsame end. Among these, in the majority of cases, are historical, geographic and cultural motives. Common to them all is the fact that our economic situation coincides with the duty of forming a single front in the battle against underdevelopment and all forms of oppression.

From all this, naturally, certain points stand out that may be deemed basic to the foreign policy of my government. Development is an aim common to Brazil and to the nations with which we endeavor to have closer relations, and the rejection of colonialism is the inevitable and imperative corollary of that aim. . . .

At this point it might be appropriate to refer to the ideological prejudices of the capitalist democracies, ever ready to decry the idea of state intervention in countries where either the state controls and governs economic growth—which has become a question of sovereignty—or nothing at all is achieved. We are not in a position to allow the free play of economic forces in our territory, simply because those forces, controlled from outside, play their own game and not that of our country.

The Brazilian Government is not prejudiced against foreign capital—far from it. We stand in dire need of its help. The sole condition is that the gradual nationalization of profits be accepted, for otherwise it no longer is an element of progress but becomes a mere leech feeding on our national effort. Let it be known that the state in Brazil will not relinquish those controls that will benefit our economy by channeling and ensuring the efficiency of our progress.

Economic imbalance is doubtless the most critical of all the adverse factors that beset the Inter-American regional system, and from it almost all others stem. My government is convinced that it is fighting for the recovery of Pan Americanism and that this must start with the economic and social fields. Politically we are trying to give shape and content to the imperative principles of self-determination and non-intervention, and it is these principles that guide us in relation to the Americas as well as to the rest of the world.

The still dramatically present question of Cuba convinced us, once and for all, of the nature of the continental crisis. In defending with intransigence the sovereignty of Cuba against interpretations of an historical fact, which cannot be controlled *a posteriori*, we believe we are helping to awaken the continent to a true awareness of its responsibilities. We stand by our position on Cuba, with all its implications. Surely the Brazilian attitude has been understood by other governments, and as it gains ground, the entire regional system shows signs of a regeneration in the assessment of the responsibilities of each member nation.

The government of the United States, through its recent aid programs, took an important step toward the revision of its classical and inoperative continental policy. We hope that President Kennedy, who is not lacking in qualities of leadership, will carry the revisions of his country's attitude to the very limit and will sweep away the considerable remaining obstacles on the road to a truly democratic, continental community.

As to Africa, we may say that today it represents a new dimension in Brazilian policy. We are linked to that continent by our ethnic and cultural roots and share in its desire to forge for itself an independent position in the world of today. The nations of Latin America that became politically independent in the course of the nineteenth century found the process of economic development delayed by historical circumstances, and Africa, which has only recently become politically free, joins us at this moment in the common struggle for freedom and well-being.

I believe that it is precisely in Africa that Brazil can render the best service to the concepts of Western life and political methods. Our country should become the link, the bridge, between Africa and the West, since we are so intimately bound to both peoples. . . .

Here I must underscore another important aspect of the new Brazilian foreign policy. My country has few international obligations: we are bound only by pacts and treaties of continental assistance, which commit us to solidarity with any member of the hemisphere that may become the victim of extra-continental aggression. We have not subscribed to treaties of the nature of NATO, and are in no way forced formally to intervene in the cold war between East and West. We are therefore in a position to follow our national inclination to act energetically in the cause of peace and the relaxation of international tension.

Not being members of any bloc, not even of the Neutralist bloc, we preserve our absolute freedom to make our own decisions in specific cases and in the light of peaceful suggestions at one with our nature and history. . . . The first step in making full use of the possibilities of our position in the world consists in maintaining normal relations with all nations. . . .

The world must be made aware of the fact that Brazil, in intensively increasing its production, is looking not only to the domestic market, but specifically seeking to attract other nations. Economically speaking, my government's motto is "Produce everything, for everything produced is marketable." We shall go out to conquer these markets: at home, in Latin America, in Africa, in Asia, in Oceania, in countries under democracy, and in those that have joined the Communist system. Material interests know no doctrine and Brazil is undergoing a period where its very survival as a nation occupying one of the most extensive and privileged areas of the globe depends on the solution of its economic problems. Our very faithfulness to the democratic way of life is at stake in this struggle for development. A nation such as ours, with 70,000,000 inhabitants and with the world's highest rate of population growth, will not permit even a slowing down of its movement toward the full utilization of its own wealth.

Development and the Northeast

Celso Furtado

As seen earlier, during the colonial period the northeast was the primary source of Brazil's wealth. After the sugar trade weakened during the eighteenth century and the capital was moved from Salvador da Bahia to Rio de Janeiro in 1763, the region declined rapidly. By the twentieth century, the northeast faced significant economic and social problems. In the 1950s, literacy rates were the lowest in the country, with over half of the population functionally illiterate, and infant mortality rates were also high, with 180 infant deaths for every 1,000 live births. Periodic droughts in the hinterlands caused waves of destitute migrants to flee to urban areas.

Consistent with his developmentalist push, in 1959 President Kubitschek established SUDENE (Superintendency for the Development of the Northeast) and tapped Celso Furtado (1920–2004) as its first director. Furtado was one of Brazil's leading economists and a prolific writer, best known for his view that underdevelopment was not a temporary stage through which economies must pass as they emerge into developed ones, but rather was a particular economic structure defined by the relative timing of industrialization. Underdeveloped countries relied on developed countries to industrialize, and thus could not industrialize in the same way. In his directorship of SUDENE, Furtado advocated not for land reform but rather for heavy federal intervention and investment in the region to subsidize industrialization. In the extracts below from an article published in May 1962, he justifies his approach and its divergence from earlier efforts, while also invoking twentieth-century visions of Brazil as divided between a backward northeast and a modern south.

After the military coup of 1964, Furtado had his political rights suspended for ten years and consequently lived in exile until 1979.

The fight in Brazil for a constructive solution to the problem of the Northeast did just not begin today. During the Empire, technical commissions were formed to address the social crises that arose from the so-called Ceará droughts, and in the nineteenth century construction of the first big public dams began. We know that in the last three quarters of the century, the Northeast has been a constant source of concern for politicians in this country, as well as a constant source of chagrin for the way in which the government has been incapable of dealing with the problem.

Notwithstanding this effort, the Northeast did not find the path to development. On the contrary, as the population grew, so did poverty and social fragility, transforming the region into the largest poverty zone in the Western hemisphere. These reflections carry a huge sense of present opportunity, as they point inexorably to the conclusion that the principal reason for this weakness has been the lack of political policies to support technical work in order to provide continuity and a needed foundation through institutional reforms, without which efforts and enthusiasm become sterile gestures. . . .

On considering this half-century of work in the harsh conditions of the Northeast, we may easily conclude that the men who established the technical guidelines did the best they could for their era. Political conditions frustrated and rendered impotent their efforts. We, the directors of SUDENE, must carefully reflect on this experience before undertaking the great struggle in which we are engaged, one that has the support of all the enlightened opinion of the country's south. Our great strategy, based on the analysis of the experience of those who preceded us, is rooted in three points. Two of them have to do with broadening the horizon toward which we are headed in order to immediately include all those elements that, one way or another, will play a role in the final decisions. The third point concerns the need to strengthen the forces that support us from behind.

In the first place, we need to approach the problem of the Northeast as a problem of development, that is, from a positive and dynamic point of view. We should avoid excessive emphasis on negative aspects of the region's complexity, such as the case of the droughts. In a large part of the Northeast, the rainy season is, on the whole, consistently irregular. When this irregularity exceeds certain limits—when the rate of rainfall hits, shall we say, 30 percent—we have a drought. A drought of huge proportions is as rare as a normal winter. Because of this, the economic development of the Northeast should assume the form of a double process of increased productivity and a progressive adaptation to regional ecological conditions.

In theory, development constitutes a multifaceted process with progressive differentiation and complementarity among different parts of the economic system. Thus, a development policy must look in multiple directions simultaneously, without ever losing a unity of purpose. This principle is especially true in the case of the Northeast, where development cannot follow conventional lines. On equal footing with the efforts of capitalization should be another effort to adapt to surroundings, even with the creation of technology. We are today convinced that for the Northeast to reach even the current level of production of the Center-South of Brazil, that is, to triple the per capita production of the region, it will be necessary to have an understanding of tropical soil that is much more complete than what we have today, both within Brazil and abroad.

In the Northeast, there are three million hectares of land with adequate rainfall that are close to the most populated zones that thus could be culti-vated, but we don't know how to take advantage of this land. However, if it were possible to use these lands, we would double the cultivated area in the region without the need to use semiarid zones. We should start with the principle that in the Northeast there are abundant untapped resources and that this failure to take advantage of them results not only from the lack of systematic mobilization but also from the fact that available technolo-gies, created for different climatic conditions, are not always effective in that region. Observed from the perspective of development, the problem of the Northeast is perhaps more serious in regions with rainfall than in semiarid ones. The emphasis on the problem of droughts made this exact diagnosis difficult. However, in the rainy regions the rate of infant mortality is higher, life expectancy is shorter, the diet of the average worker is worse. Still, it is in the regions with rainfall that natural resources are flagrantly underuti-lized and whence capital flows permanently to the rich regions of the South. Additionally, two-thirds of the Northeastern population is concentrated in these regions. It was thus necessary to confront the Northeastern problem as a whole: unemployment in urban regions, underused land in regions with rainfall, and lack of adaptation in semiarid zones. And only from the angle of economic development would it be possible to find common denominators for all these problems, attacking them simultaneously on all fronts without dispersing efforts.

The next point in our strategy is intimately linked to the first: it is not possible to solve the problems of the Northeast limiting our concerns to the public sector. We should not forget that a large portion of investment is the responsibility of the private sector. Statistical analysis has demonstrated that the Northeast is an exporter of private capital. The principal objective of a de-velopment policy should therefore be to retain resources found in the region for its own use, so that these resources are used to reproduce themselves, creating permanent employment for the population. It is a business decision to limit the promotion of public works aimed at development and set aside this important factor of change in the process of growth. This fact, in itself, distinguishes the function of SUDENE as an agent of regional development: the task of planning public works, the systematic study of natural resources, the promotion of technology research, and the development of a technical staff, that is, the task of combining direct government action with the ad-ministration of multiple incentives for private initiatives. SUDENE approved more than fifty industrial projects in the past two years, which should be considered an installation phase, permitting the Northeast to recuperate a leadership position among the regions of the country that most expanded in industrial investment in that period. We have cultivated, simultaneously, electrification and industries that will consume energy, the study of natural resources and industries that will use these resources, systems of transportation and the goods they will transport. Only in this way will we create in the region the climate of optimism necessary to preserve local capital goods and attract capital from more developed regions. The incentives I speak of are not limited to the administration of favors already provided by law. We consider it important to systematically study the principal industrial sectors in the region and assist the managers in defining their own needs. By these means, we are training all specialized personnel of the regional textile industry and attempting to restart more than sixty factories in this sector in a period of two years.

Permit me to refer now to the third point of what I called our great strategy. It addresses the necessity of always connecting technical action and political leadership. When we affirm that SUDENE is a strictly technical organization, this means that it is independent of any partisan politics. But no development plan exists without a development policy, and no policy can be effective without support from the principal centers of political power. What makes SUDENE unique is that technical questions and politics are not isolated in two distinct areas. Governors of nine states participate in its Deliberative Council, which is essentially a political authority. The President delegates the authority of its superintendent, who is also the organization's director. This is an attempt to avoid the dualism that in the past was fatal to technical authority. This unity of technical matters and politics permitted SUDENE to interact directly with public opinion. Unconnected to any partisan activity, its objectives can be submitted to the test of open conversation. Since the debate over problems of development is a rational matter and has an educative character, the great polemic that surrounds SUDENE has contributed to the formation of a regional consciousness of the difficulties it faces and the need to demand systematic and ongoing government action. The level of all political discussion in the region improved, based on the last state elections for governor, as candidates debated plans and development policies. Connecting the problem of development to the political debate was key to the support SUDENE needed from public opinion. Had we limited analysis of the region's objective problems to hermetically sealed circles, isolating from the people those issues that are called "technical problems," and had we permitted the discussion to be limited to the points of view of local politicians, we would only have repeated the past without any better possibility for survival. We made this observation from the beginning, knowing that without the total support of public opinion SUDENE would not be up to the enormous task it faces. We knew from the lessons of the past that the economic development of the Northeast demands institutional reforms that can only be calculated and executed by an agency possessing extraordinary authority in the region, and that this authority cannot be upheld through slogans and myths. It was indispensable to bring the objective discussion of the problems of development to the people, cleansing it of the easy promises of the electoral period, reclaiming confidence in those responsible for the administration of public works.

As technicians completely disconnected from partisan political conversations, the experience we have lived through in the Northeast in the last three years serves as a lesson. That lesson is that the actions of a technician do not make sense carried out in isolation. They can only be understood as part of a collective effort. In other words, in our generation the actions of a technician have a necessary social dimension. The technician will not feel fulfilled as a citizen and as a person if his effort does not achieve increased social efficacy. On the other hand, the community demands that the technician respond to the call and assume responsibility during this decisive phase of national reconstruction. Having recognized this fact, the technician cannot ignore the ultimate results of social action within which he works. On the contrary, he should participate in the definition of these ends, translating them into rational issues. In this way, scientifically trained men will be able to contribute decisively to the objectives of economic and social development, so that they do not become mere myths. The struggle for development is also a struggle for rationality in politics; only by overcoming ideological mythology can we avoid the domination of the people by demagogues and opportunists.

Translated by Emma Wohl

President João Goulart's Speech at Central do Brasil

João Goulart

On March 13, 1964, President João Goulart addressed a massive rally in front of the Central do Brasil train station in Rio de Janeiro. During his speech, Goulart announced a series of planned economic and social reforms, including the nationalization of petroleum processing plants and the expropriation with compensation of land near federal highways and rivers as part of an agrarian redistribution proposal. He also described the socioeconomic and political environment in the country and alluded to the threats he faced from opponents as he embarked on these reforms. The radical tone of the speech alarmed conservative forces and galvanized them to oust Goulart from power two and a half weeks later.

I must thank all the labor unions, supporters of this great gathering, and I thank the Brazilian people for this extraordinary meeting in Rio de Janeiro. I must also thank the unions mobilizing their members from all of the states, and I would like to direct greetings to my countrymen, who at this moment are mobilized in all corners of the country and listening on their radios or watching television. I speak to all Brazilians and not just the ones able to acquire a formal education. I speak to the millions of our brothers who give more to Brazil than they receive and are paid back in suffering, misery, and deprivation; for to earn the right to be Brazilian it is necessary to work from sunrise to sunset for the greatness of this country. As president of eighty million Brazilians, I want my words to be well understood by all our countrymen. I will speak in a direct but sincere manner without any subterfuge. This is also the language of hope, of one who wishes to inspire trust for the future, but who has the courage to face without weakness the harsh reality in which we live. . . .

It has been said, Brazilian workers, that this demonstration would be an attack on the democratic regime, as if in Brazil reactionaries were still the owners of democracy or the proprietors of town squares and streets. . . . For them democracy is not a regime in which the people have the freedom of assembly. . . . The democracy that they want to impose on us is a democracy against the unions. . . . The democracy that they want is a democracy of the privileged, a democracy of intolerance and hate. The democracy that they want, oh laborers, would abolish [the state-owned oil company] Petrobras. It is the democracy of the monopolies, both national and international, a democracy that would fight against the people, the democracy that led President Vargas to his ultimate sacrifice. . . .

Democracy, my fellow workers, is what my government is trying to achieve. . . . There is no threat more serious to democracy than the attempt to strangle the voice of the people, the voices of the people's legitimate leaders, hushing their righteous claims.

. . . From the North to South, from West to East, people clamor for reforms of its [the government's] foundation and structure, but above all for agrarian reform, which would be the equivalent of abolishing bondage for tens of millions of Brazilians who barely survive in the countryside under deplorable conditions. . . .

To those who call upon the president of the Republic to offer a tranquil word to the Nation, to those all over Brazil who hear us at this opportunity, what I can say is that we can achieve social peace only through social justice. Those who fear that the government will carry out subversive action in the defense of political or personal interests and those who expect that this government will use repressive force against the people, against their rights and demands, are wasting their time. . . . I do not regret being called subversive for the act of proclaiming—which I have proclaimed and will continue proclaiming in all corners of the nation—the necessity to revise the constitution. It is a necessity, Brazilian workers, to revise the constitution of our Republic, which no longer meets the needs of the people or the needs of the nation's development. The current constitution, workers, is an antiquated constitution because it legalizes an unjust and inhumane socioeconomic structure that is already outdated. The people want democracy to be broadened. They want an end to privilege for a minority. They want land ownership to be accessible to all and participation in political life made easier through suffrage, for all to be able to vote and run for election so that financial power may no longer intervene in elections and representation of all political currents may be guaranteed without any ideological and religious discrimination. . . .

Workers, I have just signed the [land reform decree]. . . . It is still not the agrarian reform for which we fought. . . . But it is the first step: a door that has opened toward a definitive solution to the problem of rural Brazil. . . . In this regard, agrarian reform is an imperative, not only to increase the fieldworker's standard of living, but also to create more demand for industries and better wages for urban workers. It is because of this, that it [the reform] is in the interest of the industrialists and the merchants. Agrarian reform is necessary, after all, to improve our social and economic lives, so that the country might progress in its industries and in the well-being of its people.

How can the right of authentic ownership be guaranteed if, of the fifteen million Brazilians that work on the land in Brazil, only two and a half million are the owners?

What we are attempting to do in Brazil is no different from what has been done in all the developed countries of the world. It is a step toward progress that we must accomplish and accomplish it we shall! . . .

By announcing the decree of expropriation of all private oil refineries before the people in the public square, I pay respectful homage to he who always stayed in touch with the people's needs, the great and immortal President Getúlio Vargas. . . .

In the message that I sent to the National Congress for consideration, there are two other reforms requested that the Brazilian people demand; they are required for our development and our democracy. I am referring to electoral reform, an expansive reform that allows all Brazilians eighteen or older to have a hand in deciding their destinies, that allows all Brazilians who fight for the improvement of the country to influence the glorious destiny of Brazil. In this reform, we fight for fundamental democratic principles, such that every draftee may also be eligible [to vote].

Also included in the message to Congress is a university reform, demanded by Brazilian students and particularly by the university students who come from those socioeconomic classes that stand courageously in the forefront of all national and popular movements. In addition to these measures and decrees, the government continues to examine other provisions of fundamental importance for the defense of the people, especially the common people. . . .

Today, as the nation is our witness, and with the solidarity of the people gathered in this square, which belongs to the people alone, the government, which both represents and belongs to the people, reaffirms its unwavering determination to fight with all of its strength for the reform of Brazilian society. Not only for land reform but also for judiciary reform, for ample electoral reform, for the vote for the illiterate, for the electoral eligibility of all Brazilians, for the purity of democratic life, for economic emancipation, for social justice, and for the progress of Brazil.

Translated by Lanna Leite, Molly Quinn, and Erika Manoselis

March of the Family with God for Freedom

Anonymous

Among the different groups that opposed the Goulart government were right-wing women's organizations. Along with conservative segments of the Catholic Church and anticommunist groups throughout the country, they helped organize anti-Goulart demonstrations that relied heavily on Catholic symbolism. By kneeling to pray and prominently displaying rosary beads during their demonstrations, participants symbolized the movement's defense of the supposedly traditional family and the Catholic faith. The following announcement of a series of upcoming demonstrations called the March of the Family with God for Freedom appeared as an article in the newspaper O Globo, which offered overt support to efforts to depose Goulart.

In the March of the Family the people of Rio will express their rejection of Communism.

The entities who promote the March of the Family with God for Freedom will pass out flyers stating that the movement is of a civil-religious character, destined to reaffirm the sentiments of the Brazilian people, their loyalty to democratic ideals, and their purpose of lending prestige to the regime, the Constitution, and Congress. They will protest foremost their repudiation of atheist and antinational Communism.

They ask participants in the march to sing only patriotic songs or religious hymns during the parade, avoiding any allusions to partisan individuals, groups, or societies.

So that the march may occur with a propriety compatible with a demonstration that celebrates, above all, God, Brazil, and democracy, [there should be] no signs, banners, or flyers promoting individuals or political candidates. The burning of any sort of fire is prohibited.

The movement is composed of the Association of Brazilian Ladies, the Networks of Democratic Institutions, the Social Institute, the Democratic Youth Front, the Patriotic Flank, and the Liberty Club, as well as other organizations of students, workers, and intellectuals promoting unity, awaiting the approval of their directorates. These include the following: Cross of the Rosary and Family, Women's Campaign for Democracy, Freedom of National Defense, Circles of Catholic Employees, Association of Heads of

Families, Brazilian Federation for Female Progress, Group Dedicated to the Rosary, Optimists Club, São Paulo Civic Union, Alumni Association of the Sacred Heart of Jesus, Movement of Brazilian Democratic Reaffirmation, Ex-Combatants' Groups of the FEB [Brazilian Expeditionary Forces in World War II], Federation of Assistance to Lazarus and in Defense of Lepers, Catholic Confederation of the Archdiocese of Rio de Janeiro, and others.

The program of the March of the Family with God for Freedom: April 4, Rio Claro, São José do Rio Preto; April 5, Passos, in Minas Gerais, and Presidente Prudente, in São Paulo; April 11, Taubaté, Periguí, and Botucatu; April 12, Guarantinguetá and Lorena; and April 15, Brasília.

March 28, 1964

Translated by Emma Wohl

The U.S. Government and

the 1964 Coup d'État

Various authors

As early as mid-1962, U.S. President John F. Kennedy and key figures in his adminis-tration discussed how they might best support and encourage members of the Brazil-ian military contemplating the removal of Goulart. A key figure in this effort was Lincoln Gordon, a Harvard-educated economist who served as the U.S. ambassador to Brazil during both the Kennedy and Johnson administrations. His attitudes toward Goulart reflected the Cold War climate that animated much of U.S. policy toward Brazil: he repeatedly asserted that the Brazilian Communist Party had great influ-ence in the Goulart government, whose social and agrarian reform could easily lead to a Cuban-style social revolution. As plotting within Brazil by both the military and their civilian allies developed, Gordon and his military attaché, Col. Vernon Walters, acted as intermediaries between the Brazilian generals planning the overthrow and the White House, Pentagon, and CIA who supported them. They organized efforts such as supporting anti-Goulart candidates in the 1962 gubernatorial elections, sus-pending economic aid to the federal government and channeling money to opposition political groups, among other activities.

In this series of excerpts from three cables transmitted between the embassy in Rio de Janeiro and the State Department in Washington, DC, on the eve of the coup d'état, Gordon explains why he supported the removal of Goulart. He also calls for shipments of arms and fuel supplies to help the Brazilian plotters and arranges with Washington for the dispatch of a naval detachment to side with the military in the advent of a civil war—a covert plan that would be given the code name Operation Brother Sam. The fourth excerpt comes from a White House audiotape of the conver-sation that took place between President Johnson and Undersecretary of State George Ball once the coup was underway.

Absent any significant resistance to the coup d'état, the White House halted the deployment of the naval contingency. The Johnson administration also immediately recognized the interim government of Ranieri Mazzilli, the speaker of the house, who had hastily assumed the office at 3 a.m. on April 2. This came just moments after Goulart left Brasília for Rio Grande do Sul, where he had hoped to gather his forces. Instead, the president of the senate declared the presidency vacant and Mazzilli stepped in. Less than two weeks later, a weakened Congress elected the military's choice for the presidency and one of the conspirators admired by Gordon: General Humberto Castelo Branco.

Top Secret Cable to the State Department from Ambassador Lincoln Gordon, Rio de Janeiro, March 27, 1964

. . . My considered conclusion is that Goulart is now definitely engaged on campaign to seize dictatorial power, accepting the active collaboration of the Brazilian Communist Party, and of other radical left revolutionaries to this end. If he were to succeed it is more than likely that Brazil would come under full Communist control, even though Goulart might hope to turn against his Communist supporters on the personalist model which I believe he personally prefers. . . . By all odds the most significant development is the crystallizing of a military resistance group under the leadership of Gen. Humberto Castelo Branco, Army Chief of Staff. Castelo Branco is a highly competent, discreet, honest, and deeply respected officer who has strong loyalty to legal and constitutional principles and until recently shunned any approaches from anti-Goulart conspirators. . . . Unlike the many previous anti-Goulart coup groups who have approached us during the past two-and-one-half years, the Castelo Branco movement shows prospects of wide support and competent leadership. If our influence is to be brought to bear to help avert a major disaster here—which might make Brazil the China of the 1960s—this is where both I and my senior advisors believe our support should be placed. Despite their strength in the officer corps, the resistance group is concerned about the adequacy of arms and the possible sabotage of POL [petroleum, oil, and lubricants] supplies. Within the coming week, we will be appraised of their estimates of needed arms. . . . POL needs would include . . . Navy fuel . . . together with motor fuel and aviation gasoline. Given the absolute uncertainty of timing of a possible trigger incident (which could occur tomorrow or any other day) we recommend (A) that measures be taken soonest to prepare for a clandestine delivery of arms of non-US origin, to be made available to Castelo Branco supporters in São Paulo as soon as requirements known and arrangements can be worked out. Best delivery means now apparent to us is unmarked submarine to be off-loaded at night in isolated shore spots in state of São Paulo south of Santos, probably near Iguape or Gananeia. (B) This should be accompanied by POL availabilities (bulk, packaged or both may be required), also avoiding USG [U.S. government] identification, with deliveries to await outbreak active hostilities. . . . The above two actions might suffice to secure victory for friendly forces without any overt US logistical or military participation, especially if politically covered by prompt US recognition our side as legitimate GOB [government of Brazil]. We should, however, also prepare without delay against the contingency of needed overt intervention at a second stage and also against the possibility of Soviet action to support the Communist-leaning side. . . . One possibility appears to be the detachment of a Naval task force for maneuvers in South Atlantic, bringing them within a few days' steaming distance of Santos. . . . Carrier aircraft would be most important for psychological effect.

Top Secret Cable to the State Department from Ambassador Lincoln Gordon,
March 29, 1964

Re[garding] para[graph] 3 of Saturday's [March 28] message ["To what purposes would armaments offloaded from submarine be put? How critical would small shipment this kind be to success of main military thrust? Questions also arise here about feasibility furnishing unmarked or non-US origin arms without these later being attributed to US covert operation."] purpose of unidentified arms made available soonest and if possible pre-positioned prior any outbreak of violence could be manifest, depending on unforeseeable development of events. Could be used by Para-military units working with the Democratic Military groups, or by friendly military against hostile military if necessary. Immediate effect, which we stress, would be bolster will to resist and facilitate initial success. Given Brazilian predilection joining victorious causes, initial success could be key to side on which many indecisive forces would land and therefore key to prompt victory with minimal violence. Risk of later attribution to US Government covert operation seems minor to us in relation positive effects if operation conducted with skill, bearing in mind that many things we don't do are being regularly so attributed. . . . In civil war type situation our ability to show force promptly in response appeal from politically recognized democratic side might be crucial determining factor early victory that side. I well understand how grave a decision is implied in this contingency commitment to overt military intervention here. But we must also weigh seriously the possible alternative, which I am not predicting but can envisage a real danger of defeat of democratic resistance and communization of Brazil. . . . What is needed now is a sufficiently clear indication of United States government concern to reassure the large number of democrats in Brazil that we are not indifferent to the danger of a Communist revolution here, but couched in terms that cannot be openly rejected by Goulart as undue intervention. . . .

Secret Cable to Ambassador Lincoln Gordon from the State Department,
March 31, 1964

For your personal information only, the following decisions have been taken in order be in a position to render assistance at appropriate time to anti-Goulart forces if it is decided this should be done. (1) Dispatch of U.S. Navy tankers bearing POL from Aruba, first tanker expected off Santos between April 8 and 13; following three tankers at one day intervals; (2) Immediate dispatch of naval task force for overt exercises off Brazil. Force to consist of aircraft carrier (expected arrive in area by April 10), four destroyers, two destroyer escorts, task force tankers (all expected arrive about four days later); (3) assemble shipment of about 110 tons ammunition, other light equipment including tear gas for mob control for air lift to São Paulo (Campinas). Lift would be made within 24 to 26 hours upon issuance final orders and would involve 10 cargo planes, 6 tankers, and 6 fighters. Unloading of POL by U.S. Navy tankers (item 1) and dispatch of airlift (item 3) would require further development politico-military situation to point where some group having reasonable claim to legitimacy could formally request recognition and aid from us and if possible from other American Republics. Dispatch of tankers from Aruba and of naval task force does not immediately involve us in Brazilian situation and is regarded by us as normal naval exercise.

*White House Audiotape, President Lyndon B. Johnson Discussing
the Impending Coup in Brazil with Undersecretary of State George Ball,
March 31, 1964*

BALL: We decided on the basis of the information that has come in this morning to go ahead and start a naval task force out, but with no commitment, so that it will be steaming down in that direction [toward Brazil]. It couldn't get into the area before April 10th but in the meantime we can watch the developments and see whether it should go on or not. It can be done in a way that doesn't create any kind of public stir. . . . We have instructed Gordon not to take any more contact with the civilians till we see how the situation develops as there has to be some more movement in São Paulo to make sure that this thing is going to move. We don't want to get ourselves committed before we know how the thing is going to come out. He feels that on the basis of the momentum that has been started so far, it can wait for twelve hours before anything has to be—or overnight— before we have to take any decision on what we should or shouldn't do. I think that we can see the developments and then make a judgment. . . .

JOHNSON: I think that we ought to take every step that we can, be prepared to do everything that we need to do, just as we were in Panama, if that is at all feasible. . . . I'd put anybody who had any imagination or ingenuity in Gordon's outfit. . . . We just can't take this one, and I'd get right on top of it and stick my neck out a little.

Portraits: Oscar Niemeyer

Victoria Langland

When Oscar Ribeiro de Almeida Niemeyer Soares Filho died in December 2012 just a few days short of his 105th birthday, he left behind a vast architectural legacy in Brazil and the world. Among the roughly six hundred projects he completed in his long lifetime, some of the most well-known are the headquarters of the United Nations in New York (with Le Corbusier, 1947); the Museum of Modern Art of Caracas (1955); over twenty buildings in Brasília, such as the National Congress, the Supreme Court, and the Cathedral of Brasília (1956–2012); the French Communist Party Headquarters in Paris (1965); and the Museum of Contemporary Art in Niterói (1991–96), just to name a few.

During his long, productive life he received numerous honors and awards, including the Lenin Peace Prize (1963), the prestigious Pritzker Architecture Prize (1988), the Prince of Asturias Award for Art (1989), and the Royal Gold Medal of the Royal Institute of British Architects (1998). As this formidable list of accomplishments and accolades suggests, Niemeyer helped define modern architecture in the twentieth century. A critic of orthodox modernist aesthetics, he pushed the limits of engineering to build curvaceous, airy, and playful structures and infused modernism with unmistakably Brazilian elements. In the process, he inspired generations of architects around the world through his love for aesthetic form and through his insistence that we question the relationship between architectural structures and the people and societies who inhabit them.

Born in Rio de Janeiro in 1907, Niemeyer received his early architectural training in the city's Escola Nacional de Belas Artes. He then gained important experience working as a draftsman for the firm headed by Lúcio Costa, an architect known for his efforts to infuse modern perspectives and techniques with historic Brazilian styles. The position was fortuitous for Niemeyer, as he became an important collaborator in the design of a new building for the Ministry of Education and Health in Rio de Janeiro in 1936, joining Costa's team, which included the landscape designer Roberto Burle Marx, the painter Cândido Portinari, and the French architect Le Corbusier (brought in as an advisor), as well as other up-and-coming Brazilian archi-

Oscar Niemeyer (1907–2012). Courtesy of Acervo Iconografia.

tects. Together the team made the first modernist skyscraper in the world, a building that seemed suspended in the air, perched on thin concrete pillars. It also accommodated Rio's tropical climate, as the use of plate glass and extensive, sculpted brise-soleil allowed occupants to adapt the façade to different sun and wind conditions. These modernist elements dovetailed with an enormous, cubist-style mural in the foyer created by Portinari out of traditional Portuguese blue tiles, and with the lush, tropical sculpture garden built by Burle Marx. The building, now officially called the Gustavo Capanema building, became an international architectural sensation and helped to launch Niemeyer's career, attention that only increased when Niemeyer and Costa again collaborated on the Brazilian pavilion of the New York World's Fair in 1939.

In 1940 the mayor of Belo Horizonte, Juscelino Kubitschek, hoped to use Niemeyer's talent and growing renown to encourage development in Pampulha, an area north of the city dominated by an artificial lake. Kubitschek commissioned Niemeyer to create a series of buildings—a casino, church, dance hall, and yacht club—that might inspire middle-class families to build homes in the area. The project allowed Niemeyer to experiment with what would later become his trademark curving lines, as he designed voluptuous, rounded buildings, using reinforced concrete to construct canopy roofs and bending catwalk ramps and paths. As he later wrote in his memoirs, "My architectural oeuvre began with Pampulha, which I designed in sensual and unexpected curves. This was the beginning of the plastic freedom that reinforced concrete unleashed."[1] Indeed, the sensuality of the curvilinear vaults of the São Francisco Church, along with the tiled mural of Portinari on the outside wall, so surprised and scandalized Catholic officials that they refused to consecrate the chapel for fourteen years. Throughout Pampulha, Niemeyer linked his designs to their proposed functions. For example, the dance hall is shaped by undulating, rhythmic waves that follow the contours of the lakeshore, while the yacht club balcony juts out over the water like a pier. He completed construction in 1943, the same year in which he and others were featured in an architectural exhibit at the New York Museum of Modern Art called *Brazil Builds*, a reflection of the international acclaim he was already earning and of the Good Neighbor cultural politics of the war era.

Niemeyer's rise to prominence coincided with a boom in civil construction in Brazil, and he received numerous commissions in the 1940s and '50s, from residential buildings to commercial structures, from schools to the various buildings within Ibirapuera Park in São Paulo, where he designed museums, a gymnasium, and several large pavilions. He also built a home for himself in São Conrado, Rio de Janeiro, that, according to the magazine *Architectural Review*, was the "centre of discussion" for foreign visitors to the 1953 São Paulo Art Biennale.[2] And he took the unusual step of founding an art and architecture magazine, *Módulo*, in 1955, which became a critical forum for the circulation of his and other Brazilian designers' work. It was here that one could find his own textual explanations of his developing ideas about the relationship between form and function, and about the need for a dialogue between buildings and open spaces.

As Niemeyer's career was booming, President Kubitschek announced in 1956 that the federal government would build a new capital called Brasília, to be inaugurated in 1960. After numerous architects and designers submitted bids for the project, Lúcio Costa won the position as Brasília's urban planner; Oscar Niemeyer became the chief architect; and Robert Burle Marx became the city's landscape designer.

The choice of this modernist team reflected Kubitschek's futuristic and utopian vision for the new capital, which was to herald a new beginning for the nation. Indeed, some have argued that Costa's master plan for the city embodied modernism's goal of social transformation, in which creating new spaces and patterns of social interactions in daily life could effect social change. Brasília's residential district, for example, was designed to house all government employees in the same apartment buildings and residential areas, from high-ranking officials to janitors, preventing class segregation and reducing the role of housing as a marker of status. Yet while Niemeyer was a longtime member of the Communist Party, he openly disavowed the idea of social architecture, arguing that real solutions lay beyond the architect's grasp. Instead, he proclaimed, "I am in favor of an almost unlimited plastic freedom, a freedom that is not slavishly subordinate to the reasons of any

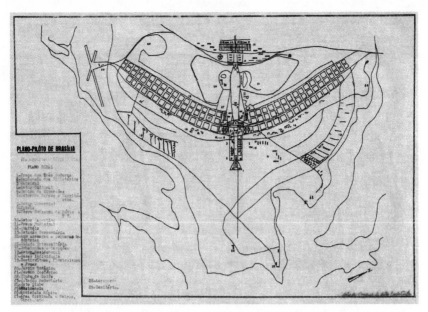

Lúcio Costa's plan for Brasília. Credit: Fundação Getúlio Vargas, CPDOC.

given technique or functionalism, but which makes an appeal to the imagination, to things that are new and beautiful, capable of arousing surprise and emotion by their very newness and creativeness: a freedom that provides scope, when desirable, for moods of ecstasy, reverie and poetry."[3] Thus for Niemeyer, the construction of Brasília allowed him considerable creative license to pursue this love for form. He designed numerous monumental buildings—public institutional structures that were also symbolic and sculptural objects, such as the National Congress, the Federal Supreme Court, and the Palácio da Alvorada (Dawn Palace) presidential residence.

Shortly after Niemeyer completed work on Brasília, the civil-military coup of 1964 and resulting military dictatorship meant that mostly anticommunist military officials occupied many of the buildings he had made there. Because of Niemeyer's Communist Party ties, he was repeatedly held for questioning by state security forces; the offices of *Módulo* were ransacked, and he soon found it impossible to secure work inside the country. Thus in 1966 he moved to France, where he reestablished his career in exile, designing buildings in Europe and Africa, such as the headquarters of the French Communist Party (begun in 1966; finished in 1980), the University of Constantine in Algeria (1965–78), and the Mondadori publishing house in Italy (1975).

When Niemeyer returned to Brazil in the 1980s as the military dictatorship was ending, he received numerous commissions, building the Sambódromo in Rio de Janeiro, where samba schools compete each Carnival season, and a monument called the Latin America Memorial, among other works. By

The Dawn Palace, Brasília's new presidential residency. Credit: Fundação Getúlio Vargas, CPDOC.

this time, his works came to embody a more deliberate call to democracy, wherein they emphasized the public within public buildings. At the Contemporary Art Museum of Niterói, for example, built between 1991 and 1996, the enormous ramp that leads into the majestic structure showcases the entering and exiting public visitors. A similarly grandiose ramp marks the museum he built in Curitiba in 2002, originally named the Novo Museu but now called the Oscar Niemeyer Museum.

By the time Niemeyer completed this museum in Curitiba, he was in his midnineties but showing few signs of slowing down, completing numerous projects in Brazil and abroad. In 2004 he lost his wife, Annita Baldo, to whom he had been married since 1928, but he married again in 2006, this time to fellow architect Vera Lúcia Cabreira. When Niemeyer turned one hundred in 2007, he began work on a cultural center in Asturias, Spain, that included four buildings and a large outdoor space. He finished the project in 2011 and participated in its inauguration via video. He also began and finished several projects in Brazil in his final years. A few years before he died, he spoke to a journalist about his legacy. "When people ask me if I take pleasure in the idea of someone looking at my buildings in the future, I tell them that this person will vanish, too. Everything has a beginning and an end. You. Me. Architecture. We must try to do the best we can, but must remain modest. Nothing lasts for very long."[4]

Notes

1. Oscar Niemeyer, *The Curves of Time: The Memoirs of Oscar Niemeyer* (London: Phaidon, 2000).

2. "Report on Brazil," *Architectural Review*, 116, no. 694 (October 1954): 235.

3. Oscar Niemeyer, "Form and Function in Architecture," in *Architecture Culture, 1943–1968: A Documentary Anthology*, edited by Joan Ockman and Edward Eigen (New York: Columbia Books of Architecture/Rizzoli International Publications, 1993), 309–13.

4. Jonathan Glancy, "I Pick Up My Pen. A Building Appears" (Interview with Oscar Niemeyer), *Guardian*, August 1, 2007.

X

The Generals in Power and the Fight
for Democracy, 1964–1985

The generals and their civilian allies who supported the military's seizure of power on April 1, 1964, offered several justifications for deposing President Goulart in their so-called revolution. They claimed that high inflation, labor unrest, and reckless fiscal policies were leading the country to an economic collapse. They insisted that the Goulart administration, as well as that of former president Kubitschek, had been corrupt and that the personal finances of former governmental figures needed to be investigated. Finally, they argued that President Goulart had come under the influence of the Brazilian Communist Party and was planning to carry out a power grab that would end in a political crisis, the seizure of the government by more radical forces, and a Cuban-style socialist revolution. The U.S. ambassador, Lincoln Gordon, who kept in close contact with the military conspirators through Col. Vernon Walters, the U.S. military attaché stationed in Brazil, agreed with this third justification. Gordon used similar arguments when advocating in favor of the coup d'état to the White House and State Department officials.

Initially, a governing junta consisting of three officials from the army, the navy, and the air force assumed power, justifying their actions through an extralegal government decree they called an institutional act. Among other measures, this act suspended the Constitution, abolished earlier prohibitions against active-duty military officers holding elected office, and ordered Congress to elect a new president within forty-eight hours through an open roll-call vote. With Congress now purged, that body duly chose Army Field Marshal Humberto de Alencar Castelo Branco, the highest-ranking military officer among the coup's conspirators, who became the new president of Brazil. He promised to clean house by wiping out government corruption and fixing the economy. The U.S. government immediately recognized the regime and offered Castelo Branco unconditional support, unblocking international aid and foreign loans that had been halted during Goulart's last two years in office. Castelo Branco promised to quickly turn the reins of power

Government troops outside the Ministry of War on April 1, 1964. Courtesy of the
Brazilian National Archive, Acervo/Fundo: *Correio de Manhã*.

over to civilians; instead the military dictatorship lasted twenty-one years
under five different military presidents.

To consolidate their hold, during the first months after the coup d'état,
the armed forces detained, arrested, and brutally interrogated an estimated
ten thousand people. In some cases, especially in the Northeast, prisoners
were tortured severely. Particularly targeted were members and supporters
of the Communist Party and other socialist and revolutionary organizations,
as well as radical trade unionists, members of the Brazilian Labor Party, peasant leaders, rank-and-file soldiers and sailors, student activists, left-wing intellectuals, and politicians, including elected officials.

The military government also initiated extensive military-police investigations of thousands of people and organizations to determine if they had
been involved in subversive activities. Tens of thousands lost their jobs and
were blacklisted. Although various groups such as students, sectors of the
military, and rank-and-file members of left-wing political parties sought to
oppose the coup d'état, neither the leadership of the Brazilian Labor Party
nor that of the Brazilian Communist Party organized any systematic resistance. This fact would later discredit them in the eyes of many people who
actively fought against the dictatorship. As a whole, the left retreated to survive and regroup.

Perhaps the easiest way to understand the complexities of the Brazilian dictatorship is by dividing the twenty-one years of military rule into three periods. From 1964 to 1968, the governments of Castelo Branco (1964–67) and his successor General Artur da Costa e Silva (1967–69) attempted to stabilize and reorganize the economy, while proclaiming their commitment to democracy. Indeed, throughout the planning and execution of the 1964 military takeover, Castelo Branco and his key coconspirators had been particularly concerned about the need to maintain political legitimacy at home and abroad. Thus, they insisted that their plan was to quickly restore the democracy that they claimed had been so threatened by Goulart. Rather than merely ruling by decree, the generals in power and their civilian allies attempted to maintain the appearances of normalcy and legality while eliminating the opposition.

As a result, in their first years in power they kept Congress open, generally maintained direct legislative elections, and permitted some forms of public protest. But they also imposed strict restrictions on the democratic process and resorted to issuing institutional acts when necessary. For example, an electoral upset in the October 1965 gubernatorial elections in Rio de Janeiro and Minas Gerais, where the opposition candidates defeated those supported by the military, led the government to issue the second institutional act. This measure and subsequent decrees dissolved existing political parties, made permanent the indirect election of the president through a congressional Electoral College, and mandated the indirect, open-ballot election of governors by the state legislatures, among other things. Another decree declared the country's major cities to be security zones and authorized the president to appoint their mayors.

To ensure a majority in Congress, the government set up an official party, the Alliance for National Renovation (ARENA), and an official opposition party, the Brazilian Democratic Movement (MDB). Meanwhile, the military retained the power to take away a citizen's political rights for ten years, an especially effective tool for influencing the state legislatures and, through them, the state governors. And in 1967 they issued a new constitution that granted the president extensive new powers. At the same time, the government attempted to hold down inflation with a series of austerity measures and wage freezes, while encouraging foreign investment in the country. With labor actions significantly restricted, Brazil offered a friendly business environment for transnational corporations.

By 1966, student and left-wing opposition to the regime had reorganized and begun to gain momentum. Protests grew in size and number the following year, despite (and even because of) the fact that student leaders were often persecuted, and the National Student Union was operating underground. Simultaneously, new cultural expressions, many antiauthoritarian in content, took hold among students and youth, many of whom embraced a culture of dissent. Some were attracted to radical Marxist ideas and looked favorably

March of 100,000 in Rio de Janeiro against the military regime in June 1968. Credit: Fundação Getúlio Vargas, CPDOC.

Funeral procession with the coffin of Edson Luis de Lima Souto, who was killed by the police in a downtown Rio demonstration protesting the quality of food at a student cafeteria. His death sparked massive protests against the dictatorship throughout the country. Courtesy of the Acervo *Última Hora*, Arquivo Público do Estado de São Paulo.

on the Cuban and Chinese revolutions as examples to be imitated in Brazil. Small clusters of students, intellectuals, workers, and rank-and-file members of the armed forces, who had been purged in 1964 for their pro-Goulart sentiment, joined underground organizations that advocated rural or urban guerrilla warfare in order to overthrow the regime and implement socialism or a radical democratic government in Brazil.

By the end of 1968, a wave of student mobilizations, wildcat strikes, and a sometimes defiant national Congress contributed to widening discontent with the regime and led the generals to issue their fifth institutional act. This act temporarily closed Congress and removed some remaining guarantees of civil rights, such as freedom of expression and due process, effectively authorizing unrestrained repression against the opposition in defiance of international public opinion. Even the Nixon administration, which supported the dictatorship, felt obliged to review U.S. aid to Brazil for a brief time, although military and economic support resumed several months later.

In the ensuing second period, under the presidency of General Emílio Garrastazu Médici (1969–74), the government systematically attacked and dismantled its opposition through heavy repression, censorship, and state-led propaganda. Using nationalistic themes, regime propaganda linked the country's economic growth directly to the government's policies, and it cast regime critics as traitors. It also relied on what historian Carlos Fico has called "non-political propaganda," presenting a view of a harmonious and prosperous Brazil with boundless optimism for its future.[1]

News of the systematic torture of political prisoners nonetheless began to circulate worldwide and led to a series of international campaigns to halt this abuse. While increasing numbers of the regime's opponents languished in jails, the huge influx of foreign capital helped grow the economy at a staggering rate of 11 percent a year. Large sectors of the middle classes that had previously grumbled about ongoing, albeit declining, inflation now basked in the new prosperity and the ability to buy more consumer goods. The Médici government's successful use of nationalistic appeals was reflected in stunning electoral victories in congressional and state legislatures. Critics, however, pointed out that the rapid economic growth, referred to by the government as the Economic Miracle, skewed income distribution in favor of the middle and upper classes, while wages remained stagnant or declined among most of the population.

By 1974, sectors of the armed forces had come to the conclusion that they could not remain in power indefinitely. They began to consider strategies for withdrawing from government without undermining their long-term economic and political goals. They also sought to prevent being held responsible for the human rights violations committed under their watch. This gave rise to the third period of military rule, from 1974 to 1985, which was marked by the inauguration of Ernesto Geisel (1974–79), the fourth general-president,

AME-O OU DEIXE-O

The bumper sticker "Brazil: Love it or leave it" was borrowed from the slogan used against antiwar activists in the United States in the late 1960s, but in Brazil it became a strongly nationalistic statement against revolutionary and other stances oppositional to the military regime.

"Nobody can stop this country" was another government slogan promoting patriotism and pride in national development. Images courtesy of Thomas Holloway.

who promised a slow, gradual, and secure transition to democracy. The decision did not signify the end of state-led repression, as 1974 witnessed the largest number of disappearances in one year, many of them revolutionary militants assassinated and disappeared in the interior region of Araguaia in the Amazonian state of Pará, and 1975 saw dozens of members of the pro-Maoist Communist Party of Brazil (PC do B) imprisoned and tortured. Nonetheless, a complex dialectic emerged between controlled liberalization from above and pressure from below to expand and speed up the democratization process. It continued under the presidency of João Figueiredo, who took power in 1979 and left office in 1985, succeeded by a civilian president.

In this final phase, as the international oil crisis of the mid-1970s sent oil prices soaring, Brazil had to borrow considerable sums from foreign banks to import needed petroleum, which caused a huge increase in inflation. In this context, the opposition MDB made momentous gains in the 1974 congressional elections, especially in urban areas and in the south-central and southern regions of the country. Emboldened, the opposition seized on each and every modest gesture of liberalization by the government to push for more political openings. Intellectuals began publishing oppositional tabloids, and news of deaths by torture and of cover-ups led to public protests in 1975 and 1976. Stu-

Opposition figures PMDB president Ulisis Guimarães (*left*), labor leader and future president Luiz Inácio Lula da Silva (*center*), and future president Tancredo Neves (*right*). Credit: Fundação Getúlio Vargas, CPDOC.

dents too returned to the streets en masse from 1977 on, demanding an end to the dictatorship and a return of their right to organize through the National Student Union, which had been suppressed soon after the military came to power in 1964. Furthermore, in the late 1970s a series of strikes by autoworkers in São Paulo, the industrial heart of Brazil, shook the foundations of the regime. Hundreds of thousands of workers defied strike prohibitions and government wage policies, reflecting the growing sense of unity and possibility among some sectors of the working class. Luiz Inácio "Lula" da Silva, the president of one of the metalworkers' unions in the industrial belt around São Paulo, assumed leadership of the strike wave that continued into 1980 and reestablished the importance of the labor movement in national politics.

Faced with a growing and increasingly united opposition that again made significant headway over the military's candidates in the 1978 congressional elections, the dictatorship adopted a divide-and-conquer approach to staying in power. It supported popular calls for an amnesty law that released most political prisoners from jail and allowed thousands of exiles to return to Brazil, including many seasoned politicians who would participate in the renewed political process. But it also included a last-minute provision of reciprocal amnesty, protecting from prosecution officials responsible for the torturing and killing of political opponents and for other human rights violations. Another law abolished the two political parties and allowed new ones to be formed and the multiparty system to resume. The reconstituted Party of the Brazilian Democratic Movement (PMDB) gathered significant support, while many members of the left also reorganized in the Workers' Party (Partido dos Trabalhadores, PT), headed by Lula. Right-wing paramilitary groups responded to this liberalization with acts of violence, including attacks on newspaper kiosks known to sell left-leaning publications, letter bombs to prominent politicians and journalists, and a failed attempt to bomb a Workers' Day celebration in Rio de Janeiro in 1981.

In 1982, in the first direct elections for governor since 1965, the new opposition parties trounced the progovernment party and also picked up a majority in Congress. Because of these democratic gains, enormous demonstrations were organized throughout the country in support of a national campaign for the return of direct presidential elections. Although the congressional vote for this measure failed by a narrow margin, the message was clear. Brazilians in small towns and large urban centers demanded a return to democratic rule.

Demoralized, sectors of the military sought to transfer power to a politician sympathetic to their interests. To their dismay, an internal dispute in the conservative promilitary party provoked a split. José Sarney, a senator from the state of Maranhão who had defended the dictatorship since 1964 and served as president of the progovernment ARENA party as well as of its successor, the rightward-leaning Democratic Social Party (PDS), shifted his allegiances. Instead of backing the PDS candidate, Paulo Maluf, he threw his support to Tancredo Neves, the presidential candidate of the opposition PMDB, and even ran as vice president for the opposition alliance. In so doing he brought with him important electoral votes. Neves, for his part, had been prime minister for eleven months under Goulart during the parliamentary system interlude. He was elected a senator from Minas Gerais in 1978 and then governor of the state in 1982. With Sarney as his vice-presidential candidate, Neves received enough votes in the congressional Electoral College to be indirectly elected president in 1984, and thus to bring the period of direct military rule to an end.

Note

1. Carlos Fico, *Reinventando o otimismo: Ditadura, propaganda e imaginário social no Brasil* (Rio de Janeiro: Fundação Getulio Vargas, 1997).

Institutional Act No. 1

Francisco dos Santos Nascimento

On April 9, 1964, the three-member military junta that temporarily took power following the coup against President Goulart issued an institutional act reaffirming the power of the 1946 Constitution while simultaneously granting the military government extensive extraconstitutional powers. These powers included, among other provisions, the authority to suspend politicians' mandates, to take away any citizen's political rights for ten years, and to rescind the tenure of military officials and government employees. In the following days, the junta released lists of those to whom it was applying these measures, including some of the most prominent names of the political left and center, such as the deposed president João Goulart and several of his diplomats and ministers, former president Jânio Quadros, numerous governors and members of Congress, and trade union and peasant leaders, as well as military officers seen as unsupportive of the decision to undertake a coup. The act was the first of what would eventually be seventeen such institutional acts and innumerable complementary acts.

The following selection from the first institutional act begins with its preamble, where readers can note the ways in which the authors drew on the rhetoric of revolution as they sought to legitimize the military seizure of power.

The Nation

It is indispensable that we define the meaning of the civil and military movement in Brazil that just opened a new perspective on the future. What happened and will continue to happen at this moment, not only in the spirit and behavior of the armed forces but also in national public opinion, is an authentic revolution.

The revolution distinguishes itself from other armed movements by the fact that it does not just express the interest and will of one group, but the interest and will of the Nation.

The victorious revolution takes possession of the exercise of Constituent Power. This [Constituent Power] manifests itself through popular election or through revolution. This is the most expressive and most radical form of Constituent Power. As such, the victorious revolution, as a Constituent Power, legitimizes itself. It dismisses the previous government and has the ability to construct the new government. It contains within itself normative force, inherent within Constituent Power. It establishes legal norms without being limited to those norms that precede its victory. The Leaders of the victorious revolution, thanks to the action of the Armed Forces and to the unequivocal support of the Nation, represent the People and in their name exercise Constituent Power, of which the People are the sole owner. The Institutional Act that today is enacted by the Commanders in Chief of the Army, Navy, and Air Force, in the name of the revolution that became victorious with the support of the Nation almost in its entirety, aims to provide to the new government that is to be instituted the indispensable tools for the economic, financial, political, and moral reconstruction of Brazil, such that it can face, in an immediate and direct manner, the grave and urgent problems on which the restoration of our nation's internal order and international prestige depend. The victorious revolution needs to be institutionalized and hastens, through its institutionalization, to limit the full powers that it effectively affords.

The present Institutional Act can only be changed by the victorious revolution, represented by the Commanders in Chief of the three wings [of the armed forces] that are currently responsible for the fulfillment of revolutionary objectives, and who are determined to prevent any impediment to these. Constitutional processes did not work to destroy the government, which was deliberately disposed toward Bolshevizing the country. The revolution dismissed this government, and only the revolution is able to define the norms and procedures in constituting a new government and granting it powers and juridical instruments that assure it the exercise of Power in the exclusive interest of the Nation. To demonstrate that we do not mean to radicalize the revolutionary process, we have decided to maintain the Constitution of 1946, limiting ourselves to only modifying the sections relating to the powers of the President of the Republic, so that this figure can complete the mission of restoring economic and financial order in Brazil and taking urgent measures intended to drain the Communist coffers, whose corruption had infiltrated not just the heights of government but also its lower administrative offices. To reduce even more the full powers with which the victorious revolution finds itself vested, we resolve to also maintain the National Congress, with limitations of its powers, as established in the present Institutional Act.

Let it be abundantly clear, then, that the revolution does not seek to legitimize itself through Congress. It receives its legitimacy through this Institutional Act, resulting from the exercise of Constituent Power, inherent to all revolutions.

In the name of the victorious revolution, and with the purpose of consolidating its victory, in order to secure the realization of its objectives and to guarantee the Country a government that is able to attend to the anxieties of the Brazilian people, the Supreme Command of the Revolution, represented by the Commanders in Chief of the Army, Navy, and Air Force resolves to enact the following:

Institutional Act

Article 1. The Constitution of 1946 and the state constitutions and their respective amendments are maintained, with the ongoing modifications of this Act.

Article 2. The election of the President and Vice President of the Republic, whose mandates will end January 31, 1966, will be by an absolute majority of the members of the National Congress, within two days after this Act, in a public session by roll-call vote.

§ 1. If a quorum is not obtained in the first vote, another will be held the next day, and whoever receives a simple majority will be considered elected; in the case of a tie, the voting will proceed until one of the candidates obtains this majority.

§ 2. No one will be ineligible for the election regulated in this article.

Article 3. The President of the Republic will be able to send proposals to amend the Constitution to the National Congress.

The proposals for constitutional amendments issued by the President of the Republic will be considered in a session of the National Congress, within thirty days from their receipt, in two sessions, with a maximum interval between them of ten days, and will be considered approved when they obtain, in both votes, the absolute majority of members of both Houses of Congress.

Article 4. The President of the Republic will be able to send proposed laws about any matter to the National Congress, which will be evaluated within thirty days from their reception in the Chamber of Deputies, and in the same time frame in the Federal Senate; if they are not, they will be considered approved.

The President of the Republic, judging it necessary, may ask that the consideration of a proposed law be done in thirty days by a joint session of the National Congress, in the form prescribed in this article.

Article 5. The right to initiate enactment of laws that create or increase public expenses falls exclusively on the President of the Republic; neither House of the National Congress may increase the expenses proposed by the President of the Republic.

Article 6. The President of the Republic, in any of the cases permitted in the Constitution, may decree a state of siege, or prolong one, for a maximum of thirty days; this act will be submitted to the National Congress, accompanied by a justification, within forty-eight hours.

Article 7. Constitutional and legal guarantees to tenure and stability are suspended for six months. . . .

Article 8. Inquiries and trials aimed at determining responsibility for crimes committed against the State or its property, or against the political and social order, or acts of revolutionary war, may be conducted individually or collectively.

Article 9. The election of the President and Vice President of the Republic, who will take power on January 31, 1966, will be held on October 3, 1965.

Article 10. In the interest of peace and national honor, and within the limits prescribed in the Constitution, the Commanders in Chief, who issue the current Act, may suspend political rights for a term of ten years and cancel federal, state, and municipal legislative terms of office exclusive of judicial evaluation of these acts.

Once sworn in, the President of the Republic, by indication of the National Security Council, may carry out the acts laid out in this article within sixty days.

Article 11. The present Act is in force from this date until January 31, 1966; all provisions stating the contrary are revoked.

Rio de Janeiro-GB, April 9, 1964.

Arthur da Costa e Silva, General of the Army

Francisco de Assis Correia de Mello,
Lieutenant-Brigadier [of the Air Force]

Augusto Hamman Rademaker Grunewald,
Vice Admiral [of the Navy]

Translated by Emma Wohl and Victoria Langland

A U.S. Senator Supports the New Military Government

Senator Wayne Morse

In the early morning hours of April 2, 1964, while João Goulart was in Rio Grande do Sul organizing his supporters, the National Congress in Brasília met in a stormy late-night session. Over the objections of Goulart's allies, the Senate president officially declared that the president had abandoned his office and vacated the presidency, ob-ligating Congress to follow constitutional procedure and name Ranieri Mazzilli, the speaker of the lower house, as interim president. At the insistence of Lincoln Gordon, the U.S. ambassador to Brazil, President Lyndon B. Johnson immediately recognized the new government. The following day Senator Wayne Morse, a Democrat from Oregon and a member of the Foreign Relations Committee, praised Johnson's decision on the floor of the U.S. Congress, although he remained an outspoken critic of the president's foreign policy in Vietnam. A year later, disillusioned with the fact that the Johnson administration had withheld information about the military takeover from members of Congress, and critical of the ongoing undemocratic measures carried out by the Brazilian regime, Morse began criticizing U.S. political and economic support for the Castelo Branco government.

It is worth noting that in November 2013, in a highly symbolic meeting that counted on the presence of family members of João Goulart, the Brazilian National Congress voted to annul the April 2, 1964, session as a form of symbolic reparation for its role in deposing the president.

April 3, 1964

MR. MORSE. Mr. President, here, again, President Johnson has acted with the same great care, calmness, and deliberation that have characterized his actions; and he deserves our thanks for the note he sent to the new President of Brazil.

I wish to make very clear that I can testify, on the basis of such knowledge as I have—and I think the members of the Senate Foreign Relations Committee were kept thoroughly briefed on all details of the developments in Brazil—that the United States in no way intervened or was responsible in any way for the action which occurred in Brazil. I am convinced that the developments there were completely Brazilian; and they were long in the making.

In the Senate's Foreign Relations Committee we have discussed this matter many, many times, and have expressed our concern over the developing thunderheads in the foreign-policy skies over Brazil. We have known for some time that Communists or, certainly, those who were advocating Communist policies, were infiltrating themselves into the administration of Goulart. That was of great concern to constitutionalists in Brazil.

Mr. President, the developments in Brazil did not result from action by a military junta or from a coup by a military junta. Instead, the overthrow of the presidency of Brazil resulted from a development in which the Congress of Brazil, acting under the Constitution of Brazil, was the guiding force, and was reinforced by a military group, which backed up the preservation of the Brazilian constitutional system. Under that constitutional system, Goulart could have remained in Brazil and could have stood trial, so to speak, in connection with charges which would have been placed against him, as provided for under the Brazilian constitutional system. But certainly the Congress of Brazil and the governors and the people of Brazil could not be expected to stand idly by and see their government and its forces gradually, step by step, turned over to a Communist apparatus.

The important point for us to note is that the new President of Brazil —and, under the Brazilian system, he will occupy only temporarily the office of President—is the one next in line under the Brazilian Constitution to occupy the office of the Chief Executive of Brazil. Furthermore, it is also interesting to note that this is not the first time he has occupied that office under somewhat similar circumstances. It is both interesting and, I believe, also somewhat ironic that the new President of Brazil was the temporary President of that country when Quadros resigned and found it convenient to leave Brazil, and Goulart then was next in line, under the constitution. However, there was some opposition to allowing Goulart to assume that office; and at that time Mr. Mazzilli, the new President of Brazil, insisted that the Brazilian constitutional procedures be followed. In my opinion, that is about all we need to know in regard to Mr. Mazzilli's faith and conviction in regard to the importance of the maintenance of a system of government by law, in keeping with the framework of the constitutional system that is binding upon his country.

In my opinion, President Johnson very appropriately waited until the legal and constitutional system of Brazil had worked its course. When we were notified that the new President of Brazil had taken office, then the warm message of the President of the United States was sent to the new President of Brazil.

It is a beautiful statement, as Senators will see, if they have not already read it. I commend and congratulate my President for that act of statesmanship.

The Brazilian Revolution

Caio Prado Júnior

Literary critic Antonio Candido defined Caio da Silva Prado Júnior (1907–90), along with Gilberto Freyre and Sérgio Buarque de Holanda, as one of Brazil's most important modern essayists. Whereas Freyre emphasized culture in his writing and Buarque de Holanda was influenced by the concepts of Max Weber, Prado Júnior believed in historical materialism. From a wealthy Paulista family, he graduated from the São Francisco Law School in São Paulo in 1928 and soon became a distinguished historian, geographer, writer, politician, photographer, and publisher. He also founded the Brasiliense publishing house in 1943. His writings helped establish a Marxist historiographic tradition in Brazil. His work focuses largely on the colonial period, which he placed within an international economic context.

Prado Júnior joined the Communist Party in 1931, and his first major text, The Political Evolution of Brazil *(1933), reflects this Marxist influence. A second important work,* The Colonial Background of Modern Brazil *(1942), was supposed to be the first volume in a series on Brazil's historical evolution, but he never completed the other volumes. In 1945, he was elected as a São Paulo state representative on the Communist Party ticket, but he lost his mandate in 1948 when the Communist Party was outlawed. In 1966, he published the polemical book* The Brazilian Revolution, *which argued that a socialist revolution was possible in Brazil, and received the Juca Pato Prize from the Union of Brazilian Writers as Intellectual of the Year. In 1969 the Second Military Court of São Paulo indicted him for "incitement to subversion" because of an interview he gave to a student newspaper about the prospects for revolutionary action in Brazil, and he served a year-and-a-half prison term.*

The following text from 1966 shows his Marxist analysis of the possibility of modernization through revolution at a moment when left-wing intellectuals were being persecuted by the military regime.

The term "revolution" includes an ambiguity (or truly many, but we focus here on the principal one) that has given rise to frequent confusion. In the sense in which it is normally used, "revolution" suggests the use of force and violence to overthrow a government and seize power by some group, social category, or other oppositional force. In this case, "revolution" has a meaning more consistent with the term "insurrection." "Revolution" also means a transformation of the political-social regime that can be, and as a rule historically has been, triggered or stimulated by insurrections. But revolution does not necessarily happen in this way. The basic meaning of the word implies transformation, but not the immediate process through which change is accomplished. The French Revolution, for example, was triggered and then accompanied by successive violent actions, especially in its early days. But this was certainly not what entirely constituted and what is properly understood as the "French revolution." Nor are, clearly, the storming of the Bastille, the peasant uprisings of July and August 1789, the march of the people on Versailles in October of the same year, the fall of the monarchy and the execution of Luis XVI, the Terror, and other incidents of the same kind. "Revolution" in its real and profound sense means the historical process signaled by successive economic, social, and political reforms and modifications that, concentrated in a relatively short historical period, yield structural transformations of society, especially of economic relations and of the reciprocal equilibrium of different classes and social categories. The rhythm of history is not uniform. It alternates between periods or phases of relative stability and apparent immobility and moments of activation of sociopolitical life and abrupt changes in which social relations are profoundly and rapidly altered. Or, more precisely, [it is a time] in which political, economic, and social institutions remodel themselves in order to improve and better attend to generalized needs that were not previously satisfied. It is these historical movements of rough transition from one economic, social, and political situation to another, and the transformations that go into effect therein, that constitute what is properly understood as "revolution."

It is in this sense that the term "revolution" is employed in the title of this book. Essentially, what it attempts to do is show that Brazil finds itself nowadays facing or awaiting one of those moments in which reforms and transformations go into effect rapidly and are capable of restructuring the life of the nation in a manner consistent with its greatest and most general needs and the aspirations of the great mass of its population, which, in its present state, are not being attended to. For many—but still, in the summary count, an insignificant minority, though they make themselves heard because leverage over those in power and economic, social, and political order rests in their hands—all is fundamentally well, only lacking (and here some minor divergences can be seen) some retouching and perfecting of the existing institutions, sometimes no more than a simple change of personnel in political and administrative positions, that the country may find a satisfactory situation and equilibrium. For the vast majority of the rest of the country, however— and even as it does not always perfectly perceive reality, incapable as it is of projecting generally and together, as a body, its dissatisfactions, desires, and personal aspirations—the work of creating a safe and satisfactory condition of existence is much more than this. Above all it is something deeper that lifts the life of the country toward a new course.

And the facts, adequately analyzed and profound, confirm this. Brazil finds itself in one of those decisive moments in the evolution of human societies in which the injustice of its basic institutions becomes clear, sensible, and sufficiently noted by all. In this situation tensions are vividly demonstrated in deep, general discontent and dissatisfaction, in friction and conflicts, many effective and others only potentially so, and tear at Brazilian life and weigh it down, without an appreciable expectation of a permanent, effective solution. This situation is at the same time the cause and effect of political inconsistency; inefficacy in all sectors and branches of the public administration; social inequalities; economic and financial crisis, which had been coming for a long time but was hidden for a short term—from one to two decades—due to speculative and chaotic material growth. Now the situation begins to show its true face; and the insufficiency and precariousness of the very structural bases in which the life of the country is rooted. This is what characterizes our modern Brazil. In addition, there is above all else the most complete skepticism and generalized disbelief regarding true possible solutions within the current order of things. Concretely, this leads, indiscernibly or not, to changes in the system, to an unbridled race to "save yourself if you can," to all people caring solely (and wrongly) for their immediate concerns and immediately trying to make the most out of the moment that may by chance pass within arm's reach.

Translated by Emma Wohl

The Myth of Racial Democracy

Abdias do Nascimento

Abdias do Nascimento (1914–2011) was a pioneering figure in the fight against racism in twentieth-century Brazil. An intellectual, an actor, a writer, a visual artist, and a politician, he had many talents, and he marshaled all of them in his lifetime struggle against racism.

Born in the town of Franca, in the state of São Paulo, to an Afro-Brazilian family, he began working at the age of six as a delivery boy. He studied accounting and received a BA in economics from the Federal University of Rio de Janeiro in 1938. He also quickly became a vocal critic of what were then conventional notions that Brazil was generally free of racial discrimination, participating in Brazil's first black political party, the Frente Negra Brasileira, based in São Paulo. He was imprisoned twice for his political activities in São Paulo, and at one point organized a theater group among fellow inmates. Once released, he moved to Rio de Janeiro, where in 1944 he formed and began directing the Black Experimental Theatre, a theater troupe that trained and employed black actors and that sought to use theater to promote racial consciousness. Among other productions, in 1956 the group staged Orfeu da Conceição, *a play by Vinicius de Moraes with music by Antônio Carlos Jobim, which transposed the Greek myth of Orpheus to a favela in Rio. Abdias do Nascimento performed in the piece, staged at the Municipal Theater in Rio de Janeiro with sets designed by Oscar Niemeyer. It was later adapted into the award-winning film* Black Orpheus.

Following the implementation of military dictatorship in 1964, Nascimento found it increasingly difficult to live in Brazil. Accepting a two-month humanities fellowship in the United States in 1968, he was outside of Brazil when the military dictatorship issued its repressive Institutional Act No. 5 and ended up remaining in the United States for the next thirteen years. During these years of exile, Nascimento accepted a number of visiting professorship positions, such as at the Yale School of Drama and Wesleyan College, before becoming a professor at the State University of New York at Buffalo, where he founded the chair in African Cultures. He also served as a visiting professor at the University of Ife in Nigeria from 1976 to 1977, deepening his involvement in the international Pan-African movement. At the same time he created strikingly bold and colorful paintings with Afro-Brazilian themes that were exhibited in galleries and shows.

Like many other exiles, Nascimento returned to Brazil in the early 1980s. Join-
ing Lionel Brizola's Democratic Labor Party, which was the only national political
party to embrace his ideas about the nature of racism in Brazil, he ran successfully
for Congress. As a federal congressman and as senator representing the state of Rio
de Janeiro between 1983 and 1999, Nascimento introduced numerous bills to combat
racial discrimination and promote affirmative action programs. He also served in the
Rio de Janeiro state government as secretary of state for human rights and citizenship
and as secretary of state for the defense and promotion of Afro-Brazilian populations.

Nascimento published the following statement in the left-wing journal Cadernos
Brasileiros *in 1968, on the eightieth anniversary of the abolition of slavery. It ap-*
peared shortly before his trip to the United States.

Now that eighty years have passed since the abolition of slavery in Brazil, it is
opportune to look objectively at the results of the law of May 13, 1888. Are the
descendants of African slaves really free? Where do Brazilian blacks really
stand in relation to citizens of other racial origins, at all levels of national life?

More than ten years ago, a reporter from a prominent Rio de Janeiro magazine asked various persons of color to respond to these questions. But the
interviews were never published, although the questions obviously remain
valid and hold the same significance, because since then nothing has changed
in the ways black people live in this country.

The abolitionist campaign stopped abruptly in 1888. . . . Abolition was a
façade: juridical, theoretical, abstract. The ex-slaves were driven to the brink
of starvation; they found only disease, unemployment, and complete misery. Not only the elites, but also all of Brazilian society closed the avenues
through which black people might have survived; they shut off the possibility
of a decent, dignified life for the ex-slaves. They created a fabric of slogans
about equality and racial democracy that has served to assuage the bad national conscience. Abroad, it presents our country as a model of racial coex-
istence; internally, the myth is used to keep black people tricked and docile.

There was a phase during which the condition of black people awakened
the interest of scholars, especially in the Northeast. But although sincere,
the intellectuals dealt with black culture as ethnographic material for their
literary and academic exercises . . . [when, instead], the situation of black
people cried out for urgent practical action to improve radically their horrible
existence. . . .

It is a characteristic of our racial democracy myth that it accurately defines
a "pathology of normality." . . . There is no exaggeration here. We remember
that Brazilians of dark pigmentation number nearly thirty million. Certain
apostles of "whitening" would like to see the extinction of black people as
an easy way to resolve the problem. . . . The white portion, or the less-black
population, would continue to monopolize political power, economic power,

Abdias do Nascimento (1914–2011), a pioneering activist against racial discrimination in Brazil. Photograph by Bia Parreiras. Courtesy of Acervo IPEAFRO (Instituto de Pesquisas e Estudos Afro-Brasileiros).

access to schools, and to well-being, thanks to the legacy of the wretched "Golden Law," which Antonio Callado has correctly dubbed "The Law of White Magic." Under the Law of White Magic, black people are as free as any other Brazilian. In practice—without any white or black magic—being black is simply this: [existence as] a racial pariah consigned to the status of a subaltern.

Why should black people be the only ones to pay for the onus of our "racial paradise"? I stand corrected. Indians, as well, have been treated in the same way. According to a study by the federal government itself, practices to liquidate indigenous peoples were employed in the 1960s. The study yanked the mask off the face of our vaunted Brazilian humanism, tempered with compassion and Christian spirit. . . .

It is imperative for human dignity and a civic duty for Brazilians to struggle —blacks and whites—to transform the concept of racial democracy into reality. Black people should organize to take up the promise deeded to them by history. This should be done without messianism, without hatred or resentment, but firmly and steadfastly in pursuit of the just place to which we are entitled. Black people should create pressure groups, instruments for direct action. In the process, we will encounter our qualified leaders. Only through dynamic organization will black people obtain equality of opportunity and the status of a better life . . . not only for Brazilian blacks, but also for all the Brazilian people.

Naturally, anything directed against the status quo runs risks. But black people run risks from the instant of their birth. Do not fear the label of "black racist," because the product of intimidation is docility. It is enough for us to know that our cause has integrity and follows our consciences as democrats and humanists. Our historical experience shows us that antiracist racism is the only path capable of extinguishing the differences between races.

Translated by Robert M. Levine and John J. Crocitti

A Brazilian Congressional Representative Speaks Out

Márcio Moreira Alves

In Brazil, 1968 was marked by massive student demonstrations and their frequent repression by the police and military, events that showcased and fueled growing opposition to the military government. The death of a student at the hands of the police in March inspired an enormous wave of protests across the country. In June, a series of particularly violent police acts against student demonstrations led church officials, musical celebrities, and others to join students in Rio de Janeiro in protest. In August, when police in Brasília raided the University of Brasília campus, dragging students and professors out of their classrooms and destroying laboratories and libraries, Congressman Márcio Moreira Alves of the opposition Brazilian Democratic Movement denounced the repression. Alves had long been a thorn in the military regime's side, investigating and denouncing state torture in 1964 as a journalist, then running for and winning federal office in 1966. Following the events in Brasília, he delivered the following speech in the Chamber of Deputies, vehemently criticizing the police action and proposing that women take up a sexual boycott against military men, an idea that harkened back to the Greek comedy Lysistrata.

Although the speech generated little public commentary at the time, it led to a firestorm within the military. Copies of the speech quietly circulated within military circles, and soon thereafter Congress received a formal request that Alves's parliamentary immunity be revoked so that he might be tried for offending the armed forces. Congress voted against the measure on December 12, and Institutional Act No. 5 was announced the following day. One of its many provisions was the closure of Congress.

Mr. President, Fellow Congressional Representatives: Everyone recognizes, or says they recognize, that the majority of the armed forces do not agree with the militaristic leadership that perpetuates violent acts and keeps this country in a state of oppression. Since the events in Brasília, I believe, we have reached a great moment of unity for democracy. This is also a moment for boycott. Brazilian mothers have already staged protests; all social classes shout their repudiation of this violence. However, this is not enough. What needs to be established—especially by women; the wives of ARENA

449

Students being arrested at the University of Brasília in 1968. Courtesy of
Acervo *Última Hora*, Arquivo Público do Estado de São Paulo.

congressmen are beginning to do this in this house—is a boycott of milita-
rism. September 7 [Independence Day] is coming up. The militaristic leadership is seeking to exploit the people's deep sense of patriotism and will
ask schoolchildren to parade alongside the torturers of students. Each father,
each mother, will have to understand that their child's presence in this parade helps the tyrants who beat them and machine gun them in the streets.
Therefore, may all of them boycott this parade! This boycott can also be
extended—speaking again of women—to the girls, to those who dance with
the cadets and date the young officers. It is necessary that today in Brazil
the women of 1968 imitate the warlike Paulistas of the Emboabas and deny
entrance to their homes to those who revile the nation. They must refuse to
accept those who keep silent and thereby serve as accomplices. Disagreeing
in silence accomplishes little. What is needed is to revolt against the abuses of
the armed forces by speaking and acting in the name of the abused.

I believe, Mr. President, that it is possible to resolve this farce, this dictatorship disguised as a democracy [*democratura*], this false understanding,
by a boycott. As long as those responsible remain silent, any and all contact
between civilians and military personnel ought to cease, because only in that
way will it be possible to force this country to return to democracy. Only in
that way will we be able to make the silent ones, those who do not support
their leaders' abuse of power, follow the magnificent example of the fourteen
officials of Crete, who had the courage and the manliness to publicly demonstrate against an illegal and arbitrary act by one of their superiors.

Translated by Victoria Langland

450   *Márcio Moreira Alves*

Institutional Act No. 5

Luís Antônio da Gama e Silva

The decision on December 12, 1968, by a majority of the Brazilian Congress to stand up to the military-civilian regime and refuse to strip Márcio Moreira Alves of his congressional immunity served as a convenient pretext to issue a new set of authoritarian decrees severely limiting democratic rights in Brazil. Immediately after the congressional vote, President Costa e Silva convened a meeting of the twenty-three-member National Security Council to approve a series of extreme measures, such as the executive's power to suspend Congress, the denial of habeas corpus for those suspected of political crimes, the expansion of press censorship, the power of the president to intervene in state and local government, and the extension of the power to deny citizens' political rights for ten years. This decree marked the beginning of the most repressive period of the dictatorship, described by many as a second coup d'état or a coup within the coup.

Article 1: The Constitution of January 24, 1967, and the State Constitutions, with the modifications contained in this Institutional Act, remain in force.

Article 2: The President of the Republic may decree recess of the National Congress, the State Assemblies, and the Municipal Legislatures, through a Complementary Act, with or without a state of siege being in force. These same bodies shall not reconvene until called to do so by the President of the Republic.

   1. If a parliamentary recess is decreed, the corresponding Executive Power shall be authorized to legislate on all matters and to exercise all the powers prescribed in the Constitutions or in the Municipal Laws.
   —During the period of recess, the federal and state Senators and Representatives and Aldermen shall receive only the fixed portion of their salaries.
   —In the case of a recess of a City Council, financial and budgetary control for those municipalities which do not have an Accounting Office shall be exercised by the respective state. The state shall also assume the role of auditor, monitoring the accounts of administrators and of those responsible for public assets and securities.

Article 3: The President of the Republic, in the national interest, may decree the intervention in the States and Municipalities without the limits set forth in the Constitution.

> Sole Paragraph: The President of the Republic shall name acting heads of the States and Municipalities; these shall exercise all of the functions and duties normally carried out by the governors and the mayors, and will enjoy all the prerogatives, term of office, and benefits established by law.

Article 4: In the interest of preserving the Revolution, the President of the Republic shall, upon consultation with the National Security Council and without the limitations established in the Constitution, have the power to suspend the political rights of any citizen for a period of ten years, and to revoke the term of office of elected federal, state, or municipal officials.

> Sole Paragraph: Federal, state, or municipal legislators whose terms of office have been terminated will not be replaced, and the parliamentary quorum will be adjusted based on the number of positions effectively filled.

Article 5: A suspension of political rights based on this act simultaneously includes the following:

1. cessation of the privileges of legal immunity by virtue of office;
2. suspension of the right to vote, or to be a candidate in labor union elections;
3. prohibition of political activities, and of demonstrations on political matters;
4. application of the following security measures, when necessary:
   a) supervised liberty;
   b) prohibition against visiting certain places;
   c) designation of a place of residence,
      1) The act that decrees the suspension of political rights may also establish restrictions or prohibitions related to the exercise of any other public or private rights.
      2) The Minister of Justice shall apply the security measures dealt with in item 4 of this article; such action shall not be subject to judicial review.

Article 6: Constitutional or legal guarantees concerning life tenure, fixed place of employment, or job security, as well as those concerning the exercise of duties for a fixed period, are hereby suspended.

1. The President of the Republic shall have the power, via decree, to dismiss, remove, forcibly retire, or place on leave any holder of the guar-

antees referred to in this article, as well as employees of autonomous agencies, public enterprises, or mixed-ownership enterprises. Military personnel, or members of the Military Police, shall also be subject to dismissal, transfer to the reserves, or forced retirement. The President, at his discretion, may safeguard the pension or benefits proportional to an employee's length of service.

2. The provisions in this article, and its first paragraph, also apply to the Federal District, the States, the Municipalities, and the Territories.

Article 7: The President of the Republic, in any of the cases prescribed in the Constitution, may decree or extend a state of siege, and define its duration.

Sole Paragraph: If the National Congress is recessed, the provision contained in 1, Article 153 of the Constitution, is dispensed with.

Article 8: The President, after investigation, has the power to decree the confiscation of property of all those who have illicitly enriched themselves while exercising public functions or office, including autonomous agencies, public enterprises, and mixed-ownership enterprises. Such action will not waive appropriate criminal sanctions.

Sole Paragraph: Property proven to be legitimately acquired shall be returned.

Article 9: The President of the Republic may issue Complementary Acts to execute this Institutional Act. Also, if necessary to defend the Revolution, the President shall adopt the measures prescribed in the subsections "d" and "e" of paragraph 2 of Article 152 of the Constitution.

Article 10: The guarantee of habeas corpus is hereby suspended in cases of political crimes against national security, the economic and social order, or the public economy.

Article 11: All actions initiated in accord with this Institutional Act, or its Complementary Acts, as well as their respective effects, are excluded from judicial review.

Article 12: The present Institutional Act becomes effective on this date, and all provisions to the contrary are hereby revoked.

Brasília, December 13, 1968,
147th Anniversary of Independence and
80th Anniversary of the Republic

Translated by Emma Wohl and Victoria Langland

Letter from the Ilha Grande Prison

Various authors

While the police had used torture to extract information from political prisoners during Getúlio Vargas's Estado Novo (1937–45), this practice gained new prevalence and meaning during the military dictatorship. Soon after the coup of 1964, the military regime employed extreme forms of physical and psychological violence to gather information about "subversive activities" and to intimidate the opposition. Under the cover of Institutional Act No. 5 of December 1968, the military and police tortured indiscriminately, as documented in reports that prisoners managed to smuggle to supporters and the press. These denunciations fueled an international campaign against human rights abuses in Brazil. The following statement, which was published in the U.S.-based antidictatorship publication Brazilian Information Bulletin, *was composed by political prisoners incarcerated on Ilha Grande, an island off the coast of Rio de Janeiro state. Signed by Marco Antonio da Costa Maranhão on behalf of thirty other political prisoners there, it was written surreptitiously inside a prison cell. As the introduction to the document explained, "One prisoner watched while another wrote. Every time a guard passed by, the paper had to be quickly hidden under a mattress." Marco Antonio da Costa Maranhão was later released from prison when a group of revolutionaries kidnapped the Swiss ambassador in order to negotiate his and others' release. The ambassador was freed and seventy political prisoners were flown safely to Chile. At the time the statement was published, Maranhão's thirty fellow signatories were still in jail.*

To: The International Press

To: The International Commission of Human Rights

To: The free people of the world and all institutions that
struggle for justice and freedom

Our voice rises from the entrails of the Brazilian dictatorship, hoping to tell people all over the world the true facts concerning the life of political prisoners of the Brazilian military regime.

Because we struggle to overcome the misery and exploitation that oppress the Brazilian people, because we struggle against the anti-national and anti-popular policy of the tyrants, we were thrown in jail.

We live desperate hours jailed in this island-prison, about 20 miles off the coastline. The growing process of destruction to which we are subjected in this prison clearly reflects the policy of individual annihilation by the penitentiary system of the Brazilian dictatorship. With higher or lower intensity, this is happening in prisons all over Brazil, generating despair.

We are confined in cells 10 feet long and 13 feet wide for 23 hours a day, being allowed only one hour in the open air when there is sunshine. All night long lights are kept on, causing nervous strain. More aggravating is the fact that we have to live in groups of three in each of these small cells.

Our relatives, who are allowed to pay us a visit once a month, are subjected to grievous hardships in order to see us. It is difficult for them to obtain transportation to get to the prison. They have to travel in old boats and in the back of old trucks. As if that were not enough, they are charged high prices (Cr$10.00 and Cr$20.00) for transportation. They go through all these sacrifices for a visit of only two hours. All this is done to hinder us from any contact with our relatives.

We live segregated from the world, from our relatives and our friends, feeling that alienation, along with loneliness, will lead to degradation and disfigurement of our humanity.

Alleging laws concerning censorship, our jailers forbid any access to culture. We are not allowed to work. Inactivity, coupled with isolation and constant terror, have generated psychic disturbances in many of our fellow-prisoners.

The director of this prison, Captain Sebastião Calheiros, is a professional torturer who is responsible for a continuous policy of terror with the aid and assistance of such aberrant guards as Adilson and Ezequiel. We are constantly subjected to provocation and, for little or no reason, are thrown into solitary confinement—dark, humid, unhealthy cells where we are kept for months. We find it imperative to mention the names of some of our cell-mates who have been subjected to this inhuman treatment: Sebastião Medeiros Filho, Nelson Eleuterio, Alúsio Ferreira Palmar, Sebastião Cornelio—these last three went mad.

We know that, by bringing to the public our tragic plight, we may be subjected to all kinds of violence by the Brazilian dictatorship. Nevertheless, the desperate living conditions we are submitted to at this moment give us little choice: either we passively accept the growing process of annihilation we are subjected to, or, while our strength is not yet thoroughly exhausted, we raise our voices, tear away the deceitful cloak of the Brazilian fascist regime, and bring truth to light.

This kind of life in jail is a continuation of the tortures applied to political prisoners during interrogation by the police officers of the dictatorship—CDO (Coordination for Internal Defense), CENIMAR (Navy Information Center), OBAN (Operação Bandeirante), PE (Military Police) and others. The "parrot's perch" (*pau-de-arara*), simulated drowning, electric shocks and many other methods used during interrogation are now replaced by isolation, provocation, threats of shooting and beatings.

Would it be too much to ask for us to be removed from this island? Would it be too much to ask for us to have a regular relationship with our relatives, friends and fellows? Would it be too much to ask for the Declaration of Human Rights to be enforced?

The only weapons we have against terror, against torture, are protest and denunciation. To protest, to denounce, we went on a hunger strike against terror, against torture and for humane living conditions.

We ask that an international commission visit this prison to find out the truth of the facts we are now bringing to light.

We ask the world to listen to us and to make us heard.

Ilha Grande, December 1970
(Signed) Marco Antonio da Costa Maranhão

The Kidnapping of the U.S. Ambassador

Various authors

A small minority of the student movement that had mobilized against the dictator-ship in 1968 embraced armed struggle to overthrow the regime. Inspired by the success-ful path to power of Cuban revolutionary leader Fidel Castro and his supporters in 1959, dissident youth groups and other former members and supporters of the Brazil-ian Communist Party organized guerrilla organizations in 1967 and 1968. Two such groups, the October 8 Revolutionary Movement (a reference to the date of the assas-sination of Che Guevara in Bolivia in 1967) and National Liberation Action (ALN), decided to kidnap the U.S. ambassador to Brazil in a dramatic show of their strength and as a propaganda measure designed to emphasize the ongoing support of the U.S. government for the regime. The militant groups also wanted to use the kidnapping to help secure the release of political prisoners then undergoing torture. After four days of captivity, the ambassador was released and fifteen political prisoners were flown to Mexico, where they received political asylum. The following manifesto articulated the demands of the revolutionary organizations.

Revolutionary groups today detained U.S. ambassador Charles Burke Elbrick, bringing him to an unnamed location in the country where they are holding him captive. This act is not an isolated episode. It adds to the innumerable revolutionary deeds already carried out: bank robberies that raise funds for the revolution and return what the bankers take from their employees and from the people; occupations of [army] barracks and police stations, where weapons and ammunition are obtained for the fight to bring down the dicta-torship; invasions of prisons, during which revolutionaries are freed so that they can return to the people's struggle; explosions of buildings that symbol-ize oppression; and the execution of hangmen and torturers.

In reality, the abduction of the ambassador is just one more act of a revo-lutionary war that advances every day and that initiated its rural guerrilla stage just this year.

With the kidnapping of the ambassador, we want to show that it is possible to defeat the dictatorship and exploitation if we arm ourselves and organize. We will appear where the enemy least expects us and disappear immediately,

Student activists and revolutionaries released from prison and flown to Mexico in exchange for the freedom of the kidnapped U.S. ambassador in September 1969. Courtesy of Acervo Iconografia.

weakening the dictatorship and causing terror and fear among the exploiters, hope and certainty of victory among the exploited.

In our country, Mr. Burke Elbrick represents the interests of imperialism that, allied with the big bosses, landowners, and national banks, maintains a regime of oppression and exploitation.

It was this alliance's interest in gaining even more wealth that created and maintained the salary squeeze, the unjust agrarian structure, and institutional repression. The kidnapping of the ambassador is therefore a clear warning that the Brazilian people will not let [the exploiters] rest and at every moment will unleash upon them the weight of their struggle. Let it be known to all that this is a struggle without truce, a long and hard fight that does not end with the exchange of one general in power for another; one that only finishes with the end of the regime of the great exploiters and with a constitution of a government that frees the country's workers from this situation in which they find themselves.

We are in Independence Week. The people and the dictatorship commemorate [the occasion] in different ways. The dictatorship promotes public events and parades, sets off fireworks, and posts propaganda. With [these displays], the dictatorship does not commemorate anything; it seeks to throw sand in the eyes of the exploited, establishing a false happiness with the objective of hiding the life of misery, exploitation, and repression in which we live. How can you hide the obvious? Can you hide from the people their own misery when they feel it in the flesh?

During Independence Week, there are two commemorations: that of the elite and that of the people, that of those who organize parades and that of those who kidnap the ambassador, a symbol of exploitation.

Translated by Molly Quinn

A Letter to Pope Paul VI

Marcos Penna Sattamini de Arruda

Among the different groups that opposed the military regime in the 1960s was Ação Popular (Popular Action), which had grown out of the left-wing Catholic student movement to embrace Marxist and later Maoist ideas by the end of the decade. Among its members was Marcos Arruda, a former seminarian born and raised in Rio de Janeiro. Trained as a geologist but blacklisted from any employment in the field because of his student activism, Arruda, under the guidance of Ação Popular, decided to find a job in a factory in São Paulo, in order to organize the working class against the dictatorship. In early 1970, he received word that a young woman who had joined an armed struggle organization wanted to leave the group and was seeking a place to hide. He met with her briefly and promised to try to assist her. She was subsequently arrested and tortured, and revealed a scheduled meeting with Arruda. Members of Operação Bandeirante (OBAN), a special government unit with private-sector funding that was set up to systematically track down and eliminate all of the radical opposition organizations, arrested Arruda, who was subjected to brutal torture and almost died while under detention. Arruda's family managed to get him out of prison, and he left the country for exile in the United States, where he was a leader in campaigns against the dictatorship while living in Washington, DC. An interview Arruda granted to the Washington Post *in September 1971 about his experiences in prison led the newspaper's editorial board to publish a hard-hitting editorial questioning the Nixon administration's support of the Brazilian generals.*

The following letter to Pope Paul VI was widely circulated as part of the international effort to denounce torture in Brazil. Written at the height of repression in his home country, it is deliberately vague about some of the circumstances leading to Arruda's arrest to protect the woman he had met and tried to help, since she remained in prison.

February 4, 1971

Your Holiness Pope Paul VI,

   Please find herewith an account of all that happened to me during almost nine months' imprisonment. . . . I was arrested on May 11, 1970 in São Paulo on my way to dinner with a young lady whom I had recently

Marcos Arruda while living in exile in the United States in the 1970s.

met. I learned afterwards that she belonged to a political organization. She had been arrested several days previously and violently tortured and taken to Operation Bandeirante [OBAN].

I was picked up even before I reached the meeting place and taken off in a car (the license plate was not an official one) by four armed policemen. We went to the OBAN headquarters. During the journey the leader of the group ordered the young lady to show me her hands so that "I could have an idea of what awaited me." She lifted her hands, which were handcuffed, and I saw that they were greatly swollen and were covered with dark purple hematomas. I learned that she had been badly beaten with a hard wooden paddle. Once the car stopped in the OBAN courtyard, they immediately began to punch and kick me in the presence of some people seated on benches in front of the main building. I was beaten as I went up the steps to a room on the top floor where they continued to slap me, hit me about the head, and bang my ears with cupped hands (telephone torture). They then took the handcuffs off and continued to hit me with their truncheons while questioning me.

They ordered me to strip completely; I obeyed. They made me sit down on the ground and tied my hands with a thick rope. One of the six or seven policemen present put his foot on the rope in order to tighten it as much as possible. I lost all feeling in my hands. They moved my knees up to my elbows so that my tied hands were on a level with my ankles. Then they placed an iron bar about eight centimeters wide between my knees and elbows and suspended me in the air by resting the two ends of the iron bar on a wooden stand so that the top part of my body and my head were on one side and my buttocks and legs on the other, about three feet from the floor.

After punching me and clubbing me, they placed a wire on the little toe of my left foot and placed the other end between my testicles and my leg. The wires were attached to a field telephone in which the current increased or decreased according to the speed at which the handle was turned. In this way, they began to give me electric shocks and continued to beat me brutally both with their hands and with a *"palmatoria"*—a wooden paddle full of holes—which left a completely black hematoma, larger in size than an outstretched palm, on one of my buttocks.

The electric shocks and the beatings continued for several hours. I arrived about 2:30 pm, and it was beginning to get dark when I practically lost consciousness. Each time that I fainted, they threw water over me to increase my sensitivity to the electric shocks. Then they took the wire from my testicles and began to apply it to my face and head, giving me terrible shocks on my face, in my ears, mouth, and nostrils. One of the policemen remarked, "Look, he is letting off sparks. Put it in his ear now." The group of torturers was under the command of Captain Albernaz and consisted of about six men, among them Sergeants Tomas, Mauricio, Chico, and Paulinho.

The torture was so serious and long-lasting that I thought I would die. I began to feel completely drained; my body was covered in a cold sweat; I could not move my eyelids; I was swallowing my tongue and could only breathe with difficulty; I could no longer speak. I tried throughout this time to think of great men who had suffered horrible things for a noble ideal. This encouraged me to fight on and not give way to despair. I felt that my hands would become gangrenous because circulation was blocked for some hours. I moaned "My hands, my hands!" and they continued to beat my hands with their clubs. I think they had lowered the bar and laid me out on the ground. They tried to revive me with ammonia, but I didn't respond. They struck my testicles with the end of a stick; they burnt my shoulders with cigarette stubs; they put the barrel of a revolver in my mouth saying they would kill me. They threatened me with sexual abuse. Suddenly, my whole body began to tremble, and I began to writhe as if shaken by an earthquake. The policemen were alarmed and called for a doctor from the first-aid post. They said I was a soldier who was feeling ill. They gave me an injection and refused to give me water although my body was completely dehydrated. They left me to sleep in the same room in which I had been tortured.

The following morning I was violently shaken by the shoulders. I realized that I was still shaking, my eyelids were shut, my tongue was paralyzed, and I felt strange muscular contractions on the right side of my face. My left leg was like a piece of wood, the front turned downward, and my toes had contracted and would not move. The small toe was totally black. After enduring many insults, I was carried to the general military hospital of São Paulo. The sole of my left foot was again forcibly struck in order to try and return it to its normal position and make it fit into my shoe. Despite shooting pains, the foot would not move. The torturers took me by the arms and legs and brought me like a sack to the courtyard where I was thrown into the back of a van.

I later learned that at the hospital they gave me only two hours to live. The military chaplain came to hear my confession. I asked the soldiers who were on guard in my room to leave us alone, but they refused. In these circumstances, the priest could only give absolution *in extremis* in case I should die. For several days I was subjected to interrogation at the hospital despite the fact that my condition had not improved. The fifth day after I was admitted to the hospital, two policemen opened up the door to my room saying, "Now that you are alone we are going to get rid of you. You are going to die . . . and one of them began to hit me about the face and body. I tried to protect myself and to cry out, but I was still shaking and could hardly move. In addition, my twisted tongue prevented me from crying out loudly. I could not see them well because my eyelids still would not move. The policeman continued to say, "No one can hold out against Sérgio Adão, you are going to die. . . ." He went out for a moment with the other person to see if anyone was coming and then returned to continue. Eventually, I managed to cry out loudly. They were frightened and left me. . . .

I remained in this general hospital for about a month and a half. During this time I was visited several times for questioning. My family had been trying to help me, and for over a month had been trying unsuccessfully to find me. I finally received a note in which they told me that they had discovered where I was. But I remained incommunicado, without permission to see my family, for five more months, and I received no visit from a lawyer throughout the duration of my detention.

When I was released from the hospital, my right eyelid was still paralyzed (it remained thus until the month of December) and I had a slight but constant shake in the shoulders, the left arm and leg; the latter, half paralyzed, could not support any weight, and I was obliged to use a broomstick for a walking stick.

I was sent back to OBAN, put in a cell, and told to write out a statement. . . . I finished this in three days, at the end of which time I was brought face to face with the young woman whom I had been on my way to meet at the time of my arrest. It was six o'clock when I was carried into the room where she was kept. They wanted me to admit the name of the organization of which they believed I was a member, and they wanted me to give the names of supposed comrades. They began to carry the young woman off into another room and gave her a strong electric shock in order to make me talk (they were afraid to torture me again in view of my poor physical condition). I heard the cries of the girl being tortured, and when they brought her back into my room, she was shaking and totally distraught. I was paralyzed with fear at witnessing such cruelty and even more terrified when they threatened to do the same to members of my family if I didn't tell them what they wanted to know. They repeated the electric shock treatment on the girl and, seeing that they were not achieving anything, decided to call the doctor to examine me physically to see if I was fit to undergo more torture. The doctor ordered certain tablets and said that I should not be given food. They brought me back to my cell and were to return for me later. Having seen that they were ready to torture the young woman again, and possibly members of my family as well, I decided to try and protect these people, and I agreed to write out another deposition.

I was carried into the room of a certain Captain Dauro, who, along with another officer, offered coffee and cigarettes for me and advised me in a comradely fashion to cooperate with them. I began by saying that I did not want to cooperate with them since they represented the institutions of force and violence, and because they used such inhuman treatment when dealing with people against whom they had no proof. They were irritated and began to torture the young woman once again in order to make me talk. Finally, they used violence on me again, along with insults and moral attacks, threats concerning members of my family, and even attempts to strangle me. They blindfolded me and pushed a revolver against my forehead—all to the same end. After several hours, they carried the young girl and me back to our cells. Major Gil, head of OBAN, and Captain Dauro, Captain Faria, jailer Robert, a huge lieutenant with ginger hair and moustache, a young feeble-looking black man, and three others, about whom I can remember nothing, took part in this torture session.

The following evening, when they came for me I was again suffering from contractions, my right side was paralyzed, I dribbled, my body twitched constantly. . . .

The next morning I was carried into court. My condition had considerably worsened and my seizures were continual and more visible. I was photographed, my fingerprints were taken, and I was then brought into a room on the same floor as the torture room. A sergeant in a military police uniform with his name band covered with a sash, interrogated me calmly for forty-five minutes. He threatened me alternately with torture and death if I refused to confess. Later, he told me that he was a doctor and knew that I would die if he permitted me to be tortured again. In the end, he gave me an injection for my spasms and told me that I ought to be taken back to the hospital. Throughout the night, I was locked up in a bathroom and was then taken to a doctor, Primo Alfredo, who had recently been arrested. Throughout the night, we heard as usual the terrible screams of people being tortured. The following morning I was once again brought to the military hospital.

Two days later my condition began to worsen, and I lost consciousness and became delirious; this condition lasted more than ten days. I learned afterwards what had happened during that period.

. . . It is clear that my case is not exceptional, as such events have become commonplace during the last few years in Brazil.

. . . I thank your Holiness for your interest and the action taken in an attempt to secure my release. I beg you to do the same for the other thousands of men and women who suffer the same treatment in Brazil and in other countries, . . . unfortunate human beings who continue to be tortured.

Marcos Penna Sattamini de Arruda

Two Presidents at the White House

Various authors

The visit of General Emílio Garrastazu Médici, Brazil's president from 1969 to 1973, to the Nixon White House in December 1971 symbolized the ongoing support that the U.S. government had offered the authoritarian regime since 1964. While the two heads of state exchanged toasts inside, several dozen clergy and human rights activists protested the meeting in the park across from the White House. These activists displayed images of political prisoners who had been tortured alongside a thirty-foot banner with a slogan that stated, "Stop U.S. $ Complicity with Brazilian Torture." Leading newspapers, such as the Washington Post *and the* New York Times, *published scathing editorials denouncing the torture of political prisoners.*

The warm exchange of greetings during this state visit reflects the uncritical endorsement by the Nixon administration of the Brazilian regime. The first remarks below are from President Nixon. President Médici responded in Portuguese; his remarks were translated by an interpreter. On December 9, 1971, at the conclusion of President Médici's meetings with President Nixon, White House press secretary Ronald L. Ziegler read the final agreed-upon statement at his regular news briefing.

Statement by President Nixon

Mr. President, Mrs. Médici, and our very distinguished guests from Brazil and from the United States of America:

It is always a very special occasion when the largest country in South America and the most populous country in North America meet, as they do today, on a state visit. But this occasion is distinguished from other occasions in which the leader of Brazil and the leader of the United States have met, whether here or in that country.

Brazil is a country that, for us in the United States, has always been one of great promise, great mystery, great excitement, and I think the description of Brazil which is contained in one section of its national anthem perhaps tells us why Brazil has such a special meaning to those of us in the United States who look to this great country to the south and think of its future.

As I recall, Brazil is described there as a great sleeping giant lying eternally in a magnificent cradle. That was true of Brazil 150 years ago, when it had

President-General Médici and President Nixon at the White House in 1971. Courtesy of the Richard Nixon Presidential Library and Museum.

its independence, and the United States was the first country in the world to recognize its independence. It was true of Brazil 100 years ago, 50 years ago, maybe even 25 years ago, or 10 years ago. But it is not true today.

The giant is awakened. The people of Brazil know it. The people of the world are discovering it, and the visit of the President of Brazil to this country will tell this message to our people and tell it better, also, to the people of the world. This great giant is now awake—100 million people, unlimited natural resources, developing now not only on the coast, the beautiful cities that we all know, but developing, due to the leadership of our guest of honor tonight and those who have worked with him, developing the heartland of the country through highways and cities and exploration such as was only dreamed of before, but now is being actually done.

This has meant that Brazil and all of its promise that people have dreamed about through the years is now being realized. The international historian, Arnold Toynbee, in 1934, wrote that Brazil's possibilities would be unlimited once it had the leadership in its government that would attract the kind of investment from its own people and from abroad that would explore and develop its resources. And I think the greatest tribute that I can pay to our distinguished guest tonight is that in the brief time that he has been President of Brazil there has been more progress than in any comparable time in the whole history of that country.

This is a great record. It is one which the people of Brazil thank him for. It is one that we, his very good and devoted and dear friends from the north, also respect him for, and we, in our country, Mr. President, welcome the opportunity to work with this great giant of the south, no longer sleeping, very much alive, with its future so unlimited.

Working with you as the leader of that country—because we know that as Brazil goes, so will go the rest of that Latin American Continent—the United States and Brazil, friends and allies in the past, and as this dinner tonight reaffirms, strong and close personal and official friends today, we shall work together for a greater future for your people, for our people, and for all the people of the American family, for which we have a special place in our hearts.

I know that in that spirit all of us would like to reaffirm our affection for Brazil, for its people, for the American family, by raising our glasses to the health of our distinguished guest, the President of Brazil.

Statement by President Médici

Mr. President, Mrs. Nixon:

In the words of Your Excellency, I find not only a gesture of fraternal welcome but also the determination to preserve and to strengthen the traditional solidarity that exists between our homelands.

My wife and I, and all the members of my party, shall always cherish unforgettable memories of the fellowship that is prevailing here this evening, of the joy that permeates these moments, thanks to the generous hospitality of Mrs. Nixon and yours, Mr. President.

Here we are, Mr. President, to engage in a frank conversation between friends, to exchange views and share experiences, to reminisce about the past of common struggles, to discuss the problems of the present, and particularly to formulate long-range plans for the future. Here we are to carry out a joint effort in establishing a new point of departure mutually beneficial for the relations that have always been peaceful between the two nations which we represent.

We met at length this morning, fully aware that our points of view are not always coincident. We did not, however, lose sight for a single moment of this objective of trying to harmonize them and integrate them in the broadest cooperation which is not only beneficial for both countries, but it is also important for the handling and the solving of the problems, problems of the hemisphere as well as worldwide problems.

Our friendship has undergone the tests of both war and of peace, and the United States always knows that it will find in Brazil a loyal and independent ally. Brazil cannot display indifference and apathy in the presence of new events and new circumstances, in the presence of a reality which is ever changing and above which we must rise in order to build a new world order in the spheres of political, diplomatic, economic, financial, and monetary activity.

We must approach this new world without preconceived ideas and without inflexible positions. And what seems imperative to us is that this new world order must also bring about an entirely new phase of peace, justice, and progress for all the members of the family of nations.

The Brazilian and American voices which are blending around this table are all imbued with the same feeling of friendship, and they share an equal yearning for achievement. These voices do not find it difficult to make themselves heard and understood and fully appreciated. These are voices which are joining in common purposes, still without giving up their own identity, which is autonomous and spontaneous.

It is on the basis of reciprocal trust, of mutual respect, and equality of rights that we are going to preserve the great friendship, a friendship which is indicated to us and imposed upon us by common interests.

It is in this spirit, and with these thoughts in mind, that I ask all those present here to raise their glasses in toasting the health of Mrs. Nixon and the President of the United States of America, and also toasting the greatness and the happiness of the great American Nation which was born and which has been prospering under the aegis of freedom.

Statement Read by White House Press Secretary Ronald L. Ziegler

The visit of President Médici to Washington provided an excellent opportunity for conversations in depth between the Heads of State of two of the largest and most populous nations in the Western Hemisphere. Talks between President Médici and President Nixon were conducted in an atmosphere of warm friendship, and both agreed that recent world developments made their frank exchanges most timely and mutually profitable.

Their discussions covering the broad aspects of the international situation were particularly significant and timely in the light of President Nixon's upcoming meetings with other world leaders.

There was an exchange of evaluations and views on many of the issues of world significance affecting, as they do, the interests of both nations. They reviewed action taken and contemplated to bring greater order to the international monetary system to further international trade and development.

The two Presidents consulted closely on important hemispheric issues, recognizing the need for continuing and intensified cooperation among the nations of the region with respect to economic and social development, as well as their common security interests. They agreed that the primary goal of an era of peace and prosperity for the region can be achieved only by co-operation which in turn must be founded on the principles of freedom and self-determination.

The Presidents extensively reviewed relations between the United States and Brazil. Bilateral relationships embracing all facets, including common security interests, and political, economic, military, scientific and cultural matters were discussed in the spirit of the traditionally close and friendly ties between the two countries.

The meetings provided an excellent basis for continued and intensified co-operation between the two nations over a wide range of matters which both Presidents considered of primary importance.

The two Presidents also discussed the impressive economic progress made by Brazil under the leadership of President Médici, progress which has marked Brazil as one of the most rapidly developing nations of the world.

The conversations were particularly marked by the two Presidents' mutual grasp and understanding of problems and issues facing both nations. Their talks provided not only an opportunity for a review of past and present relations, but, importantly, established a firm basis for continuing consultations in the future on world, hemispheric, and bilateral problems of mutual concern.

National Security and the Araguaian Guerrillas

Ernesto Geisel and Germano Arnoldi Pedrozo

Because of censorship, very few people in the early 1970s knew that the Brazilian Army was carrying out a massive military operation near the Araguaia River in the Amazonian state of Pará against militants from the pro-Chinese PC do B, the Communist Party of Brazil. The group had split from the pro-Soviet Communist Party in 1962, and had been trying for several years to organize a rural guerrilla movement in the region. Military security forces learned of the existence of this group in 1972, and soon thereafter the army began combat operations.

Superior numbers overwhelmed the guerrillas, who had just over seventy combatants. Their familiarity with the rugged terrain and their contacts with community members, however, meant that they mounted a good deal of resistance. In response, the army used overwhelming force in its efforts to annihilate the group. Most of the guerrillas were killed in combat or murdered after capture, their bodies secretly buried in Araguaia. The military cloaked the entire counterinsurgency operation in silence.

The following tape-recorded conversation between Ernesto Geisel and his old friend and head of security, Lieutenant-Colonel Germano Arnoldi Pedrozo, of the CIE (Army Intelligence Center), took place three days after Geisel's election to the presidency by the Electoral Congress. It offers a rare glimpse into the thinking of the military hierarchy about Araguaia.

GEISEL: Come here. How is that operation over in Altamira?

PEDROZO: Over in Xambioá? I have the impression that it is proceeding as planned. Some two or three months remain to complete it.

G: But have they achieved something yet?

P: Presently they have caught almost thirty.

G: Thirty?

P: Thirty. What was more or less estimated was in the order of 180, 200.

G: And those thirty, what did they do? Were they liquidated? As well?

P: As well.

G: Oh?

P: Some in the same action. And others later, in captivity. There's no way around it.

G: And the others? They do not liquidate them because it's pointless?

P: No. Because they cannot catch them. . . .

G: And the populace?

P: The populace was brought around by them a long time ago. . . .

G: The populace was not aware of these deaths, was it?

P: They ought to be; they ought to be because the action occurs in the presence of the woodsmen and then [the news] spreads. But they now know, General, what matters is that they now know in their hearts that most are terrorists, subversives. In the beginning they organized an ambush of the district police station to steal weapons; they killed a police officer. The populace was indignant. So they lost some of that support from the locals.

G: That was foolish on their part.

P: It was, because they counted on the support. The locals are very ignorant.

G: The first rule of guerrilla warfare is to have the support of the populace.

P: They are trapped fair and square because of this. They lost support. They had storage places with provisions and medicine. Many of these storage places have been discovered; they were deactivated. They practically do not have any resources. They stopped receiving money. They received it constantly; each month they received it.

G: Where did it come from? The Cubans?

P: No, it was from people who brought it personally to the area.

G: Where was their center, their leadership, in São Paulo?

P: Their directions come from the PC do B, the Communist Party of Brazil. And they had in the area a member of the so-called military committee. He basically supervised their work in that area. That commission had people from Rio and São Paulo that took turns. The commission ought not to be functioning any more. They are virtually alone, abandoned. They do not receive money; they do not have the support of the locals. The majority lives in survival mode in the forest. I imagine two, three more months . . . despite the fact that they still have not caught the leader, one Osvaldão [Osvaldo Orlando da Costa].

G: Who was it?

P: Osvaldão. A fellow almost two meters tall, a reserve officer of the CPOR [Center for the Preparation of Reserve Officers], lieutenant. That one has been in that area for six years.

G: But he should be easy to find.

P: Ah, but he is buried there in the forest. He has an exit. The region is very difficult. If he sets out into Araguaia he has a means to escape. It is an enormous area; there are no means of communication. . . . The location is there on the map. You will see there are three, four shacks in a clearing in the middle of the forest.

G: What is their end game?

P: They are attempting to form a free zone.

G: But if they hardly have a population . . .

P: I have the impression that they brought people there from outside, to take advantage of the small number of locals and bring in people from outside; beyond this, they are training. . . .

G: How did they get there, by the river?

P: By the river. Normally they would enter through São Geraldo, a small city near Xambioá . . . on the edge of Araguaia.

Translated by Emma Wohl

What Color Are You?

National Household Sample Study, Brazilian
Institute of Geography and Statistics

The document below is an alphabetical listing of the terms people used to identify their skin color in the 1976 National Household Sample Study. Unlike the national census, where census takers in years past had determined whether respondents should be classified according to one of the five official color categories (i.e., as white, black, indigenous, yellow, or brown), in this study researchers asked the respondents themselves to identify their skin color through an open-ended question that let them use any description they wished. They did so using 135 different terms.

This collection of colors points to Brazil's racial complexities. Racial definitions based solely on biological criteria—such as the one-drop rule employed in the United States—have historically been less dominant in Brazil. And postabolition Brazil never had the kind of race-based laws that were common in the United States and South Africa and that required highly specified systems of racial classification. Instead, a more ambiguous and fluid understanding of race prevails in Brazil, often expressed in terms of color. Defining one's color, though, includes considering a wide mix of phenotypic criteria, such as eye color and hair texture, one's socioeconomic situation, the specific context in which the definition is produced, and even the regional setting. As the singer Caetano Veloso once said, "[Gilberto] Gil is a mulatto who is dark enough to be called black even in Bahia. I'm a mulatto who is light enough to be called white, even in São Paulo. But his eyes are much lighter than mine." Such indeterminateness allows for some flexibility in the brokering of color, such that some people can negotiate their own terms and uses of these criteria in some contexts. Yet one's own identification of color may not always align with the views of outside observers, and racial discrimination rests on this understanding.

Self-identification may also reflect one's response to the socially produced understandings associated with particular skin colors. In the list below, the multiple terms signifying "white" make clear the persistent importance of whiteness as an ideal or social aspiration, rather than as a stable color definition, demonstrating its continued social power. Even more numerous are terms that signify a racial mixture, such as the many variations of moreno, *illustrating how many people identify with the dominant narratives of racial mixture. Nonetheless, note too how many of the self-*

ascribed terms for nonwhites are either derogatory, related to food, related to animals, or imply some kind of outsider status.

Despite the seeming diversity of colors invoked in this list, 95 percent of respondents self-identified using one of six colors, and forty-five of the 135 colors noted were used by only one or two people. Thus the 82,577 Brazilians who responded to the survey certainly used a large number of creative terms to describe their skin color, but their responses do not suggest an outright rejection of racial categories based on skin color nor of racially discriminatory attitudes.

1. *acastanhada* (chestnut-like)
2. *agalegada* (like a Spaniard from Galicia)
3. *alva* (white)
4. *alva-escura* (dark white)
5. *alvarenta* (whitish)
6. *alvarinta* (whitish)
7. *alva-rosada* (pinkish white)
8. *alvinha* (a little white)
9. *amarela* (yellow)
10. *amarelada* (yellowed)
11. *amarela-quemada* (burnt yellow)
12. *amarelosa* (yellowish)
13. *amorenada* (tannish)
14. *avermelhada* (reddened)
15. *azul* (blue)
16. *azul-marinho* (navy blue)
17. *baiano* (from the state of Bahia)
18. *bem-branca* (very white)
19. *bem-clara* (very light)
20. *bem-morena* (very tan)
21. *branca* (white)
22. *branca-avermelhada* (reddish white)
23. *branca-melada* (honey white)
24. *branca-morena* (tanned white)
25. *branca-pálida* (pale white)
26. *branca-queimada* (sunburned white)
27. *branca-sardenta* (freckled white)
28. *branca-suja* (dirty white)
29. *branquiça* (whitish)
30. *branquinha* (a little white)
31. *bronze* (bronze)
32. *bronzeada* (bronzed)
33. *bugrezinha-escura* (dark little Indian)
34. *burro-quando-foge* (fleeing donkey)

35. *cabocla* (mixture of white and Indian)
36. *cabo-verde* (Cape Verde)
37. *café* (coffee)
38. *café-com-leite* (coffee with milk)
39. *canela* (cinnamon)
40. *canelada* (cinnamony)
41. *cardão* (thistle colored)
42. *castanha* (chestnut)
43. *castanha-clara* (light chestnut)
44. *castanha-escura* (dark chestnut)
45. *chocolate* (chocolate)
46. *clara* (light)
47. *clarinha* (a little light)
48. *cobre* (copper)
49. *corada* (reddened)
50. *cor-de-café* (coffee colored)
51. *cor-de-canela* (cinnamon colored)
52. *cor-de-cuia* (calabash colored)
53. *cor-de-leite* (milk colored)
54. *cor-de-oro* (gold colored)
55. *cor-de-rosa* (pink)
56. *cor-firma* (translation uncertain)
57. *crioula* (term originally meant Brazilian-born slave; here meant black)
58. *encerada* (waxy)
59. *enxofrada* (sulfurous)
60. *esbranquecimento* (almost white)
61. *escura* (dark)
62. *escurinha* (a little dark)
63. *fogoio* (fire colored)
64. *galega* (a Spaniard from Galicia)
65. *galegada* (like a Spaniard from Galicia)
66. *jambo* (*jambo* fruit, sometimes called a rose apple in English)
67. *laranja* (orange)
68. *lilás* (lily)
69. *loira* (blonde)
70. *loira-clara* (light blonde)
71. *loura* (blonde)
72. *lourinha* (little blonde)
73. *malaia* (Malaysian)
74. *marinheira* (foreigner [in the northeast, a Spaniard from Galicia])
75. *marrom* (brown)
76. *meio-amarela* (semiyellow)
77. *meio-branca* (semiwhite)

78. *meio-morena* (semitan)
79. *meio-preta* (semiblack)
80. *melada* (honeyed)
81. *mestiça* (mixture of white and Indian)
82. *miscigenação* (miscegenation)
83. *mista* (mixed)
84. *morena* (tan)
85. *morena-bem-chegada* (very tan)
86. *morena-bronzeada* (bronzed tan)
87. *morena-canelada* (cinnamon-like tan)
88. *morena-castanha* (chestnut-like tan)
89. *morena clara* (light tan)
90. *morena-cor-de-canela* (cinnamon-colored tan)
91. *morena-jambo* (*jambo* fruit tan)
92. *morenada* (tanned)
93. *morena-escura* (dark tan)
94. *morena-fechada* (very dark tan)
95. *morenão* (very dark tan)
96. *morena-parda* (brownish tan)
97. *morena-roxa* (purplish tan)
98. *morena-ruiva* (reddish tan)
99. *morena-trigueira* (wheat-colored tan)
100. *moreninha* (a little tan)
101. *mulata* (mixture of white and black)
102. *mulatinha* (a little mixture of white and black)
103. *negro* (black)
104. *negrota* (young black)
105. *pálida* (pale)
106. *paraíba* (from the state of Paraíba)
107. *parda* (brown)
108. *parda-clara* (light brown)
109. *polaca* (Polish)
110. *pouco-clara* (a little light)
111. *pouco-morena* (a little tan)
112. *preta* (black)
113. *pretinha* (a little black)
114. *puxa-para-branca* (leaning toward white)
115. *quase-negra* (almost black)
116. *queimada* (burnt)
117. *queimada-de-praia* (tanned on the beach)
118. *queimada-de-sol* (tanned by the sun)
119. *regular* (regular; nondescript)
120. *retinta* (very dark black)

121. *rosa* (rose)
122. *rosada* (pinkish)
123. *rosa-queimada* (burnished rose)
124. *roxa* (purplish)
125. *ruiva* (redheaded)
126. *russo* (Russian)
127. *sapecada* (toasted)
128. *sarará* (light-skinned with light-colored kinky hair)
129. *saraúba* (like a white meringue)
130. *tostada* (toasted)
131. *trigo* (wheat)
132. *trigueira* (wheat colored)
133. *turva* (opaque)
134. *verde* (green)
135. *vermelha* (red)

Second-Wave Brazilian Feminism

Editors of Nós Mulheres

The process of political liberalization in the mid-1970s presented possibilities for new social movements to emerge that challenged traditional notions of race, gender, sexuality, and social norms. A dialogue began among female Brazilian political exiles living in Europe, who had become influenced by feminist ideas, and many women activists in Brazil who had been involved in underground activities against the dictatorship. In 1975 a group of women founded the newspaper Brasil Mulher *and published twenty issues between that year and 1980. The next year, another collective of women began publishing* Nós Mulheres, *which also articulated a feminist agenda and published eight issues between 1976 and 1978. One of the debates among supporters of a women's movement in Brazil was about how to advance feminist ideas when many in the opposition sought to focus on ending the dictatorship. The feminists countered that specific questions related to the oppression of women were intimately tied to issues of social justice, democracy, and the end of authoritarian rule. The following editorial was published to mark the first anniversary of* Nós Mulheres, *noting the successes and challenges of the newspaper's efforts.*

After a long period of silence, in about 1973 new groups formed around democratic ideas, once again using the right to social criticism. In 1975, the International Women's Year, the debate about the oppression of women intensified. It was in this climate of emerging enthusiasm that, in May 1976, a year ago, we prepared the first issue of *Nós Mulheres* [*We Women*]. It was the first time that we had created a newspaper, hence [we operated in] a climate of confusion and insecurity. But even in the midst of this confusion, we retained a clear objective: to create a newspaper for working women, mothers, housewives of the working-class neighborhoods of São Paulo, for students, professionals, intellectuals. A forward-looking journal that had room to discuss the oppression of women. A newspaper that would argue that the situation of Brazilian women was destined for failure, according to some, or was ridiculous according to others. Even among ourselves there were reservations about using the term "feminist," since it had become a worn-out word. At times it seemed that it was easier to close one's eyes to oppression and be satisfied with the small bits of freedom given us, or to seek personal solutions with the false idea that other women are oppressed but we have overcome this problem.

The group Nós Mulheres was formed around the idea of creating a feminist newspaper. Most of us didn't even know each other, just as we didn't know what feminism meant to the rest of the group. Slowly, in what at times was a painful process, we got to know each other. We respected opinions that were different from ours; we accepted the slowness of the way in which decisions had to be made by the whole group; we developed a way of working together. It was a long process in which some women left, and others approached us. We left a cold and damp basement and moved to a sunny and open room where we currently work. A baby was born, and two are on the way. And like a newborn, we overcame the greatest of difficulties during the first year. We're learning to walk.

In this first year, we made contacts with other groups in São Paulo and feminist groups in Rio, Belo Horizonte, Salvador, Recife, and Porto Alegre. The movement grew, which is a tendency in this historical moment when one can no longer tolerate the violation of human rights. We grew so much that we celebrated March 8, International Women's Day, a date that was virtually unknown in Brazil two years ago. This year the celebration took place in several locations in the city with the participation of over a thousand working women, domestic workers, housewives, mothers, students, and intellectuals. We grew so much that the National Congress has initiated a parliamentary investigation into the situation of women in Brazil. And although it is common practice when there is no solution to a problem to appoint a parliamentary investigating committee, the fact is that the inferior status of women is no longer a taboo subject as such, and [is] an officially recognized matter.

There is hope, however. Even when we are fighting against the lack of freedom of expression in the political system, we are carrying out our work. (And for this reason, we have had support among broad sectors of the press.) Even though we are confronting many financial problems, we've managed to survive. We know that as long as there is an oppressed woman, there will be no freedom. As long as our eyes still see poverty in the favelas, entire families living on the streets, images of seminude women on magazine covers and hanging on walls in offices; as long as there are hungry and abandoned children, locked in their rooms while their mothers are working; as long as there is prostitution, no woman will be free. We know this, and this is our cause. Having overcome initial difficulties, a female comrade has written, "Today it's possible to think about me without forgetting about you, or all of us; it's possible to think of all of us without feeling that I am disconnected from the broader struggle; it's possible to think about politics without having to forget about me or about us. And this is much more than a beginning."

Translated by James N. Green

LGBT Rights and Democracy

Aguinaldo Silva

As the political climate liberalized in 1977, a handful of gay intellectuals, journalists, writers, and artists decided to publish Lampião da Esquina, *a monthly newspaper directed at homosexuals that offered a political and cultural critique of ongoing discrimination against nonnormative sexual practices and gendered behavior. The name of the monthly, which literally meant "street-corner lamppost," was also a tongue-in-cheek reference to Virgulino Ferreira da Silva (1897–1938), better known as Lampião, a hypermasculine Robin Hood figure and rural bandit from the Brazilian northeast.*

The editorial in the first issue, "Leaving the Ghetto," called on gay men to leave what the author considered the insular and isolating world of bars, saunas, and homosexual sociability—referred to as the ghetto—and interject themselves into public debates about sexuality and oppression. The publication of Lampião da Esquina *encouraged the formation of* SOMOS *(We are): Group of Homosexual Affirmation, Brazil's first gay and lesbian rights organization in São Paulo, as well as a dozen other groups throughout the country. The publication largely addressed issues of gay men but also included cover stories related to the discrimination against lesbians, Afro-Brazilians, transvestites, transsexuals, and other marginalized social groups. Although* Lampião *folded in 1981, its publication represented a founding moment for what would become an extremely dynamic lesbian, gay, bisexual, transgendered, and transsexual movement in Brazil.*

Brazil, March 1978. Favorable winds are blowing in the direction of some sort of liberalization of the national landscape. In an election year, the press broadcasts promises of a less rigid Executive Power, speaks of the creation of new political parties and of amnesty. An investigation into the proposed alternatives allows one to discern an "opening" of Brazilian discourse. But a homosexual newspaper, why?

The easiest answer would be one that would show us wielding an exotic flag of "tolerance," digging more deeply inside the walls of the [gay] ghetto, and endorsing—upon "coming out"—the isolated position that the Great Homosexual Conscience is reserved for those who don't pray according to its catechism, which befits the perpetuation and functioning of the ghetto.

Cover of the first issue
of *Lampião da Esquina*.

Our response, however, is this: it is necessary to say "no" to the ghetto and, consequently, to leave it. What interests us is destroying the stereotypical image of the homosexual that portrays him as a being who lives in the shadows, who prefers the night, who faces his sexual preference as a kind of curse, who is given to exaggerations, and who always stops short of any attempt at becoming a thoroughly self-actualized human being because of this primary factor: his sexuality is not what he would wish for.

To do away with this stereotypical image, *Lampião* does not intend to weep over our daily oppression or to act as an escape valve. It will simply serve as a reminder that a statistically significant part of the Brazilian population, by shouldering the stigma of being unable to reproduce sexually in a society that is frozen in Judeo-Christian mythology, must be characterized as an oppressed minority. And fundamentally these days a minority needs a voice.

This minority is not interested in the positions of those who have remained a part of the Establishment in which they become court jesters and who have declared themselves free of all discrimination, and with access to ample opportunities. What *Lampião* demands in the name of this minority is not only that we "come out" and be accepted. What we want is to recapture the status that all societies built on macho foundations have denied us. Homosexuals are human beings and as such have a right to fight for complete self-actualization.

To this end, we will be found monthly in every newspaper stand in the country, speaking of current events and attempting to clarify the homosexual experience in all aspects of society and human endeavor. We also intend to go further, giving a voice to all groups that are unjustly discriminated against—blacks, Indians, women, and ethnic minorities in Kurdistan. We say "Down with the ghettos and pariahs, masking themselves as the Establishment."

Speaking of discrimination, fear, the forbidden, or silencing, we will also talk freely of sexuality and its positive and creative qualities, attempting to discuss issues that impact this very concrete reality and the lives of (possibly) millions of people.

We intend to show that the homosexual refuses for himself and for other minorities the blemish of caste and the assignment of higher or lower social class. He doesn't want to live in ghettos or to raise flags that stigmatize him. He is neither one of the chosen nor one of the cursed. His sexual preference must be seen within a psychosocial context as just one of many features that form his character. *Lampião* is very clear about what will inform its struggle. We pledge to delegitimize the concept that some would like to attach to us—that our sexual preference can negatively affect our performance within the world in which we live.

Translated by Caroline Landau

The Movement for Political Amnesty

Various authors

In 1975, Terezinha Zerbini founded the Feminine Movement for Amnesty with the goal of winning broad-based support to pressure the government for the release of political prisoners and the return of exiles to Brazil. The organization strengthened networks of relatives of political prisoners, exiles, and the political opposition. In the following years, the demand for a broad, general, and unrestricted amnesty became a slogan written on banners at all public events, demonstrations, and even soccer matches. In 1978, activists founded the Brazilian Amnesty Committee to unite local committees throughout the country and press for an amnesty law. The first document below is the statement of principles presented at the first National Amnesty Congress held in São Paulo in November of that year.

João Figueiredo, the fifth general-president, signed an amnesty bill in August 1979 that released political prisoners and allowed exiles to reenter the country, with the exception of those involved in armed actions resulting in deaths. (Many of those prisoners or exiles saw their lengthy sentences reduced soon thereafter, allowing them to leave prison or return to Brazil.) However, the law also contained a provision that pardoned people involved in crimes conexos, or related crimes, a euphemism for government officials or employees who had tortured or killed political detainees. In 2010, the Brazilian Supreme Court upheld this provision in the law, in contravention of an Inter-American Human Rights Court ruling that the Brazilian state cannot grant amnesty to government officials involved in enforced disappearances of other crimes against humanity.

Minimum Action Program of the Brazilian Amnesty Committee

1. *Total and Absolute End to Torture.* Denounce tortures and protest against them, through all possible means. Denounce the torturers publicly and fight for their criminal responsibility. Investigate and denounce publicly the existence of entities, divisions, apparatuses, and vehicles of torture and fight for their total and absolute eradication.

2. *Freedom for Political Prisoners and Return of Those Hunted, Forcibly Retired, Banned, Exiled, and Persecuted for Political Reasons.* Publish the identity, loca-

tion, and situation of all those imprisoned, hunted, banned, forcibly retired, exiled, and persecuted due to political motivations. Fight for their freedom, for their return to the Nation, and for the resumption of their civil, professional, and political lives.

3. *Transparency about the Situation of Disappeared Persons.* Support the fight of family members and other interested parties in the clarification of the whereabouts of those citizens who were disappeared for political reasons.

4. *Reinstatement of Habeas Corpus.* Fight for the reintroduction of habeas corpus for all political prisoners; denounce all attempts to annul or obstruct this right and protest such attempts by all means.

5. *End of Arbitrary and Inhumane Treatment of Political Prisoners.* Investigate conditions to which all political prisoners are subjected. Denounce arbitrary acts committed against them and organize a means to protest and repudiate them. Demand liberalization of prison legislation. Fight against silencing of political prisoners.

6. *Revocation of the National Security Law and End to Repression and Punitive Norms against Political Activity.* Fight, through judicial and political means, against all coercive and punitive norms, exceptional or not, that impede the free exercise of the right of speech, meeting, association, protest, and partisan political activity. Denounce—and organize public demonstrations against—all forms of repression, legal or not, that aim to intimidate, threaten, restrain, or punish those who try to exercise those rights. Fight for the revocation of the National Security Law.

7. *Support for the Struggles for Democratic Rights.* Support the pronouncements, demonstrations, campaigns, and struggles of other social sectors, bodies, and entities that promote the same ends expressed in this Letter of Principles and in this Minimal Program of Action. Support the struggles of family members of those imprisoned, hunted, forcibly retired, banned, exiled, and persecuted for political reasons for their immediate freedom or return [to Brazil], to regain the memory of their existence, to denounce the tortures and arbitrary and inhumane treatment in prison where they were, are, or will be victims. Support the struggles of trade unions, professional unions, and associations of salaried employees and workers in general against the economic exploitation and political domination to which they are subjected and for freedom and autonomy of unions, for the right to organize in workplaces, for the right to meet, associate, protest, and strike. Support the struggles against all forms of censorship and closure of the press, theater, cinema, music, artistic expression, production and distribution of art and science, in defense of broad freedoms of information, thought, opinion, and criticism, and the freedom to acquire and use knowledge. Support student movements for better learn-

Student protest against the dictatorship at the Pontificate Catholic University of Rio de Janeiro in 1977. Courtesy of the Arquivo Nacional, Acervo/Fundo: Serviço Nacional de Informações da Rede de Informações e Contrainformação do Regime Militar no Brasil (1964–85).

ing conditions, for the right to organize, and for the right to create and run representative bodies. Support the struggles of all people for better living and working conditions, for better salaries, against the rising cost of living, for better nutrition, living, transportation, education, and health. Support the activities of parties and representatives that endorse those same struggles. Denounce and repudiate all attempts to impede, distort, obstruct, mischaracterize, and repress the struggles of the CBA/SP (Brazilian Amnesty Committee) and other sectors, organizations, and bodies that identify with the principles and objectives proclaimed here.

Amnesty Law (1979)

Law no. 6,683 of August 1979.

The President of the Republic: I make it known that the National Congress decrees and I sanction the following law:

Article 1. Amnesty is granted to all those who, in the period between September 2, 1961, and August 15, 1979, committed political crimes or ones related to them, who committed electoral crimes, those who had their political rights suspended, official and contracted employees of the state administration or institutions linked to the state, employees of the legislative and judicial branches, members of the military and union leaders and representatives, duly punished in Institutional and Complimentary Acts.

§ 1—For the purposes of these articles, related crimes are considered those crimes related in whatever way to political crimes or politically motivated crimes.

§ 2—Those who were convicted for crimes of terrorism, assault, kidnapping, or violation of the person are exempt from the benefits of amnesty.

§ 3—Wives of members of the military who were dismissed by the Institutional Acts will have the right to request reinstatement in order to receive pensions, following the requirements of Article no. 3. . . .

Article 7. Amnesty will be granted to employees of private businesses who, due to their participation in a strike or whatever action to demand their rights according to existing legislation, were fired from their jobs or removed from administrative positions or positions as union representatives.

Article 8. Amnesty will be granted in relation to infractions or penalties arising from the failure to complete military service obligations of those who, during the period of recruitment, found themselves exiled or prevented from registering.

The provision in this article applies to dependents of those granted amnesty.

Article 9. Union leaders and representatives will have the benefits of amnesty if they were punished under the Acts referred to in Article 1, or if they suffered disciplinary punishment incurred through absence from service in that period, provided it did not exceed thirty days; this also applies to students.

Article 10. Under the terms of Article 2, rehabilitated civil servants and members of the military will have their leaves of absence from active service counted, subject to the provisions in Article 11.

Article 11. This law, aside from the rights expressed in it, will be used to enact any other law, including those relating to salaries, credit, wages, restitution, delays, reparations, promotions, or reimbursements.

Article 12. Those granted amnesty who joined a legitimately constituted political party will be able to return and be elected in party conventions to occur one year from the enactment of this law.

Article 13. Within thirty days, the Executive Power will issue a decree regulating this law.

Article 14. This law will go into effect on the day of its publication.

Article 15. Provisions to the contrary are to be repealed.

Brasília, August 28, 1979; the 158th year since
Independence and the 91st year of the Republic
[President] João Figueiredo

Translated by Emma Wohl

Lula's May Day Speech to Brazilian Workers

Luiz Inácio Lula da Silva

The military regime's wage and labor policies relied on a compliant trade union move-ment. The Institutional Acts, the National Security Law, and labor legislation cre-ated a series of political and legal barriers that discouraged workers from going on strike and demanding wage increases or better working conditions. However, by the mid-1970s a new generation of trade union leaders and rank-and-file activists had emerged who were less willing to comply with government restrictions. When union leaders discovered that Delfim Netto, the minister of planning, had doctored the rate of inflation statistics in 1973 and 1974 to keep down automatic cost-of-living wage ad-justments, they decided to confront the regime. In 1978, metalworkers from the indus-trial belt around the city of São Paulo organized a wildcat strike that demanded a 34.1 percent increase in their salaries to cover lost back wages and successfully negotiated a settlement with the major auto companies. The work stoppage, led by Luiz Inácio Lula da Silva, the president of one of the largest unions in the area, set off a three-year strike wave throughout the country that challenged the government's economic and labor policies and catapulted Lula, as he is known, to national prominence. In the midst of labor mobilization, the military regime passed a law abolishing the two of-ficial political parties and legalizing a multiparty system. Lula played a decisive role in founding the Partido dos Trabalhadores (Workers' Party), which eventually gained national strength and elected two presidents in the first decades of the twenty-first century: Lula and Dilma Rousseff. The selections from the speech below come from a rally held during the 1979 metalworkers' strike in the greater São Paulo area.

Comrades:

The time has arrived to look forward and see what is happening in our land. They say that inflation has been caused by the wages of working people. Over the past fifteen years they have held down our wages, and yet inflation has continued at the same high rate as it was before 1964. The transnational corporations did away with the sacred rights workers once cherished. They ended what was once held so dear, job stability, and instead implemented a severance fund, which only makes it easier for bosses to fire their employees. And let us remember all the riches we have given to Brazil only to be kicked in the pants.

Lula leading the 1979 metalworkers' strike in São Paulo. Courtesy of Acervo Iconografia.

All of you know that ten years ago it was very different. Ten years ago we had lawyers, we had teachers, we had medical doctors, we had public-sector workers, we had journalists and so many other professions that sought to distance themselves from manual laborers. Thank God for the political awakening of the Brazilian worker, the political awakening of all who earn wages, and for their opposition to the state of misery that the government has created for all of those who depend on wages to get by.

It is because of this that today, on the first of May 1979, we can say that we are living in the greatest moment the Brazilian working class has ever known. We say enough is enough when public-sector workers are awarded raises of 30 percent only to see 20 percent taken away, with the result that these workers receive only 8 percent increases in actual salary.

Enough is enough when we look at the situation of garbage collectors, those who pick up the trash of the owners of the Pacaembu Stadium and then return home only to find that they don't have enough money to buy food and are forced to survive on the food they find in the waste they collect. Enough is enough when we see bus drivers whose only option is to protest. Enough is enough when we see teachers who are driven to protest. Why do we find ourselves in this state of hunger, pushed to scream and yell at the top of our lungs, not just to ask for the right to strike, but to take our rights back and actually go on strike? Not just to ask for the freedom and autonomy of trade unions but to force the freedom and autonomy of trade unions?

They think that they will destroy the [labor] movement in the ABC [an area in greater São Paulo] by intervening in our union, yet they forget that a union is not a building; a union is the worker inside the factory and the laborer in the public square. The metalworkers of the ABC region know that we have agreed to wait until the thirteen (of May) before taking any further action. Sunday, the thirteenth, we will have a meeting, and we want just as many people to show up as we have today. Because, if they don't increase our salaries, on the fourteenth at midnight the ABC will again go on strike.

We will march forward, we will continue to confront [our enemies], and we will again go on strike—and some newspapers and magazines publicly affirm this—if we go on strike again they will use mortar guns on us here in São Bernardo do Campo. To confront the tanks in São Bernardo, every single worker should bring their wives and their children to the streets to show that our struggle is much more serious than the stupidities that some speak of.

In closing, comrades, I would like to ask all workers, from all the different labor sectors, that when the boss denies your demands, the only weapon you use is to stop the machines. I would like all my comrades to understand that every day we discuss this with all of the different labor sectors and, in so doing, we see that the bosses do not agree [with our perspective]; but this does not bother me, because, one more time, we will show them that, in the end, the Brazilian working class will have the final word.

To conclude, comrades, I would like to say that every single worker should keep in mind, and tell your children, tell your wives, that today our movement is leading Brazilian society as a whole and that nobody resents us, with the exception of the bosses and some public officials. All of Brazilian society is on our side, and all believe that the time has come to assume our rights, or, should I say, take our rights and walk with our heads held high. We all know that the Volkswagen factory arrested four workers this past Friday, and tomorrow we will show everyone that these workers should be freed. However, the principal slogans continue to be the slogans of the ABC. I believe this for all of us: nobody will have to work an additional hour until we win an increase in our salaries.

Everybody should be prepared to budget what they have, because if we don't get our raise, we will go on strike. If they think that by taking over the union our resolve will be crushed, they don't understand our conviction. . . .

Translated by Natan Zeichner

Portraits: Caetano Veloso and Gilberto Gil

James N. Green

In 1962, the Brazilian sound of bossa nova burst onto the American music scene, popularized by Stan Getz and Charlie Byrd's album *Jazz Samba*. Robert Farris Thompson, *Saturday Review*'s music critic, noted, "Qualitatively higher by light years than the rock-and-roll replications of the twist, an elegant countertrend, 'samba jazz' has been slowly taking shape in supper clubs and dancehalls of a few of our nation's cities. Fragile and still exploratory, the new genre nevertheless bears the marks of careful development and refinement, stamping it as perhaps the most promising popular phenomenon of the decade thus far." Guitarist Byrd enthusiastically declared, "I seriously think that the bossa is the best movement going on in popular music anywhere in the world."[1]

Byrd, Herbie Mann, and other American jazz musicians had toured Brazil in 1960 and brought back the new, cool, contained, soft, and seductive sound with them. Byrd shared a record of João Gilberto, one of bossa nova's creators, with saxophonist Stan Getz, and they cut an album featuring the best of the Brazilian genre. One of the songs, "Desafinado" (Off-key), won Getz a Grammy for Best Solo Jazz Performance. The music received a five-star review in *Downbeat* magazine, shot to the number one position on the *Billboard* pop chart, and sold hundreds of thousands of copies.

Just as the bossa nova boom started to wane in 1964, Getz produced an album with João Gilberto titled *Getz/Gilberto* that featured Astrud Gilberto, João Gilberto's wife, singing in English. The recording introduced American audiences to Tom Jobim and Vinícius de Moraes's 1962 hit "A garota de Ipanema." With English lyrics by Norman Gimbel, "The Girl from Ipanema" won a Grammy for best song and became an international sensation. In 1966, Sérgio Mendes furthered this Brazilian musical craze with his album *Sérgio Mendes and Brasil 66*. For the next decade, Mendes popularized a bubbly upbeat blend of bossa nova and American pop that marketed Brazilian music and culture as imbued with unending joy and happiness.

The bossa nova craze in the United States was a rare phenomenon, somewhat like a similar fascination with Carmen Miranda during and immedi-

Caetano Veloso during a concert in the late 1960s. Credit: Fundação Getúlio Vargas/
CPDOC.

ately after World War II, when Brazilian musicians and singers managed to
break into the U.S. and European markets. Whereas U.S. music—jazz, big
band, pop, rock and roll, rap, and so on—has permeated the Brazilian air-
waves and influenced generations who listen to music that is sung in English,
the opposite transmission of culture has been much more precarious.

Caetano Veloso and Gilberto Gil are among the recent exceptions. The
two Brazilian singers have become international stars and part of the galaxy
of performers whose music has circulated globally since the 1980s. Gil's and
Veloso's sounds have distinctly Brazilian flavors, yet they are laced with international influences from the United States, Europe, Africa, Latin America,
and the Caribbean. Among the most popular singers in Brazil in the 1960s and
'70s, they both continue to perform and create new sounds. No one musical
style or performer can represent a period or a generation, but one cannot understand the late 1960s and early 1970s in Brazil or cultural production under
the military regime without knowledge of these two masterful performers.

Caetano Veloso was born in 1942 in Santo Amaro da Purificação in the
state of Bahia. In 1960, his family moved to the capital of Salvador, where he
became enamored of bossa nova and the work of João Gilberto and learned to
play the guitar. There he began creating music that would become part of a
new musical genre that combined and drew on many traditions from folk to
protest, from regional to international. Although it is difficult to categorize
Brazilian popular music, as it came to be known, its songwriters have a "keen

ability to combine compelling melodies, rich harmonies, varied rhythms, and poetic lyrics."[2] Veloso's mellifluous voice, charming personality, and sophisticated lyrics immediately won him a faithful following.

Like Veloso's family, Gil's parents also moved from a small town in Bahia to the capital, where Gil continued to show a talent for music that had manifested itself at a very young age. Of African descent, Gil was the son of a medical doctor and a schoolteacher. His mother encouraged his interest in music, and he learned to play the accordion until he heard a bossa nova hit by João Gilberto on the radio. He immediately abandoned the accordion for the guitar. Gil met Veloso and his sister, Maria Betânia, who would also become a nationally acclaimed singer, at the Federal University of Bahia, where they circulated among poets, musicians, artists, and other creative people. Like Veloso, he mixed sounds, introducing music and instruments from the northeast into a repertoire that also became influenced by rock and roll.

Both moved to São Paulo, where they explored their musical careers, and quickly became part of a new generation of successful young performers. For that reason, they were invited to the 1967 Song Festival. In 1965, television stations and record companies began organizing song festivals to attract viewing audiences and market their labels. The contests among different performers and their compositions were broadcast in front of live audiences. Following a tradition from the days of live radio, the public cheered their favorite singers and booed those they disliked. The song festivals became a space where different musical tastes, the talents of composers, and the performances of singers could be disputed in public.

In the festivals of 1965 and 1966, protest songs that either openly or indirectly criticized the military regime won top places in the song competitions. Their success reinforced a notion among many youths that songs should be imbued with political content. Then, in 1967, Caetano Veloso and Gilberto Gil shook the festival audience with something new. The two songwriters presented entries in the contest that experimented with unusual lyrics and new sounds. The style was Brazilian but also influenced by rock and roll. Rather than being explicitly political, the lyrics captured moments of everyday life, from a stroll through the city to a romantic tragedy in a park that seemed divorced from any larger critique of the military regime.

Caetano Veloso's entry in the 1967 festival, "Alegria Alegria," combined complex, disjointed lyrics with eclectic references to popular culture and with the sounds of the electric guitar. The song charmed some in the audience and shocked others, who considered the seemingly apolitical theme, the lyrics, and the instrument all "alienated" manifestations of U.S. and European influences on Brazilian culture. Nationalist sentiment rejected the electric guitar as a form of cultural imperialism, and many in the audience booed his song. Gilberto Gil's entry, "Sunday in the Park," while performed on an acoustic

Gilberto Gil with the Filhos de Gandhy Carnaval group in Salvador, Bahia. Photograph by Sayonara Moreno. Courtesy of Agência Brasil.

guitar, used African musical instruments and had a lyric structure quite different from what had become the standard fare of Brazilian popular music.

Gil's and Veloso's performances at the 1967 Song Festival contributed to founding a new cultural movement that year known as Tropicália that also contributed to innovations in theater, poetry, and art. It drew on many influences, among them the modernist notion of *antropofagia* that had been proclaimed by bohemian Paulista intellectuals in the 1920s (see part VII, "The Cannibalist Manifesto"). Like the modernists, this new movement argued that the role of the artist is to appropriate international influences and remake them into something that combines both Brazilian and foreign elements but is completely new and different. To many politicized students, the lack of a clear antidictatorship message in Veloso's work was disturbing. The next year, 1968, Veloso's decision to perform disjointed electric rock at the festival in a song titled "It's Prohibited to Prohibit," in reference to a slogan of the French student protests that had just taken place, provoked boisterous outcries from the audience. Once again, students accustomed to folk or protest music played on an acoustic guitar denounced the use of the electric guitar and the absence of an overtly antiregime message.

Yet Veloso and Gil had tapped into a vibrant new antiauthoritarian sentiment in Brazil, as the armed forces had ramped up their repressive apparatus against the radical opposition. Although not linked to the left-wing groups that bore the brunt of post-1968 repression, Veloso and Gil's cultural politics of libertarianism challenged the generals' chauvinism and conservative morals, which deemed their music and performances subversive. As a result, in early 1969 they were arrested, imprisoned for fifty days, and then prohibited from performing in Brazil. They decided to leave the country for exile in London.

Veloso later described his time in England as melancholic. He produced an album that expressed tremendous longing for Brazil. Gil, on the other hand, used his time in London to immerse himself in the music scene, connecting with Caribbean and African performers and absorbing their sounds and styles into his music. Both returned to Brazil in the early 1970s and had a profound effect on cultural shifts taking place in the country during the slow process of liberalization that began in 1974. Gil promoted Afro-Caribbean music in Brazil, and Veloso pushed the limits of traditional gender roles in androgynous performances that questioned normative notions of masculinity. Both continued to reinvent themselves and their music as the decades passed.

Notes

1. Robert Farris Thompson, "The 'Bossa Nova' from Brazil," *Saturday Review* 45 (September 15, 1962): 42.
2. Chris McGowan and Ricardo Pessanha, *The Brazilian Sound: Samba, Bossa Nova and the Popular Music of Brazil* (Philadelphia: Temple University Press, 1998), 75.

XI

Redemocratization and the New Global Economy, 1985–Present

During the past three decades, Brazil has witnessed many intense political and social dramas. Popular mobilizations and new social movements emerged during the 1970s to challenge authoritarian rule and many exclusionary practices. Traditional institutions, political alignments, and economic interests also remained as the country moved to consolidate democratic rule.

In 1984, the surprise departure of Senator José Sarney from the prodictatorship party to join the opposition tipped the balance of power in the congressional Electoral College. The moderate political approach of presidential candidate Tancredo Neves positioned him to win the support of sectors from both the left and the right. With Sarney as his pick for vice president, Neves allayed the fears of many conservatives who were leery of the opposition coming to power. On January 15, 1985, the congressional Electoral College cast 480 votes for Neves, thereby electing him president.

On the eve of his inauguration, however, Neves suddenly became ill. He was hospitalized and underwent surgery. Because he was unable to assume the presidency, Sarney was sworn in on March 15, 1985, as vice president and then immediately became acting president. The nation came to a standstill as people closely followed the news about Neves's seven operations and were saddened at each announcement of his deteriorating condition. He died on April 21, and Sarney assumed the presidency.

Sadness over Neves's death was augmented by the fact that a long-term supporter of the military dictatorship was now at the helm of the state. Moreover, an economic crisis quickly turned public opinion against Sarney. Over the previous decade, the military regime had accumulated an enormous foreign debt of 100 billion dollars, and inflation soared in 1986. Sarney attempted to contain rising prices through the Cruzado Plan, which created a new currency, froze prices on goods and services, and restrained wage increases through controlled incremental adjustments. This halted price increases for a time, and the opposition party, the Party of the Brazilian Democratic Movement, swept the gubernatorial races of 1986. Soon thereafter, price caps were

Impeachment vote of President Fernando Collor de Mello in the Chamber of Deputies. Photograph by Roosevelt Pinheiro. Courtesy of Agência Brasil.

removed and inflation again surged. The Cruzado Plan led to a drastic reduction in foreign reserves. In 1987, Brazil had to declare a moratorium on paying the foreign debt.

The military's exit from power also created the political opportunity to write a new Brazilian constitution. The country's last charter had been imposed on the Congress by the military in 1967. Those members of Congress elected in 1986 received a mandate to write a new one. Proceedings began in 1987, and the body was dominated by a large coalition of moderate political parties. The final version guaranteed direct elections for president, vice president, and legislative bodies; guaranteed illiterate people the right to vote; gave sixteen- and seventeen-year-olds optional voting privileges; ended censorship; increased revenue sources for states and localities; and ensured property rights. Yet the National Constituent Assembly also blocked proposals presented by political and social movements for land reform and other democratic rights.

The presidential elections of 1989 pitted the former union leader Luiz Inácio Lula da Silva against Fernando Collor de Mello, the charismatic governor from the state of Alagoas. Collor ran on a campaign promising to eliminate government sinecures. He also sought to discredit Lula due to his lack of formal education beyond primary school. Collor won in the second round and spent considerable time during his first year in office attempting to combat hyperinflation. He also began implementing a neoliberal policy of selling off state-owned industries to private interests, a process that would increase during subsequent presidencies.

Then, a little more than a year into his term, Collor was involved in a massive corruption scandal, accused of collecting enormous sums of money through an associate in exchange for political influence. As he had campaigned on an anticorruption platform, these charges were particularly damning. When a congressional investigation discovered evidence supporting these claims and news of his personal extravagance surfaced, popular outrage erupted.

Those who most colorfully expressed this sentiment were university and high school students who demonstrated against him in the streets. Many of them painted their faces with the green and yellow of the national flag or, at times, with black as a sign of mourning. Hence they became known as the *caras pintadas* (painted faces). As impeachment proceedings moved against Collor, student protests, and their similarity to the antidictatorship protests of 1968, became symbols of a renewed Brazilian democracy. The television network giant Globo's airing of a new miniseries on the student protests of 1968, *Anos Rebeldes* (Rebel years), prompted references to the similarities between these two moments. Fearing imminent impeachment, Collor resigned in December 1992, providing a legal and peaceful outcome to the political crisis.

Collor's vice president, Itamar Franco, a former senator from Minas Gerais, assumed office but faced serious economic problems as inflation reached 1,100 percent in 1992 and surged to 2,400 percent the following year. During his administration, Franco appointed Fernando Henrique Cardoso, senator from São Paulo and a former left-wing sociologist who had lived for many years abroad during the military regime, as his minister of foreign affairs and then minister of finance. Cardoso and a team of economists implemented a plan that created a new currency, the *real*, and drastically held down inflation. After years of staggering jumps in prices, the economic stability that resulted from Cardoso's policies easily guaranteed his election in 1994, with 54 percent of the votes in the first round against left-wing opposition leader Luiz Inácio Lula da Silva.

Although Cardoso had been a moderate social democrat during his years as a sociologist and as a political figure in the Brazilian Democratic Movement, he moved to more pragmatic, and some would say more conservative, positions in the 1990s while a leader in the Brazilian Social Democracy Party. As president he aligned himself with a center-right coalition in Congress that pushed through an amendment allowing a second presidential term. Again, in 1998, Cardoso won easily in the first round against Lula with a margin of 53 to 37.1 percent.

The social and labor movements that had gained strength in the 1970s and '80s picked up steam throughout the 1990s. Feminists won major victories by

Presidents Fernando Henrique Cardoso (*left*) and Michel Temer (*center*) with São Paulo governor Geraldo Alckmin (*right*). Photograph by Beto Barata. Courtesy of Agência Brasil.

shifting public policy on many questions related to women's rights. Activists forced the government to adopt a progressive approach to AIDS prevention and treatment, and an LGBT movement emerged with increasing visibility during this period. Afro-descendant activists challenged national myths regarding racial equality and tolerance, and began pushing for affirmative action programs. Environmental groups organized throughout the country, as did the Movement of Landless Rural Workers, which demanded agrarian reform. Brazil became internationally known for its diversity of political and social movements that fought to expand democratic and social rights for its citizens.

During his two terms in office, Cardoso oversaw the privatization of many state-owned industries, including the National Steel Company, the Vale do Rio Doce mining company, and Telebras, the national telephone company. These measures provoked a bitter national debate between those who wanted to open the economy to the free market and those who considered the state-owned companies Cardoso privatized a national legacy that should remain in the hands of the state, where they could more effectively contribute to national development.

After three failed presidential bids, Lula da Silva, the leader of the Workers' Party, launched his fourth campaign in 2001 with a much more moderate program. In the runoff campaign against his opponent, José Serra of the Brazilian Social Democracy Party, Lula issued a "Letter to the Brazilian

People" to reassure the nation that he would not implement radical economic or social policies if elected president. He earned 61.3 percent of the votes cast.

In office, Lula pledged to carry out a series of social programs to distribute money and resources to the poor and the struggling middle classes. Some of these initiatives had begun under the Cardoso presidency, but Lula expanded them and won considerable popularity with their implementation nationwide. One such initiative, Bolsa Família (Family grant), a cash-transfer program, reached an estimated 12 million families or 46 million people a year. During the Lula administration, Brazil's macroeconomic performance was so robust that the country at one point inched up to being the sixth largest economy in the world. Yet Lula's choice of some centrist ministers and his moderate economic policies earned him criticism among sectors of the left. A vote-buying scandal, known as *mensalão* because of monthly payments to members of Congress to ensure a majority that could implement Lula's political agenda, reached members of his inner circle but did not tarnish his personal popularity. In 2006, Lula won a second term against the center-right coalition led by the Brazilian Social Democracy Party.

Lula's foreign policy initiatives included challenging international trade rules that Brazil argued unfairly favored the Global North. His administration also campaigned to increase the country's prominence through participation in international agencies, including lobbying for a permanent seat on the UN Security Council. The selection of Brazil to host the World Soccer Cup in 2014 and the Olympics in 2016 also added to Lula's popularity. He left office as perhaps the most popular president in Brazilian history.

Lula's handpicked successor was his chief of staff and former minister of mines and energy, Dilma Rousseff. She had participated in the armed struggle against the military regime in the 1960s and early '70s and later joined the moderate social democratic left. Running on a campaign to continue the social programs and economic policies of her successor, she defeated José Serra in the 2010 elections. Although she garnered considerable popular support in her first two years in office, largely for continuing to implement programs initiated under Lula's administration, her popularity slipped as mobilizations erupted in June 2013 against the rising cost of transportation, inadequate health and education programs, and excessive expenditures for new and remodeled soccer stadiums for the upcoming World Cup. A weakening economy also undercut her popularity. The dominant tone of the 2013 demonstrations expressed frustration that the Workers' Party–led government coalition had not fulfilled all of its promises to improve the quality of life of ordinary citizens. However, within the mobilizations there was an undercurrent of direct opposition to Rousseff's rule that called for her to step down.

In the first round of the 2014 presidential elections, Dilma Rousseff ran a tight race against the former environmental minister, Marina Silva, and Aécio Neves, former governor of the state of Minas Gerais and the candidate

Presidents Dilma Rousseff and Lula da Silva at the 2014 election victory celebration. Photograph by Fabio Rodrigues Possebum. Courtesy of Agência Brasil.

Proimpeachment forces protesting in front of the Palácio do Planalto, the presidential palace, dressed in green and yellow, the colors of the Brazilian flag. Photograph by Wilson Dias. Courtesy of Agência Brasil.

of the Brazilian Social Democracy Party. In the runoff election, voting was polarized, and Rousseff beat out Neves by a 3.3 percent margin, the smallest since direct presidential elections were reenacted in 1989.

At the same time that the country was deeply divided around the presidential elections, Sérgio Moro, a federal prosecuting judge, launched a series of corruption investigations known as Operation Car Wash, which uncovered evidence that high-ranking officials of Petrobras, the state-owned oil company, were involved in skimming off millions of dollars in contract kickbacks and other illicit schemes involving most of the country's major construction companies. Recently approved plea-bargaining measures encouraged entrepreneurs of leading companies to become state witnesses. They provided evidence of corruption schemes between politicians and corporation heads, with some of that money ending up in undeclared campaign coffers of the country's major political parties. The daily news about this alleged corruption, some of it linked to members of the Workers' Party, fueled public sentiment against Dilma Rousseff's presidency, and center and right-wing forces organized nationwide mobilizations throughout 2015 demanding her impeachment. Yet formal accusations against Rousseff stalled in the Chamber of Deputies until Eduardo Cunha, the president of that body and a leader of the Party of the Brazilian Democratic Movement, which formed the largest bloc in Rousseff's multiparty congressional coalition, was himself accused of corruption. Annoyed by the fact that the Workers' Party voted against him in the lower house's ethics commission, Cunha turned against Rousseff and accepted impeachment charges alleging that she had carried out irregular budgetary procedures.

The Chamber of Deputies temporarily removed Rousseff from office in April 2016 and recommended an impeachment trial in the Senate. Vice President Michel Temer, also of the Party of the Brazilian Democratic Movement, and who had also publicly turned against Rousseff earlier in the year, assumed the presidency, a major boon to his and Cunha's party. Temer then shocked the nation by appointing an all-white and all-male cabinet, which included over a half-dozen politicians under corruption investigations. In August 2016, the Senate voted to remove Rousseff from office, although she retained her political rights. Temer immediately began to implement a political agenda that included, among other measures, reformulating Brazilian labor legislation and regulations related to the country's national social security and retirement systems. In subsequent 2017 Car Wash investigations, Lula was convicted of illicitly receiving an apartment from a construction company and sentenced to twelve years in prison. His case was still under appeal at this writing, but the Clean Slate Law barred him from running in the 2018 presidential elections, although he was leading in the polls.

The ouster of Rousseff and the conviction and imprisonment of Lula

Mobilization in Recife, Pernambuco, against the impeachment of Dilma Rousseff. Her supporters characterized her removal from office as a coup d'état. Photograph by Sumaia Vivela. Courtesy of Agência Brasil.

have further polarized political discussions in Brazil. Defenders of the former presidents argue that the judiciary has wielded excessive and arbitrary power, focusing only on alleged misdeeds of politicians of the center-left while largely ignoring similar illegal activities by other politicians, including President Temer and Senator Aécio Neves, both of whom supported Rousseff's removal from office. Left-wing critics also contend that the upsurge in mobilizations against Rousseff and the recent Workers' Party–led governments reflect a rejection of many of the social programs carried out in the last decade by those threatened by the shift in the country's social and economic relations. Defenders of the impeachment and the Car Wash investigations praise the efforts to rout out political corruption and blame the recent rise in unemployment and inflation on mismanagement of the economy by the previous government. A minority in that camp supports the return to military rule.

As this publication goes to press, it is impossible to predict the next political developments in the country. This should not be a surprise to anyone who has studied Brazilian history and followed closely the contents of this *Reader*. Unexpected events and twists and turns in history have been a hallmark of the country's past. Movements advocating social justice and inclusion remain a constant. For many years, observers have noted that the electoral victories of the Workers' Party have brought an end to the effectiveness of social movements as vehicles of critical opposition from the left. Yet mobilizations that took place in mid-2013 challenge this assertion. Others have held that Brazil will never manage to close the social and economic gap between the rich and poor and address the legacies of slavery, social hierarchies, and the politics of exclusion. Following the evolution of these issues as Brazil takes its place among the fast-developing nations of the twenty-first century will provide scholars with much to study and fascinating material to analyze and share in the future.

Forty Seconds of AIDS

Herbert Daniel

The first reported case of AIDS in Brazil occurred in 1982. The disease was immediately associated with homosexuality, and a series of extremely negative stereotypes about gay men and transvestites circulated in the media. Throughout the 1980s and into the 1990s, however, activists worked with public health officials to forge a national AIDS policy that included explicit educational campaigns about safer sex and the prevention of infection, the widespread distribution of condoms, free state-financed treatment programs, and pressure on the international pharmaceutical industry to make drugs inexpensive and readily available by threatening to break the patents and issue low-cost generic alternatives. This campaign was largely successful.

Two former revolutionary opponents of the military dictatorship played an important role in these efforts to change state policy and social attitudes. Herbert "Betinho" de Souza, a hemophiliac, won widespread sympathy when he announced he had AIDS. Another early activist who pressured the Brazilian government and the medical profession to adopt progressive AIDS policies was Herbert Daniel, a former medical student and guerrilla leader who, soon after discovering that he was HIV positive in 1989, founded one of the first support groups for people living with HIV/AIDS (see "Portraits" in this part). The following essay captures the anxiety and anger of those who confronted the disease when many in the medical profession still retained prejudices toward those with the virus.

Deep down I believe in the conventional. It's very hard, it's too heavy a blow, it's a difficult shock to hear, it's an earthquake, and it's the start of a journey with no return. No one, in fact—that is what I believed—is prepared to receive a piece of news like this one. At least that's what I thought until I myself received this piece of news. You have AIDS. I got the news and it actually was the start of a journey. I understood then, and not without irony, that no journey in life has a return and that life is exactly this: the possibility of an eternal second chance, which always is before us. The best place in the world is here. And now.

Not that I was prepared. No one ever is. I began preparing myself, as everyone does, for my new conditions for living. Conditions for living, I repeat, to make it perfectly clear that I don't mean the circumstances of a predetermined and forcibly imposed death. I learned right away, during the health crisis that led to the painful diagnosis of my condition, that I am not an "aidetic" (an AIDS-ish person). I only have AIDS. As for what I am, I continue to be what I am not and never was, [namely] a continuing possibility that I, as others, am from day to day.

Yet I wasn't unprepared. I was alive. I am alive. The most frightening thing, and I write these pages in protest, was the absolute unpreparedness of the doctor who gave me the news. He was unprepared. The illustrious representative of a fossilized style of medicine that has more in common with terrorism than science, he was not prepared to deal with people, whether they were ill or not—he was prepared to deal with machinery, bacteria, torture, and murder.

Some stories don't happen to everyone. This is one such story, worth telling, because it happens to many and involves a plot whose threads weave through our bodies.

I got sick. For many reasons, I didn't believe that I could have AIDS. Not the least of them was the fact that I refused to accept such a drastic hypothesis. After all, we never believe the "worst." And AIDS is always presented as the "worst thing." Besides, I didn't feel, nor do I feel now, that I have the "worst thing in the world." (There are worse things. I lived through worse things. Dictatorship. The loss of liberty. Exile. Going underground. Mass murder and torture. Remember the years of authoritarianism? I say this without wanting to take any seriousness away from AIDS, but merely to place it in due perspective. It isn't the "worst thing that can happen to a person." It is a tragic situation. It is a disease; it is not a melodrama.)

Although many things about my body might have made me suspect that I had the disease, I didn't imagine it for me—mainly because what I was seeing in myself didn't correspond to the typical "patterns" of the disease. Another thing I have learned is that every case is a case in itself, and that the medical definition of AIDS is a theoretical generalization. It must be discussed not only in terms of signs and symptoms, but also from the standpoint of the great myths of "incurability" and "fatality." I still don't mean to diminish the seriousness of AIDS. It is, for the moment, incurable. It is fatal. But it is not only that. Or principally, AIDS is not "essentially" that, as the prophets of fear and discrimination would have us believe.

In short, I didn't suspect that I could have AIDS because I didn't "look like" a person who was sick with AIDS. Now, glancing in the mirror, I know what a person who is sick with AIDS looks like. By the way, this is an exercise that anyone can do in front of the mirror, to see the famous face of AIDS. (I also learned that, although my "personal" case is peculiar to me, nothing leads me to suppose that mine is different from all the other cases. This is an epidemic. We are a multitude. We are living a story of our time. And it will be up to our time to find an answer to this phenomenon).

In an emergency, I sought out a "doctor" (the quotes are used so as not to offend other worthy professionals, like those who treated me with such solidarity later on). I didn't know him, but I had recommendations as to his "technical competence." A huge mistake! The technical competence of a doctor should be measured by his humanism, not by how well he has been trained to respond with conditioned reflexes. What's more, even technically he soon proved to be a charlatan. I won't say his name. There are many others just like him. He is most valuable as a symbol. Divulging his name solves nothing, since it might even lead him to believe I want to start some sort of polemic. And that might even end up adding to his vanity.

In any event, I trusted him to tell me what evil was tormenting me. What patient doesn't make this sort of transference? During the examination, he left me seated for half an hour, naked, on the table, after taking a sample of my saliva for analysis. Dizzy with fever, with visible signs of a pneumonia that had prostrated me, I waited.

He came back, ordered me to dress and told me in three sentences that I had pneumonia of the type caused by *Pneumocystis carinii*, "a sure indication of an immunological deficiency." He was going to prescribe a medication (which he did, but in the wrong dosage); afterward I was to undergo a test which would reveal the "other disease" (as he euphemistically called it) that had led me to have pneumonia. . . .

Certainly, in that instant, many things that were happening in my body became clear to me. I did not doubt his diagnosis. I didn't doubt (why should I?) when he told me that he had seen the protozoa. I simply felt a shock that anyone can easily imagine.

So, in exactly forty seconds the "doctor" gave me the news; he gave me a prescription, charged me forty thousand *cruzados* and dispatched me from his office. Signing the check was a difficult task, principally because I had to control my trembling hands.

(Some days later, in rather different circumstances, it was confirmed that I had AIDS, but that the reason for my prostration had been glandular tuberculosis. I very probably never had the pneumonia that he had diagnosed. He very probably "saw" homosexuality, as so many "doctors" have come to do.)

Forty seconds. That was the amount of time that he gave me to absorb the news. It was sufficient time, above all, to give me the horror of seeing, in that clinical indifference, perhaps a certain touch of cruelty: could he not be taking "vengeance" on me because I was a homosexual and deserved to be punished? Possibly. One can never guess what sort of sexuality—or behavior —such a "doctor" actually has.

Horror—that was exactly what I felt. I had before me a diagnostic device, a dehumanized medical apparatus that could suddenly entangle me in its machinery and lead me to something even more terrible than AIDS: in the place of death as a vital experience, I faced the indignity of an empty, hospitalized death. Above all, I feared the future, which that monstrosity foresaw for me. I knew that I would become subject to a series of infections and, as such, I was afraid of becoming subjected to the infernal machinery directed by this pack of dehumanizing specialists.

I have AIDS. It is a corporeal experience about which I still have a great deal to say. But is has nothing to do with the illness I had there, in the eyes of that "doctor."

I left that office deeply troubled. Forty seconds of AIDS! I had escaped. Cláudio, my companion, was waiting for me out here. My friends were waiting for me. Life was waiting for me. I freed myself from the frightful disease that had killed me for forty seconds. I escaped—with the conviction that it is necessary to free other sick people from this trap. Real AIDS is something far too serious to be treated by "doctors," by that brand of medicine that AIDS came to prove has failed.

What's left is life. Forty seconds at a time. Intensely.

Affirmative Action in the Ministry of Foreign Affairs

Celso Lafer

In the 1980s, activists from the United Black Movement against Racial Discrimination, among others, as well as historic Afro-descendant leaders such as Abdias do Nascimento, continued to call on the Brazilian government to carry out official programs to overcome the systemic legacies of racism and discrimination. But public officials were slow to respond. Some politicians and intellectuals argued that policies such as affirmative action were mechanical implementations of U.S. programs that did not take into account historical differences between the two countries. Some also argued that they would reify essentialized notions of race in a country of complex racial mixture and diversity.

Slowly, proponents of concrete affirmative action programs gained ground. While today many universities have implemented affirmative action programs, one of the first efforts was inaugurated during the government of Fernando Henrique Cardoso in 2002. It entailed establishing scholarships for people of African descent to prepare them for the highly competitive entrance exams for admission to the Rio Branco Institute, the professional school for those seeking entry into the diplomatic corps of the Ministry of Foreign Affairs (Itamaraty). In the following speech, Celso Lafer, the minster of foreign affairs, explains the reasons for this government program.

His Excellency, Ambassador Ronaldo Sardenberg,
Ministry of Science and Technology

His Excellency, Professor Paulo Sérgio Pinheiro,
Secretary of State for Human Rights

Professor Esper Cavalheiro, President of the National Council on Research

Mr. Carlos Moura, President of the Palmares Foundation

Minister João Alminio, Director of the Instituto Rio Branco

In a ceremony that took place yesterday, May 13, in the Presidential Palace (Palácio do Planalto), the President of the Republic [Fernando

Henrique Cardoso] signed a decree that instituted a national affirmative action program designed to promote the principle of diversity and pluralism in filling federal public administrative posts and in service contracts with government bodies.

In the same ceremony, the President of the Republic launched the Second National Human Rights Plan that stipulated 518 goals in the area of civil, political, economic, social, and cultural rights. Said plan reinforces the means to fight against discrimination experienced by society's most vulnerable. The National Affirmative Action Plan and the Second National Human Rights Plan broaden the concept of equality, foreseen in the Brazilian Constitution, making it more in tune with social and political changes and above all adjusting to the new dimensions of rights and citizenship that characterize democratic societies. It is an inclusive policy that favors diversity and the representation of different social and racial groups in the exercise of the relevant functions of the State and society.

The Affirmative Action Program of the Rio Branco Institute is in perfect alignment with the measures announced yesterday by the President of the Republic. Its basic objective is to increase the equality of opportunity in accessing a diplomatic career. With it, Itamaraty is taking another step on its path of democratization and the search for excellence.

As President Fernando Henrique Cardoso stated in the ceremony when giving the National Human Rights Award in December of last year, we need "to have a diplomatic corps that is a reflection of our society, that is multicolored, and it is unacceptable that Brazil presents itself abroad as a white society, because it is not one."

Twenty scholarships to pursue a diplomatic career will be given to Afro-descendant candidates to prepare for the Rio Branco Institute entrance exams. There will also be a concern for gender parity. Applicants may apply for scholarships from today until June 20.

We are taking one more step toward democratization. Already in 1852, Paulino José de Souza, the Viscount of Uruguay, created the public competition for consular officials which today would be a diplomatic career. Since then many innovations have been introduced with the general tendency toward democratization: creating the Rio Branco Institute, incorporating women into the diplomatic corps in the 1950s, holding exams throughout the country and in eleven state capitals, and beginning this year allowing people to apply through the internet.

If we want to attract the best, we can't allow candidates to be excluded because of racial discrimination or financial limitations that curtail their educational opportunities, or because people don't have sufficient resources to prepare adequately for the entrance exam. Afro-descendants and the poor who manage to receive a university degree, overcoming many obstacles, in truth show an extraordinary capacity. It is among them that we will choose and grant these scholarships, broadening the base of recruitment for the entrance exam, and thus reinforcing the tradition of excellence in the Rio Branco Institute. We also hope that the results of this program contribute to making our diplomacy more representative of the different segments that make up Brazilian society.

The affirmative action program of the Rio Branco Institute will not be limited to the terms of this agreement. We are carrying out a major effort to disseminate the information about this entrance exam so that it reaches all social classes and regions of the country. Candidates from indigenous communities can especially benefit from special attention through the sending of bibliographic material by diplomats on a volunteer basis. We are carrying out an effort so that young women diplomats transmit information about this career to potential candidates. We are doing this because we understand that women are still underrepresented in Itamaraty.

One cannot lose sight of the fact that the implementation of an inclusive policy that favors diversity and representation of different racial and social groups in Brazilian public administration will provide benefits for the country. During the time that practices of racial discrimination were prevalent in Brazil, one of the strategic errors of the States and the business sector was precisely not offering effective educational and employment opportunities for certain segments of the population who suffered discrimination.

Overcoming the problem of discrimination will not happen without definitively ending what [Joaquim] Nabuco called "the work of slavery," which persists more than a century after emancipation as a characteristic trait of Brazilian society.

The events celebrated yesterday in the Palácio do Planalto and today in the Rio Branco Institute represent a fundamental step in that direction. They signify, above all else, the definitive end to the neutrality and indifference of public power regarding the situation of racial inequality in Brazil.

The government of President Fernando Henrique Cardoso has promoted a broader discussion about the racial question in the history of our country. One of the main conclusions that the government reached is regarding the imperfection of public policies that are supposed to be universal as a way of ensuring rights to those individuals and groups who are socially and economically unequal. Although indispensable for the combat of discriminatory practices, such universalistic policies tend to prove insufficient to overcome the historical framework of racial inequality among whites and blacks in Brazil.

For these reasons, the Brazilian State is determined to avoid the deepening of inequality, to promote actions destined to ensure formal equality among individuals that is already present in our constitutional system, and to continue progressively expanding in the direction of protecting and defending the particular rights of groups socially disfavored and discriminated against.

The document that we sign is consistent, therefore, with the policy of the government, as conducted in the highest echelons by President Fernando Henrique Cardoso. It is consistent with our responsibilities as a signee of the International Convention for the Elimination of Racial Discrimination, and involves a partnership with Itamaraty, the Ministry of Justice, the Ministry of Culture, and the Ministry of Science and Technology.

We hope that one day the degree of democracy achieved by Brazil will make affirmative action unnecessary. But the fact is that today it responds to an urgent imperative. Itamaraty and the Rio Branco Institute will not stand by with their arms crossed waiting for the situation to change on its own.

Thank you very much.

Translated by James N. Green

A Young Voice from the MST

Cristiane

Since its foundation in the mid-1980s, the Movement of Landless Rural Workers (Movimento dos Trabalhadores sem Terra, MST) has constituted the largest social movement in Brazil and one of the most influential in Latin America. The MST tries to redress Brazil's unequal rural landholding system and high rates of rural poverty by pressing for agrarian reform. Agrarian reform suffered important legal setbacks during the writing of the 1988 Constitution, which in turn fueled the militancy of the MST. The movement is best known for staging highly organized land occupations in which groups of MST families take over privately owned but unproductive land, setting up assentamentos, *or encampments—communities of homes, collective kitchens, medical centers, schools, and so forth. The MST also demands urban attention to rural problems by blocking highways, thereby halting the delivery of agricultural products to cities. They also demand* pedágios *(tolls) from drivers or undertake* saques *(looting) of cargos, using these resources to fund the organization.*

These activities have not gone uncontested, and MST members have been violently attacked by private security forces and the police. The most notorious of these incidents occurred on April 17, 1996, in Eldorado dos Carajás, Pará, when the military police opened fire on an MST group, killing nineteen people and injuring more than sixty. Local TV reporters captured some of the violence on video, while later investigations revealed that some victims were shot in the back of the head or bludgeoned to death with their own farming tools. Such an example of atrocious human rights abuses created an uproar in Brazil and abroad at the time.

At the one-year anniversary of this massacre, MST members staged a commemorative march from three different points within Brazil to the capital of Brasília. Thousands walked together for weeks through blazing sun or pouring rain in order to participate. Among them was fourteen-year-old Cristiane, whose words below give one young girl's view of life as a poor rural Brazilian, both before and after her family became involved with the MST. As this document is the edited transcription of an oral interview, Cristiane's narrative is not always as linear as a written memoir, but her perspective as someone whose life has been profoundly impacted by the MST is clear.

My name is Cristiane. I am from [the state of] Mato Grosso do Sul, from the city of New Acre, where my parents are currently *assentados* [people living on an *assentamento*]. I was born in 1983, in the city of Dourados. . . . I lived in that city, and my father worked on a farm near there. He worked as a *bóia-fria* [a day laborer, nicknamed *bóia-fria*, or "cold lunch," because these workers typically bring their own lunch, which is cold by the time they eat it] so that we could survive. . . . My mother also worked on the farm, taking care of livestock. . . .

Working as a *bóia-fria* is like this: you had to get up really early in the morning . . . and then you'd go to the corner and catch a ride on the truck that went to the fields. . . . The first time I went to work as a *bóia-fria*, I lost all my illusions. I remember it was a Friday, and we couldn't go to school that day without a uniform and a textbook. And since I didn't have the money to buy those things, I went to work. And the first day you really feel it! It is really, really, awful the first day you start working, isn't it?

I was nine years old—eight going on nine. . . . We were going to the fields in the truck and it was full of people, of *bóia-frias*. . . . And a police truck passed us as we were going. And they talked to us like this:

"Hey, Dog Killers! . . ."

They yelled at us like that. Yes! Because, for them, "dog killers" is the way they talk about human beings. . . . And then they fired three shots into our truck! I was with my brother and my dad. My dad pushed us down . . . [but] there was another boy who was also working to support himself. . . . He tried to look, and the last shot—an explosive bullet—hit him in the head! He fell on a woman's lap, and we thought he was sleeping, that he was crouching down, but then her skirt started to get stained with blood and she started to scream! After that the driver turned around. We went back, went to the hospital, but it was too late, he was already dead. . . .

I was still a kid then, but I felt remorse about that. I still feel it today. I couldn't look at police . . . nor dead people. . . . I had all of that stuck in my head. And in the statement [the police] gave afterward, they said they had engaged in conflict with a thief, but that wasn't the case! He was a worker who was going to work! It was my first ever day of work and this is what happened. . . . I never forgot it. I cried . . . for three days. . . . They had a demonstration in front of the City Courthouse, but it was such an isolated event. There was no real organization to do more. This all took place in Dourados, so it had no wider repercussion. It was isolated. It was one day, and by the next day it meant nothing to the authorities. The police were not arrested, and even today the police have gone unpunished.

. . . We undertook our first occupation on May 16, 1992, at the Santarém farm, which is owned by a rich landowner from this state. Most of the land in the area is his. . . . We left Dourados at midnight to do this occupation. We did the occupation in the early morning hours on a Saturday. We stayed there all day that Saturday. We stayed the night at the farm, and Sunday in the early morning, the police came with a preliminary eviction notice.

Activists from the Movement of Landless Rural Workers in Brasília demanding access to land. Photograph by José Cruz. Courtesy of Agência Brasil.

What most moved me, and what kept us from having conflicts with the police, was that [when the police arrived] we were singing the Brazilian national anthem! Because those of us at the farm weren't timid! We sang the Brazilian national anthem, and that moved the police who had their weapons in their hands, you know? [But] they had no way of shooting at unarmed people who were singing the Brazilian national anthem. Unarmed, just with farming tools!

. . . They gave the eviction order and we left the farm . . . in the rain, really heavy rain! It soaked all of our things. My sister was four, I was nine, my brother twelve. She got lost in the midst of all the police and they didn't do anything, they just laughed! And her, so little, and all wet with rain . . . but we found her. We left there, traveling at night. They dispersed our organization. . . . They sent some of us to BR 163 [a highway between Mato Grosso and Pará], which is close to the city of Brilhante. . . . We made huts [there], and stayed there in our encampment.

So it was like this: we stayed on the median of the BR, less than a hundred meters from the road! . . . It was very crowded where we were. At the back of the encampment we built a really big, really pretty camp and also built a school . . . [but] it was really hard for us to stay at that place. . . . We had to go fetch water at a river . . . except that the mayor of the city—who is also a big landowner—dumped all the sewage in the river! . . . So no one could drink the water! The only thing we could do with it was wash our clothes. . . . [But] in school we learned a lot of things. They talked about [local] government officials so that we could learn to fight for our rights. Because, when I first entered the movement, I didn't talk with anyone! I was a very unfriendly child, very fearful. I had a lot of fear of the police. I was scared of those people who really are equal to us, you know? So I talked very little. It was here, in the movement, that I learned to talk, to be able to express my feelings. It was here that I even learned to sing!

We stayed in that encampment on the side of the BR for one year. At the end of the year, we decided to undertake another occupation, in another city, on a farm where the farmer planted marijuana and transported illegal lumber. He is a foreigner: so Brazilian lands are in the hands of foreigners. . . . Other families had undertaken an occupation of this land once before. . . . They had conflicts with the police! Some were injured, others maimed. . . . For that reason, some of their group gave up. We got together with those who had remained and undertook a second, unified occupation. In that occupation, we were peaceful: in less than twenty-four hours the judge brought the eviction order and there wasn't time to move our things onto the farm. . . . We had to leave.

We requested authorization to stay on a plot of land near the farm. And from that plot we undertook eleven occupations of the farm. . . . From one week to the next we would undertake an occupation and then leave peacefully. We would grab our things, cross over the fence [that surrounded the farm], and stay close to the river. . . . It was always like this: we'd go and come back, go and come back, go and come back . . . and they would always clear us out!

So, on that farm, where we had camped so many times, we decided to occupy part of the plot. We set up an occupation there. Even helicopters passed by! And the day that they were going to evict us, we all went to the site. We said, "If the police come, we are not going to leave! We are going to try to resist! Now, if they want to enter into conflict, then we will leave." And we decided to really stay, to stay three years on that farm, just occupying, occupying, occupying. Occupying and going back.

. . . The guy who worked for the foreigner, who spoke Portuguese—he was the one who undertook all the negotiations—came [one day] to look things over. . . . He took some pictures of all of our crops. We had planted lots of things and were going to suffer a lot of loss [if we were forced to leave]. He took the photo, brought it to the state INCRA [National Institute for Colonization and Agrarian Reform] office, and we were not evicted. There were still some other efforts to dislodge us, as there still are, but they have not been able to. . . .

That was five, almost six, years ago. And now we're big, aren't we? We entered the movement when we were small. And we worked, studied. . . . Now I'm in the seventh grade! [Right now during this march] I am missing class, but since the school is within our encampment, if I write a report about this for my teacher, it will earn me a very good grade, because I am fighting for everyone! For the rights of those who aren't here, right? But, if I were still living in the city, this wouldn't be an acceptable justification. . . .

I can see, can clearly differentiate, what my life was like before and after I entered the movement. Look, so much changed! Because in the city, there were days when we had no food! When we went hungry! Now, here in the movement, since we moved to the encampment, we never go without eating. . . .

So my life is very different because I created a vision and solidarity through my other fellow participants in the movement: when I had, I gave to others; when they had, they gave. . . . When we all had some kind of general need, when everyone was without something, we found an alternative, for example setting up *saques* or *pedágios*. I would stand there, with the little rope [stretched across the road], asking for money. Then, along with other people, you can keep that up. Thanks to God, in the Movimento Sem Terra I never went hungry. . . . Here, within the Movimento Sem Terra, I have been able to have a better vision of my rights [than if I had stayed in the city], to learn more. Because it's no use going to school when you're hungry, because you don't learn anything! In the MST, I learned lots, lots, lots. I learned lots!

Translated by Victoria Langland, Page Martell, and Lonny Ivan Meyer

World Social Forum Charter of Principles

Various authors

As people around the world in the late 1990s began looking for new models of democratic governance and popular political participation in the shadow of globalization, they increasingly looked to Brazil, especially to the city of Porto Alegre in Rio Grande do Sul. In 1989, that city began experimenting with participatory budgeting, in which citizens helped determine how the city allocated its financial resources, and the program became a model for many other communities in Brazil and abroad. Thus when Brazilian activists, in coalition with social movements from other countries, sought to establish an alternative to the World Economic Forum in Davos, Switzerland, Porto Alegre became an ideal host city. It first played host in January 2001, gathering around twelve thousand people from across the globe to discuss alternative visions of globalization and integration under the slogan Another World Is Possible. At its conclusion, Brazilian organizers drew up the following charter of principles, defining the nature and goals of the World Social Forum. As of this writing, there has been a World Social Forum every year since its founding, now alternating among various cities worldwide.

The committee of Brazilian organizations that conceived of and organized the first World Social Forum, held in Porto Alegre from January 25 to 30, 2001, after evaluating the results of that Forum and the expectations it raised, consider it necessary and legitimate to draw up a Charter of Principles to guide the continued pursuit of that initiative. While the principles contained in this Charter—to be respected by all those who wish to take part in the process and to organize new iterations of the World Social Forum—are a consolidation of the decisions that formed the governing rules for the Porto Alegre Forum and ensured its success, they extend the reach of those decisions and define orientations that flow from their logic.

1) The World Social Forum is an open meeting place for reflective thinking, democratic debate of ideas, formulation of proposals, free exchange of experiences, and networking for effective action by groups and movements of civil society that are opposed to neo-liberalism and to domination of the

Participants at the 2005 World Social Forum in Porto Alegre use an enormous earth-shaped balloon to symbolize the global importance of their political agenda. FreeImages.com/Heliton Oliveira.

world by capital and any form of imperialism, and are committed to building a planetary society directed towards fruitful relationships among human-kind and between it and the earth.

2) The World Social Forum at Porto Alegre was an event localized in time and place. From now on, in the certainty proclaimed at Porto Alegre that "Another World Is Possible," it becomes a permanent process of seeking and building alternatives, which cannot be reduced to the events supporting it.

3) The World Social Forum is a world process. All the meetings that are held as part of this process have an international dimension.

4) The alternatives proposed at the World Social Forum stand in opposition to a process of globalization commanded by the large multinational corporations and by the governments and international institutions at the service of those corporations' interests, with the complicity of national governments. They are designed to ensure that a globalization based on solidarity among the people will prevail as a new stage in world history. This will respect universal human rights, and those of all citizens—men and women—of all nations, as well as the environment in which they live, and will rest on democratic international systems and institutions at the service of social justice, equality and the sovereignty of peoples.

5) The World Social Forum seeks only to bring together and interconnect organizations and movements of civil society from all countries of the world; it is not intended to be a representative body for worldwide civil society.

6) The meetings of the World Social Forum do not deliberate on behalf of the World Social Forum as a body. No one, therefore, will be authorized, on behalf of any of the meetings of the Forum, to express positions claiming to be those of all its participants. The participants in the Forum shall not be called on to take decisions as a body, whether by vote or acclamation, on declarations or proposals for action that would commit all, or the majority, of them and that propose to be taken as establishing positions of the Forum as a body. It thus does not constitute a locus of power to be disputed by the participants in its meetings, nor does it intend to constitute the only option for interassociation and action by the organizations and movements that participate in it.

7) Nonetheless, organizations or groups of organizations that participate in the Forum's meetings must be assured the right, during such meetings, to deliberate on declarations or actions they may decide on, whether singly or in coordination with other participants. The World Social Forum undertakes to circulate such decisions widely by the means at its disposal, without directing, hierarchizing, censuring or restricting them, but as deliberations of the organizations or groups of organizations that made the decisions.

8) The World Social Forum provides a pluralistic, diversified, non-religious, non-governmental, and non-party context for deliberation that, in a decentralized fashion, interconnects organizations and movements engaged in concrete action at levels from the local to the international to build a better world.

9) The World Social Forum will always be a forum open to pluralism and to diversity of activities and ways of engaging of organizations and movements that decide to participate in it, as well as a diversity of genders, ethnicities, cultures, generations and physical capacities, providing they abide by this Charter of Principles. Neither party delegations nor political organizations shall participate in the Forum. Government leaders and members of legislatures who accept the commitments of this Charter may be invited to participate in a personal capacity.

10) The World Social Forum is opposed to all totalitarian and reductionist views of economy, development and history and to the use of violence as a means of social control by the State. It upholds respect for human rights, the practices of real democracy, participatory democracy, and peaceful relations; for equality and solidarity, among individuals, ethnicities, genders and peoples, and it condemns all forms of domination and all subjection of one person by another.

11) As a forum for debate, the World Social Forum is a movement of ideas that prompts reflection and the transparent circulation of the results of that reflection in order to influence the mechanisms and instruments of domination by capital, on means and actions to resist and overcome that domination, and on the alternatives proposed to solve the problems of exclusion and social inequality that the process of capitalist globalization, with its racist, sexist and environmentally destructive dimensions, is creating internationally and within countries.

12) As a framework for the exchange of experiences, the World Social Forum encourages understanding and mutual recognition amongst its participant organizations and movements, and places special value on the exchange among them, particularly on all that society is building to center economic activity and political action on meeting the needs of people and respecting nature, in the present and for future generations.

13) As a context for interrelations, the World Social Forum seeks to strengthen and create new national and international links among organizations and movements of society, that, in both public and private life, will increase the capacity for non-violent social resistance to the process of dehumanization the world is undergoing and to the violence used by the State, and will reinforce the humanizing measures being taken by the action of these movements and organizations.

14) The World Social Forum is a process that encourages its participant organizations and movements to situate their activities in various venues, from the local level to the national level, to seek active participation in international contexts, as issues of planetary citizenship, and to introduce onto the global agenda the change-inducing practices that they are using to experiment in building a new world of popular solidarity.

Approved and adopted in São Paulo, on April 9, 2001, by the organizations that make up the World Social Forum Organizing Committee, approved with modifications by the World Social Forum International Council on June 10, 2001.

The Bolsa Família Program

Various authors

One of the most important social programs in Brazil today is the Bolsa Família, or Family Grant, a system of conditional cash transfers for poor families. Inaugurated by President Lula in 2003, it was the centerpiece of his campaign against poverty and was considered central to his prolonged electoral success.

Through Bolsa Família, families earning less than US$70 a month receive a monthly cash subsidy; those with children who attend school, or women who are currently pregnant or breast-feeding, receive additional subsidies per each qualified child (up to five per family). In order to reduce corruption and bureaucratic graft, the executive branch pairs directly with municipalities in running the program, bypassing state governments. Moreover, since this is an entitlement program, politicians have little ability to disperse funds for electoral purposes, and the amount that families receive is registered on a public website. Recipients are given a debit card called a Cartão Cidadão (Citizen card), so that funds may be credited directly. The cards are issued to the primary female member of the family, when possible. The following excerpts from interviews with two women from Araçuaí, Minas Gerais, who participate in Bolsa Família exemplify how the program has transformed the lives of some of Brazil's poorest populations.

Dona Helena, Age Thirty-One

[Bolsa Familia] is very good. It rescued us, as they say, because before the grant we went hungry, to be honest, because it was difficult. For me who doesn't have a husband, who has this throng of kids, to take care of them out here in the country, [getting to be a part of] Bolsa Família was worrying for me, but once it came out I was relieved. It helps me buy their school materials, to buy rubber sandals for them.

If you didn't have the grant, do you think you would go hungry?
We would go hungry; we would still be going hungry.

What do you think about [the cards] being in women's names, and not in men's names? Do you think that's good or bad?

It's good, because if it were in men's names, if they got the funds, I think they wouldn't let [their families] lack for anything, but, I don't know, we wouldn't have their privilege of being responsible for the money. Even when the guys work, they don't pass the money over to women's hands. They want to, I don't know, give things out grandly: I'm going to buy this; this money is mine, I'm the one who worked for it; I'm the one who earned this money; this is coming in my name. So, I don't know. Sometimes a guy would put off buying a pair of rubber sandals for his own children in order to, I don't know, spend the money on other things. Because men, not all of them, but most of them, have weak heads; they take the money and go to a bar to have a good time.

Do you think voting helps you? Does it change anything or does it not change things?

It doesn't just change things for me, it changes things for everyone, but voting helps, right? It's that people don't know how to choose. Sometimes I vote for a candidate thinking he's a good candidate, but in the end he's the worst candidate ever. But I think it helps, yes.

Dona Palmira, Age Thirty-Three

I think Bolsa Família is good because without it I would have died of hunger with my children . . . because what people earn around here is very little. I work three days a week to earn twenty-five *reais*. Three days to earn twenty-five *reais*.

What kind of work do you do?

Maid work, doing everything.

Twenty-five reais?

For the three days. The woman of the house pays me. Three days without tears. Those three days that I go to work, I clean, I cook, I iron, I tidy up the house. You can do the math and see how much I earn per day.

Not even nine reais. . . .

She told me that's all she can afford. I said, "I accept." So, it's twenty-five *reais*. I said, I'll go so as not to sit around doing nothing. I don't like to sit around doing nothing, no, not at all. My boy wakes up in the morning and wants bread—what am I supposed to do? I have no other way of buying it. His father doesn't help. He's disappeared off the map, the father of all three of them. So, what am I going to do? I'm going to work to earn twenty-five *reais*, ten *reais*, and if they say to me, I'm going to give you nine *reais*, will you come and wash our clothes today? I'm going to go and wash their clothes.

Translated by Victoria Langland

Music, Culture, and Globalization

Gilberto Gil

Since the early 1960s, Gilberto Gil has been at the forefront of creative thinking about Brazilian culture (see "Portraits" in part X). In 2003, President Luiz Inácio Lula da Silva appointed the internationally acclaimed songwriter and musician as minister of culture. Despite the fact that a majority of Brazilians have some African heritage, Gil was only the second person who identified himself as black to be appointed to a Cabinet post. The following reflection about Brazilian culture in the age of globalization explains Gil's understanding of the complex dialectical relationship between national and international cultural production. It has been slightly edited to clarify the original translation from Portuguese to English.

Take a look at the cover of my album "Parabolicamará." It has a picture of my daughter Maria carrying a parabolic antenna made of straw on her head:

> Before the world was small
> Because Earth was big
> Today the world is too big
> Because Earth is small
> Of the size of a parabolicamará antenna
> É, turn of the world, camará
> É, world turns, camará

I recorded this song in 1991. It has the same title as the album with the picture of my daughter carrying—the same way the women in Africa and in Brazil do—a basket shaped as an antenna on her head. At that time, it was still unusual to hear the word globalization. I named the album Parabolicamará to call the attention to some of the aspects of a future globalization that I contemplated and even desired, in a tragicomic manner, as someone who embraces everything that happens.

Parabolicamará brings together the word parabolic, the type of antenna that can be seen everywhere, even in the poorest corners of Brazil, and the word camará, the name the players of capoeira, the afro-american playful martial art, have chosen to call their singing and dancing partners, "camaradas."

Cover of Gilberto Gil's album *Parabolicamará*.

The chorus "É, turn of the world, camará" I borrowed from a very common verse present in any capoeira gathering. It is a way of singing about the vastness of the world, which also brings the certainty that the world comes and goes, and that in the next turn—as in the choreographed turn of the dance-fight—the player who today loses can become the winner. Everything changes, all the time. And only those who understand change can conquer, or achieve victories, which are always partial. When I was writing the song I was thinking about the history of capoeira. Once I went to visit Macau. A few years ago, in Macau, there was a Portuguese boy teaching capoeira to the kids from Angola. The world certainly turns and each turn it becomes more complex.

People say that capoeira was conceived in Angola, but was born in Brazil. No one knows for certain its history. Yet it seems to be a truly Brazilian invention, built upon African elements, like samba. Today Brazilians teach capoeira in Africa, in Portugal and in many other countries. The students spread the art through the rest of the world. It is a sport, an art and even a spiritual practice, which is part of human heritage, just like judo, fencing or Thai boxing. Search for capoeira on the Internet. I looked it up on Google: there are more than 6 million pages. Very few compared to the 71 million pages concerning samba, or the 92 million about reggae, or the 371 million about jazz. Yet, it is a number that keeps growing.

There was no cultural policy on the part of the Brazilian government, or on the part of the global cultural industry to disseminate capoeira to the world. It happened without official support, in a decentralized fashion, like a virus spreading through all continents.

I like to contemplate phenomena like these. We, those who produce cultural policies for our governments and for our international institutions, have a lot to learn observing them. In my view we have to identify them, solidify them, make stronger what already exists and is produced with more or less spontaneity by the people in their creative sharing or partaking. This seems to me more efficient than trying to impose from the top down forms of behavior that try to tell the nations what they must be, or what they must continue to be. These events of non-programmed cultural sharing demonstrate that many forces are in play concerning the culture of the planet, and that speaking merely about the homogenization that takes place always and everywhere is perhaps simplifying the reality too much.

Am I being naïve? I know very well about the other side of the coin, the terrible power relations that make original cultures disappear every day and impose standards of consumption on the planet for the benefit of those envisaging easy profits. But I want to face the challenge that the global cultural industry is proposing to us—I am part of this industry too—trying to use its power for my artistic goals. I am still not sure whether I was successful in creating my own space inside its laws. But I am still cultivating this strange and provocative experience of bringing together ideas that seemed bound to be eternally separated. Just like parabolic and camará. I like to see the world echoing just like the head of a *berimbau*. I like to connect the differences.

Because I radically support this particular worldview, I have been criticized and booed many times. When I was very young, in the 60's, and I was starting to become famous in Brazil, I was booed by a crowd of university students because I performed in a concert together with a rock group. These students thought that electric guitars could destroy the authentic Brazilian culture. But I always thought of culture as open-ended, as an open source software. Collaboration and exchange with the other, and perpetual cultural cannibalism, both are part of the vitality of cultures, and the possibility of free exchange must be preserved against any effort to impose restrictions. Maybe I think like this because I have lived for a long time beside the sea. I will try to explain clearly everything I said. I apologize if this might seem repetitive:

Seaside
Common place

Beginning of the walk
To another place.

Among the various aspects of being human, one leads to two very different, but complementary, perspectives, about our place on the planet: the condition of being from the seaside or being from the countryside. I am from the seaside. Even though I spent my childhood in the countryside, I grew up with a longing for the seaside. More specifically, I am from the city of São Salvador by the Bay of All Saints, Brazil. This category in which I belong creates a notion of belonging in the world with eyes focused on the horizon. Seated by the beach, looking at the sea, the "transcendental cinema," as sung by Caetano Veloso, when I was still a child, I traveled through all the oceans, I found harbor in all ports, sitting down firmly, but my soul wandered without destination. The continental tends to look suspiciously upon this being, who seems frivolous and too much of a dreamer, because it [the inhabitant of the shore] is a more solid creature, with more profound roots planted in his homeland, with a clear notion of paths and limits.

As an inhabitant of the harbor, of the back-and-forth of the waves and of ideas, I grew up Brazilian, a word with ambiguous and mysterious meanings. Searching for certainties, I turned myself to the countryside, paulistas and paulistanos, mineiros das gerais, amazons, sertanejos. As an artist, I was moved by what I called my people and I sang their hardships. With my agitated seaside spirit, however, I did not resist the temptation of synthesis, and I shuffled the destiny of some with the condition of others; I mixed chiclets with bananas, and, in Bonsucesso, a poor neighborhood in Rio de Janeiro, which is another seaside city in Brazil, I took an express train which took me away from poor Brazilian surroundings to the world, throwing me beyond the year 2000:

The express 2222 started
Departing from Bonsucesso and beyond
The express 2222 started from Central do Brasil
Departing from Bonsucesso to beyond the year 2000

As I mentioned before, when I played the rhythms of the Brazilian countryside with the electric guitar of the Beatles and of the Rolling Stones, I shocked the shorebound spirits of my country. The consequence was that I was considered a threat to national security. Tropicalism was my child, my destiny, and my space of affirmation as a Brazilian.

Today, when a lot has been said about globalization, which is not exactly what I was singing in Parabolicamará, when homogeneity is deeply feared, when wars are once again waged under the pretext of protecting certain values considered superiorly human, I think of my Portuguese ancestors, who "from the Western Portuguese beach . . . were expanding faith, the empire, and were devastating the barbarous lands of Africa and of Asia." And I think of how this was a reason for pride to the poet Camões. I think of my African ancestors, men and women from the seaside, looking at the Atlantic, which meant commerce, riches, disgrace, slavery and nostalgia. I think one of the results of all of this is the Brazil of today, with its peculiar alloy of tragedy and celebration of life. History, just like God, uses sinuous and elusive forms to write its text.

Elsewhere I have declared I am not afraid of being Brazilian. We are what we are, in spite of ourselves, whether this proves favorable or unfavorable to us. Just like another Portuguese poet with eyes turned toward the sea, I always knew I am not one, I am many. If this poet, meaningfully named Pessoa, once felt nostalgia for the lost empire, it was not because of mundane power, but because of another silent reason, one that could inhabit the fields of Ancient Greece, or express itself in the language of the Bretons, or celebrate the small river of its village. Everything was possible, if the soul was not small.

When suspicion of national hegemonies was spreading out through the world, like a good man from the seaside, I was prepared. And in my condition as a man, I recognized my female half; in my condition as a heterosexual, I contemplated my homosexual sensibility; in my condition as a black, I praised my soul of all colors; in my condition as a believer, I embraced the belief in all gods. As a politician, I saw in environmentalism the possibility of overcoming our immediate pettiness and of providing a cosmic dimension to our actions in society. Today, as Minister of Culture in my country, I see in the idea of culture the possibility of dealing with the Brazilian human being in all dimensions, embedded in the environment of Brazil, always nature and culture. As an artist and as a citizen of the world, I see in culture the space for countries to share faiths, races, sexualities, values, in the cacophony of its differences, in the antagonism of its incompatibilities, in the generosity of a common place, something that has never existed, but has always been dreamed of by those who let their gaze be lost in the horizon.

The vocation of the boy of Salvador of All Saints, navel-tied to the mother land but with the vagabond soul of sailor, follows me to all the ports where I find harbor, allowing me to talk in the international language of music about a certain people, that inhabit a certain place, and about a common place, where we are all equal in our immeasurable differences.

The Inaugural Speech of Brazil's First Female President

Dilma Rousseff

On January 1, 2010, Dilma Rousseff became Brazil's first female president. The daughter of a left-wing Bulgarian immigrant and a schoolteacher from Minas Gerais, Rousseff grew up in a comfortable upper-middle-class home in Belo Horizonte, where she spent hours in her father's library reading his extensive collection of books. In 1965, while in high school, she joined a clandestine revolutionary organization that adopted the strategy of organizing a guerrilla movement to overthrow the military dictatorship. Forced to flee to Rio de Janeiro in 1969, she operated underground until she was arrested in January 1970. She was tortured for two weeks and then sentenced to three years in prison for violating the National Security Act.

After her release in 1972, she moved to Porto Alegre in southern Brazil to be near her partner, Carlos Araújo, who remained incarcerated. In the late 1970s she completed her college degree in social sciences and began a political and administrative career, first as a member of the Democratic Labor Party and then as a member of the Workers' Party. She served as secretary of education and communication in the state government of Rio Grande do Sul and then was tapped by newly elected president Luiz Inácio Lula da Silva to be the minister of mines and energy. When a scandal erupted in the Lula administration, forcing his chief of staff to resign, Rousseff assumed that position, acting as the political coordinator between the legislative and executive branches of government. She became Lula's handpicked successor to run as the head of the Workers' Party–led coalition in the 2010 presidential elections. She defeated José Serra, her center-right opponent, by 56 to 44 percent in runoff elections.

Her impeachment in 2016 for alleged budgetary improprieties polarized the nation. These extracts from her inaugural speech lay out the main priorities for her first administration, from 2011 to 2014, and echo the optimism of those who heralded the election of Brazil's first female president. In her remarks she mentions the "presalt," oil deposits on the coast of Brazil that have been discovered below a thick layer of salt on the ocean floor. The proceeds from these oil reserves promise significant income for government investment in social programs.

. . . I would like to direct this speech to all Brazilians, my friends from all over Brazil. It is an immense joy to be here tonight. I have received from millions of Brazilians a mission, perhaps the most important mission of my life.

And this fact, in a larger sense, is a demonstration of the democratic advancement of our country, because for the first time a woman will preside over Brazil. I have already noted, therefore, my first postelection commitment: to honor Brazilian women so that this fact, until today uncorrected, becomes a natural event that can repeat itself and expand into businesses, civil institutions, and representative entities in all parts of our society. Equality of opportunity between men and women is an essential principle of democracy.

I want fathers and mothers to be able to look into the eyes of their daughters and say, "Yes, a woman can." My joy is even greater for the significance that the presence of a woman in the Presidency of the Republic gives to the sacred path of the vote, the democratic decision of the voter, the most elevated exercise of citizenship.

For this reason, I note here another commitment to my country: valuing democracy in all of its dimensions, from the right to opinion and expression to the essential, basic rights of nourishment, employment, income, decent housing, and social peace.

I am going to ensure the most ample and unrestricted freedom of the press, the most ample freedom of religion, the discerning and permanent observation of human rights so clearly sacred in our own Constitution. I will guarantee our Constitution, the greatest duty of the President of the Republic.

In the long journey that brought me here, I was able to speak to and visit all of our regions. What most gave me confidence and hope was the immense capacity of our people to seize an opportunity, as small as it may be, as simple as it may be, and with it construct a better world for them and for their family. The capacity of our people to create and to strive is simply incredible.

For this reason, I here reemphasize the fundamental commitment that I have maintained and reiterated throughout this campaign: the eradication of poverty and the creation of opportunities for all Brazilians. I emphasize, however, that this ambitious goal will not be achieved only through the will of the government. This will is important, but our goal is to reach out to the nation, to businessmen, to churches, to civil entities, to universities, to the press, to governors, mayors, and all good people of our country. . . .

Brazil is a generous land and always returns in twofold every seed that is planted with a loving hand and a look to the future. My conviction in assuming the goal of eradicating poverty does not come from a theoretical certainty, but from experience lived within our government, the government of President Lula, in which immense social mobility was achieved, making possible today a dream that always appeared impossible. . . .

I do not count on the strength of developed economies to propel our growth. For this reason our own market, our own savings, and our own economic decisions become even more important.

I am far from saying with this that we intend to close the country to the world; on the contrary. We will continue advocating for the opening of commercial relations, the end of the protectionism of rich countries that impedes poor nations from fully realizing their vocations, and against the currency war that occurs today in the world. But it is necessary to recognize that we will have great responsibilities in a world that still is confronting the challenges and effects of a financial crisis of great proportions and that needs the help of mechanisms not always adequate, nor always balanced, for the return to growth. . . .

We will responsibly take care of our economy. The Brazilian people will no longer tolerate inflation, which is an irresponsible solution for instability. The Brazilian people do not accept governments that spend more than what is sustainable. For this reason, we will make all efforts to improve the quality of public spending, simplify and reduce taxation, and improve the quality of public services.

But we reject the view that adjustment should fall on social programs, essential services to the population, and necessary investments for the good of the country. We will seek elevated rates of long-term development that are socially and environmentally sustainable.

To do this, we will ensure public saving, meritocracy in the civil service, the excellence of public service, and the improvement of all mechanisms that free the entrepreneurial capacity of our entrepreneurs and our people.

I will encourage microenterprise to establish millions of individual and family businesses. I will expand the limits of "super simple" [taxation] and construct modern mechanisms of economic improvement as our government, the government of President Lula, did in civil construction and electrical production, with the law of business recovery, among other measures.

The regulatory agencies will have full support to act with determination and autonomy aimed at the promotion of innovation, healthy competition, and the effectiveness of regulated sector control. We will always clearly present our plans of governmental action.

We will bring to public debate the big national issues and always treat with transparency our goals, results, and difficulties. But, above all, I want to reaffirm our commitment to the stability of the economy and economic rules, signed contracts and set achievements.

We will treat the proceeds of our natural resources always with thought to the long term. For this, I will work with Congress for the approval of a presalt social fund and a regulatory framework model for sharing [the profits gained from] presalt [oil extraction]. Through these means, we will realize many of our social objectives. We reject ephemeral spending that leaves future generations only debt and hopelessness.

The presalt social fund is a long-term social fund to support current and future generations. It is the most important fruit of a new model that we propose, the model of sharing, that reserves to the people of this country the most important portion of the riches gained from the exploration of presalt [oil fields]. We will not transfer our wealth out of the country to leave only the crumbs to our people.

I committed myself in this campaign to improving the quality of education and health services. I committed myself to improving public security and combating drugs that hurt families and compromise our children and youth. I reaffirm these commitments. I will name ministers and a highly qualified team to achieve these objectives. But I will also personally follow actions in these important areas for the country's development. . . .

I said during the campaign that those most in need—children, youth, the disabled, the unemployed worker, the elderly—would have all of my attention. I reaffirm here this commitment. Michel Temer and I were elected by a coalition of ten parties and the support of leaders of various other parties. With them I will construct a government in which professional capacity, leadership, and a disposition to serve the country will be fundamental criteria. I will value the professional staff of public administration, independent of party affiliation.

I also direct this speech to opposition parties and to the sectors of society that were not with us in this campaign. I extend a hand to them. From me there will be no discrimination, privileges, or collusion. From my inauguration on, I will be president of all Brazilians, respecting differences of opinion, belief, and political orientation.

Our country still needs to improve the conduct and quality of politics. I want to engage, together with all parties, in political reform that elevates republican values that advance our young democracy. At the same time, I clearly affirm that I will value transparency in public administration. There will be no tolerance for mistakes, deviance, and poorly done work.

I will be strict in the defense of the public interest at all levels of my government. The organs of control and oversight will work with my support without ever pursuing adversaries or protecting friends. . . .

I thank the Brazilian and international press and all of their employees for their coverage of the electoral process. I do not deny that some of the things spread by the press saddened me, but as someone who has risked her life fighting for democracy and the right to free opinion, like many others among us who dedicated our youth to the right to free expression, they and I are natural lovers of freedom. I said and now repeat that I prefer the noise of a free press to the silence of dictatorships. Critics in a free press help the country and are essential for democratic governments, pointing out mistakes and bringing up necessary contradictions. . . .

Now, after the election, we know it is time to get to work. After the debate on projects, it is time for unity. Unity for education, unity for development, unity for the country. Together with me were elected new governors, new senators, new federal congresspeople. While also congratulating all of the state legislators elected in the first round, I invite them all, independent of party affiliation, to join in determined, effective, and energetic action for the future of our country, with the conviction that a Brazilian nation will achieve exactly the size, exactly the greatness measured by that which we together do for her.

I embrace each and all of my friends.

Translated by Molly Quinn

The June Revolts

Marcos Nobre

During the first two and a half years of her presidency, Dilma Rousseff retained enormous popularity among the electorate, with a positive approval rating that hovered between 65 and 70 percent, even surpassing Lula's popularity in some polls. Though the economy was slowing down as exports slumped, and inflation began to pick up, there was a general sense of optimism about her administration and the country's future. Moreover, the government was preparing for the 2014 World Soccer Cup and the 2016 Olympic Games, which had brought considerable international attention to the country. Then, a series of relatively small protests in São Paulo organized by the Movement for Free Passes, which opposed a recent rise in bus fares and proposed instead a form of government subsidies and tax restructuring that would render public transportation free, met brutal police repression. Within days, millions of people took to the streets across the country to protest a wide variety of grievances. The following essay by Marcos Nobre, a professor of philosophy at the State University of Campinas (UNICAMP) and a senior researcher at the CEBRAP think tank, offers an analysis of this nationwide upheaval within the historical context of the changes since the late 1980s. In the essay, Nobre traces a longer history of protests and corruption, and points to the importance of the media and its role in producing scandals, as well as to the persistent gulf between public opinion and the political system.

In seven days, between June 13 and 20, 2013, two myths were undone that persist in the imagination when one speaks of Brazil: that of a country of soccer and that of a land without open political conflicts. In the midst of the Confederations [Soccer] Cup, millions of people took to the streets to demonstrate their nonconformity.

To what end? That is the main question.

July 2013 bore a multitude of demands, frustrations, and aspirations. The fight against an increase in fares on public transportation and the opposition to megasporting events (the World Cup, the Olympic Games) catalyzed dissatisfactions of a much different order. Public transportation is an example of inefficiency, poor quality, and exorbitant prices. The construction for the Cup and the Olympics left a trail of violations of rights and made the population question their supposed benefits. The violent police repression of the earliest protests in the country triggered an even larger wave of mobilization, as much in defense of the constitutional right to demonstration as against actions by the police. Thus, a series of demands came together in these initiatives.

No type of unified narrative came out of these protests as a model. It is not about one movement, but several. Therefore, the interpretations diverge about what in fact happened as well as about the meaning of what happened. The significance of the revolts is not given and set, but will continue to be constructed, in the streets, and in different attempts at systematization and explanation.

The dynamics of organization are different in different parts of the country, in each city, in each part of the city where protests occur. Demonstrations surge like eruptions, large, small, isolated, united. When people unite in huge masses, demonstrations take the form of waves. Depending on the wave, the march can have different, irreconcilable meanings.

The June Revolts did not have leaders, podiums, or discussions. The marches formed, divided, and reunited without an established script. They came together through social networks and the word-of-mouth of text messages. They were not revolts directed against this or that party, this or that public figure. They were revolts against the system, against "all there is."

The June Revolts were surprising, but not a bolt of lightning in a blue sky. In no moment since the decline of the military dictatorship (1964–85) did society stop protesting. Strikes, occupations, resistance to police action, and demonstrations did not cease. Neither did demands that were material in nature, like inflation (the high cost of food, especially), the poor quality of employment, or the high price of public transportation. But it also seems clear that those individual elements do not explain the reasons for the revolt.

The June Revolts revealed a whole new democratic political culture that had formed the basis of society and had invaded the streets. An unknown number of discussion groups, in person and virtual, emerged and multiplied. The mass demonstrations opened the way for an impressive number of smaller, localized protests to spread throughout the country. The demands and marches proliferated, calling attention to neighborhood and street problems, local, regional, national, global problems, all at the same time.

As in other political eruptions around the world, this enormous democratic vitality seems not to fit into a political system; it hardly seems to fit in an entirely self-organized society. There are so many generous impulses that do not fit inside a system like the limiting (but democratic) movement that tries to institutionalize demonstrations in a new configuration. Losing one of the two critical dimensions of the democratic experience would mean losing its deepest meaning.

However, despite the self-organizing impetus of the new political groups that began the demonstrations, the June Revolts did not aim for an abolition of the boundary between society and the political system. Its vision was that of a radical reform of that system.

From the point of view of the political system, the reaction was one of confusion. Accosted in the streets, politicians went out in search of a hierarchical organization with leaders and clear demands, whom they could debate like technocrats, with spreadsheets and budgetary laws. They did not find what they were looking for. They did not understand, could not understand what was happening. For twenty years, this system functioned well enough to blind itself to the power in the streets, and it could not understand how the streets had invaded politics with so little ceremony.

The first and most precarious form of this blindness was the forced unity against the military dictatorship and its two tolerated parties, one in power and the other in opposition. In the 1980s, the party that had halted absolute power over the political process, the PMDB [Party of the Brazilian Democratic Movement], successor to the official opposition party during the dictatorship, imposed an indispensable union of all "progressive" forces in order to uproot authoritarianism. With the exception of the Workers' Party (PT), all the parties participated in the indirect election of 1985, in the so-called Electoral College, controlled by the forces of the dictatorship.

Tancredo Neves, of the PMDB, was elected president. When he died in April of the same year without having taken power, he left in charge his vice president, José Sarney, a historical source of support to the dictatorship. Even with Sarney as president, "progressivism" continued to represent the official ideology of a tepid transition to democracy, controlled by the dictatorial regime in crisis and agreed upon by an elitist political system.

The first crisis faced by this conservative arrangement occurred during the Constituent Assembly, when the forced unity turned away from social movements and organizations, unions, and popular assemblies that did not fit in the strict channels of open politics. Under the command of a nonpartisan superbloc containing the majority of PMDB representatives, the political system found a way to neutralize them, betting on the absence of a unified agenda and a party (or alliance of parties) that would streamline the hopes of the reformists.

The first form of blindness was that of the political system's disregard for society, which was named PMDBism, in memory of the party that led the transition to democracy. But at the same time it gave birth to a set of forces of social transformation in opposition to that same PMDBism, which always had referred back to the political fight the Constitution promulgated in 1988.

The forced unity of progressives continued to prevail in the fight for the impeachment of President Collor in 1992. But the postimpeachment period left behind the unifying ideology of the progressive forces, giving rise to a second form of PMDBism. It was upheld as an indisputable truth that President Fernando Collor de Mello had fallen because he did not have sufficient support in Congress, because he lacked the ability to govern. The unquestionable need for overwhelming majorities that could block movements like that of impeachment was born. Thus, the system preserved itself without changing, strengthening its logic of stopping large transformations, repressing differences under a new forced unity.

Beginning in 1993, the channels of expression of the forces in opposition to PMDBism narrowed. The power of the streets was replaced, little by little, by the clamor of public opinion. And public opinion was replaced by the opinion of the media. To make the system change, in the little ways that were possible, it was necessary to produce intensive denunciation campaigns vocalized by the media. The "tools of blindness" were being produced, tested, and perfected, being utilized in the course of two consecutive mandates for Fernando Henrique Cardoso (1995–2002). In that period, the forces in opposition to PMDBism worked on translating media campaigns into terms of institutional action: creation of the Parliamentary Investigation Commissions (CPIs), appeals to the Federal Supreme Court (STF), mobilizations and demonstrations of localized and limited protest.

Change only came with "scandals," which are difficult to produce because they demand a continuous exposure of reported acts, with redoubling and constant growth of new elements. And, above all, change depended on the filter of the highly oligopolistic media of the country. With time, even this now limited resource of denunciation lost force. Leading the forces of opposition, the PT reoriented its strategy and began to prioritize the conquest of federal power, through the election of Lula in 2002, in place of betting on the social mobilization of the masses. Beginning in the Cardoso government, few denunciations were successful to the point of becoming scandals and provoking significant changes in the system. Denunciations only succeeded and had institutional consequences when done in public disputes among allies inside the governing "supermajority."

Despite the establishment of the PT, after 1989, as an excellent representative of anti-PMDBism, the same customs repeated themselves in the period of Lula's presidency (2003–10), with the scandal known as the *mensalão* in 2005. It consisted of a political operation of illegal fund-raising to finance local and regional candidates in the 2004 municipal elections. Nineteen Congressmen were investigated in the Federal Legislature, six of them from the PT. Four confessed before the beginning of the investigation. The majority were absolved of the accusation at the parliamentary level. Three representatives were impeached. The judicial proceedings resulted in Penal Action 470, judged by the Supreme Court in the second half of 2012.

Leading a minority government until 2005, the first since 1992, the government of Lula saw itself accosted by the ghost of impeachment and adhered to the PMDB's idea of constructing a parliamentary supermajority. After the *mensalão* scandal, in the remainder of the Lula period, the development of the

PMDB's tools of blindness reached completion, continuing in use even more ostentatiously under the presidency of Dilma Rousseff, beginning in 2011.

From then on, the clamor of public opinion could not affect even a slight opening in the blindness of the political system. Ever more questioned in its role and work, the large traditional media stopped fulfilling the role of channeling dissatisfaction. The nation seemed to have conformed to the blindness of the PMDB, and there was no other form of protest capable of piercing the blockade.

That is, until June 2013 and the unconditional rejection of PMDB blindness, a common thread amid the diversity of the protests. The novelty is that this rejection was not expressed in a unified manner, like the forced unity of progressivism that held sway until the impeachment of Collor. The rejection of the ways of the PMDB came from all sides and was directed against numerous aspects of the political system. Because of this, too, the June Revolts represent a great advance: they show that the agenda is no longer that of the transition to democracy, in which economic and political stability were at play, but rather of the deepening of democracy. This, among many other things, encompasses the decisive challenge to leave behind the political culture of the PMDB.

Translated by Emma Wohl

Portraits: Herbert Daniel

James N. Green

The slow-motion return to democratic rule that took over a decade and the subsequent consolidation of democracy in Brazil relied on many kinds of actors. A considerable number had initiated their political activities in opposition to the military regime in the 1960s, and they continued to engage in social change after the return to democracy in the late 1980s and beyond. Such is the case of Herbert Eustáquio de Carvalho (1946–1992), known as Herbert Daniel, whose activism bridged generations, political movements, and visions for the transformation of Brazilian society.

Herbert, born to a lower-middle-class family in 1946, was one of thousands of that generation who in the late 1960s chose a radical response to the military regime's repressive actions of 1964. He became a student activist, then a member of a guerrilla organization that kidnapped the German and Swiss ambassadors in 1970 and demanded the release of 110 political prisoners in exchange for the diplomats' freedom. When his clandestine organization was decimated and he was hiding underground, he met Cláudio Mesquita, who later became his lifetime partner. While in exile, he challenged the revolutionary left's homophobic attitudes. A decade later, when he discovered that he was HIV positive, he helped reinvent public discourse on AIDS in Brazil.

Herbert's father, grandfather, and later his brother were all members of the military police in the state of Minas Gerais. Partly descended from slaves on his father's side and from Italian immigrants on his mother's, he lived a simple life in Belo Horizonte. Shy but brilliant, he learned to read at an early age and excelled in school. He loved culture, art, and films. In 1965, he easily passed the rigorous entrance exam to enter medical school at the Federal University of Minas Gerais.

Herbert became immersed in student politics almost from the first day of classes. In the midst of mobilizations against the recently installed military regime, he gravitated toward revolutionary politics. Che Guevara's writings about the Cuban Revolution convinced Herbert and many others that rural guerrilla warfare was the only possible strategy that could successfully topple the military dictatorship and establish a new socialist government that would guarantee economic and social justice.

Yet while he increasingly embraced Marxist ideas, he experienced tremendous personal turmoil because of his erotic and romantic same-sex desires. For a time he hid his feelings from other student activists while secretly having furtive trysts with young men he happened to meet on the streets or in the city's municipal park. Eventually homophobic norms prevailed, and he decided to repress his sexual desires in order to participate in a revolutionary organization that took the name Commandos of National Liberation (COLINA).

In 1968, Herbert participated in demonstrations against the dictatorship in March and supported a major strike of workers in April. He was arrested in May for participating in a sit-in at the medical school to protest the government's detention of student activists. During the second half of that year, while members of his group were preparing for guerilla actions, he represented COLINA in meetings held in Rio de Janeiro and São Paulo to discuss its merger with revolutionary groups in other parts of the country.

Herbert and his colleagues were convinced that the dictatorship's days were numbered in 1968. When the minister of justice announced on the radio the closure of Congress and the suspension of democratic rights on December 13, 1968, they mistakenly thought that it signified the military's weakening grip on the country.

In early 1969, the police arrested members of COLINA that had participated in a double bank robbery in a town near Belo Horizonte. The action was designed to raise funds to set up rural guerrilla activities. Herbert and others, including Dilma Rousseff, immediately fled to Rio de Janeiro and lived there underground. In June of that year, a newly constituted joint organization, Revolutionary Armed Vanguard (Palmares), managed to hoist the safe of the mistress of the former governor of the state of São Paulo. It contained 2.6 million dollars. The group's financial problems were over; their political problems were not.

While Herbert and his fellow revolutionaries believed they would soon be victorious, they miscalculated the socioeconomic climate of Brazil at the time. Newfound economic prosperity among the middle classes undermined opposition to the regime. Nationalist discourse linked to Brazil's victory at the 1970 World Soccer Cup in Mexico also boosted the dictatorship. An effective government-sponsored propaganda campaign represented the revolutionaries as dangerous terrorists who threatened Brazil's political stability and social order. An efficient use of torture of political prisoners dismantled organizations and demoralized supporters.

Even though the revolutionary organization he had helped found had split, with dozens of members arrested, tortured, and assassinated, he remained undeterred. In January 1970, he joined eighteen other revolutionaries in a military training operation in the remote countryside of southern São Paulo. Detected and surrounded by the army, he and most of the group managed to

Herbert Daniel (1946–1992) during his political exile in Paris. Courtesy of Geny Brunelli de Carvalho.

slip out of the region and back to Rio de Janeiro. There he joined other militants to kidnap the German ambassador. In exchange for his freedom, forty revolutionaries, many of whom had been close friends of Herbert's from his student days, were flown to Algeria. Herbert later remembered that when he saw the news of their release on television, it was the happiest day of his life.

Undeterred and by this time a member of the leadership of the People's Revolutionary Vanguard, he participated in yet another political kidnapping. This time it was the Swiss ambassador, and the demand was the release of seventy prisoners. The military dragged out negotiations for forty days, finally meeting the revolutionary organization's demands, and the released prisoners were flown to Chile. But his organization was decimated. Herbert, who by this time had assumed the underground name Daniel, suddenly found himself isolated and alone. One by one the remaining comrades in his organization were arrested or killed.

Hidden in an apartment for four long months, he began to reevaluate his past political actions, and especially his decision to remain celibate in order not to act on his sexual desires. Then, by chance, Cláudio Mesquita walked into his life. He offered to hide Daniel, and the two immediately became friends. They shared their personal stories and each admitted to the other his homosexual desires.

The two, still only friends, avoided arrest during Carnival in 1973, escaped to another city where they decided to open a disco, and finally fled the country in September 1974 to Portugal, where a revolution was taking place. In Portuguese exile, they began a relationship that lasted almost twenty years. Once again the energy generated by 1968, reaffirmed by events in revolutionary Portugal, ignited Herbert's political passions. This time he worked as journalist in a traditional women's magazine that had been turned into a radical feminist publication.

When the revolutionary process in Portugal stalled and the country turned rightward, Herbert and Cláudio departed for Paris to find work and construct a life together. Paris was the center of the Brazilian exile community in Europe, but Herbert and Cláudio avoided the endless meetings and debates about the future of revolutionary politics in Brazil. There was one noted exception. The Artists' Committee of the Brazilian Amnesty Commission in Paris proposed holding a debate about homosexuality. The idea split the revolutionary ranks of the exile community, but it nevertheless took place at the Casa do Brasil, the modernist center for Brazilian students. During the meeting of a hundred or so gathered revolutionaries, Daniel made a complex theoretical presentation about homosexuality and the homophobia of the left. The event provoked an intense debate among the Brazilian left with ripple effects that crossed the Atlantic Ocean.

Herbert returned from exile in 1981 and helped to reinvent the politics of sectors within the Workers' Party ticket by proposing new debates about racism, sexism, homophobia, and the destruction of the environment. At the same time, he had become a published writer and playwright. After an unsuccessful bid as an openly gay candidate for the state legislature in 1986, Daniel joined the Brazilian Interdisciplinary AIDS Association (ABIA), a foundation doing research and education on HIV/AIDS, as a writer and editor.

In 1989, he discovered that he had AIDS. With the same energy he had used to fight against the dictatorship, he took up the cause of forcing the newly constituted democratic government to adopt a progressive AIDS policy. Drawing from the knowledge that he had acquired as a medical student and his experience as a seasoned political activist, he published essays and appeared on national television to talk about living with AIDS. He presented a simple slogan: the cure for AIDS is solidarity. He emphasized that people living with HIV/AIDS should not be treated as if they had received a death warrant, and that support of family and friends was essential for combating the disease. His political message about AIDS reached an international audience before he passed away in March 1992. Cláudio, his lifelong partner, died two years later of a heart attack.

From student activist to revolutionary guerrilla, political exile, openly gay candidate, and AIDS activist, throughout his life Herbert Daniel remained at the cusp of radical social change. He also represented a bridge between the radical Marxist ideas of the 1960s and the feminist, LGBT, and environmental movements of the 1980s and beyond. The synthesis of his political experiences accumulated over several decades in a unique approach to challenging homophobia and discrimination against people living with HIV/AIDS marks him as an extraordinary figure among those committed to creating a democratic and equalitarian society.

Suggestions for Further Reading

We have chosen a selection of works on Brazil in English that will supplement the documents contained in this volume. They include English translations of works originally written in Portuguese. Some of these selections cover periods that extend beyond the section divisions in the *Reader* or a single topic.

General

Alberto, Paulina L. *Terms of Inclusion: Black Intellectuals in Twentieth-Century Brazil.* Chapel Hill: University of North Carolina Press, 2011.

Beattie, Peter M., ed. *The Human Tradition in Modern Brazil.* Wilmington, DE: Scholarly Resources, 2003.

Bethell, Leslie, ed. *Brazil: Empire and Republic, 1822–1930.* Cambridge: Cambridge University Press, 1993.

Bethell, Leslie, ed. *Colonial Brazil.* Cambridge: Cambridge University Press, 1991.

Bishop-Sanchez, Kathryn. *Creating Carmen Miranda: Race, Camp, and Transnational Stardom.* Nashville: Vanderbilt University Press, 2016.

Bruneau, Thomas C. *The Political Transformation of the Brazilian Catholic Church.* Cambridge: Cambridge University Press, 1974.

Conniff, Michael L., and Frank D. McCann Jr., eds. *Modern Brazil: Elites and Masses in Historical Perspective.* Lincoln: University of Nebraska Press, 1979.

Conrad, Robert Edgar. *Children of God's Fire: A Documentary History of Black Slavery in Brazil.* Princeton, NJ: Princeton University Press, 1984.

Dean, Warren. *With Broadaxe and Firebrand: The Destruction of the Brazilian Atlantic Forest.* Berkeley: University of California Press, 1995.

Degler, Carl N. *Neither Black nor White: Slavery and Race Relations in Brazil and the United States.* Madison: University of Wisconsin Press, 1971.

Eakin, Marshall C. *Becoming Brazilians: Race and National Identity in Twentieth-Century Brazil.* New York: Cambridge University Press, 2017.

Ferreira, Roquinaldo. *Cross-Cultural Exchange in the Atlantic World: Angola and Brazil during the Era of the Slave Trade.* New York: Cambridge University Press, 2012.

Freyre, Gilberto. *The Masters and the Slaves: A Study in the Development of Brazilian Civilization.* Berkeley: University of California Press, 1986.

Green, James N. *Beyond Carnival: Male Homosexuality in Twentieth-Century Brazil.* Chicago: University of Chicago Press, 1999.

Hahner, June E. *Emancipating the Female Sex: The Struggle for Women's Rights in Brazil, 1850–1940*. Durham, NC: Duke University Press, 1990.

Hemming, John. *Amazon Frontier: The Defeat of the Brazilian Indians*. Cambridge, MA: Harvard University Press, 1987.

Hemming, John. *Red Gold: The Conquest of the Brazilian Indians*. Cambridge, MA: Harvard University Press, 1978.

Johnson, Paul C. *Secrets, Gossip, and Gods: The Transformation of Brazilian Candomblé*. New York: Oxford University Press, 2002.

Lesser, Jeffrey. *Immigration, Ethnicity, and National Identity in Brazil, 1808 to the Present*. New York: Cambridge University Press, 2013.

Metcalf, Alida. *Family and Frontier in Colonial Brazil: Santana de Paraíba, 1580–1822*. Austin: University of Texas Press, 1992.

Miki, Yoko. *Frontiers of Citizenship: A Black and Indigenous History of Postcolonial Brazil*. New York: Cambridge University Press, 2018.

Nascimento, Elisa Larkin. *The Sorcery of Color: Identity, Race, and Gender in Brazil*. Philadelphia: Temple University Press, 2007.

Nazzari, Muriel. *Disappearance of the Dowry: Women, Families, and Social Change in São Paulo, Brazil, 1600–1900*. Stanford, CA: Stanford University Press, 1991.

Pinho, Patricia de Santana. *Mama Africa: Reinventing Blackness in Bahia*. Durham, NC: Duke University Press, 2010.

Rogers, Thomas E. *The Deepest Wounds: A Labor and Environmental History of Sugar in Northeast Brazil*. Chapel Hill: University of North Carolina Press, 2010.

Sadlier, Darlene J. *Brazil Imagined: 1500 to the Present*. Austin: University of Texas Press, 2008.

Schwartz, Stuart B. *Slaves, Peasants, and Rebels: Reconsidering Brazilian Slavery*. Urbana: University of Illinois Press, 1996.

Schwartz, Stuart B. *Sugar Plantations in the Formation of Brazilian Society, 1550–1835*. New York: Cambridge University Press, 1985.

Seigel, Micol. *Uneven Encounters: Making Race and Nation in Brazil and the United States*. Durham, NC: Duke University Press, 2009.

Serbin, Kenneth P. *Needs of the Heart: A Social and Cultural History of Brazil's Clergy and Seminaries*. Notre Dame, IN: University of Notre Dame Press, 2006.

Skidmore, Thomas E. *Black into White: Race and Nationality in Brazilian Thought*. Durham, NC: Duke University Press, 1993.

Skidmore, Thomas E. *Brazil: Five Centuries of Change*. New York: Oxford University Press, 2010.

Weinstein, Barbara. *The Color of Modernity: São Paulo and the Making of Race and Nation in Brazil*. Durham, NC: Duke University Press, 2015.

Wolfe, Joel. *Autos and Progress: The Brazilian Search for Modernity*. Oxford: Oxford University Press, 2010.

Part I. Conquest and Colonial Rule, 1500–1579

Metcalf, Alida C. *Go-Betweens and the Colonization of Brazil, 1500–1600*. Austin: University of Texas Press, 2005.

Staden, Hans. *Hans Staden's True History: An Account of Cannibal Captivity in Brazil*. Durham, NC: Duke University Press, 2008.

Part II. Sugar and Slavery in the Atlantic World, 1580–1694

Anderson, Robert Nelson. "The Quilombo of Palmares: A New Overview of a Maroon State in Seventeenth-Century Brazil." *Journal of Latin American Studies* 28 (1996): 545–66.

Baerle, Caspar van. *The History of Brazil under the Governorship of Count Johan Maurits of Nassau, 1636–1644*. Gainesville: University Press of Florida, 2011.

Bradley, Peter T. "The Portuguese Peril in Peru." *Bulletin of Spanish Studies: Hispanic Studies and Researches on Spain, Portugal and Latin America* 79, no. 5 (2002): 591–613.

Cohen, Thomas M. *The Fire of Tongues: António Vieira and the Missionary Church in Brazil and Portugal*. Stanford, CA: Stanford University Press, 1998.

Groesen, Michiel van. *Amsterdam's Atlantic: Print Culture and the Making of Dutch Brazil*. Philadelphia: University of Pennsylvania Press, 2017.

Part III. Gold and the New Colonial Order, 1695–1807

Barickman, B. J. *A Bahian Counterpoint: Sugar, Tobacco, Cassava, and Slavery in the Recôncavo, 1780–1860*. Cambridge: Cambridge University Press, 1998.

Boxer, Charles R. *The Golden Age of Brazil*. Berkeley: University of California Press, 1969.

Furtado, Júnia Ferreira. *Chica da Silva: A Brazilian Slave of the Eighteenth Century*. Cambridge: Cambridge University Press, 2009.

Kiddy, Elizabeth W. *Blacks of the Rosary: Memory and History in Minas Gerais, Brazil*. University Park: Pennsylvania State University Press, 2005.

Langur, Hal. *The Forbidden Lands: Colonial Identity, Frontier Violence, and the Persistence of Brazil's Eastern Indians, 1750–1830*. Stanford, CA: Stanford University Press, 2006.

Maxwell, Kenneth. *Conflicts and Conspiracies: Brazil and Portugal, 1750–1808*. Cambridge: Cambridge University Press, 1973.

Soares, Mariza de Carvalho. *People of Faith: Slavery and African Catholics in Eighteenth-Century Rio de Janeiro*. Durham, NC: Duke University Press, 2011.

Wadsworth, James E. *Agents of Orthodoxy: Honor, Status, and the Inquisition in Colonial Pernambuco*. Lanham, MD: Rowman and Littlefield, 2007.

Part IV. The Portuguese Royal Family in Rio de Janeiro, 1808–1821

Barman, Roderick J. *Brazil: The Forging of a Nation, 1789–1852*. Stanford, CA: Stanford University Press, 1988.

Bethell, Leslie. *The Abolition of the Brazilian Slave Trade: Britain, Brazil, and the Slave Trade Question, 1807–1869*. Cambridge: Cambridge University Press, 1970.

Schultz, Kirsten. *Tropical Versailles: Empire, Monarchy, and the Portuguese Royal Court in Rio de Janeiro, 1808–1821*. New York: Routledge, 2001.

Part V. From Independence to the Abolition of the Slave Trade, 1822–1850

Bieber, Judy. *Power, Patronage, and Political Violence: State Building on a Brazilian Frontier, 1822–1889*. Lincoln: University of Nebraska Press, 1999.

Frank, Zephyr L. *Dutra's World: Wealth and Family in Nineteenth-Century Rio de Janeiro*. Albuquerque: University of New Mexico Press, 2004.

Graham, Richard. *Feeding the City: From Street Market to Liberal Reform in Salvador, Brazil, 1780–1860.* Austin: University of Texas Press, 2010.

Karasch, Mary C. *Slave Life in Rio de Janeiro, 1808–1850.* Princeton, NJ: Princeton University Press, 1987.

Kraay, Hendrik. *Race, State, and Armed Forces in Independence-Era Brazil, Bahia, 1790s–1840s.* Stanford, CA: Stanford University Press, 2001.

Luna, Francisco. *Slavery and the Economy of São Paulo, 1750–1850.* Stanford, CA: Stanford University Press, 2003.

Mosher, Jeffrey C. *Political Struggle, Ideology and State Building: Pernambuco and the Construction of Brazil, 1817–1850.* Lincoln: University of Nebraska Press, 2008.

Read, Ian. *The Hierarchies of Slavery in Santos, Brazil, 1822–1888.* Stanford, CA: Stanford University Press, 2012.

Reis, João José. *Slave Rebellion in Brazil: The Muslim Uprising of 1835 in Bahia.* Baltimore, MD: Johns Hopkins University Press, 1993.

Part VI. Coffee, the Empire, and Abolition, 1851–1888

Barbosa, José Carlos. *Slavery and Protestant Missions in Imperial Brazil: The Black Does Not Enter the Church, He Peeks.* Lanham, MD: University Press of America, 2008.

Barman, Roderick J. *Citizen Emperor: Pedro II of Brazil.* Cambridge: Cambridge University Press, 1999.

Barman, Roderick J. *Princess Isabel of Brazil: Gender and Power in the Nineteenth Century.* Wilmington, DE: SR Books, 2002.

Beattie, Peter M. *The Tribute of Blood: Army, Honor, Race, and Nation in Brazil, 1864–1945.* Durham, NC: Duke University Press, 2000.

Bell, Stephen. *Campanha Gaúcha: A Brazilian Ranching System, 1850–1920.* Stanford, CA: Stanford University Press, 1998.

Borges, Dain. *The Family in Bahia, 1870–1945.* Stanford, CA: Stanford University Press, 1992.

Costa, Emilia Viotti da. *The Brazilian Empire: Myths and Histories.* Rev. ed. Chapel Hill: University of North Carolina Press, 2000.

Dias, Maria Odila Silva. *Power and Everyday Life: The Lives of Working Women in Nineteenth-Century Brazil.* New Brunswick, NJ: Rutgers University Press, 1995.

Graden, Dale Torston. *From Slavery to Freedom in Brazil, Bahia, 1835–1900.* Albuquerque: University of New Mexico Press, 2006.

Graham, Richard. *Britain and the Onset of Modernization in Brazil, 1850–1914.* New York: Cambridge University Press, 1968.

Graham, Richard. *Patronage and Politics in Nineteenth-Century Brazil.* Stanford, CA: Stanford University Press, 1990.

Graham, Sandra Lauderdale. *Caetana Says No: Women's Stories from a Brazilian Slave Society.* New York: Cambridge University Press, 2002.

Graham, Sandra Lauderdale. *House and Street: The Domestic World of Servants and Masters in Nineteenth-Century Rio de Janeiro.* Cambridge: Cambridge University Press, 1988.

Hanley, Anne G. *Native Capital: Financial Institutions and Economic Development in São Paulo, Brazil, 1850–1920.* Stanford, CA: Stanford University Press, 2005.

Holloway, Thomas H. *Policing Rio de Janeiro: Repression and Resistance in a 19th-Century City*. Stanford, CA: Stanford University Press, 1993.

Kiddleson, Roger A. *The Practice of Politics in Postcolonial Brazil, Porto Alegre, 1845–1985*. Pittsburgh: University of Pittsburgh Press, 2006.

Kirkendall, Andrew J. *Class Mates: Male Student Culture and the Making of a Political Class in Nineteenth-Century Brazil*. Lincoln: University of Nebraska Press, 2002.

Lewin, Linda. *Politics and Parentela in Paraíba: A Case Study of Family-Based Oligarchy in Brazil*. Princeton, NJ: Princeton University Press, 1987.

Needell, Jeffrey. *The Party of Order: The Conservatives, the State, and Slavery in the Brazilian Monarchy, 1831–1871*. Stanford, CA: Stanford University Press, 2006.

Pessar, Patricia. *From Fanatics to Folk: Brazilian Millenarianism and Popular Culture*. Durham, NC: Duke University Press, 2004.

Reis, João José. *Death Is a Festival: Funeral Rites and Rebellion in Nineteenth-Century Brazil*. Translated by H. Sabrina Gledhill. Chapel Hill: University of North Carolina Press, 2003.

Russell-Wood, A. J. R. *Slavery and Freedom in Colonial Brazil*. Oxford: Oneworld, 2002.

Santos, Martha S. *Cleansing Honor with Blood: Masculinity, Violence, and Power in the Backlands of Northeast Brazil, 1845–1889*. Stanford, CA: Stanford University Press, 2012.

Schwarcz, Lilia Moritz. *The Emperor's Beard: Dom Pedro II and the Tropical Monarchy of Brazil*. Translated by John Gledson. New York: Hill and Wang, 2004.

Stein, Stanley J. *Vassouras, a Brazilian Coffee Country, 1850–1900: The Roles of Planter and Slave in a Plantation Society*. Princeton, NJ: Princeton University Press, 1985.

Toplin, Robert Brent. *The Abolition of Slavery in Brazil*. New York: Atheneum, 1972.

Part VII. Republican Brazil and the Onset of Modernization, 1889–1929

Albert, Bill. *South America and the First World War: The Impact of the War on Brazil, Argentina, Peru and Chile*. Cambridge: Cambridge University Press, 1988.

Andrews, George Reid. *Blacks and Whites in São Paulo, Brazil, 1888–1988*. Madison: University of Wisconsin Press, 1991.

Besse, Susan K. *Restructuring Patriarchy: The Modernization of Gender Inequality in Brazil, 1914–1940*. Chapel Hill: University of North Carolina Press, 1996.

Butler, Kim D. *Freedoms Given, Freedoms Won: Afro-Brazilians in Post-abolition São Paulo and Salvador*. New Brunswick, NJ: Rutgers University Press, 1998.

Carvalho, José Murilo de. *The Formation of Souls: Imagery of the Republic in Brazil*. Translated by Clifford E. Landers. Notre Dame, IN: University of Notre Dame Press, 2012.

Caulfield, Sueann. *In Defense of Honor: Sexual Morality, Modernity, and Nation in Early-Twentieth-Century Brazil*. Durham, NC: Duke University Press, 2000.

Chazkel, Amy. *Laws of Chance: Brazil's Clandestine Lottery and the Making of Urban Public Life*. Durham, NC: Duke University Press, 2011.

Diacon, Todd A. *Stringing Together a Nation: Cândido Mariano da Silva Rondon and the Construction of a Modern Brazil, 1906–1930*. Durham, NC: Duke University Press, 2004.

Font, Mauricio. *Coffee and Transformation in São Paulo, Brazil*. Lanham, MD: Lexington, 2010.

Hochman, Gilberto. *The Sanitation of Brazil: Nation, State, and Public Health, 1889–1930*.

Translated by Diane Grosklaus Whitty. Champaign: University of Illinois Press, 2016.

Holloway, Thomas H. *Immigrants on the Land: Coffee and Society in São Paulo, 1889–1934*. Chapel Hill: University of North Carolina Press, 1980.

Lesser, Jeffrey. *Negotiating National Identity: Immigrants, Minorities, and the Struggle for Ethnicity in Brazil*. Durham, NC: Duke University Press, 1999.

Levine, Robert M. *Vale of Tears: Revisiting the Canudos Massacre in Northeastern Brazil, 1893–1897*. Berkeley: University of California Press, 1992.

Love, Joseph L. *The Revolt of the Whip*. Stanford, CA: Stanford University Press, 2012.

McCann, Frank D., Jr. *Soldiers of the Pátria: A History of the Brazilian Army, 1889–1937*. Stanford, CA: Stanford University Press, 2004.

Meade, Teresa A. *"Civilizing" Rio: Reform and Resistance in a Brazilian City, 1889–1930*. University Park: Pennsylvania State University Press, 1997.

Mehrtens, Cristina. *Urban Space and National Identity in Early Twentieth-Century São Paulo: Crafting Modernity*. New York: Palgrave Macmillan, 2010.

Schwarcz, Lilia Moritz. *The Spectacle of the Races: Scientists, Institutions, and the Race Question in Brazil, 1870–1930*. New York: Hill and Wang, 1999.

Scott, Rebecca, ed. *The Abolition of Slavery and the Aftermath of Emancipation in Brazil*. Durham, NC: Duke University Press, 1988.

Smith, Joseph. *Unequal Giants: Diplomatic Relations between the United States and Brazil, 1889–1930*. Pittsburgh: University of Pittsburgh Press, 1991.

Topik, Steven. *The Political Economy of the Brazilian State, 1889–1930*. Austin: University of Texas Press, 1987.

Topik, Steven. *Trade and Gunboats: The United States and Brazil in the Age of Empire*. Stanford, CA: Stanford University Press, 1996.

Wolfe, Joel. *Working Women, Working Men: São Paulo and the Rise of Brazil's Industrial Working Class, 1900–1955*. Durham, NC: Duke University Press, 1993.

Woodard, James P. *A Place in Politics: São Paulo, Brazil, from Seigneurial Republicanism to Regionalist Revolt*. Durham, NC: Duke University Press, 2009.

Part VIII. Getúlio Vargas, the Estado Novo, and World War II, 1930–1945

Blake, Stanley E. *The Vigorous Core of Our Nationality: Race and Regional Identity in Northeastern Brazil*. Pittsburgh: University of Pittsburgh Press, 2011.

Conniff, Michael. *Urban Politics in Brazil: The Rise of Populism, 1925–1945*. Pittsburgh: University of Pittsburgh Press, 1981.

Dávila, Jerry. *Diploma of Whiteness: Race and Social Policy in Brazil, 1917–1945*. Durham, NC: Duke University Press, 2003.

Davis, Darién J. *White Face, Black Mask: Africaneity and the Early Social History of Popular Music in Brazil*. East Lansing: Michigan State University Press, 2009.

Dulles, John W. F. *Vargas of Brazil: A Political Biography*. Austin: University of Texas Press, 1967.

Eakin, Marshall. *Tropical Capitalism: The Industrialization of Belo Horizonte, Brazil*. New York: Palgrave, 2001.

Fischer, Brodwyn. *A Poverty of Rights: Citizenship and Inequality in Twentieth-Century Rio de Janeiro*. Stanford, CA: Stanford University Press, 2008.

Garfield, Seth. *Indigenous Struggle at the Heart of Brazil: State Policy, Frontier Expansion, and the Xavante Indians, 1937–1988*. Durham, NC: Duke University Press, 2001.

Hertzman, Marc A. *Making Samba: A New History of Race and Music in Brazil*. Durham, NC: Duke University Press, 2013.

Hilton, Stanley E. *Brazil and the Great Powers, 1930–1939*. Austin: University of Texas Press, 1977.

Lesser, Jeffrey. *Welcoming the Undesirables: Brazil and the Jewish Question*. Berkeley: University of California Press, 1995.

Levine, Robert M. *Father of the Poor? Vargas and His Era*. Cambridge: Cambridge University Press, 1998.

McCann, Bryan. *Hello, Hello Brazil: Popular Music in the Making of Modern Brazil*. Durham, NC: Duke University Press, 2004.

McCann, Frank D. *The Brazilian-American Alliance*. Princeton, NJ: Princeton University Press, 1973.

Otovo, Okezi. *Progressive Mothers, Better Babies: Race, Public Health, and the State in Brazil, 1850–1945*. Austin: University of Texas Press, 2016.

Tota, Antonio Pedro. *The Seduction of Brazil: The Americanization of Brazil during World War II*. Translated by Lorena B. Ellis. Austin: University of Texas Press, 2009.

Weinstein, Barbara. *For Social Peace in Brazil: Industrialists and the Remaking of the Working Class in São Paulo, 1920–1964*. Chapel Hill: University of North Carolina Press, 1996.

Williams, Daryle. *Culture Wars in Brazil: The First Vargas Regime, 1930–1945*. Durham, NC: Duke University Press, 2001.

Zweig, Stefan. *Brazil: Land of the Future*. Riverside, CA: Ariadna, 2000.

Part IX. Democratic Governance and Developmentalism, 1946–1964

Castro, Ruy. *Bossa Nova: The Story of the Brazilian Music That Seduced the World*. Translated by Lysa Salsbury. Chicago: A Cappella, 2000.

Dávila, Jerry. *Hotel Trópico: Brazil and the Challenge of African Decolonization, 1950–1980*. Durham, NC: Duke University Press, 2010.

Erickson, Kenneth Paul. *The Brazilian Corporative State and Working-Class Politics*. Berkeley: University of California Press, 1977.

French, John. *The Brazilian Workers' ABC: Class Conflict and Alliances in Modern São Paulo*. Chapel Hill: University of North Carolina Press, 1992.

French, John. *Drowning in Laws: Labor Law and Brazilian Political Culture*. Chapel Hill: University of North Carolina Press, 2004.

Holston, James. *The Modernist City: An Anthropological Critique of Brasília*. Chicago: University of Chicago Press, 1989.

Leacock, Ruth. *Requiem for Revolution: The United States and Brazil, 1961–1969*. Kent, OH: Kent State University Press, 1990.

Levine, Robert M., and José Carlos Sebe Bom Meihy. *The Life and Death of Carolina Maria de Jesus*. Albuquerque: University of New Mexico Press, 1995.

Skidmore, Thomas E. *Politics in Brazil, 1930–1964: An Experiment in Democracy*. New York: Oxford University Press, 2007.

Weis, W. Michael. *Cold Warriors and Coups d'Etat: Brazilian-American Relations, 1945–1964*. Albuquerque: University of New Mexico Press, 1993.

Welch, Cliff. *The Seed Was Planted: The São Paulo Roots of Brazil's Rural Labor Movement, 1924–1964*. University Park: Pennsylvania State University Press, 1999.

Part X. The Generals in Power and the Fight for Democracy, 1964–1985

Alvarez, Sonia E. *Engendering Democracy in Brazil: Women's Movements in Transition Politics*. Princeton, NJ: Princeton University Press, 1990.

Alves, Maria Helena Moreira. *State and Opposition in Military Brazil*. Austin: University of Texas Press, 1988.

Archdiocese of São Paulo. *Torture in Brazil: A Shocking Report on the Pervasive Use of Torture by Brazilian Military Governments, 1964–1979 / Secretly Prepared by the Archdiocese of São Paulo* [Brazil, Nunca Mas]. Translated by Jaime Wright; edited with a new preface by Joan Dassin. Austin: University of Texas, Institute of Latin American Studies, 1985.

Black, Jan Knippers. *United States Penetration of Brazil*. Philadelphia: University of Pennsylvania Press, 1977.

Burdick, John. *Looking for God in Brazil: The Progressive Catholic Church in Urban Brazil's Religious Arena*. Berkeley: University of California Press, 1993.

Calirman, Claudia. *Brazilian Art under Dictatorship: Antonio Manuel, Artur Barrio, and Cildo Meireles*. Durham, NC: Duke University Press, 2012.

Cowan, Benjamin A. *Securing Sex: Morality and Repression in the Making of Cold War Brazil*. Chapel Hill: University of North Carolina Press, 2016.

Dunn, Christopher. *Brutality Garden: Tropicália and the Emergence of a Brazilian Counterculture*. Chapel Hill: University of North Carolina Press, 2001.

Dunn, Christopher. *Contracultura: Alternative Arts and Social Transformation in Authoritarian Brazil*. Chapel Hill: University of North Carolina Press, 2016.

Flynn, Peter. *Brazil: A Political Analysis*. London: Ernest Benn, 1978.

Green, James N. *Exile within Exiles: Herbert Daniel, Gay Brazilian Revolutionary*. Durham, NC: Duke University Press, 2018.

Green, James N. *We Cannot Remain Silent: Opposition to the Brazilian Military Dictatorship in the United States*. Durham, NC: Duke University Press, 2010.

Hanchard, Michael George. *Orpheus and Power: The "Movimento Negro" of Rio de Janeiro and São Paulo, Brazil, 1945–1988*. Princeton, NJ: Princeton University Press, 1994.

Huggins, Martha K. *Political Policing*. Durham, NC: Duke University Press, 1998.

Huggins, Martha K., Mika Haritos-Tatouros, and Philip G. Zimbardo. *Violence Workers: Police Torturers and Murderers Reconstruct Brazilian Atrocities*. Los Angeles: University of California Press, 2002.

Kirkendall, Andrew J. *Paulo Freire and the Cold War Politics of Literacy*. Chapel Hill: University of North Carolina Press, 2010.

Langland, Victoria. *Speaking of Flowers: Student Movements and the Making and Remembering of 1968 in Military Brazil*. Durham, NC: Duke University Press, 2013.

Lesser, Jeffrey. *Discontented Diasporas: Japanese Brazilians and the Meaning of Ethnic Militancy, 1960–1980*. Durham, NC: Duke University Press, 2007.

Parker, Phyllis. *Brazil and the Quiet Intervention, 1964*. Austin: University of Texas Press, 1979.

Pereira, Anthony W. *The End of the Peasantry: The Rural Labor Movement in Northeast Brazil, 1961–1988*. Pittsburgh: University of Pittsburgh Press, 1997.

Sattamini, Lina Penna. *A Mother's Cry: A Memoir of Politics, Prison, and Torture under the Brazilian Military Dictatorship.* Translated by Rex P. Nielson and James N. Green, with an introduction by James N. Green. Durham, NC: Duke University Press, 2010.

Serbin, Kenneth P. *Secret Dialogues: Church-State Relations, Torture, and Social Justice in Authoritarian Brazil.* Pittsburgh: University of Pittsburgh Press, 2000.

Skidmore, Thomas E. *The Politics of Military Rule in Brazil, 1964–85.* New York: Oxford University Press, 1988.

Veloso, Caetano. *Tropical Truth: A Story of Music and Revolution in Brazil.* New York: Alfred A. Knopf, 2002.

Part XI. Redemocratization and the New Global Economy, 1985–Present

Albuquerque, Severino. *Tentative Transgressions: Homosexuality, AIDS, and Theater in Brazil.* Madison: University of Wisconsin Press, 2004.

Alves, Maria Helena Moreira, and Philip Evanson. *Living in the Crossfire: Favela Residents, Drug Dealers, and Police Violence in Rio de Janeiro.* Philadelphia: Temple University Press, 2011.

Atencio, Rebecca. *Memory's Turn: Reckoning with Dictatorship in Brazil.* Madison: University of Wisconsin Press, 2014.

Baiocchi, Gianpaolo. *Militants and Citizens: The Politics of Participatory Democracy in Porto Alegre.* Stanford, CA: Stanford University Press, 2005.

Baiocchi, Gianpaolo, ed. *Radicals in Power: The Workers' Party (PT) and Experiments in Urban Democracy in Brazil.* New York: Zed, 2003.

Caldwell, Kia Lilly. *Negras in Brazil: Re-envisioning Black Women, Citizenship, and the Politics of Identity.* New Brunswick, NJ: Rutgers University Press, 2007.

Covin, David. *The United Black Movement in Brazil, 1978–2002.* Jefferson, NC: McFarland, 2006.

Daniel, Herbert, and Richard Parker. *Sexuality, Politics and AIDS in Brazil: In Another World?* London: Falmer, 1993.

Dehesa, Rafael de la. *Queering the Public Sphere in Mexico and Brazil: Sexual Rights Movements in Emerging Democracies.* Durham, NC: Duke University Press, 2010.

Edmonds, Alexander. *Pretty Modern: Beauty, Sex, and Plastic Surgery in Brazil.* Durham, NC: Duke University Press, 2010.

Fishlow, Albert. *Starting Over: Brazil since 1985.* Washington, DC: Brookings Institution Press, 2011.

French, Jan Hoffman. *Legalizing Identities: Becoming Black or Indian in Brazil's Northeast.* Chapel Hill: University of North Carolina Press, 2009.

Gay, Robert. *Popular Organization and Democracy in Rio de Janeiro: A Tale of Two Favelas.* Philadelphia: Temple University Press, 1994.

Hockstetler, Kathryn, and Margaret E. Keck. *Greening Brazil: Environmental Activism in State and Society.* Durham, NC: Duke University Press, 2007.

Keck, Margaret E. *The Workers' Party and Democratization in Brazil.* New Haven, CT: Yale University Press, 1992.

Kingstone, Peter R., and Timothy J. Power. *Democratic Brazil Divided.* Pittsburgh: University of Pittsburgh Press, 2017.

Klein, Misha. *Kosher Feijoada and Other Paradoxes of Jewish Life in São Paulo.* Gainesville: University Press of Florida, 2012.

McCann, Bryan. *The Throes of Democracy: Brazil since 1989*. London: Zed, 2008.

Mitchell-Walthour, Gladys L. *The Politics of Blackness: Racial Identity and Political Behavior in Contemporary Brazil*. New York: Cambridge University Press, 2018.

Nunn, Amy. *The Politics and History of AIDS Treatment in Brazil*. New York: Springer, 2008.

O'Dougherty, Maureen. *Consumption Intensified: The Politics of Middle-Class Daily Life in Brazil*. Durham, NC: Duke University Press, 2002.

Ondetti, Gabriel. *Land, Protest, and Politics: The Landless Movement and the Struggle for Agrarian Reform in Brazil*. University Park: Pennsylvania State University Press, 2008.

Parker, Richard. *Beneath the Equator: Cultures of Desire, Male Homosexuality, and Emerging Gay Communities in Brazil*. New York: Routledge, 1999.

Paschel, Tianna S. *Becoming Black Political Subjects: Movements and Ethno-racial Rights in Colombia and Brazil*. Princeton, NJ: Princeton University Press, 2016.

Penha-Lopes, Vânia. *Confronting Affirmative Action in Brazil: University Quota Students and the Quest for Racial Justice*. Lanham, MD: Lexington Books, 2017.

Perry, Keisha-Khan Y. *Black Women against the Land Grab: The Fight for Racial Justice in Brazil*. Minneapolis: University of Minnesota Press, 2013.

Power, Timothy J. *The Political Right in Postauthoritarian Brazil: Elites, Institutions, and Democratization*. University Park: Pennsylvania State University Press, 2000.

Purcell, Susan Kaufman, and Riordan Roett, eds. *Brazil under Cardoso*. New York: Americas Society, 1997.

Scheper-Hughes, Nancy. *Death without Weeping: The Violence of Everyday Life in Brazil*. Berkeley: University of California Press, 1992.

Smith, Christen A. *Afro-Paradise: Blackness, Violence, and Performance in Brazil*. Urbana-Champaign: University of Illinois Press, 2016.

Telles, Edward. *Race in Another America: The Significance of Skin Color in Brazil*. Princeton, NJ: Princeton University Press, 2004.

Tranjan, J. Richard. *Participatory Democracy in Brazil: Socioeconomic and Political Origins*. Notre Dame, IN: University of Notre Dame Press, 2016.

Weyland, Kurt. *Democracy without Equity: Failures of Reformism Brazil*. Pittsburgh: University of Pittsburgh Press, 1996.

Wolford, Wendy. *This Land Is Ours Now: Social Mobilization and the Means of Land in Brazil*. Durham, NC: Duke University Press, 2010.

Brazil in the Movies

This is a brief selection of films about Brazil with English subtitles that have historical, political, social, or cultural content.

Abdias Nascimento. Director: Aída Marquez, 2011. Documentary about the life of Abdias do Nascimento, who was an Afro-Brazilian leader, actor, playwright, artist, poet, founder of Brazil's Teatro Experimental do Preto (Black Experimental Theater) and Museu de Arte Negra (Museum of Black Art), and finally a politician, elected to the Brazilian Federal Chamber of Deputies in 1983 and 1987, and serving in the Brazilian Senate from 1997 to 1999.

Abdias Nascimento: 90 Years, Living Memory. Director: Elisa Larkin Nascimento, 2006. This video documents the life of Brazilian black activist Abdias do Nascimento through footage of panels, conferences, ceremonies, and international colloquia.

Abril despedaçado (Behind the Sun). Director: Walter Salles, 2001. In 1910 northeastern Brazil, impoverished farmers wage a tragic blood feud with a neighboring clan.

Anjos do arrabalde (Angels of the Outskirts). Director: Carlos Reichenbach, 1987. Drama about the lives of three teachers in the poor outlying neighborhoods of São Paulo.

O ano que os meus pais saíram de férias (The Year My Parents Went on Vacation). Director: Cao Hamburger, 2007. A boy is left alone in a Jewish neighborhood of São Paulo by his revolutionary parents at the height of political repression in 1970, when Brazil is competing in the soccer World Cup.

Antônia. Director: Tata Amaral, 2007. A soulful look into the lives of four women living on the outskirts of São Paulo, Brazil. Determined to escape their poverty-stricken lives, they learn that out of struggle come strength and the courage to continue on.

O assalto ao trem pagador (Assault on the Pay Train). Director: Roberto Farias, 1962. Based on a true story of a train robbery in Rio de Janeiro, 1960.

Assim era a Atlântida (That Was Atlântida). Director: Carlos Manga, 2007. Documentary about the Brazilian burlesque *chanchada* films of the 1950s from the archives of Atlântida, the main studio specializing in the genre.

Baile perfumado (Perfumed Ball). Directors: Lírio Ferreira and Paulo Caldas, 1986. Using some footage from the 1930s, this story describes how a filmmaker befriended the northeastern outlaw Lampião and filmed his exploits.

O Bandido da Luz Vermelha (The Red Light Bandit). Director: Rogério Spanzerla, 1968. A crime film based on the life of a burglar known as the Red Light Bandit, which is a representative work of *cinema marginal*.

Batismo de sangue (Baptism by Blood). Director: Helvécio Ratton, 2007. Brazil was ruled by military dictatorship from 1964 to 1985. In the 1960s, some Dominican friars support leftist organizations, but they are arrested and tortured by the chief of political and security police, who is trying to arrest the leader, Carlos Marighella.

Bay of All Saints. Director: Annie Eastman, 2012. The stories of Geni, Jesus, and Dona Maria, three single mothers, and their families living in Salvador, Bahia, shape this film's narrative as they confront uncertainty and insecurity.

Beijo na boca (Kiss My Mouth). Director: Jacira Melo, 1987. Interviews with street prostitutes in urban Brazil.

Brava gente brasileira (Valiant Brazilian People). Director: Lúcia Murat, 2001. In 1788, Portuguese colonizers, dazzled and tormented by the vision of the New World, confront indigenous people, whose land is invaded and their tribes decimated.

Brazil: A Report on Torture. Director: Saul Landau, 1971. Documentary with former Brazilian political prisoners in exile in Chile about their experience while imprisoned by the political police.

Brazil in Black and White: Skin Color and Higher Education. Directors: Mike Dewitt and Adam Stepan, 2007. New affirmative action quotas for higher education in Brazil launch a controversial dialogue about race and identity. Five college candidates from diverse backgrounds compete for a spot at the University of Brasília.

Bye bye Brasil. Director: Carlos Diegues, 1980. This film follows a troupe of carnival-type entertainers traveling through the backlands at a moment in the 1970s when Brazil is going through significant economic and social change.

Cabra marcado para morrer (Twenty Years Later). Director: Eduardo Coutinho, 1984. Originally a planned 1964 feature film about a Peasant League leader who was assassinated by landowners, the director returns twenty years later to shoot new footage of some of the actors and crew.

Capitães da Areia (Captains of the Sands). Directors: Cecília Amado and Guy Gonçalves, 2011. The life and adventures of a gang of abandoned street kids known as Capitães da Areia (Captains of the Sands), in Salvador, Bahia, during the 1950s.

Carandiru. Director: Héctor Barbendo, 2003. A reconstruction of the October 2, 1992, prison riot known as the Carandiru Massacre and set in São Paulo's House of Detention.

Carlota Joaquina, Princesa do Brazil (Carolota Joaquina, Princess of Brazil). Director: Carla Camurati, 1994. A comic parody of the history of early nineteenth-century Brazil, as the Portuguese royal family flees Napoleon's troops and sets up the capital of the Portuguese Empire in Rio de Janeiro.

Carmen Miranda: Bananas Is My Business. Director: Helena Solberg-Ladd, 1995. Using archival footage, film fragments, interviews, and dramatic reenactments, this documentary goes behind the scenes to convey the life story of Carmen Miranda, the Brazilian Bombshell.

Os carvoeiros (The Charcoal Workers). Director: Nigel Noble, 1999. Documentary about the life of charcoal producers and the desperate poverty they endure.

O caso dos irmãos Naves (Case of the Naves Brothers). Director: Luis Sérgio Person, 1967. Based on the real story of two brothers who are arrested and after being tortured confess to a crime that they did not commit.

Cazuza—O tempo não pára (Cazuza—Time Doesn't Stop). Directors: Walter Carvalho and Sandra Werneck, 2004. Biographical film about rock singer Daniel de Oliveira, known as Cazuza, his meteoric rise to success, and his death from AIDS.

Central do Brasil (Central Station). Director: Walter Salles, 1998. Touching story about the friendship of a young boy and a jaded middle-aged woman.

O cheiro do ralo (The Smell of Sex). Director: Heitor Dhalia, 2012. A pawn shop proprietor buys used goods from desperate locals—as much to play perverse power games as for his own livelihood, but when a beautiful woman and a backed-up toilet enter his life, he loses all control.

Cidade de Deus (*City of God*). Directors: Katia Lund and Fernando Meirelles, 2003. Built in the 1960s, Cidade de Deus (City of God) is a sprawling housing project built to keep the poor as far as possible from Rio's glamorous beaches and resorts. By the 1980s, it has degenerated into a dangerous war zone and a place of poverty, drugs, and crime.

Cine Holliúdy. Director: Halder Gomes, 2013. Set in the 1970s in northeastern Brazil, when more and more people had TVs. A theater owner and his wife are worried that their business will fade and the art of cinema will die.

Cinema, aspirinas e urubus (*Cinema, Aspirins and Vultures*). Director: Marcelo Gomes, 2005. A road movie about a German man who goes to northeastern Brazil in 1942 to sell aspirin.

Conceição: Autor bom é autor morto! (*Conception: A Good Author Is a Dead Author*). Director: André Sampaio, 2007. A group of young people are drinking in a bar and trying to choose a story for the movie they have decided to make. The film follows the highlights of the conversation and develops the backgrounds of the motley crew of characters.

Corações sujos (*Dirty Hearts*). Director: Vicente Amorim, 2012. In 1945, Japan surrendered and World War II was over, but for 80 percent of the Japanese community in Brazil, Japan had won the war and defeat was merely American propaganda. The few Japanese immigrants that accepted the truth were persecuted or assassinated by their own countrymen, causing the start of a new, private war.

Corumbiara. Director: Vincent Carelli, 2009. In 1985, Marcelo Santos denounced a massacre of Indians in Glebe Corumbiara, and Vincent Carelli filmed what remained of the evidence. Santos and his team took years to find survivors. This film reveals the results of this search and the Indians' side of events.

The Cross and the Crossroads. Director: Brian Brazeal, 2004. Documentary about Candomblé, an Afro-Brazilian religion, as practiced in Bahia, Brazil.

De passagem (*Passing By*). Director: Ricardo Elias, 2003. Story about two friends who grew up together in the slums of São Paulo and the different paths their lives have taken.

Deus e o diabo na terra do sol (*Black God, White Devil*). Director: Glauber Rocha, 1964. A classic of the Cinema Novo (New Cinema) movement set in the dry backlands of the Brazilian northeast, the film addresses the sociopolitical problems of the region.

O dia que durou 21 anos (*The Day That Lasted 21 Years*). Director: Camilo Tavares, 2012. The story behind the 1964 coup that with U.S. support turned Brazil into a dictatorship for twenty-one years.

Diário de uma busca (*Diary of a Search*). Director: Flavia Castro, 2012. The director tells the story of her father, Brazilian activist and journalist Celso Afonso Gay de Castro, whose life was intertwined with the political struggles that shattered Latin America starting in the 1960s.

Doce Brasil holandês (*Sweet Dutch Brazil*). Director: Monica Schmiedt, 2011. A documentary that looks behind the nostalgia that some Brazilians feel about the period when the Dutch ruled the northeastern part of the country between 1630 and 1654.

Dois perdidos numa noite suja (*Two Lost in a Dirty Night*). Director: José Joffily, 2004. Set in New York, this is the story of a couple, Tonio and Paco, two illegal immigrants from Brazil. Tonio misses his family and Brazil, and tries to stay a step ahead of the U.S. authorities, but is arrested and about to be deported. Paco, a performer, is focused on achieving success and recognition.

Dona Flor e seus dois maridos (Dona Flor and Her Two Husbands). Director: Bruno Barreto, 1976. Comedy based on a novel by Jorge Amado set in Salvador, Bahia, in 1940 about a woman whose gambling, partying, and drinking deceased husband comes back from the dead after she marries a respectable middle-class pharmacist.

Dzi Croquettes. Directors: Tatiana Issa and Raphael Alvarez, 2009. A documentary about the Brazilian drag cabaret troupe Dzi Croquettes in the early 1970s, whose gender and sexual taboo-breaking performances were influential as a subversive means of cultural resistance to the military dictatorship.

Edifício Master. Director: Eduardo Coutinho, 2002. The daily lives and routines of thirty-seven families living in a huge twelve-story building in Copacabana, Rio de Janeiro.

Eles não usam Black-Tie (They Don't Wear Black-Tie). Director: Leon Hirszman, 1981. Story of a working-class São Paulo family that faces its own conflicts during a strike.

Entreatos: Lula a 30 dias do poder (Intermission: Lula Thirty Days from Power). Director: João Moreira Salles, 2004. The movie was filmed during the first and second rounds of the 2002 presidential elections and offers a unique portrait of the working-class leader who became the president of Brazil.

É proibido fumar (No smoking). Director: Anna Muylaert, 2010. A chain-smoking guitar teacher in her forties craves a romantic relationship. When a musician moves into the apartment next door, she sees the possibility of turning her lonely life around. Instead, she finds herself involved in a love triangle leading to a jealous rage.

Os Fuzis (The Guns). Director: Ruy Guerra, 1964. In the poverty-stricken northeast, a holy man urges peasant pilgrims to venerate an ox deemed sacred to end a drought while a group of soldiers are dispatched to thwart the plundering of a storehouse by starving peasants.

Gabriela. Director: Bruno Barreto, 2004. Story of a middle-aged bar owner in Brazil whose passionate romance with young Gabriela sends sparks flying in a town where sex and politics are the main diversions.

Garrincha: Alegria do povo (Garrincha: The Happiness of the People). Director: Joaquim Pedro, 2007. A look at the legendary Brazilian soccer star Garrincha during the heyday of his career in the early 1960s.

Grandma Has a Video Camera: "Life in the U.S. Is Good but It Is Bad. Life in Brazil Is Bad, but It Is Good." Director: Tânia Cypriano, 2007. This documentary is about a family of Brazilian immigrants living in the United States. From enchantment to disillusionment, from idealization to conformity, firsthand images and voices depict how they struggle to establish a place that they can consider home.

A guerra dos canudos (The Battle of Canudos). Director: Sérgio Resende, 1996. Epic film about the conflict between a poor community in northeastern Brazil at the turn of the twentieth century led by a charismatic religious leader that ends up being attacked and destroyed by the federal government.

O homem que virou suco (The Man Who Became Juice). Director: João Batista de Andrade,

1980. A working-class poet who arrives in São Paulo from the northeast is confused
with a worker who has killed his boss.

A Hora da Estrela (*Hour of the Star*). Director: Suzana Amaral, 1985. Film adaptation of
Clarice Lispector's book with the same name about the ultimate loneliness of a
woman within modern mass society.

Ilha das Flores (*Island of the Flowers*). Director: Jorge Furtado, 1990. A whimsically
presented but bitterly ironic exploration of values, the food supply, and the poverty
that requires people to search for food in garbage.

Os inconfidentes (*The Conspirators*). Director: Joaquim Pedro de Andrade, 2005.
Dramatization of the ill-fated plot by a group of Brazilian military officers, poets,
and intellectuals to overthrow the Portuguese Crown and establish a Brazilian
independent republic in 1789, inspired by Rousseau and the success of the American
Revolution.

Inocência (*Innocence*). Director: Walter Lima Júnior, 2005. In the nineteenth century,
a country girl is seduced by a young doctor who's staying at her house for a few
days, caring for her, and tries to hide the forbidden romance from her father, who
disapproves of the relationship.

Iracema: Uma transa amazônica (*Iracema: An Amazonian Love Affair*). Directors: Jorge
Bodansky and Orlando Senna, 1975. Countering official propaganda, this film
documents the social problems and deforestation of the Amazon region during the
dictatorship through the story of a young prostitute and a truck driver who travel
along the Transamazonian Highway.

It's All True. Directors: Orson Welles, Norman Foster, Richard Wilson, Bill Krohn,
and Myron Meisel, 1993. Orson Welles's producers shelved his ambitious Brazilian
film project, which was part of the U.S. government's Good Neighbor Policy. This
documentary features the story of the film's making and unmaking, including
previously unknown footage.

Jogo de cena (*Playing a Scene*). Director: Eduardo Coutinho, 2008. Following a newspaper
ad, ordinary women tell part of their life stories to director Eduardo Coutinho,
which are then reenacted by actresses, blurring the barriers between truth, fiction,
and interpretation.

Latitude zero (*Zero Latitude*). Director: Toni Venturi, 2003. A pregnant woman abandoned by her lover runs a bar in the remote countryside and is joined by a fugitive
from justice who worked with her former lover.

Lavoura arcaica (*To the Left of the Father*). Director: Luiz Fernando Carvalho, 2001. Based
on a novel by Raduan Nassar, a young man battles with his obstinate father and
leaves the farm for the city. His return shatters the family's confining life.

A lira do delírio (*The Lyre of Delight*). Director: Walter Lima Jr. A participant in a Carnival
group is kidnapped and killed. A police reporter attempts to solve the crime while
also investigating the murder of a homosexual man.

Lisbela e o prisioneiro (*Lisbela and the Prisoner*). Director: Guel Arraes, 2004. Romantic
comedy in which a man, on the run after an affair with a hitman's wife, falls in love
with a woman who loves movies and is engaged to a man from the country trying
to pass as a cosmopolitan Rio native.

Lúcio Flávio, o passageiro da agonia (*Lúcio Flávio: The Agonized Passenger*). Director:
Hector Babenco, 2009. Story of Brazilian bank robber Lúcio Flávio, who fascinated

some people in Rio de Janeiro during the 1970s for his bold robberies and spectacular escapes, and also because he was thought to be intelligent and politically aware.

Lula's Brazil. Director: Gonzalo Arijon, 2005. When Luiz Inácio da Silva, a former metalworker, won the Brazilian presidency in 2002, popular hopes for social change galvanized the nation. This film examines his successes and failures within the context of his election promises.

Macunaíma. Director: Joaquim Pedro de Andrade, 1969. This funny, free-wheeling adaptation of a masterpiece of Brazilian modernism reflects the simultaneous triumph of *tropicalismo* and onset of the military dictatorship.

Madame Satã (Madame Satan). Director: Karim Aïnouz, 2002. Born to former slaves and traded at the age of seven by his mother for the price of a mule, João Francisco dos Santos, one of the most famous drag queens of the 1930s, battled all stereotypes on the mean streets of Lapa, Rio de Janeiro.

Matou a família e foi ao cinema (Killed His Family and Went to the Movies). Director: Júlio Bressane, 1969. A film that criticizes sensationalist newspapers for their banal treatment of violence and sexual exploitation, but also references torturers who killed oppositionists and went home in peace.

Memórias do cárcere (Memoirs of Prison). Director: Nelson Pereira dos Santos, 1984. Based on the autobiographical novel of writer and leftist Graciliano Ramos's experience in prison during the Vargas era in the late 1930s and '40s.

Memórias do cativeiro (Memories of a Slave). Directors: Guilherme Fernández and Isabel Castro, 2005. This film was produced based upon the oral testimonies that descendants of slaves have given to the Oral History and Image Laboratory of the Fluminense Federal University.

Meu pé de laranja lima (My Orange Tree). Director: Marcos Bernstein, 2012. Zezé, almost eight years old, is a storyteller. His favorite refuge is a sweet orange tree on which he can unload all the bad things that happen to him, all the good news, and all his secret tricks. Then he strikes up an unlikely friendship with the town's eccentric.

Morte e vida severina (The Death and Life of a Severino). Director: Walter Avancini, 2011. An imaginative interpretation of João Cabral de Melo Neto's celebrated poem about the different ways people face life and death through the saga of Severino, a poor guy living in the back country of the northeast who leaves for Recife in search of a better life.

Mutum. Director: Sandra Kogut, 2007. A boy who lives in a simple house in the countryside witnesses the intense drama and problems of his parents, grandmother, siblings, and relatives.

Uma noite em 67 (A Night in 1967). Directors: Renato Terra and Ricardo Calil, 2010. Documentary about the 1967 Song Festival held in São Paulo, featuring young Chico Buarque, Caetano Veloso, Gilberto Gil, Roberto Carlos, Edu Lobo, and Sergio Ricardo.

Noite Vazia (Men and Women). Director: Walter Hugo Khouri, 1965. Two friends take two prostitutes for a night of pleasure. But the night turns out to be frustrating for all involved, as much bitterness is revealed in their conversation and attitudes, uncovering their anguish and deeper feelings, and the emptiness of their lives.

Odô yá! Life with AIDS. Director: Tânia Cypriano, 1997. Story of how Candomblé, a

Brazilian religion of African origin, has become a source of strength and power for a group of AIDS sufferers.

Olga. Director: Jayme Moniardim, 2005. Drama based on the life of German-born Olga Benário Prestes, wife of Brazilian communist leader Luís Carlos Prestes and herself a revolutionary militant, who is deported from Brazil to a German concentration camp in the 1930s.

Ônibus 174 (Bus 174). Directors: José Padilha and Felipe Lacerda, 2002. An award-winning examination of the tragic series of events that followed a desperate bus hijacking in Rio de Janeiro in 2000 that turned deadly when a SWAT team took evasive action against the hijacker.

A opinião pública (Public Opinion). Director: Arnaldo Jabor, 1967. Documentary about middle-class people in Rio de Janeiro in the 1960s in which they disclose their fears, aspirations, and political alienation.

Orfeu (Orpheus). Director: Carlos Diegues, 1999. Remake of *Orfeu Negro (Black Orpheus)*, retelling the Greek legend of Orpheus and Eurydice.

Orfeu Negro (Black Orpheus). Director: Marcel Camus, 1959. Set in Rio de Janeiro, the story is an adaptation of the Greek legend of Orpheus and Eurydice that takes place during Carnaval.

O padre e a moça (The Priest and the Girl). Director: Joaquim Pedro de Andreade, 1965. A newly ordained priest arrives in a rural town and meets an influential merchant and his concubine. She and the priest end up running away together.

O pagador de promessas (The Given Word). Director: Anselmo Duarte, 1962. This drama is a political and social commentary about a peasant farmer who vows to carry a cross into the local church if his injured donkey is cured. When the miracle happens, he attempts to carry out his promise, but everything starts to go wrong.

Um passaporte húngaro (A Hungarian Passport). Director: Sandra Kogut, 2008. The film documents the experience of the Brazilian director's attempts to obtain a Hungarian passport.

Peões (Metalworkers). Director: Eduardo Coutinho, 2006. Filmed during Luiz Inácio Lula da Silva's presidential campaign, the film examines the personal histories of anonymous workers who were involved alongside Lula in labor strikes in the late 1970s.

Pixote: A lei do mais fraco (Pixote [small child]: *The Law of the Weak)*. Director: Héctor Babenco, 1980. Story of Pixote, a young boy who is used as a child criminal in muggings and drug transport.

Pra Frente, Brasil (Go Ahead, Brazil!). Director: Roberto Farias, 1982. Fictional story of a man mistakenly arrested by a group linked to the military dictatorship during the 1970 World Cup soccer match.

Preto contra branco (Black against White). Director: Wagner Morales, 2004. The film discusses racial preconceptions in Brazil, using as a point of reference a soccer game played between two neighborhoods in São Paulo, divided up into the black team and the white team.

O que é isso companheiro? (Four Days in September). Director: Bruno Barreto, 1997. Political drama based on the 1969 kidnapping of the U.S. ambassador in Rio de Janeiro by a group of young revolutionaries demanding the release of political prisoners being tortured by the military police.

Que horas ela volta? (*The Second Mother*). Director: Anna Muylaert, 2015. The daughter of a maid moves into the house of the wealthy family for whom her mother works, to study for the entrance exam to the University of São Paulo, provoking tensions of all sorts.

Quilombo. Director: Carlos Diegues, 2005. A romanticized account of Palmares, the largest community of runaway slaves, or *quilombo*, in eighteenth-century Brazil, which for years resisted Portuguese domination.

Quilombo Country. Director: Leonard Abrams, 2005. This documentary provides a portrait of rural communities in Brazil that were either founded by runaway slaves or began from abandoned plantations.

O rei da noite (*King of the Night*). Director: Hector Babenco, 2009. In São Paulo, we see the life of a young man through the decades as he lives a Don Juan existence, courting three sisters and having an affair with a pretty young prostitute.

Os residentes (*The Residents*). Director: Tiago Mata Machado, 2010. In a series of short vignettes, we follow several Brazilian men and women through various surreal encounters.

Rio, 40 graus (*Rio, 100 Degrees F*). Director: Nelson Pereira dos Santos, 1955. A precursor to the Cinema Novo films of the 1960s, this semidocumentary follows five poor Rio de Janeiro children working as peanut vendors and selling their wares throughout the city.

Salve geral (*Time of Fear*). Director: Sérgio Rezende, 2010. The widowed mother of an incarcerated teen begins working for a criminal organization that operates from within the São Paulo state penitentiary system.

Santiago. Director: João Moreira Salles, 2006. Sensitive documentary about Santiago Badariotti Merlo, the butler for the parents and family of the film's director for thirty years, who was also an eccentric lover of film, theater, music, and history.

São Bernardo. Director: Leon Hirszman, 1972. Based on the novel of the same name by Graciliano Ramos, it tells the story of a farmer and landowner who is tortured by his personal desires and ambitions.

São Paulo, Sociedade Anônima (*São Paulo: Anonymous City*). Director: Luis Sérgio Person, 1965. The film follows the life of a middle-class man from São Paulo during the development of the automobile industry in the late 1950s and his existential crisis amid the industrialization process.

O som ao redor (*Neighboring Sounds*). Director: Kleber Mendonça Filho, 2012. Life in a middle-class neighborhood in present-day Recife takes an unexpected turn after the arrival of an independent private security firm, which brings a sense of safety, but also a good deal of anxiety, to a culture that runs on fear.

Tatuagem (*Tattoo*). Director: Hilton Lacerda, 2013. Set in Recife in the later years of the military dictatorship, it follows the story of a theatrical troupe that performs shows full of debauchery and nudity.

Terra em transe (*Entranced Earth*). Director: Glauber Rocha, 1967. This political allegory is about a young poet and journalist who is persuaded by his lover to become involved in politics. He fights against two corrupt politicians, a populist governor and a conservative president, both of whom were at one time his friends.

Toda nudez será castigada (*All Nudity Shall Be Punished*). Director Arnaldo Jabor, 1973. This drama based on Nelson Rodrigues's play by the same name portrays the hypocrisy of traditional middle-class families.

Topografia de um desnudo (Topography of a Nude Person). Director: Teresa Aguiar, 2011. In
   1968, Rio de Janeiro is preparing for a visit from Queen Elizabeth II. A journalist
   investigates the death of beggars and stumbles on a plan to kill them to clean up the
   city.

Transeunte (Passer-by). Director: Eryk Rocha, 2010. Expedito is an older man who loses
   touch with life and wanders the streets of Rio de Janeiro, listening to the conversations around him. Eventually he begins to accept invitations to start his life over.

Tropa de elite (Elite Squad). Director: José Padilha, 2007. Drama about BOPE (Special
   Police Operation Battalion), an elite corps of the military police designed to fight
   drug lords and police corruption in Rio de Janeiro.

Tropa de elite 2: O Inimigo Agora é Outro (Elite Squad: The Enemy Within). Director: José
   Padilha, 2010. Sequel to the 2007 film *Tropa de Elite*, it continues the story of BOPE
   and its relationship to law enforcement and politics.

Urbania. Director: Flavio Federico, 2009. Two men, a taxi driver and an old blind man,
   rediscover the city of São Paulo.

Vale a pena sonhar (It's Worth Dreaming). Director: Stella Grisotti and Rudi Böhm,
   2003. Apolônio de Carvalho, the subject of this documentary, fought alongside
   republicans in the Spanish Civil War, participated in the French Resistance against
   the Nazis, struggled against the Brazilian military dictatorship, and was the first to
   register with the Workers' Party.

Veias e vinhos: Uma história brasileira (Blood and Wine: A Brazilian Story). Director: João
   Batista de Andrade, 2006. A Brazilian family living through the political turmoil
   of the 1950s and the following two decades, from the president's suicide to the
   establishment of martial law, tries to find hope in the tragedy of everyday life.

O velho: A história de Luiz Carlos Prestes (The Comrade: The Life of Luiz Carlos Prestes).
   Director: Toni Venturi, 2008. This film documents the life of the controversial
   leader of the Brazilian Communist Party and includes commentaries by journalists,
   historians, family members, and former communist activists interwoven with rare
   historical film footage.

O veneno da madrugada (The Evil Hour). Director: Ruy Guerra, 2007. A small town is
   disturbed by anonymous notes delivered during the night, telling the secrets of its
   inhabitants.

Vidas sêcas (Barren Lives). Director: Nelson Pereira dos Santos, 1963. Based on the novel
   by Graciliano Ramos. A family and their dog struggle to survive in the drought-
   stricken northeast.

Vlado: Trinta anos depois (Vlado: Thirty Years Later). Director: João Batista de Andrede,
   2005. This documentary tells the story of journalist Vladimir Herzog, who was
   tortured and then killed while imprisoned during the repressive years of the Brazilian military dictatorship.

Acknowledgment of Copyrights and Sources

Part I. Conquest and Colonial Rule, 1500–1579

"Letter to King Manuel I of Portugal," by Pêro Vaz de Caminha, in *Portuguese Voyages 1498–1663*, edited by Charles David Ley (New York: Dutton, 1947), 42–45, 53–54, 56–59.

"Captaincy Charter Granted to Duarte Coelho," by King Dom João III, from a 1534 charter, in *História da Colonização Portuguesa do Brasil*, edited by Carlos Malheiro Dias (Porto: Litografia Nacional, 1924), 3:311–13.

"Letter from a Jesuit Friar," by Manuel da Nóbrega, July 5, 1559, Letter 32 to Tomé de Sousa, from *Cartas do Brasil e Mais Escritos do P. Manuel da Nóbrega (Opera Omnia)* (Coimbra: Por Ordem da Universidade, 1955), 316–54.

"Impressions of a French Calvinist," by Nicolas Barre, from "Cartas de N. B. [Nicolas Barre]. Enviadas entre fevereiro e maio de 1556," in *Copie de quelques lettres sur la navigation du chevallier de Villegaignon es terres de la Amerique oultre "Aequinoctial"* (Paris: Chez Martin le Ieune, 1557), 18–21.

"Indigenous Experiences of Colonization," by Eduardo Viveiros de Castro, from "O mármore e a murta: Sobre a inconstância da alma selvagem," in *A inconstância da alma selvagem e outros ensaios de antropologia* (São Paulo: Cosac e Naify, 2002), 183–87. Used by permission of Eduardo Vivieros de Castro.

"On Cannibals," by Michel de Montaigne, from chapter 30, "Of Cannibals," in *Essays of Michel de Montaigne*, book 1, translated by Charles Cotton, edited by William Carew Hazlitt (London: G. Bell, 1905), 146–48.

"On the Customs of the Indians of the Land," by Pero de Magalhães Gândavo, from "Capítulo Sétimo: Da condição e costumes dos índios da terra," in *Tratado da Terra do Brasil: História da Província Santa Cruz* (Belo Horizonte: Itatiaia, 1980), 57.

"A Description of the Tupinambá," by anonymous, from "Extracto," *Revista do Instituto Histórico e Geographico do Brazil*, vol. 1, 2nd ed., no. 3 (1839), 201–28.

"History of a Voyage to the Land of Brazil," by Jean de Léry, from *History of a Voyage to the Land of Brazil, Otherwise Called America*, translated by Janet Whatley (Berkeley: University of California Press, 1990), 56–59, 67.

"Portraits: Hans Staden," by Victoria Langland.

Part II. Sugar and Slavery in the Atlantic World, 1580–1694

"Letter from a Portuguese Trader," by Francisco Soares, from "A letter of Francis Suares to his brother Diego Suares dwelling in Lisbon, written from the river of Jenero in Brasill in June 1596," in *The Principal Navigations, Voyages, Traffiques, and Discoveries of the English Nation, made by sea or over-land to the remote and farthest distant quarters of the earth at any time within the compasse of these 1600 yeeres*, edited and translated by Richard Hakluyt (Glasgow: MacLehose and Sons, 1904), 9:39–43.

"Exploration of the Amazon," by Father Cristóbal de Acuña, from "New Discovery of the Great River of the Amazons," in *Expeditions into the Valley of the Amazons, 1539, 1540, 1639*, translated by Clements R. Markham (London: Hakluyt Society, 1857), 61–103.

"The Inquisition in Brazil," by various authors, from "Confissão de Frutuoso Álvares, Vigário de Matoim, no Tempo da Graça em 29 de Julho de 1591," and "Confissão de Jerônimo Parada, Estudante, Cristão-Velho, na Graça, em 17 de Agosto de 1591," reprinted in *Confissões da Bahia: Santo ofício da inquisição de Lisboa*, edited by Ronaldo Vainfas (São Paulo: Companhia das Letras, 1997), 45–51, 86–89.

"Excerpts from the Sermon on the Rosary," by António Vieira, from *Obras completas do Padre António Vieira, Sermões*, 15 vols. (Porto: Livraria Chardon, 1907–9), 12:301–34, translated and reprinted in *Children of God's Fire: A Documentary History of Black Slavery in Brazil*, by Robert Edgar Conrad (University Park: Pennsylvania State University Press, 1994), 163–74.

"The Sugar Industry," by Giovanni Antonio Andreoni, from "The Agricultural Wealth of Brazil in the Cultivation of Sugar," in André João Antonil, *Brazil at the Dawn of the Eighteenth Century*, translated by Timothy J. Coates, completing a partial translation begun by Charles R. Boxer (Dartmouth: Tagus, 2012), 15–16, 39–42, 43–44. Reprinted by permission of Lilly Library, University of Illinois, Bloomington, Illinois, Tagus Press, and Carla Boxer Vecchio.

"The Dutch Siege of Olinda and Recife," by Ambrósio Richshoffer, from *Diário de um soldado as Índias Ocidentais*, translated by Alfredo de Carvalho (Recife: Laemmert, 1897), 56–60.

"An Eyewitness Account of the First Battle of Guararapes," by Francisco Barreto de Meneses, from *Documentos dos Arquivos Portugueses que Importam ao Brasil*, no. 2 (Lisbon: Oficina Gráfica, Secretariado Nacional da Informação de Portugal, 1944–45), reprinted in E. Bradford Burns, *A Documentary History of Brazil* (New York: Knopf, 1966), 76–80.

"Two Documents in the War against Palmares," by various authors, from "Relação das Guerras Feitas aos Palmares de Pernambuco no Tempo do Governador D. Pedro de Almeida de 1675 a 1678," *Revista Trimensal do Instituto Historico, Geographico e Ethnographico do Brasil* 22, no. 2 (1859): 303–29; "Condições Ajustadas com o Governador dos Paulistas Domingos Jorge Velho em 14 de Agosto de 1693 para conquistar e destruir os negros de Palmares," *Revista Trimensal do Instituto Historico, Geographico e Ethnographico do Brasil* 47, part 1 (1884): 19–24.

"*Bandeirantes*," by anonymous, from "Informação do Estado do Brasil e de suas Necessidades," in *Revista Trimensal do Instituto Historico, Geographico e Ethnographico do Brasil*, 25 (1862): 473.

"Portraits: Count Johan Maurits von Nassau-Siegen," by James N. Green.

Part III. Gold and the New Colonial Order, 1695–1807

"The Brazilian Gold Rush," by Antonio Giovanni Andreoni, from "The Development and Wealth of Brazil by Gold Mining," in André João Antonil, *Brazil at the Dawn of the Eighteenth Century*, translated by Timothy J. Coates, completing a partial translation begun by Charles R. Boxer (Dartmouth: Tagus, 2012), 147–48, 152–53. Reprinted by permission of Lilly Library, Indiana University, Bloomington, Indiana, Tagus Press, and Carla Boxer Vecchio.

"The Minas Uprising of 1720," by anonymous, from "Relação do Levantamento que Houve nas Minas Geraes no Anno de 1720, Governando o Conde de Assumar D. Pedro D'Almeida," *Revista Trimensal de História e Geografia* 3, no. 11 (October 1841): 275–81.

"Expulsion of the Jesuits from Brazil," by King Dom José I, from *Documents about the extinction of the Jesuits, Codex 784* (1773–1801), September 9, 1773, Nossa Senhora da Ajuda Palace, Ajuda, Portugal.

"Portugal, Brazil, and *The Wealth of Nations*," by Adam Smith, from chapter 6, "Of Treaties of Commerce," and chapter 7, "Of Colonies," in *An Inquiry into the Nature and Causes of the Wealth of Nations*, book 4, *Of Systems of Political Economy*, compiled by Edwin Cannan (London: Meuthen and Co., 1904), 56–75.

"Poems from Baroque Minas," by various authors, from Tomás Antonio Gonzaga, "Marília de Dirceu," in *Marília de Dirceu* (São Paulo: Livraria Martins, 1972), 3–7; Cláudio Manuel da Costa, "Sonnets," in *Poemas de Cláudio Manuel da Costa* (São Paulo: Editôra Cultrix, 1966), 33–36.

"Tiradentes's Sentence," by Queen Maria I of Portugal, from "A sentença da Alçada," April 18, 1792, in Lúcio José dos Santos, *A Inconfidência Mineira: papel de Tiradente na Inconfidência Mineira* (São Paulo: Escolas Profissionais do Lyceu Coração de Jesus, 1927), 615.

"The Tailors' Revolt," by Luís Gonzagas das Virgens e Veiga, from "Avizo ao Clero, e ao Povo Bahinense," pamphlet, Autos de Devassa da Conspiração dos Alfaiates Collection (ADCA), Arquivo Público do Estado da Bahia, 37; "Luís Gonzaga das Virgens e Veiga to Dom Fernando José de Portugal e Castro, Governor of Bahia, 18 Dec. 1792," letter, Autos de Devassa da Conspiração dos Alfaiates Collection (ADCA), Arquivo Público do Estado da Bahia, 116.

"Letter from a Sugar Mill Owner," by João Rodrigues de Brito, from João Rodrigues de Brito et al. to Dom João de Saldanha da Gama Melo e Torres, Governor of Bahia, 1807, *Cartas Econômico-Políticas Sobre a Agricultura e Comércio da Bahia*, edited by Waldir Freitas Oliveira (Salvador, Bahia: Federação das Indústrias do Estado da Bahia, 2004), Series FIEB Documentos Históricos, no. 2, 84, 85–87, 88–90, 97–99, 101, 105.

"Portraits: Chica da Silva de Oliveira," by Victoria Langland.

Part IV. The Portuguese Royal Family in Rio de Janeiro, 1808–1821

"The Royal Family's Journey to Brazil," by Thomas O'Neill, from "Proceedings of the Squadron under the Command of Adm. Sir Wm. Sidney Smith, &c.," in *A Concise and Accurate Account of the Proceedings of the Squadron under the Command of Rear Admiral Sir Will. Sidney Smith, K.C. in Effecting the Escape, and Escorting the Royal Family of Portugal to the Brazils* (London: R. Edwards, Crane Court, Fleet Street, 1809), 26–27.

"Letter from a Son in Brazil to His Father in Portugal," by Luíz Joaquim dos Santos Marrocos, excerpted from letters to his father, written on April 12, 1811, and September 27, 1820, in *Cartas do Rio de Janeiro, 1811–1821* (Lisbon: Biblioteca Nacional de Portugal, 2008), 77–78, 498.

"Treaty between Portugal and Great Britain," by various authors, from *Treaty of amity, commerce and navigation, between His Britannic Majesty and His Royal Highness the Prince Regent of Portugal, signed at Rio de Janeiro the 19th of February 1810* (London: A Strahan, Printers-Street, Gouigh Square, 1810).

"Rio de Janeiro's First Medical School," by Count of Aguiar, from "Criação do curso de Cirurgia na Santa casa de Misericórdia do Rio (1813)," in *Catálogo das obras impressas no século XVII: A colecção da Santa Casa da Misericórdia de Lisboa* (Lisbon: Santa Casa da Misericórdia de Lisboa, Arquivo/Biblioteca, 1994).

"The Influence of the Haitian Revolution in Brazil," by Paulo José Vianna, from a letter to the Marquis of Aguiar, 1815, National Archive, Rio de Janeiro, GIFI 6J-79.

"Petition for Pedro I to Remain in Brazil," by anonymous, from *Gazeta do Rio*, Supplemento de No. 11, January 24, 1822, 69–71.

"Speech Given at the Cortes (National Assembly) of Lisbon," by Diogo Antônio Feijó, from a speech delivered during the April 25, 1822, session, printed in the *Diário das Cortes: Geraes, Extraordinarias e Constituintesda Naçao Portugueza* (Lisbon: Impresa Nacional, 1822), 5:952–53.

"Portraits: Empress Maria Leopoldina of Brazil," by Lilia Moritz Schwarcz.

Part V. From Independence to the Abolition of the Slave Trade, 1822–1850

"On the Declaration of Brazilian Independence," by Padre Belchoir Pinheiro de Oliveira, from *D. Pedro I e o Grito da Indepêndencia*, edited by F. Assis Cintra (São Paulo: Companhia Melhoramentos, 1921), 213–17.

"Acclamation of Pedro as Emperor of Brazil," by José Martins Rocha, from *Correio Brasilense*, no. 175 (December 1822): 578–79.

"On Slavery," by José Bonifácio de Andrada e Silva, from *Projetos para o Brasil* (São Paulo: Companhia das Letras, 1998), 45, 65.

"From the Journal of Maria Graham," by Lady Maria Dundas Graham Callcott, from *Journal of a Voyage to Brazil, and Residence There, during Part of the Years 1821, 1822, 1823* (London: Longman et al., 1824), 276–81, 317–18.

"Portugal Recognizes the Brazilian Empire," by Charles Stuart, Luiz José de Carvalho e Mello, and Barão de Santo Amaro, from "Tratado de Amizade e Aliança entre el-Rei o Senhor D. João VI e D. Pedro I, Imperador do Brasil, feito por mediação de Sua Majestade Britânica, assinado no Rio de Janeiro a 29 de Agosto de 1825, e Ratificado por parte de Portugal em 15 de Novembro e pela do Brasil em 30 de Agosto do dito ano," http://dai-mre.serpro.gov.br/atos-internacionais/bilaterais/1825/b_2/.

"The Malê Revolt," by João José Reis. Courtesy of João José Reis.

"How to Write the History of Brazil," by Carl Friedrich Philipp von Martius, from *Jornal do Instituto Histórico e Geográfico Brasileiro*, no. 24 (January 1845): 389–411.

"Scenes from the Slave Trade," by various authors, from *African Repository and Colonial Journals*, September 1841; Thomas Nelson, *Remarks on the Slavery and Slave Trade of the Brazils* (London, 1846); João Dunshee de Abrantes, *O Captiveiro* (Rio de Janeiro,

1941), in Robert E. Conrad, *World of Sorrow: The African Slave Trade to Brazil* (Baton Rouge: Louisiana State University Press, 1986), 45–47. Courtesy of Ursula Conrad.

"Cruelty to Slaves," by Thomas Ewbank, from *Life in Brazil; or, a Journal of a Visit to the Land of the Cocoa and the Palm* (New York: Harper and Brothers, 1856), 437–40.

"The Praieira Revolution Manifesto to the World," by Antônio Borges da Fonseca, from *Diário Novo* (Pernambuco), January 1, 1849, 1.

"Portraits: José Bonifácio de Andrada e Silva," by Lilia Moritz Schwarcz.

Part VI. Coffee, the Empire, and Abolition, 1851–1888

"Memoirs of a Settler in Brazil," by Thomas Davatz, from *Memórias de um colono no Brasil (1850),* translated by Sérgio Buarque de Holanda (São Paulo: Livraria Martins, 1941), 47–52.

"*O Guarani,*" by José de Alencar, from *The Guarany,* translated by James W. Hawes, serialized in *Overland Monthly and Out West Magazine* (San Francisco) 21, no. 127 (July 1893): 193–96.

"The U.S. Civil War and Slave Rebellions in Brazil," by Francisco Primo de Souza Aguiar, official letter sent by the president of the province of Maranhão to the minister of justice, Francisco de Paula de Negreiros Sayão Lobato, December 13, 1861, Brazilian National Archives, Rio de Janeiro, Série Justiça, GIFI 6J 108.

"The Slave Ship," by Antônio Frederico de Castro Alves, from "O Navio Negreiro," in *Vozes d'Africa, Navio Negreiro, Cantico do Calvario* (Rio de Janeiro: Livraria Academica de J.G. de Azevedo, 1880), 11–22.

"Victims and Executioners," by Joaquim Manuel de Macedo, from *As Vítimas-algozes* (Rio de Janeiro: Typ. Americana, 1869), 1–11.

"The Republican Manifesto," by members of the Republican Party, from *Saga: A Grande História do Brazil Império: 1840–1889,* vol. 4 (São Paulo: Abril Cultural, 1981), 233.

"Law of the Free Womb," by José Maria da Silva Paranhos and Princess Isabel, Law No. 2040 of September 28, 1871, from *Coléção de Leis do Império do Brasil,* vol. 1 (Rio de Janeiro: Typographia Nacional, 1871), 147.

"Early Brazilian Feminism," by Francisca Senhorinha da Motta Diniz, from *O sexo feminino,* October 25, 1873, translated by June E. Hahner, in *Emancipating the Female Sex: The Struggle for Women's Rights in Brazil, 1850–1940* (Durham, NC: Duke University Press, 1990), 211–13.

"Letters to the French Mineralogist Claude-Henri Gorceix," by Emperor Dom Pedro II, from Dilma Castelo Branco Diniz, "Cartas inéditas de Dom Pedro II A Henri Gorceix: Tradução e comentário," *Caligrama* (Belo Horizonte) 15, no. 1 (2010): 130–34.

"Selections from *Abolitionism,*" by Joaquim Nabuco, from *Abolitionism: The Brazilian Antislavery Struggle,* translated and edited by Robert Conrad (Urbana: University of Illinois Press, 1977), 9–11, 18–19.

"A Critique of José de Alencar's *O Guarani,*" by Joaquim Maria Machado de Assis, from *Obra Completa de Machado de Assis,* 2nd ed., vol. 3 (Rio de Janeiro: Nova Aguilar, 2008), 1310–13.

"Abolition Decree," by Princess Isabel and Rodrigo Augusto da Silva, Law No. 3,353, May 13, 1888, from *Diário Oficial da União Seção* 1 (May 5, 1888): 1.

"Portraits: Emperor Dom Pedro II," by Lilia Moritz Schwarcz.

Part VII. Republican Brazil and the Onset of Modernization, 1889–1929

"Hymn of the Proclamation of the Republic," by José Joaquim de Campos da Costa de Medeiros e Albuquerque and Leopoldo Miguez, from *Diário Oficial da União* (Rio de Janeiro), January 21, 1890, 10.

"The Human Races," by Raimundo Nina Rodrigues, from *As raças humanas e a responsibilidade penal no Brasil* (Rio de Janeiro: Ed. Guanabara Waissman Koogan, 1894), 30–35.

"*Os Sertões* or Rebellion in the Backlands," by Euclides da Cunha, from *Rebellion in the Backlands* (Rio de Janeiro: Laemmert, 1902), 475–76, translated by Samuel Putman (Chicago: University of Chicago Press, 1975), 475–76. Reprinted by permission of the University of Chicago Press.

"The Owner's Pastry Shop," by Joaquim Maria Machado de Assis, from *Esaú e Jacó* (Rio de Janeiro: H. Garnier, 1904), translated by Helen Caldwell (Berkeley: University of California Press, 1965), 160–64.

"Revolt of the Whip, *A Revolta da Chibata*," by João Cândido Felisberto and Bulcão Vianna, from *A revolta da Chibata*, 2nd ed. (Guanabara: Editoria Letras e Artes, 1963), 149–50, 179.

"Three Types of Bureaucrats" (Três gênios da secretaria), by Afonso Henriques de Lima Barreto, from *O homem que sabia javanês e outros contos* (Curitiba: Polo Editorial do Paraná, 1997).

"On the Mestizo in Brazil," by João Batista Lacerda, from "Sobre os mestiços no Brasil," paper presented at the First World Congress on Race, London (July 26–29, 1911), in Lilia Moritz Schwarcz, "Previsões são sempre traiçoeiras: João Baptista de Lacerda e seu Brasil branco," *História, Ciências, Saúde-Manguinhos* 18, no. 1 (Rio de Janeiro, March 2011).

"Demands of the São Paulo General Strike of 1917," by Proletarian Defense Committee, from "A Conflagracão," *O Estado de São Paulo*, July 12, 1917, 1.

"Brazil and World War I," by anonymous, from "Navio brasileiro é afundado, Brasil entra na Guerra," *Estado de São Paulo*, April 12, 1917, 2.

"The Cannibalist Manifesto (Manifesto Antropófago)," by Oswald de Andrade, from "O Manifesto antropófago," *Revista de Antropofagia* 1, no. 2 (June 1928), translated by Leslie Bary, *Latin American Literary Review* 19, no. 38 (July–December 1991): 38–47. Reprinted by permission of the *Latin American Literary Review*.

"*Macunaíma*," by Mário de Andrade, from *Macunaíma: O herói sem nenhum caráter* (São Paulo: Martins, 1978).

"Revolutionary Manifestos from the Tenentes Revolts," by various authors, from "Um Communicado dos Chefes do Movimento," *O Estado de São Paulo*, July 10, 1924, 1, reprinted in Cyro Costa and Eurico de Goes, *Sob a metralha: Historico da revólta em São Paulo de 5 de julho de 1924: Narrativas, Documentos, Commentarios, Illustrações* (São Paulo: Ed. Monteiro Lobato, 1924), 56–60; "Moção dos Militantes Operários ao Comitê das Forças Revolucionárias" (July 1924), reprinted in *Alvorada Operária: Os Congressos Operários no Brasil* (Rio de Janeiro: Mundo Livre, 1979), 332–34.

"An Essay on Brazilian Sadness," by Paulo Prado, from *Retrato do Brasil: Ensaio sôbre a tristeza brasileira* (São Paulo: Companhia das Letras, 1997), 130–61.

"Portraits: Tarsila do Amaral," by Victoria Langland.

Part VIII. Getúlio Vargas, the Estado Novo, and World War II, 1930–1945

"From the Platform of the Liberal Alliance," by Liberal Alliance, in Paulo Bonavides and Roberto Amaral, *Textos políticos da história do Brasil*, vol. 4 (Brasília: Senado Federal/Subsecretaria de Edições Técnicas, 1996), 19–54.

"Prestes's Declaration about the Liberal Alliance," by Luís Carlos Prestes, from "Manifesto em Maio de 1930," in Paulo Bonavides and Roberto Amaral, *Textos políticos da história do Brasil*, vol. 4 (Brasília: Senado Federal/Subsecretaria de Edições Técnicas, 1996), 168–72. Courtesy of Anita Prestes.

"*The Masters and the Slaves*," by Gilberto Freyre, from *The Masters and the Slaves: A Study in the Development of Brazilian Civilization*, translated by Samuel Putnam (Berkeley: University of California Press, 1986), 3–5, 7, 9–11, 13–14, 23–24, 71.

"Speech by the First Woman Elected to Congress in Brazil," by Carlota Pereira de Queirós, from "República dos Estados Unidos do Brasil," in *Anais da Assembleia Nacional Constituinte: Organizados pela Redações dos Anais e Documentos Parlamentares*, vol. 11 (Rio de Janeiro: Imprensa Nacional, 1936), 268–81.

"Manifesto of the National Liberating Alliance," by Luís Carlos Prestes, from "Manifesto de Julho da ALN," *A Platéa*, July 6, 1935. Courtesy of Anita Prestes.

"The Cordial Man,' by Sérgio Buarque de Holanda, from *Em Raízes do Brasil* (1936; reprint, São Paulo: Companhia das Letras, 1995), 208–21.

"Vargas and the Estado Novo," by Getúlio Vargas, from "No limiar do ano de 1938," December 31, 1937, Biblioteca da Presidencia da Republica.

"Rubber and the Allies' War Effort," by various authors, from Joseph L. Apodaca, "Can the Americas Live Alone?," *Agriculture in the Americas* 1, no. 1 (February 1941): 1–6; Edgar R. Burkland, "Speaking of Rubber . . . ," *Agriculture in the Americas* 1, no. 1 (February 1941): 7–11.

"Portraits: Patrícia Galvão (Pagú)," by James N. Green.

Part IX. Democratic Governance and Developmentalism, 1946–1964

"Telenovelas in Constructing the Country of the Future," by Esther Hamburger. Courtesy of Esther Hamburger.

"The Oil Is Ours," by Getúlio Vargas, from *Diário Oficial da União*, Section 1 (October 3, 1953), 16705.

"An Unrelenting Critic of Vargas," by Carlos Lacerda, from "O Sangue de um Inocente," *A Tribuna da Imprensa*, August 5, 1954, 1. © Estate of Letícia Lacerda. Courtesy of Cristina Lacerda Simões Lopes and Sebastião Lacerda.

"Vargas's Suicide Letter," by Getúlio Vargas, CPDOC, Fundação Getúlio Vargas.

"The Life of a Factory Worker," by Joana de Masi Zero, interview by Edson de Oliveira Balotta, São Paulo, September 6, 1996.

"Operation Pan America," by Juscelino Kubitschek, from "Aide Memoire Sent by the Government of Brazil to Governments of Other American States, August 9, 1958," in Council of the Organization of American States, Special Committee to Study the Formulation of New Economic Measures for Economic Cooperation, vol. 1, *Report and Documents, First Meeting, Washington, D.C. November 17–December 12, 1958* (Washington, DC, 1959), 29–31.

"Excerpts from *Child of the Dark*," by Carolina Maria de Jesus, from *Child of the Dark: The Diary of Carolina Maria de Jesus*, translated by David St. Clair (New York: Penguin, 2003), 43–44, 57, 75–77, 149–50, 154.

"Education as a Practice of Freedom," by Paulo Freire, from *Education for Critical Consciousness* (New York: Seabury, 1974), 42–44, 46–49.

"Letter of Manumission for the Brazilian Peasant," by Francisco Julião, from "Carta da Alforria do Camponês," *A Liga* 6 (1963): 4.

"Brazil's New Foreign Policy," by Jânio Quadros, from *Foreign Affairs* 40, no. 1 (October 1961): 19–27. Permission conveyed through Copyright Clearance Center, Inc.

"Development and the Northeast," by Celso Furtado, from "A luta pelo Nordeste e a estratégia da Sudene," *A Defesa Nacional* 49, 574–75 (Rio de Janeiro, May–June 1962), reprinted in *Arquivos Celso Furtado: O Nordeste e a saga da Sudene, 1958–1964* (Rio de Janeiro: Contraponto, 2009), 171–72, 174–78. Courtesy of Centro Celso Furtado.

"President João Goulart's Speech at Central do Brasil," by João Goulart, from Hélio Silva, *1964: Golpe ou contragolpe?* (Rio de Janeiro: Civilização Brasileira, 1975), 457–66.

"March of the Family with God for Freedom," by anonymous, from "Marcha da família, com Deus, pela liberdade," *O Globo*, March 28, 1964, http://www.gedm.ifcs.ufrj.br/documentos_lista.php?page=5&ncat=1.

"The U.S. Government and the 1964 Coup d'État," by various authors, from Top Secret Cables to the State Department from Ambassador Lincoln Gordon, Rio de Janeiro, March 27, 1964; March 29, 1964; Secret Cable to Lincoln Gordon from State Department, March 31, 1964; State Department Files, National Archives II, College Park, Maryland; President Lyndon B. Johnson Discussing the Impending Coup in Brazil with Undersecretary of State George Ball, March 31, 1964, White House Audio Tapes, Lyndon B. Johnson Presidential Library, Austin, Texas.

"Portraits: Oscar Niemeyer," by Victoria Langland.

Part X. The Generals in Power and the Fight for Democracy, 1964–1985

"Institutional Act No. 1," by Francisco dos Santos Nascimento, from *Diário Oficial da União*, section 1, April 10, 1964, 3217.

"A U.S. Senator Supports the New Military Government," by Senator Wayne Morse, from *Congressional Record: Senate*, April 3, 1964, 6851–52. Courtesy of Roberta Nioac Prado.

"*The Brazilian Revolution*," by Caio Prado Júnior, from *Clássicos sobre a Revolução Brasileira*, edited by Caio Prado Júnior and Florestan Fernandes (São Paulo: Editora Expressão Popular, 2000), 25–53. Courtesy of Roberta Nioac Prado.

"The Myth of Racial Democracy," by Abdias do Nascimento, from *Cadernos Brasileiros* 10, no. 47 (May–June 1968): 3–7. Courtesy of Elisa Nascimento.

"A Brazilian Congressional Representative Speaks Out," by Márcio Moreira Alves, from *Anais da Câmara dos Deputados* 23 (Brasília, 1968), 432–33.

"Institutional Act No. 5," by Luís Antônio da Gama e Silva, from *Diário Oficial da União*, December 13, 1968.

"Letter from the Ilha Grande Prison," by various authors, from *Brazilian Information Bulletin*, no. 4 (July 1971): 11–12.

"The Kidnapping of the U.S. Ambassador," by various authors, from "Manifesto," in

Manifestos Poliíticos: Do Brasil contemporâneo, edited by Lincoln de Abreu Penna (Rio de Janeiro: E-papers, 2008), 334–38.

"A Letter to Pope Paul VI," by Marcos Penna Sattamini de Arruda, from Amnesty International, *Report on Allegations of Torture in Brazil* (Palo Alto, CA: Amnesty International West Coast Office, 1973). Reprinted by permission of Amnesty International.

"Two Presidents at the White House," by various authors, from "Toast of the President and President Médici of Brazil," no. 383, December 7, 1971, in Richard M. Nixon, *Richard Nixon: 1971: Containing the Public Messages, Speeches, and Statements of the President* (Washington, DC: Office of the Federal Register, National Archives and Records Service, 1972).

"National Security and the Araguaian Guerrillas," by Ernesto Geisel and Germano Arnoldi Pedrozo, recorded conversation, January 1974, cited in Elio Gaspari, *A Ditadura Escancarada* (São Paulo: Companhia das Letras, 2002), 402–4.

"What Color Are You?," from National Household Sample Study, Brazilian Institute of Geography and Statistics, 1976.

"Second-Wave Brazilian Feminism," by editors of *Nós Mulheres*, from *Nós Mulheres*, no. 7 (March 1978).

"LGBT Rights and Democracy," by Aguinaldo Silva, from "Saindo do Gueto," *Lampião da Esquina*, no. 0 (April 1978): 2.

"The Movement for Political Amnesty," by various authors, from Carta de Princípios da Comitê Brasileira de Anistia, São Paulo, 1978, Fundação Perseu Abrão Archive; Law no. 6,683 of August 28, 1979, *Diário Oficial da União*, section 1, 12265.

"Lula's May Day Speech to Brazilian Workers," by Luiz Inácio Lula da Silva, from Luis Flavio Rainho and Osvaldo Martins Bargas, *As lutas operárias e sindicais dos metalúrgicos em São Bernardo (1977–1979)*, vol. 1 (São Bernardo do Campo, SP: Associação Beneficente e Cultural dos Metalúrgicos de São Bernardo do Campo e Diadema, 1983), appendix 33, 232–33. Courtesy of Luiz Inácio Lula da Silva.

"Portraits: Caetano Veloso and Gilberto Gil," by James N. Green.

Part XI. Redemocratization and the New Global Economy, 1985–Present

"Forty Seconds of AIDS," by Herbert Daniel, from *Vida antes da morte, Life before Death* (Rio de Janeiro: Abia, 1994), 46–49. Courtesy of Geny Brunelli de Carvalho.

"Affirmative Action in the Ministry of Foreign Affairs," by Celso Lafer, from Press Release no. 223, Assesoria de Impresna do Gobinete, Ministéro das Relações Exteriores, May 14, 2002.

"A Young Voice from the MST," by Cristiane, from Andrea Paula dos Santos, Suzana Lopes Salgado Ribeiro, and José Carlos Sebe Bom Meihy, *Vozes da Marcha pela Terra* (São Paulo: Edições Loyola, 1998), 36–39, 42, 44, 48–49.

"World Social Forum Charter of Principles," by various authors, from World Social Forum International Council, June 10, 2001, http://www.universidadepopular.org/site/media/documentos/WSF_-_charter_of_Principles.pdf.

"The Bolsa Família Program," by various authors, from Walquiria Leão Rego and Alessandro Pinzani, *Vozes da Bolsa Família: Autonomia, dinheiro e cidadania* (São Paulo: Editora UNESP, 2013), 126–27. Courtesy of UNESP.

"Music, Culture, and Globalization," by Gilberto Gil, mirrors.creativecommons.org/
    msoffice/GilbertoGil-en.doc. Courtesy of Gilberto Gil.
"The Inaugural Speech of Brazil's First Female President," by Dilma Rousseff, www
    .brasi.gov.br/noticias/arquivos/2011/01/10/leia-interga-do-discurso-de-posse-de-
    dilma-roussef-no-congresso.
"The June Revolts," by Marcos Nobre. Courtesy of Marcos Nobre.
"Portraits: Herbert Daniel," by James N. Green.

Every reasonable effort has been made to obtain permission. We invite copyright
holders to inform us of any oversights.

Index